READINGS IN ADVERTISING

Current Viewpoints on Selected Topics

READINGS IN ADVERTISING

Current Viewpoints on Selected Topics

James E. Littlefield
Professor of Business Administration
University of North Carolina
at Chapel Hill

WEST PUBLISHING CO.
St. Paul · New York · Boston
Los Angeles · San Francisco

Library of Congress Cataloging in Publication Data
Main entry under title:

Readings in advertising.

    1. Advertising—Addresses, essays, lectures.
I. Littlefield, James E.

HF5821.R37   659.1'08   75–10010

ISBN 0–8299–0030–6

TO MY MOTHER

*

PREFACE

READINGS IN ADVERTISING is designed primarily for supplementary use in a course which provides an introductory view of advertising. It is designed to provide depth to some areas (advertising management and social issues in advertising are examples) which are not covered well in the popular advertising textbooks and to help the reader obtain currency in the general field of advertising. The book should be of interest to instructors in Schools of Journalism as well as Schools of Business because articles are presented for people interested in managing advertising as well as those interested in preparing advertisements and campaigns.

It should also be of interest to practitioners in retail, manufacturing, and service organizations and to those in advertising agencies because it brings together a number of writers from several publications not normally a part of the practitioner's reading list.

Not all areas covered in an introductory advertising textbook are covered in this readings book. Some of the omitted topics seem to be covered well enough already; others do not have supplementary readings available. An attempt has been made to present provocative articles and to present both sides of particular issues. A few of the articles are from several years ago; most are rather current. All have been chosen from the standpoint of providing background material to the person wishing to increase his knowledge of advertising preparation and management.

The reader will note a section on the future of advertising. Although all of these prognostications certainly will not be correct, they should provoke thought and provide material for interesting class discussions. A number of questions have been provided at the end of each article throughout the book, to start these discussions.

I am indebted to Professors Rollie Tillman, Jr. and Jay E. Klompmaker of the University of North Carolina at Chapel Hill and William G. Nickels of the University of Maryland for their thoughtful comments and suggestions regarding chapter placement and selection of specific articles. Also, I appreciate the help of Ms. Sayeste Daser and Mr. Dario Galindo with the end-of-chapter questions. Errors of omission or commission, however, remain mine.

James E. Littlefield

TABLE OF CONTENTS

†

READINGS IN ADVERTISING

Current Viewpoints on Selected Topics

PART I

THE CONSUMER AND COMMUNICATION

No one really knows yet what advertising does to the consumer. This statement may shock the reader, but it is true. To be sure, some steps have been made toward identifying advertising's effect on the consumer, but much has yet to be learned.

Advertising does work, of course, of that there is no doubt. Perhaps this lack of doubt itself impedes the progress toward learning just how advertising affects the consumer and, in turn, how the consumer affects advertising.

It is a truism, and therefore probably true, that the key to this knowledge lies in studying consumer behavior and the process of communication. This section presents articles on what advertising does for the consumer, how it is necessary to segment the market before preparing advertising messages, how and why consumers respond to advertisements as they do, how businessmen in particular view advertising, and how advertising is different from other forms of communication.

Part I starts off with an article "What Does Advertising Do for the Consumer?" The reader should evaluate the statements made in the article in terms of his own perceptions of what advertising does for him.

O'Toole and Cone present different approaches to the same question, that of segmenting the market for advertising messages. Communication, is a difficult task at best, and both of these readings can add to the understanding of this task.

Weilbacher and Kanter report on how and why consumers respond to advertisements. As might be expected, consumers have diverse reactions. Interestingly, only 5% of the advertisements were categorized as offensive when all types of ads are considered. However, when one breaks the ads down into product classes, 56% of the liquor ads and 19% of the cigarette ads were considered offensive.

Greyser and Reece report on a survey of businessmen and their attitudes toward advertising. While still respecting advertising as a selling tool, businessmen are increasingly uneasy about other aspects such as truthfulness and social impact.

Contrary to common belief, Preston and Scharback conclude in the last reading in this section that people may perceive more in advertisements than is actually there. People apparently perceive messages differently when presented in advertisements than when written in the form of other types of communication.

1

Reprinted by permission from JOURNAL OF ADVERTISING, Vol. 2, No. 2, pp. 22-27.
Copyright 1973 by Board of Directors, JOURNAL OF ADVERTISING.

I-1

WHAT DOES ADVERTISING DO FOR THE CONSUMER?

Sub-Council on Advertising and Promotion of the National Business Council for Consumer Affairs

I. INTRODUCTION

Advertising is a subject about which many people have strong opinions. It is one of our most visible forms of communication and people tend to have highly personal reactions to it.

On the other hand, how advertising works is not really visible at all, and while there is much speculation about it, is not well understood.

The National Business Council for Consumer Affairs thought it might be useful to give you the opportunity to review some of the basic factual and conceptual information on advertising as this is understood through research and hard practical experience by professionals in the field.

You may find it different from what you normally hear about advertising.

Every observer of advertising, of course, has personal reactions to advertising, but what is discussed here has to do with the basic nature of advertising and what is known about the dynamics of its operation.

The fundamental reason why advertising

is used is that it is the most inexpensive way for a marketer to communicate with a consumer about his products. This has enabled many marketers to employ an evergrowing production force to provide an increasing number of products to an expanding consumer market. It is generally accepted that this has been of enormous value in promoting the business health of the country and is of major importance in supporting a full employment economy.

But this is only one of the dimensions of advertising.

Advertising is much more complex than this. It is at once a creative art, a science, a business and a social institution.

It is, therefore, not surprising that different people view advertising differently. How advertising is perceived depends on the perspective of the viewer and what he focuses on in perceiving it.

The Marketer (how it sells product)
The Production Worker (how it provides and sustains jobs)
The Advertising Technician (how it communicates)
The Psychologist (how to use it effectively)

2

The Economist	(how it affects free competition and the economy)
The Social Observer	(how it affects society and life values)
The Art-Form Observer	(how aesthetic it is)
The Government Observer	(how honest it is)
The Consumerist	(how informative it is)
The Consumer	?

Those most directly concerned with advertising know that all advertising is not equally effective, but that when used well, it is a clearly positive force.

Outside observers tend to see advertising as more negative than positive. The core of their concern is the consumer, the vast majority of whom rarely voice their opinions about the fundamental workings of the market place.

In expressing concern about the role of advertising in the consumer's life and the need to protect the consumer from possible ill effects from advertising, critics sometimes portray the consumer a rather unintelligent, rather gullible, rather helpless...ingesting and acting on advertising like a robot. They do not often see the consumer as receiving meaningful help from advertising.

One need only think about oneself (since we are all consumers in addition to our regular jobs) to know this portrayal is not accurate. Certainly, this is not the consumer to whom the marketer advertises.

The objective of this presentation is to give you the picture, drawn from consumer research, of how the consumer perceives and uses advertising and to establish that the service advertising performs for consumers is at least comparable in value to the service it performs for manufacturers.

II. ADVERTISING AND THE CONSUMER

The two generalizations--"advertising" and "consumers" each encompass a very broad spectrum.

"Advertising" includes all kinds of messages about products and services emanating from different sources (manufacturers, retailers, etc.) and delivered through all media (TV, radio, magazines, newspapers, outdoor, transportation posters, direct mail, skywriting, bus benches, store circulars, coupons, etc.).

"Consumers" are men, women and children; all ages, incomes and educational levels; all geographic areas in the country; all races, creeds and colors; using all manner of products and services ranging from soup and cola drinks to insurance and cars.

All advertising cannot possibly be of interest to all consumers (though all advertising will be of interest to some consumers--and all consumers will be interested in some advertising).

Though advertisers attempt to target their message to its intended audience, a penalty of mass media is that this cannot be done with precision. The result--a high volume of advertising to every consumer, a daily parade of several hundred products and services, more than anyone could possibly want, afford or even use.

Isn't this a wasteful process? Isn't it confusing to the consumer? It's neither, and the key to why it's not lies with consumers and what they do with advertising to turn it into a valuable tool for themselves.

Because this is a personal process-- different for every consumer and for every buying problem, let's narrow the field down to one kind of consumer (a housewife), one kind of advertising (national advertising in major media), and one kind of environment in which it operates (the supermarket).

The supermarket today is the major outlet for nationally advertised food and
related household products. Though
not generally recognized, the relationship between national advertising and
supermarkets is a very close one, and
it is unlikely that supermarkets
could exist as we know them, were it
not for national advertising which encourages a high level of consumer demand and the required traffic into
the stores.

Major social and economic changes have
occurred in the past 10 years and today's housewife--and the consumers she
represents--reflect these changes.

Only 10 years ago, more than half of
all women 25 and over had not finished
high school. In 1971, not only are
more than half (57%) high school graduates, but 20% have gone on to college. The proportion of college age
women (20-21) who have had some college is almost 40%.

So, today's housewife is better educated than consumers of the past. She
also has more money to spend. Her
family income (1971) was $9,012--or
about $175 a week.

According to an extensive study done
by the Kroger Company in Cleveland a
few years ago, the typical supermarket
customer is 41 years old and represents
a family of four--husband, wife and two
children. She is an experienced homemaker, though her needs keep changing
as her family grown and matures.

At the time of the study she spent 18%
of her income for food and household-
related items spread out into three
shopping trips per week. At current
income levels ($175 per week), she is
probably spending between $30 and $35
a week now.

She does her major food shopping once
a week in a large supermarket where

over 7,000 brands, varieties and sizes
of items are available for purchase--of
which 1,500 (22%) were not there a year
ago (A.C. Nielsen Company) and 3,500
(55%) were not there 10 years ago
(*Progressive Grocer*). The rate of new
product influx means that every week
she shops there are some 30 products
that were not there the week before,
while almost as many products that were
there a week ago are not there now.

She is generally knowledgeable about
brands from her trial and use of them,
but is interested in the advertising
for food and household products because
of her need to know. However, like
everybody else, she receives far more
advertising messages than she can possibly use every day. How does she cope
with this?

The answer is very simple. She does
with advertising exactly what she does
with excesses of information received
from any source (too much news, too
many facts, too much entertainment, too
much gossip, etc.)--she notices what
she wants to notice and ignores, over-
looks, or forgets the rest.

As clearly pointed out in the 1971 Marketing Science Institute report on advertising, a person accomplishes this
by two principal methods:

1. *Selective perception*--a way of
screening out of her mind information
that is not of any interest. By selective perception, she notices:
 Women's products more than men's or
  children's
 Product classes she uses more than
  those she doesn't
 Among products she uses, brands she
  likes more than those she dislikes;
  new brands more than old brands;
  new advertising more than old advertising
 Sees advertising more clearly when
  she is about to buy

Selective perception operates in every
field. The tennis player doesn't notice

much about golf. But the golf player does. It enables people to perceive from their environment what they want to perceive.

2. *Message filter*--a matter of the content of advertising and its personal relevance to her.

She tends to check what she reads and hears against her previous experience, her existing knowledge and attitudes and her personal value system. Only a very few advertisements can come through this filter because:
Many add nothing to her knowledge
Some say something new but conflict with her knowledge or beliefs
A few say something new that links up to her knowledge or beliefs.
If so:
She will listen more carefully
Remember it better
Perhaps even plan to look for the advertised product at the store

These two methods effectively remove from her active involvement most of the messages she receives. However, survival of an ad through the filter process does not imply that she "believes" the message. A desire to "try" the product is a tentative acceptance and desire for more complete information.

Brought up from childhood with advertising, the consumer recognizes that advertising is a partisan representation of a product, not a complete textbook description. To evaluate the product, she must see it and use it.

However, advertising has performed its function if it gets the consumer to "want to try."

The best possible action one could get out of willingness to try is exactly that--trial. But even that doesn't always happen. Let's follow our supermarket customer to the store. (Ten million transactions of the type we are about to describe occur in super-

markets daily.)

THE TRIP TO THE SUPERMARKET

Our housewife arrives by car, has given thought to meal planning for the week and knows from store ads (which she regularly reads) what the special prices are today. She doesn't shop from a list, but knows what she must have, what she'd like to have, and has a few notes in her head about what she wants to look at.

In 22 minutes, she selects 28 items for a total cost of $15 at the check-out counter (Kroger study updated to reflect 1971 income).

Let's look in the cart and ask her a few questions. Six of the items are fresh meat, fruit or vegetables which have required no brand choice. Twenty-two are branded items, most of which she also bought last time. She continues with these, not because of the advertising, but because she has used them before and is satisfied with the brands.

A few of the items are brand switches-- and represent her experiments for the week. Let's go back on one of these-- a new brand of freeze-dried coffee and see what went through her mind and why she made the switch.

THE COFFEE DISPLAY

Over 50 different brand, types and sizes of coffee are displayed in the coffee section. Our shopper normally buys Brand A's regular drip grind coffee. In the past she's tried some other regulars, some instants and some freeze-dried, and now she's heard about new freeze-dried Brand X described in the advertising as "a man's coffee."

Her husband happens to be fussy about coffee, and never really happy with any of the brands of coffee she's tried. So she's going to look at it.

Will Brand X be there? Is it available in the right size? At the right price? In an attractive package? In this particular case, the answer was "yes" on all counts, and she bought it because her husband "may like it..."

This becomes a trial encouraged by advertising. She takes it home and uses it for tomorrow's breakfast. If her husband doesn't like it, next week she'll be back to Brand A. If he doesn't notice any difference, it's also likely she'll be back to Brand A because that's her habitual behavior. But if there is something better about Brand X she'll make a more informed judgment in favor of Brand X next week.

How many people will this same ad interest in buying the product? How many wives have husbands who don't like their coffee? Not many--but it's significant to this consumer, since she solved a problem this way.

HOW ADVERTISING WAS USED

Let's think about what we've just seen here. Has advertising dominated the consumer? Or has the consumer dominated advertising? How has she used advertising? We have seen that:

The consumer does what no advertiser can do for her.
   She limits the amount of information she receives and extracts what is potentially useful to her.

The consumer does what no government agency can do for her.
   She checks the products against her wants, her purchasing power and her family needs and preferences

The consumer does what no retailer or manufacturer can do.
   In a very real sense, she governs the market place by her action of buying what she feels to be relevant to her family life.

The consumer emerges as a careful, intelligent and efficient shopper whose basic criterion in shopping is essentially her satisfaction with products.

Advertising plays an important role in this by directing her attention to possible ways she may achieve even more satisfaction.

The real role of advertising in the consumer's life thus emerges:
   Advertising tells the consumer what's available; offers a parade of suggestions on how she may spend her money; and gives her the freedom to accept or reject these options as she wishes.

Critics of advertising have largely misunderstood this function. They have been so pre-occupied with the role of advertising as a selling tool for the manufacturer that they have failed to see it as an important buying tool for the consumer.

And they have been so concerned with the possibility that advertising can manipulate the consumer that they have failed to see the strength of the consumer.

On the other hand, every advertiser concerned with the success of his advertising has developed a very healthy regard for the consumer. He does a great deal of consumer research. He knows his advertising must reflect the realities of the consumer's life, or the consumer will pay no attention to it. He knows his advertising must reflect the realities of his product, or the consumer will not continue to buy. He knows he can never take the consumer for granted, for there is no such thing as a totally loyal customer. And he knows that in our fast-changing environment, he competes not only with products that are similar to his but with all products, new and old, that compete for the consumer's dollar. He recognizes that a free competitive market place depends on the principle that producers submit themselves to the choice of the public and that buyers can choose for themselves according to their preferences.

In broad strokes, this applies to all types of products and services--tangible and intangible--low cost or high cost--frequently or rarely purchased. Advertising presents the options and the consumer selects in light of the physical, social, psychological and economic realities of his or her own life. If he feels he needs more information, he will seek it out. In the final step, he chooses what he feels suits his needs best.

III. THE SOCIAL CRITICISMS OF ADVERTISING--and how they are modified by this view of how the consumer uses advertising in the market place

Advertising leads people to buy what they don't need

Most people today have incomes and spending power beyond the necessities of life. They "want" as well as "need"? Did our supermarket shopper "need" the coffee she bought or did she want it? And if she "wanted" it, wouldn't the least expensive coffee do? Obviously not. The fact is that spending habits change as income changes and yesterday's "wants" become today's "needs."

Advertising over-persuades

Advertising can only suggest. Our shopper did try a product suggested by advertising, but will never buy it a second time if she perceives it to be inferior.

Advertising will not work effectively if the product is not fully competitive in value--product quality and price considered. Nor will it work effectively if the product does not deliver what the advertising promised.

Advertising is misleading, sometimes false

No reputable advertiser deliberately misleads the consumer. Many advertisers go so far as to conduct tests to make sure that consumers perceive from an ad exactly what was intended and nothing more. Nevertheless, in any field of endeavor, there are some dishonest practitioners. There are laws to cope with this, and in addition, the advertising industry is organized for self-regulation. Moreover, the consumer herself, is a formidable regulator.

Advertising creates a barrier to small, innovative companies who may be able to bring the consumer better products

One need only look at the list of names of such smaller companies and the successes they have had in the market place to realize that the consumer recognizes and supports product quality without concern for whether a company is large or small.

Scott's Liquid Gold
Sara Lee Bakeries
Hudson Pulp and Paper
Chun King
Green Giant
Colt 45 Malt Liquor
Getty Oil

These companies all used advertising to make the consumer aware of their existence and were not handicapped by the fact that they competed with advertising giants.

The consumer, by seeking information

from advertising and choosing to buy or not to buy, encourages competition and forces all companies--large and small--to improve products, bring out new ones, find new ways to use old products and generally to keep the market place up-to-date.

Advertising deals in marginal differences between products

When consumers have discretionary income, they are inevitably looking for values beyond the basic necessities of life. They are looking for improved products, extra utilities, new amenities, even luxuries...

The addition of countless minor product improvements one on top of the other results in constant, steady upgrading in the quality and convenience of consumer goods.

Advertising deals in satisfactions that are irrelevant and of little interest to most people

People buy products, but their purpose is to obtain satisfactions.

It is the difficulty of advertising that in using mass media, advertising has to parade in front of the total population a series of product satisfactions which, for any given product, will interest possibly 20%, but which may be uninteresting and perhaps even boring for the remaining 80%.

Different kinds of people, different generations, different income and educational levels all have different ideas about what are worthwhile satisfactions.

Further, and most important, the range of human satisfactions is very great and those that appeal to one person are viewed with distaste by another.

Industry responds by making a wide range of products to meet every taste. If industry did not do this, and consumers did not have options from which to choose, much of the value and enjoyment of their increased spending power would be lost.

It is interesting to note that the critics of advertising rarely feel that they have been over-persuaded, led to buy something they don't need or can't afford or proved to be irrelevant to them. They assume this happens because they are resistant to advertising while others are vulnerable. They observe that they don't react to advertising much, but believe others do.

The truth is that we are all resistant to advertising that does not relate well to our needs, problems and desires. Yet all of us can and do react to advertising that talks our language and speaks to our personal needs, problems and desires.

If we can recognize that all advertising is not meant to be useful to all consumers, we will have come a long way.

We can then see that when the right ad reaches the right person--the person for whom it is intended--both the manufacturer and the consumer benefit equally.

This in essence, is advertising at work --a balanced view of both the economic and social benefit of advertising and the reason why it has persisted over the years despite its many critics.

But even this does not yet present the full picture of the benefits that flow to the consumer because of advertising. Consider:

Advertising makes possible high-value, low-unit-cost production, which is the single most important factor contributing to low cost for the consumer.....

Some economists argue that advertising raises prices because the end cost to consumer includes the expense of advertising. What they fail to realize is that if a manufacturer were not assured of a market through effective advertising, he could not justify the large capital outlay required for large-scale manufacturing. Without this, he could not offer the product to consumers at the low cost associated with mass production.

Advertising encourages the introduction of new and improved products in the market place. Without advertising, how would the manufacturer bring his new product to consumer attention? And how much time might elapse before consumers were aware that their options in buying were widened, and perhaps improved?

Advertising makes it possible for consumers to find new products they're interested in at their local retail store. No intelligent retailer will invest his limited capital in an untried new product unless he has some reason to believe that it will move off his shelf. If he knows that an effort will be made through advertising to encourage initial consumer trial, he is willing to stock the product and give it a chance to prove itself.

Advertising makes brand name shopping possible, which is one of the most effective consumer protection mechanisms ever devised. In his brand name, the manufacturer puts his reputation on the line and assures consumers of both the quality and uniformity of his product, whenever or wherever they shop.

Advertising supports our free press, our magazine industry and our broadcast industry. Without advertising, these communications media would never have reached their present level of growth, their present low cost to consumers, and their present importance in consumers' lives.

——— ——— ———

Consumers do not give much thought to these relationships, yet they benefit from them every day in genuine ways.

The point we want to make is that advertising is of service both to business and the consumer, and it is erroneous to think of advertising's value only in terms of business.

Further, there is a built-in discipline in the market place that arises from the interaction of business and the consumer. A manufacturer cannot succeed with advertising unless he understands his consumers and satisfies their desires. If he does not do this the consumer will not pay attention to his advertising or buy his products.

It is fortunate that this is so, because the sheer volume of retail activity in this country--which runs into hundreds of millions (and perhaps billions) of transactions every day--makes the market virtually unpoliceable on any other basis.

No government agency, no matter what its budget or number of employees, can possibly "protect" the consumer on this magnitude of transactions. Only the combination of an informed and critical customer, and an honest businessman can possibly do it. And fortunately, that is the way it usually is.

One further point. Advertising is not a static institution. It evolves as society evolves. It is not the same force today that it was yesterday. And tomorrow, we may be sure, it will be different still.

Its discipline, though, will remain the same--to serve the public--to serve the consumer--because only in this way can it justify its existence.

DISCUSSION QUESTIONS

1. Consider the following two statements:
"Advertising has dominated the consumer."
"The consumer has dominated advertising."
Does one come closer to the truth than
the other?

2. "Advertising encourages the introduction of new and improved products in
the marketplace." Discuss how a consumer may benefit genuinely from this
relationship in his everyday living.

Reprinted by permission from JOURNAL OF ADVERTISING; Vol. 2. No. 2, pp. 32-34.

I-2

ARE GRACE SLICK AND TRICIA NIXON COX THE SAME PERSON?

John E. O'Toole

Stop and think. Have you ever seen them together?

Absurd as the question may seem, it points up a dilemma faced in agency creative departments today whenever we try to make advertising out of the inadequate information we often receive.

Say you're a copywriter trying to reach, interest and persuade a certain kind of prospect. Here is the definition of that prospect you might receive from the combined intelligence of the client, the media and your research department.

A woman, 25 to 35 age group. Family income over $15,000. Urban. Working. College graduate. Let's say a college like Finch in New York. 2 to 3 members of household. White. Probably comes from an upper-income family herself with professional or executive father who belongs to Republican Party.

Okay. That's far more information than you'd normally get, but let's err on the side of the devil. We have that prospect pretty well defined now, right?

Sure. It's Tricia Nixon Cox, married

in a beautiful White House ceremony and exemplifying the straight life.

It's also Grace Slick, of Jefferson Airplane, who isn't into marriage but gave birth two years ago to a daughter who was originally named god, but whom Miss Slick now refers to as China.

So there's your prospect. And there's the kind of non-information we've been working with for far too long. As a result, I think this industry has made advertising that's not as effective as it could be. Furthermore, and here I crawl recklessly out on the limb, it's contributed to an erosion of public confidence in advertising that could endanger our livelihoods.

Because I think that the most serious threat to advertising is the diminishment of confidence, belief and, indeed, acceptance of advertising on the part of the public to whom we speak.

Not that I believe consumers were ever truly enamored with advertising. But the magnitude of their negative feelings today and the vocal expression of them can't be shrugged off. You've seen the numbers. Starch finds more than 65% of their sample believing that advertising makes people buy things they don't need,

45% maintaining that "most advertising nowadays tries to deceive people rather than inform them."

Lou Harris had 21% of his 1956 sample expressing "a great deal of confidence in advertising leadership." Last year it was down to 13%.

And ORC found 47% of the people with a low approval of business and advertising back in 1965. Last summer it was up to 60%.

Meanwhile, almost anyone who wants to hang out a shingle as a consumerist can attract an immediate following by attacking advertising. And CROC, the Committee for Rejection of Obnoxious Commercials, is in its third year with an ever-growing membership.

Anyone who still sees the consumer as a passive and static set of demographics is reading these events the way General Custer read his intelligence reports.

It's this frame of mind, this set of attitudes, that's at the core of the more tangible troubles besetting us today. For without an increasing rejection of our activities and growing acceptance of theirs, the lobbyists for government regulation of advertising and the opportunistic consumerists and the anti-advertising press would have no platform from which to weave their fantasies about the "manipulated consumer."

Furthermore, I think that the blame for this sad set of circumstances can be laid at no other doorstep than our own. The kind of thinking that terminates in the conclusion that Tricia Nixon Cox and Grace Slick are identical is the kind of thinking that's making people laugh at, curse at or yawn at much of the advertising they see today.

Where did we go wrong? Take a look at some fairly recent historical events that bewildered us so at the time.

Consider them in terms of what they were leading to: the Revolution of the individual.

The fifties and sixties in our country saw society become increasingly depersonalized. As the population grew, urban areas congested. Half of us jammed ourselves into less than 1% of the land mass. And we found ourselves more and more part of a crowd.

On the highways, in grocery stores, on commuter trains, in front of a TV set, the feeling kept growing that you, as an individual, were becoming less important. Less real.

Computers came along to reduce us all to numbers instead of names. And by the sixties, there was a growing national sickness that was loosely labeled "identity crisis." The inevitable reaction was already taking place. People began dressing and growing hair and finding non-work activities to say something about themselves. They began forming liberation groups: black, feminist, gay, consumer, anything. They began sounding off.

They began saying something in their responses to mass communications. Television viewing started to drop off among the generation that had grown up with the tube. Mass circulation magazines began to have serious problems and, one by one, they all died. But meanwhile, special interest and life style publications like *Sports Illustrated*, *Sunset*, *Playboy*, *New York* and *TV Guide* flourished.

What people were saying was simply this: "I'm not part of a crowd, I'm a person. Pay some attention to me and what I need. Or else." They were saying it to governments, to industries, to advertising. But advertising didn't listen. For the most part, it continued to look at people in terms of demographics rather than as individuals united by common attitudes or lifestyles or perceptions of themselves.

It continued to discount their intelligence in favor of some vast common denominator. It continued to shout at a crowd rather than talk to persons.

Some of the Pavlovian techniques of television advertising made sales, but at the expense of that credibility, that acceptance which is the soil in which advertising flourishes.

It was a kind of strip-mining for which we're beginning to pay the price now. And the price--should it turn into popular support of government regulation--is frighteningly high.

But it doesn't have to go that far. Not if we all go right to where the problems started--the individual--and find our new opportunities there.

We must have research data that lets us adapt our advertising to the Revolution of the individual, shows us how to approach our prospect on a one-to-one basis, helps us communicate with persons instead of people.

Some advertising agencies--Foote, Cone & Belding being one--are placing more and more emphasis on segmentation research. By dividing that audience up, not necessarily by age and income but in terms of certain basic attitudes they share, you arrive at a much more human, personal understanding of your prospect.

Secondly, we're all doing a lot more group sessions with consumers. Focus groups have long been maligned by research professionals because they're quantitatively inadequate and results are unprojectable. All that's probably true. But group sessions are invaluable, nonetheless. They are personal dialogues with consumers. About products, about concepts, about advertising.

We've also found it beneficial to put good researchers right in the creative groups to let them become working partners in the creative process.

But the most critical area--and the one in which a new approach can do most to mend that tattered public acceptance-- is in the nature of our ads and commercials.

The basic attitude toward the consumer from which the idea starts has to be rooted in the Revolution of the individual. The people who create the messages have to do so with a single human being in mind, with an understanding of that person's attitudes and way of life, with a regard for his or her sense and sensibilities.

What we don't need is the kind of implicit contempt for the consumer's intelligence that will substitute white tornadoes for human communication. That will seriously pose situations like a man who doesn't recognize his old girl friend because she's wearing a new Cross-Your-Heart Bra. That will bludgeon the masses into submission with meaningless mnemonic devices rather than communicate in personal terms with another human being.

What we do need is more recognition of that paradoxical truth that guided the great communicators from Homer to Robert Frost--that the way to move millions is to talk to one single person.

With the kind of information we work with today, it's difficult. But it's being done. In several ways.

One way is to recognize that a single product may have different benefits depending on the life-style of the individual you're addressing.

An advertiser that brings this off beautifully is Levis. Honig, Cooper & Harrington speaks personally about different benefits of Levis jeans to totally different persons when they advertise in *Seventeen* and when they appear in farm publications.

But sometimes a product is so simple it has only one benefit. And that benefit is not, in itself, associated with a particular life-style or attitude. That single message can still be executed in a way that clearly tells a certain person that an advertiser is talking directly to her.

For instance, every ad for Kotex tells exactly the same product story and promises the same benefit: confidence. But confidence is perceived in different ways by different women. Consequently, the model, wardrobe, situation and mood are not the same in *McCall's* as they are in *Cosmopolitan* or, of course, in *Essence*.

It can be done in television, too. From commercial to commercial, Dial soap executions show different human beings how a single benefit of a single product has meaning and importance in each of their lives.

But quite often the nature of the product or its distribution or its budget make either of those personal approaches unfeasible. That's when the writer is really tested and where too many fail.

Two commercials that clearly didn't fail are N.W. Ayer's spot for the Bell System's Long Distance Service called "Heart-to-Heart Talk" and one for Hallmark by Foote, Cone & Belding called "What A Day." The latter has appeared only on the *Hallmark Hall of Fame* but has achieved wide recognition nonetheless.

Both of those spots found a common denominator, but it wasn't demographic. And it wasn't an irrelevant gimmick. Being unable to segment the mass audience, the writers made a personal statement to another human being that struck a chord because it was so human, so true or so important. And when the chord is struck in one, the vibrations reverberate in millions.

Those writers realized another truth that's so simple and yet so widely ignored: that advertising isn't about products, it's about a person's life and how a product can fit into that life to make it better.

This is advertising designed to get into someone's heart not under his skin. It's advertising that helps build a business rather than make a one-time sale.

And it's advertising that people like. But I advocate it not solely for that reason. I think this kind of attitude toward the consumer is now essential for the survival of our business. Because advertising that people like will soon be the only kind of advertising they'll stand for.

DISCUSSION QUESTION

---

1. "Advertising isn't about products, it's about a person's life and how a product can fit into that life to make it better." Do you believe that this is a practical guideline for effective communication in the case of advertising agencies? Discuss.

I-3

WHEN ADVERTISING TALKS TO EVERYONE

Fairfax Cone

When publicly contemplating the future of almost anything, there is nothing safer than to see in it all manner of drastic change, even to the point of disaster. Then, if trouble comes, the viewer with alarm can smugly regard the situation that he has predicted and be called a wise soothsayer. If, on the other hand, the prophet of crack-up and breakdown turns out to be wrong, no one is hurt, and he need only say that his timing was off or that vastly changed circumstances made the difference. I am going to take the long chance.

If we are indeed entering an era of news monopoly in terms of both national and world news, it seems more than likely that regional and local news services actually will be increased. The development of small-town and suburban community newspapers at a time when many big-city newspapers have ceased publication has been a phenomenon of the last two or three decades. Now, with local cable television coming to communities of all sizes, it can be predicted that this new emphasis on local news and interests will be intensified.

A recent broadcasting event in Newport Beach, California, illustrates this.

The cable television station there invited thirty candidates for public offices ranging from the U.S. Senate to the local village council to tell their stories in terms of their own interests. All accepted with the result that hundreds of citizens of this small southern California seaside community for the first time saw candidates in the light of their own problems.

In much the same way, I believe we are entering a time when much advertising also will become more local and more meaningful. Advertising aimed precisely at what might be termed need-groups promises a new and welcome relevancy.

When advertising tries to talk to everyone, the result is no different than it is when any other form of communication is aimed at the largest possible audience. The days of yellow journalism at the turn of the century are an example. The heyday of the great mass magazines in the 1950s is another. Neither could last, for audiences tire of unchanging fare, and either break up into separate interest groups or find new sources for their enlightenment and their entertainment. Both of these developments are occurring in broadcasting at this moment, and their effect on advertising will be profound.

15

One of the unhappy concomitants of today's television, with its enormous time and production costs for advertising, has been the unwillingness of many major advertisers to depart from commercial routines that have proved to be successful economically, no matter how wearisome they may be to millions of viewers. It is a demonstrable fact that one's reaction to almost any advertising message breaks down into two parts: the form in which the message is presented and the promise itself. The result is that the form may be, and often is, a subject of ridicule (e.g., the white tornado that blows through the kitchen or the eye-winking plumber who clears a clogged drain with nothing more than a sprinkling of powder that is available from your nearest friendly grocer), while the proposition that is made for the product involved is totally accepted.

If this sounds impossible, or even improbable, I can only explain it in terms of noises to which one becomes accustomed to the point of not hearing them at all, while a special sound of much lesser intensity comes through loud and clear. However, this is hardly an excuse for the foolishness that makes so many commercial minutes seem ugly and interminable.

The trouble lies in the lack of creative ability in the people in advertising agencies and production studios, and among the advertisers, who are caught between two deadly dilemmas. One is to follow the leader with the implausible dramas of fun and games at the sink or in the bathroom or laundry; the other is to try anything at all that is different--for that reason alone. Of the two, it is questionable which is harder to take if one pays attention.

Both, however, may well be headed for the discard, for paying attention to the commercials is no longer a requirement of the television experience. In the beginning it was said, and it was probably true, that viewers gladly accepted the advertising as a reasonable price of admission to the shows they watched. But the audience has become more sophisticated. There has developed a little mechanism in the brain of almost every one of us that can automatically shut off our attention to a point where only certain sounds come through: mostly product names and promises and pertinent details of unusual services.

To be sure, there are exceptions to the general low interest in commercial messages. Some are full of fun and the fun is to the point. Others, such as commercials for many food and household products, present demonstrations that help the homemaker with her relentless job. Still others substitute dramatic facts for throaty claims for automobile tires and batteries and insurance, etc.

The changes that one can foresee in advertising in the next few years, and that should make much of it more attractive and useful for everyone concerned, are becoming apparent in an about-face in advertising philosophy that will bring it into line with growing interest in the consumer as an object of concern and respect and not a faceless, nearly mindless purchasing unit. To say this another way, I believe the impersonality is going out of advertising much as I believe that it is going to be replaced in business for the very good reason that this works both ways: Customer loyalty simply cannot be maintained by an impersonal supplier, and business and advertising must, in the long run, depend on that loyalty. That they must also earn it is the reason for the inevitable changes.

The alternative is the complete breakdown of an imperfect system. The imperfection may be the result of growth and standardization, and the temporary subjugation of the individual during a period of great economic change and concentration of power. Whatever the reason, no one can doubt that as a nation we have arrived at a time when skepticism may be our most outstanding characteristic. Viet Nam is only one reason for this. Rightly or wrongly, the maturing generation believes that we have been lied to and manipulated by business and government, and even in our educational and legal systems, and the young men and women who supply this generation with its conviction and strength see advertising as one of the worst sins of a venal establishment. Nor is this a question particularly of dishonesty or sharp practice. Unhappily, these evils are largely taken for granted. The overriding objection is to the mass appeal of advertising at a time when all the emphasis our young people can muster is on individuality. There is a thing called life-style that simply cannot be dictated by anyone--advertisers least of all.

This will unquestionably mean more special-interest publications, both magazines and community news organs (either printed or electronically reproduced), with special-interest advertising. Still, the biggest change will probably be in television and television advertising, where the messages for many products and services will be delivered almost as professional buyers' guides by a nationwide corps of competent local authorities who will evaluate and recommend products and services according to their own standards and experience. Products of only general interest (or those lacking interest at any given moment, such as analgesics) will continue to be advertised over the networks in national news and sports programs and the more popular comedy and variety and dramatic hours.

Despite considerable speculation to the contrary, it seems unlikely that either pay television or the cassette will mean the end of the big variety or dramatic programs or the ace news commentators as we have come to expect these from the networks. For one

thing, entertainment that one must pay for must be a good deal better than entertainment that is free, and this may be hard to come by for more than a few hours in any week, for the costs will be considerable. Also, news cannot be canned; it must be contemporaneous. On the other hand, hundreds of independent cable television stations are going to compete, and successfully, I believe, with the run-of-mine programs by offering a conglomerate of special interest features for limited but extremely receptive audiences.

Cable television was introduced as a means of establishing or improving physical reception in remote areas, and this it has done very successfully. While no one knows precisely what its effect will be in metropolitan centers, where reception is satisfactory for the most part and where there is already a choice of channels and programs, the likelihood is that it will become not so much an extension of television as we now know it, but an essentially new medium.

It is not difficult to imagine the attraction of a station that performs service to the community by broadcasting purely local news and commentary and an almost unlimited number of programs of unique interest. The key factor, of course, is the freedom of the cable station operator from the demands for a large audience by any advertiser, for his audience is made up of paid subscribers. Such advertisers as there may be, and I expect there will be many, will be satisfied with any reasonable, and reasonably priced, audience whose special interest they share.

This, then, is where the greatest change in advertising is likely to take place. In recent years, most large advertisers increasingly have aimed their messages at the largest available audiences at the lowest possible cost per thousand. This led to the disastrous circulation races among the mass magazines, the strain of which caused the demise of half a dozen of them, and a gradual diminution in the number of daily newspapers. Neither could compete successfully with a medium that was wholly advertiser-supported and adored by advertiser and public alike. This was in television's long honeymoon stage. Today many an advertiser is beginning to wonder whether the large audiences are really worth the total expenditures involved, no matter how low the cost per thousand. The questions arise partly out of a desire to save money and so increase profits and partly out of a determination to talk only to one's most logical prospects. Clearly, such a change in advertising strategy should dictate a much more thoughtful and much less blatant use of all advertising media.

It is safe to say that television is today the principal source of news as well as entertainment for the majority of American families. If this presaged a monopoly of either one by a monolithic television system, I would be fearful of the result. But I think the imminence of community cable television negates the possibility, in the very same way that it promises advertising that is less dictated and confined by formula.

It is necessary here to remember that all advertising is not alike either in its making or intention. Manufacturers' advertising, for the most part, an-nounces innovations and product changes and improvements, and this advertising appears mostly in magazines and on television and radio. The advertising of retailers, which is concerned primarily with the values in those products in terms of style, size, price, etc., makes up the bulk of newspaper advertising, except for want ads.

The changes that I foresee will have little or no effect upon the division of advertising between the various media. It should stay much as it is, with only some diversion of special-interest advertising from the general magazines to the growing list of special-interest publications.

On the other hand, I believe that advertising may be greatly changed by still another factor. With two-way communication established between receivers and cable stations, whereby subscribers may dial requests for any information under the sun, which will be available by computer, it is unlikely that consumer reports will not be included. No service could be more natural or have greater effect upon advertising. For the reply to the subscriber's query and the advertising that floats freely through the air on the same subject must allow no disparity. Both must serve the recipient in his own best interest.

This is something that advertisng has always promised to do. But the promise has not always been kept. In large measure, it may now be.

DISCUSSION QUESTIONS

---

1. Discuss the changes that have taken place in the television advertising audience in the last few years and the changes that are likely to take place in the foreseeable future.

2. Do you believe that special-interest publications will gradually replace mass media to the extent that television will diminish in value as a powerful communication medium? Discuss

From the AAAA STUDY ON CONSUMER JUDGMENT OF ADVERTISING, 1965, 4A's, 200 Park Ave. N.Y. Reprinted by permission of William Weilbacher, who is Executive Vice President of Dancer Fitzgerald Sample, Inc.

I-4

CONSUMER RESPONSE TO ADVERTISEMENTS

William M. Weilbacher

What are the reactions of the public when actually confronted with a daily diet of advertisements? There are three major findings in this study concerning how consumers respond to individual advertisements.

1. Consumers do *not* pay attention to all the advertisements to which they are physically exposed. The evidence is that a great many of the consumer's physical opportunities for exposure to advertising do not result in the engagement of his attention.

2. When an advertisement *does* engage the consumer's attention, it is very likely not to strike him as *annoying* or *offensive*, but it is not very likely to strike him as *enjoyable* or *informative*, either.

3. Advertisements which offend some, may annoy others, but these same advertisements may also inform some and even entertain others. We found no unanimity among consumers about individual advertisements: one consumer's annoyance is another's entertainment, another's information, and another's offense. Furthermore, many consumers may pay no attention to these very same advertisements.

Let us examine each of these major findings in more detail.

CONSUMER ATTENTION TO ADVERTISEMENTS

In seeking to measure consumer response to advertisements, our purpose was to determine how the consumer reacts to specific, individual advertisements. In a broader context, we wanted to know whether consumers may be complacent about *advertising* in general but indignant about *particular ads*. We wanted to know whether they like advertis*ing* but dislike advertise*ments*.

Mr. Cohen has reported how we tried to find out. Respondents used a hand counter to record those advertisements --from magazines, newspapers, radio, and television--which made a conscious impression on them in the course of an assigned half-day period.

Further, whenever the respondent saw or heard an advertisement that he considered annoying, enjoyable, informative or offensive, according to the detailed definitions supplied to him, he made a special note of it on the advertising record cards provided for this purpose.

So, we have a record of the advertisements in four major media which engage the consumer's attention. In addition, there is a further record of those advertisements which he considers annoying or offensive, and informative or enjoyable.

It should again be emphasized that there is no necessary connection between the data produced by this new procedure and the sales effectiveness of advertising. Our sole concern in this procedure was to measure attitudinal response to advertisements as advertisements. And of major importance, too, was our desire to provide the consumer a natural and easy way to pick out the offensive and annoying advertisements he found.

What reactions do consumers have to individual advertisements?

First, the average consumer reports having seen or heard about 38 advertisements during his counting period. Since each consumer counts for only half a day, this figure can be doubled--76 advertisements--to estimate the number of ads which might be counted in an entire day. (Except where noted below, the half day figures are presented, since they represent the direct information from any respondent.)

These counter totals tell us very clearly that consumers do not consciously react to a very high proportion of the advertisements to which they are actually physically exposed. The attraction of attention--as expressed by pressing the counter--occurs considerably fewer times in a day than there are physical opportunities. Apparently, the consumer has developed defenses against many opportunities to attend to advertisements; he has trained himself to pay attention *only* under certain limited sets of circumstances.

We can examine these data on several

demographic dimensions. For example, Exhibit 1 shows the number of ads counted on the basis of sex and age. While women count more ads than do men,

Exhibit 1

ADS COUNTED BY SEX AND AGE

All people	38
By sex	
Men	35
Women	40
By age	
18-24 years	34
25-34 years	39
35-49 years	42
50-64 years	38
65 years and over	31

and while both younger and older people count fewer ads than do others, these variations are not of great magnitude. When consumers' ad counts are analyzed on the basis of the individual's favorability toward advertising (Exhibit 2) again there is not a great deal of

Exhibit 2

ADS COUNTED BY FAVORABILITY TO ADVERTISING

All People	38
Favorable to Advertising	37
Unfavorable to Advertising	44
Mixed	37
Indifferent	37

variation.* It is interesting to note, however, that people who are unfavorable to advertising tend to count some-

---

*While there is relatively little variation in total counting among *groups* of consumers, the counts reported for *individuals* do vary considerably--from 0 to over 100.

what more ads than average. There is a suggestion here that people unfavorable to advertising tend to have rabbit ears: they seem to be somewhat more sensitive to the ads to which they are exposed.

To repeat, the major conclusions about the counting of advertisements are 1) *many physical opportunities for exposure to advertising are missed by consumers,* and 2) there is relatively little variation in the counting of advertisements among different demographic groups of consumers.

CONSUMER REACTION TO ADVERTISEMENTS

To measure the reactions of consumers to specific, individual advertisements, we turned to the data on those counted ads which were further categorized as annoying, enjoyable, informative, or offensive.

Our respondents singled out an average of six advertisements in their half day period for such further categorization. That is to say, of the 38 ads which are counted by the average respondent, about 16% are considered annoying, enjoyable, informative, or offensive; 84% are judged to be in none of these categories, and are counted by our respondents without further comment.

The fact that 84% of the counted advertisements were not further categorized does *not* mean they made no impact on consumers. Quite the reverse--*every counted advertisement, by definition, has crossed the threshold of consumer awareness.* (Donald Kanter will report below on an effort to learn more about why these advertisements are not further categorized.)

How do the 16% of the (counted) advertisements which *are* further categorized

break down into the four categories? As shown in Exhibit 3, of those advertisements which were further categorized, a strong majority were seen as

Exhibit 3

BREAKDOWN OF CATEGORIZED ADVERTISEMENTS

Average total ads counted	38
Not categorized - 32 ads - 84%	
Categorized - 6 ads - 16%	
Annoying - 1.4 ads	
Offensive - 0.3 ads	
Enjoyable - 2.1 ads	
Informative - 2.2 ads	

either informative or enjoyable: an average of 2.2 were called informative and 2.1 enjoyable. The average consumer considered 1.4 advertisements annoying and 0.3 advertisements offensive. (These counts, it should be remembered, were for half a day.) *Thus, when we use the 9,325 advertisements singled out by our respondents as a new base of 100%, 23% of these ads were considered annoying, 36% enjoyable, 36% informative, and 5% offensive.*

So, we see that when an advertisement *does* engage the consumer's attention enough to make him click the counter, it is very likely not to strike him as annoying or offensive, but it is not very likely to strike him as enjoyable or informative, either. Overall, among the rather small group of ads actually categorized, the odds are better than 2 1/2 to one that the consumer will be informed or entertained, rather than offended or annoyed.

DIVERSE REACTIONS TO ADVERTISEMENTS

We have seen that of the categorized advertisements, 23% were seen as annoying, 36% were called enjoyable, 36% informative, and 5% offensive. *What about variations in this pattern by product category?* The 9,325 categorized ads were divided into 78 standard industry product classifications. In making this classification, we attempted to develop relatively broad categories for product classifications where relatively few advertising dollars are expended, and more detailed and sensitive groupings for product classifications where relatively more advertising dollars are spent.

Of the 78 different classifications, a total of five produced more annoying and offensive advertisements than enjoyable and informative ones. Let us review these five product groups, shown in Exhibit 4.

Exhibit 4

ANALYSIS OF NEGATIVELY CATEGORIZED PRODUCT GROUPS

	Annoy- ing	Offen- sive	Enjoy- able	Infor- mative
All Advertise- ments	23%	5%	36%	36%
Liquor	13	56	23	8
Soaps & Detergents	55	4	21	20
Dental Supplies & Mouthwashes	47	3	23	27
Depilatories & Deodorants	45	6	20	29
Cigarettes	37	19	36	8

Liquor

The liquor classification generated an abnormally high proportion of advertisements categorized as *offensive*, although relatively few liquor ads were seen as *annoying*. This stems basically from the fact that *people who consider liquor advertising offensive are largely those who believe the product should not be advertised at all*. For contrast, beer advertisements generate only 19% *offensive* categorizations (still above average), only an average level of *annoying* ads, and a very high (54%) proportion of *enjoyable* advertisements.

Dental Supplies
Soaps & Detergents
Depilatories & Deodorants

While a high proportion of *annoying* advertisements are generated by each of these products, *offensive* ads are at about average levels. The balance of the advertisements for these classifications are split about evenly between *enjoyable* and *informative*.

Cigarettes

The cigarette product group generates an above-average level of *both annoying* and *offensive* advertisements, an average level of *enjoyable* ads, and very few *informative* ads. It should be noted that this study was conducted *after* the release of the Surgeon General's report on cigarette smoking.

To repeat, these five classifications are the only ones which, in this study, yielded more ads characterized by consumers as *annoying* or *offensive*, than ads characterized by consumers as *enjoyable* or *informative*. What about the remaining 73 classifications? Space does not permit treatment of all 73, but let us examine five of them, drawn to represent products for which there are heavy advertising expenditures. These are shown in Exhibit 5.

Canned & Packaged Foods
Major Appliances

Both these categories generate a much

Exhibit 5

ANALYSIS OF SELECTED PRODUCT GROUPS OF HEAVY ADVERTISING EXPENDITURE

	Annoying	Offensive	Enjoyalbe	Informative
All Advertisements	23%	5%	36%	36%
Canned and Packaged Foods	9	2	59	30
Major Appliances	7	1	13	79
Gasoline and Oil	23	2	20	55
Toilet Soaps Medicines and Proprietaries	38	5	17	40

higher level of *informative* and *enjoyable* advertisements than do other product groups. Of particular interest are the very low levels of *annoying* and *offensive* ads in both these categories. Canned and packaged food advertising produces a high proportion of *enjoyable* ads, and the appliance category generates a high proportion of *informative* ads.

Gasoline & Oil
Toilet Soaps

Gasoline and Oil advertising generates a very high level of *informative* advertisements. Toilet Soap advertising produces a very high level of *enjoyable* advertisements. Both these categories are at or below, the average for *annoying* and *offensive* advertisements.

Medicines and Proprietaries

This is a classification frequently alleged to produce more than its share of advertising which offends. The data show that Medicines and Proprietaries produce a considerable, and above average amount of *annoying* advertisements, only an average amount of *offensive* ads, and a relatively large amount of *informative* ads. However, advertisements for this product group are considerably less likely to be categorized as *enjoyable* than the average of all advertisements.

The most important point to be made from this analysis of individual product classifications is that there are no blacks and whites in consumer response to advertising from particular product classifications.

✓ While the Canned and Packaged Foods classification enjoys a substantial amount of enjoyable and informative advertising, there are ads from this product group which are offensive to some consumers, and annoying to others.

✓ Medicines and Proprietaries produce more than their share of annoying advertising. At the same time, in this product category, there are advertisements which some people consider enjoyable and others think are informative.

Thus, there is no ground for any particular product group to be monolithically tarred with the brush of offensiveness. Truly, the evaluation of advertising depends upon the eye of the beholder. What is one man's annoyance is another's information. What is one man's offense is another's enjoyment. And, as we have seen earlier, by far the greatest proportion of advertisements which make a conscious impresion on the consumer are considered to be in *none* of these categories.

This extremely important finding is further underlined when data for individual brands within product groups are analyzed. I do not plan to take you into the detail of brand-by-brand analysis here. But I can summarize for you the findings in these product categories which generated enough individual brand responses for meaningful analysis. The pattern which emerges is the same as for product groups: *There is no uniformly negative or positive response to advertisements for individual brands.* The annoying, offensive, entertaining, informative pattern does vary from brand to brand, but the general pattern is

that to some a brand's advertisements may be annoying, to others enjoyable, to others informative, and to still others offensive. And many consumers may take no note at all of the very same advertisements.

Having now seen *how* the public reacts to advertisements themselves, let us turn to an analysis of *why* they react to ads the way they do.

DISCUSSION QUESTIONS

1. Do the major findings of the study imply that most advertising makes no impact on consumers? What would be a reliable measure of impact of an advertisement? Discuss

2. "The evaluation of advertising depends upon the eye of the beholder." Discuss the significance of this conclusion for an advertiser who seeks the consumer's attention.

From the AAAA STUDY ON CONSUMER JUDGMENT OF ADVERTISING, 1965, 4A's, 200 Park Ave. N.Y. Reprinted by permission of Prof. Kanter, who is Chairman of Marketing at the University of Southern California.

I-5

WHY CONSUMERS REACT TO ADVERTISEMENTS AS THEY DO

Donald Kanter

Having gathered information on the relative proportions of advertisements consumers classify as annoying, enjoyable, informative, or offensive--or none of these--the research team wanted to go beyond these numbers in their understanding of the ways in which Americans react to the advertisements they see and hear. We wanted to know *why* people classified advertisements the way they did.

To achieve this further understanding, consumers were asked to tell, in their own words, what there was about the advertisements they categorized that made the ads either annoying, enjoyable, informative, or offensive. In addition, through interviewer probing, richer and more detailed responses were gathered. The interviewer did this by turning to each recorded advertisement in the respondent's advertising record book, and queried the respondent on the reasons behind his classification.

This report reviews the reasons given by consumers for favorable and unfavorable categorization, discusses an approach to understanding why advertise-

ments are not categorized at all, and relates favorable and unfavorable categorizations to product usage and brand attitude.

FAVORABLE CATEGORIZATIONS

Let us start by examining the favorable categories.

First, what were the reasons why consumers classified advertisements as *informative*? These informative advertisements account for 5.8% of those which consumers counted, and 36% of those categorized.

Exhibit 1 shows pointedly, as might be expected, that advertisements which teach something about the product, its functions, or its price is the leading reason for advertisements being classified as informative.

Nevertheless, some other reasons are volunteered by consumers in their explanation of why they consider certain advertisements to be *informative*.

√ Advertising which creates personal

25

Exhibit 1

REASONS WHY CERTAIN ADVERTISEMENTS
WERE CONSIDERED.....*INFORMATIVE*

<u>Learned something from the advertising</u> (About the product/about the function/about price)	87%
<u>Created personal involvement</u> (With situation being advertised/with product's problem-solving advantages)	34
<u>The advertising was truthful</u> (I know the product/the product lives up to claims/it was straight- forward)	27
<u>Other answers</u>	2
"It was <u>just informative</u>" or no further answer	12
	162%*

*Percents add to more than 100% due to multiple mentions

involvement, which creates a "you-are-there" feeling, is also considered informative.

√ Advertising which is considered to be truthful is also categorized by some as informative. People square the contents of the advertisement with their first-hand knowledge of how the product or brand really functions.

This everyday life comparison of advertising claims with relevant personal experience is a fact of consumer life continually revealed in this study.

What are the reasons why certain advertisements were considered by consumers to be *enjoyable*? The advertisements in this category constitute 5.5%

Exhibit 2

REASONS WHY CERTAIN ADVERTISEMENTS
WERE CONSIDERED.....*ENJOYABLE*

<u>Enjoyed advertising treatment itself</u> (Music/attractiveness/humor/actors)	65%
<u>Enjoyed identification with advertising situation</u> (Person in advertisement was like me/had my problems/it made me want to use the product now)	21
<u>Enjoyed product advertised</u> (It's my kind of product/I use the product)	20
<u>Enjoyed the advertising information</u> (Learned how to use product/ learned new features)	9
<u>Enjoyed straight-forward presentation</u> (No exaggeration/low-key story)	8
<u>Other answers</u>	11
"It was <u>just enjoyable</u>" or no further answer	10
	144%*

Percents add to more than 100% due to multiple mentions.

of those counted, and 36% of those categorized.

As shown in Exhibit 2, several reasons stand out:

√ The advertising treatment itself--music, appearance, humor, the actors--is the major reason why certain advertisements were considered enjoyable. The way in which the advertising story is told thus can be a source of enjoyment to consumers.

√ The phenomenon of personal identification with the advertising situation can be enjoyable to some consumers. (Recall that this was an element of informative advertising also.)

√ Some consumers classified advertisements as enjoyable because the advertising squared with their knowledge of the product.

UNFAVORABLE CATEGORIZATIONS

So much for the advertisements which consumers feel favorably about. Let us turn to the reasons which lead consumers to have negative reactions to advertisements.

Why were certain advertisements considered to be *annoying*? The annoying category accounted for 3.7% of the total number of advertisements counted, and 23% of those categorized.

As Exhibit 3 shows, the most important reason advertisements are classified as *annoying* is that they contradict experience with or knowledge about the product. This means that consumers feel some advertisements are false, have misleading claims, or exaggerate. The consumer is vigilant in his comparison of advertisements with his version of reality.

Some advertisements were also considered to be annoying because of their advertising treatment, some because consumers felt they were intellectually

Exhibit 3
REASONS WHY CERTAIN ADVERTISEMENTS
WERE CONSIDERED.....*ANNOYING*

Contradicts experience with or knowledge about the product (Disbelief/false, misleading claims/exaggeration)	37%
Advertising treatment itself (Too loud, long/announcer, actors/ music/irritating, boring confusing)	33
Intellectually unsettling or unworthy (It's absurd, silly, stupid/ it talked down to me/trivial, meaningless same sales points as other ads)	25
Repitition of ad (Seen it too often)	20
Moral reservations (About the product/not for children	10
Other answers	8
"It was just annoying" or no further answer	5
	138%*

* Percents add to more than 100% due to multiple mentions

unsettling or unworthy, and some because of continued repetition of the same ad.

Note that among the annoying advertising treatments are some which can also serve as a source of enjoyment; announcers' voices and music are examples.

Fairly low on the list are those advertisements which a few people feel should not be seen by children or should not be advertised at all.

Exhibit 4 shows the reasons why certain advertisements are considered *offensive*. These constitute less than 1% of all advertisements counted, and only 5% of those categorized.

There are, however, some clear-cut reasons why consumers put them in this category. Just as in advertisements which are considered annoying, the contradiction of experience with or knowledge about the product plays the biggest role. Once again, we see the vigilant consumer comparing advertising claims with his own life experiences. Not readily fooled, he uses

his experience with products as a major criterion for his evaluation of advertisements. Exaggeration and untruths can annoy and/or offend him.

Moral reservations about the product class and a product's potential harmful effect on children are important reasons for offensive categorizations. (Note that these were relatively unimportant reasons in appraising annoying ads.) Also, some advertisements are so intellectually or emotionally unsettling, or are so frequently repeated, that some consumers categorize them as offensive, rather than the less severe annoying.

UNCATEGORIZED ADVERTISEMENTS

The research team was also interested in why advertisements were not categorized at all. Accordingly, a pilot study was conducted, using a subsample of 210 consumers.

These respondents performed a slightly

Exhibit 4

REASONS WHY CERTAIN ADVERTISEMENTS
WERE CONSIDERED.....*OFFENSIVE*

Contradicts experience with or knowledge about the product (False/disbelief/exaggeration)	34%
Moral reservations (About product class)	28
Children should not see it (Bad for children)	22
Advertising treatment itself (Announcer, actors/too long, music)	20
Intellectually unsettling or unworthy (Silly/patronizing)	12
Emotionally unsettling (Depressing/repulsive)	8
Repetition of ad (Seen it too often)	7
Other answers	8
"It was just offensive" or no further answer	2
	141%*

* Percents add to more than 100% due to multiple mentions.

Exhibit 5

REASONS WHY CERTAIN ADVERTISEMENTS
WERE.....*NOT CLASSIFIED*

<u>Sameness</u> (Nothing special about it/all advertisements for product class the same)	22%
<u>No interest in product class</u> (Don't use or like it/not in the market for it)	20
<u>Advertising treatment itself</u> (Poorly done/no imagination)	14
<u>Have seen enough</u> (Already seen it)	11
<u>Other answers</u>	19
<u>Can't remember</u>	6
<u>Don't know</u>	19
	111%*

*Percents add to more than 100% due to multiple mentions.

different version of the task. Instead of recording an advertisement only when it would be categorized as annoying, enjoyable, informative, or offensive, respondents recorded information and feelings about every fifth advertisement counted, whether or not the advertisement was otherwise salient to them. Then, respondents were probed in detail on all advertisements which they did not categorize as annoying, enjoyable, informative, or offensive: "Why do you say there was nothing special about the ad?"

Information on a total of 1,320 uncategorized advertisements was obtained using this technique.

Exhibit 5 shows the reasons why certain advertisements were considered to be more or less *neutral*.

It is clear that the consumer's lack of personal interest in the product and sameness in advertising treatment are the major reasons responsible when advertisements make no impression beyond being counted. Consumers are discriminating and selective about the advertisements they choose to observe.

ATTITUDES AND PRODUCTS

What is the relationship between (1) the ways in which advertisements were categorized and (2) respondents' usage of the products advertised, and attitudes toward the brands advertised.

Exhibit 6 shows the categorization data broken down by whether or not respondents used (or owned) the product advertised.

Clearly, advertisements seen as *enjoyable* or *informative* tend to be those for products which the respondent owns or uses.

When one considers that a key reason for categorizing an advertisement as *informative* is that it provides information on new products, the 60% 'yes' figure may represent an understatement of those who would *like* to own the product. Ads categorized as *offensive* show an opposite tendency: non-users are the majority.

Further light on these relationships is revealed by Exhibit 7, depicting the relationship between advertisement

---

Exhibit 6

PRODUCT USAGE AND AD CATEGORIZATION

Product Usage	Enjoyable	Informative	Annoying	Offensive	All Advertisements
Yes, use	68%	60%	50%	27%	59%
No, don't use	26	33	43	67	34
Don't know	6	7	7	6	7
Base:	(3,423)	(3,368)	(2,126)	(408)	(9,325)

(Base is number of advertisements, not respondents)

Exhibit 7

BRAND ATTITUDE AND AD CATEGORIZATION

	Enjoyable	Informative	Annoying	Offensive
Base: Number of Advertisements	2,320	2,063	1,069	130
"If you use (or own) this kind of product, which best describes how you feel about buying the brand advertised?"	%	%	%	%
My favorite brand; I prefer it over all others	29	29	9	2
A brand I like better than most others	28	26	11	8
A brand I like about as well as any others	32	30	31	24
A brand that will do if nothing I like better is available	5	6	22	18
A brand I wouldn't buy	2	2	21	40
No opinion	4	7	6	8

---

categorization and brand attitude.

Brands which are preferred by consumers tend to have advertising which is favorably classified by consumers. In contrast, those brands which are least preferred tend to have advertisements which are classified relatively unfavorably.

Whether brand preference causes favorable advertising responses or vice versa is unknown: there is, however, a strong relationship between the two. This suggests that it is wiser to produce advertising that is informative or enjoyable than it is to produce advertising which is annoying or offensive.

CONSUMER DEFENSES

We find that the big defects people see in some advertisements are *the contradiction of experience, unreality, and repetition.* On the other hand, favorable reactions to advertisements seem to derive from the fact that they square with consumers' reality, inform, amuse, or make for what might be called "the shock of personal recognition."

In a sense, the reasons why consumers feel that some advertisements are annoying or offensive constitute the resistances they have to being sold in general. They are aware that advertising seeks to persuade, and they are unwilling to be gullible. Awareness of the consumers' vigilance and standards in judging advertising is valuable knowledge for wise advertisers.

It is important to remember that consumers are reality-oriented. The world of products is part of their everyday life--and when advertising has irrelevant fantasy and absurd selling propositions, the consumer senses this. The consumer relates the contents of advertising to his experience. He is strongly and knowledgeably product-rooted in his evaluation of advertisements.

This touches on one of the most important issues with which the study is involved: What "defenses," if any, do consumers have against the expert blandishments of advertising? In the judgment of the research team, *the myth of the defenseless consumer can be laid to rest.*

In addition to having built-in resistances to being sold by advertising or in person, he views sales messages through a filter of doubt, prior experience--and not a little boredom and disinterest. *He "protects" himself* from the blind acceptance of advertising as he does from other promises and panaceas he is proffered.

DISCUSSION QUESTIONS

1. Discuss the reasons why certain advertisements may be considered by consumers to be favorable or unfavorable.

2. What is the relationship between (a) the ways in which advertisements were categorized and (b) respondents' usage of the products advertised.

3. What protections, if any, does the consumer have from a blind acceptance of advertising?

I-6

BUSINESSMEN LOOK HARD AT ADVERTISING

Stephen A. Greyser

√ In cases of deceptive advertising, the Federal Trade Commission is considering penalties that would force advertisers to devote part of their own paid time and space to admitting the wrongdoing to the public. The FTC also wants to halt advertising it questions while an investigation is in process, rather than only after investigations, judgments, and appeals.

√ Consumer-causes advocate Ralph Nader is calling out for full substantiation of advertising claims.

√ Regarding food advertising aimed at children, nutrition investigator Robert Choate has urged restrictions on claims of product superiority and nutritional content, a limit to the number of food commercials per hour in "kiddie TV," and elimination during those hours of proprietary drug messages and the like.

√ Not satisfied with the banishment of cigarette commercials from television, some critics now want health warnings in all cigarette ads.

√ Media rate structures are again under investigation to see whether they unfairly benefit large advertisers.

√ Accusations continue in Washington circles that advertising is an important element contributing to "monopoly power and monopoly profits" on the part of many major advertisers.

Increasing attacks on advertising that have manifested themselves in proposals for further administrative and legal restrictions on it, and a growing din of public criticism of advertising's volume and content--these raise questions about the role and impact of advertising both as a tool of business and as an institution in our society. Such questions encompass advertising in its functional economic roles as well as its "side effects" in terms of social consequences.

Content--the ads themselves--is an important consideration both in general and with regard to particular techniques and campaigns. Also relevant is the perceived need for regulation--what kind and by whom. These and associated questions warrant fresh exploration, particularly among those who pay for advertising and in whose behalf it functions, the business community.

Despite the stake of business in advertising, relatively little has been done to learn about businessmen's ideas and

attitudes about the subject. Nine
years ago HBR published a study of
what executives think about advertising.[1] Because of changes that have occurred since then--such as the increasing volume of advertising, the emergence
of consumerism, and evolving regulatory
patterns--HBR's editors decided that
the 1962 inquiry needed updating.

An eight-page questionnaire, similar
to that used in the original study,
was completed by some 27% of the cross
section of the nearly 10,000 HBR subscribers to whom it was mailed (for details, see the ruled insert below).
The high rate of return of the lengthy
and complex instrument and the many
handwritten comments appended to the
questionnaire forms give evidence of
the subject's interest and importance
to executives of widely varying backgrounds. The respondents (see Exhibit
1 for their profile) include many with
job assignments in industries where advertising is of modest or little importance, as well as executives with
more experience in the field.

The responses show a continuing strong
respect for advertising, particularly
in its economic functions. But more
executives question advertising's impact and power in the social role than
was true in 1962, and the content of
advertising draws some ringing criticism. To use the language of the title
of the 1962 report, the executive community's assessment of advertising today contains less *yes* and more *but* than
nearly a decade ago.

STUDY METHODOLOGY

The questionnaire employed consisted
principally of clusters of agree-dis-
agree statements topically related in

---

[1] Stephen A. Greyser, "Businessmen Re
Advertising: 'Yes, But...'" (Problems
in Review),May-June 1962, p. 20.

subareas of advertising (economic,
social, and so on). In addition, a
number of ranking and check-off questions were included.

Although most of the questions were
identical to those in the 1962 study,
there were several major additions to
the questionnaire (and some deletions
on the ground of lack of current relevance). One addition sought executives'
views regarding the media in which they
are most likely to find ads they react
to favorably and unfavorably. Another
new section asked businessmen to recall
specific advertising campaigns which
they found particularly good or bad.
There were some new questions treating
other aspects of truth in advertising.

An important element of the study was
the two-sided approach to the exploration of most issues. This is a systematic application of questions worded
in alternate forms and administered to
split halves of the sample, in order to
probe both sides of a given issue fairly and to overcome problems associated
with the wording and presentation of
many attitude research questions in a
single instrument. For example, wording itself has been known to influence
the nature of responses to individual
questions. Also, an overbalance of
positively or negatively presented
statements can affect the direction of
responses.

To reduce the uncertainties connected
with these problems, we first phrased
in alternate forms the statements to be
used in the questionnaire--one oriented
favorably toward advertising, the other
unfavorably. Then we selected the statements for each section so that each of
the two forms of the questionnaire contained roughly even numbers of favorably and unfavorably worded statements.
Thus, each form of the questionnaire
was balanced between statements favorable and unfavorable to advertising,
and each statement appeared in both a
favorable and an unfavorable form. This
procedure enabled us to draw inferences

Exhibit 1

PROFILE OF HBR SUBSCRIBERS RESPONDING

Management position

Top management	= chairman of the board; board member; owner; partner; president; division or executive vice president; vice president; treasurer; secretary; controller; general manager; general superintendent; editor; administrative director; dean; and assistants thereto.	34%
Upper-middle management	= functional department head (e.g., advertising, sales, brand manager, production, purchasing, personnel, engineering, etc.)	33
Lower-middle management	= assistant to functional department head; district manager; branch manager; section manager; etc.	15
Nonmanagement	= all others employed in business	11
Professional	= doctor; practicing lawyer; practicing CPA; professor; consultant; military officer; government official; union official; clergyman; etc.	7

Job function

Accounting	6%
Advertising	4
Engineering; R & D	13
Finance	9
General management	39
Marketing (other than advt.)	19
Labor relations; personnel	5
Production; other	5

Education

High school	2%
Some college	11
Bachelor's degree	33
Graduate school	54

Company's annual sales

Under $1 million	12%
$1 - $10 million	19
$10 - $25 million	10
$25 - $100 million	15
$100 - $500 million	16
Over $500 million	28

Importance of advertising to company

Very important	28%
Rather important	33
Not particularly important	20
Rather unimportant	10
Very unimportant	9

Industry

Manufacturing consumer goods	14
Manufacturing industrial goods	27
Advertising; media; publishing	4
Banking; investment; insurance	11
Construction; mining; oil	5
Defense industry	3
Education; social services	6
Government	4
Management consulting	10
Personal consumer services	2
Retail or wholesale trade	7
Transportation and public utilities	5
Other	2

Relative size of company in industry		Age		Advertising-marketing experience	
Very large	34%	Under 30	18%	Present job in advertising	5%
Larger than most	30	30-39	34	Present job in marketing	26
About average	19	40-49	29	Previous job in either	13
Smaller than most	12	50-59	15	No advertising or marketing	
Very small	5	60 or over	4	experience	56

from comparisons of agreement with fav-orable statements and disagreement with unfavorable statements, and vice versa.

As noted, we sent the two forms of the questionnaire to split halves of the sample. The demographic characteris-tics of the respondents to each form are remarkably similar--as was true in the 1962 study--and the response rates are also virtually identical.

An additional methodological probe was employed in exploring advertising's social dimensions (see the section *Social influence*). In this area, par-ticularly, there is often confusion between the *power* of an entity (that is, its capability) and the *direction* of that power (that is, whether its capability is a force for good or evil). So we asked respondents to react to the statements in this area in two ways-- first on whether it was true or false, then on whether, if true, this was a good or a bad thing.

Study Highlights

Here are the major findings of the new study, followed by more extensive analy-sis in the indicated sections:

√ Businessmen today take a somewhat more critical stance than they did nine years ago. This is true in areas of advertising's economic role, its social impact, and its perceived truthfulness. In assessing advertis-ing, executives also seem to be ap-plying broader criteria than tradi-tional business efficacy alone. (See

the section on *Changing perspectives*.)

√ Executives still almost unanimously agree that advertising is essential to business and that the public places more confidence in advertised products than in unadvertised ones. (See *Overall appraisal*.)

√ Respondents think that advertising speeds the development of markets for new products, helps raise our standard of living, and results in better products. And they acknowledge that large reductions in advertising expenditures would decrease sales-- for business in general *and* for their own companies. (See *Economic issues*.)

√ If advertising were eliminated, busi-nessmen claim, selling expenses would have to go up. On the other hand, executives think too much money is spent on advertising. They probably would agree with that statement more strongly if they only knew exactly how much is spent--an amount they now grossly underestimate. (See *Adver-tising's bill*.)

√ Businessmen agree--more strongly than they did in 1962--that advertising has an unhealthy influence on children and that it persuades people to buy things they do not need. Also, fewer (though still a majority) believe that people pay more attention to ad-vertising today than before. Execu-tives look with disapproval on most of advertising's effects in the social area. (See *Social influence*.)

√ The percentage of businessmen who think that ads present a true picture

of the product declined sharply--
from more than half to less than one
third. Moreover, the sample finds
people in ads quite different from
the way people really are. Although
businessmen agree that advertising
is on a higher plane than it was a
decade ago, in some areas they think
standards have slipped. Specifically, they notice a greater proportion
of ads that irritate and insult the
public's intelligence--and their own.
(See *Standards & content*.)

✓ Reacting in their role as consumers,
businessmen consider direct mail and
television as the media having the
largest proportion of annoying and
offensive ads. Trade publications
receive the best ratings overall.
(See *Media and Campaigns*.)

✓ While executives generally believe
in codes of ethical practices for
their own industries, they think that
advertising has an even greater need
for such codes--but also that advertising would be less able to enforce
a code internally than their own industries could. The favored mode
is a group of industry executives
plus other community members. The
code should force advertisers to
substantiate their claims. In addition respondents single out elimination of untruthful and misleading
ads as the most important form of
self-improvement advertising should
undertake. (See *More regulation?*
and Action steps.)

✓ Executives overwhelmingly credit per-
sosons in the advertisng field for advertising's achievements, but also
blame them principally for its faults.
While those closest to advertising
also are seen as sharing the burden
for making improvements in ads, the
respondents place the primary responsibility for improvements on corporate top management. (See *Scoreboard*.)

✓ Not surprisingly, those surveyed
whose jobs are in the advertising

field are more generally favorable
toward it than are executives in general. Between the two, but striking
an independent path, are executives
whose jobs are or were in marketing.
These differences in attitudes are
especially apparent with respect to
advertising's social implications and
its standards. (See *Admen's view*.)

CHANGING PERSPECTIVES

What are the major changes since 1962
in executives' attitudes toward advertising? First--and most general--is
a stance somewhat less favorable; on
most key issues, opinion has moved some
5 to 10 percentage points toward an
anti-advertising position.

(This shift to a small extent may be a
function of the composition of the sample compared with that of 1962. There
are fewer consumer goods executives and
substantially more consultants; the
former group tends to be somewhat more
pro-advertising, the latter slightly
less. Some 3% fewer say their assignments are in the advertising or marketing function, while 5% more are in engineering and R & D jobs; the former
are considerably more pro-advertising,
the latter rather less so. Some of
these changes in composition, of course,
are natural reflections of changes in
the character of the management population over the past nine years.)

The most significant changes in attitudes, however, are far more dramatic:

In the economic area--where executives
customarily give an almost blanket en-
dorsement--advertising is still seen
as having predominantly positive effects. But 15-20 percentage-point
declines are recorded on such issues
as whether advertising results in
better products, raises our standard
of living, and results in higher or
lower prices.

In the social area, executives question

advertising's influence, and in some instances are very critical of it. The perceived negative impact on public taste and unhealthy effect on children show an increase of 15 percentage points. Furthermore, as in 1962, businessmen see advertising as having a powerful influence for persuasion, an influence they regard unfavorably.

The area of ad content generates sharper criticism than was the case nine years ago. Most notable is the 24 percentage-point decline in the proportion of executives--now only about one third--who agree that "in general advertising presents a true picture of the product advertised."

One reason for these changing perspectives no doubt is the "behavior" of advertising. But a significant part of the explanation may well be rooted in changes in the context in which businessmen assess advertising. These changes relate particularly to today's greater perceived appropriateness of evaluating business activity not only in business terms but also in terms of societal implications. Thus, more than two thirds of our respondents disagree with the philosophy that "advertising's sole justification should be returning a profit to the advertiser."

Further evidence of this broader perspective comes in responses to paired questions on the issue of advertising's responsibility for the effects of the products it promotes. Almost half (49%) agree that admen should be held accountable, and 73% disagree with the premise that admen have no responsibility in the area.

An important related element of the changing environment is consumerism. About 4 out of every 5 persons sampled think that "consumerism will lead to major modifications in advertising content."

OVERALL APPRAISAL

Executives agree almost unanimously that advertising is necessary. More than 90% say it is essential for business in general, while some 73% also indicate that it is essential for their own companies. The change since 1962 in this endorsement has been slight-- one of degree rather than substance. Whereas 80% of those responding in 1962 indicated "strong agreement" with the statement that advertising is necessary to business, this figure has dropped down to 67% now.

More than three quarters agree that society is better off with advertising than without it. This is nearly as many as in 1962, despite the strong criticism of advertising that has been voiced since that time.

An overwhelming 90% feel that the public has more confidence in advertised products than in unadvertised ones, and 68% of this group say that they strongly agree with this statement. In the latter category, however, some erosion has taken place; nine years ago about 81% of the respondents indicated "strong agreement."

ECONOMIC ISSUES

From at least as far back as the 1930s, observers have questioned the economic influences of advertising. Many of the issues raised then are still being discussed today. Exhibit 2 summarizes opinion on several of these economic questions, both from the new study and from 1962.

We used dual-phrased questions, tapping both sides of each issue and administered to split halves of the sample (see the ruled insert on pages 33 and 35 for explanation). The respondents to each form of the statement were virtually identical demographically, so it can be assumed that dissimilar response patterns indeed represent different perceptions of a particular

37

Exhibit 2

ADVERTISING AND CERTAIN ECONOMIC ISSUES

	Alternatives	Percentage of 1971 respondents who said:			Percentage of 1962 respondents who said:		
		Agree	Can't say	Disagree	Agree	Can't say	Disagree
Development of markets for new products	Speeds it	94%	2%	4%	95%	3%	2%
	Slows it	9	7	84	6	5	89
Effect on products for the public	Better ones	55	9	36	76	7	17
	Poorer ones	10	11	79	8	7	85
Effect on standard of living	Raises it	67	12	21	83	8	7
	Lowers it	7	8	85	4	5	91
Effect on prices	Lower prices	35	16	49	54	13	33
	Higher prices	49	10	41	28	9	62
Advertising one brand against another	Not wasteful	68	10	22	66	10	22
	Wasteful	26	10	64	23	8	68
Reductions in ad expenditures would decrease sales	Large reduction	72	12	16	*	*	*
	Small reduction	22	26	52	22	27	51
To hasten recovery in a recession	Moderate decrease in advertising	8	18	74	*	*	*
	Moderate increase in advertising	42	20	38	*	*	*

* No comparable statement

issue when it is presented in two ways.

New product stimulus: In the area of new product marketing, advertising is perceived as making its highest functional contribution to the economy. Executives are almost unanimous in agreeing that "advertising speeds the development of markets for new products" (and in disagreeing with the statement that it slows such development).

In addition, 90% of the respondents believe that "it would be almost impossible today to introduce a new consumer product without advertising." They find this less true for launching

an industrial product: only 63% agree in this case.

General influence: One charge critics make is that large sums of money spent on advertising enable some companies to sell products that may be inferior to those made by smaller competitors who cannot afford these marketing costs. Thus, it is argued, advertising prevents consumers from getting the best products. This contradicts the traditional idea that manufacturers are more likely to develop new and better products because of advertising. The reasoning here is that they use this tool to sell efficiently large enough quantities to recover research costs in a reasonable period of time.

Businessmen believe that "advertising results in better products for the public," but they are considerably less likely to say so now than they were nine years ago. As can be seen in Exhibit 2, this 21 percentage-point change in attitude is not matched on the reverse form of the question, where respondents still overwhelmingly reject the notion that advertising results in *poorer* products.

Another traditional argument in advertising's behalf is that it helps raise our standard of living. Here, again, some erosion of support has occurred since 1962. While executives are still quick to reject the anti-advertising statement, they are less enthusiastic about endorsing the favorable ones.

On the always thorny issue of effect on prices, a dramatic change in attitude is evident. Just about half of the respondents deny that advertising lowers prices, and the same proportion think that it results in higher prices. This is considerably different from the case in 1962. Interestingly, executives in consumer goods companies are slightly more likely than others to say "higher prices."

Company economics: Few managers think that "small reductions in advertising expenditures would decrease sales." However, nearly three fourths of them believe that large cuts in the ad budget would have this effect.

Opinion is divided as to the helpfulness of a slight increase in advertising in hastening recovery from a recession. On the other hand, there is little agreement with the belief that a moderate *decrease* can hasten recovery. Executives appear to favor a policy of at least holding the line. This viewpoint is supported by independent research data confirming that "industries which do not cut back on their adver-

tising during a recession...do much better in sales and profits than those that do cut."[2]

Finally, HBR asked businessmen whether "advertising's value would be better recognized if its effects could be more precisely measured." The findings reiterate the strong position taken in 1962; some 86% of the respondents believe this is true.

Generally speaking, the results do indicate a strong reinforcement of executives' beliefs in advertising's economic validity and impact for businesses. However, the support is weaker than in 1962 regarding some of advertising's economic influences.

ADVERTISING'S BILL

Slightly more than half of HBR's respondents say that too much is spent on advertising--an increase of 15 percentage points from 1962. Paralleling this, approximately an equal number disagree that too little is spent. A substantial 27%, however, disagree that too much is spent for advertising. This seems to indicate a belief that to some extent advertising expenditures are "about right."

Executives seem uncertain as to whether money allocated for advertising is well spent--they disagree with *both* sides of this issue (see Exhibit 3). Perhaps they are saying that while company money is not wasted, it could be managed more carefully.

Nearly 7 out of 10 executives think that "it would take more money in substitute selling expenses" to replace advertising expenditures.

Respondents were asked for their "best guess as to how much money was spent on advertising in the United States last year," and the responses were

---

[2] Buchen Advertising, Inc., Advertising in Recession Periods (Chicago, 1970).

Exhibit 3

OPINION ON EFFECTIVENESS OF
ADVERTISING DOLLAR

Statement	Percentage of respondents who:		
	Agree	Can't say	Disagree
Most of the money allocated for advertising is well spent	28%	22%	50%
Most of the money allocated for advertising is wasted	25	12	63

grouped into categories. Exhibit 4
shows a very wide range of estimates.

The generally accepted answer--accord-
ing to the traditional McCann-Erickson
estimates, now developed by Robert J.
Coen for *Marketing/Communications* maga-
zine--is $19.5 billion in 1969 and
$19.7 billion in 1970. As the line
with the arrow indicates, only 8% of
the answers are in the territory.
(Note that only 9% would be added to
this group if the range were broadened
to extend from $15 billion to $30 billion.)

This result parallels the findings of
the 1962 study, in which only 20% of
responding executives were near the
correct figure of $12 billion.

Those whose current assignment or background is in advertising and marketing
evince a slightly better knowledge of
advertising's bill. Some 26% of them
give estimates within the $15-billion
to $30-billion range.

SOCIAL INFLUENCE

Advertising has felt some particularly
bitter stings in the social area in
the years since HBR's previous study.
While social criticism has always been
directed at advertising,[3] it has intensified in the past decade.

Businessmen's views in important social
issues are summarized in Exhibit 5. We
asked respondents to rate a statement

in two ways: first on whether it was
true or false, and then on whether, if
true, this was good or bad. As reflected in the exhibit, what is seen
as true is not always seen as good,
and vice versa.

An alleged detrimental social impact of
advertising is that it "leads to uniformity of taste among consumers."
Slightly more than half of those surveyed agree that this statement is true.

[3] For a historical review of such cri-
ticism, see Raymond A. Bauer and Stephen
A. Greyser, *Advertising in America:The
Consumer View* (Boston, Div. of Research,
Harvard Business School, 1968),Ch. 2.

Exhibit 4

HOW MUCH MONEY IS SPENT ON
ADVERTISING

Annual amount	Percentage of respondents citing
$30 billion or more	15%
$21 - $29.9 billion	4
$18 - $20.9 billion ←——	8
$15 - $17.9 billion	5
$10 - $17.9 billion	17
$5 - $9.9 billion	14
$1 - $4.9 billion	28
Less than $1 billion	9

Note: Arrow points to generally
accepted figure.

Exhibit 5

ADVERTISING"S SOCIAL INFLUENCES

| Issue | Alternatives | Percentage of respondents who say: | | | | | |
| | | This is: | | | If true, this would be: | | |
		True	Don't know	False	Good	Don't know	Bad
Effect on taste among consumers	Leads to uniformity	51%	10%	38%	6%	19%	75%
	Leads to diversity	67	10	23	79	17	4
Impact on public taste	Downgrades it	41	13	46	2	7	91
	Improves it	37	15	48	74	15	11
Influence on children	Healthy	17	16	67	68	13	19
	Unhealthy	57	13	30	1	4	95
Amount of attention paid to it	More than ever	54	19	27	47	32	21
	Less than ever	31	12	57	25	23	52
Persuades people to buy things they don't need	Seldom	17	3	80	56	13	31
	Often	85	3	12	7	17	76
Persuades people to buy things they don't want	Seldom	50	5	45	66	14	20
	Often	51	7	41	3	9	88

On the other hand, two thirds agree that advertising leads to *diversity* of taste. A likely explanation is that advertising encourages many people to want the same things (uniform taste), but it tries to satisfy customers by providing many products and many brands within product categories (diversity).

Closely linked is the question of what influence advertising has on the level of taste. Executives seem to believe that advertising neither upgrades nor downgrades public taste; the response patterns for both forms of the question are similar. The important finding here is the change from 1962, when the results showed a majority of executives convinced that advertising improves public taste.

The businessmen seem to go along with critics who attack advertising's effect on children. While two thirds of those responding disagree that advertising has a healthy influence on children, some 57% go even further and affirm that the influence is unhealthy. This represents a 13-15 percentage-point increase from the anti-advertising "rating" of 1962.

A majority of executives still believe that "people today pay more attention to advertising than ever before," but the proportion has declined somewhat in the past nine years. More important, the percentage of respondents who think that this is good has dropped even more.

On the related issue of how effective advertising is, compared with a decade ago, similar results are evident. There is little change in the percentage finding this assertion true or false; however, the proportion of executives who think it is good that advertising is *less* effective has doubled, and the percentage thinking it is good that advertising is *more* effective has declined from 52% to 41%.

HBR also inquired as to how persuasive they think advertising is. Nearly all respondents believe that "advertising often persuades people to buy things they don't need." They are more evenly split (just about 50-50) on the notion that advertising can seduce consumers, that it "often persuades people to buy things they don't want." Note that regardless of whether advertising is viewed as having such power, to have it is seen as bad.

Overall, businessmen seem to look less favorably on the social effects of advertising's capabilities than they did in 1962.

STANDARDS & CONTENT

One of the most dramatic changes in opinion uncovered by this study deals with views of the truthfulness of ads. Only 30% of the respondents believe that "advertisements present a true picture of the product advertised"; 60% agree with the reverse form of the statement. That 30% represents a decline of 24 percentage points since 1962, the largest single shift in attitude from the previous study. Perhaps it helps to explain some of the anti-advertising sentiment noted elsewhere; businessmen apparently find it hard to feel as much economic satisfaction with advertising when so many question its content.

Nevertheless, businessmen think that standards of advertising today are slightly higher than they were a decade ago. Some 43% say standards are higher; 26% say "about the same"; and 31% rate them lower. Comparable figures in 1962 were: 40%, higher; 36%, about the same; and 24%, lower.

Managers also were asked to compare their views of ads today with those they held a decade ago on certain at-tributes. Their reactions to these categories of content are given in Exhibit 6.

The "problem ads" most frequently cited as having increased--those which insult the intelligence and those which irritate--are the same two problem areas most criticized by executives in 1962.

Ads with too little information receive the highest number of "about the same" responses, despite criticism on this point from other quarters. Furthermore, a plurality of respondents believe there is a *smaller* proportion of ads with invalid or misleading claims than ten years ago.

Managers do not feel that "most people in ads are pretty much like the way people really are." Only one respondent in ten agrees with this statement. This is one area where both sexes seem to get equal treatment. Two separate questions show that fewer than one in five think advertising accurately portrays the roles of men, and of women, in our society.

A frequent cause of annoyance is not so much the format or content of the ad, but its repetition. Three fourths of the executives believe that "repetition has been substituted for imagination in much of today's advertising."

Another irritant is the hard-sell promotion that pounds its message home. According to respondents, this type of irritation is not necessary to sell; 9 out of 10 agree that "soft-sell advertising *does* sell goods." On a related issue, however, the businessmen just about split evenly on whether the most effective TV commercials are the most annoying.

In summary, the sample singles out the truth dimension and the irritating qualities of ads as major detrimental aspects of content. Otherwise, there is only a slightly less favorable perception of content than in 1962.

Exhibit 6

CHANGE OF ATTITUDE RE ADVERTISING
CONTENT: NOW VERSUS TEN YEARS AGO

Compared with ten years ago, would you say there is a greater, a smaller, or about the same proportion of...	Percentage of respondents who answer:		
	Smaller proportion	About the same proportion	Greater proportion
Ads with invalid or misleading claims	38%	30%	32%
Ads which themselves are in bad taste	29	25	46
Ads for objectionable products	21	38	41
Ads which insult the *public's* intelligence	20	28	52
Ads which insult *your* intelligence	18	25	57
Ads with too little information	19	46	35
Ads which are irritating	18	28	54

MEDIA & CAMPAIGNS

It is insufficient to consider the standards of advertising content without referring to the context--that is, the media--in which ads appear. Some products might be viewed as "objectionable" on television but not in an adult-oriented magazine. A newspaper ad that seems low in informational content might be considered differently on a billboard.

Most criticism of irritating ads, the amount of advertising, and information content is voiced from a consumer vantage point. So HBR asked executives in their role as consumers to assess the major media in terms of the proportion of ads that they find annoying, enjoyable, informative, and offensive,[4] In addition, they were asked to give their perceptions as to the overall amount of advertising in each medium.

The scale used to rate media ranged from very low (1) to very high (5). Exhibit 7 shows the mean scores recorded.

---
[4] These categories are the same as those used with consumers in the nationwide study reported by Raymond A. Bauer and Stephen A. Greyser, op. cit.

Not surprisingly, businessmen treat their own trade publications most kindly. This medium receives the highest score for the proportion of ads that are enjoyable and informative, the lowest ratings for annoying and offensive ads, and the second lowest rating on overall amount of advertising. Consumer magazines receive the next most favorable ratings, followed by newspapers.

At the other extreme lies direct mail, with the worst image in the areas of annoying, enjoyable, and offensive ads. Television's image is not much better-- except for the fairly high score it receives for enjoyable commercials.

In the category of overall amount of advertising, no medium has a mean of less than 3, and TV is singled out with an average of 4.24. This dubious distinction must in part be the result of interruptions in programs caused by commercials. (Television actually carries *less* advertising than most other media. Even during crowded time periods, commercials are limited to 16 minutes per hour--just under 27%. This is well under the 40%-50% figure toward which many magazine publishers strive and less than half the amount found ir most newspapers.)

Exhibit 7

MEDIA RATING SCORES

Nature of ads	Mean rating on 1-5 scale						
	Consumer magazines	Direct mail	Newspapers	Outdoor	Radio	Television	Trade publications
Annoying	2.09	3.89	2.19	2.81	3.21	3.72	1.62
Enjoyable	2.91	1.45	2.32	2.10	2.20	2.50	2.95
Informative	2.85	2.05	2.73	1.66	1.95	2.06	4.03
Offensive	1.87	3.14	1.91	2.22	2.50	3.06	1.35
Overall amount of advertising	3.49	3.77	3.48	3.25	3.65	4.24	3.39

Good ads & bad ads: The respondents told HBR what campaigns they consider to be particularly good and particularly bad. These campaigns--mostly from late 1970--are summarized in Exhibit 8 by product category, with the exception of a few brand names that stand out.

Nearly one third single out the 1970 Alka-Seltzer campaign as a favorite. (Interestingly enough, Miles Laboratories, maker of Alka-Seltzer, recently received much unfavorable comment in the advertising trade press for firing the agency that created these ads, reportedly because of unsatisfactory sales results.) Many executives also cite Volkswagen ads favorably.

When asked to identify campaigns they dislike, executives usually cite product categories rather than specific brands. Nonetheless, one brand, Winston cigarettes, draws enough mentions to rate a place of its own.

HBR compared the campaigns selected by those respondents whose current jobs are in advertising with those mentioned by other executives. More admen say they like the Alka-Seltzer commercials than do other managers--40% versus under 30%. Admen are also 50% more likely to name an automobile or car rental promotion as a favorite than are other businessmen (21% versus 14%), but they are only half as likely to

list a public service campaign.

In general, persons in advertising like more campaigns than do other executives. In the case of particularly bad promotions, a higher percentage of admen than nonadvertising respondents are annoyed by soap and detergent ads. The opposite is true for cigarette ads and ads for toothpastes and mouthwashes.

MORE REGULATION?

A clamor for greater regulation of advertising is part of the context in which this study was conducted, as we have noted. It is important (and only fair) to point out that voices from within the advertising fraternity have been among those calling for change. Perhaps the best-known proposal is that advanced by American Advertising Federation chairman, Victor Elting, for an industry review board combined with a media agreement not to run advertisements that fail to obtain the board's approval.

HBR's questions to executives covered many issues in this important area, especially on the *what* and *why* of such regulation.

First, is there a need for more regulation? One underlying reason why many executives seem to be answering *yes* to this question is their growing conviction that public faith in advertising

Exhibit 8

VIEWS OF 'GOOD' AND 'BAD'
ADVERTISING CAMPAIGNS

Campaigns	Percentage of respondents mentioning
Campaigns considered "good"	
Alka-Seltzer	30%
Volkswagen	27
Other automobiles and car rentals (e.g., Volvo, Dodge, American Motors, Avis)	15
Public service/interest ads (e.g., antismoking, Peace Corps, clean air and water)	7
Foods and beverages (e.g., Pepsi, Coca-Cola, Sunsweet prunes, Kraft)	8
Cigarettes (especially Benson & Hedges, Marlboro)	5
Airlines (Eastern, United, American, etc.)	4
Other (e.g., local banks or stores, corporate institutional)	19
Campaigns considered "bad"	
Winston (cigarette brand)	11
Other cigarettes (specific brand mentions or all of this type)	19
Soaps, detergents, other household cleaning products (generic or brand names)	15
Deodorants and other personal products (e.g., feminine hygiene sprays, cosmetics, shaving products)	11
Toothpastes and mouthwashes	5
Beer and liquor	1
Political advertising	3
Remedies (e.g., headache, stomachache, or sleeping pills; patent medicines; cold remedies)	8
Other (e.g., toys, underwear, auto dealers)	25

is eroding. Indeed, some 42% (compared with 28% in 1962) go so far as to agree that "the public's faith in advertising is at an all-time low." (Only 38% disagree, compared with 54% in 1962.) Moreover, only 15% say "the public's faith in advertising is at an all-time high" (68% disagree!), whereas nine years ago opinion on this statement was 31% agree, 50% disagree.

Also, the businessmen today more sharply criticize advertising people in terms of their recognition of public responsibility than was the case in 1962. About half agree with the view that, on the whole, admen in their activities fail to recognize their accountability, up 12-15 percentage points from nine years ago.

One way of formalizing approaches to responsibility in business practice is with industry codes of ethical practices. Businessmen in the past have generally favored such standards for their own industries.[5]

We asked our sample to consider the desirability of ethical codes, and how best to enforce them, for their own industries as well as for advertising. While the respondents may have known little or nothing about whether adver-

----
[5] See Raymond C. Baumhart, S.J.,"How Ethical Are Businessmen?"(Problems in Review),HBR July-Aug. 1961, p. 6.

Exhibit 9

OPINIONS ON CODES OF ETHICAL PRACTICES
1971 VERSUS 1962

| Questions | Percentage of respondents answering: | | | |
| | For all practices in your own industry | | For all of advertising | |
	1971	1962	1971	1962
A. How do you feel about the idea of a general code of ethical practices?				
Excellent idea	46%	41%	53%	50%
Good idea	22	22	24	24
Fair idea	11	11	12	11
Poor idea	12	15	10	12
Already has a code	9	11	1	3
B. If such codes were drawn up, who should enforce them?				
Management of each company (i.e., self-enforcement)	26%	38%	20%	32%
A group of executives from various companies within the industry	27	32	19	28
A group composed of industry executives plus other members of the community	34	22	47	32
A government agency	9	4	10	5
Other	4	4	4	3

tising needs a code (or, for that matter, whether it already has one), their answers can be taken as indicating their opinions as to whether a code for advertising--and stricter enforcement of any codes--is more or less desirable than codes for their own industries.

Their opinions, shown in Exhibit 9, ascribe a greater need for regulation and for stronger enforcement procedures to advertising than to their own fields. Moreover, compared with 1962, more executives think the idea of such codes is "excellent" or "good," and fewer think that enforcement at the company or industry level is most appropriate.

The most striking finding in Exhibit 9 is that the preferred mode of enforcement would consist of a group of industry executives plus other member of the

community. The respondents see this as especially desirable in enforcement of advertising codes, perhaps because advertising impinges so broadly on the public. While only a very small proportion of the sample opts for government enforcement of such standards, more than half (59%) also agree that "if advertising can't keep its own house in order, the government will have to."

'Shape up': Reinforcing these views are results from a number of separate but related questions. For example, a majority (58%) of executives think that "self-regulation for advertising can't be genuinely effective," which is slightly more than the percentage agreeing with this statement in 1962. Only 19% of all respondents (but 55% of those in advertising jobs) claim any knowledge of present self-regulation efforts in advertising.

A large proportion of the sample (more than 70%) take the position that advertising needs stronger policing of its content. Furthermore, 90% agree that advertisers should be forced to substantiate their claims. In light of recent debates on this matter, it is noteworthy that this is one of the most widely held opinions in the current study, and that almost as strong a view was taken in 1962--albeit coupled at that time with a somewhat less critical reaction to ads than is the case now.

Of course one explanatory factor, representing a major force that has emerged in the marketing environment in the last decade, is consumerism. About 80% of our respondents think consumerism will lead to major modifications in advertising content, and 86% consider this to be a good thing.

In sum, businessmen clearly are saying to advertising that there is a need to "shape up," especially in terms of content. They look favorably on consumerism as an environmental force conducive toward this end, and they urge stronger codes of ethical practice in advertising, with less reliance on self-enforcement and intra-industry enforcement.

Let us now look in more detail at executives' recommendations for action on the part of advertising.

ACTION STEPS

HBR asked its sample for suggestions for action which advertising could undertake--ideally and realistically-- to overcome criticism. As was true nine years ago, the recommendation offered most frequently in both situations is to increase truth in advertising (see Exhibit 10).

This view is summed up by one respondent from Kentucky, who says advertisers should "report truthfully, without under- or overstatements." The

Exhibit 10

WHAT SHOULD ADVERTISING DO TO OVERCOME CRITICISM?

Suggestions	Percentage of respondents citing:	
	Ideally	Realistically
More truth	21%	18%
More taste	7	9
More truth *and* taste	4	3
Self-enforced regulation; ethical code	11	12
Provide more information	8	7
Do a better job	2	3
Do nothing	1	1
Other comments	16	17

assistant treasurer of a meter manufacturer aptly explains the difference between ideal and realistic goals. Ideally, he says, advertising should "be honest"; realistically, it should "be a 'little' honest."

Comments relating to the tastefulness of ads come from a number of executives. A representative quotation from the vice president-operations of a New York consulting firm is: "Reduce oversimplification and insulting of the user's intelligence."

The second largest number of suggestions relate to increased self-regulation and establishing an industry code of ethics. Typical was this recommendation from the president of a Connecticut consumer goods company: "Form an ethics committee to regulate misleading and poor-taste advertising."

More pessimistic about the industry's ability to police itself, a New York ad agency account executive calls for "self-regulation (ideally), government regulation (realistically)." In agreement, the advertising-sales promotion manager of a New Jersey chemical

Exhibit 11

SPECIFIC FORMS OF SELF-IMPROVEMENT
ADVOCATED FOR ADVERTISING

Activity	Percentage of respondents who say:	
	Should be undertaken	Is most important
Eliminate untruthful or misleading ads	91%	56%
Establish and enforce a code of ethics	65	14
Upgrade the intellectual level of ads	62	11
Increase the information content of ads	59	11
Work only for reputable companies or products	42	4
Become more efficient as a business	23	3
Other	4	2

company postulates a kind of Gresham's Law: "It needs regulation so that meaningful, worthwhile advertising is not drowned out by the illiterate shrieks that constitute the bulk of present advertising."

"Become more informative" and "provide more facts" are recommendations from another group of managers. Still others believe that the best thing the industry can do to overcome criticism is simply to learn to do its job better. "Learn to measure effectiveness," remarks the general manager of an Ohio measurement and control systems manufacturer.

A small number of respondents believe advertising should just ignore its critics. As the vice president of a New Jersey retailing firm puts it, "It can't overcome all criticism and shouldn't try to."

The frequently advanced notion of a public information program to be undertaken by the industry was treated in a separate question. If such a program were to be pursued, some 75% of those responding believe that "advertising's role and function in our economy" should be emphasized. And a secondary theme, which gains 65% support, would highlight "efforts to curb objectionable advertisments." Supplementing and

reinforcing these views are executives' recommendations for "specific forms of self-improvement" for advertising. Responses to a checklist of such activities to improve advertising appear in Exhibit 11.

SCOREBOARD

Whose job is it to stimulate these improvements? Who gets the most credit for advertising's achievements and blame for its faults? What groups in society are seen as most antagonistic toward advertising, best able to help or hurt it, the ones to which the industry should pay most attention?

Businessmen place primary credit, blame, and responsibility for improvement in advertising's situation with the same groups as they did in 1962. But a larger percentage of respondents cite more groups in each category now. The largest increase, 21 percentage points, comes in the number of executives charging the government with the burden of improving advertising. Exhibit 12 presents the current views.

The government, along with the public and our economic system, receives very little credit or blame for advertising's condition. Advertising agency people and company advertising departments lead both of these lists. These same

Exhibit 12

WHERE SHOULD CREDIT AND BLAME LIE?

| | Percentage of respondents citing: | | |
Location	Credit for achievements	Blame for faults	Responsibility for improvement
Advertising agency people	81%	81%	81%
Our economic system	35	34	21
The government	8	16	42
Media people	46	54	63
The public	18	33	45
Company advertising departments	69	74	74
Company top management	52	67	88

groups are perceived as being very much accountable for changing advertising, but on this dimension top management moves into first place. Respondents believe that *those who set campaign policy*--and approve advertising's piece of the company budget--*are best able to ensure that advertising shapes up.*

Executives rate our economic system last in terms of responsibility for improving advertising. But in a separate question HBR asked whether "the faults of advertising are inherent in our economic system"; some 40% of the respondents say *yes*, suggesting that most of advertising's problems are of its own making.

Some ad industry proponents have claimed that advertising--as the most visible marketing tool--receives an undue amount of criticism, that it serves as a scapegoat for business in general. Executives disagree. All but 15% say that "criticism of advertising stems more from advertising itself than from hostility toward the whole economic system."

Are some groups in society more antagonistic toward advertising than others? Businessmen say *yes*, citing opinion leaders among the public (whoever they may be) and the public in general (see

Exhibit 13).

But, they go on to say, these groups have less power to help or hurt advertising than does the business community. Government leaders are also viewed as having considerable power, a change from 1962 when they ranked only fourth on this issue.

The finding most clearly evident in Exhibit 13, however, is that fully three quarters of the respondents believe that advertising should pay most attention to the public. Businessmen apparently are saying that the success or failure of advertising depends in large part on how well it listens to those whom it is trying to reach.

ADMEN'S VIEW

Not surprisingly, those whose present jobs are in advertising (some 5% of the total surveyed) look more favorably at it than do persons outside the field. To illustrate, some 85% of those in advertising generally disagree that "society is worse off with advertising than without it," compared with only 47% of other respondents.

Although only 42% of nonadvertising executives think that today's advertising standards are higher than a decade ago, some 70% of those in the field

Exhibit 13

HOW DO VARIOUS GROUPS IN OUR SOCIETY
RELATE TO ADVERTISING?

Group	Percentage of respondents who find this group:		
	Most antagonistic	Most powerful	The one advertising should pay most attention to
The business community	16%	64%	57%
Clergymen	24	6	8
Educators	46	12	17
Government leaders	43	50	27
Opinion leaders among the public	53	40	49
People in advertising itself	12	45	23
The public in general	52	46	75

Note: Respondents could check more than one group in each column.

believe this is so. Perhaps one reason why admen hold this favorable view is that more than half of them maintain that ads *do* present a true picture of the products advertised--a percentage double that for other managers.

Admen, like most other people in wanting their work recognized, believe that consumers pay more attention to advertising than ever before; 70% think that this is true, compared with just over 50% for others. What is more, an equally high percentage, 71%, think this is good, while only 55% of others think so. And whereas only 37% of businessmen outside the field say that advertising's ability to add psychological attributes to products is a good thing, some 63% of those in advertising approve it.

Quite naturally, admen have different ideas about the kind of regulation the industry needs--and greater knowledge of present regulatory efforts. Some 17% of the "outsiders" claim to know of any ad industry self-regulation, but 55% of those in the field do. What is surprising is that 45% of those who supposedly are governed by such regulation do not know that it exists.

Admen are no different from other respondents in approving the idea of an ethical code. They are much more likely to vote for enforcement by company management, however. Three quarters of them state that self-regulation can be genuinely effective, compared with 42% of other respondents.

Admen are more than twice as likely as others (54% versus 26%) to disagree that too much money is spent on advertising. Depending on their jobs, respondents view impact on prices differently. About 65% of those in advertising believe that it results in lower prices, as against 34% of the rest.

CONCLUSION

In what is being called "the age of accountability," advertising has been put under the spotlight--as have many institutions and business practices. Perhaps because it touches the public in so many ways and throughout the day, advertising seems to be receiving a constant barrage of criticism from both activists and the public. What can, what should, advertising do about it?

Such a straightforward question is, unfortunately, not subject ot a simple answer. This is in part because of the number of component institutions involved in the creation, approval, and transmission of advertising--that is, the company-advertiser, agency, and media. Thus there is no single entity that, in fact, *is* "advertising."

In part it is because the issues are often very complex. For example, in a legal system that is adversary-rooted, should (as has been proposed) a party be forced not only to testify against himself but to subsidize dissemination of the testimony? Or, if advertisers get together to monitor and control content, is this a form of collusion?

In spite of such questions and difficulties, certain suggestions do emerge from this analysis of what the business community thinks and says about advertising today. The survey findings clearly point to rising expectations for advertising's performance held by the business community itself, expectations reflecting a changing--wider--context in which advertising is being assessed.

The main direction of executive finger pointing is at advertising content. This, it seems, is a zone which is most in control of those in advertising. Content can be policed at its place of birth, and hence it is rather more susceptible to change than, say, economic factors.

For example, advertisers--via top management directive--and agencies can shun the frequent practice of "legal limits" activity. Rather than trying to wend a way over, under, around, and through legal boundaries, an advertiser could focus on what's right for the consumer (or, more properly, for various kinds of consumers). Such steps, among others, would represent behavioral change that would also help rebuild consumer confidence in advertising.

The concluding comments of the 1962 HBR study referred to the challenge and opportunity of making improvements in advertising. The task of the advertising fraternity's responsible members to "weed out those in their midst whose activities bring opprobrium upon all of advertising" drew special attention. At that time, such action was characterized by the word "hopeful," to avoid encouraging outside regulation.

Today the "challenge and opportunity" perhaps should be replaced by "challenge and necessity." The objective is not only to inhibit restrictions that might be inflicted on advertising by those with little understanding of its operations. But also, from a very selfish point of view, it is to prevent any further "devaluation" of advertising as an important business tool.

DISCUSSION QUESTIONS

1. Discuss the reasons why businessmen might be increasingly uneasy about truthfulness and the social impact of advertising.

2. Do you believe that advertising has an unhealthy influence on children? Why or why not?

3. Businessmen consider direct mail and television as the media having the largest proportion of annoying and offensive ads. Which media do you consider most annoying and offensive, less annoying and offensive? Why?

4. What changes would you recommend for advertising to improve the attitudes of businessmen?

I-7

ADVERTISING: MORE THAN MEETS THE EYE?

Ivan L. Preston

This article reports experimental results suggesting that people may perceive messages differently when written in the form of advertisements than when written in the form of other types of communications.

The study is based on an earlier experiment which found that people often perceived as part of an ad's content certain statements which they invalidly believed to be implied by the ad's literal content (Preston, 1967).

The tendency toward illogical thinking was so strong that it prompted the question of whether perception of advertising may operate differently from the way perception of other messages operated.

Might the illogical attribution of content be less in evidence when other messages were used? Might people, rather than observing the same behavioral laws for all communication forms, adopt perceptual conventions when examining ads which they do not apply when perceiving other message forms? And will a model of advertising perception eventually be required in order to properly specify characteristics not adequately covered by general communication models?

Preston (1967) exposed subjects to ads, then exposed them to accompanying sets of statements which included some illogically derived from the ads' contents. The subjects were asked to label each statement as an accurate or inaccurate restatement or paraphrase of what the ad stated or implied.

For example, a Bell Telephone ad said, "You'll get a royal welcome when you call Long Distance." The logically invalid statement was that if you don't call long distance, then you are sure of not getting a royal welcome. This involves a false conversion of propositions: if a message says "If X then Y," it is invalid to think that it implies either "If Y then X" or "If not-X then not-Y."

By the rules of logic, the invalidly drawn statements could not be considered accurate restatements of the ad's literal content. But when a subjuct accepted an invalid statement as accurate, it apparently became, for him, as much a part of the message's perceived content as if it were literally contained therein. The number of times that this happened was unexpectedly high: 65 percent.

Upon obtaining this finding, the experimenter found himself beleaguered in attempting to explain it. The original assumption had been that copywriters deliberately wrote ads so as to make illogical conclusions more likely.

The Geritol case was cited, in which people were not told that they actually had tired blood, but were encouraged by wording and tone to assume that the ad was really telling them this.

Though some responsibility for this happening was placed upon the advertiser, the experimenter assumed that illogical conclusions were primarily the reader's own responsibility and were avoidable through careful reading and thoughtful reasoning.

The subjects, however, demurred. Upon having the project explained, several commented that it was by no means true that they reasoned poorly. One might pass this off as a protective stance, but it was hard to deny the alternate explanation they presented. They argued, simply, that what they perceived the ad as saying was what the advertiser would have liked to say, or liked the reader to conclude--and attribution of such statements to the ad's perceived content was perfectly valid and logical beyond question. Would not Bell Telephone, for example, like you to think that you'll get that "royal welcome" *only* if you call long distance? Of course they would. And Geritol, equally so, would like you to think you have tired blood. Therefore, it was "logical" to see the ads as saying these things, even though such perceived content could not be attributed logically to the ads' literal contents.

In addition, it might also be regarded as logical to see ads saying all sorts of things which are not strictly logical according to the classical rules developed by Aristotle. This would follow from general public understanding of advertising as including flights of fancy rather than adhering strictly

to cold facts. To understand that advertising is "poetry" in a sense, that it is emotionally-oriented, is to expect it to be something other than strictly logical.

Meanwhile, other forms of communication would not have these expectations attached to them. Though most communicators and communicatees stray from formal logic to some degree, there is reason to believe that advertising strays much farther than other sorts of messages.

The principal issue of the present study, then, is whether the earlier results were due to (1) the reader's careless logic or (2) a perceptual framework which incorporated his possibly very sensible expectations about what advertisers want to tell their readers. At stake as well is the issue of whether perception of advertising is different in important respects from the perception of other communication forms. These two issues may be examined simultaneously as follows.

If more illogical behavior is found with advertising than with the other forms, it would suggest that people's reasoning about ads is based on quite sensible (although special!) assumptions about the nature of advertising, and is not illogical after all. It would also suggest that a model of advertising perception should be developed which accounts for various advertising characteristics which general communication models do not employ.

If no difference in "illogical" behavior is found between advertising and other forms, it would leave open the question of why such behavior occurred (careless reasoning would remain the principal hypothesis), and it would provide no evidence of a need to develop an advertising perception model.

The experiment reported below examined these possibilities by testing people's comparative tendencies to accept

53

"logically invalid" statements after reading messages prepared variously in the forms of advertisements, newspaper stories, business memoranda, and personal letters.

SELECTION OF MESSAGES

From the advertisements used in the earlier study, 12 were selected for which subjects had shown strong tendencies to accept the illogical statement. The original selection of 45 ads is discussed in Preston (1967).

The content of each of the 12 ads was reconstructed into the form of news stories, business memoranda, and personal letters. Ideally, the exact words would have been rearranged, thus altering form without changing content. In practice this was not possible; for example, the slogan "Bayer works wonders" seemed so unlikely to be contained in a personal letter that it was changed to "Bayer worked wonderfully for me."

Although it would have been best to vary only the form of communication, the experiment must be regarded as comparing messages which vary not only in form but also in content to the degree that it interacts inseparably with form. Nonetheless, content was essentially preserved in all forms, and special pains were taken to assure this for those portions of content referred to in the five test statements accompanying each ad.

Additional content, not included in the ads, was added as required in order to make the news stories, memos, and letters appear real. Especially for letters, it seemed necessary to include much material irrelevant to the product message. Letter writers *do* occasionally mention products among their comments, but would not devote a large portion of a letter to that.

The content of each message was presented on a separate typed sheet. This was done for the ads as well as for the other message forms. For each ad, all verbal content was recorded and identified as headline, body copy, caption, etc., and all illustrations were thoroughly described. At the top of each message was a label which identified the form of the message; news stories, memos, and letters were described as genuine.

Each subject in the experiment was exposed to one form of each of the 12 messages, with three messages presented in each of the four forms. Order of messages and selection of forms were made randomly for each subject.

STATEMENTS ACCOMPANYING MESSAGES

For each of the 12 messages, subjects were given a set of five statements; they were to specify each as an "accurate" or "inaccurate" restatement or paraphrase of what was stated or implied in the message content.

Two of these statements were defined by the experimenters as accurate restatements; one was a simple paraphrase of the content and the other was a logically-valid derivation from it.

The other three statements were defined as inaccurate; they included a logically invalid derivation from the message content, a statement directly negated by some portion of the message, and a statement called "independent" which was about the product but otherwise unrelated to anything stated in the message (neither true nor false, neither validly nor invalidly derived). These statements were the same used in the earlier study, and are described at length in Preston (1967).

PROCEDURE

One hundred and five students were the subjects. A test booklet was submitted to each subject, which contained a page of instructions followed by the 12 messages and the set of five statements accompanying each.

Following data analysis, a questionnaire was prepared which explained the true purpose of the experiment and summarized the results. The purpose of the questionnaire was to obtain subjects' explanations about why the results occurred as they did.

STATISTICAL RESULTS

Principal findings (Table 1) were the mean percentages of times subjects called the logically invalid statement an "accurate" restatement of the message content for each of the four types of messages. With each subject exposed to three examples of each type of message, the datum for a given subject for a given message was the total number of "accurate" claims (zero to three). Therefore, the base was 105 for each message form, 420 for the entire experiment.

A two-way analysis of variance, "subjects" x "messages," with one observation in each cell, was performed on these data. "Subjects" served as a control variable. The F ratio obtained for message effects was 6.96 (3,312 df), significant far beyond conventionally tabled probabilities.

Post-hoc comparisons among the various pairs of means showed that advertisements were significantly higher in acceptance of logically invalid restatements than each of the other message forms. In addition, letters were significantly higher than news stories.

Table 1

THE LOGICALLY INVALID STATEMENT

Type of message	Mean percentage of times called "accurate"
Ads	62.53
Letters*	54.30
Memos*	50.80
News stories*	48.57
Total	54.04

* Mean percentage for letters, memos, and news stories combined was 51.22 (N = 315).

No other comparisons of means showed significant differences.

Additional findings concern the other four types of statements which subjects described as "accurate" or "inaccurate" (Tables 2, 3, 4, and 5). Analyses of variance similar to that reported above found significant results only for the logically valid statement: $F = 4.08$, $p = .007$.

Post-hoc comparisons performed for the logically valid statement found no differences when comparing each single

Table 2

THE TRUE STATEMENT

Message	Mean percentage of times called "accurate"
Letters	84.13
Memos	83.81
Ads	83.17
News stories	79.05
Total	82.54

mean to the other; the only significant post-hoc comparison was between the combination of ads and news stories and the combination of memos and letters, which was significant at the .05 level.

Table 3

THE LOGICALLY VALID STATEMENT

Message	Mean percentage of times called "accurate"
News stories*	62.23
Ads*	60.63
Letters†	52.37
Memos†	51.10
Total	56.59

* Mean percentage for news stories and ads combined was 61.27 (N = 210).
† Mean percentage for letters and memos combined was 51.73 (N = 210).

Table 4

THE INDEPENDENT STATEMENT

Message	Mean percentage of times called "accurate"
Ads	18.41
Letters	18.10
News stories	18.10
Memos	15.87
Total	17.62

Table 5

THE FALSE STATEMENT

Message	Mean percentage of times called "accurate"
News stories	9.52
Letters	8.25
Ads	6.35
Memos	5.08
Total	7.30

DUSCUSSION AND FURTHER ANALYSIS

The hypothesis that "illogical behavior may be greater with advertising than with other forms of communication was supported by experimental responses to the logically invalid statement. Acceptance of this statement averaged over 11 percent more for ads than for the other forms.

If this "illogical" behavior were caused strictly by faulty reasoning, it should have occurred equally often for all communication forms. Because it did not, it was assumed instead that it happened because people looked at advertisements in a different way. The illogical statements were advantageous to the advertiser (Bell Telephone would enjoy having us believe that we *must* call ahead by long distance), and subjects apparently were more willing to assume that the advertiser "meant to say" such a statement than that other communicators did.

This conclusion is also supported by results for the logically valid statement, in which the subject's tolerance of what the communicator "meant to say" would produce a specification of "accurate" rather than "inaccurate."

Though demonstrating it less strongly for these statements, subjects again showed this tolerance more with ads than with letters or memos (though not significantly different than news stories). In doing so, they produced fewer errors of logical reasoning (i.e., fewer specifications of "inaccurate") rather than more, and this strengthens the suggestion that the observed behavior stemmed more from subjects' approaches to the various message forms from their logical reasoning *per se*.

Additional relevant information, revealing the perceptual framework within which subjects viewed the messages, was provided by the post-experimental questionnaire. Of 105 subjects, 102 said they had no trouble seeing that the messages were of the various types, and 99 said they identified each message as being of the type the label said it was. Seventy said they accepted each of the messages as being a legitimate example of that type of message. Of the 35 who questioned the legitimacy, 29 said letters with product contents seemed hard to believe.

When asked whether they were affected by the fact that the messages took different forms, 68 of 105 answered "no." This suggests there was little awareness of the differential responses they actually made.

When respondents were asked why they labeled an inaccurate statement as accurate 54 percent of the time, this question did not produce surprising responses. The question, rather, was used primarily to set subjects up for questions which probed why the differential response to advertising occurred.

Answers to these questions were consistent with the earlier report of Preston (1967) that many subjects felt their "illogical" responses were actually quite logical. One of the themes found in the answers was that people see advertisements as purposeful in ways different from the purposefulness of other message forms. Some comments were:

"Ads are designed to create favorable responses, rather than just communicate."
"Ads call for you to make a decision --the other messages don't."
"With other messages it is someone else's problem--the ad usually makes it *my* problem."
"Advertising is not a passive form of communication. It demands some action on your part."

The communication form most clearly different from advertising in this way would be news stories, which are generally seen as imparting information and not calling for a response. Memos and letters do at times call for a response, and the ones in this study certainly appeared to do so. Apparently, the subjects were discussing memos and letters not as they appeared in the study but as they had perceived them in previous experience. In any event, they were emphasizing that ads virtually always call for a decision or response, while other forms do not.

This calls to mind the philosophical point that all communication requires a response in the sense that the communicator is attempting to have something to do with someone else's response toward the message topic (Taplin, 1960). Nonetheless, the subjects clearly observed a difference--they saw ad writers as being far more concerned with this than the writers of other messages.

A second theme in the questionnaire answers was that advertising not only calls for a response but, in addition, makes it quite clear to the reader just what that response is. Again, this contrasts with other forms in which specification of possible response is far less clear.

The result of being aware of a specific desired response is that the reader tends to see the advertisement, in contrast to other message forms, as making the strongest possible statements which will support that response. This meant, in the study, perceiving the ad to be stating certain things which actually were not a part of its literal content. Of course, the latter was done for the other message forms as well in 51 percent of cases, but the additional 11 percent for advertising might be attributed to the reader's tendency to see the ad as strongly urging the specific desired response.

It may be useful, therefore, to incorporate this assumption into models of advertising perception or advertising communication. Such assumption has not been established in general communication models because, in most communications, a topic (product or whatever) may be mentioned favorably without the reader instantly believing that the purpose is to produce sales or some equally strong favorable response. The reader of other message forms does not perceive the source as being necessarily partial to the outcome; therefore, he does not tend so strongly to see the message making positive claims.

An interesting implication of this suggested model change is that it appears to contrast with certain beliefs the public presumably claims about its handling of ads. The conventional wisdom on this matter is that many citizens report they are intolerant of much ad content and, therefore, discount the statements made therein. But this study appears to demonstrate expansion rather than contraction of perceived ad content--seeing more rather than seeing less--showing a certain tolerance rather than intolerance.

A number of subjects hinted at this possibility in their answers:

"Due to something of an unconscious receptiveness of advertising's conditioning process, we have often not questioned the logic behind the statements offered in ads. I think people are more in the groove of thinking constructed by advertising, rarely questioning good ads."

"Maybe we've come to expect so much exaggeration in ads that we're liable to assume that they meant to say it that way even if they didn't in so many words."

"I think we try to figure out what the ad is getting at and then accept it even if illogical."

"One is ready to accept illogical content because this is what is expected of ads."

"The reader knows the illogical statements are over-generalizations and false, yet they are accurate as far as what the advertiser hopes to imply."

That there may be a difference between what people are aware of and not aware of in their response to advertising was suggested by one subject in this way:

"Despite the subconscious effects ads have, people are consciously more hesitant or disbelieving of advertising statements."

The tolerance and expansion of perceived content, in other words, may happen only at a low level of awareness. At a higher level of awareness, meanwhile, he may demonstrate the more conventional stereotyped intolerance and contraction of content.

Thus, one might hypothesize a model showing expansion of perceived ad content at an unconscious level, followed by contraction of perceived content at the conscious level. People may discount what they think they see, but what they think they see may be greater than the literal content to which they are actually exposed. The result could be that the public is far more tolerant of advertising than it thinks it is.

SUMMARY

It was found that apparently illogical behavior observed in an experimental situation occurred more in response to advertising than in response to other communication forms. This difference may be due not to illogical thinking *per se* but, rather, to sensible expectations which people make about the content of ads. Because they know what the advertising would like to say, they tend to see the ad actually making such statements even when it does not literally do so.

The data have illustrated several facets of what appears to be a set to perceive advertising in certain ways not applicable to the perception of other communication forms. Of special interest is the emerging idea of a tolerance for advertising which contrasts with conventional views of the public's reactions to this communication medium. Perhaps people are really more tolerant of advertising than they suppose themselves to be, with their unconscious behavior tending to counteract the conscious intolerance they often express in their public statements about advertising.

Though it can be argued that the data clearly show the phenomena which was discussed, it seems fairer to suggest that the reader treat these ideas as hypotheses rather than confirmed findings. By regarding the work as hypothesis-forming rather than hypothesis-testing, the interpretation may have gone somewhat beyond the date.

But the purpose has been to produce questions as well as answers. Perceptual sets toward advertising, tolerance of advertising, and the possibly distinctive characteristics of an advertising communication model may be important things to ask further questions about.

REFERENCES

Preston, Ivan L. Logic and Illogic in the Advertising Process. *Journalism Quarterly*, Vol. 44, No. 2, pp. 231-239.

Taplin, Walter. *Advertising: A New Approach*. Boston: Little, Brown, 1960.

DISCUSSION QUESTIONS

1. "People often perceived as part of an ad's content certain statements which they invalidly believed to be implied by the ad's literal content." Does the study suggest good reasons why the above hypothesis may hold true?

2. Does the study imply anything which contrasts with the conventional view of the public's reactions to advertising?

PART II

SOCIAL ISSUES IN ADVERTISING

"All advertising in the United States was stopped at 10 o'clock this morning.

The nation's more than 6,600 commercial radio stations, stunned by the loss of their only revenue, announced plans immediately to suspend operations indefinitely.

All of the nearly 700 commercial television stations, also financed solely by advertising, are expected to go dark in a matter of days.

The major radio-TV networks have announced an imminent halt in all services.

The nation's newspapers and magazines, primarily dependent on advertising revenue, are trying desperately to adjust.

Many newspapers hope they can hang on--by trimming the size of editions and doubling or tripling prices to subscribers. Most magazines were pinned to the wall and ceased publication.

Hundreds of thousands of people in advertising, broadcasting, and the print media are looking for jobs--or soon will be. They will be joined shortly by thousands more employed in program production, equipment manufacturing, and similar allied industries."[1]

The quotation is the first part of a booklet published by the National Association of Broadcasters, a trade association of firms in the broadcast industries. The booklet goes on to state the differences in the amount of time a worker must spend in New York City versus Moscow to earn enough to purchase such items as a pound of butter, a man's shirt, and a pair of women's hose. One of its conclusions is: "Remove the keystone (advertising) and the entire economy could come crashing down as suddenly as the Roman Empire tumbled in another era."[2]

Ignoring the fact that the collapse of the Roman Empire was caused by a series of complex factors and it took centuries, is advertising really so important to the economy, or is it the bane of our existence as some critics might charge? This section of the book contains a number of articles which provide thoughts on this question. The articles come from people in government, universities, and the advertising industry. This may be the section of the book which engenders the most discussion because it contains the most controversial points of view.

[1] Taken from a booklet published by the National Association of Broadcasters in 1972, "Advertising STOPPED at 10 o'clock." [2] Ibid.

II-1

ADVERTISING AND CONSUMERISM

Virginia H. Knauer

Several weeks ago in his regular column for *Advertising Age*, E.B. Weiss asked the following: "Did you know that on campus right now a popular pastime is to ridicule TV commercials? It has become a hilarious game played by both sexes. That hilarity cloaks deep resentments."

While it may be the "in" thing on campus to laugh at ads, others find the subject not so amusing.

Take the American public for instance. In a recent Harris poll based on interviews with 1,648 households, the public gave advertising a 12 percent confidence rating, the lowest among 16 major institutions.

The attitude of many women toward advertising is particularly critical. In a recent survey, the New York Chapter of the National Organization for Women found that a very large proportion of 1,200 ads depicted women as "domestic adjuncts," "demeaned housekeepers," "dependent on men," "submissive," "sex objects," and "household functionaries."

A study by *Good Housekeeping* of the attitudes of 1,000 women towards advertising showed that 40 percent believed that "the modern woman is insulted by women-directed commercials, and it's time broadcasters realized the days of talking down to her were over."

Similarly, a survey of advertising by the YMCA of Buffalo and Erie County in New York in conjunction with the State University College of Buffalo gave heavy adverse ratings to ads for Confidents, Feminique, Mitchum, Wonderbread, Gladbags, Playtex, Colgate, and Geritol.

Men have had their say about advertising, also. The Committee for the Rejection of Obnoxious Commercials (CROC) handed out "Lemmy" awards to ads showing a child with only one cavity, the girl whose boyfriend didn't recognize her because of her new bra, the father who wore a crown on his head after using a certain margarine, and the barrel-chested actor who brags from his bed that he hasn't used his deodorant all day.

Serious criticism has come from such organizations as the Institute for Public Interest Representation, a public interest law group at the Georgetown University Law Center. The Institute analyzed the documentation for 59 television ads and found that 41 were

not substantiated by data submitted to
the Federal Trade Commission.

Even businessmen are critical. In 1971,
a poll taken of 2,700 subscribers to
the *Harvard Business Review* showed that
only 30 percent of the respondents believed that advertisements presented
a true picture of the product advertised. That 30 percent represented a
drop of 24 percent since a similar
poll taken in 1962.

What has gone wrong?

In the first place, not everything is
wrong. There are a number of ads
which are not only great examples of
creativity but which are also informative and communicate on a level which
is respectful to the viewing audience.

BP Oil Corporation found that its ads
created an enormous demand for its
"BP Miser" booklets: 1.5 million were
given out in the first three months of
the campaign, and BP ordered a new
booklet with a two million printing
for the next phase of the campaign.
BP executives based this ad program on
research which showed that the buying
public wanted something more than
puffery. And the campaign resulted in
a substantial increase in "trial"
purchases.

American Motors Corporation attributes
its big spurt in sales to its new
"Buyer Protection Program" which relies
heavily on tasteful, informative ads.
And according to *Advertising Age*,
Ford's "Listening Program" broke all
records in terms of viewer and reader
response. Hunt-Wesson's sales increased
25 percent in two months after introduction of its "We'll Help You Make It"
program.

Family Health Magazine recently gave a
number of awards to advertisers who
gave nutrition information and education to the consumer in their ads. Recipients included Giant Food, Inc., the
Florida Citrus Commission, Borden,

Kellogg, and PVO International. Sears,
Roebuck and Co. proudly announces the
data for its claims are available for
anyone who wishes to examine these records. Volkswagen and Alka-Seltzer ads
are known for their entertaining, good
humor, and Kraft consistently produces
agreeable ads. There are, of course,
many other ads beyond these which consumers find tasteful, informative and
appealing.

With so many advertisers doing so well
in sales by those approaches, why is
it that there still remains a glut of
garbage advertising? What factor or
factors separate those who consistently
communicate on a dignified, informative
level from those advertisers who believe
in low level appeals.

To get at the answers to these questions,
I have talked with advertising experts
in and out of government--officials
from the Federal Trade Commission, advertising associations, advertising
agencies, clients, and private lawyers
representing clients in trouble.

All these experts made the same central
observation: The final say on the advertising message belongs to the client's
management. To say this is not to ne-
gate the responsibility or the role of
the agency. To the contrary, judging
from some of the outstanding examples
I have seen, an agency can often persuade a skeptical client to accept the
high road rather than the low one.
However, as a vice president of one advertising agency told me, "the agency
does not lead the client, the agency
follows the client."

To my way of thinking, there are more
than enough convincing arguments in
favor of "high road" ads. In an *Advertising Age* article, Kenneth Mason,
group vice president for Quaker Oats, is
quoted as saying, "By pitching their
sales messages continually below the
level of intelligence of the best
audiences, ad people are finding that
they have largely lost those audiences

and that advertising is, in many cases, beginning to prove enormously inefficient."

Besides the question of efficiency and effectiveness, there is the real danger of receiving a tarnished corporate image due to adverse consumer response. As I have mentioned, we have already seen several examples of organized opposition to tasteless ads, and we are very likely to see increased opposition in the future. Why take such risks when they are not necessary?

Of course, I recognize that there are some clients and some agencies who are convinced that garbage ads sell better. In the December 25 issue of *Advertising Age*, the executive vice president of a major advertising firm literally brags about all the adverse criticism he received over a toilet paper ad. All the adverse criticism from *Time Magazine*, from consumer groups, from *Variety*, and other important sectors didn't bother the client either. It is this basic Babbit-type philosophy which is doing so much harm to the advertising profession, a point made by Edward G. Gallagher, Executive Vice President of N.W. Ayer and Son in the same issue. Too many in the advertising profession Mr. Gallagher maintains, are "looking, sounding, and selling in a outmoded manner, out of step with the new attitude of today and tomorrow, a new attitude of a growing majority of American consumers who will increasingly look on him and his works with annoyance and some contempt, or, worse, with amusement."

Foote, Cone, and Belding made the same point a little differently in a recent Wall Street Journal ad: "Some of the Pavlovian techniques of television advertising made sales, but at the expense of credibility, that acceptance which is the soil in which advertising flourishes. It was a kind of strip-mining for which we are beginning to pay the price now."

What about the progressive firms? What special characteristics do they generally share? In my discussions with advertising experts, these traits were paramount:

1. A finely tuned social sensitivity.
2. Solid communications with their national associations.
3. The knowledge that mature ads sell and sell very well.
4. A carefully spelled out policy on what constitutes honest and tasteful advertising.

This latter point, to my mind, is most important. The National Business Council for Consumer Affairs' Sub-Council on Advertising and Promotion recommended such a policy in an advertising report issued this past September. The Council said:

"1. The chief executive officer of the corporation should be involved in the development of the statements of advertising and promotion policy and procedures.
"2. The statements should be reduced to writing.
"3. The statements should be disseminated to all individuals involved in the organization's advertising and promotion functions.
"4. The statements should be made available to interested individuals outside of the organization.
"5. The statements should be subject to continuing review and revision."

The Council's recommendations were indirectly endorsed in a "Truth in Advertising" report in 1972 by the American Management Association. Said the AMA, "Companies that desire a high degree of honesty, that have clear-cut and definite objectives, that have communicated to their agency exactly what they expect will no doubt have fewer problems, if any, with the FTC, consumers, and its sales objectives."

Why more companies do not have their advertising policy clearly written out is rather puzzling. Data presented by the AMA indicates that only about 20 percent of the companies have set forth their policies in writing.

With a well thought out advertising policy, businesses can demonstrate their commitment to responsible advertising communications. A written policy can keep a firm from getting into trouble with government and consumer groups while at the same time help accomplish sales objectives.

I have examined the policies of several firms mentioned in the National Business Council's advertising report. Here are excerpts from some outstanding policies:

"Advertising should avoid the use of claims whose validity depends upon fine interpretation of meaning."

"It is the basic principle of the company and of the law that advertising shall be honest in fact and in spirit."

"Advertising shall not claim nor promise by implication any product performance or characteristic which is not fully supported by test or research data or other similar factual information."

"The test of whether anything is permissible in advertising under our policy is to ask: 'Is it the truth? Is it believable? Is it in good taste?'"

A written policy, of course, isn't a sure guarantee of consumer or government satisfaction with the final product. But it is an important first step.

It's a step which must be taken if business wants to communicate on the level the public desires, if business doesn't want its advertising to be laughed at, not only in the college dorms, but in American homes.

Businessmen and advertisers should be horrified at the 12 percent confidence rating given to advertising in the recent Harris poll. This poll shows that advertising is being judged today by the public on more than the criteria of "does it sell?"

Commenting on the poll and the adverse criticism of advertising by consumers, Foote, Cone, and Belding has said, "Anyone who still sees the consumer as a passive boob is reading these events the way Custer read his intelligence reports."

Those firms which base their arguments for poor taste ads purely on the "selling" yardstick are displaying their insensitivity to the public.

They are saying, in essence, that they will give the public not what the public wants, but what the corporation wants the public to have.

They are saying, in essence, that they believe in the "sucker born every minute" pitch.

Fortunately, there are others who have a different point of view. There are a number of businesses and advertisers who know that the public wants a different message, a message which says, in effect, that business thinks well of people.

The future is not with the Babbitts or the P.T. Barnums. It's with those businessmen and advertisers who present their products to consumers in a manner which clearly demonstrates respect for them as individuals and appreciation for their continued business.

DISCUSSION QUESTIONS

1. It is reported that confidence ratings of advertisements score low as alertness on the part of consumers increases. Discuss what, in your opinion, constitutes credibility in advertising?

2. How should firms take into account the increasing impact of consumerism in setting up their advertising policies?

Reprinted by permission from ADVERTISING AGE; 23 October, 1972, pp. 71-2, 74, 78.

II-2

ADVERTISING MEETS ITS ERA OF SOCIAL ACCOUNTABILITY

E. B. Weiss

The era that "could not happen" is here--the era of advertising's social accountability.

I predict that if by 1980 advertising does not adequately reflect the required social accountability, it will not merely face stifling regulation, but will be deeply enmeshed in it.

Unfortunately, advertising's present crawling pace toward social accountability, when measured against the frenetic pace of our new society, is hardly cause for optimism.

The American Management Assn., in a preface to one of its research studies into the social aspects of marketing, remarked: "Some companies refuse to believe that they are forcing consumers and government into the advertising arena by not recognizing that they have created a credibility gap and a communications barrier between themselves and the consumer.

"There is some evidence to suggest that consumers are being impatient with misleading and deceptive advertising, tired of being treated like pawns in a market grid box, of being intellectually abused by a bombardment of degrading advertisements."

In *Advertising Age* last Oct. 25, a marketing executive declared: "By pitching their sales messages continually below the level of intelligence of the best audiences, ad people are finding that they have largely lost these audiences, and that advertising is, in many cases, beginning to prove enormously inefficient."

A study released last April by the American Assn. of Advertising Agencies shows how serious the problem is today (a problem in no way diminished by current Four A's ultra-conservatism). Of 9,000 students from 177 universities and colleges who were asked whether they considered advertising believable "some of the time," a shocking 53% told the Four A's that they did. That is hardly justification for complacency-- especially since "some of the time" obviously made that a loaded question. Could a reasonable respondent answer "never" when asked that loaded question? Well--47% did precisely that!

Moreover, 57% thought that more government regulation should be imposed on the advertising industry. Surely that clearly indicates that, in their opinion, even "some of the time" does not constitute very much of the time.

Right here the gravity of the situation becomes apparent, since these students of 1972 will constitute advertising's primary audience in the 1980s.

The reasons for disapproving of advertising often cluster around the conclusion that it is a social pollutant, not a malevolent economic instrument. But social pollutants generally are no more highly esteemed by our new society than are today's environmental pollutants.

The accelerating debate about advertising and its proper position in our modern society involves social, moral and ethical issues. This dialog cannot be wholly divorced from economic issues--but economic questions are secondary.

In 1967, Leo Burnett appealed to the Four A's for studies of the "economic and social effects of advertising, which I believe are long overdue."

If the Four A's is deeply concerned about the "economic and social effects of advertising," that attitude did not come through at its 1972 annual conference. The major conclusion of that conference was that all advertising needs is more advertising extolling advertising's social and economic virtues!

Yet Kenneth Mason, a vice-president of Quaker Oats Co., has recently said that for the past two decades, advertising has been seriously lacking "in terms of ethics, in terms of contributions to society, and perhaps even in terms of economic efficiency."

Certainly, as the more knowledgeable segments of our society (who now control, or will in the future control the major share of disposable income) increasingly question advertising's social contributions to our society, advertising's economic efficiency must be impaired. Moreover, the evidence suggests that, as a direct consequence, more sophisticated yardsticks for

measuring advertising will be demanded by more advertisers.

And that suggests that, by 1980, advertising will contend with serious budget problems if it has not made ads more socially acceptable, because the farther advertising drops behind our new higher social standards, the smaller the return per dollar invested in advertising.

CAR DEALERS BAN PUFFERY

I am reminded in this connection that on July 1, the automobile dealers of Wisconsin took an uncharacteristic step: They eliminated puffery from their ads.

This action was required under the state's new Motor Vehicle Trade Practice Code. But its inclusion in the code was proposed voluntarily by the dealer's own organization, the Wisconsin Automotive Trade Assn. The Wisconsin rule specifically states, "Terms such as 'best,' 'less,' and 'greater' and other superlatives and comparatives indicate puffery and are prohibited unless there is detailed proof for such claim."

Canada will be clamping down on puffery under new legislation. A recent step in this same direction is implicit in the suggestion of Commissioner Mary Gardiner Jones of the Federal Trade Commission that: "There is no such thing as a category of opinion statements that deserve legal exemption merely because no one would believe them or rely on them."

Ad Age columnist William Tyler reported that 1970s top ad campaigns contained less information than before (AA, March 22, 1971). The trend has moved since then toward the ultimate--no information at all--giving us what *Advertising Age* has called the "Latest ad gimmick-- no-advertising advertising." That editorial conclusion was based on a wave of gasoline advertising that dodged all formula claims because of fears of an FTC crackdown involving advertised claims for identical products.

Traditionalists in advertising claim that critics' base of support is so small that the problem is not a major one. Only naive students of public opinion would follow that line of reasoning. After all, experience has proved time and again that "causes" sponsored by small groups of activists can suddenly explode on a large scale.

CHOATE CEREALS BLAST CHANGES MINDS

Consider, for example, the variations in response to a poll in which mothers would be asked if they approved of advertisements for presweetened cereals for their children. If such a poll had been conducted in the early spring of 1970, mothers would have given overwhelming approval to cereal advertising.

However, after the Robert Choate cereal blast, the degree of tolerance vanished overnight. Yet that blast was ignited by just *one* critic.

The new advertising strictures emerging from our sophisticated society were dramatically demonstrated when a Houston real estate company agreed to provide equal promotion of both predominantly white and predominantly black real estate subdivisions in newspaper advertising. It also agreed to put 10% of its ad budget into black media for the next year--under a consent decree obtained by the Justice Department.

The decree resolved a housing discrimination suit filed in February in which the government charged that the Suburban Homes Realty Co. created racially segregated neighborhoods by its sales practices, and by advertising and media usage that steered prospective home

buyers to areas in which their race was predominant.

A Justice Department official said that the company ran ads for predominantly white subdivisions in general media, and advertised predominantly black subdivisions only in black media. He said that this is the third or fourth time the Justice Department has required a land sale company to spend 10% of its ad budget to back both black and white subdivisions in black media. The decree also requires the company to include an equal housing opportunities slogan in all of its advertising and promotional material.

HOW TO GEAR PROFIT TO SOCIAL NEEDS

That decree explains why a large consumer goods corporation is experimenting with an office of consumer affairs, whose primary objective will be to achieve a more socially accountable marketing program. Its directives include establishment of (1) a task force to develop profit opportunities in existing and new products that will relate to the new social values of our society, (2) a genuine consumer panel to provide continuing playback on the social reactions to the corporation's marketing and advertising programs (the panel will be exposed to advertising before it runs as well as after), and (3) programs for working with the various consumer organizations--national, state and local.

Clearly, the expectations of American society have begun to rise at a faster pace than advertising's social performance. Yet some advertising executives --maybe the majority--derive comfort from the conclusion that the new social pressures bedeviling advertising are merely a temporary phenomenon sired by massive urban decay, environmental pollution, etc.

The cold reality, however, is that society is demanding a radical redefinition of the responsibility of private enterprise. Never have critics of our business institutions criticized such a broad range of business policies and practices, in such large (and still mounting) numbers.

Advertising, the most visible function of free enterprise, inevitably becomes a prime target in this broad sweep toward social responsibility.

Industry equates "private" enterprise with "free" enterprise. But the public is saying that industry--and especially advertising--has abused its freedom.

Industry may remain private nonetheless. But it will continue to lose still more of its traditional freedom--advertising especially, because it is so constantly, so annoyingly visible to the public.

Addressing himself to advertising's new environment, Paul Harper, chief executive of Needham, Harper & Steers, said: "Just as surely as our cities are being enveloped in smog and other filth, so is communications environment becoming more cluttered and obscured. The public is beginning to react with confusion and indifference to this deluge. We are faced with a growing consensus among congressmen, other government officials, and organized segments of the public that advertising is both wasteful and unnecessary."

ADVERTISERS 'INTRUDING EXCESSIVELY?'

Yet the total number of TV and radio commercials per hour continues to increase. Magazines are now permitting advertisers to intrude excessively by means of gatefolds, inserts, loose cards, pop-ups. The ratio of editorial

matter to ads continues to be slashed. And newspapers, especially on Sunday, are loaded with many irritating odds and ends of advertising.

Even the virtuous *New York Times* on Sunday makes its contribution to solid waste pollution with its sheer bulk, and to reader irritation with its special advertising supplements.

Apathy, boredom and indifference created by advertising are economic as well as social evils. The advertising business, consequently, will--in time--be less able economically to justify advertising that flagrantly disregards public time, convenience, privacy and intelligence.

Will it be impossible for advertising to remain adequately persuasive under the new social imperatives? Well, right now 85% of advertising messages don't persuade, because they are seen by unseeing eyes or heard by tuned-out ears and minds--and another 5% to 10% of ad messages, although registering, are not believed.

So the advertising industry must ask itself: Can advertising, under self regulation or imposed regulation, possibly achieve poorer results than it does right now?

Could even dull, informative advertising bomb worse than presumably scintilating advertising today?

In July, 1971, our prestigious Committee for Economic Development published a landmark study of the new social responsibilities of business. That study includes this conclusion:

"Over-all, a clear majority of the public thinks corporations have not been sufficiently concerned about the problems facing our society. Two-thirds believe business now has a moral obligation to achieve social progress, even at the expense of profitability."

That road leads to government regulation. Since advertising shows so little inclination to reform itself, it is probable that, by 1980, advertising will be regulated to a shattering degree.

The up-coming generation are now seniors in high school. The most talented of this group--a million or so--will cut an even wider swath in society than their immediate predecessors--who have cut both deep and wide.

Those million high school seniors will become advertising's target as the end of the 1970s approaches. What will happen when these bright young people step out of their colleges and universities? I am sure they will not accept ideas that are presented in advertising in the context of the lowest common denominator.

Young advertising talent could redeem advertising in the future--if it were not hobbled by the Establishment at the higher executive levels.

CYNICAL ABOUT ADS AT AGE FIVE

The young generation has been reared on a vast cynicism concerning traditional marketing and advertising. Time and again I think of that 1971 Harvard study that disclosed that, by five years of age, children exposed to television commercials are already cynical about advertising. If advertising fails to make adequate changes --how will these children respond to advertising when they mature?

Many of our young people read only their underground publications--listen only to their underground radio. They are exceedingly intolerant of advertising programs that do not match their intellectual and social standards.

How will industry advertise in 1980 to

18-to-30-year-olds who are sophisticated (and skeptical) of advertising?

Sweeping guidelines designed to take note of the social consequences of children's TV advertising have been formulated by the Assn. of National Advertisers.

The ANA, which, according to *Ad Age*, has been cool to over-all industry strictures, is now moving to set special standards for advertising directed toward children--partly as protective reaction against the crusading mothers of Action for Children's Television.

The ANA's main thrust in these guidelines is toward advertising, but implicit throughout is the ANA's concern for television programming as well.

The ANA urges advertisers to capitalize on the potential of TV to foster understanding and impart knowledge by supporting programs that go beyond entertainment values; it also suggests that "children's hour" advertisers keep in mind social standards such as friendship, equality and generosity.

REGULATION? TOY ADS GET IT FIRST

The question of social values is approached by the ANA from several other directions. It is suggested that ads accentuate the positive aspects of society rather than portraying violence or appealing to fear; parents or other child guidance figures should not be shown in a disdainful fashion.

Advertising directed at children will be the first broad category of advertising (after cigarette advertising) to be severely regulated. Already some toy advertisers are dropping advertising aimed directly at children, and are using adult programs and media for appeal to parents.

Step-by-step restrictions on toy advertising will provide advertising with a preview of the way in which other product classifications and services will be regulated. Vitamin pill advertising aimed at children is now under attack.

The White House Conference on Children proposed to the President that commercials shown during children's programming be clustered. Will the "cluster" concept now be broadly adapted for adult programs because of the public aggravation over excessive TV advertising?

The review board of the National Assn. of Broadcasters recently amended its TV code to reduce by 25% the time devoted to commercials and other non-program material during weekend television programs for children. This means that the amount of non-program time in children's programs shown between 7 a.m. and 2 p.m. on Saturdays and Sundays will drop from 16 to 12 minutes per hour.

Will non-program time then be reduced on some sports programs? In short, each of these real and potential restrictions on advertising should persuade advertisers to ask, "What's next?" I don't doubt there will be more and more of these restrictions.

WILL TAX BREAKS REPLACE AD REVENUE?

Action for Children's Television has filed a formal petition with the FCC to remove all advertising during children's peak viewing times, and to compel stations to carry a minimum of 14 hours of children's programming per week. They propose that lost revenues resulting from the advertising ban would be made up to networks and local stations via tax breaks.

Will this concept of media tax breaks

as a device for curtailing advertising take hold? Never doubt that an aroused public can bring it about if advertising continues to dodge social accountability. And important segments of our society are at the stage of anti-advertising militancy.

More toy campaigns directed to children will be pre-tested with panels of mothers. And if the mothers turn thumbs down, the advertising won't run. What product category will be next?

It is startling to learn that business executives now tend to be almost as cynical as the more knowledgeable segments of the public about advertising other than their own. This was brought out conclusively in two Harvard Business School studies made ten years apart and reported in depth in the *Harvard Business Review* for May-June, 1971.

That study concluded that, in ten years, business executives' conclusions about advertising have deteriorated dramatically. They continue to respect advertising as a marketing tool, but now entertain serious doubts about its truthfulness and socially beneficial impact. They see a negative impact on public taste and a socially undesirable effect on children.

They complain about the repetitive factor in advertising, that it persuades the public to make unnecessary purchases, that irritating and insulting ads are more common. Only 30% rate advertising as truthful.

CRITICISM IMPLIES AD POWER

Point by point, these business executives were critical of advertising's social disamenities for precisely the same reasons advanced by other critics of advertising, including the young generation. I find this both amazing --and hopeful.

Ironically, underlying a substantial amount of the criticism of advertising's persuasive powers is an assumption that advertising is extremely powerful. Yet logic suggests that advertising is less "powerful" in 1972, in the true meaning of that term, than has been the case as far back as the 1950s.

There is small reason to conclude that this deterioration in advertising's overall ability to persuade will even stabilize over the next few years. This is precisely why more sophisticated systems for measuring the total impact of advertising are just now be-demanded by advertisers. These new measurement systems must include an evaluation of advertising's social impact--a social audit for advertising.

Advertising displays only a painfully slow reaction to these new social postures, despite the obvious fact that the opinion molders of our new society feel that advertising is morally, ethically and esthetically offensive. It was not extraordinary, therefore, to note in January that the National Advertising Review Board stated it would extend its interests to areas of "taste" and "social responsibility." (But by September, progress in these directions by NARB had been minimal.)

The public is asking for higher and higher standards in *all* commercial communications. The press is responding to some degree. So is broadcasting in its documentaries and some newscasts.

But advertising has lagged in responding to this social demand. This is one of the origins of "counter advertising."

Counter advertising promises to mushroom. As it increases, it will function as a curb on advertising volume, as well as a corrective influence on ad content. Beyond doubt, it will be abused--many nonsensical demands for counter advertising will be generated. But the blunt fact is that the public increasingly will become less tolerant of one-way communication--and advertising has been just almost 100% one-way.

COUNTER ADVERTISING WILL INCREASE

I predict that some advertisers, in the future, will allocate a part of their advertising budget to finance the public's right to two-way communication. This counter advertising will be sponsored by advertisers as a free public forum. Perhaps some of these advertiser-financed counter-advertising programs will adapt for public communication the panel concept that some advertisers are using right now for private communication with representative groups of the public. It is also possible that large foundations may underwrite counter advertising in the way that church groups, stockholders, are now challenging the social responsibility of some corporations.

Sponsorship of counter advertising is one example of ways in which advertisers can become more socially accountable.

The overriding question in this area is whether advertising adequately reflects the values of our new society. Most sophisticated observers label advertisers and marketers not as creators of new values, but as exploiters of old values.

TV CLUTTER TO GOVERNMENT REGULATION

There's no doubt that TV clutter is one of the biggest thorns in advertising's side these days--and since it involves public complaints about invasion of its right to privacy it becomes a social issue.

At the American Advertising Federation meeting in Washington in May, three prominent executives--an advertiser, an agency man, and the chief public member of the National Advertising Review Board--railed against TV clutter as the biggest abomination facing advertising today.

It seems clear that TV commercial clutter irritates consumers to the point that they automatically react negatively to almost any commercial. Moreover, that resentment carries over to advertising in other media.

Jock Elliott, chairman of Ogilvy & Mather, said: "Today the over-commercialization of television has become an abomination, an affront to all of us. The irritation of endless program interruptions prejudices people against advertising in general."

Kenneth Mason, group vp-grocery products, Quaker Oats Co., pulled out research to show that most of the audience for six highly rated TV shows didn't recall what was being advertised. With the typical consumer exposed to 300 commercial messages per day, Mr. Mason remarked: "No wonder 97% of the people we asked had no idea who the advertisers were in the shows they had been watching."

I conclude that neither television nor other forms of advertising will curb their excesses voluntarily. Therefore, it seems safe to prophecy that some time between 1975 and 1980, TV commercials will be placed under several types of restrictions, very likely patterned after some of those now in effect for European television.

NEW CLIENT: GOVERNMENT COUNTER ADS

I have already predicted that counter advertising will multiply with each of the remaining years of the '70s. Now I suggest that advertising boutiques will create some of these counter campaigns, and that the total impact will be to further muddy the already too muddied image of advertising.

Indeed, I think it is quite likely that, because of rising public pressure, government will vote funds for counter advertising, and advertising will be taxed to provide funds for counter advertising. In this event, counter ad campaigns may be sizable enough to attract large agencies.

Counter advertising has already persuaded some advertisers to make their advertising more socially acceptable, and may wind up making a contribution to the future of advertising.

The auto industry has learned that government, prodded by an informed electorate, can even compel an industry to design its product to conform with government regulations. Five years ago, I predicted this--but I'm stunned nonetheless.

Government is entering still more deeply into the very guts of the marketing function. Government control of advertising by the toy industry, the advertising of identical products, advertising to create additional demand for energy during a looming energy crisis will multiply by 1980 to a degree that will compel advertising and marketing executives to wonder whatever induced them to complain about advertising restrictions in 1972.

General Mills' report to stockholders makes this significant point of policy: "Any competitive or comparative statement to be made about any product or service must be supported. Each manager responsible for a product is also responsible for the preparation of claims and the development of adequate substantiation for them where necessary." This is one phase of social accountability that will become fairly general in the years ahead.

Fortunately or unfortunately--depending on your viewpoint--major segments of our knowledgeable and affluent shopper population are becoming the "sovereigns of the marketplace"--as advertising labeled them while they were still pawns in the marketplace. This great shift from pawns to something closer to participatory democracy (if not sovereignty) is the great revolution now being shaped by our new society. It will not dominate the total marketplace by 1980--but it will have become a potent force, compelling changes in advertising policy and practice in the public interest.

We hear a good deal currently about "positioning" products. I suggest that products will also be positioned for social accountability. Johnson & Johnson, in its new marketing strategy, plans a program designed to locate areas of greatest consumer dissatisfaction with all the company's consumer products. That's a splendid example of using a social audit to achieve improved service to the public--and improved profit performance.

ACCOUNTANTS WAY AHEAD OF US

If corporate responsibility for social problems is to be meaningful, business will have to develop new ways of measuring progress. Virtually all of the indices of business activity currently in use are based on volume. Improved social accounting is needed if the corporation itself, as well as the public, is to be in a position to appraise the corporation's contributions to the betterment of our society.

The accounting profession currently contends with some of the same problems. But the accountants are moving far more purposely toward social accountability than are advertising and marketing.

The American Institute of Certified Public Accountants has been told that accountants must be responsible not only to corporate management, but also to investors, creditors, labor, consumers, scholars and the government.

The advertising industry must become at least equally socially alert--and soon.

TIME IS RUNNING OUT

All industry faces social accountability, but advertising, because of its visibility, more so than any other segment of business. Time is indeed running out, and if advertising doesn't reform, I predict there will be anti-advertising demonstrations before 1980 that could rival some of the anti-Vietnam demonstrations.

I conclude that:

√ Any corporation of size must expect its free enterprise privileges to shrink at an accelerated pace.

√ The larger the share of market controlled by a corporation, the smaller its free enterprise privileges.

√ Just as the public's right of privacy has been diminished, so will the corporate right of privacy diminish.

Those three basics of social accountability will be even more applicable to larger advertisers.

I point out, as an omen of the future, that the California Department of Insurance has ordered all health insurance advertisers to submit newspaper,

magazine and TV advertising to the
department "at least 30 days prior to
the printing commitment date." Who
will be next?

DISCUSSION QUESTIONS

1. Discuss the implications of increased government regulation in the
advertising industry as a means of
evoking increased social accountability.

2. Assuming that corporations do in
fact come to be concerned with social
problems, how would the management and
organization for advertising in a
company be affected? What would be
the new measures of effectiveness in
advertising?

Reprinted by permission of JOURNAL OF ADVERTISING RESEARCH; October, 1973, Vol. 13, No. 5, pp. 9-12. Copyright 1973, by the Advertising Research Foundation.

II-3

WHAT IS DECEPTIVE ADVERTISING?

Tom Dillon

If you run an advertisement which says, "Your wife will enjoy this new mink coat now on sale for $1,200," and, acting on this representation, I buy the coat and subsequently believe that my wife really didn't love it, I do not think I have been deceived.

On the other hand, if I buy this coat, and, regardless of my wife's affection for it, it turns out not to be mink but rabbit, I have been deceived. I have relied on an objectively ascertainable material fact relating to a decision to purchase, and I certainly have recourse to the law.

The legislation that created the Federal Trade Commission is obviously based on the assumption that each and every consumer should not be obligated to so defend himself against this type of deception. Therefore, the Commission was empowered to begin proceedings against an advertiser whose advertising had the capacity to deceive as described above.

I can't imagine any honest man who does not want to prevent this kind of advertising and who does not support legislation that would be effective in doing so. And, indeed, for many, many years since its original founding, the FTC has proceeded vigorously against all kinds of businesses which have made such deceptive representations.

It is true that the vast portion of these cases involved relatively small businesses. Many were businesses offering mail-order courses, falsely labeled wearing apparel, crooked repair services, and fly-by-night retailing schemes. Very rarely were the Federal Trade Commission's attentions directed to large national advertisers, although there were certain outstanding cases. What the Commissioners did was hard work which produced few national headlines.

In the late 1960s, this hard work drew increasing fire of criticism from political sources. In substance, the charge was that the FTC was only catching little fish and letting the big fish get away. While it was out chasing firms that were sticking little old ladies for $3,500 remodeling jobs that were never completed, big national advertisers were going unscathed.

Now, this is a very attractive notion to many people. If you believe that advertising depends upon deception for its efficacy, then the larger the advertising budget, the larger the deception. Thus, the little old lady, who mistakenly perceives in advertising that there should be one more meatball in her can of nationally advertised food product, is more to be pitied than if she were the victim of a $3,500 house remodeling fraud. Thus, one arrives at the notion of determining the gravity of offense by multiplying it by the number of dollars involved in the advertising.

After 1969, the thrust of FTC investigative procedures was toward the big national advertisers and their presumed deceptive practices. Now, as the investigators must have found out to their dismay, it is not easy to find national advertisers using the deceptive techniques of crooked mail-order firms, fly-by-night remodeling companies, and sly furriers.

For when the politician says that the small fish are being pulled in and the large fish are escaping, it might not have ever occurred to him that the small fish were piranhas and the large fish were largely inoffensive whales.

For had they examined the logic behind deceptive advertising, it would be clear why this is true. Deceptive advertising is only valuable to someone in a position to make one sale and thereafter not care whether he ever gets the buyer's business again. In other words, deceptive advertising is only economically practical in a hit-and-run business.

For virtually all national advertising, the cost of making a sale through advertising is prohibitive, unless the trial purchase results in a satisfied customer who comes back over and over again, thus amortizing the cost of the original advertisement.

This is true whether it is automobiles, food, beverages or over-the-counter drugs, airlines, or, indeed, any product or service that might likely be found among the hundred largest adver-

tisers. On the other hand, the man who wants to run a classified ad to sell his house or who has a business so small that he can move his operations from place to place or can collapse his business and set it up under some other name has no such concern.

It must have been rather distressing when the Commission investigators directed themselves toward the largest advertisers in this country—for the type of deception in advertising that the ordinary person perceives as deception is not, as I have indicated, utilized by major advertisers for sound economic reasons.

How, then, can the investigator produce his quota of cases? Well, in the first instance, by changing the plain meaning of the word "deception" so that practices hitherto not perceived as being deceptive would be included.

Until the FTC's new policy of deception was adopted, it had not been anyone's idea that it would be possible to be accused of deception if there was no possibility of anyone's being deceived in a way that would be relevant to the purchase of the product or service.

For example, for many years photographs were taken of lovely glasses of beer and freehand drawings were made of the same. Photographing beer is not as easy as some might think. It is hard, under the strong lights of photography, to maintain a head on the beer long enough to do the work. Therefore, for half a century photographers took pictures of beer, using for the head other materials. They came out in the actual photograph looking just like the head on the beer, but were, in fact, not made of beer at all. The natural assumption was, and not an unreasonable one, that if a man bought the beer and poured the glass and was unable to distinguish between the illustration in the advertisement and the beer in his glass, he had not been deceived.

However, under the new policies of the Commission, this is clearly a deceptive practice, whether or not the viewer is able to find any discrepancy between the product as it appears in the advertisement and as it appears in real life. Indeed, the Commission's staff has gone so far as to reject evidence that the consumer understands that kind of photography for what it is--even in some cases where consumers have expressed the opinion that the real product looks a good deal better than the advertised representation!

Now this policy of extending the meaning of deception, in the absence of any real existing deception, has opened up for the Commission a wide field of action. One reflects that every candidate for President of this country since the time of Eisenhower has had in his TV broadcasts a make-up man on the set apply material that will make him appear on the television screen substantially as he might appear to the viewer in person. The present principles of the Commission would regard this as a deceptive practice. The fact that the candidate's appearance in real life is consistent with the television representation is not a defense against any artificial steps taken on the set. I estimate that the effect of this new concept of deception is merely to raise costs and lengthen the time taken to prepare advertising. If one has an oven commercial and shows a turkey being roasted on one set and being eaten on a dining-room set, one had better be very sure that the exact same bird is shown in both shots. For however irrelevant to the purchase of an oven this may be, it is under present circumstances the valid basis for a complaint.

The next development needed to produce enough cases for the FTC was the idea that all statements made in advertising must have zero defects. In other words, if there is any circumstance, no matter how remote, that the statement might under a single condition or

under rather improbable conditions be untrue, then that must be disclosed.

This is a real Catch-22 device in that it is difficult to make any kind of unequivocal declarative sentence in which there is not the potential for endless footnotes and explanations covering every possibility under which it would not be true.

For example, take some known scientific fact. Let us suppose that I state that the boiling point of water is 212° F. While that is largely true throughout the inhabited areas of the U.S., it is certainly not true in Denver, where at the altitude of 5,280 feet, water boils at a good deal lower temperature. It is also not the correct figure if salt or other things are added to the water. It is also not true if the water is heated in a pressure cooker. Thus, if one wants to look hard and far enough for an exception to a statement, one can establish that hardly anything is true in each and every case which may be cited. One can spin this logic out, and it has been spun out in wonderful ways. One can state, for example, that the claim a cleaning detergent will clean a shirt is not true of shirts that are not dirty.

It may be, as a result of the fact that almost everyone in the FTC has a legal backgrounds, that it is possible they believe that an advertisement is a contract and that it should in complete fairness read like a life-insurance policy.

The unfortunate part of this concept is that there is a laudable desire on the part of the Commission to make advertising more informative. But if every statement of fact is subject to the criterion that it must be absolutely and unequivocally true under each and every case that can be conceived of, then the practical effect is to eliminate statements of fact, as each additional fact contains a threat of litigation.

The third concept that seems to be gaining acceptance among regulators is that the consumer and advertising exist together in a vacuum utterly protected from any outside input in the way of common sense or other personal knowledge of communication. Now, indeed, if advertising were the only contact that the consumer had with the real world of products and services, this might be tenable. But it is manifestly absurd to set up logical systems based on the assumption that after seeing a 30-second commercial for an automobile, I or anyone else without any further investigation would phone the dealer and have the car delivered. The idea that the consumer's mind is a blank tablet upon which the advertiser writes the only message seems to be a persistent notion. This theoretical consumer apparently has no friends to discuss matters with and has never in his lifetime experienced an opportunity to gain any knowledge.

This seems unusual in a country with the highest standards of education in the history of the world.

I have carried in my pocket for many years a small penknife which occasionally comes in handy. I am appalled to think where the present logic of the Commission's concepts would lead one if that were to be nationally advertised. Although I use it for opening letters and packages and such, it certainly can be used to slit someone's throat. It has the potential hazard that I could leave it in the crib with the baby. I could also kill myself by trying to cut a 117-volt extension cord with it. Moreover, the purchaser should be warned that it is not suitable for cutting linoleum and roast beef or for slaughtering hogs. If you think these are farfetched, it may be that you have not read as much of the testimony given before the Commission as I have.

Strangely enough, even with these addi-tional concepts of deception, complaints against national advertisers have not proceeded too well, and it is evident that new and additional concepts of deception will be needed.

They extend to such matters as deception being constituted by advertising which might induce the consumer to purchase something which in the Commission's opinion is not conducive to long-range social benefit. Thus, we have the Commission not only having administrative and judicial functions, but self-appointed legislative functions as well. And a legislative determination of the long-range social goals of our country must be one of the most difficult subjects any enormously wise legislative body ever had to determine.

To accomplish all these things, we have a regulatory body with an annual budget of some $30 million which, as often is pointed out, is hardly enough to put salt on the tail of crooked furriers and house remodelers, much less rascally people who are running mail-order schools out of garrets. Those who are preying on the poor and ignorant in transactions involving hundreds of thousands of dollars are now left to practice their wiles under the amazing theory that they will be frightened by the penalties exacted on great national advertisers. This must cause great delight to the grafters and bunko artists who use advertising in their schemes.

If you think I exaggerate the situation, I direct your attention to a release made by the FTC in November 1970 in which they did an analysis of the source of complaints made to the Commission and the Commission's regional offices. Of some 8,800 complaints on the part of consumers, only six percent were categorized as relating to advertising. How much of that do you suppose is national advertising? How many are those big fish that certain politicians want the FTC to catch?

Well, I am afraid we may never find out.

The 4As has asked under the Freedom of Information Act that the nature of the six percent of complaints by the consumer against advertising taken in this survey be revealed. That request has been refused.

Now why would that request be refused? Would it be possible that, among the 8,800 complaints to the FTC, there were few, if any, involving the 100 largest advertisers? Is it just possible that the problems that the consumer has with advertising are not problems with the big fish but with the piranhas? But there is no need to speculate about this because it would be very simple to find out the truth.

I would like to make what I believe to be a constructive suggestion that we find out directly from the consumer what the consumer's problems are with deception in advertising. I suggest that we do not rely alone upon the theorization of academics, the convoluted thoughts of legal minds, or the shrill outcries of professional "consumerists."

There is today no great technical problem, as there might have been when the FTC was founded, in determining from the consumer precisely the frequency and importance of deception to which he is exposed by advertising of all kinds. It is a simple problem for any well-designed consumer research.

With this as a base, it would be possible for the Commission to direct its resources in the areas which are giving the consumer the most trouble. We can go from hypothesis to actuality. We can go from finespun thinking about the values of American life to carrying out the plain mandate of Congress to protect the consumer from deception. We can also find out what part advertising plays in the total of all deceptive practices with which the consumer is involved. We don't have to do this by amateur methods such as sending out law students to interview Washington, D.C. housewives. It can be done professionally and accurately, and the results can form a basis of determining just what facilities and procedures the FTC needs to prevent deception. I think it not unlikely that such an investigation would call for an upward revision of the budget assigned to the FTC. But surely this is a better outcome than having the FTC, because of budget limitations, concentrate its small resources on areas of advertising with which the consumer may be having very little difficulty, indeed.

This may very well lead to a more intelligent examination of the structure of the process by which the Federal Trade Commission enforces the Federal Trade Commission Act.

DISCUSSION QUESTIONS

1. Based on Dillon's article and your experience and judgment, what do *you* think is deceptive advertising? Why?

2. What impact has the Federal Trade Commission had on advertising? Has it been beneficial or has it hindered advertising?

II-4

THE MORALITY (?) OF ADVERTISING

Theodore Levitt

This year Americans will consume about $20 billion of advertising, and very little of it because we want it. Wherever we turn, advertising will be forcibly thrust on us in an intrusive orgy of abrasive sound and sight, all to induce us to do something we might not ordinarily do, or to induce us to do it differently. This massive and persistent effort crams increasingly more commercial noise into the same, few, strained 24 hours of the day. It has provoked a reaction as predictable as it was inevitable: a lot of people want the noise stopped, or at least alleviated.

And they want it cleaned up and corrected. As more and more products have entered the battle for the consumer's fleeting dollar, advertising has increased in boldness and volume. Last year, industry offered the nation's supermarkets about 100 new products a week, equal, on an annualized basis, to the total number already on their shelves. Where so much must be sold so hard, it is not surprising that advertisers have pressed the limits of our credulity and generated complaints about their exaggerations and deceptions.

Only classified ads, the work of rank amateurs, do we presume to contain solid, unembellished fact. We suspect all the rest of systematic and egregious distortion, if not often of outright mendacity.

The attack on advertising comes from all sectors. Indeed, recent studies show that the people most agitated by advertising are precisely those in the higher income brackets whose affluence is generated by the industries that create the ads.[1] While these studies show that only a modest group of people are preoccupied with advertising's constant presence in our lives, they also show that distortion and deception are what bother people most.

This discontent has encouraged Senator Philip Hart and Senator William Proxmire to sponsor consumer-protection and truth-in-advertising legislation. People, they say, want less fluff and more fact about the things they buy. They want description, not distortion, and they want some relief from the

---

[1] See Raymond A. Bauer and Stephen A. Greyser, *Advertising in America:The Consumer View* (Boston:Div. of Research, Harvard Business School, 1968), see also Gary A. Steiner, *The People Look at Television*(New York:Alfred Knopf, 1963).

constant, grating, vulgar noise.

Legislation seems appropriate because the natural action of competition does not seem to work, or, at least not very well. Competition may ultimately flush out and destroy falsehood and shoddiness, but "ultimately" is too long for the deceived--not just the deceived who are poor, ignorant, and dispossessed, but also all the rest of us who work hard for our money and can seldom judge expertly the truth of conflicting claims about products and services.

The consumer is an amateur, after all; the producer is an expert. In the commercial arena, the consumer is an impotent midget. He is certainly not king. The producer is a powerful giant. It is an uneven match. In this setting, the purifying power of competition helps the consumer very little--especially in the short run, when his money is spent and gone, from the weak hands into the strong hands. Nor does competition among the sellers solve the "noise" problem. The more they compete, the worse the din of advertising.

A BROAD VIEWPOINT REQUIRED

Most people spend their money carefully. Understandably, they look out for larcenous attempts to separate them from it. Few men in business will deny the right, perhaps even the wisdom, of people today asking for some restraint on advertising, or at least for more accurate information on the things they buy and for more consumer protection.

Yet, if we speak in the same breath about consumer protection and about advertising's distortions, exaggerations, and deceptions, it is easy to confuse two quite separate things--the legiti-

mate purpose of advertising and the abuses to which it may be put. Rather than deny that distortion and exaggeration exist in advertising, in this article I shall argue that embellishment and distortion are among advertising's legitimate and socially desirable purposes; and that illegitimacy in advertising consists only of falsification with larcenous intent. And while it is difficult, as a practical matter, to draw the line between legitimate distortion and essential falsehood, I want to take a long look at the distinction that exists between the two. This, I shall say in advance--the distinction is not as simple, obvious, or great as one might think.

The issue of truth versus falsehood, in advertising or in anything else, is complex and fugitive. It must be pursued in a philosophic mood that might seem foreign to the businessman. Yet the issue at base *is* more philosophic than it is pragmatic. Anyone seriously concerned with the moral problems of a commercial society cannot avoid this fact. I hope the reader will bear with me--I believe he will find it helpful, and perhaps even refreshing.

WHAT IS REALITY?

What, indeed? Consider poetry. Like advertising, poetry's purpose is to influence an audience; to affect its perceptions and sensibilities, perhaps even to change its mind. Like rhetoric, poetry's intent is to convince and seduce. In the service of that intent, it employs without guilt or fear of criticism all the arcane tools of distortion that the literary mind can devise. Keats does not offer a truthful engineering description of his Grecian urn. He offers, instead, with exquisite attention to the effects of meter, rhyme, allusion, illusion, metaphor, and sound, a lyrical, exaggerated, distorted, and palpably false description. And he is thoroughly applauded for it, as are all other artists, in whatever medium, who do precisely this same thing successfully.

Commerce, it can be said without apology, takes essentially the same liberties with reality and literality as the artist, except that commerce calls its creations advertising, or industrial design, or packaging. As with art, the purpose is to influence the audience by creating illusions, symbols, and implications that promise more than pure functionality. Once, when asked what his company did, Charles Revson of Revlon, Inc. suggested a profound distinction: "In the factory we make cosmetics; in the store we sell hope." He obviously has no illusions. It is not cosmetic chemicals women want, but the seductive charm promised by the alluring symbols with which these chemicals have been surrounded--hence the rich and exotic packages in which they are sold, and the suggestive advertising with which they are promoted.

Commerce usually embellishes its products thrice: first, it designs the product to be pleasing to the eye, to suggest reliability, and so forth; second, it packages the product as attractively as it feasibly can; and then it advertises this attractive package with inviting pictures, slogans, descriptions, songs, and so on. The package and design are as important as the advertising.

The Grecian vessel, for example, was used to carry liquids, but that function does not explain why the potter decorated it with graceful lines and elegant drawings in black and red. A woman's compact carries refined talc, but this does not explain why manufacturers try to make these boxes into works of decorative art.

Neither the poet nor the ad man celebrates the literal functionality of what he produces. Instead, each celebrates a deep and complex emotion which he symbolizes by creative embellish-

ment--a content which cannot be captured by literal description alone. Communication, through advertising or through poetry or any other medium, is a creative conceptualization that implies a vicarious experience through a language of symbolic substitutes. Communication can never be the real thing it talks about. Therefore, all communication is in some inevitable fashion a departure from reality.

EVERYTHING IS CHANGED...

Poets, novelists, playwrights, composers, and fashion designers have one thing more in common. They all deal in symbolic communication. None is satisfied with nature in the raw, as it was on the day of creation. None is satisfied to tell it exactly "like it is" to the naked eye, as do the classified ads. It is the purpose of all art to alter nature's surface reality, to reshape, to embellish, and to augment what nature has so crudely fashioned, and then to present it to the same applauding humanity that so eagerly buys Revson's exotically advertised cosmetics.

Few, if any, of us accept the natural state in which God created us. We scrupulously select our clothes to suit a multiplicity of simultaneous purposes, not only for warmth, but manifestly for such other purposes as propriety, status, and seduction. Women modify, embellish, and amplify themselves with colored paste for the lips and powders and lotions for the face; men as well as women use devices to take hair off the face and others to put it on the head. Like the inhabitants of isolated African regions, where not a single whiff of advertising has ever intruded, we all encrust ourselves with rings, pendants, bracelets, neckties, clips, chains, and snaps.

Man lives neither in sackcloth nor in sod huts--although these are not notably inferior to tight clothes and overheated dwellings in congested and

polluted cities. Everywhere man rejects nature's uneven blessings. He
molds and repackages to his own civiliz-
ing specifications an otherwise crude,
drab, and generally oppressive reality.
He does it so that life may be made for
the moment more tolerable than God evidently designed it to be. As T.S.
Eliot once remarked, "Human kind cannot bear very much reality."

...INTO SOMETHING RICH AND STRANGE

No line of life is exempt. All the
popes of history have countenanced the
costly architecture of St. Peter's
Basilica and its extravagant interior
decoration. All around the globe,
nothing typifies man's materialism so
much as the temples in which he preaches
asceticism. Men of the cloth have not
been persuaded that the poetic self-
denial of Christ or Buddha--both men
of sackcloth and sandals--is enough to
inspire, elevate, and hold their flocks
together. To amplify the temple in men's
eyes, they have, very realistically,
systematically sanctioned the embelish-
ment of the houses of the gods with the
same kind of luxurious design and expensive decoration that Detroit puts
into a Cadillac.

One does not need a doctorate in social
anthropology to see that the purposeful
transmutation of nature's primeval
state occupies all people in all cultures and all societies at all stages
of development. Everybody everywhere
wants to modify, transform, embellish,
enrich, and reconstruct the world
around him--to introduce into an otherwise harsh or bland existence some
sort of purposeful and distorting al-
leviation. Civilization is man's attempt to transcend his ancient animal-
ity, and this includes both art and
advertising.

...AND MORE THAN 'REAL'

But civilized man will undoubtedly deny

that either the innovative artist or
the *grande dame* with *chic* "distorts
reality." Instead, he will say that artist and woman merely embellish, enhance,
and illuminate. To be sure, he will
mean something quite different by these
three terms when he applies them to
fine art, on the one hand, and to more
secular efforts, on the other.

But this distinction is little more
than an affectation. As man has civilized himself and developed his sensibilities, he has invented a great
variety of subtle distinctions between
things that are objectively indistinct.
Let us take a closer look at the difference between man's "sacred" distortions and his "secular" ones.

The man of sensibility will probably
canonize the artist's deeds as superior
creations by ascribing to them an almost cosmic virtue and significance.
As a cultivated individual, he will almost certainly refuse to recognize any
constructive, cosmic virtues in the
productions of the advertisers, and he
is likely to admit the charge that advertising uniformly deceives us by
analogous techniques. But how "sensible" is he?

AND BY SIMILAR MEANS...

Let us assume for the moment that there
is no objective, operational difference
between the embellishments and distortions of the artist and those of the
ad man--that both men are more concerned
with creating images and feelings than
with rendering objective, representa-
tional, and informational descriptions.
The greater virtue of the artist's work
must then derive from some subjective
element. What is it?

It will be said that art has a higher
value for man because it has a higher
purpose. True, the artist is interested
in philosophic truth or wisdom, and the
ad man in selling his goods and services.
Michelangelo, when he designed the

Sistine chapel ceiling, had some concern with the inspirational elevation
of man's spirit, whereas Edward Levy,
who designs cosmetics packages, is interested primarily in creating images
to help separate the unward consumer
from his loose change.

But this explanation of the difference
between the value of art and the value
of advertising is not helpful at all.
For is the presence of a "higher" purpose all that redeeming?

Perhaps not, perhaps the reverse is
closer to the truth. While the ad man
and designer seek only to convert the
audience to their commercial custom,
Michelangelo sought to convert its
soul. Which is the greater blasphemy?
Who commits the greater affront to life
--he who dabbles with man's erotic ap-
petites, or he who meddles with man's
soul? Which act is the easier to judge
and justify?

...FOR DIFFERENT ENDS

How much sense does it really make to
distinguish between similar means on
the grounds that the ends to which they
are directed are different--"good" for
art and "not so good" for advertising?
The distinction produces zero progress
in the argument at hand. How willing
are we to employ the involuted ethics
whereby the ends justify the means?

Apparently, on this subject, lots of
people are very willing indeed. The
business executive seems to share with
the minister, the painter, and the poet
the doctrine that the ends justify the
means. The difference is that the
businessman is justifying the very commercial ends that his critics oppose.
While his critics justify the embellishments of art and literature for
what these do for man's spirit, the
businessman justifies the embellishment of industrial design and advertising for what they do for man's purse.

Taxing the imagination to the limit,
the businessman spins casuistic webs of
elaborate transparency to the self-
righteous effect that promotion and advertising are socially benign because
they expand the economy, create jobs,
and raise living standards. Technically,
he will always be free to argue, and he
will argue, that his ends become the
means to the ends of the musician, poet,
painter, and minister. The argument
which justifies means in terms of ends
is obviously not without its subtleties
and intricacies.

The executive and the artist are equally
tempted to identify and articulate a
higher rationale for their work than
their work itself. But only in the improved human consequences of their efforts do they find vindication. The
aesthete's ringing declaration of "art
for art's sake," with all its self-
conscious affirmation of selflessness,
sounds hollow in the end, even to himself, for, finally, every communication
addresses itself to an audience. Thus
art is very understandably in constant
need of justification by the evidence
of its beneficial and divinely approved
effect on its audience.

THE AUDIENCE'S DEMANDS

This compulsion to rationalize even
art is a highly instructive fact. It
tells one a great deal about art's purposes and the purposes of all other communication. As I have said, the poet
and the artist each seek in some special
way to produce an emotion or assert a
truth not otherwise apparent. But it is
only in communion with their audiences
that the effectiveness of their efforts
can be tested and truth revealed. It
may be academic whether a tree falling
in the forest makes a noise. It is *not*
academic whether a sonnet or a painting
has merit. Only an audience can decide
that.

The creative person can justify his
work only in terms of another person's
response to it. Ezra Pound, to be sure,
thought that "...in the [greatest]
works the live part is the part which
the artist has put there to please
himself, and the dead part is the part
he has put there ... because he thinks
he *ought* to--i.e., either to get or
keep an audience." This is certainly
consistent with our notions of Pound
as perhaps the purest of twentieth-
century advocates of art for art's
sake.

But if we review the record of his
life, we find that Pound spent the
greater part of his energies seeking
suitable places for deserving poets to
publish. Why? Because art has little
merit standing alone in unseen and un-
heard isolation. Merit is not inherent
in art. It is conferred by an audience.

The same is true of advertising: if
it fails to persuade the audience that
the product will fulfill the function
the audience expects, the advertising
has no merit.

Where have we arrived? Only at some
common characteristics of art and advertising. Both are rhetorical, and
both literally false, both expound an
emotional reality deeper than the
"real"; both pretend to "higher" purposes, although different ones; and
the excellence of each is judged by
its effect on its audience--its per-
suasiveness, in short. I do not mean
to imply that the two are fundamentally the same, but rather that they both
represent a pervasive, and I believe
universal, characteristic of human
nature--the human audience *demands*
symbolic interpretation in everything
it sees and knows. If it doesn't get
it, it will return a verdict of "no
interest."

To get a clearer idea of the relation
between the symbols of advertising and
the products they glorify, something
more must be said about the fiat the

consumer gives to industry to "distort"
its messages.

SYMBOL & SUBSTANCE

As we have seen, man seeks to transcend
nature in the raw everywhere. Everywhere, and at all times, he has been
attracted by the poetic imagery of some
sort of art, literature, music, and
mysticism. He obviously wants and needs
the promises, the imagery, and the symbols of the poet and the priest. He
refuses to live a life of primitive
barbarism or sterile functionalism.

Consider a sardine can filled with
scented powder. Even if the U.S.
Bureau of Standards were to certify
that the contents of this package are
identical with the product sold in a
beautiful paisley-printed container,
it would not sell. The Boston matron,
for example, who has built herself a
deserved reputation for pinching every
penny until it hurts, would unhesitat-
ingly turn it down. While she may deny
it, in self-assured and neatly cadenced
accents, she obviously desires and needs
the promises, imagery, and symbols produced by hyperbolic advertisements,
elaborate packages, and fetching fash-
ions.

The need for embellishment is not confined to personal appearance. A few
years ago, an electronics laboratory
offered a $700 testing device for sale.
The company ordered two different front
panels to be designed, one by the engineers who developed the equipment and
one by professional industrial designers. When the two models were shown
to a sample of laboratory directors
with Ph.D.'s, the professional design
attracted twice the purchase intentions
that the engineer's design did. Obviously, the laboratory director who
has been baptized into science at M.I.T.
is quite as responsive to the blandishments of packaging as the Boston matron.

And, obviously, both these customers

define the products they buy in much more sophisticated terms than the engineer in the factory. For a woman, dusting powder in a sardine can is not the same product as the identical dusting powder in an exotic paisley package. For the laboratory director, the test equipment behind an engineer-designed panel just isn't as "good" as the identical equipment in a box designed with finesse.

FORM FOLLOWS THE IDEAL FUNCTION

The consumer refuses to settle for pure operating functionality. "Form follows function," is a resoundingly vacuous cliche' which, like all cliche's, depends for its memorability more on its alliteration and brevity than on its wisdom. If it has any truth, it is only in the elastic sense that function extends beyond strict mechanical use into the domain of imagination. We do not choose to buy a particular product; we choose to buy the functional expectations that we attach to it, and we buy these expectations as "tools" to help us solve a problem of life.

Under normal circumstances, furthermore, we must judge a product's "nonmechanical" utilities before we actually buy it. It is rare that we choose an object after we have experienced it; nearly always we must make the choice before the fact. We choose on the basis of promises, not experiences.

Whatever symbols convey and sustain these promises in our minds are therefore truly functional. The promises and images which imaginative ads and sculptured packages induce in us are as much the product as the physical materials themselves. To put this another way, these ads and packagings describe the product's fullness for us; in our minds, the product becomes a complex abstraction which is, as Immanuel Kant might have said, the conception of a perfection which has

not yet been experienced.

But all promises and images, almost by their very nature, exceed their capacity to live up to themselves. As every eager lover has ever known, the consummation seldom equals the promises which produced the chase. To forestall and suppress the visceral expectation of disappointment that life has taught us must inevitably come, we use art, architecture, literature, and the rest, and advertising as well, to shield ourselves, in advance of experience, from the stark and plain reality in which we are fated to live. I agree that we wish for unobtainable unrealities, "dream castles." But why promise ourselves reality, which we already possess? What we want is what we do not possess?

Everyone in the world is trying in his special personal fashion to solve a primal problem of life--the problem of rising above his own negligibility, of escaping from nature's confining, hostile, and unpredictable reality, of finding significance, security, and comfort in the things he must do to survive. Many of the so-called distortions of advertising, product design, and packaging may be viewed as a paradigm of the many responses that man makes to the conditions of survival in the environment. Without distortion, embellishment, and elaboration, life would be drab, dull, anguished, and at its existential worst.

SYMBOLISM USEFUL & NECESSARY

Without symbolism, furthermore, life would be even more confusing and anxiety-ridden than it is with it. The foot soldier must be able to recognize the general, good or bad, because the general is clothed with power. A general without his stars and suite of aides-de-camp to set him apart from the privates would suffer in authority and credibility as much as perfume packaged by Dracula or a computer designed by Rube Goldberg. Any ordinary soldier or civilian who has ever had the uncommon experience of being in the same shower with a general can testify from the visible unease of the latter how much clothes "make the man."

Similarly, verbal symbols help to make the product--they help us deal with the uncertainties of daily life. "You can be sure ... if it's Westinghouse" is a decision rule as useful to the man buying a turbine generator as to the man buying an electric shaver. To label all the devices and embellishments companies employ to reassure the prospective customer about a product's quality with the pejorative term "gimmick," as critics tend to do, is simply silly. Worse, it denies, against massive evidence, man's honest needs and values. If religion must be architectured, packaged, lyricized, and musicized to attract and hold its audience, and if sex must be perfumed, powdered, sprayed, and shaped in order to command attention, it is ridiculous to deny the legitimacy of more modest, and similar, embellishments to the world of commerce.

But still, the critics may say, commercial communications tend to be aggressively deceptive. Perhaps, and perhaps not. The issue at stake here is more complex than the outraged critic believes. Man wants and needs the elevation of the spirit produced by attractive surroundings, by handsome packages, and by imaginative promises. He needs the assurances projected by well-known brand names, and the reliability suggested by salesmen who have been taught to dress by Oleg Cassini and to speak by Dale Carnegie. Of course, there are blatant, tasteless, and willfully deceiving salesmen and advertisers, just as there are blatant, tasteless, and willfully deceiving artists, preachers, and even professors. But, before talking blithely about deception, it is helpful to make a distinction between things and descriptions of things.

THE QUESTION OF DECEIT

Poetic descriptions of things make no pretense of being the things themselves. Nor do advertisements, even by the most elastic standards. Advertisements are the symbols of man's aspirations. They are not the real things, nor are they intended to be, nor are they accepted as such by the public. A study some years ago by the Center for Research in Marketing, Inc. concluded that deep down inside the consumer understands this perfectly well and has the attitude that an advertisement is an ad, not a factual news story.

Even Professor Galbraith grants the point when he says that "... because modern man is exposed to a large volume of information of varying degrees of unreliability ... he establishes a system of discounts which he applies to various sources almost without thought ... The discount becomes nearly total for all forms of advertising. The merest child watching television dismisses the health and status-giving claims of a breakfast cereal as 'a commercial.'"[2]

This is not to say, of course, that Galbraith also discounts advertising's effectiveness. Quite the opposite: "Failure to win belief does not impair the effectiveness of the management of demand for consumer products. Management involves the creation of a compelling image of the product in the mind of the consumer. To this he responds more or less automatically under circumstances where the purchase does not merit a great deal of thought. For building this image, palpable fantasy may be more valuable than circumstantial evidence."[3]

Linguists and other communications specialists will agree with the conclu-

----

[2] John Kenneth Galbraith, *The New Industrial State* (Boston: Houghton Mifflin Co., 1967), pp. 325-326.
[3] Ibid. p. 326.

sion of the Center for Research in Marketing that "advertising is a symbol system existing in a world of symbols. Its reality depends upon the fact that it is a symbol ... the content of an ad can never be real, it can only say something about reality, or create a relationship between itself and an individual which has an effect on the reality life of an individual."

CONSUMER, KNOW THYSELF

Consumption is man's most constant activity. It is well that he understands himself as a consumer.

The object of consumption is to solve a problem. Even consumption that is viewed as the creation of an opportunity--like going to medical school or taking a singles-only Caribbean tour --has as its purpose the solving of a problem. At a minimum, the medical student seeks to solve the problem of how to lead a relevant and comfortable life, and the lady on the tour seeks to solve the problem of spinsterhood.

The "purpose" of the product is not what the engineer explicitly says it is, but what the consumer implicitly demands that it shall be. Thus the consumer consumes not things, but expected benefits--not cosmetics, but the satisfactions of the allurements they promise; not quarter-inch drills, but quarter-inch holes; not stock in companies, but capital gains; not numerically controlled milling machines, but trouble-free and accurately smooth metal parts; not low-cal whipped cream, but self-rewarding indulgence combined with sophisticated convenience.

The significance of these distinctions is anything but trivial. Nobody knows this better, for example, than the creators of automobile ads. It is not the generic virtues that they tout, but more likely the car's capacity to enhance its user's status and his access to female prey.

Whether we are aware of it or not, we in effect expect and demand that advertising create these symbols for us to show us what life might be, to bring the possibilities that we cannot see before our eyes and screen out the stark reality in which we must live. We insist, as Gilbert put it, that there be added a "touch of artistic verisimilitude to an otherwise bald and unconvincing narrative."

UNDERSTANDING THE DIFFERENCE

In a world where so many things are either commonplace or standardized, it makes no sense to refer to the rest as false, fraudulent, frivolous, or immaterial. The world works according to the aspirations and needs of its actors, not according to the arcane or moralizing logic of detached critics who pine for another age--an age which, in any case, seems different from today's largely because its observers are no longer children shielded by protective parents from life's implacable harshness.

To understand this is not to condone much of the vulgarity, purposeful duplicity, and scheming half-truths we see in advertising, promotion, packaging, and product design. But before we condemn, it is well to understand the difference between embellishment and duplicity and how extraordinarily uncommon the latter is in our times. The noisy visibility of promotion in our intensely communicating times need not be thoughtlessly equated with malevolence.

Thus the issue is not the prevention of distortion. It is, in the end, to know what kinds of distortions we actually want so that each of our lives is, without apology, duplicity, or rancor, made bearable. This does not mean we must accept out of hand all the commercial propaganda to which we are each day so constantly exposed, or that we must accept out of hand the equation

that effluence is the price of affluence, or the simple notion that
business cannot and government should
not try to alter and improve the position of the consumer vis-a'-vis the
producer. It takes a special kind of
perversity to continue any longer our
shameful failure to mount vigorous,
meaningful programs to protect the consumer, to standardize product grades,
labels, and packages, to improve the
consumer's information-getting process,
and to mitigate the vulgarity and op-
pressiveness that is in so much of
our advertising.

But the consumer suffers from an old
dilemma. He wants "truth," but he
also wants and needs the alleviating
imagery and tantalizing promises of
the advertiser and designer.

Business is caught in the middle.
There is hardly a company that would
not go down in ruin if it refused to
provide fluff, because nobody will buy
pure functionality. Yet, if it uses
too much fluff and little else, business invites possibly ruinous legislation. The problem therefore is to
find a middle way. And in this search,
business can do a great deal more than
it has been either accustomed or willing to do:

√ It can exert pressure to make sure
  that no single industry "finds
  reasons" why it should be exempt
  from legislative restrictions that
  are reasonable and popular.

√ It can work constructively with
  government to develop reasonable
  standards and effective sanctions
  that will assure a more amenable
  commercial environment.

√ It can support legislation to provide the consumer with the information he needs to make easy comparison between products, packages, and
  prices.

√ It can support and help draft improved
  legislation on quality stabilization.

√ It can support legislation that gives
  consumers easy access to strong legal
  remedies where justified.

√ It can support programs to make local
  legal aid easily available, especially to the poor and undereducated who
  know so little about their rights and
  how to assert them.

√ Finally, it can support efforts to
  moderate and clean up the advertising noise that dulls our senses and
  assaults our sensibilities.

It will not be the end of the world or
of capitalism for business to sacrifice
a few commercial freedoms so that we may
more easily enjoy our own humanity.
Business can and should, for its own
good, work energetically to achieve this
end. But it is also well to remember
the limits of what is possible. Paradise was not a free-goods society. The
forbidden fruit was gotten at a price.

DISCUSSION QUESTIONS

1. Senators Hart and Proxmire want to
sponsor consumer protection and truth
in advertising legislation. They argue
"people want less fluff and more fact
about things they buy." Do you feel
that if companies provide more "fact"
and less "fluff" in their advertising
they would sell more? Why?

2. Is Levitt for or against advertising?
Why do you say so?

II-5

ARE NEW FTC ADVERTISING POLICIES INHIBITING COMPETITION?

Yale Brozen

No one would argue that the FTC should not attempt to stop fraudulent advertising. This activity probably does not do great harm to consumers. It is even possible that the costs imposed fall short of the resulting benefit, although no one knows whether or not this is the fact.

Before going into recent FTC activities which do a positive disservice to consumers, it should be mentioned that there are those who believe that the FTC involvement in the deceptive advertising arena is not worth the effort, particularly in view of the alternative remedies available which would continue to be available even if the FTC were abolished. Professor Richard Posner, at the University of Chicago Law School, for example, has said

> A ... fundamental question, ... rarely put because the answer strikes most people as self-evident, is whether there ought to be a government agency that prosecutes sellers who try to mislead consumers. Even in the absence of any legal remedies, it is unclear that deception would be markedly more frequent than it is. Good preventives against deception are to be found in the incentive of the consumer to exercise reasonable care and

common sense in purchasing, in the incentive of sellers not to antagonize customers, and the incentive of competitors of deceptive advertisers to give consumers prompt and accurate information in order to correct any misrepresentation that might cause a substantial diversion of their sales.

The last point is too little stressed. In other areas of discourse we posit a market place of ideas in which good ideas can be expected to prevail in open competition with bad. One could quite reasonably take a similar approach to advertising. Individuals probably know a good deal more about household products than about political questions. If we trust them to evaluate competing and often fraudulent claims by political candidates, we should also trust them to evaluate competing product claims. Since other sellers, like rival candidates, have every incentive to counter the misleading representations of a competitor, there seems little danger that false claims will not be exposed. Nor is it clear that occasional, transitory misrepresentations are entirely a bad thing. If a false claim elicits a substantial increase in sales, the industry has learned something about consumer demand, and competitors of the false advertiser will have an incentive to develop a product about which the claim can be truthfully made (1).

However, I do not propose to abolish the FTC--despite the excellent case that has been made for this suggestion --but to urge that it mend its ways. I wish to propose that the FTC stop doing those things which raise the costs of supplying consumers, which restrict the flow of information to buyers, which stifle competition, and which tend to bottle up some of the innovations that would otherwise become available.

SUBSTANTIATION OF ADVERTISING CLAIMS

Let's begin with a recent case brought by the FTC in the area of advertising claim substantiation. In July of last year the Commission ruled, in a face-saving opinion when it dismissed its complaint against Pfizer Un-burn, that the record did not indicate that Pfizer had showed conclusively that it had a reasonable basis for its Un-burn claims --but neither did it indicate that the FTC's staff had showed conclusively that it didn't.

The case against Pfizer Un-burn advertising was brought on the basis that the advertised claims were not supported by "well founded scientific tests." Exactly what does that mean? Pfizer had claimed that its sunburn ointment "relieves pain fast" and that it "actually anesthetizes nerves in sensitive sunburned skin." The FTC asserted that Pfizer had no evidence substantiating these claims.

Pfizer maintained that the general state of medical knowledge and medical literature both agreed that the two key ingredients in Un-burn performed in the manner claimed. The company maintained

that there was every reasonable expectation that its formulation would perform in the manner indicated in the medical literature given the formulations with which the medical profession had had experience.

The FTC ruling, in effect, states that this was not a reasonable basis for Un-burn's claims. Since the same opinion states that it is unfair [to competitors] to make a product claim "without a reasonable basis for making that claim," this implies that any product which is formulated or designed on the basis of information in medical or other scientific literature will not be able to defend itself against complaints about unsubstantiated claims despite the availability of such information. A supplier evidently will have to replicate the relevant testing (using his product) instead of relying on the information already produced by previous scientific testing.

There are two consequences of the fact that this case was brought and of the ruling in this case that worry me. First, if past scientific testing must be replicated whenever anyone prepares to bring a product to market, the cost of preparing to offer a product will be increased, without any appreciable gain to the consumer, by the replication of tests already performed. Either of two things will happen. Prices which might otherwise fall will tend to stay high because manufacturers will have to have a higher price to cover the cost of all this additional, duplicate testing. Some potential competitors of existing products will not bother to bring competing products to market because such testing will make the cost too high to allow this to be an economic investment. Existing products will, then, in many instances, be given "grandfather rights" to the market because of this "barrier to entry" erected by this FTC ruling.

The FTC, founded to keep markets competitive is becoming an instrument for preventing competition. It is imposing unwarranted and unnecessary costs on potential entrants, cutting the amount of potential entry into the market, and leaving current producers free to increase prices above levels which would previously have attracted additional competition.

A second aspect of this case is, perhaps, even more worrisome. The Un-burn case was a test to see how far the law could be stretched to serve the crusading zeal of the FTC staff. There was no precedent for its contentions. The staff was not arguing that Pfizer's claims were untruthful. It is contended only that Pfizer lacked scientific tests for the truthfulness of its claims.

Pfizer was puzzled as to why it was selected as a defendant to such charges. It believed that medical literature and experience showing that Un-burn's ingredients had been used safely and effectively for seventy years were a "reasonable basis for the claim." Also, products using the same ingredients and making the same claims had preceded Unburn on the market. Pfizer was puzzled as to why it had been selected for what could only be regarded as harrassment.

Given this precedent, firms better bring out only those new products to compete with established products from which they can expect revenues sufficient to cover not only costs of production and distribution—they had better expect to generate enough revenues also to cover the costs of defense against harassment if they do any advertising informing consumers about the merits of their brand. Otherwise, don't bother bringing out the product. Again, this can only be regarded as an FTC activity which will reduce entry and make the market less competitive.

Before the FTC proceeds further in the arena of substantiation of advertising claims, it should draw back and evaluate its policy a bit more carefully. What costs is it imposing? Are these extra costs likely to reduce the com-

petitiveness of the market or raise the costs of operation to the point where the higher prices consequent upon this activity more than offset any gain to consumers? If substantiated information is worth so much to consumers, won't current or potential competitors find the voluntary provision of substantiation sufficiently attractive to consumers that this will become a competitive marketing tool without any action on the part of the FTC? If such substantiation is not provided, does this not mean that consumers don't find this variety of information worth the cost and that the FTC should not be forcing suppliers to engage in activities which consumers don't find worth their cost?

HASTY ISSUANCE OF PROPOSED COMPLAINTS

Turning away from FTC activities in the substantiation arena, let me briefly mention the costs imposed by the FTC's tendency to rush into issuing some proposed complaints half cocked. The proposed complaint concerning the Zerex can-stabbing commercial has received wide publicity and needs little discussion here. The main point to be made is that the proposed complaint was issued six weeks before FTC investigators visited the DuPont laboratories to discover whether there was any basis for the complaint. Instead of issuing a proposed complaint which then has to be dropped after investigation is undertaken, investigations should be made before issuing a complaint proposal.

The FTC itself should have suspected that there was little ground for the complaint. It had received a number of letters from members of the Auto Radiator Repair Association asserting that Zerex damaged radiators. Now why should anybody in the repair business complain about a product that was generating business? It might be suspected that the product was performing as claimed in stopping small leaks and that repairers were complaining because their business was dropping--not increasing.

THE SHARED MONOPOLY IN CONCENTRATED INDUSTRIES DOCTRINE

Let me turn to some other doctrines recently adopted by the FTC which it is using to try to make new law. Again, these are doctrines which, if the FTC staff prevails, will cause markets to become less competitive and will increase prices.

In the complaint recently issued against the cereal industry, the FTC complains that the cereal industry is concentrated--that is, the biggest four firms producing RTE cereals in the United States have a very large share of the market--and it complains that the cereal industry does a lot of advertising. This, argues the FTC, should be called illegal. High concentration they believe should be designated as illegal because, says the FTC staff, it leads to tacit, if not explicit, collusion and causes high prices. It offers no evidence to support its contention that there is tacit collusion (shared monopoly) in the cereal industry nor does it content that there is explicit collusion. It just believes that anyone in his right mind in a highly concentrated industry will engage in tacit collusion.

This is a little like contending that if anyone has made love to my wife, I must have shot him--even if there is no body to demonstrate that someone has been shot. After all, wouldn't any husband in his right mind shoot any thief who steals his wife's love? This analogy approximates the level of support offered by the FTC for its contention that high concentration should be ruled a violation of the antitrust laws.

The people who argue for making high concentration illegal--as proposed by the White House Antitrust Task Force in 1968 and since supported by Senators Harris and Hart in bills offered in Congress--have always puzzled me. It seems to me that any firm winning a large share of the market in competition with others trying to do the same thing must be offering a superior product at attractive prices. It must be doing a better job for consumers than its competitors. Breaking up such a firm or threatening any firm with divestiture if it wins a large share of the market seems to say that no firm should offer such a good product or such low prices that a major share of the buyers in a market will prefer dealing with it. In other words, it seems to say to firms, "compete, but don't do too good a job for consumers. Don't pass on so much of the benefit of innovations or cost saving that many many consumers will prefer buying from you."[1]

The hostility to concentration by an agency which says it is serving consumers surpasses my understanding. I am nonplussed by this attitude in the FTC staff.

---

[1] Richard Posner indicates that limits on market share above which mandatory deconcentration would be applied would result in *less* competitive behavior. "The threat of dissolution may...have a serious disincentive effect. Firms may hold back from expanding sales to the point at which they would become subject to dissolution under the statute, even if they are more efficient than their competitors.""Oligopoly and the Antitrust Laws:A Suggested Approach." 21 *Stanford Law Review* 1562 (1969).

THE ADVERTISING "BARRIER TO ENTRY" DOCTRINE

The second doctrine urged by the FTC staff in the cereal case is that the advertising done by the cereal companies shuts out would-be entrants who would otherwise find it worthwhile entering cereal production and marketing. They believe that advertising is a method of cementing the loyalty of customers, that it is a barrier to entry by potential suppliers of RTE cereals, and that the cost of advertising adds to the cost of operation and is passed on to customers in higher prices. Break up the cereal companies into several companies, urges the FTC staff, and the amount of advertising will drop and the price of cereals will decline.

Let us examine those contentions. First, does advertising create loyalties impossible for new entrants to erode and thereby erect a barrier to entry? The simple answer is that *advertising does exactly the opposite. Advertising is used to create disloyalty*. Firms don't advertise to get the customers they already have. That is obviously a foolish waste of money. They advertise to get the customers they don't yet have. They try to let people know they have a product--a product which may satisfy their desires better than those for which they are now spending their money. Firms use advertising to make customers of other products *disloyal*. A business advertises when it has what it believes as a better product. It shouts to the world, "Don't be loyal to those other brands and other products. Here is a product about which you may not know. Come try it."

Any firm offers a product which it hopes will be so satisfactory to some consumers for the price that they will come back and buy again and again. It is the *product* which creates loyalty. No advertising is going to hypnotize anyone into repeatedly purchasing an unsatisfactory product. All advertising can do is get the customers a firm does not yet have to come try the product. All it can do is create disloyalty. Then the product better deliver or the advertiser will find that the customers he has attracted will spread the word about how unsatisfactory the product is and he will be dead--killed by his own advertising. That is why superior products are extensively advertised and inferior are not (2).

Advertising--far from being a barrier to entry--is a means of entry. It is new products or old products being introduced into new markets which are extensively advertised. Studies have been done showing that the more intensively advertised products have more product turnover and shorter lives than the less intensively advertised products. This is a direct refutation of the notion that advertising is a barrier of entry. These studies show that it is a means of entry.

But what about the contention that advertising is costly and that the consumer is forced to pay higher prices to cover the cost of advertising. If there were less advertising, would not the price of products fall?

This is a little like saying that products that use much electricity in their production would be less costly if we cut the amount of electricity used. If you cut down on electricity, you would have to resort to steam engines or mules to supply the power to drive the machinery. Electricity is used because it is cheaper than using other sources of power. Cutting the use of electricity would raise the cost of the product.

Similarly, advertising is used because it is cheaper than other methods of marketing and distributing the product. (It has even served to cut manufacturing cost by flattening marked seasonal swings. Cold cereals and soft drinks formerly tended to fade out of the market in the winter time. Consumption had very high peaks in the summer. Advertising helped to fill those winter valleys and cut the costs of maintaining idle capacity for summer use). Before the advent of television advertising, the cereal industry used costly methods of marketing and distribution. Costs of delivery by panel truck to store door and stocking of shelves by driver salesmen along with other marketing and shipping costs ran to 35% of the wholesale price. Since TV advertising has become available to effectively and efficiently inform consumers, pool car shipment and warehouse distribution has become feasible. The driver-salesman has been eliminated. Marketing-distribution costs have fallen to 26% of the wholesale cost of the product, judging by the experience of one major RTE cereal producer.

Not only has advertising saved costs for the manufacturer by being substituted for more costly means of distribution--it has also saved costs at the retail level. The more intensively advertised cereals--and other products-- sell for lower mark-ups. The retailer finds them cheaper to handle. The pre-sold consumer takes less of the retailer's time. The pre-sold product has a higher volume per foot of shelf space or square foot of display room and higher volume per salesman or clerk. As a result, the product can be handled at the retail level at a lower mark up.

Advertising does not add to costs--it saves cost. Reducing advertising by placing arbitrary limits on it would be more likely to result in higher prices for consumers than lower prices.

Finally, suppose the FTC breaks up the major cereal companies. Are the pieces going to advertise less than their predecessors? Judging from the data gathered by the National Commission on Food Marketing for 1964, smaller companies spend more on advertising per dollar of sales than the Big 4. In 1964 (when the average level of cereal advertising was 50% higher than currently), the Big 4 spent 15% of sales on advertising while smaller firms spent 20% (3). Judging by these data, breaking up the major firms would result in an increase in advertising cost, not a decrease, without producing any additional values for consumers.

With a friend like the FTC, the consumer has no need of enemies.

REFERENCES

(1) Posner, Richard, "Separate Statement of Richard A. Posner." American Bar Association Commission on the Federal Trade Commission (1969).

(2) U.S. Federal Trade Commission, *Chain Stores: Quality of Canned Fruits and Vegetables* (1933): Philip Nelson, "Advertising as Information" (unpublished paper, 1972).

(3) National Commission on Food Marketing. *Studies of Organization and Competition in Grocery Manufacturing.* Technical Study No. 6. pp, 208, 210.

DISCUSSION QUESTIONS

1. If the FTC persists in requiring expensive data and tests on products, what inflationary effects will it have? What could happen to the advertising business as a whole?

2. Do you believe that the FTC is inhibiting competition? Explain.

Text of speech delivered at the Eastern Annual Conference of the 4A's in June of 1972. Reprinted by permission of the author.

II-6

WHAT IS AN ADEQUATE SUBSTANTIATION?

Robert A. Skitol

I'd like to talk about substantiation of claims and offer some thought on the Commission staff's experience in administering the Commission's substantiation program.

Everyone seems to agree that advertising claims should be based on some form of substantiation. Claims should not be created out of thin air, and the public has a right to expect some form of supporting data before claims are made.

This consensus ends, however, and controversy begins when the contention is made that the making of a claim, without adequate substantiation should be deemed unlawful. What the advertiser may consider adequate to support a particular claim, may be something quite different from what the FTC would consider adequate, which in turn may be something less than what Ralph Nader, Senator Morse, or the advertiser's competitor would consider sufficient.

These divergent views present problems for advertisers and agencies that wish to act responsibly, but presently lack guidance as to what is considered adequate for various types of advertising claims. Some degree of guidance may soon be available in the Commission's

final decision in the Pfizer litigation, which hopefully will clarify the relevant legal principles governing this question.

It would be foolish, however, to expect this one decision to tell advertisers exactly what is necessary in the way of substantiation to support every possible type of claim. The problem seems to be that different kind of claims require not only different kinds of data or evidence, but also different levels or standards of proof in order to be considered by the FTC or its staff adequately substantiated.

Given the great variety of advertising claims and the present lack of standards for determining what is adequate, I'm afraid I am not capable of doing the job assigned to me in the original notice for this conference. That notice stated, that, and I quote: "The government spokesman will tell us as clearly as possible what type and scope of substantiation should be developed."

Well, my inability to provide this information suggests that the notice was a deceptive advertisement.

I will see to it that no charges are pressed by the FTC, if you in turn will permit me to just offer a few general thoughts, about the Commission's experience in running our program.

I think the logical place to begin would be with a brief summary of what the Commission has done so far. The Commission's experience includes several cases which are in the process of being litigated.

The first case of importance was, of course, Pfizer, in which we have charged that it is unfair and deceptive to represent that Un-burn will provide relief from sunburn pain without prior substantiation in the form of adequate and well-controlled scientific studies or tests.

The next major case then was the Commission's proposed complaint against Sugar Information, which is the trade association for the sugar industry. That case involved an alleged representation that consumption of sugar and foods containing sugar before meals is an effective means of reducing human weight and maintaining reduced weight.

It is our contention that, and I quote from our complaint: "There existed at the time of said representation, no reasonable basis to support that claim." The recently issued complaints against analgesics advertising indicate our view that claims of therapeutic superiority for any brand of aspirin should not be made unless and until the validity of any such claim has become "established," in the sense that there exists no substantial question as to the validity of any such representation.

These same complaints challenge various mood claims made for analgesics, on the ground that such claims lack a reasonable basis in the form of competent and reliable scientific evidence to support such representations.

As you can see, we seem to be using different standards and different substandards, and I hope we have rational

distinctions. Finally, we have challenged ads for Control Data's computing program and courses. Ads based on the claim that there is now or will be an urgent need or demand for trained people in the field of electronic data processing, which respondent's training is designed to meet. It is our contention in those cases that respondents have no reasonable basis for making this claim and that the only reasonable basis for such claims would be competent and reliable statistical evidence obtained prior to the making of such statements.

Now in addition to its work on these pending cases, the Commission staff has devoted a great deal of effort to implementation and evaluation of the first several rounds of the advertising substantiation program. The Commission's decision to institute a program of obtaining as substantiation for public scrutiny on a public record, was based on the following five policy considerations:

√ First, public disclosure can assist consumers in making a rational choice among competing claims.

√ Two, the public's need for this information is not being met voluntarily.

√ Three, public disclosure can enhance competition by encouraging competitors to challenge advertising claims which have no basis in fact.

√ Four, the knowledge that documentation or the lack thereof, will be made public, will encourage advertisers to have on hand adequate substantiation before claims are made.

√ And, finally, the Commission has limited resources for detecting claims which are not substantiated by adequate proof. By making documentation available to the public the Commission can be alerted by consumers, businessmen and public interest groups to possible violations of Section V.

Under this program, the Commission has obtained from advertisers and placed on the public record, or is in the process of obtaining for the public record, ad substantiation for six product categories. Automobiles, air conditioners, electric shavers, television sets, cough and cold remedies, and tires.

Chairman Kirkpatrick recently testified before a subcommittee of the Senate Commerce Committee, on the Commission's experience under this program, and he submitted a staff report which evaluates the results of the first few rounds. Chairman Kirkpatrick expressed a number of reseravtions about the success of this program in light of the stated objectives and these reservations are also reflected in the staff's report.

The major disappointment thus far, has been the apparent failure of consumers, competitors, public interest groups and others to take full advantage of the availability of the documentation submitted for study and analysis. Unless these groups come in and scrutinize the material and convey the results to the public, the stated twin objectives of education and deterrents simply will not materialize.

A few groups have devoted a great deal of effort to some of the rounds thus far, particularly in connection with the automobile material. Much more is needed, however, in order to make the program work in the manner that was originally contemplated.

The Commission's staff is presently taking steps to encourage a more active interest and participation by consumer groups and academic communities. The staff would also like to encourage and is taking steps in exploring ways to encourage more interest on the part of advertisers, who might find it profitable to evaluate the data submitted by their competitors and to then contribute to the objectives of this program

by challenging competitors' claims in their own advertising.

Until very recently, advertisers were barred from this kind of advertising or at least there was an impression that this kind of advertising was off limits by restrictive policies of two or three TV networks. In response to a request by the Commission's Bureau of Consumer Protection, those networks have agreed to change these policies so that advertisers are now free to challenge competing ad claims.

Whether advertisers will actually do so remains to be seen. Mutual forebearance to attack competing claims has been a tradition, strong tradition for the past many years, based on the excuse, and I use the word "excuse" intentionally,--of avoiding litigation on charges of false disparagement of competitor's products.

There can be no liability, however, for truthful refutation of competing claims, based on the inadequacy or non-existence of substantiation. It seems to me that vigorous challenges to competing advertising claims, would be fully consistent with how the competitive process is supposed to work.

Moreover, it would be most desirable from a public policy viewpoint, since it would help to provide the consuming public with useful information about competing products. Finally, given the rising tide in current tone of consumerism in this country, I would think that ads which take this approach would prove quite effective from the advertiser's point of view.

Commission staff attorneys have attempted to evaluate the documentation received in each round of the substantiation program, in an effort to assess the extent of inadequacy of substantiation. The Staff Report to Congress indicates the results of this evaluation. A serious question was raised by Commission Staff, with regard to the adequacy of the data, with regard to 30% of all claims involved.

Another 30% involved documentation that was so technical that it was beyond the ability of Commission Staff attorneys to evaluate on their own. It was so technical that special expertise is essential before making any judgment as to its adequacy.

The highly technical nature of this substantiation was not the advertiser's fault, of course, and no negative inference was intended by this observation. In light of these conclusions, however, the Commission Staff is compelled to consider litigation against the most serious instances of inadequate substantiation in material received thus far.

We are also exploring a variety of ways to obtain the expertise needed to evaluate all of the data beyond our comprehension. Given this picture of the Commission's active interest in the quality and extent of substantiation available to support ad claims--what should advertisers and agencies do to avoid questions being raised about the substantiation for their claims?

The first and most obvious suggestion to be made is that compilation and analysis of substantiating data should routinely occur prior to the airing of every new claim, rather than waiting until the FTC takes you by surprise with a 6-B order. Of course, when I use the word claim--that requires substantiation, I mean an objectively verifiable claim as opposed to mere puffing.

However, it is clear from our experience in the substantiation program that some claims which advertisers consider puffing, will be deemed objectively verifiable by the FTC and its staff. It's clear that permissible puffing covers less territory today than it did a few years ago. In reviewing new campaigns and preparing substantiation

before dissemination, advertisers and agencies would be well-advised to take a narrow view of the puffing concept, to resolve all doubts in favor of insisting that adequate substantiation exists to support a new representation.

One related problem concerns the real or imagined distinction between claims made explicitly, and claims which are made by implication only. The Commission Staff's experience in the substantiation program indicates that some advertisers will have extensive and impressive substantiating data to support explicit claims, but very little if any documentation to support representations that are fairly implied in their advertising.

Sometimes this happens because the advertiser disagrees with out judgment that an implied claim exists in the advertising in question. At other times, it happens because the advertiser simply did not expect to be asked to substantiate mere implications.

Regardless of the reason for this problem in the past, advertisers and agencies would be well-advised to take account of the need for adequate substantiation to support representations which may not be explicit but which are clearly implied in their advertising.

After having determined precisely what are the objectively verifiable claims that are contained expressly or implied in proposed new advertising, the advertiser and agency then must assess the adequacy of the data in support of each claim. One fundamental problem at this point, particularly for the people at the ad agency I would think, will be that the data will often be too technical for laymen to comprehend.

As I suggested before, this is a problem that presently faces the FTC staff, and we're attempting to get technical help from a variety of sources. An advertising agency, however, should be able to get all the help it needs from the technical staff of the advertiser client, and I would think that an agency should expect a client to translate technical data into a form that is meaningful to non-experts, and into a form that permits the agency personnel to make a rational and independent judgment regarding the adequacy of substantiation to support a proposed claim.

Assuming that the data is effectively translated in a way that is comprehensible to agency personnel, the question still remains as to whether that material is adequate. The data in connection with most ad claims will probably be in the form of laboratory tests, clinical studies or statistical surveys and it will be necessary to make some judgment as to the scientific validity of the results.

I would be unreasonable to expect agency personnel to be capable of spotting all of the possible flaws or deficiencies in test procedures or protocols, which may detract from the validity of the test or study results.

On the other hand, it is not at all unreasonable to expect agency people to develop some awareness of some obvious defects that are sufficiently serious to render a test or a study worthless as support for an ad claim. Often study protocols, particularly if designed by the advertiser's own personnel, introduce elements of inherent bias that make the results unreliable.

Sometimes test procedures will be uncontrolled, in the sense that no steps are taken to eliminate or reduce the effects of chance factors. Another basic problem may be that the test subjects or the study sample or the test conditions are not representative of consumers generally, or of normal consumer experience.

Whatever may be the basic defect or deficiency, if it is sufficiently serious to invalidate the results, then it's quite clear that the proferred test or study cannot be considered adequate substantiation. It seems to me, that advertising agencies as well as the FTC should be making very substantial efforts at the present time to develop among its own staff some basic knowledge of the basic principles of proper scientific testing and procedures.

A related problem concerns the difficulty of interpreting--a related problem concerns the difficult task of properly interpreting test or study results. It appears that valid tests are sometimes misinterpreted, intentionally or otherwise, and used to support claims which go substantially beyond the claims which may legitimately be made on the basis of those test results.

This would not happen as often as it does, if advertising agency personnel were armed with knowledge of the basic principles of proper interpretation of test results, including some ability to analyze statistics.

It will often not be sufficient to have a test or study that supports a proposed claim, even if the test or study is scientifically valid. If there is reason to believe that the proposed claim involves a matter of some controversy, then it becomes important to make some effort to examine whatever conflicting tests or studies may exist.

While the advertiser's study or test standing by itself may appear to constitute a reasonable basis for making a given claim, it may be unreasonable to rely on that basis in the face of more reliable or extensive conflicting tests or studies.

Moreover, even if the advertiser's data is equally reliable and equally extensive as the conflicting data, the existence of contrary evidence may impose upon the advertiser an obligation to avoid phrasing the claim in a manner that implies that it is established fact. And, in some cases to affirma- tively disclose the existence of the conflicting data or contrary point of view.

Even when there is no conflicting data, it may be unreasonable to rely on the advertiser's own test or study if the test or study--although valid and reliable when first performed has be- come questionable with the passage of time, and with new developments in a relevant field of science. The fact that an advertiser's only substantia- tion consists of a test or study which is twenty years old, should be a sig- nal to the ad agency that some special scrutiny of the situation is warranted.

The agency should want to know why the only evidence is twenty years old. Whether, or to what extent the data may fail to reflect the current state of knowledge in the applicable disci- pline, and whether there have been any subsequent tests or studies that prod- uce contrary results.

Some people have suggested that the Commission's new militance with regard to substantiation will have the effect of deterring advertisers from making objective claims, so that advertising will become increasingly mood-oriented and generally less informative.

A regulatory policy which has the ef- fect of deterring informative advertis- ing surely would be of questionable value to the public. However, I do not believe that the Commission's concern with ad substantiation is subject to this criticism.

First, advertising claims which lack adequate substantiation should be deterred. They are conveyers of mis- information rather than of reliable and useful product information. Second- ly, any inclination on the part of ad- vertisers to avoid objective claims in their ads, will be effectively countered by two related forces. The first is the growing demand by the consuming

public for ads that convey hard infor- mation, the kind which is needed to make rational choices among competing brands of goods and services.

Given the increasing sophistication and increasing militance of a large segment of the consuming public, the old kind of mood advertising, with no informative content, will be less and less effective from the advertisers standpoint.

The second force that will operate against any trend toward mood advertis- ing, is the FTC's ability and resolve to require advertisers to disclose es- sential facts about their products, facts which are necessary to an in- formed purchase decision.

The Commission's new concern with ad substantiation will be effectively complemented by its vigorous efforts, increasingly in the future, to ensure that advertising performs its intended function in the marketplace, the func- tion of conveying product information in a way that promotes competition among sellers and rational purchasing patterns by the consuming public.

Thank you.

DISCUSSION QUESTIONS

1. Has the Federal Trade Commission gone far enough in requiring substan- tiation of advertising claims? Has it gone too far? Explain.

2. What should advertisers and agencies do to avoid questions being raised about the substantiation for their claims?

II-7

ADVERTISING AND
THE FEDERAL TRADE COMMISSION: A REPOST

James J. McGaffrey

Last spring, Louis Harris conducted a study of consumerism under the auspices of the late-lamented Life Magazine. I think at least one of the major conclusions is fascinating. More than *eight out of every ten* people interviewed expressed the conviction that government regulation and watchdogging is a desirable thing when it comes to protecting the consumer against shoddy merchandise, exorbitant pricing, false advertising representation, misleading packaging and the rest. But of this same group, *six out of ten* professed the worry that *over*-regulation by government could seriously disrupt the very business on which the economic health of the country depends.

It's this seeming paradox that I believe we'll be living with as far ahead as the eye can see. Yet it is nowhere near being an unsolvable problem. I think the panic about it exhibited in some quarters is pretty silly, because in the main--*except* for the lunatic fringe--what advertising is being asked to do is not something out of the ordinary. About this lunatic fringe, more anon.

Burns Roper put it very well while speaking about a recent study his organization conducted for one of our clients.

He said that the responsibility of business and advertising in today's climate should be governed by the principle of enlightened self-interest--that success and prosperity will be achieved by being *candid, forthright, accountable* and *responsive*. "In its simplest terms," says Mr. Roper, "*self-interest takes into account the interests of others.*"

If you can come to this point in your thinking, it's then easy to acknowledge and justify the relevance of certain government action to prevent abuses which are harmful, not only to the general public, but also to business itself. By the same token it's a short step from this to serious private action taken to initiate the elimination of such abuses and excesses, instead of resisting such elimination.

But I'm often alarmed at the tendency on some fronts to pitch the baby out with the bathwater. Daniel Yankelovich phrased it pretty succinctly for me in a recent magazine article, when he said:

"Put in my own terms, while we don't argue with responsible outcries for social change and the elimination of commercial abuses, we *do* take issue, however, with the chorus of self-serving and irresponsible suggestions

104

of individuals and pressure groups, *and the reaction of government to such suggestions*, when they lack factual basis or proper regard for the consequences."

Apparently a majority of the American people agree with that.

It has often been said that truth--like beauty--is in the eye of the beholder. And truth in advertising is no exception. If I had 10¢ for every different view I've heard recently on what it is, I'd be able to offset a few enthusiastic--but thoroughly whimsical--investment adventures.

In fact, the people who appear to be most concerned with the subject these days--the organized consumerists and the government and advertising people themselves--can't even seem to agree on what advertising is.

In this connection, I came across a rather remarkable speech the other day. It was given by a man named Gerald Thain, whose job is Assistant Director for National Advertising, Bureau of Consumer Protection, Federal Trade Commission.

Mr. Thain delivered this speech--"Consumerism and the Regulation of Advertising: The American Experience"--at the International Conference on Consumerism in London on Wednesday, October 11, 1972.

One of the things that makes the speech remarkable is that, at the outset, Mr. Thain thus assures his audience:

"The opinions I will express are my own and should *not* be taken as the *official* views of the FTC or any individual Commissioner."

I suppose I should say the same before going any further, but I know--as I'm sure Mr. Thain knew last October 11th--that it's difficult, if not impossible, to speak in public "non ex cathedra"

when one is a government agent or an officer of a trade association as I am.

So I have to assume that somebody higher up in the FTC gave him the green light to make this speech, and that its substance--in the main--represents the thinking, if not the formal policy of that organization.

While neither Mr. Thain nor I may have the *total* support of our respective groups, I assure you that our words are more than off-the-cuff observations of professionals.

The second remarkable thing about Mr. Thain's speech is contained in the following:

"First, I want to state my personal view of the proper role of advertising in an economy based on competition, such as that in the U.S. I believe that the proper function of advertising in such a system is to provide information or, more fully, to provide relevant, meaningful information about the advertised product, from which consumers may make a rational determination as to whether they wish to buy the product."

He continues:

"I have occasionally been met with cries of outrage from some members of the business and marketing communities when I stated this view. *Their response was that the purpose of advertising is to persuade, not inform.*

Now, this is a serious disagreement. It's at the root of a lot of the complications in the government-business relationship today.

I know it's an old gambit to revert to the dictionary, but I did it anyway. On my thesis that the purpose of advertising is *advocacy* or *persuasion*, here's what the good book has to say:

Advocacy is: "active support, as of

a cause."
And to *advocate* is: "to speak in favor of; to recommend."
By the same token, an *advocate* is: "an intercessor, supporter, or defender."
To persuade is "to cause someone to do something by means of argument, reasoning or entreaty," or "to win over someone to a course of action by reasoning or inducement."

O.K., so that's what we in it believe advertising is all about. But what is the definition of advertising *itself*, according to the lexicographers?

The dictionary defines *advertising* as: "proclaiming the qualities of a product or business *so as to increase sales*." And further, it says that *an advertisement*: "is necessarily designed to attract public attention or *patronage*."

Very clear, I think. And completely at odds with Mr. Thain's wishful thinking. Surely of *all* people, he and the rest of the 30-some attorneys who work in the Division of National Advertising ought to understand this. The French word for lawyer is "avocat." And it's somewhat ludicrous to think of F. Lee Bailey presenting a properly-balanced and fully-informational case when he's desperately trying to save a client from a long tour in the pokey.

In short, we have no interest in Mr. Thain--or anyone else--redefining the purpose and responsibility of the business we're in, any more than we'd be presumptious enough, however sorely tempted, to tell the lawyer what *his* role in life is.

Because I found this particular speech fascinating as a clear report of what FTC has been doing in the proper (and sometimes over-eager) exercise of its vested powers, and because I think it represents such a clear blueprint for future activity in this respect, I'd like to devote the remainder of this piece to discussing what the man said

and how we in the advertising business feel about what he said.

To begin with, Congress rightly endowed the FTC with non-static responsibility. Its mandate, going back to its founding in 1914, is to stay aware of and be governed by new principles, new laws, a changing society, changing advertising techniques and the rest.

But I do *not* believe that this provides support for power grabbing beyond the intentions of the Congress or for the promulgation of schemes which are designed to harass business and which are as dangerous as they are crackpot.

One of the ideas advanced by Mr. Thain in his October 11th speech could be called the "Large Advertiser/Giant Killer" thesis. As an example of the Commission's intention to make advertising regulation "more planned and programmatic" than in the past he pointed to its recent concentration on major campaigns by major advertisers--those with significant impact on the public. All perfectly logical, in the sense of utilizing most effectively the efforts of 1400 full-time employees and the nearly $25 million it takes to run the animal, but somewhat suspect when you recognize the *enormous* interest the proprietors at FTC have in assuring the public that they're doing their jobs-- and *then* some--and aren't afraid of the biggest dragons around. It would be hard to say which came first--efficient operation or guaranteed publicity. I have my personal views on the subject.

Mr. Thain's second major point has to do with the expansion of FTC's authority beyond the specifications of the FTC Act. It's here that one begins to wonder where it will all stop. He says this:

"The language of the Act, and the case law which has developed interpreting the Act, clearly establish that the Commission may attack practices which may *not* be unfair to competitors in the traditional anti-trust sense, and may *not* be, in a traditional sense, deceptive or misleading with regard to consumers, but which are simply *unfair* in their impact on consumers. (The Congress) left the Commission free to determine *within broad limits* what new or different kinds of trade practices should be forbidden because they are unfair to the consuming public."

Now, I don't think you need any particular legal training, or even a terribly sharp mind, to realize that, if this view is valid, it can cover a great many elements of government regulation we have barely begun to dream of.

Thain says he expects this doctrine to develop in the future into "one of the Commission's most important legal tools." His staff is beginning to look at areas in which it could be applied--"areas such as advertising that associates a product with strongly-held social values, when in fact the product has no significant relationship to such values." (I guess an example here might be advertising for Cadillac or Rolls Royce.) And certain advertising where the need for mature and sophisticated analysis can't occur, because ordinary people aren't intelligent enough to make such an analysis. (Ted Sorenson recently called this thinking "the most patronizing kind of paternalism.")

Next Mr. Thain got to the subject of "corrective advertising" and announced the Commission's intention to promote this new remedy as "a means of depriving false advertisers of the fruits of their unlawful conduct." He says: "Presumably a consumer's reevaluation of the correct information will result in the shifting of sales from the false advertiser to his competitors. The remedy is *not* intended to deprive a false advertiser of sales per se, but *only* sales which were gained through unlawful advertising. *The intention is to restore competitive conditions*

to where they would have been if no false advertising had existed."

Now *there's* one for the books. This says in effect that 25 percent of a new campaign by a *presumed* previous sinner for one year will establish equilibrium in the market and penalize the sinner for *only* that business gained as a result of his *presumably* false advertising appeal!

I know it sounds incredible, but these people really believe that things happen that way. And through the device of the consent decree, they're in the process of persuading advertisers to go along with them, on the grounds that it's cheaper than a long, drawn-out lawsuit. What I suspect is that such advertisers *know* it won't work. And what I further suspect is that the whole scheme was born out of the Commission's patent inability to tackle major problems rapidly, thereby letting the culprit continue with whatever it was he was doing for an extensive period of time without penalty.

Mr. Thain next talks about FTC's advertising substantiation program, which began a little over a year ago and is designed to provide a source from which consumers can obtain exhaustive information about product performance--information to which the consumer might not otherwise have access. Its usefulness to competitors and to consumerist organizations is also obvious.

He notes that the substantiation program has been subject to "some criticism." Well, he's right, although little of it has come from our side of the fence. Advertising's view of this particular maneuver is that as long as *confidential* or *proprietary* information won't be leaked to competitors and to others who would profit unfairly from it, it is a perfectly legitimate arrangement --something that we in the business invariably do anyway before preparing advertising for the public media.

But the Commission, which I have found abnormally sensitive to *any* criticism of *any* kind by *any*body, has been getting heat on this from someone, because they sent their emissaries to New York a couple of months ago for the stated purpose of checking industry reaction to the substantiation program. In reality, it was a thinly-veiled need to defend the idea which has cost hundreds of thousands of dollars even in the short period in which it has existed and which hardly anybody makes use of.

Then the man got to counter advertising --that delicious, screwy scheme which is giving the FCC fits these days. I don't tend to worry about it very much, because the thing is so asinine that even in a world of asininity and illogicality, it hasn't got a chance.

Probably most of you know how the counter advertising question came about. It's a direct offshoot of the Fairness Doctrine which the FCC applied to cigarette advertising five or six years ago, and which resulted in the on-air appearance of anti-smoking commercials, mainly sponsored by the American Cancer Society.

The FCC thought it was being careful in specifying that this was "a unique situation." A once-in-a lifetime proposition.

As it turned out, this was a naive view indeed. And the FCC has spent the ensuing years wishing to high heaven that it had never applied the Fairness Doctrine to *any* advertising and wondering how to avoid future confrontations on the subject.

A while back, the FTC leaped into the fray by recommending to its sister agency a counter advertising program creating "open available time" for *paid* counter advertising and "free access in prime time" for the discussion *in commercials* of controversial issues raised by paid commercials--all this

in what they call "certain carefully defined circumstances."

Thain supports this by saying: "Advertising today is largely a one-way street. Its usual technique is to provide only *one* aspect of any story. It's probably the only form of *public discussion* where there presently exists no *public debate*."

And here, in this short space of time, we've gone full-circle. *Again* the man is arguing that advertising should *not* be an advocate, that it should *not* try to persuade for the purpose of creating sales, that it *is* a form of "public discussion." If you ever wonder why things can sometimes get confusing, this is a marvelous case in point.

Before winding up his speech, Mr. Thain underscores the fact that the Commission has designed "programs to increase its own knowledge in the area of product advertising." He refers to the FTC hearings on advertising of Fall-1971, and applauds "the large body of information which promises to be of great assistance to the Commission in the exercise of its duties."

Well, I'd trade the twenty-nine volumes of printed testimony and analysis they're likely to get for *one or two grains of common sense* on the part of the Commission and its staff in the upcoming months. The fact that they can support corrective and counter advertising without an apology or even cracking a smile makes it seem as if the 4 1/2 days we spent down here in the Fall of 1971 were somewhat wasted. *One* of the reasons we were invited to come was to help them in their jobs. The other clearly was to try to educate them on what the *real* world of business and advertising is all about.

Mr. Thain concludes his treatise with the statement that:

"Consumers not only can expect us to continue our efforts but, indeed, to expand them with diligence and energy."

You can *bet* on it. But I often wonder who all these "consumers" are who whisper in Mr. Thain's ear. How *many* of them are there?

Are they the *same* consumers with whom most of *us* have to deal, day-in and day out? Or is Thain just reacting to the plaintive bleatings of people whose views of life in America make Don Quixote sound like history's most practical man? They lack any semblance

of what a Bahamian friend of mine likes to refer to as "Mother's Wit."

Keep in mind that our elected representatives and their appointees are merely human beings. There are good ones and bad ones, heroes and bums, brains and dummies. We owe them every respect and willingness to cooperate when they're dealing with us on legitimate matters of law and the public interest. We owe them *nothing* but sharp loud rebuttal when they're wrong in taking us to task, or when they're careless with the facts.

DISCUSSION QUESTION

1. The article refers to a Louis Harris study: "More than *eight out of every ten people* interviewed expressed the conviction that government regulation and watch-dogging is a desirable thing when it comes to protecting the consumer against shoddy merchandise, exorbitant pricing, false advertising representation, misleading packaging and the rest. But of this same group, *six out of ten* professed the worry that *over* regulation by government officials could seriously disrupt the very business on which the economic health of the country depends." With which point of view do you agree? Explain.

Reprinted by permission of Harry Henry and THE ADVERTISING QUARTERLY; September, 1973, pp. 24-31. Dr. Henry is a visiting Professor of Marketing Communications at the Cranfield School of Management and of Marketing at the University of Bradford.

II-8

ADVERTISING AND THE ENVIRONMENT

Harry Henry

The two concepts 'Human Environment' and 'Advertising' do not have any logical relationship with each other. But since the people who are currently making most noise about environmental problems are the same sort of people who for many years have made no secret of their hostility to advertising, it is hardly surprising that the concepts should be linked together by them. Business men cannot ignore the problem, since although the groups concerned are small and unrepresentative they are highly vociferous, and can bring to bear on governments an influence out of all proportion to their numbers.

Perhaps it would be well to begin by reviewing the function of advertising, and by systematising what it actually does (as opposed to what it is sometimes supposed to do). The function of advertising can be described very simply: it is to inform. In the case of the press, the process of communicating information is required by two sets of people, and paid for by them quite separately. The reader wishes to be informed about what is happening in the world--though this is frequently for the purposes of entertainment rather than for any useful purpose, and a large proportion of the news is so trivial that it might just as well

be fictional. For this the reader pays the publisher for a copy of the newspaper. At the same time, the advertiser wants to communicate with the reader, as part of his overall marketing effort, and *he* pays the publisher for this facility by buying advertising space. Although the advertisements are paid for by the advertiser, evidence we have from all over the world indicates that the advertising is regarded by the reader as an essential part of the total package of information he is buying.

CONCEPT TESTING

I have said that the function of advertising is to inform, but of course it is also concerned to *persuade*; and it is upon this aspect that the critics of advertising seize, by attempting to make a distinction between information (which they consider acceptable) and persuasion (of which they disapprove). The distinction is not one which can logically be made, particularly in the field of action-directed information: you cannot meaningfully describe a product, or even a political platform, without drawing attention to its advantages.

110

This problem comes sharply into focus when, in the fields of product innovation or development, we attempt what is known as concept-testing--that is to say, describing a new idea and gathering the reactions to it of likely customers or consumers. Unless some attempt is made to include some element of persuasion in the description, by highlighting its more attractive qualities, there is no way of making the test realistic by simulating what will be said in the shop by the assistant, or what will be said by consumers talking to each other, or what the customer will discover for himself once he has tried the product.

Advertising, indeed, is no more than a part of the selling process, essentially doing no more in large and developed markets than is done by the merchant personally selling his wares in the village market-place. Certain constraints are essential, of course; society must be protected against false and fraudulent claims, either in the direct selling situation or in advertising, and most developed countries have controls of one sort or another to ensure this. The only country which has really lagged behind here is the U.S., which is why there has been created there that violent backlash of 'consumerism,' the reverberations of which are causing some temporary annoyance in the rest of the world. But advertising may be regarded as simply a lubricant of selling, enabling the processes of the exchange of goods and services to operate more smoothly in a form suitable to the great population aggregates in which we live today.

Another of the essential functions of advertising is the speeding-up of innovation. This is not to say that advertising can ever make people do what they do not want to do, or create apparent needs which do not really exist. This, as we shall see a little later, it cannot do. What it can provide is a greater awareness of new products and services, more quickly than would

be the case if potential consumers had to rely on word-of-mouth or imitation, and thus create faster those economies of scale which help in more efficient production and a more rapid reduction in costs and prices.

FALSE DATA

Advertising, by providing a wider dissemination of information, can help to speed up the processes of change. What it cannot do is to *force* change in respect of products and services which will not satisfy some real need, be it actual or latent, or physical or psychological, or which do not offer a benefit appropriate to the present state of the concerned society or market. All of us who have anything to do with commerce or marketing know this to be true, despite the arguments of Professor Galbraith and his followers--arguments which are usually based on false data, or on a misinterpretation of the data resulting from pure ignorance.

It is not difficult to think of large numbers of examples of major changes in behavior patterns resulting from improvements in production technology which are totally independent of advertising or marketing. The spread of the bicycle through the underdeveloped world, for example, is a consequence of the fact that a bicycle is a very useful thing to have--and this is perhaps the one single technological development in the last 100 years whose results have been wholly beneficial. It owes nothing to advertising. Another development, the transistor radio, is nothing like so harmless: it is a major contribution to noise-pollution, and wherever you go throughout the world you will see teenagers holding transistor radios to their ears for fear of missing some seconds of a pop record which they have heard 20 times already--and as often or not they are riding a bicycle at the

111

same time! But, again, the development of this product is in no sense a result of advertising. The really major source of noise-pollution, the aerophane, has developed because people find it convenient to fly; air travel would have reached something like its present level if no airline had ever advertised.

In Russia today, while there is no advertising for cars, my colleagues tell me that the average Soviet citizen is just as anxious to own a car as is any other member of a developed economy-- and is prepared, if he is allowed, to spend three or four years' wages in order to get one. Advertising is no stimulant here: the stimulus is the benefit of having a car, which anybody can see for himself. At the same time, when in consequence of their absurd system of production planning the Soviet chiefs find themselves left with large quantities of badly designed, badly made, inefficient and unattractive consumer durables such as refrigerators, they resort to advertising in an attempt to get rid of them. Advertising is, in fact, regarded by them as a method of shaping demand to conceal major production planning errors: if there is a way of doing this, the industrial companies in the free world, who also make major production planning errors now and again, have not yet discovered it, and would dearly like to know how to do it.

MARKETING 'MAGICIANS'

One of the further difficulties we encounter, however, is that although businessmen know that advertising cannot sell an inefficient or unwanted product or service, our own governments and bureaucrats and most academics cannot understand this. I myself have had numerous encounters with Government Ministers and senior civil servants who firmly believe that their failure to make the public act as they want is entirely due to their own deficiencies in advertising, and that if only they can persuade the magicians of marketing and advertising to work on their behalf they will be able to assume full control. The nonsense in this belief is easily enough seen if we consider dictatorships or totalitarian societies. In such states nothing can be read or heard in the press, on posters, on radio or television, which does not have the full authority of a government, exercising total control over all media of communication. Yet such governments cannot even exist without the whole elaborate machinery of secret police, terror, prison camps, and firing squads: in some cases, indeed, dictatorships have to call in further instruments of repression from --outside. The whole weight of the state behind propaganda--which is only a special form of advertising--cannot sufficiently influence the minds of men. It is therefore not unreasonable to ask how far the limited and often contraacting activities of individual manufacturers and traders can do anything material towards the enslavement of the human mind.

I have discoursed at some length on the nature and functioning of advertising in order to provide a background against which to view those types of social and economic behavior which have any major impact on the human environment. We may now turn to this aspect of the matter, which can be considered under four main heads:

1. those activities which are regarded as deleterious to the environment;
2. the effect of advertising on consumption-patterns, and hence on production-patterns;
3. advertising as a direct pollutant of the environment;
4. advertising as a mental pollutant.

Let us turn first, therefore, to a brief review of those activities which are regarded as harmful to the environment. I would interject here that, although I am personally not much in sympathy with the more extreme environmentalist and conservationist lobbies, I am not here concerned to examine the validity of their arguments: I am interested only in the relationship between them and the processes of advertising--or, rather, to see if there is in fact any relationship. The main categories can be summarised as the exhaustion of natural resources; direct pollution; noise pollution; and what may be called 'the spoiling of the natural heritage.'

The exhaustion of the world's resources is worried about mainly in terms of mineral resources--coal, oil, metals, and the like. The pressure on these is a direct result of the world demand for a continuously higher level of material welfare, but I have already argued that this demand at the general level is affected by advertising to only the smallest degree, if at all.

Minerals, once extracted and used, are for the most part lost for all time (though some measure of recovery and recycling is possible). But this does not apply to crops, either animal or vegetable, except in certain circumstances. It is true that overfishing is putting in danger some species of whale: it is also true that a high proportion of whale-meat finishes up in Great Britain, in tins, as food for cats and dogs. But though pet foods are heavily advertised here, we have no evidence that the greater tendency to use them is a *result* of this advertising: it is almost certainly due for the most part to changes in the general dietary patterns of the British (with far more use for human consumption of those parts of cattle and sheep previously regarded as fit only for animal consumption), to the disappearance of the horse, and to the rises in world prices of ordinary meat which are themselves a function of the world's increasing affluence. The attempt by

our government, shortly after the end of the last war, to persuade the British to eat whale-meat, though heavily promoted by advertising, met with no success at all.

One particular resource, which is a crop but tends to be regarded by the environmentalists as exhaustible, is timber, for which the principal world use is the making of paper. It is sometimes said that to produce a single edition of the New York Sunday Times requires the felling of (I forget how many) acres of forest. It is further argued that, since the New York Sunday Times is 80% advertising, advertising is therefore responsible for the despoiling of the world's forests. But forests cut down can be, and are, replanted: if demand ever outstrips supply, prices of timber and wood-pulp will go up, and the world will turn to other materials such as plastics-- though insofar as these are more indestructible they may give rise to further pollution problems.

MATERIAL WELFARE

Our second problem area is direct pollution, through the deliberate or accidental discharge of oil and chemicals, thermal effects, vehicle exhausts, disposal of radio-active waste, and the like. These are all a consequence of an increasing standard of material welfare, on which (as we have seen) the effect of advertising is negligible. This is not to say they should not be controlled: simply, they have little or no connection with advertising. Where a relationship *may* be thought to exist is in respect of packaging materials which I will return to shortly.

Reference has already been made to the problem of noise pollution--which environmentalists usually refer to in connection only with aircraft and with

vehicles. Again, these are a consequence of a rising level of material
welfare, and have nothing to do with
advertising. If I were asked to choose
between the noise of an aeroplane overhead carrying people about their business with speed and comfort, and a
hairy youth bellowing protest-songs
about pollution to the noise of an
electric guitar, my choice would invariably be the former. But this is
perhaps a personal view.

The most intractable problem arises in
relation to what we have described as
'the spoiling of the natural heritage,'
which is usually thought of in terms
of the physical beauty of the country-
side. Here we have a real dilemma: a
beautiful beach, for example, is only
beautiful so long as it has no people
and buildings on it. But if nobody
comes to it it is not beautiful, because nobody can see it: as soon as
people come to enjoy it, they spoil
it. In a feudal or aristocratic society the problem hardly arises; the
aristocrat may build himself a villa
in exquisite taste, to which the common people are allowed to come only as
servants, and the beauty remains un-
spoiled, though enjoyed by only a tiny
minority of people. In a democratic
society, however, this is not longer
possible--everybody has the right to
come, and as soon as they do so it is
spoilt. All this, though, has nothing
to do with advertising. In a similar
situation, the caves at Lascaux in
France have had to be closed because
the breath of thousands of tourists
was ruining the Cro-Magnon wall-paint-
ings. At the same time it may be noted
that some of the major works of antiquity,
particularly in Greece, are not subject
to this problem. The Acropolis at Athens,
the temple compound at Delphi, the hospital complex at Epidouros, are not
spoilt by the presence of people: they
were built for thousands of tourists
(though in those days they were called
pilgrims), and can absorb them quite
happily.

EFFECTS ON CONSUMPTION

Let us now turn to the second of our
four main heads: the effect of advertising on consumption patterns and hence
on production patterns. We have already
seen that a number of consumption patterns, and still more of production
patterns, may reasonably be regarded as
detrimental to the environment. How
far this is an acceptable price to pay
for increasing material welfare is a
matter of priorities, which in democratic societies cannot be determined
by a small, highly privileged and self-
appointed elite. But we have also seen
that, despite a number of unsubstantiated
claims to the contrary, there is no evidence that these patterns are materially affected by advertising in any except the shortest of runs, and that most
evidence is in the opposite direction.

My third category was concerned with
advertising as a *direct* pollutant of
the environment--that is to say, the
extent to which the physical attributes
of advertising have this effect. We
are concerned here essentially with the
intrusive nature of advertising, and
this varies according to the particular
medium involved, so we must consider the
various media separately. Undoubtedly
the media which are considered the most
intrusive are commercial radio and television. But here we come to the problem of priorities in the allocation of
resources. State broadcasting systems,
non-commercial, are paid for out of taxa-
tion, and are very expensive to run.
Increased choice--through more channels
--can only be provided by the state at
the cost of increased taxes, and governments are usually well aware that this
solution is politically unacceptable.
Instead, *commercial* channels are author-
ised, paid for by advertising. Of
course, the consumer pays for even
these indirectly, since they ultimately
enter into the costs of the goods and
services he purchases--in Britain it
amounts to rather less than one half of
one percent of consumer expenditure--

but this the electorate find acceptable. At the same time, if the citizen chooses to use one of the commercial channels he is entering into an
implicit contract to expose himself
to the advertising it carries, and cannot logically complain of intrusions.

There are very few countries in which
he does not have a choice, even if
this means switching off the set for
half an hour a day, and the development of community antennae, cable TV
and pay-TV are now giving him the
choice even in the U.S. Of course, in
nearly all countries there are government controls on the proportion and
timing of commercials, but this is not
the best solution--the very simple rule
is, 'If you don't like commercials,
don't use the commercial channels.'
The remedy, if the viewer really objects to the disease, is in his own
hands.

Posters are a different matter: there
is no real way of avoiding these, and
certainly posters along rural highways
in countries such as Italy and the U.S.
cannot be regarded as other than intrusive and detrimental to the environment, though even in the U.S. they are
not permitted on parkways. In most
countries, however, governments have
taken steps to restrict this type of
use, and have confined them to urban
environments where they are wholly in
place and indeed a positive advantage.
It is interesting to observe how British
architects, after many years of excluding posters from their designs for new
business and shopping centres, are now
taking particular pains to include them
as a means of giving more colour and
life to the local environment. And if
you have ever seen Moscow, a city virtually without advertising except for
the occasional propaganda poster, you
will appreciate the positive contribution which posters make to the general
appearance of a city.

GENERAL LAWS

Of course, most advertising is found
in the press, where it might be regarded
as unavoidably intrusive. But years of
research into the role of advertising
in the press have produced two basic
general laws. The first is that, since
people are highly selective in what they
read on a page, if they are not interested in the advertising they simply do
not look at it--their own defense mechanisms, on the principle of what is
called selective perception, protect
them from intrusion. The second is
that they are just as interested in the
advertising as in the editorial--in
frequent cases much more so; and this
is because they welcome the information
contained in the advertisements as being of specific use to them in the conduct of their daily affairs, which is
not always true of the editorial. To
return to Russia, *Pravda* is undoubtedly
the dullest newspaper in the world, and
though Russians read it because they
have nothing else it would not last
five minutes against the competition of
the sort of newspaper we have in the
free world--largely, I would suggest,
because of its absence of advertisements.

I referred earlier to the question of
the pollution caused by packaging materials, and we may now consider this.
The non-returnable bottle, and the can,
undoubtedly create a pollution problem
greater than that of the returnable
bottle. They are, however, more efficient and cheaper; and the same consideration applies in the case of plastic containers, where the pollution
problem is worse and will remain so until somebody develops a satisfactory
bio-degradable plastic. Once again we
face the question of values and priorities, which applies with equal force to
the problem of wrapping and packaging
material made of paper and plastic.
But if products are more elaborately
packaged than they used to be, this is
because it provides better protection
against spoilage and breakage.

Finally, we come to our fourth cate-
gory--advertising as a 'mental pollutant.' The argument here is that advertising creates spurious wants for
which there is no real justification,
and creates levels of dissatisfaction
among the under-privileged which lead
to social unrest. We have already seen,
however, that advertising is incapable
of creating a demand where no actual
or latent consumer need exists: the
products it helps to sell may be regarded by some people as trivial, but
the people who want them have every
right to regard them as significant.
As for the creation of dissatisfaction,
while it is true that the American
negro (the usual example) sees on television commercials a number of products
and living styles beyond his financial
reach, he also sees them in shop windows, in the houses he enters in a
service capacity, in every film he at-
tends, in the programme contents of
television and the press, and indeed
in the whole environment in which he
lives. To suggest that his envy arises
solely, or even mainly, from the advertising component of that environment
is totally untenable.

In this connection it is interesting
to consider the 'cargo cults' of sav-
age Africa and of the islands and arch-
ipelagos of south-east Asia and north-
ern Australasia. Typically these
emerged in the days of European colon-
ialism: the indigenous populations,
seeing ships arriving laden with
desirable goods which their European
masters took without apparently working for them, came to the conclusion
that these were gifts from the gods,
intended for the natives, which the
Europeans were stealing; from this
there arose their belief that some day
the gods would send a ship laden with
a glorious cargo which they could have
for themselves. The point of this
anthropological reference is simply
that there was no advertising, no commercial radio or television, no posters
or cinema advertising, to create this
dissatisfaction: it arose from the
sight of the products alone. Mankind
is much of a muchness in its basic
reactions and desires, whatever the
colour of its skin or the level of its
education. Possibly the environmentalists
would be a little better informed if
they had more knowledge not only of the
working of economic systems but also of
history, sociology and anthropology.

DISCUSSION QUESTIONS

1. The author writes, "...the function
of advertising is to inform, but of
course it is also concerned to persuade;
..." What distinction is there between
these two issues? Which do you feel is
more important from the point of view
of the seller?

2. In your judgment, what is the effect
of advertising on the environment?

Reprinted by permission from ADVERTISING AGE; 12 March, 1973, pp. 4A, 4B, 78A, 78B.

II-9

ADVERTISING AND THE PUBLIC INTEREST

John A. Howard and James Hulbert

This chapter suggests recommendations on FTC policy and procedures in connection with advertising and consumer problems. To illustrate our recommendations, some of the FTC's current procedures and policies will be discussed. Some of the recommendations will involve proposals for basic consumer research for, without such, objective solutions to some problems are unlikely--perhaps impossible. FTC policies will be discussed in relation to those of other public and private agencies affecting the consumer.

FEDERAL TRADE COMMISSION

The Federal Trade Commission bears the primary responsibility for federal regulation of advertising.

The Bureau of Consumer Protection, which initiates recommendations to the commission, has evaluated ads (usually intuitively), primarily in terms of the truthfulness criterion. By "intuitive," we mean that the bureau generally cannot articulate how it reached its judgment. In the evaluation process, three levels of intuitive judgments are involved: (1) Whether--and when--a claim is a claim, as explained in Chapter Five, in the discussion of actual vs. implied claims; (2) whether the claim is true or false; (3) whether the claim, as a matter of law, is deceptive. The fact that these judgments are made intuitively does not imply that they are wrong. Others may be inclined to question these judgments, particularly, however, if they do not understand the process by which the judgments were made. Where possible, we propose objective criteria, the application of which can be articulated and understood by the commission, its staff, industry, and consumers.

RECOMMENDATIONS IN TERMS OF CRITERIA

Our purpose is to make recommendations in terms of the criteria of optimal conditions of choice, described in Chapter Eight, with respect to advertising practices. We shall deal separately with special audiences.

TIMELINESS

We believe that advertising does well on this criterion; thus, regulation is not necessary. Obviously, it is in the

interest of the advertiser to conform
to this criterion.

INTELLIGIBILITY

Intelligibility is the capacity of the
ad to clearly transmit its meaning to
the consumer. The ad industry has experts in writing comprehensible ads;
but, as Allen C. Rosenshine has pointed
out, it has not always been possible
for an agency to enforce the discipline
to secure such intelligibility in its
ads.

We do not believe it is necessary to
regulate this characteristic *per se*.
It is in the advertiser's self interest
to produce intelligible messages. In-
advertent failures in communication
should occur less frequently as creative people come to view the consumer
in a more detailed and accurate way,
and as basic research enables us to
articulate more fully the consumer's
response to advertising.

Where omissions in incomplete comparatives result in an incomprehensible
message, the problem can be considered
as an aspect of truthfulness. Incomplete comparatives--sometimes referred
to as "open-ended claims"--are not intelligible; for example, "Brand X is
better." Better than what?

The Bureau of Consumer Protection must
be concerned with the intelligibility
criterion in producing corrective ads.

RELEVANCY

Casual observation suggests to us that
the industry's performance is less than
adequate on the criterion of relevancy.
However, such systematic evidence is
lacking.

The commission has moved increasingly
in the direction of affirmative disclosure: cigarets, octane, care of
apparel, phosphate, and analgesics.

Mr. Robert Pitofsky has indicated that
he expects affirmative disclosure to be
an "important regulation" in the future.
This direction raises the question of
what information should be disclosed.
We believe the answer is "relevant" information. As discussed in Chapter
Eight, relevant information is information pertaining to the attributes by
which the consumer conceptualizes the
brand, as well as the purchasing and
use situation, in order to make his decision. If credible, this information
molds the consumer's comprehension of
the brand and his attitudes--personal,
self concept, and impersonal--as developed in Chapter Four. This view assumes that the consumer knows enough
about the product class (not necessarily
the particular brand) to be able to conceptualize all brands in it so as to
meet his needs.

• A more representative judgment of an
ad than that obtained by current commission practice, could be from a *survey* of consumers. (This should not be
confused with the past practice of
bringing in consumer witnesses to testify.) Representativeness would be gained
with a consumer survey, but the judgment
would still be intuitive. Thus, an intuitive link in the means-end chain
would still exist. Also, such a practice encounters the usual operating research handicaps of cost and delay.

As described in Chapter Eight, we believe this criterion is now fully operational. The commission can determine,
by research, what are the specific
choice criteria which consumers use to
evaluate brands in the particular product class. Like many tools, this one
can be sharpened, and additional research may be able to make its application more economical. Until such research is done, we recommend that this
criterion be used only as an adjunct to
defining deception that arises due to
omission of relevant information.

The relevancy criterion is particularly
"researchable" because it has a theo-

retical counterpart in the theory of
consumer behavior. This counterpart--
the attitude construct--specifies the
facts which must be quantified. From
a sample of consumers, attitude dimensions can be elicited by fairly standard means. Information that conveys
meaning about these dimensions can be
called "relevant."

Aside from cost and time involved in
collecting the data, there are two
limitations upon this ideal approach.
First, consumers may not be well
enough informed to know how to best
conceptualize the brand in their own
interest. We do not, however, believe
these cases are numerous within the
general population. Yet, in some
cases (like diet, where even the experts disagree), such lack of knowledge may be frequent. Second, in the
case of a radically new brand, consumers
have not yet learned to conceptualize
it.

COMPLETENESS

In many cases, advertising does not
include as much information as it
should. According to this criterion,
all of the commission's affirmative
disclosure cases are deficient. The
criterion, however, must be carefully
defined.

The industry fears the use of this
criterion. Weil pointed out that
completeness could be used to prevent
a company from advertising characteristics which competing brands share to
an equally satisfying degree (Weil
T1951).

Even Mr. Maxwell Arnold, who seemed
less fearful of regulation than some
industry representatives, expressed
concern here: Except in the cases of
drugs and cleaners, "a product should
not have to spend money to advertise
its drawbacks, in the sense of informing consumers how it may be inferior
to the competition or deficient in

desirable benefits" (Arnold T1861,1862).
Andrew Kershaw, president of Ogilvy &
Mather, put it epigrammatically: "The
truth, nothing but the truth, but not
the whole truth." Mr. Pitofsky made it
clear that a product is not expected to
advertise its deficiencies, except for
reasons of health and safety.

We believe that an advertiser should be
permitted, in a product class where all
brands are identical, to name a benefit
of his brand without being required to
say that competitors' brands also have
such a benefit--unless he claims uniqueness for his brand. The consumer benefits because he can believe that this
brand has the benefit. His uncertainty
is relieved, and his confidence is increased. In the case of an important
purchase, uncomfortable tension is relieved. This advertising service to
the consumer usually goes unnoticed by
the critics. The consumer is then free
to search for more information, if he
wishes to do so.

• We believe that advertisers should
think in terms of the consumer's total
information requirements, and design
their marketing strategies and plans to
be consistent with these needs. The
marketing task becomes more complex,
yet the more astute marketers are already doing this, in a more or less intuitive way. It is implicit in the
media mix decision. The complexity occurs, in part, because of the difficulty of coordinating market activity so
that a given consumer has a high probability of observing two separate
pieces of information in reasonable
proximity in time. For example, he
sees an ad on television today, and
goes into the retail store tomorrow
where the brand is displayed.

We do not know whether this criterion
is operational for the commission; that
is, whether it can be objectively applied. If it is not, however, it would
not be a major research undertaking to
make it so.

119

TRUTHFULNESS

The activities of the commission have
proven that some ads are untruthful
and deceptive. From casual observation,
it would appear that substantial progress has been made in the last two
years toward improving this characteristic. The effort should be continued.
However, self-concept advertising has
been excluded in the past. It should
now be included.

Substantial basic research should be
devoted to making the criterion operational.

ACCURACY OF TARGET AUDIENCES

Does the advertiser accurately identify
his target audience, and is he able to
beam his messages to only the desired
audience? Although companies devote a
great deal of effort toward identifying the "best" market segments, in
terms of growth and profit, significant research evidence suggests that
such efforts are not very precise.

It may be that an advertising message
is deceptive for one audience, but not
for another. This difference is dramatically shown with children. Younger
children, because of their less dis-
criminative capacities, are more inclined to take ads at their face value
than are older children or adults. Although a claim that others believe a
particular brand is superior might be
perfectly true for an ad going only to
owners of the brand, such an advertising effort does not contain the normal
problems connected with defining accurately an advertiser's target audience.

In most cases, we do not see the inability of an advertiser to identify
his audience accurately, and to reach
it with precision as a serious issue.
The capacity to accurately identify
his audience would provide the advertiser with an incentive to develop im-

proved ways of identifying and reaching
his intended audience. However, we are
not concerned, except in the case of
special audiences, with "waste circulation"; that is, the unintended viewing
the ad, or the intended not doing so.

SPECIAL AUDIENCES

The problems associated with special
audiences can be divided into two groups:
(1) those best dealt with by self regulation; (2) those in which government
should be involved.

In the hearings, stereotyping was of
concern to spokesmen for ethnic minorities and women. As indicated in Chapter
Six, we deplore such stereotypes. Indeed this is an area where self regulation can prove its effectiveness. We
want this report to contribute to an
enhanced sensitivity on the part of
the industry and its self-regulatory
bodies, to issues of stereotyping.

Based upon an extensive discussion in
Chapter Six, we do not believe that the
other problems of special audiences
will be solved by the action of industry alone. First, let us discuss the
child audience, with specific reference
to television.

· The young child in America spends a
great deal of time watching television.
Consequently, the medium has developed
special offerings to appeal to him--
notably, "Saturday morning" television.
As we stated in Chapter Six, there is
only a limited amount of existing evidence regarding effects of television
on young children. What evidence does
exist, however, is internally consistent
and agrees with laboratory evidence.
Children, six and under, have less capacity to discriminate, both perceptually
and cognitively, than do older children.
These younger children discriminate
less between advertisement and program.
They are not warned by the due, "a commercial." They are more credulous and
less able to sort the relevant from

the irrelevant.

Given that these young children do not discriminate between ad and program, what should be done? Proposals have ranged from placing a ban on children's television to making no change and continuing with the present system. We believe that each of these extremes is too simplistic. To provide an adequate answer to the question, we must make some judgment about the effects of advertising on the child. We must also deal with the heterogeneous viewing patterns of children. We believe there is less of a problem with children six years and over. An adequate answer must reflect the fact that these children will view television in any case, and advertisements may be a factor in teaching them how to be consumers.

There is, also, the question of parental responsibility. If television advertising is injurious to young children, should we not expect their parents to prevent them from watching it? Or should parents be expected to make use of television time by employing it to teach their children the arts of buymanship? Are mothers irresponsibly using television as an electronic "Baby sitter?" At one time, our society looked upon the unemployed and the aged as being irresponsible because they did not provide for themselves. Sensing an analogous shift of values here, we believe that there is a substantial desire for the government to accept this responsibility for it to limit the possibility of the young child viewing television ads.

We propose the following: First, evaluative criteria should be rigorously applied to all advertisements broadcast during the "children's programing" hours. Truthful ads can contribute to developing a child's ability to make good consumer decisions; untruthful ones cannot. Completeness should be applied to ensure that comparatives are not abused, and that qualifiers

(where applicable) are clearly stated. Intelligibility should be applied to ensure that ad content (particularly qualifiers) is understood by the child audience. Relevance should be applied to the appeals used. The relevance criterion will be more difficult to apply to children, however, because their cognitive structures are less sharply differentiated than adults. The use of testimonials and self-concept appeals should be discouraged in such advertising.

• Second, we believe that the broadcaster should make the distinction between program and commercial more perceptible. A brief, video signal (as used in Britain), and perhaps an added voiceover, would make this distinction clearer. Also, we believe that the program personalties (cartoon or otherwise) should not be used in the commercials.

The issue of advertisement-free programing for young children is controversial. We believe that the primary responsibility for controlling the viewing habits of younger children lies with the parents. However, we believe that the networks should aid parents in their task of selecting what their children should watch. Thus, third, rather than a complete advertising ban, we believe there should be a period of time (one hour seems appropriate) set aside on an experimental basis by each network staggered on Saturday mornings, when programs to the very young (under six years of age) should be shown for three hours without commercial interruptions. We recognize the progress which has been made in this area. Programs such as "Sesame Street" and "Mister Rogers" are network in terms of the availability; and they offer the type of commercial-free choice we are concerned about. However, our proposal is much broader in its implications.

• By clearly announcing this advertisement-free period, parents concerned about the effects of advertising to

121

young children would be able to ensure
that their children could watch television without being exposed to advertising. This is an ideal. Even on an
experimental basis, there would be
problems of implementation (such as
preventing local stations from "cutting
in" local advertising). However, the
experiment would provide an opportunity
to find out to what extent the parents
did take advantage of such an idea.
For those parents who do not take advantage of such an advertising-free
television period, we could find out
why, and develop a better policy if
such seems called for. The approach
would, also, avoid the networks presenting an image of intransigence--an
image which is not appropriate for an
industry so visibly impinging upon the
public interest.

In Chapter Six, we stated that the
needs of the poor and the disadvantaged
were a special case of a general information gap. One gap in the consumer's
knowledge is how to go about lodging
complaints, and to seek satisfaction
for grievances. How many consumers
know about the Direct Mail Advertiser
Assn.'s "Certified Service?" How many
know about the American Advertising
Federation--Council of Better Business
Bureaus local advertising review boards?
How many know of the Natioanl Advertising Division of the Council of Better
Business Bureaus and the National Advertising Review Board? The sincerity
of industry's self-regulatory efforts
remains difficult to judge as long as
consumers remain ignorant of their
availability. We believe that more efforts should be made to close this gap:
to make consumers, in general, and the
poor and the disadvantaged, in particular, more aware of the mechanisms that
have been established to seek their
feedback. We believe the Advertising
Council could make a great contribution
in this area. We are delighted that
the council has developed, and is executing, an advertising campaign urging
consumers to make use of the local
better business bureaus.

IMPLEMENTATION

The criteria have a number of current
implications for public policy. We believe that their future implications
will be substantially stronger and more
comprehensive than they are now. They
do not necessarily imply a more stringent policy, however, in the future.
Let us develop these current implications.

Ad substantiation is an effective way
of implementing the truthfulness criterion. However, the continuing ad
substantiation program, as applied to
particular industries, must be distinguished from the ad substantiation requirements imposed upon a particular
company.

The ad substantiation program should be
reviewed in order that the experience
gained from it can be utilized fully in
future activity.

• Some criticize the FTC's substantiation program, saying that the consumer
does not want the information. A trade
paper reporter recently wrote, "Consumers apparently aren't greatly interested in obtaining reports of claim
substantiation, if Colgate-Palmolive
Company's experience is a good example."
Colgate-Palmolive had advertised the
availability of a forty-three page report, from a private testing laboratory,
which stated that Ajax was superior to
competitors on certain dimensions.
Only 300 requests for the pamphlet had
been received in the first three weeks.
Several thoughts can be raised about
the validity of the reporter's conclusions. First, being able to obtain the
report may, in itself, have favorably
affected the consumer's judgment of the
brand. Second, forty-three pages is
extensive reading. (In this case, the
laboratory required that the company
make available the entire report.) Advertisers often refer orally to instances where consumers have refused to
read ads with relevant information; but,
systematic evidence to support these

statements is lacking. We believe that supporting analysis is often a sample of the total population, instead of those who are "in the market" for the product class, so that much of the sample does not need information.

• Individual substantiation should be a widely used practice, and the information should be in relevant terms. We believe that the consumer will be well served by such substantiation. Industry will also learn more about the true needs of the consumer, as well as how to avoid regulations. Mr. [Robert] Choate writes, "Substantiation cannot deal scientifically with the attractions of a toy, the sound of a record, or the smell of a drink." We believe that, in most cases, it is possible to make adequate measure of these subjective phenomena. However, it is more difficult with younger children.

As it is not feasible to require all probable violators to substantiate, we recommended that cases be selected at random in order to keep the offenders "off guard." We believe that using "the biggest" or "the most flagrant" advertisers to serve as examples, in establishing the principle of requiring certain ads to be substantiated to others, is not as effective as taking a more direct "fear-of-getting-caught" approach. A random selection should increase the effectiveness of proceeding against individual companies.

Corrective advertising should be continued until better evidence is obtained, regarding its relative merits, vis-a-vis other procedures for improving truthfulness. There may be cases where corrective advertising is a more appropriate remedy than ad substantiation; for example, where the untruthful ad has been especially effective in misleading the consumer. Such conjecture, however, should not be the basis of policy.

• Finally, some arrangement is desirable to bring together, intermittently, over an extended period of time, representatives of industry, representatives of consumers, and representatives of the commission. We believe that consumer advertising is an element of a vital socioeconomic process, which transmits technology to the consumer and creates investment opportunities that add to the level of employment. Also, we believe that advertising can serve the consumer much more effectively than it does at the present time. The cost of tinkering may be high, but the benefits could also be high. We think the case-by-case approach is too slow, too piecemeal, and leads to too much uncertainty for industry, and to too much delay in meeting the consumer's needs. This examination could not only develop better ways of regulating advertising, but it could serve to codify existing rules.

The commissioners displayed imagination, and a sense of honest inquiry, in holding the hearings. Industry, also, is to be complimented for investing resources in order to effectively explain to the commission how advertising functions. The hearings served to correct some false premises on both sides. We recommend that this productive effort be extended over a period of at least three years, and perhaps five years.

• The innovations in policy, represented by the commission's responsiveness to consumerism, have raised many problems that could be partially alleviated. We must always expect some tension, however, between the regulated and the regulator. Once consumer representatives understand better the nature of the industry, and the constraints it imposes upon management; and management representatives better understand the consumer problems; and both better understand the commission's problems, we believe that each can make constructive recommendations as to how regulation can contribute to the consumer's information needs. By using the concepts of Chapter Four, the interested parties can separate value from fact, and discover whether it is value that separates them, or assumption about fact. Some fact questions may be answered on the spot. Where this cannot be done, more research is necessary. We are confident that new, more effective ways of regulating can be developed. The "cooling-off period" in sales arrangements is an illustration of how to deal with a problem that would have been difficult, if not impossible, to attack directly. For example, prohibiting the salesman from practicing high-pressure tactics. Analogous kinds of solutions might be created for advertising.

• The arrangements should be systematic and formalized. The organization should be a joint, permanent, fulltime staff of three responsible people. These people would report to the director of the bureau. They should be housed in the FTC building. One member should be a regular commission employe of status; another should be a respected member from the public or consumer side and, perhaps, financed by outside foundation or government funds. The third person should be from industry, and paid by industry-- perhaps an experienced product or marketing manager.

The function of this unit is to structure the problem of regulating advertising so as to bring to bear current ideas, and a flow of research findings. The group should be free to bring in the variety of experts needed. The results of the ad substantiation program could be vital grist.

The goal of the unit would be to determine fully, as the criteria are implemented, the probable consequences of the criteria of optimal conditions of information for the consumer. It would determine the extent to which the criteria are consistent with industry's interest. Therefore, with development and education, the findings of the group could become self enforcing. An important question is how their policy implications can be implemented, without damaging the socio-

economic process of product innovation.

Every three months, the staff should report to a committee composed of the bureau director, public representatives, and second-level corporate executives from the advertisers, the agencies, and the media. Every six months, it should report to the commissioners--a selected, continuing group of public representatives and chief operating executives of corporations in the industry (advertisers, agencies and media).

The commission has several mechanisms available for administrative interpretations of the statute. One or more of these might be used to carry out the joint commission-consumer-industry program proposed here, as well as the regulations that would emerge from it. We do not know the advantages and disadvantages of each mechanism, but we are confident the commissioners do.

EDUCATION OF THE PUBLIC

The commission should formulate policies for developing a consumer education program. The role that Congress and court decisions have assigned the commission is not understood by the public. The commission is severely handicapped in its relations with consumers because of its adjudicative role. For this reason, some would question whether the commission should concern itself with explaining its programs to consumers and other members of the public. We believe it should.

The commission, because of its great consumer activity and visibility, receives many complaints. Most involve issues at the local level, such as retail advertising. Only a small proportion of consumer complaints are directed at *national brand advertising*. If its area of jurisdiction were better understood among consumers, it could be more effective. It would, also, be criticized less by consumers for being ineffective.

The FTC regional offices currently devote more effort to performing useful functions in relating to consumers on a local basis than they did in the past. This effort should be strengthened.

Public addresses by commission and staff members contribute immensely to achieving closer relations with consumers. However, these do not provide the systematic consumer input to commission thinking that other ways do.

• In addition to the general public, the work of the bureau could be facilitated and improved if a sophisticated segment of the public understood its problems; for example, home economists, high school teachers of consumer courses, and interested university faculty members, particularly in economics, law and marketing. These should be considered a technical advisory group. Arrangements should be made to relate them to the activities of the Bureau of Consumer Protection. The receptivity to new ideas that we have seen among members of the staff causes us to emphasize the potential of this relation. Annual meetings with the commissioners could further serve this function. Perhaps the group should be divided into specialist committees, and work on a committee basis.

As with most regulative activity, industry groups tend to be better organized, and supported with greater resources, than are consumer groups. The annual budget of the Consumer Federation of America, for example, is infinitesimal compared to many of the industry groups. As a consequence, industry organizations have more technical expertise and can be more useful than consumer groups in giving technical advice.

We appreciate that increased effort has been devoted by the commission to increasing the amount and nature of contacts with the consumer groups. We believe that this effort should be intensified.

OPERATING RESEARCH

Congressman John D. Dingell pointed out (T6) that Congress, in creating the commission, envisioned both formal adjudicative powers and fact-finding functions. He noted that the commission's Bureau of Economics has come to be "recognized as one of the federal government's leading gatherers of information relating to economics and trade practices." By implication, the commission has not done as well on the consumer side.

We recommend that a behavioral research department be established to help provide answers to immediate operating problems. Operating and basic research can be roughly distinguished, according to the criterion of immediate usefulness. Operating research is intended to be immediately useful in helping to provide answers to operating and planning questions. Basic research is to develop knowledge that can be used, at some future time, in answering operational questions. Operating research could take a number of directions.

One of the most difficult questions is: "When is a claim a claim?" We believe that this question could be answered by a small survey of consumers. The general idea of the question, simplistically stated, would be: "What claims about the brand does this ad convey to you?" The response would be a measure of information retained. Obviously, there are technical questions of sample size, reliability, and validity; but, reasonable reules concerning such can be worked out.

• Having introduced one area of operating research to provide some sense of the intended meaning of the term, let us examine one of the problems relating to commission policy with respect to information. If the commission frequently subpoenas company market research, and uses it as evidence against the company, will companies reduce their research efforts? We believe a company

should be free to use its own judgment,
with respect to the risk it takes. If
it wishes to make decisions on less
information, it should have this option. If it believes the research is
likely to be subpoenaed, and used as
evidence, it may feel it is necessary
for it to go beyond what it would do
in terms of its own needs. When a
company makes a risky decision, and
finds it wrong, it can (to a substantial extent) contain the undesirable
effects of the bad decision. This capacity is shown in new product development by forms of concept testing, test
marketing, and national "roll-outs."
In some cases, only the company can
have relevant data; for example, if the
point at issue can be evaluated only by
data from the more distant past, from a
time earlier than when the case was being brought. Research, which provides
only data current long after the event,
may not be helpful. How frequently the
commission's needs for past or current
data would be evidenced is something
we do not know.

• At some point, operating research
should be applied to deception. We believe that it is unwise for the commission to continue to rely solely upon
its court-endowed expertise in the area
of truthfulness. Even if the defen-
dants do not begin to bring forward
empirical evidence on deception (which
we suspect they may), the use of judi-
cially conferred expertise may arouse
suspicions which more objective evidence would avoid. We believe the commission has not been questioned for
two reasons: First, because of the
strong moral support in American society for the principle of truth,
which will not apply to the other
evaluative criteria; second, the cases
in most instances have been fairly obvious. The public will demand increasingly stringent enforcement. As this
occurs, borderline cases will multiply.

Operating research should be applied
whenever relevancy of information is
an issue. As the commission has moved

to require the advertiser to take a
more affirmative role (as in the case
of octane ratings in gasoline, and the
care of clothing, in the case of apparel), the question of relevancy has
become more significant. Because operational criteria can be developed for a
particular product class, operating research is feasible. The issue of relevancy may become sharper if substantiation of self-concept advertising is
required.

For all other criteria of optimal conditions of consumer choice that we have
recommended, operating or basic research
will be required in developing the
necessary objective subcriteria.

FOOD AND DRUG ADMINISTRATION

"The apparent intent of Congress was
that the jurisdiction of the two agencies (FTC and FDA) be mutually exclusive...The courts, however, created a
broad area of overlapping jurisdiction
...The FDA regulates the labeling of
food, drugs, and cosmetics, and the advertising of prescription drugs. The
FTC regulates the advertising of food,
non-prescription drugs, and cosmetics,
together with the advertising and some
of the labeling of other products."*
A formal arrangement has been developed
between the two agencies to exchange
information whenever there are overlapping problems.

With the growing emphasis upon diet and
modern foods, labeling--especially
among foods--has become an increasingly
important item. As advertising is
judged more and more in terms of the
consumer's total information requirements, jurisdictional problems may be
sharper. For example, the application
of the completeness criterion to a food
or drug manufacturer's communications

* 80 Harvard Law Review 1005 (1967).

program would require a considerable amount of coordination between the FDA and the FTC.

FEDERAL COMMUNICATIONS COMMISSION

The Federal Communications Commission is responsible for the programing of broadcast media. The Federal Trade Commission is responsible for advertising on the program.

Advertisers believe, with some evidence, that the media program content influences the nature of advertising effect. We do not see this as a major problem in obtaining optimal conditions of choice for the consumer.

EXECUTIVE OFFICE

The Office of the President, through its Office of Consumer Affairs, has exerted substantial influence in shaping federal consumer policy. Its function has been to explore the nature of the consumer problem, and to strive to exercise political leadership in this area. The office has served a useful purpose in contributing to optimal conditions of choice for the consumer.

ROLE OF LEGISLATION

Should the industry not cooperate in the arrangement to bring the commission, consumer representatives, and advertising industry representatives together in a formal, joint, continued examination of the consumer problem as related to advertising, or if the commission finds itself unable to perform this

assignment, the spirit of the consequences of the recommendation should be embodied in legislation. The potential of these discussions is more difficult to obtain legislatively than by the commission. The issues are subtle, not well understood, and wide differences sometimes separate the three parties. Nevertheless, we believe that congressional procedures could be used here. Our optimism springs from the fact that congressional procedures carefully applied were effective in formulating the Investment Company Act of 1940 for another industry. The advertising by industry, as a whole, is not in as much disrepute as were the mutual funds; but, there is the common element of the low credibility of their advertising.

We believe there is a need for something like the Moss Bill (S. 1753), to finance essential basic research in those aspects of consumer behavior that bear on the issues discussed here. We do not believe that sufficient funds will be available from private sources to carry out this task. The implications of this need will be discussed in a later section.

We hope that the members of Congress will continue to monitor the consumer situation as it evolves, in order to avoid crisis legislation. Unfortunately, consumer interests are diffuse and of low salience. Any individual is typically more concerned about his job --his productive effort--than he is about his consuming activities. He typically works at a single job, but he consumes many products. Consequently, he tends not to organize as a consumer and not to support legislation in this interest. Only when consumer activists work through the press to raise the salience of the issue and thus widen the scope of the conflict among the various interests, does action tend to occur. Individual legislators perform this activist role, as do non-legislators.

JUDICIAL PROCEDURE

Generally, the judiciary is beyond the scope of this report. Its strong role in shaping consumer policy, however, was seen in Chapter Seven.

ROLE OF CONSUMER INTEREST GROUPS

The formation of many consumer groups in recent years, as well as the strengthened Consumer Federation of America, has endowed the consumer with increased effectiveness in pursuing his goals. But, consumers are not well-organized, and it is difficult to reach them with relevant information which can strengthen their efforts.

> The major disappointment (with the ad substantiation program) has been the apparent failure of consumers, competitors, public interest groups and others to take advantage of the availability of the documentation submitted for study and analysis. Unless these groups come in and scrutinize the material and convey the results to the public, the stated twin objectives of education and deterren(ce) simply will not materialize.[1]

The two great handicaps to effective political power that consumers face--diffusiveness and lack of salience--could be overcome substantially with greater organization.

The mass media are helpful. But mass media depend upon the dramatic, which is, by definition, temporary on any given issue. Consumers are unaware of the efforts of some companies to deal effectively with consumer complaints. If they were aware, their attitudes toward the company could become more favorable. And thus, the company would be rewarded. As it is, the company's incentive to provide these systems is greatly reduced. The market system does not operate adequately.

Earlier, we stressed the need for an underlying rationale to consumer efforts. We believe this lack of a philosophical basis has been a handicap to consumer organization. Throughout this report, we have emphasized the consumer choice aspect of that rationale. It is obviously important. Implied in the rationale is the role of the consumer (as a countervailing power) in achieving equal status with industry and labor to exercise freedom. The consumer's powers are not adequate to give the commission the support--particularly, the consistent and stable support in Congress--that is needed to offset other interest groups, and to provide a framework for the commission to perform most effectively.

INDUSTRY'S ROLE

There are at least two aspects of industry's role: First, what each company can do individually to further optimal conditions of choice for the consumer; second, what companies organized together can do.

Each company, acting alone, can have a substantial effect upon optimal conditions of choice for the consumer. The consumer orientation implied by the marketing concept, however, is more complex than one might have thought a decade or two ago. First, except for the existence of some contrived alternative, the consumer can only communicate about his feelings by his purchasing behavior. If what he wants does not appear on the market, he has no

---

[1] R.A. Skitol, "What is an Adequate Substantiation?", A.A.A.A.Eastern Annual Conference, New York, June 5, 1972, p. 5.

opportunity of rejecting or accepting it, and showing his preference. Second, if it *does* appear on the market, given the current state of market research practices, it is by no means easy for the seller to discover *why* the consumer has accepted or rejected the product.

One of the contrived ways for the market mechanism to be suplemented is for the consumer to write a letter to the company. However, only a small proportion of consumers will do this. Company organization has not always been conducive to encouraging such actions. Why should a brand manager spend time worrying about the letter when the problem is probably in the factory? And, further, there is no reward--no incentive--for the brand manager to concern himself with consumer mail ... better to put his efforts to activities that pay off, in terms of his professional goals. This lack of incentive for attention to consumer needs is less true of new products than of ongoing products.

• In recent years, however, some companies devoted substantial effort to developing an effective complaint-handling procedure. A major packaged goods company reports that it received 114,000 letters in 1971, as compared with 87,000 in 1961. About 40,000 of these in 1971 were complaints, which the company estimated averaged about one complaint for every 150,000 packages sold. A staff of twelve people answer these letters. "Once a week a full report on incoming product complaints is sent to each product division, along with samples of any defective products ... over-all the mail, both inquiries and complaints, is much more specific and sophisticated than it was a few years ago."[2] More specifically, monthly reviews of product complaints are made for each brand, with

_____
[2] General Foods and the Consumer, a report to the Senate Commerce Committee, June 30, 1972, pp. 21-22.

copies going to the brand manager, his superior (the marketing manager), the vice-president of marketing services, and others. If there is an increase in complaints, the report is reviewed by the marketing manager with the brand manager. At that time, the two attempt to work out a satisfactory solution as quickly as possible.

Another feedback to management on how well the company is serving the consumer's requirements can be market research. However, we believe that, in its current state, market research is not as useful in this role as it might be. First, this is not generally viewed by managers and researchers as one of its functions. Second, market research has been weakened by the lack of a theoretical underpinning to provide the manager and researcher with a way of articulating the consumer's information needs. We believe the specialization of labor--particularly between the client, the agency, and the media--demands a better articulation of the nature of the consumer than has been true in the past. This fuller articulation can become the basis for improved market research, and better feedback to management.

• Third, some observers believe that market researchers have less interaction with management today than they did a decade or so ago. As one puts it: Market research has become institutionalized. There has been the rise of extensive mathematical techniques, the technician is unable to explain to laymen how these techniques work, nor is he able to persuade management to leave such details to him to worry about. This problem is not unique to market research. It characterizes all relations with the specialist in an organization.

Fourth, higher management has not thought through what it does, and [what they] should expect of market research and how to evaluate it. There are some indications, however, that higher management is now recognizing the problems and thinking about solutions.

Fifth, ad agencies are playing a decreasing role in market research. The client has tended to take over this function, and to turn more to outside suppliers for data collection. For many companies, this is a learning period.

Finally, unless this market research feedback is supported by the company's incentive system, its implications for action are likely to be ignored.

• Joint efforts by companies contribute, in a major way, to the consumer's optimal conditions of choice. The outstanding example may be the National Advertising Review Board. It currently exhibits substantial growing pains, illustrated by its early unwillingness to make its findings and results public (even to the industry), as a guide to those people preparing ads. If it should develop effective procedures, it could contribute substantially to relieving the burden of the commission. It can clear out the underbrush of mild deception. It can aid in bringing to industry a growing understanding of the need to regulate advertising.

We wish to make two points on the role of self regulation: First, the National Review Board is likely to have a major impact only insofar as there is a strong commission policy operating. Second, as the procedures now provide, the extreme cases will have to come to the attention of the commission.

We believe the future of the industry depends upon developing credibility for advertising. Because the industry has so much to gain, we urge that its leadership cooperate with the commission in developing a set of norms for the criteria of optimal conditions of choice. These standards should clarify existing regulations and other issues discussed in connection with en-

forcement of commission policy. Such standards must be worked out with great thought and care.

The better business bureaus, national and local, have been rejuvenated and are better supported. Their efforts to monitor consumer complaints, and to analyze them in meaningful terms, can provide essential information to all interested parties, reduce the conflict among the interested parties, and encourage rational policy making. If effective, they can be especially useful at the local level, where most consumer complaints arise and where they must be dealt with. We have the impression, however, that local advertising review boards are not being established as rapidly as is desirable.

Finally, the advertising industry (through its Advertising Council) has, for many years, run public interest campaigns of great variety, magnitude, and skill. Its current campaign, urging the consumer to consult his local better business bureau when a problem arises, could be a significant aid to the commission in providing optimal conditions of choice for the consumers. Whether the better business bureaus have the necessary machinery established, and whether their criteria will be adequate, remains to be seen. They have accepted a difficult assignment.

STATE AND LOCAL GOVERNMENTS

State consumer agencies have, with exceptions, become increasingly effective. Some states have installed "hot lines," where consumers can call toll free and register their complaints. In some large cities, consumer agencies indicate the contribution that can be made in strengthening consumer protection. The greatest number of consumer problems exist at the local level. As indicated in Chapter Two, a large pro-

portion of advertising is local advertising. There would seem to be great
opportunity for the three agencies--
the commission, the state, and local
units--to cooperate on particular
cases. The local agency can, through
cases and attendant publicity, render
the consumer's information problem
more visible and salient. This can
stimulate the activist (both in and
out of Congress), and the development
of consumer organizing activity.

BASIC RESEARCH

Recurring themes throughout the report have been (1) our limited understanding of advertising effects upon
the consumer, and the corrollary;
(2) the need for research. Such research would narrow the differences in
views, because most of the differences
seem to be matters of fact, rather
than of value. It has been our persistent premise that better research will
cause companies to exhibit advertising
practices more consistent with the consumer interest because they will find
that it is to their own interest to do
so. We believe that companies have
been misled by the undue stress on the
recall criterion for evaluating ads.
The truth of this premise must be veri-
fied.

To create this body of research is a
task of major magnitude. Since the
commission is an operating agency, we
do not believe that it is their role
to finance this research. But we do
believe that the commission should encourage the research by cooperating in
every way possible, other than by offering financial support. In some
areas of basic development, the underlying disciplines of economics, psychology and sociology will be required.
Sums will be required that only the
federal government can provide over a
substantial period--perhaps two to

three decades. This is why we are sympathetic to Sen. Moss' proposal to establish a National Institute of Advertising, Marketing & Society.

The surface has hardly been scratched.
We have presented a theory of consumer
behavior, and formulated evaluative
criteria in terms of it. This is an
important and essential first step.
Yet, we cannot even classify ads in any
systematic way: An ad is an ad is an
ad. The ability to classify ads is an
essential condition to comprehensive,
systematic application of consumer
theory to policy problems. There will
be many institutional barriers, both
inside and outside government agencies,
to this kind of research. First, it
must have a strong, applied tone, and
applied work is not looked upon favorably. Second, because it will require
the development of basic behavioral
science ideas there will be opposition
to its being done in the context of
marketing. Third, because of the academic unrespectability of advertising
as a research topic, there will be more
opposition. It is essential that this
research be accomplished quickly in
order to enlist some of the best scientists from the basic disciplines.

• We can be optimistic that rapid progress can be made. In most areas of
science, an underlying theory has proven
to be essential to quick development.
Progress in empirical research of the
past decade is largely summarized in
the structure of consumer behavior, described in Chapter Four. This structure
provides that essential underlying
theory. This report puts that theory
to work on public policy issues of advertising. It is not complete. But,
it puts the parts together, and it has
been tested enough to indicate that it
has a substantial degree of validity.
The power of this over-all organizing
franework, represented by the theory,
is illustrated by the discussion of advertising repetition in Chapter Five.
It was shown that the effects of repetition depend upon a variety of conditions.

These conditions can be specified within the theory. We believe that this
complexity is the typical condition
when advertising is studied in the
natural market setting, as opposed to
the laboratory.

The task is two-fold. First, it is
necessary to develop an understanding
of human response to communication in
a real-world market environment. Second, the criteria for evaluating ads
in terms of this behavior must be made
operational. These are the intuitive
links in the means-end chain of values
that constitute our philosophical rationale. These must be replaced by
explicit links.

We now examine the nature of the research task in terms of specific major
areas; however, these are more illustrative than comprehensive, and are
described in lay language instead of
scientific terms.

ADVERTISING AND MOTIVATION

One of the most serious charges against
advertising is that "it causes people
to buy things they don't need." In a
society which places a high value on
individual freedom, we interpret this
charge to mean that, as a minimum, advertising stimulates consumers to buy
more of a product class than they
otherwise would. If this is not so,
the problem of regulating advertising
can be substantially delimited for the
normal consumer. If it is so, the
problem becomes more complex. The
answer is important.

When the research issue is defined in
these more concrete terms, we believe
it can be answered without great difficulty. Current methodology is adequate.

If the research issue is broadened,
however, to deal with such a statement
as "advertising causes the consumer to
be more materialistic," it becomes more

difficult--and, perhaps, impossible--
to research with available methodology.

CONSUMER'S DEFENSELESSNESS

It is often alleged that consumers are
defenseless against advertising and,
as a consequence, they are victimized.
In Chapter Four, it was our conclusion
that consumers are remarkable "tuner-
outers" of the irrelevant. Consumer
victimizing, therefore, could arise
only under a peculiar set of conditions.
It is conceivable, however, that tele-
vision-viewing is characterized by those
peculiar conditions. Because of the
importance of the issue and the perva-
siveness of the belief in it, we believe it deserves high research priority.

What are the conditions that might render the consumer defenseless? Some
need--such as the sight of an empty
coffee jar--can trigger the relevant
set of motives, and these interrupt the
ongoing act, at least temporarily.
Here, we are speaking of the same mechanisms that operate in terms of the
criterion of timeliness. If the relevant set of motives is triggered and if
the motives are of low absolute intensity, the consumer will take information into his long-term memory, even
though the information was *irrelevant*
to the original task. Implied is that
this would occur only when the motives
energizing the ongoing act were also of
low intensity; in other words, when the
person is in a relaxed state. Otherwise, they would not be replaced by a
set of low-intensity motives in his
hierarchy. Taking in irrelevant information is the essence of the latent
learning controversy that raged in experimental psychology in the 1930s and
1940s. The issue was whether or not
people could learn--take in information
--when they were not rewarded for learning. Dr. Krugman referred to "advertising by emphasis," which is with "similar inexpensive and less involving"
products (T208). He indicated that,
under these conditions, advertising

might cause a consumer to buy an "un-wanted product." To explore the sig-nificance of latent learning for the problem of whether television adver-tising causes consumers to take in ir-relevant information, is a major re-search undertaking.

VULNERABILITIES OF CHILDREN

Research should be continued and ex-panded in the effects of television advertising on children up to age twelve. As we have indicated, the children age six and under concern us the most. We believe this age group deserves the most attention.

Researching children, especially those six and under, is difficult. New, more rigorous methodologies must be developed.

DECEPTION

We believe that normal adults are, to some extent, capable of protecting themselves from deception. There is some evidence that, although consumers may take in less dependable informa-tion, they are less affected by it than they are by dependable informa-tion. To know more specifically what this level of self-protectiveness is would be useful in designing policy. Also, it could remove the necessity for the commissioners to call upon their court-endowed expertise. We be-lieve this would render the decisions more palatable to some. But until better scientific evidence is avail-able, the use of the court-endowed expertise is essential.

Substantial related research has been done in the area of credibility. New methodology enables us to deal with complex systems. These should facili-tate the development of new knowledge in the deception area.

INFORMATION NEEDS OF CONSUMERS

Research effort should be directed to the broad issue of the information needs of the consumer. We tend to view the problem in a quite restricted sense; for example, the truthfulness of adver-tising. We need a broader conceptuali-zation from which to work. For example, with CATV developing, we need to evalu-ate its role in supporting optimal con-ditions of choice for the consumer. It is a problem in the sociology of com-munication.

SUMMARY AND CONCLUSIONS

In the first part of this final chap-ter, we developed our recommendations for the Federal Trade Commission. For the benefit of the general reader, and to provide perspective, we examined the commission's regulation of advertising in the context of other agencies--gov-ernmental and non-governmental--that can also contribute to providing opti-mal conditions of choice for the con-sumer.

Let us summarize our recommendations. We presented six criteria which should serve as the basis for evaluating ad-vertising. The example we used was set forth in the context of the relevancy criterion, because we believe it is--at present--the only fully operational criterion of the set. Other criteria will require operating research, and even basic research to render them op-erational. Only truthfulness is com-pletely within current rules as a regu-lative criterion. We believe its ap-plication should be extended to self-concept ads. Completeness and rele-vance should, as is current practice, be used in a limited way to support the application of the truthfulness cri-terion.

The younger child--six and under--con-

stitutes a special audience. We recommended that the criteria be rigorously applied to television advertising to this age group. Accuracy of
target audiences may raise particular
problems here. We recommended that a
signal indicate the shift from program
to commercial, and that each network
should experimentally make available a
one-hour program each Saturday morning
free of commercials. The free hours
should be staggered among the three
networks, to provide three continuous
hours of viewing free of commercials.

• As for enforcement of advertising
rules, we believe that cases should be
selected at random. Corrective advertising should be continued, at least
until it is determined whether it is
more or less effective than ad substantiation. Finally, assuming consumers
and industry will cooperate (and we
are confident they will), the commission should provide a vehicle whereby
the commission, consumer and industry
can evaluate current ways of regulating advertising. Its objective would
be to determine the consequences of
applying the criteria of optimal conditions of consumer choice.

We discussed how such a body should be
organized, but we leave open the particular legal form that its recommendations might take.

Greater attention should be given to
public education in terms of the general public, a small sophisticated public, and organized consumer and industry groups.

The commission should institutionalize
its receptivity to behavioral research
by establishing a well-staffed, operating research unit analogous to the
Bureau of Economics.

Aspects of advertising mentioned by
others have not been touched upon.
For example, we do not believe problems
of intrusiveness and clutter should be
dealt with by the commission. The

question of whether or not advertising
is productive is often raised. We believe that it can be in a social sense,
and usually is, though substantially
less than it might be. Advertisers
sometimes complain that advertising is
criticized when, in fact, the product
is bad, not the advertising. Mr. Weil
stated that it was "the confusion of
the advertising with the product" (T
1949). If so, the advertising may have
promised something the product cannot
deliver, and the advertising deserves
to be criticized.

• Let us turn now to the issue of coordination between various agencies,
with an interest in the consumer's conditions of choice. The cross-agency
perspective is one way of looking at
the problem, although we believe it
will be increasingly important in the
years ahead. Another perspective
stressed repeatedly in the hearings,
and described in Chapters Three and
Four, is that advertising is only one
element of the marketing mix. Other
elements, such as price, salesmen, and
merchandising, influence the consumer.
We urged that in the regulation of advertising, the consumer's total information requirements must be considered
--not just advertising's contribution
to them. This, in turn, will require
a high degree of coordination between
the agencies and institutions involved.

A third perspective is time--the dynamics of the consumer's information problem. As an example, let us consider
food products. In the last two years,
new vocabularies have evolved for describing the nutritional aspects of
food. These vocabularies are not only
words. They provide new dimensions by
which the consumer will (and should)
conceptualize a food. Who is to be
responsible for providing the background
information the consumer will need to
utilize these new facts? The consumer
learning problem will be enormous. In
terms of the theory presented in Chapter Four, the nutritional situation
poses a case analogous to that of a

134

radically new product. Understanding
the dynamics of this process is essential to regulating advertising in such
a way as to meet adequately the consumer's information requirements in
the face of rapid innovation. It is
this motivation process which brings
the benefits of technology to the
consumer, and creates the investment
opportunities necessary to full employment.

To deal with the consumer's conditions
of choice, in each of the great variety
of situations spawned by the dynamism
of modern markets, will not be an
easy task. It will demans a higher
degree of communication and coordination among interested parties than has
previously existed. The FTC's hearings
on advertising practices represented a
quantum improvement in opening up
these channels. It is our earnest hope
that this report will further the same
end.

DISCUSSION QUESTIONS

1. Do you believe children should be
permitted to view television ads?
Why or why not?

2. Which of the regulatory agencies
discussed should have the most influence over advertising? Why?

Reprinted by permission from MARQUETTE BUSINESS REVIEW; Spring, 1975.

II-10

THE ADVERTISING COUNCIL: A MODEL FOR SOCIAL MARKETING?

Thomas V. Greer and William G. Nickels

The Advertising Council is a private, nonprofit organization which conducts national advertising campaigns for the public good. Its objectives are two-fold: (1) to help improve the welfare of the American people as a whole, and in so doing demonstrate to the public that the advertising community is concerned with the public welfare; and (2) to show that advertising is a powerful force for public service.

As a socially oriented marketing organization, The Advertising Council provides an excellent model for studying the potential contribution of marketing to other nonprofit social organizations. This paper discusses The Advertising Council's programs in an attempt to assess the strengths and weaknesses of its marketing efforts. Such an analysis will provide guidelines for improved social marketing programs in other organizations.

ness for the continuing economic sluggishness and on the advertising industry in particular for alleged waste. It was an attempt to demonstrate the validity and strength of advertising by using it explicitly in the public interest. Established in December, 1941, and first named the War Advertising Council, it devoted itself to government support throughout World War II. In 1945 the name was changed to The Advertising Council and emphasis shifted to the country's peacetime problems. The organization continues today, utilizing advertising as a social force on a national level. In 1971, The Council was the second largest advertiser in business magazines. That was the third consecutive year that the various media contributed more than $450,000,000 of traceable advertising space and time to The Council's campaigns.[1]

BACKGROUND

The Advertising Council grew out of the depression of the 1930s as an effort to counter the blame put on busi-

[1] Background data were obtained from various publications of The Advertising Council. Such information is available in The Advertising Council, Inc., 1971 *Annual Report*. New York, 1972.

SOCIAL CAMPAIGNS OF THE COUNCIL

Currently, The Advertising Council is sponsoring advertising campaings in support of governmental, religious, charitable, educational, and other social agencies. The diversity of The Council's efforts becomes apparent when one reviews its major campaigns:

ACTION (Peace Corps, VISTA, Retired
   Senior Volunteer Program, Service
   Corps of Retired Executives, and
   Office of Voluntary Action)
Aid to Higher Education
American Red Cross
Consumer Information
Continue Your Education
Cost of Living Campaign
Drug Abuse Information
Food, Nutrition, and Health
Forest Fire Prevention
Help Prevent Crime
Help Fight Pollution
Jobs for Veterans
Minority Business Enterprise
National Alliance of Businessmen
Population (Planned Parenthood)
Rehabilitation of the Handicapped
Religion in American Life
Support for American POW/MIA in
   Southeast Asia
Technical Education and Training
The Advertising Council Campaign
Traffic Safety
United Community Campaigns
United Negro College Fund
U.S. Savings Bonds

The list includes programs bearing on many of our national social problems. In 1971, The Advertising Council initiated or continued 25 major campaigns and supported the programs of 75 national causes. Organizations seeking The Council's support must meet the following criteria:

√ If the client organization is a fund raising one, The Advertising Council takes into consideration whether or not it currently meets the standards of The National Information Bureau.

√ The project is non-commercial, non-partisan politically, and not designed to influence legislation.

√ The project is national in scope, or sufficiently national, so that the bulk of the national media audience has an actual or potential interest in it.

√ The appeal for support is one properly made to Americans generally. The project will not be rejected because it is in the interest of one group if it has such wide appeal; but it will be rejected if the appeal for participation is limited to special groups.

√ The project is of sufficient seriousness and public importance to justify treatment before the national media audience.

The ruling out of local and regional campaigns by The Council is believed to severely handicap many causes that are meritorious and perhaps more stressful than some national matters. Furthermore, neatly-packaged national public service messages from The Advertising Council may displace the time that might otherwise be used by the local community. The concentration on national problems that pervades The Advertising Council's criteria is thus the subject of much criticism. The Council's leaders have indicated that they recognize this problem. The 1971 Annual Report of The Council has a report from the Chairman and President which states that, "The swiftly changing nature of our society creates many opportunities for new ventures which can help ameliorate and solve some of our most pressing national, regional and local problems." Apparently, regional and local problems are receiving some consideration for future efforts.

ORGANIZATION OF THE COUNCIL

The Council has a Public Policy Committee which reviews and makes recommendations on proposed campaigns. However, campaigns originating with departments of the Federal Government, where the public interest has been established by an Act of Congress, are not subject to their review. This procedural favoritism for proposals on subjects covered by Acts of Congress is also subject to criticism and may need reviewing by the committee.

The Public Policy Committee reports to a board of directors composed of 85 representatives from advertising, communications, business, and sponsoring member organizations of The Council. Member organizations include the American Association of Advertising Agencies, the American Business Press, the Association of National Advertisers, the Bureau of Advertising, the Magazine Publishers Association, the National Association of Broadcasters, and the Outdoor Advertising Association of America. It is readily apparent that The Council has the support of the best advertising talent in the nation.

Once a campaign idea is accepted, the Association of National Advertisers appoints a project director, who is usually a marketing vice-president or advertising director from a national company. He works with the client and the advertising agency and coordinates activities with The Council. The American Association of Advertising Agencies invites an agency to handle the campaign. At the same time, The Council appoints one of its staff members as campaign manager, whose job is to provide general liaison. The client is the authority on accuracy and emphasis of content. The services of the project director are donated by his employer. The advertising agency also contributes its managerial and creative services, except for materials used or furnished the media.

Coordination of campaign participants, the client, advertising agency, media, and project director from industry, is enormously complicated. The process is further complicated because the work proceeds on a voluntary basis and the efficiencies that normally prevail in a client-agency relationship are diluted. This loosely aligned organization structure makes the planning, organization, coordination, and control of The Council's social campaigns more difficult than those for most business organizations. Everyone involved in The Council's campaigns appears to be dedicated to these social efforts, however, and the resulting advertising is as good as one could reasonably expect given these circumstances.

SOCIAL ADVERTISING VERSUS SOCIAL MARKETING

Because The Advertising Council receives its greatest support from advertising organizations, there is a tendency for all of its social campaigns to be *advertising* campaigns rather than *marketing* campaigns. Many of the advertising agencies that volunteer their assistance for these campaigns have the expertise for providing a broad range of marketing services, but the services they provide are largely limited to creative copy writing. The divided responsibilities between the client, the agency, the project director, and The Council leave no one in charge of establishing goals and measuring results. As a consequence, the campaigns of The Advertising Council are largely one-way influence attempts that may or may not be effective.

The social marketing process calls for marketing research and the subsequent development of a well-conceived product and appeals moving through mass and specialized communication media and through paid agents and voluntary groups to reach targeted audiences.[2] Present attempts by The Advertising Council lack the marketing research, product design, and goal orientation necessary for comprehensive social marketing programs.

CURRENT CRITICISM

Any marketing program must begin with an analysis of the needs and wants of society. Social organizations must respond to those needs and wants with programs such as those supported by The Advertising Council. There has been some question recently about the kind of programs being sponsored by The Council. In a speech before the American Association of Advertising Agencies, David McCall said that, "Many of its campaigns are addressing subjects that seem peripheral at best in 1972."[3]

The various media give much space and time to public service messages. Much time was freed by the elimination of cigarette advertising from television, in that the time given to anti-smoking commercials is now available for other social causes. McCall implied that The Advertising Council wrongfully siphons off almost all of this *pro bono publico* space and time that the nation's media make available. He also said that The Council's insistence on dealing with national problems is improper, since "the problems of the nation are overwhelmingly local." He concluded, "Now is the time for the Advertising

Council to disband."[4]

Sid Bernstein from *Advertising Age* concurs with McCall and said in his column, "By the time a 'cause' filters through its (The Council's) carefully organized mechanism, it is likely to be extremely non-controversial."[5] He finds locally directed social marketing much more effective. He concludes that social marketing should be substituted for today's social advertising. He wrote, "Maybe we should stop all public service advertising that is just *advertising*, and save this useful tool for use with well-rounded, well conceived campaigns designed to accomplish a carefully thought out, specific goal--a measurable goal, achievable within a predetermined time period."[6]

In a recent article Thomas Asher was critical of The Advertising Council's domination of the media. Asher said that, "The effect of The Council's lock on public service advertising is to prevent the people who rarely gain access to the mass media--without engaging in some form of extraordinary protest activity--from using the public airwaves and print media to launch even a modest attack."[7]

Midge Kovacs has also expressed some criticism of The Advertising Council for not supporting women's rights as expressed by the National Organization

---

[2] Philip Kotler and Gerald Zaltman, "Social Marketing: An Approach to Planned Social Change," *Journal of Marketing*, Vol. 35 (July, 1971), p. 12.

[3] A paper from the 1972 annual meeting of the American Association of Advertising Agencies titled, "Advertising and Society--A New Creative Challenge,"

American Association of Advertising Agencies, copyright, 1972.

[4] Ibid.

[5] Sid Bernstein, "Whither the Ad Council?" *Advertising Age*, Vol. 43 (April 10, 1972), p. 16.

[6] Ibid.

[7] Thomas Asher, "Smoking Out Smokey the Bear." *Journalism Review*, January 1972.

for Women (NOW).[8] Such criticism reflects a growing concern about The Council's programs.

Criticism of The Advertising Council, therefore, does not center on its attempts to promote social causes. The real criticism is directed at its selection process, its lack of concrete goals, its advertising versus marketing emphasis, and its national versus regional and local programs. In short, The Advertising Council is being criticized for having a poor marketing program. It has done a rather routine job of promoting itself as well as the causes it supports. But that is no reason to call for disbanding! What is called for is a realignment of priorities such as that which occurred in 1970. At that time, The Council had "a review of what we are doing, what we could be doing that we're not doing, and what can give way."[9] In 1970, The Council introduced nine new campaigns: Help Stop Pollution; Drug Abuse; Minority Business Enterprise; Population Size Control; Voluntarism; Jobs for Veterans; Food, Nutrition, and Health; the 1970 Census; and Pakistan Relief. These programs were in response to the felt social needs of that time. Perhaps it is time for another review with special attention to local problems.

IMPLICATIONS FOR SOCIAL MARKETING

The Advertising Council is one of the oldest official social marketing agencies in the United States. Its experi-

[8] Midge Kovacs, "Women's Rights Drive Gets Off the Ground," *Advertising Age,* September 25, 1972, pp. 73-74.

[9] Statement by Robert Keim, President The Advertising Council, in "Ad Council Reviews ts Priorities," *Broadcasting,* June 22, 1970, pp. 76-78.

ences should guide other social organizations in their attempts to market themselves and their services. Charitable, religious, educational, health political, and other social organizations are competing for dollars and attention in an increasingly complex marketing environment. Those that survive will do so partially because of a marketing program designed to meet the needs of a dynamic society.

The primary lesson to be learned is that social advertising is only one phase of social marketing. Many social organizations have attempted to advertise their services or their needs for money and support without changing their programs, without researching the market, and without establishing definite goals. Like The Advertising Council, these groups are being challenged as not being relevant, flexible, or responsive to today's social environment. Further analysis of The Advertising Council may reveal other lessons which could be applied to social organizations in general.

SOME AVENUES FOR RESEARCH

The Advertising Council is relatively unresearched. In a sense, it could be a working laboratory for marketing. Without harm to its over-all mission or day-to-day operations, it could lend itself to investigation that could possibly improve its own performance and that of the total social communications process and contribute significantly to the marketing discipline. The potential contribution is micro-economic, macro-economic, social, and behavioral.

Several suggestions can illustrate the scope of potential research. What are the differential response rates of the *media* to particular types of appeals and straightforward communications from The Advertising Council or from the clients through The Council? What are the differential response rates of the American population to the campaigns; and do they vary by medium? Is the success of The Council in affecting attitudes as great, or potentially as great, as its success at raising money? What are the indicated shapes of the decay curve? How large are the donations of the several media relative to selected indexes, such as sales volume, profits, or investment? What is the transferability of The Council's experience to other nations and cultures? How is the image of marketing affected by the work of The Advertising Council and other public service advertising?

By researching The Advertising Council, educators, consultants, and practi-

tioners could learn much about the problems of designing and implementing social marketing programs. The Advertising Council has the potential of providing an effective model for social marketing in general. The programs it sponsors cover almost every phase of social problems--from health, education and welfare to drug abuse, crime, pollution, and population control. Research findings would be of tremendous help to The Advertising Council in designing future programs. Such work would also help The Council reach its objectives of improving the welfare of the American people as a whole and demonstrating to the public that the advertising (marketing) community is concerned with the public welfare.

DISCUSSION QUESTIONS

1. What is *your* assessment of the work of The Advertising Council? Explain.

2. Can you suggest improvements in The Council's operations?

3. Should The Council's Public Policy Committee review campaigns originating with departments of the federal government? Why or why not?

PART III

THE MEDIA OF ADVERTISING

The part of advertising with which most readers of this book will be very familiar is the media. Most of us read a newspaper at least occasionally, watch television, listen to an automobile radio, or at the very least, we are exposed to billboards while driving or car cards while taking a bus or subway. We are so familiar with the media, in fact, that we tend to take them for granted.

Because most U.S. homes have television, and because the set (increasingly, U.S. homes are multiple-set homes) is turned on so much of the time, we may forget that in most markets in the world, the most important medium, in terms of total advertising dollars spent, is newspapers. Television is second, but in most world markets a poor second. Other media do not command much in the way of advertising dollars, trade magazines, for example, but they often can be extremely important to the advertiser of a particular product or service. The manufacturer of a part used in rubber processing machinery, for example, may spend a very small amount of money advertising in the rubber and tire industry trade papers, but it may do him a tremendous amount of good by reminding engineers and purchasing agents in the rubber companies of his existence and brand name so that when his salesmen call they will find it easier to get a hearing.

This part of the book starts with an article by Frank Kemp which outlines the principles of media selection, gives some measure of the magnitude of each major medium, and explains some of the language of media selection as well as the media research organizations. The other selections in the section deal with the major media, newspapers, television, radio, magazines, but also with some of the more or less off-beat media, direct mail, specialty advertising, and outdoor, most of which are not covered well in textbooks and the trade press.

The last article in this section has an international slant; it outlines and discusses the latest available figures for major media in sixteen nations around the world. It also lists the total advertising expenditures in the twenty-one nations leading in advertising.

From A HANDBOOK FOR THE ADVERTISING AGENCY ACCOUNT EXECUTIVE; 4A's, Inc., 1969
Addison-Wesley (Reading, Mass.). Reprinted by permission from the publisher.

III-1

SOME IMPORTANT THINGS I BELIEVE A YOUNG ACCOUNT REPRESENTATIVE SHOULD KNOW ABOUT MEDIA

Frank B. Kemp

In a large agency like ours, people must function cooperatively. We are all specialists, but to work effectively, we must be both familiar with and respectful of the abilities of other specialists.

We don't expect our younger account men to learn everything there is to know about media, nor to take individual responsibility for their brand's spending. We do expect them to learn everything that will help the Media Department work more effectively for their brands.

The first thing, therefore, that a young account representative should realize is that the Media Department is a service department and should be used at all times on all questions or problems relating to media. The less time the account man personally devotes to media questions and media representatives, the more time he will have for overall brand supervision.

FUNDAMENTAL RULES

Company Geography The account representative should acquaint himself with the physical layout of the Media Department and the specific location of the people working on his account.

Company People This may be academic, but the account representative should be sure of knowing the media people working directly on his account and the heads of the various inter-department groups. He should avoid, at all costs, the situation whereby the head of the media research group suddenly appears in a client meeting and introductions have to be made to the account representatives as well as the client.

Company Manners The account representative should release assignments as soon as they are received. He should not hold a job on his desk for ten days and then expect the Media Department to complete it overnight.

All requests should be in writing, giving details and due dates. On extended analyses or projects, the account representative should review such assignments with his media supervisor before requesting the job in writing. Meetings or due dates should never be set until the people involved have been consulted.

MEDIA KNOWLEDGE ON SPECIFIC BRAND

The account man should be completely conversant with the Brand, Marketing, and Copy strategies from which his media plan was developed. In this way, he will know the reasons why his brand uses the various media. When agency management or client ask why the brand is not in Sunday supplements, the account man should have the reason at his finger tip.

The account representative should elicit everyone's aid in tightening up his brand's marketing profile. Definitive market data will contribute to a more efficient and effective media plan. He should be aware of his brand's philosophy on spending by areas. Is the brand spending advertising dollars as earned, or is the brand overspending specific areas as a business building plan?

The account representative should commit to memory his brand's media appropriation and, if possible, how it was determined. He should be prepared, at all times, to comment on the specifics of the brand's media plan for spending the appropriation. It is not necessary for him to know each insertion date or spot time-of-broadcast in individual cities, but the account man should know whether *Time* or *Newsweek* or both magazines are being used, as well as the space units and annual frequency. He should know the spot frequency range (i.e., 2-4 announcements per week in 33 markets) and the specific network programs on which his brand participates. In addition, the account executive should be prepared to comment, in general terms, on the media activities of major competitors.

He should explore whether the brand can profitably employ media testing--there are very few brands that cannot. The account representative should initiate thinking on brand/account tests; therefore, it is important to learn the rudiments of such testing methods. All tests have limitations, but some are impractical or almost impossible, and the account man should know the difference.

Again, on media testing, the account representative should bear in mind that some media tests may seem farfetched, but it does not hurt to ask questions. He should step right in and question the advisability and/or desirability of alternate media test plans.

If "sacred cows" are part of an account man's media plan, he should be in a position to identify them and give reasons why. If his brand is running ads in the client's favorite magazine, he should be aware of it. But, "sacred cows" should be checked out periodically to avoid a situation whereby several years later the client, of all people, asks "What the devil are we doing in that magazine?"

MEDIA SELECTION

Although the account representative is not expected to develop media plans, it is helpful to understand the basis of media selection. There are two principal factors:

1. The people or market which is to be reached; and

2. The nature of the message which is to be conveyed.

The procedure is:

√ To obtain as precise as possible a definition of the market to be reached

--to learn the demographic characteristics of the most logical sales prospects in terms of age, sex, income, occupation, location, etc. (This information is obtained from various sources--client, account people, research, and the agency's market development section.)

√ To learn from the creative department the basic copy strategy and copy requirements, such as ad size and color needs for print media, and commercial length for broadcasting media.

√ To ascertain whether there is need for seasonal or geographical emphasis.

√ To determine the size of the appropriation.

With this information, the person responsible for developing the basic media plan relates these factors to the ability of various media to--

1. Match their audience characteristics to the profile of the market objective; and

2. Adapt themselves in physical format to the copy requirements.

The final stage in the architecture of this basic planning rests heavily on judgment factors. Within a given budget, a media plan is three dimensional. These dimensions are coverage, frequency, and ad size. If coverage is the principal objective, then frequency and/or ad size will be sacrificed. It follows that if frequency is the brand's principal objective, then coverage and/or ad size will be sacrificed. These are the areas of judgment.

Although it may be self-evident, a word of caution--the logical media combination decision is arrived at sequentially within the data supplied as outlined. Any change of information at any step may materially change the conclusions reached. This is why the account rep-

resentative should make certain his contributions are not subject to change.

——— ——— ———

The mechanics of selecting specific media within each of the major media categories should be of little concern to the account executive. This is a job for the media buyers--specialists who devote full time to studying the comparative merits of the individual media.

A suggestion to the young account representative is in order at this point.

Although it is desirable to know as much as possible about all advertising subjects, there is a pitfall in devoting too much time to the business of making his own media appraisals or listening to the sales arguments of media representatives. The fallacy in so doing is readily apparent. If, for example, he listens to the presentation of one major medium, the time and effort required is wasted unless he hears the arguments of all competing media. The time and study required for proper assimilation of the presentations of many media in this variegated field will detract from an account executive's basic job. It is obvious that the more time the account executive spends in attempting to learn the ramifications of media buying, the less time he can spend on account executive work. Rely on the media specialist.

A knowledge of the wide scope of media availabilities in this country will help to orient the account man's perspective on the number and variety of media in the U.S., as shown in the following table:

5,124 Commercial radio stations (AM & FM) (3,950 AM stations)

2,680 Business (or trade) publications

1,588 Daily newspapers

723 Outdoor plant operators

560 Sunday newspapers

539 TV stations

753 Consumer magazines

350 Color comic sections

283 Farm publications

300 Sunday magazine sections

The preceding list may be categorized generally as "major media" and it is in these media that all but a very small percentage of billings are placed. However, the variety of secondary media is extensive and includes such items as car cards, station posters, skywriting, tops of egg cartons, and matchbook covers.

Each of the major media has its own set of advantages and disadvantages with which the account executive should be familiar. It would be impracticable, in the space permitted, to list all of these factors in relation to each of the media, but some of the principal points are these:

Business Publications Enable the advertiser to pinpoint his approach to logical prospects in business, industry, or the professions with relatively little waste circulation. They serve a unique purpose in that they address themselves to the management, technicians, or professionals in each field. No general consumer magazine is designed to do this.

Consumer Magazines The outstanding advantages in consumer magazines are length of life, audience selectivity, editorial climate (conducive to thoughtful consideration of an advertising message), high quality color reproduction, and regional coverage opportunities. The disadvantages in magazines are the inflexibility of long closing dates, the lack of action and sound,

and the absence of localized appeal.

Newspapers Newspapers, both daily and Sunday, deliver an important coverage penetration in their respective markets --within every segment of the market-- in cities and suburbs--reaching people of every age and income level--in every part of the country. Newspapers are local in all respects--can be purchased on a market-by-market basis--and investment and coverage can be tailored to fit specific market needs. Newspaper closing dates are the shortest in print media, and ads can be inserted or changed practically overnight. The disadvantages are short life and high out-of-pocket cost for truly national coverage.

ROP Color is available in most papers, but the quality of reproduction is poor. High quality color can be obtained via pre-printing in most papers, but because of press slippage, a "wallpaper" type of layout must be used. A few papers are now equipped to handle accurate cut-off pre-prints (Spectacolor) and these do provide high quality reproduction of normally designed ads.

Outdoor Similarly to other media, outdoor can be used on a national scale. Or, as a local medium, outdoor can be tailored in scheduling and coverage to meet special sales problems in individual markets. The medium has a long life and the standard poster period of 30 days offers the opportunity for repeat exposures. The combination of large physical size and full-color reproduction enables an advertiser to make a dramatic presentation. However, the outdoor audience is in motion (copy must be brief) and it is generally nonselective, with exposure to all economic and social classes. Out-of-pocket cost is high--the purchase of a one-month average showing in all U.S. markets is over one million dollars.

Radio Radio's principal advantage is its ability to produce advertising messages at a low cost-per-thousand. Its disadvantage lies in the fact that its audience has become dispersed and fragmented (because of the dominance of TV), to the point where it is both difficult and expensive to achieve effective actual coverage of a desired market segment. Also, the lack of visual presentation militates against its use for many products and services.

Sunday Magazine Sections There are mainly Rotogravure Supplements distributed with Sunday newspapers. Because of this distribution arrangement, supplements provide the depth of local market coverage which newspapers offer. They also provide a reasonably efficient method of obtaining good four-color reproduction in selected markets. Supplements have many of the characteristics of consumer magazines but they do not enjoy as long a life, nor do they provide a generally uniform coverage in all areas--they tend to provide a high level of coverage in distributing cities but relatively insignificant or no coverage in non-distributing markets.

Television The great attributes of this medium lie in the fact that an advertising message can be presented visually with action, demonstration, and oral persuasion. The medium is almost universally available (94% of U.S. homes own one or more TV sets). Three principal networks, ABC, CBS and NBC, offer the most efficient means of using the medium nationally. Where select local market coverage is the objective, spot purchases or local programming fill the need. Programs can be selected, either nationally or locally, whose known audience characteristics best meet the profile of the market target. The principal disadvantage is the short life of a TV message.

Finally, the young account representative should keep up-to-date on general media developments either through the

trade press or conversation with the Media Department. Included in such surveillance should be such subjects as growth of: Color TV, CATV systems, regional and test market magazine availabilities, and Spectacolor avails.

COSTS

The account man should also have some idea as to the costs of those media elements that are likely to be considered for his own particular product. In broad terms, the account representative should be aware of the fact that one million dollars will *not* buy a prime time network show for 52 weeks. It will *not* buy 52 four-color spreads in the *Playboy* magazine. One million dollars will buy so many one-minute commercials on a prime time network show or so many four-color spreads in *Playboy*. It would be helpful to the young account executive to carry a card or slip of paper summarizing basic national media costs. The account man should not arbitrarily agree (with client) to cancel advertising unless he has prior knowledge of the effect that such cancellation will have on discounts.

CIRCULATION AND AUDIENCE

It will also be helpful to the young account man to develop a "feel" for circulation and audience numbers. As an example, he should know the approximate number of TV homes that view a high-rated evening program--10 to 15,000,000. Be aware that a magazine delivers over 5,000,000 circulation and not 500,000. It is not expected that the circulations of all magazines, supplements, newspapers, and homes reached by TV programs be known. However, one should know the difference between 1,000,000 and 10,000,000.

MEDIA RELATIONS

The account man should rely on the Media Department to negotiate all program, spot and print ad positions. Many good time periods and magazine positions have *not* been offered to specific clients because the media knew in advance that they were to receive the business.

Media have restrictions on the type of advertising that they will accept. As an example, hard liquor advertising cannot appear in broadcast media--the *Readers Digest* will not accept liquor or tobacco products, etc. Account men working on such accounts should be familiar with such restrictions.

ADVERTISEMENT UNITS

The account man should know and understand the Media Department's philosophy on the economics of color vs black-and-white, full pages vs fractional pages, 20-seconds vs minute length commercials, etc., in addition to knowing the creative philosophy. The account executive should be knowledgeable on the subject of commercial length and the various print ad sizes:

Television In spot TV, the most common commercial lengths are ID's (8 or 10 seconds), station breaks (20 seconds and 30 seconds), and minute commercials. The commercial most used in network television is one minute; however, different commercial lengths can be employed depending on total time purchased and commercial length desired. It is important to know that, in general, television programs are purchased on a long-term basis and cannot be cancelled overnight but TV spots and participations can.

The account man should be aware that there are three basic types of television programs--the local program, syndicated program, and network program.

A local program is one originated and produced (generally live) by an individual station--e.g., newscasts.

A syndicated program is produced on film or tape by a commercial studio and sold to individual advertisers or stations in separate markets.

A network program (live, film, or tape) originates in a network studio and is simultaneously fed by micro-wave links to the various stations affiliated with the network.

If television is a major part of a plan, the account executive should be familiar with four-week audience and frequency data. He should also know how the data are obtained.

Newspapers Daily and Sunday newspapers across the U.S. are not all similar to the "home town" newspaper. The new account executive should ask his print buyer to obtain newspapers from 10 or 15 different cities and see for himself the differences which exist. He certainly will never be expected to know the different papers city by city, but he should have an appreciation that there are differences. Along the same lines, the new account executive should take advantage of every opportunity to be exposed to the various media in the cities which he visits. If at all possible, tune in to the local TV station(s), radio station(s), and read the local newspaper(s). Better still, visit the local station(s) and paper(s), but don't try to negotiate.

Outdoor Regardless of the possible use of outdoor, all new account executives should, at some point in their initial career, "ride" an outdoor plant. This means devoting a full day with the owner or representative of an outdoor advertising company (plant) and being taken to the locations of the available 24-sheet posters.

Magazines Magazine ads have a long closing date and, consequently, a four-color page scheduled for August cannot be cancelled in July. Coupon returns and write-in promotion offers perform best in print media. The obvious reason is that with print, the reader is provided with the coupon or entry blank, whereas in broadcasting, the viewer, at a specific time, must be prepared with pencil and paper.

The account man should have a knowledge of the availability of farm publications--ranging from state farm papers to regional farm publications and national farm magazines.

The account man should be conversant on regional magazine availabilities, split-runs, and special units.

Supplements Sunday supplements are a an important advertising medium and the account executive should learn the difference between a roto and letterpress supplement, local vs nationally syndicated supplement, and magazine vs comic supplement.

Roto vs Letterpress - In brief, this refers to the type of printing and paper used. Roto supplements offer excellent reproduction because of printing method and coated paper. Letterpress supplements employ newsprint stock; consequently, the reproduction leaves a great deal to be desired.

Local vs National - In brief, local supplements are edited and published by individual newspapers and can be purchased locally. The nationally syndicated supplements (i.e., *This Week*, *Parade*, etc.) are, from an editorial standpoint, national in interest and are distributed by select newspapers across the U.S.

Magazine vs Comic Supplements - Magazine supplements are the nationally syndicated supplements and local roto/letterpress supplements; the comic section of the Sunday newspaper represents the comic supplement.

MEDIA RESEARCH

The new account representative should develop a working knowledge of the major media research services subscribed to or used by the agency. This would include such research as Nielsen, ARB, Pulse, Simmons, Trendex, Starch, etc. Each agency will probably have its own philosophy as to the circumstances under which these services might be used and their limitations. A brief description of some of these services follows:

ARB (American Research Bureau) Reports local ratings, homes reached, audience composition in most TV markets twice a year (November and March). Large markets have additional reports. Also reports national ratings and national audience composition. Information gathered by means of diaries.

NSI (Nielsen Station Index) Reports local television ratings and shares in most television markets, homes reached and audience composition. A diary method.

NTI (Nielsen Television Index) Measures national television ratings in two forms: *Pocketpiece*, issued bi-wekly, includes ratings and shares and homes reached of all network programs. Information is obtained by means of audimeters attached to respondents' sets. *Bluebook*, issued bi-monthly, includes demographic breakouts of program audiences, cumulative audience, minute-by-minute audience, and audience flow.

Fast MNA's (multi-network area) are issued weekly, and report ratings based on 30 markets common to the three networks.

Nielsen also provides a national television audience composition report based on diaries.

Pulse Measures (1) local and network television programs (audience composi-

tion, demographic characteristics),
(2) local radio ratings, (3) Negro
radio ratings. Uses roster-recall
method.

Simmons   Annual report on the audiences
of mass and select magazines and television programs as well as duplication
and audience characteristics data.
Television viewing patterns and product usage among magazine readers are
also provided. Personal interview
method.

Starch   Provides ad readership data
and audience characteristics for the
major consumer magazines and Sunday
supplements.

Trendex   Measures the following for
nighttime network programs: Ratings,
audience composition, program selection
data, sponsor and/or brand identification, etc. Uses the telephone coinci-
dental method.

*Alfred Politz, Inc. and Audits & Sur-
veys, Inc.*   Are frequently employed
by various media to do special media
studies.

MEDIA REFERENCE TOOLS

The young accunt representative
should school himself with the standard
reference tools used by the Media Department. The client shouldn't receive
a blank look when he refers to BAR.
Some of the standard reference tools
which are used by the majority of Media
Departments follow:

ABC   (Audit Bureau of Circulations) An
independent organization, sponsored by
publishers, agencies, and advertisers,
that is devoted to auditing the circulation records of member publishers of
periodicals with paid circulation.

ABP   (American Business Press) Reports

annual investments of approximately
1,600 companies in business papers.
Dollars are either reported by advertisers or estimated by ABP. The report
is limited to companies investing
$50,000 or more.

ACB   (Advertising Checking Bureau)
Checking service for newspaper advertising. Tear sheets, linage and/or
expenditure reports provided, but must
be ordered in advance.

BAR   (Broadcast Advertisers Report)
Monitors all network television advertising activity. Also monitors local
television during certain weeks in 75
markets. A special report called INA-
BAR covers costs of all network television programs.

Brad Vern Reports   Record of advertising space run in business papers.
Listed by advertiser in alphabetical
order. Each report includes five years,
current plus four preceding.

BPA   (Business Publications Audit) A
non-profit, tripartite corporation,
sponsored by publishers, agencies and
advertisers, which audits qualified
circulation for business publications.
The circulation may be paid or free, or
a combination of both paid and free.

Lloyd-Hall   Provides data on editorial
lineage appearing in 63 national consumer magazines. The information is
shown by a number of classifications
such as food, fiction, health, etc.

LNA   (Leading National Advertisers,
formerly P.I.B.) Publishes monthly
cumulative reports of schedules and expenditures in 90 national magazines and
six supplements, by advertisers and
product.

Media Records   This service provides
lineage by advertisers and products
run in 408 daily and Sunday newspapers
in 140 cities, showing totals on 172
classifications of national advertising.

151

N.W. Ayer & Son Directory Provides a listing of all newspapers and periodicals published in the U.S.

Rorabaugh Spot TV activity on 342 stations in 218 markets. Published quarterly six to eight weeks after the fact. Shows total number and type of spot used during quarter by product and market. Also shows total gross expenditures by company and product.

SRDS (Standard Rate and Data Service) It is from these books, which are issued monthly, that advertising rates (along with a great deal of other basic data) are obtained. There are individual books covering daily and Sunday newspapers, consumer magazines and farm publications, business publications, spot television, spot radio, network television/radio, and ABC weekly newspapers.

MEDIA BUREAUS

All account men should know the functions of the service and promotion bureaus of the various media--MPA, TvB, RAB, B of A, etc. A brief description of some of these bureaus follows:

ANPA (American Newspaper Publishers Association) Advisory association for the welfare of newspapers. Acts as a clearing house of information, including agency credit ratings.

Bureau of Advertising (Bureau of Advertising of the American Newspaper Publishers Association, Inc.) To promote the broader and more effective use of newspaper advertising by providing to advertisers and agencies a wide variety of research and market analysis services, and by providing retail advertising planning aids to staffs of member newspapers.

MAB (Magazine Advertising Bureau, Inc.) To promote magazines as an advertising medium; to serve advertisers, agencies and publishers as headquarters for information about magazine advertising.

MPA (Magazine Publishers Association) Concerned primarily with the mechanical and financial problems (other than credit ratings) of the publishing business. Advisory association for the welfare of magazines. Delves into all matters relating to publishing, including postal regulations and circulation methods.

NAB (National Association of Broadcasters) A trade association of radio and television stations and networks and allied suppliers, significant mediawise for its code of program and advertising standards.

RAB (Radio Advertising Bureau) Radio counterpart of TvB.

TvB (Television Bureau of Advertising) An all-industry sales and promotion organization designed to secure larger advertising appropriations for television and to promote more effective use of the medium.

MEDIA GLOSSARY

Obtain a copy of a glossary of media terms and begin committing them to memory. Such glossaries are available from several advertising trade journals. As an example, listed below are some terms which should be known by all account men and media people:

Broadcasting

adjacency	bonus
affidavit	channel
annual plan	confirmation
billboard	contiguous rate

cross-plug   product protection
delay   quota
four-week reach   rating
ID   satellite
network option time sectional feed
omission   share
over-commerciali-   station break
  zation   triple spotting
penetration   viewers-per-set
pre-emption

Print

agate line   gatefold
audience - primary gutter
  & secondary   inserts
best food or drug line rate
  day   makegood
bleed   milline
cancellation date net audience
closing date   optional combina-
cover position   tion
cumulative audience position request
delivered circula- publisher's state-
  tion   ment
flat rate   rate base
full position   ROP
forced combination spread

DISCUSSION QUESTIONS

---

1. What are meant by "frequency," "reach,"
and "size"? What is their significance in planning media schedules?

2. About which aspects of media planning should a young account executive
be thoroughly knowledgeable? Why?

3. Describe the basic steps in the
media selection procedure. Why should
an account representative become
familiar with them?

Reprinted by permission from ADVERTISING AGE; 21 November, 1973, pp. 66-72.

III-2

NEWSPAPERS ARE NATION'S BIGGEST MEDIUM

Advertising Age

Beset by ever-mounting production costs, shifting population centers, the ubiquitous TV screen, paper shortages and government pressures, newspapers nevertheless manage to prosper as they maintain their status as the nation's biggest advertising medium.

Daily newspapers finished 1972 with $7 billion in advertising revenues, up 13.2% from 1971, according to the Newspaper Advertising Bureau.

This No. 1 rank as the largest medium in the U.S. continues even though the number of daily newspapers is well below the alltime high. Fewer papers are doing more business.

In 1972, there were 1,761 newspapers published in the U.S., up from 1,749 in 1971. The high point for U.S. dailies was reached in 1915 when 2,442 papers were in circulation. The downward trend leveled off in the late 1930s and has remained fairly steady since then. In 1935, for example, there were 1,749 dailies, the same as in 1971. Evening dailies increased from 1,425 to 1,441 last year. Morning newspapers declined to 337 from 339. Sunday newspapers increased from 590 to 603.

In the past ten years, 185 newspapers closed through suspension, merger or changeover to weekly frequency. But 191 new dailies began operations in that same decade.

Daily circulation set a record in 1972, at 62,510,242, up nearly 300,000 papers per day. Sunday circulation dipped, however, largely because weekend editions were no longer being counted as a Sunday paper.

√ The daily newspapers' share of the total advertising outlay of $23.1 billion coutinued to increase in 1972, moving up to 30.3% from 30.2%.

Why such strength in the newspaper medium? Audits & Surveys Inc. carried out a survey in 1971 that came to the following conclusions:

"1. Daily newspaper readership is high (77%)--as high as ever during more than a decade of surveys.

"2. Daily readership is heavy among diverse segments of the population, but provides the heaviest coverage among upscale, well-educated groups both in terms of the over-all reach of the paper and in terms of reading more than one paper.

154

"3. Newspaper reading is a day-in, day-out activity, a daily need, and consequently a schedule of weekday issues accumulates high frequencies rapidly.

"4. The vast majority of readers are delivered to every type of page in the paper ... The average page, excluding classified, stands an 84% chance of being opened by the reader.

"5. Because readership and frequency of readership are both high, and because most pages of the paper are opened by the readers, reach and frequency of various kinds of pages is also high over a series of issues.

"6. The high page opening and the high reach and frequency are reflections of high involvement with the daily paper. Readers set aside special times of the day for their papers, and they almost all turn through all the pages, generally in their homes.

"7. Readership of Sunday papers is also high (67%), though not at the same level as weekday papers, since a smaller number of papers publish on weekends.

"8. Saturday readership is 58%, and in the course of four weeks a Saturday paper reaches almost eight out of ten adults at least one time.

"9. Newspapers are an action medium. Readers act and react, clipping, talking, writing in response to what they see in the paper.

"10. As part of the active process of newspaper reading, the advertising is consulted and attended to by people in the market, both for food and groceries and for the variety of other items that make up the purchases and purchase planning on a single day.

"11. Classified ad reading is high, despite the fact that the classified section tends to present the facts in their 'purest' form, with little or no art work, catchy headlines, or entertainment value."

A REACH OF 85%

A study of newspapers by N.W. Ayer & Son's media department found that while the ratio of circulation to households has declined from 128 pages per 100 households in 1945 to 96 papers per 100 households in 1971, newspapers continue to reach about 85% of the population each week. Ayer found that the loss is in duplication of readership. The advent of TV, the rising standard of living and increased leisure time activity, the movement of populations to suburban newspapers, and increased single copy costs (from 2¢ to 3¢ to 5¢ to 7¢ to 10¢ to 15¢) are seen as factors in the decline of the circulation-to-households' ratio.

But the Ayer report noted, "Newspapers still reach virtually everyone. The average newspaper is bigger than ever and circulations continue to rise."

Classified advertising remains the fastest-growing part of newspaper advertising. Included in the classified category are contract ads, real estate, automobiles, industry, dealer ads, help wanted/situations wanted, merchandise offerings, business opportunities. In 1972, classified grew to about $2 billion, up 19%.

The backbone of the medium is local advertising, which amounted to nearly $4 billion last year, up 11%. Local advertising comes from local department stores, neighborhood drug store, movie houses, supermarkets, services, etc.-- anything offered for sale locally. Advertisers who sell from one location but not at retail--a dairy, bakery, local brewery--are "general" advertisers, counted in the local category.

1970 NATIONAL ADVERTISING IN NEWSPAPERS

by percent breakdown

Classification	%
Alcoholic beverages	6.9
Amusements	0.4
Educational	0.6
Farm and garden	1.4
Foods	11.8
Hotels and resorts	3.6
Household furniture, furnishings	0.7
Household supplies	1.7
Housing equipment	1.5
Industrial	1.7
Insurance	2.4
Jewelry, silverware	0.3
Medical	1.7
Miscellaneous	6.9
Professional and service	0.6
Public utilities	2.7
Publishing and media	6.8
Radio, TV sets and phonographs	1.9
Sporting goods, cameras, photo supplies	1.1
Tobacco	2.0
Toilet requisites	2.1
Transportation	9.7
Wearing apparel	2.3
Automotive	29.2
National total	100.0

source: Media Records Inc.

✓ The smallest newspaper ad category is national, which amounted to $927,-000,000 in dailies last year, up about 10%. A national advertiser is one who offers a product or service for sale in more than one place. Distribution may be regional or national; merchandise is sold through a variety of retail outlets in more than one community. Local and national advertisers generally deal with different rate cards, and the newspaper industry justifies the difference by noting that local businessmen are steadier, place their ads direct (without agency commission) and without an advertising sales representative's commission. National rates, therefore, are higher, averaging as much as 60% more than local rates.

Three classifications lead the national advertising spenders in newspapers: Automotive, food, transportation. Automotive (which includes gasoline and tires as well as cars) represents 19.4% of the total, or $179,720,000, down from a 25% share ten years ago. Part of this share-of-market decline is due to the growth of other categories, such as tobacco (aided by the ban on broadcast advertising that saw cigaret companies invest $86,000,000 in newspapers last year, up from $16,500,000 in 1970, the pre-ban year), publishing and media, mail order and others.

Behind automotive, with an 11% share of the national ad total in newspapers, is transportation (airways, bus, tours, rail, ship) at $103,363,000 and rising. Food advertising is third, $103,138,000, also 11% of the total, and down from $122,115,000 in 1969. The three categories also lead in terms of ad linage.

BY 1980: $10 BILLION

Leo Bogart, exec vp-general manager of the Newspaper Advertising Bureau, is on record with a prediction that total annual newspaper ad revenues may exceed $10 billion by the end of the decade. By 1980, he said, local ad revenue should reach $5.2 billion; classified should be at $3.7 billion, and national at $1.5 billion. And these are his minimum figures.

The local vs national, or dual, rate is a source of conflict for the newspaper business. Most retail, or local advertising, is handled directly between the store and the newspaper, with the space contracted for at an annual rate. This annual rate is far below the rate the national advertiser pays. The national advertiser, it is held, is twice removed

THE GROWTH OF NEWSPAPER ADVERTISING
AND THE U.S. ECONOMY

Index of Growth (1946 Base)

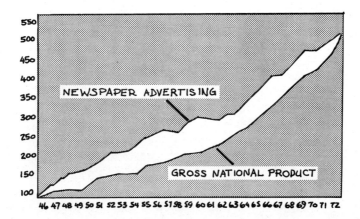

from the newspaper. There is the ad
agency, handling most of this business
on the basis of a 15% commission. And
there is the publisher's sales representative, who solicits national advertising for a 10% commission. Newspapers justify the higher national rate
on grounds that the national advertiser's dollar represents only 75% of received revenue.

Discounts are available, however. They
are offered on the basis of quantity,
time or frequency. The basic amount
upon which the cost of an ad is calculated, the highest rate against which
discounts are figured, is the "open
rate." This is the rate for a one-
time appearance of an ad. Thus, if
the newspaper's open rate is 50¢ per
line, the cost goes down as the number
of lines used during the course of the
year goes up. The discount schedule
is included in the newspaper's rate
card.

√ The open rate will be charged if the
ad is scheduled as run-of-paper (r.o.p.)
--to appear anywhere in the paper, or
"best available position." The adver-

tiser who insists on placing his ad in
a specific part of the paper--adjacent
to the TV listing, on the sports page,
or near the stock tables--will pay extra for the privilege. This is known
as "preferred position," warranting a
"premium" rate. Publishers with morning and afternoon papers, or weekday
and Sunday editions, will offer special
combination prices, or discounts, to
their advertisers.

Information on rates in metropolitan
dailies are usually quoted on a basis
of so-much-per-agate line. In smaller
dailies, and weeklies, the rates are
generally quoted by the column inch.
The *Standard Rate & Data Service* Books
contain information on newspaper rate
cards. This includes the newspaper's
key advertising personnel, name of sales
rep, addresses, commission and discount
information, general newspaper policy
on advertising, rates for b&w, color;
cancellation notice policy, split-run
(less than full circulation) advertising,
classified ad rates, mechanical measurements, circulation information, etc.

Year	Local Advertising (millions of dollars)	National Advertising (millions of dollars)	Total Newspaper Advertising[1] (millions of dollars)	Index	Gross National Product[1] (billions of dollars)	Index
1946	$ 247.8	$ 910.5	$1,158.3	100.0	$ 210.7	100.0
1947	335.6	1,139.4	1,475.0	127.3	234.3	111.2
1948	393.7	1,355.9	1,749.6	151.0	259.4	123.1
1949	475.7	1,440.0	1,915.7	165.4	258.1	122.5
1950	533.4	1,542.2	2,075.6	179.2	284.6	135.1
1951	548.9	1,708.8	2,257.7	194.9	329.0	156.1
1952	562.4	1,910.4	2,472.8	213.5	347.0	164.7
1953	642.7	2,002.1	2,644.8	228.3	365.4	173.4
1954	635.1	2,060.2	2,695.3	232.7	363.1	172.3
1955	743.3	2,344.5	3,087.8	266.1	397.5	188.7
1956	788.9	2,446.7	3,235.6	279.3	419.2	199.0
1957	809.7	2,473.6	3,283.3	283.5	442.8	210.2
1958	768.7	2,424.1	3,192.8	275.6	444.5	211.0
1959	826.2	2,719.8	3,546.0	306.1	483.7	229.6
1960	836.1	2,866.7	3,702.8	319.7	503.7	239.1
1961	802.3	2,820.8	3,623.1	312.8	520.1	246.8
1962	781.6	2,899.8	3,681.4	317.8	560.3	265.9
1963	764.9	3,039.0	3,803.9	328.4	590.5	280.3
1964	848.0	3,300.0	4,148.0	358.1	632.4	300.1
1965	869.4	3,587.1	4,456.5	384.7	684.9	325.1
1966	975.0	3,920.0	4,895.0	422.6	749.9	355.9
1967	936.0	4,006.0	4,942.0	426.7	793.9	376.8
1968	990.0	4,275.0	5,265.0	454.5	865.0	410.5
1969	1,059.0	4,694.0	5,753.0	496.7	931.4	442.1
1970	1,040.0	4,810.0	5,745.0	495.9	976.8	463.6
1971	1,140.0	5,110.0	6,250.0	539.6	1,150.4	545.9
1972	1,240.0	5,720.0	6,960.0	600.8	1,152.1	546.7

[1] All data are in current dollars, as of each year.
Source: U.S. Department of Commerce. McCann Erickson, Inc.

HOW IT'S MEASURED

Newspapers measure space in column width and lines (top to bottom) and there are 14 lines to the column inch. In describing the size of an ad, one may say 200 lines by three columns, or 200 on three. Thus, a 2"x2" ad is 28x 2, or "28 on two," or a 56-line ad (28 multiplied by 2).

There are tabloid-size pages (usually five or six columns wide and 200 lines deep, or 1,000 to 1,200 lines per page), and standard-size pages (eight columns by 280-330 lines).

Ads are accompanied by an insertion order that states the date, or dates, for the ad to appear, the size of the ad, position requested, and the rate. The order also states how the ad plate, mat or mechanical (pasteup of the complete ad) will arrive at the newspaper. Contract terms are also noted, if applicable.

Insertion orders are left with the ad-

vertiser to fill in when he signs a
contract with the newspaper. The space
contract deals with rate terms and the
duration of the contract. If the advertiser doesn't run all the linage
specified in his contract, he is charged
a short rate, or the difference between the rate earned and the rate contracted for. Example: The advertiser
contracted to run 10,000 lines a year
and actually used 6,000 lines. He
would be charged at the 5,000-line
rate, assuming the paper has no 6,000-
line rate.

✓ An index that relates ad rates to
circulation is the milline rate, the
cost per agate line per million of
circulation. This rate is determined
by multiplying the line rate by
1,000,000 and dividing by the circulation figure. This index has two desig-
nations: Miniline (minimum discount
level) and maxiline (maximum discount
level of advertising.

The cost per line per million circulation for national advertising in daily
newspapers in 1972 amounted to $6.71,
compared with $5.02 in 1962. (When
converted to 1972 dollars, however, the
1962 milline rate becomes $6.92, the
Newspaper Advertising Bureau points
out in stating that comparatively speaking, newspaper advertising cost less
last year than it did ten years ago.)
The $6.71 milline rate is the total
cost of an ad using all dailies in the
country. The combined milline rate
for national advertising in all Sunday
newspapers came to $5 in 1972, compared
with $3.68 in 1962 (or $5.08 in terms
of '72 dollars).

BILLIONS FOR CO-OP

Maximil and minimil rates are computed by allowing for the cash discount
of 2% on the net, in addition to the
15% agency commission. Thus, these

rates are computed by multiplying the
paper's open line rate, or discounted
line rate, by .983.

Another newspaper ad category is cooperative advertising, the money an advertiser will supply to a retailer on
condition that the retailer advertises
a specific product or service. About
$3 billion a year is made available in
co-op funds, and $1.5 billion of this
amount goes into newspapers. About
$500,000,000 goes into radio and TV and
the rest is unused, representing lost
potential for media.

National advertisers are encouraged to
offer co-op funds to retailers because
it enables them to avoid the higher
national ad rate. Co-op plans range
from 50% to 100% of the ad's cost. In
order to maintain an orderly marketplace, Federal Trade Commission guidelines require advertisers to offer the
same proportionate allowance to every
retailer, to play no favorites.

The job of auditing co-op advertising
is a mammoth one, and a number of companies are involved, encouraging the
use of co-op programs and auditing
these programs in the marketplace. Such
companies include the Advertising Checking Bureau, Pinpoint Marketing, and BMC
Marketing.

✓ Newspaper rates also have differentials for different classes of advertisers, such as motion picture, travel,
book and legal advertising. In the
Chicago Sun-Times, for example, the
open rate is $2.31 (scaled down to $1.82
in bulk contract), but a resort and
travel ad in the Sunday edition carries
a $1.59 open rate; lawn and garden ad,
$1.48; stamps, coins, antiques, $1.85,
and radio-TV stations, $2.10.

An increasingly popular part of the
newspaper advertising business is the
preprinted insert, both the "stuffed"
(placed into the issue unattached to a
page) and the roll-fed. Inserts reached
a volume of 11.8 billion in 1972, up

almost 50% in three years.

Of this figure, about 10.6 billion were stuffed preprints, according to Newspaper Preprint Corp., and the remainder were roll-fed Hi-Fi and Spectacolor inserts. Hi-Fi is a preprinted full-color "wallpaper" insert supplied in roll form to the newspaper and fed and collated into a normal press run. Spectacolor, also roll-fed and full-color, differs from Hi-Fi in that it has borders at top and bottom of the page. Stuffed inserts rose about 18% in Sunday and daily papers by volume, with weekdays showing bigger percentage increases. Most stuffers are multi-page (four or more pages), and about 17% are the card type. National advertisers' average per insert order is up to about 225,000 while the local advertisers' order dipped to 120,000 in 1972, according to Newspaper Preprint.

√ The use of r.o.p. color in newspapers, like Hi-Fi and Spectacolor, has been on the rise. In 1972, 1,153 newspapers offered black and three colors (and 1,498 offering black and one color) to their advertisers. The number of Hi-Fi papers rose to 1,550 and Spectacolor rose to 432 in 1972.

The premium for r.o.p. color advertising ranges from 17% to 62%, depending on the number of colors and the size of the ad. Hi-Fi and Spectacolor ads generally cost more than twice as much as a regular b&w page since the cost of the paper, printing and special handling is added into the cost. A Hi-Fi ad campaign in newspapers with a 10,000,000 total circulation would cost about $181,875 according to the N.W. Ayer study. Space would cost $80,000; add $7,000 for extra printing cylinders required by the printer; $86,250 for printing and paper (estimated at $750 per 1,000 press run and an additional 15% over average circulation), and $8,625 for shipping (about 75¢ per 1,000 copies shipped). Ayer notes that color advertising "almost pays for itself" in the additional

readership it achieves.

The use of color in weekday and Sunday supplements is one element noted in the optimistic forecasts about newspaper advertising. Other reasons given by industry officials deal with the consumerism movement, which entails providing more information to shoppers; population trends, growth of local advertising, aided by national advertisers finding new ways of approaching prospects on a market-by-market basis; the clearly-defined newspaper market, and the growing availability of private label branded items in local markets, which should force brand name advertisers to advertise more in those markets.

The 603 Sunday newspapers published in the U.S. generally include a magazine section for their readers. The leading supplements are *Family Weekly* (nearly 300 newspapers), circulation averaging nearly 10,000,000; *Parade*, (more than 100 papers and a circulation of 18,000,-000; Metropolitan Sunday Newspapers, known as *Sunday*, with some 45 papers and a circulation exceeding 23,000,000; *Tuesday*, distributed to black communities in nearly 25 major cities as part of such newspapers as the *Detroit News*, *Dallas Times Herald* and the *Oakland Tribune*, has a circulation of about 2,300,000. In addition, locally-edited newspaper-distributed magazines may be purchased individually, by markets. Some examples: *Santa Barbara News-Press* with *Your Weekend*; *Waterbury* (Conn.) *Republican Magazine*; *New York Times* magazine; *Salt Lake City Tribune's Home Magazine*.

√ The nationally distributed supplements have their own sales staffs to solicit ads. The supplements are sold to distributing newspapers on a 1,000-unit basis and the newspapers share in the ad revenue on the basis of their circulation. A one-time page rate, b&w, for *Parade*, in the full *Parade* network, is $64,185; for a four-color, inside page, the rate is nearly $79,000.

The national supplements offer combination rates for regional buys. *Family Weekly*, for example, offers 26 market regions and *Parade* offers five "target group" buys.

SALESMEN AND REPS

Newspapers use their own sales forces, usually headed by the advertising director, who, in turn, supervises the classified ad manager; retail or local ad manager, and national ad manager. Much of the classified ad volume comes in by telephone, or through the front door as walk-in business. The paper's sales staff will call on local accounts and often help prepare ads for businessmen. The salesmen also work up material about the paper's readership, although the larger dailies invest money for professionally-prepared market research. The NAB supports newspapers with "how to" seminars on local and national advertising, co-op programs, and data on newspaper audiences.

For national advertising, it is customary for the national ad manager to work through one or more newspaper representative companies. These reps work for non-competing newspapers and call on advertisers and agencies in an effort to sell space in the distant paper. Newspaper chains maintain national sales offices in major cities, as do some of the largest of the metropolitan dailies. Some of the larger newspaper rep firms are Branham-Moloney, with offices in 17 cities; Sawyer-Ferguson-Walker, with offices in 10 cities; Ward-Griffith; Story & Kelly-Smith Inc.; Mathews, Shannon & Cullen.

In addition, some sales organizations represent country weeklies, suburban and community newspapers, ethnic papers, college newspapers, comics section groups, such as *Puck-The Comic Weekly* and *Metro Sunday Comics*.

Puck represents 116 newspapers; *Metro* has 67 papers. There are, as with Sunday magazines, independent newspaper comics sections that can be bought individually by markets by advertisers. There are black newspapers in major cities; also many religious weeklies and a growing number of neighborhood weeklies in the larger cities.

√ Newsprint consumption is a prime indicator of daily newspaper progress, since, in effect, it must measure circulation and advertising. U.S. newsprint consumption last year reached a record 10.2 billion tons, or 7% more than 1971, the largest annual increase in history. There is growing concern about a newsprint shortage and industry observers see a dangerously tight supply situation developing.

Meanwhile, newsprint prices continue to increase. Higher newsprint costs, with increasing costs throughout the industry, are spurring efforts by publishers to harness the new technology for newsprint production. One new system, by Sperry Univac and others, involves a visual display terminal that is linked to a typesetting computer. Copy is typeset after being stored, for varying lengths of time, in memory files. The system is used for classified and display advertising copy as well as news copy.

All this is a long way from the May 8, 1704, edition of the *Boston News Letter*, which carried the first paid ad in an American newspaper. The ad sought a customer for an estate at Oyster Bay, N.Y. By Sept. 21, 1784, the first daily newspaper in this country, the *Pennsylvania Packet & Advertiser*, carried four pages and managed to fill 10 or 16 columns with ads offering real estate, advising of ship sailings, rewards for stolen goods, and Bibles for sale.

√ It has been onward and upward ever since. Today, the strength of the newspaper as an advertising vehicle is seen

161

in many ways. It offers geographic flexibility, since advertisers can select and reach specific markets. They can adjust their copy and ad schedules to a season, a region, a regional economy, to regional tastes and customs.

Studies show that newspaper readership peaks in the middle-age groups when people's interest in news and civic affairs is greatest. As they become older and less active, readership drops off. But readership is greatest among the upper socio-economic groups, in the large metropolitan and suburban areas.

Newspapers are growing fatter. Where the average paper with a circulation of 50,000 or more totaled 23 pages in 1946, with 12.6 pages of advertising, today the total is 52 pages, with 32.6 pages of advertising.

In the words of N.W. Ayer's media study: "With the advent of greater public interest in the world about us, there has been a growing interest, need and desire for newspapers on the part of their readers."

DISCUSSION QUESTIONS

1. Why have newspapers been able to enjoy their apparent success?

2. What prospects do you foresee for the future of newspaper advertising in the U.S.A.? Explain.

TELE/SCOPE; Vol. 5, No. 3, June, 1972. Reprinted by permission from Tele-Research Incorporated.

III-3

THE TELE-RESEARCH STUDY OF TELEVISION VS MAGAZINE ADVERTISING

Tele/Scope

Recently the three major television networks announced the results of a study conducted for them by Tele-Research, Inc. regarding the relative selling effectiveness of magazine ads and television commercials. This study is probably one of the most significant research projects ever undertaken on the subject of advertising effectiveness, and represents a major contribution to the field of media research.

The study was conducted with over 4,000 respondents, and extended over a period of almost a year. As with all Tele-Research studies, the primary criterion of "advertising effectiveness" was the degree to which exposure to the test advertising caused consumers to spend their own money to actually purchase the advertised products in the real-life marketplace.

In the near future, a full report of the complete findings of this research will be issued by the project's sponsors: ABC, CBS, and NBC. Meanwhile, because of the great number of inquiries that T/R has received regarding the results of this study, the key findings are summarized in this issue of Tele/Scope.

The major portion of this research utilized the standard T/R technique to test 12 matched pairs of television commercials and magazine ads for various food and non-food supermarket products. Each "pair" of magazine/TV ads was minutely matched in terms of both copy approach and sales points. In many cases the voice-over of the TV commercial was identical to the print copy; in some cases the same models and actors were used both on film and in print. The products included in the study were Bounty Paper Towels, Breck Shampoo, Campbell's Chunky Soup, Cold Power Detergent, Del Monte Canned Pineapple, Ivory Liquid, Jell-O 1-2-3 Dessert, Lysol Spray Disinfectant, Maxim Freeze-Dried Coffee, Moisturelle Liquid Lathering Cleanser, Nabisco Premium Saltine Crackers and Tang Instant Breakfast Drink.

The magazine ads were all full-page, four-color. The matched TV commercials were all in color; eleven were 30 sec. commercials, one was 60 sec. (approximating the current 30"/60" mix).

Using the standard T/R in-the-market-place testing technique, supermarket shoppers were assigned to one of three basic groups, with all groups carefully matched in terms of demographic characteristics, brand preferences and other relevant traits.

√ *The Control Group* received T/R's booklet of various cents-off coupons, but was not exposed to any advertising, either magazine or TV.

√ *The Magazine Group* received identical cents-off coupons, but also viewed some of the test magazine ads before going into the store to shop.

√ *The TV group* received identical cents-off coupons, but also viewed some of the test TV commercials prior to shopping.

With this research design, the different rates at which the three separate groups purchased the test products provides a direct measure of the effectiveness of the advertising, since this is the only variable which differentiates the three groups.

Table 1 summarizes the results obtained in this phase of the research.

In all twelve cases, the test TV commercial generated more sales for the advertised product than its magazine ad counterpart. The smallest advantage that TV demonstrated was 49%, while the largest TV advantage was 130%. On the average, exposure to magazine advertising produced an increase of 9.6 purchases per each 100 shoppers. Exposure to TV advertising produced an average increase of 17.5 purchases per 100 shoppers. Overall, therefore, exposure to TV advertising generated 82% more purchases than exposure to magazine advertising.

In addition to the major portion of the research (summarized above and in Table 1), two smaller-scale sub-studies were also conducted.

Table 1

Product	A. Number of Purchases Per 100 Shoppers Not Exposed to Advertising	B. Additional Purchases Per 100 Shoppers Exposed to Magazine Advertising	C. Additional Purchases Per 100 Shoppers Exposed to TV Advertising	D. TV Advantage Over Magazine $\frac{C - B}{B}$
A	28.8	22.5	33.5	48.9%
B	9.7	3.1	4.8	54.8%
C	11.3	3.8	6.1	60.5%
D	16.7	9.2	15.2	65.2%
E	12.3	6.1	10.6	73.8%
F	26.0	8.0	14.3	78.8%
G	19.0	9.2	16.6	80.4%
H	23.0	9.8	18.3	86.7%
I	17.3	6.0	11.7	95.0%
J	29.0	11.3	22.6	100.0%
K	28.7	14.3	29.4	105.6%
L	23.5	11.2	25.8	130.4%
Average	20.4	9.6	17.5	82.3%

1. COLOR VS B&W COMMERCIALS

In one of these special sub-studies, TV commercials were shown in color to owners of color TV sets, and shown in B&W to owners of B&W sets. The results from the two groups were then combined, weighting monochrome and color in the ratio that color set penetration existed nationally at the time of the study.

Under these conditions, the selling effectiveness advantage of TV over print was 72%.

2. PROGRAM AND EDITORIAL CONTEXT

In the second of these special sub-tests, TV commercials were embedded in a segment of the "Tonight Show," and the counterpart magazine ads were placed in a stripped-down, simulated issue of *Life* magazine.

With both media, viewing advertising within an editorial or program context resulted in a decrease on selling effectiveness. The effectiveness of the print ads, however, was curtailed more than the effectiveness of the TV commercials. The magazine ads which had been embedded in the simulated *Life* generated an average of 6.2 additional purchases for the advertised products per each 100 viewers. The TV commercials shown within the context of the Tonight Show segment produced an average of 15.0 additional purchases per 100 viewers; or, an advantage in the selling effectiveness of TV over print of 142%.

The results of this particular sub-study were also analyzed by taking only regular readers of *Life* as the magazine-exposed group, and regular viewers of the Tonight Show as the commercial-exposed group. Under these conditions, the selling effectiveness of the magazine ads dropped quite sharply, while the effectiveness of the TV commercials dropped barely at all. TV's advantage over print, under

these special conditions, rose to 207%.

Under different sets of test conditions, therefore, the advantage of TV advertising over print advertising would seem to vary. Under the most adverse conditions (i.e., B&W set owners viewing TV commercials in B&W) TV was 72% more effective than magazine advertising in generating sales for the advertised product. Under the most advantageous conditions, TV commercials proved to be 207% more effective than the matched magazine ads. Under no conditions did magazine advertising sell the advertised product more effectively than TV.

All factors considered, the 82% TV advantage which emerged in the major portion of the study would seem to be a fair, impartial assessment of the relative selling effectiveness of these two media.

DISCUSSION QUESTIONS

---

1. Which other measures of advertising effectiveness could have been used in the study? Why is it important to be able to evaluate the effectiveness of advertising?

2. Describe the conclusions of this study. How reliable are these results?

Reprinted with permission. SALES MANAGEMENT; February 1, 1971, pp. 32-36.

III-4

'NOW' RATIO: SEXY, SEGMENTED, & SELLING LIKE MAD

Sales Management

On the second floor of a two-story frame building tucked away in a private alley in Greenwich Village, Julian Cohen, 31, flicks some switches on a recording studio console. What follow are four variations of a 60-second commercial for du Pont Cantrece nylon panty hose: soul, for a young black audience; bubble-gum rock, for early teens; modified country and western, for a young blue-collar audience; and hard-rock, for a young general audience. "Each commercial has the same message, but for a different audience," says Cohen, president of year-old No Soap Radio Ltd., one of a growing number of hip, young radio production companies. "And each audience is reached by a specific type of station."

In essence, Cohen is saying that in today's ultra-segmented radio, station and programming are synonymous; whatever market segment an advertiser wants to reach is reachable through at least one dominant station in any major market.

The Cantrece commercials, which du Pont hosiery division advertising manager Frank Oswald claims were highly successful in reaching girls under 24, form a single instance of how radio is being used as a marketing tool, and why it

is so successful. In the language of the young people who put radio back in the big time, it is the one mass medium that knows where its head is at. While television and mass magazines suffer dwindling audiences, skyrocketing costs, and identity problems, radio is establishing itself as an economical, efficient, flexible medium entirely in tune with the times.

Says Robert Alter, executive vice president of the Radio Advertising Bureau (RAB), which member stations budget for $1.5 million a year, "We have changed from a living room society into one that's mobile and diverse. Radio moves with people and offers selectivity. Advertisers have found that when every buck counts, they can hit whom they want when they want to."

As radio men will be the first to admit, now that things are going so well, they haven't always had it so good. The shock wave created by television in the early 1950s put radio into a swoon from which it very nearly didn't recover. The massive advertiser defection to television had station managers virtually giving away time, while programming formats were changed more often than disc jockeys' phonograph needles. At the start of the 1960s, smart radio men saw several lights at the end of the tunnel, namely a glut of cars, a generation of adolescents with a completely new, mobile life-style, the transistorized radio, and rock music, which spoke directly to the young. "Rock music revived radio," says No Soap's Cohen. "Rock was relevant to the kids, and if you're relevant to youth, you can sell to them."

In its current incarnation, radio has something for everyone, advertiser and listener alike. Radio's numbers alone are more than impressive. According to RAB estimates, there are 320 million radio sets in 62 million homes and 80 million cars. RAB points out, in fact, that there are 58% more radios in the U.S. than there are people. Further, 51% of the population owns transistor radios, for which they spent $200 million on batteries in 1969. RAB's Bob Alter, who spends most of his time feeding these and many more figures to advertisers, adds, almost unnecessarily, "We have enough numbers to back our claims of reach."

In radio, listeners literally have a movable feast. The dial of an AM/FM radio can have as many as 40 signals in a major market like New York, Chicago, or Los Angeles, most of them offering vertical programming (e.g., all-news, hard rock, country, soul, Spanish or other ethnic, or classical). Because radio stations can promote themselves literally every couple of minutes by mentioning their call letters after each record (as does WABC, New York's top hard-rock station), listeners can dial to whatever suits them. In Los Angeles, for example, someone listening to rock on KDAY is likely to switch to KFWD, an all-news station, for a traffic report, which he knows is broadcast every 10 minutes.

Advertisers skew (a favorite radio word meaning concentrate) their messages to the audience's listening, indeed living, habits. Within the past five years, early morning and late afternoon, bet-

ter known as "drive time," have become to radio what 7-11 pm are to television --prime time. After drivers, who are likely to have listened to Bob Steele of WTIC, Hartford, John Gambling, WOR, New York, or J.P. McCarthy of WJR, Detroit, get to work, advertiser emphasis switches to housewives preparing to attack the supermarkets. The noon hour also is heavy radio listening time, after which it tapers off until late afternoon drive time. Does it end here? Not by a long shot. Three pm to midnight are the prime FM hours, especially for the young people who are goading once-stodgy FM stations into programming--often in stereo--an increasing quantity of "progressive" (socially significant, anti-establishment) rock. For the adults, evening is TV time, which radio men also use to their advantage by urging advertisers to synergize their TV campaigns with frequent radio commercials.

There are, of course, variations to this theme. In agricultural and rural areas, farm stations like KMMJ, Grand Island, Neb., and WNAX, Yankton, S.D., provide livestock and grain prices regularly. On WSMB, New Orleans, U.S. Steel advertises steel tubing to oil well operators. In the Boston area, electronic firms use radio for recruitment advertising.

With its sharply defined audiences, its generous variety of programming, and its still-economical rates (which range from $5 a minute on a struggling FM outlet to $260 a minute for a market's top "morning man," like WOR's John Gambling), what advertiser in his right mind would resist radio?

The answer, by indications over all of 1970 and the first month of this year, is that a rising number of advertisers are running to radio. Even without cigarettes and a soft economy, radio revenues are expected to rise about 4% this year; within this increase, spot radio sales--commercials bought by national advertisers--are expected to

167

rise 8% above 1970 and total $385 million. A sampling of heavy investors in radio this year reads like a blue book of packaged goods marketers. For the first half alone, estimates are that Sterling Drug plans to spend $2 million; General Foods nearly $3 million; Coca-Cola more than $4.5 million; Colgate, around $4 million; PepsiCo, around $4 million; and American Home Products, still unable to get television approval for its Preparation H hemorrhoid remedy, is increasing its outlay to more than $6 million. Sears, Roebuck came into radio last year with about $25 million, almost overnight qualifying as radio's top advertiser.

The reasons marketers like radio generally come down again to youth appeal and segmentation. "We use radio to reach specific target audiences." says Jerry Schoenfeld, Coca-Cola account executive at McCann-Erickson. Coke, with a radio budget estimated at $8 million in 1969, is one of the top 10 radio users. Its radio targets, says Schoenfeld, are general youth, ethnic consumers (mainly Latin and black), and housewives, who respond well to pricing information.

Gilette tells essentially the same story, emphasizing its use of contemporary AM stations to reach young people. So far, says a Gilette official who, like many involved in intensely competitive radio advertising, prefers to remain anonymous, the toiletries maker has steered away from FM. "But," he adds, "we're looking at it more closely because we suspect it attracts a better class of audience." Like many radio advertisers, Gilette still is far from satisfied with audience listenership data, which is far from exact because so much radio is heard outside the home.

Walter Masters, which handles Austin Nichols' Charles Heidsieck of Dreher Advertising, New York, champagnes, has in the past year turned to FM to reach what he describes as a "more educated

RADIO ADVERTISING EXPENDITURES

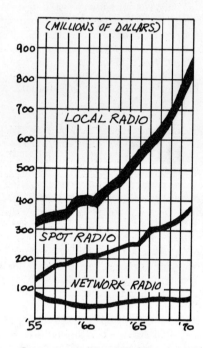

Source: Radio Advertising Bureau

and somewhat more affluent audience" that either ignores or pays little attention to television. Like many others, Masters' main gripe about radio is its lack of scientific audience data.

At last month's National Retail Merchants Assn. (NRMA) convention in New York, a session attended mainly be department store executives, radio representatives seemed to be behind every pillar of the vast New York Hilton. Largely, they argued that department stores could increase reach and frequency without substantially increasing their ad budgets. Michael Hauptman, manager of retail sales development for ABC-owned radio stations, insists that department stores stay with newspapers more out of habit than anything else. "Department store managements feel locked into newspapers," he says, "because their advertising departments

DAYTIME IS RADIO TIME
AVERAGE QUARTER-HOUR RATINGS
MONDAY-FRIDAY, 6 AM - MIDNIGHT

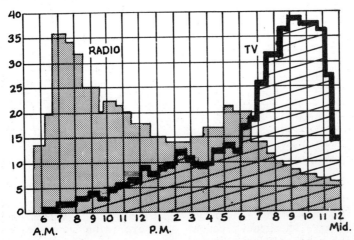

Source: John Blair & Co.

and agencies don't know how to advertise on radio." Stations are pitching the same message to retailers as they are to packaged goods marketers: radio offers efficiency through segmentation, and radio is the medium most in touch with young spenders.

Ironically, radio runs into the most static at ad agencies. RAB's Bob Alter, who already has stated that radio has sold itself to marketing people through its research, says the medium still must sell itself creatively. "The last big objection to radio comes from the creative people at ad agencies," he says. "TV-oriented creative types scoff at radio because they can't 'show' a radio commercial like they can a print ad or a television reel." No Soap Radio's Cohen goes further. "Agencies have no skill at radio commercials." he says. "The 30-year-old creative man grew up with TV and isn't equipped to put imagery into sound alone."

Interestingly, 20 years after television commercials were deprecated for being radio commercials that showed the announcer, many of today's radio commercials are denounced as TV commercials without visuals. Shepard Kurnit, chairman of DKG, Inc., which is heavily into radio with Getty Oil and Remington Electric razors and hot combs, says the recent agency practice of teaming copywriters and art directors has inhibited the creation of good radio commercials. "Tell a copywriter to come up with a radio commercial," says Kurnit, "and all of a sudden he can't get creative ideas from his art director." Norman Tate, a creative director at Ted Bates Co., says he is urging young creatives to sharpen their radio skills. "When any of them object that radio isn't a creative enough medium for them," says Tate, "I remind them that radio never held back Stan Freberg."

Radio never held back Martin Solow either. President of Solow-Wexton Advertising, New York, Solow has at least

as many creativity awards as Arnold
Palmer has golf trophies. "To me,
radio was always the theater of the
mind," says Solow, who numbers among
his radio accounts Vita Herring (with
which he made advertising history with
his Beloved Herring Maven), Carlsberg
Beer, and KLH home entertainment systems. "Radio is an enormously visual
medium. It's still uncluttered enough
to make a good commercial noticeable."

Creative problems aside, agencies have
other objections to radio. Many feel,
for example, that relatively low time
rates and radio ad budgets yield too
little revenue to justify a strong
creative effort. Another complaint is
the paper work that accompanies spot
radio buys. "There are 6,000 radio
stations, many of them with 24-hour
broadcast days," says an agency account
supervisor. "The clerical detail that
accompanies radio buys eats substantially into radio profits." A further objection, also administrative, is that
there still is no reliable procedure
for monitoring radio spots. The problem of commercials not being aired due
to preemption or just plain neglect by
the station has prompted Gray Advertising to start a missed-spots study.

With all its success, radio risks the
same problems that beset magazines and
TV a few years back. "Radio may be
getting trapped by the numbers game
that hurt the magazines," says a corporate ad manager who would rather not
be identified. "All stations are aggressively promoting the same audience
--the in-car commuter, the housewife,
the affluent young person, and they're
doing this with some claims that are
harder and harder to believe." Also,
some fear that radio will lose one of
its most desirable features--uncluttered
commercials. "Radio's popularity may
cause stations to follow TV with clutter," warns Martin Solow. "I'd hate
to see it happen, since I feel certain
that back-to-back, 20-second commercials will hurt TV seriously."

There is no question that radio is enjoying its finest hours since Jack
Benny sold Jell-O. It picks out an
audience and attaches itself to it like
a pilot fish, going along wherever the
listener goes. It offers the advertiser
flexibility, and, intelligently used,
drives home the message introduced by
television advertising. In its present
collective frame of mind, radio feels
attractive to every type of advertiser.
Judging from the sophisticated marketing
radio has shown over the last couple of
years, who knows? Maybe it's true.

DISCUSSION QUESTIONS

1. Differentiate between the nature of
local, spot, and network radio.

2. What strengths and weaknesses of
radio as an advertising medium have
been identified in the article?

3. "Radio time is daytime." Explain.

III-5

THE THINKING MAN'S MEDIUM

Roy E. Larsen

During the fifty years of my career in publishing, the function of general interest and informational magazines in American society has been radically changed by the advent of new communications media, by the rise of millions to affluence, by the vastly increased formal education of our people, and by the growing complexities of our private, national and international lives.

When I was in knee breeches, there was no radio, I was out of college for some years before Al Jolson sang "Mammy" in the first talking motion picture. I had lived through two world wars and the Great Depression before there was television. My contemporaries and I may not have realized it fully at the time, but we were witnessing forward strides in communications comparable to the giant stride of Gutenberg five centuries earlier.

Each of these new media, of course, offered alternative means for the public to get part of the information and entertainment it wanted, and each was therefore awarded a portion of the public's attention time, which before had been devoted mostly to print media. Each of the new media prospered as it deserved, and is continuing to prosper.

The arrivals of radio fifty years ago and television twenty-five years later were unquestionably blessings for mankind--but they were also traumatic experiences for all print media, and especially for the editors and publishers of general interest magazines. After all, for about 100 years magazines had been the principal bearers of entertainment and certain kinds of information into the home. The new media that invaded our nation's castles without bothering to ring twice were regarded by some--not including myself--as interlopers and upsetters of apple carts. Our industry fought them tooth and nail as they came, but they refused to go away. It was years in each case before we admitted that they were here to stay and that each had virtues print media did not have. Try as we might, for instance, no magazine could rival the hilarious silences of a Jack Benny on radio or the sense of participation we all felt as TV showed us man's first step on the moon.

If you will forgive what seems to be boasting--because it is--I was one of the first to use an electronic medium--radio--as a means of promoting a magazine. Some of you may remember "The March of Time"--on radio or in motion pictures--which dramatized some of the news to be found in the magazine and enticed some thousands of radio listeners to become subscribers to *Time*. As circulation manager of the magazine during that Depression period, my motto was: "If you can't beat 'em, use 'em."

Later on, as president of Time Inc., and in recognition of the great virtues of TV as a new communications medium, I recommended that our company get a piece of the new action by going into TV ourselves. We did, to the extent possible by law, and we have not been sorry. I might add that we have also invested quite heavily in the *next* generation of electronic communication, currently known as cable TV, and are seriously exploring video cartridges.

Although the competition between magazines and TV as advertising media is still going on, it seems to me that a lot of general interest magazines, including those in which I have been active, wasted a lot of effort and money during the late Fifties and Sixties in trying to meet TV head on in a battle for the advertising dollar. For a while there--too long a while, it now appears--we argued almost exclusively in terms of audience size and cost per thousand readers or viewers. We got into some pretty fancy arithmetic on that gambit, and wasted a lot of our energies in internecine warfare. Finally, it dawned on us--as it had twenty-five years before with radio-- that numbers should not be the name of the game. It is true, of course, that TV is a fantastic mass medium, capable of reaching practically everyone with a set of eyes and ears. It is also true that several magazines regularly reach audiences far larger than do regular television offerings. The *significant* competitive fact, however, is not the mere size of the audience but the characteristics of that audience. It is not just the eyes and ears that count; what is between them is equally important.

Much to the joy of publishers, research has shown beyond question that the people who read significant magazines are the thinking men and women of our time. The magazine audience is a select audience, including a high percentage of people with the most resources, education, and influence. The magazine audience includes the generals and captains and lieutenants of the Command Generation--and the top revolutionaries as well. It includes a high percentage of the involved ones, the people who will lead other people wherever we are going.

We live, of course, in a participatory democracy, where all men are equal under the law and in their chances at heaven. But we also live in an Orwellian world where some animals are "more equal than others." Given the vagaries of the DNA molecule, some men seem born to lead and some to follow. Some are participators in the passing parade and some are spectators. It is to those whom chance has made more equal than others, to those who lead, and to those who participate that the better magazines particularly address themselves. No one is excluded, of course. Everyone who can stand the heat of the kitchen is welcome. But the selection of the audience for magazines is not really made by publishers; it is made by readers who voluntarily give their attention to editors because they hope to learn.

This elite audience for magazines-- thinking men and women--are testifying with hard cash as to how important magazines are to them. The voluntary circulation of the better magazines, despite sharply increased costs to the reader and despite the temptations of more spectacular media, has increased steadily. Certain kinds of people want magazines because they need them, because they feel magazines can help them in their personal and professional lives.

The journalistic medium that offers the highest protein content, and to which

readers bring their most serious attention, is the news-oriented magazine. Before they open such a magazine, readers know what they have a
right to expect. They have the right
to a hard, keen, skeptical, yet benign
look at the world's performance, reported urbanely and illuminated by
flashes from the past and blips from
the future. They expect the correspon-
dents, writers, researchers, and editors who have gathered and checked the
facts, written them up, and pointed
them up to have thrown out the fluff
and the empty calories, and to have
preserved the essence in its proper
sweet and sour sauce. They expect
these professionals to have argued a-
mong themselves about the significance
and implications of what has happened,
and to have had the courage at least
to intimate what readers should make
of it all and severally. In short,
thinking people look to news-oriented
magazines for the kinds of information
and the sophistication of judgment they
need for the strategic part of their
personal planning--and often of their
business thinking, too.

I do not have to enumerate the problems
on which we all would probably appreciate some help and guidance. The
cities. The environment. Drugs. The
race problem. Poverty. The Indo-china
war. The war in the Middle East. The
good life. The midi skirt. Boredom.
Any one of us could list fifty problems
of our time, each vying for the top of
the list.

But events are not all that is happening. There is also occurring a kind
of electrical phenomenon, something of
the kind usually blamed on global fields
of magnetic force, sun-spots, or subtle
emanations from moon rocks. Its name
is polarization. In their attitudes
on major questions, major groups of our
people seem to have withdrawn as though
by magnetism to the extremes of their
positions so as not to be bothered with

any such nonsense as finding a middle
ground with anyone else. Parents have
withdrawn to their pole and gaze frigid-
ly out at their children raising hell
at their pole, and at their own parents
complaining of neglect in California.

White people gather at the white pole,
increasingly wrapped in snow, and black
people gether at the black pole, wrapped
in impatience. Other polarizations involve consumers and manufacturers,
strictly private enterprisers and would
be socialists, Bible thumpers and the
sons of Cain, women's liberationists
and male chauvinists. I suppose the
ultimate polarity is between dyed-in-
the-wool conservatives and wild-eyed
liberals, the one group crying for the
imposition of order and the other for
revolution.

Many polarized people believe they are
the sole custodians of answers and that
all the answers are simple. But today's
problems are not simple, and they will
not yield to shallow analysis and instant or emotional solutions. Whether
we like it or not, life in the Seventies
is unprecedentedly complicated. What
seems simple is complex; what seems
obvious is subtle. In fact, anything
that seems to be, probably isn't.

There is considerable evidence that
millions of people--especially many of
our youth--have become inclined toward
simplistic solutions to complicated
problems, because for years they have
seen problems dramatically presented
and neatly solved on television within
a thirty-minute period, minus commercials. Millions have been tempted to
the fantasy that reality is something
either black or white, good or bad,
desirable or reprehensible--never anything in between. And millions are inclined to believe, on the evidence of
Dan'l Boone or *Mission Impossible*, that
the good guy always beats the bad guy
in the end.

Clearly, there is additional information to be provided if our society is

to meet its sophisticated problems in a sophisticated way, if the people who pull levers in polling booths are to pull the right ones for the right reasons.

All media are addressing themselves to this need, and doing it well. The protein content of both radio and TV is higher than ever before; I've never seen more thoughtful beards and shining pates on the tube. The better newspapers are now concerned not only with hard news but with its soft implications. And magazines of an informational nature have become increasingly cerebral, as befits the most sophisticated medium of all.

Thought, of course, is the most sophisticated action of which man is capable. Deep thought is work, and it is done best when the mood is there, time is available, and distractions are absent.

One trouble with the electronic world of Marshall McLuhan is that it does not stay put to await the convenience and the mood of the viewer; it puts on its show by the clock and goes away. Except in sports, McLuhan's world offers no instant replays, and the puzzled listener's "How's that again?" goes forever unanswered. A magazine, on the other hand, is a patient and thoughtful thing that will bide its time for the convenience of the reader. It can answer the "How's that again?" by offering replay at the flick of an eye or finger.

It would appear that our society's solution to current problems will be wise or willful, simplistic or knowing, largely in direct relation to the way in which magazines continue to help guide thinking people through the complexities of an ever-changing world.

DISCUSSION QUESTIONS

1. Describe the nature of magazines as an advertising medium.

2. What is the nature of competition, cited in the article, between television and news magazines? Which medium do you believe is more effective in news coverage? Why?

Reprinted by permission from ADVERTISING AGE; 4 June, 1973, pp. 76-77.

III-6

CLASSIC SALES LETTERS NEVER SEEM TO DIE-- OR FADE AWAY

Bob Stone

What are the magic ingredients of a sales letter which go to make it a classic?

In an effort to find out, let's look at two proven classics and one which will predictably become a classic.

KIPPLINGER'S BOOM OR BUST LETTER

Be there a reader of *Advertising Age* who has not received this letter, with update, from Kiplinger one, five, ten times or more over the past 12 years? One would certainly think the theme would have long run its course.

But Stanley Mayes, assistant to the president of Kiplinger Washington Editors, reports that over a half billion mailings using the boom-or-bust theme have traversed the U.S. mails over the past 12 years. And it isn't that Kiplinger hasn't tried to beat this letter. They've tested scores of letters against the classic. But every time they count the subs, boom-or-bust wins again!

Why? I've got a theory, and my theory

is, the lead of the letter is *irresistible*! Let's look at the lead and put the likely reactions of the reader in parenthesis.

NEW BOOK (great) AND MORE INFLATION (ouch) AHEAD ... and What YOU Can Do About It (ah--a solution for *me*.)

There's the promise of good news, a warning of bad news and the promise of a solution *for the reader* ... all in the lead. You've just got to read on. And millions do!

THE FAMOUS 'WIDOW' LETTER

For longevity, there's perhaps no match for *Barron's* famous "widow" letter, which rates high as one of the alltime classics.

The late Les Davis, of Dow Jones fame, told me that season after season the "widow" letter outperformed every letter tested against it. By the year 1952 he estimated some people had received this classic letter up to 50 times, with updates in copy. And years after Les' passing, the "widow" letter

STANLEY R. MAYES ASSISTANT TO THE PRESIDENT

THE KIPLINGER WASHINGTON EDITORS, INC.

1729 H STREET, NORTHWEST, WASHINGTON, D. C. 20006   TELEPHONE: 298-6400

THE KIPLINGER WASHINGTON LETTER THE KIPLINGER TAX LETTER
THE KIPLINGER AGRICULTURAL LETTER THE KIPLINGER FLORIDA LETTER
THE KIPLINGER CALIFORNIA LETTER THE KIPLINGER EUROPEAN LETTER
CHANGING TIMES MAGAZINE

MORE BOOM AND INFLATION AHEAD...and What YOU Can Do About It

Over the next 10 years, inflation will continue to gallop along at
nearly twice the rate of the 1960's...despite all efforts to roll it back.
And business will continue to boom, easily overcoming short range down-
turns, because the long term direction of the economy is significantly UP.

This may be hard for you to accept under today's conditions. But
the fact remains that those who DO prepare for more boom ahead will reap
big dividends for their foresight...and avoid the blunders others will make.

You'll get the information you need for this type of
planning in the Kiplinger Washington Letter...and the
enclosed form will bring you the next 26 issues of
this helpful service on a try-out basis. The fee:
Less than 54¢ per week...$14 for the next 6 months.

During the depression, in 1935, the Kiplinger Letters warned of
inflation and told what to do about it. Those who heeded their advice
reaped rich rewards.

Again, in January of 1946, the Letters renounced the widely-held
view that a severe post-war depression was inevitable. Instead they predicted shortages, rising wages and prices, a high level of business. And
again, those who heeded their advice were able to avoid losses, to cash in
on the surging economy of the late 40's, early 50's and mid-60's.

And now, regardless of short-range prospects, Kiplinger foresees
still more boom and inflation in the years just ahead. And our weekly Letters
to clients are pointing out profit opportunities...and also dangers.

The Kiplinger Letter not only reports, analyzes and interprets current developments, but gives you advance notice of new government programs...
political moves and their real meaning...money policy...foreign affairs...
investments...union plans and tactics...employment...wages...anything that
will have an effect on you, your job, your personal finances, your family.

To try the Letter for the next 6 months, just check and return the
enclosed form with your payment...or ask us to bill you or your company
later. Either way, the sooner you do this, the quicker you'll profit from
the penetrating forecasts, judgments and advice in each weekly issue.

Sincerely,

Stanley Mayes
Assistant to the President

SAM:kmb

A CLASSIC LETTER, Kiplinger has mailed over a half billion in a 12-year period, and the boom-or-bust theme with its "irresistible" lead is still coming up a winner.

was still *Barron's* control letter!

Here is the platform of this classic letter, 1952 version.

"DEAR FRIEND OF BARRON'S:

"Back in 1925, *Barron's* published an article suggesting how $100,000 might be well invested in securities for a widow with two small children.

"The plan was based on a set of ten rules for investors, stated in the article.

"The securities (stocks and bonds), all picked in accordance with the first seven of the ten rules, are today worth $227,000.

"The stocks are worth $176,000--over three times their original value of $51,000.

"Average annual income, for the entire twenty-eight years, has exceeded $6,900.

"Income for 1952 was $10,532.

"So here you have the story to date of how a list of securities, compiled in the third year of Calvin Coolidge's Presidency, weathered the wild twenties, the woeful thirties, and World War II-- *yet without benefit of the important interim supervision provided for in the last three of the original ten rules*.

"We have now reprinted these ten rules in a little *Barron's* booklet, with interpretative comment on each rule.

"As a piece of printed matter, the booklet is slight; takes you but a few minutes to read.

"But I believe you will agree, its every word is pure gold.

"You'll not only welcome the ten rules for their immediate value, I venture to predict you'll also come back to them repeatedly in the future--for their help on your ever-present problem of safeguarding what you have and making it grow and produce for you.

"But you can't buy this booklet. It's not for sale.

"*I would like you to accept it* in return for a little favor I want you to do. A pleasant easy courtesy that I think will interest you.

"*Barron's*, as you probably know, is a national financial weekly--the only one affiliated with Dow Jones, the world's largest, fastest business news-gathering organization."

WHY THE LETTER BECAME A CLASSIC

The balance of the letter described *Barron's* thoroughly as *the source* for investment insight, told the reader he could cancel after seeing two issues or accept a three-month introductory subscription at a special price. The booklet with the ten rules was free, regardless.

Let's try to analyze why this letter became a classic.

1. The letter was directed at people known to have an interest in stocks, bonds and other investments.

2. That explains why the story of the fabulous return on the widow's investment drew keen interest within the reader audience.

3. The dramatic story is related to following *seven of the ten rules* offered to the prospective subscriber. (Implied additional benefit to be derived from the last three of the original

McGovern
For President
410 First Street, S.E., Washington, D.C. 20003

Mr. John Doe Fill-In
123 Main Street
Anywhere, U.S.A.

Dear Mr. Fill-In:

Can George McGovern defeat Richard Nixon?

There is no doubt about it.

And he will do it the same way he won the nomination.

With the same courage and common sense on the issues that won him one smashing victory after another in the primaries.

With the same superb volunteer organization that won the admiration even of veteran political leaders -- and joined now by the workers of the Democratic Party.

And with the same outpouring of financial support from thousands of Americans who are weary of the Vietnam war and the neglect of our own society.

That's where you come in.

We are hoping that a total of one million Americans will eventually contribute to the campaign and become members of our McGovern Million Member Club.

Meanwhile, as in the primaries, we must depend most on those who care the most. We have reason to believe that you are one of them.

So while others might give only once to the McGovern campaign, we would like to ask those of you who are especially aware and committed to give more than once.

That's the only way we can be sure of being able to compete with Nixon's huge campaign war chest, bulging with large contributions from anonymous influence-seekers.

One of our friends has come up with an ingenious idea for making it easier to make a multiple contribution.

You can send us four checks all at the same time, but date the second check Sept. 1 -- the third check Oct. 1 -- and the fourth check Nov. 1. Then our campaign treasurer will not deposit your second, third, and fourth checks until their effective dates.

If you like the idea, you can use either your own checks or the enclosed blank checks with your name and address already imprinted on them.

This will enable you to make a monthly contribution without having to remember to do so, and will save us the postage and clerical costs involved in contacting you again.

With the help of people like you, Senator McGovern has already accomplished the impossible. The half-way point to the presidency has been passed. Now let's go all the way!

Sincerely yours,

Gary Warren Hart
Campaign Director

A COPY OF OUR REPORT FILED WITH APPROPRIATE SUPERVISORY OFFICE IS (OR WILL BE) AVAILABLE FOR PURCHASE FROM THE SUPERINTENDENT OF DOCUMENTS, UNITED STATES GOVERMENT PRINTING OFFICE, WASHINGTON, D.C. 20402.

George McGovern's successful campaign for the presidential nomination against overwhelming odds was made possible in part by the special devotion of many contributors who donated more than once.

Now you can help elect McGovern in the same way.

By contributing monthly between now and Election Day (November 7) you can multiply the power of your support tremendously.

To make it easy for you, here are four blank checks dated 30 days apart.

If you'll fill out all four and send them to us now, our campaign treasurer won't deposit your second, third, and fourth checks until their effective dates. (Or you can use your own printed checks, of course). This will enable you to make a monthly contribution without having to be reminded.

P.S. Another way you can help is to send us names and addresses of 4 friends whom you believe would also contribute if asked.

Just fill out the form at right.

McGovern for President
410 First Street, S.E.
Washington, D.C. 20003

Mr. John Doe Fill-In
123 Main Street
Anywhere, U.S.A.

_____ 1972

PAY TO THE ORDER OF   McGovern for President $_____

THE SUM OF _____ DOLLARS

YOUR CHECKING ACCOUNT BANK

BANK ADDRESS   SIGNATURE

CITY   STATE   YOUR CHECKING ACCOUNT NUMBER

Mr. John Doe Fill-In
123 Main Street
Anywhere, U.S.A.

_____ 1972

PAY TO THE ORDER OF   McGovern for President $_____

THE SUM OF _____ DOLLARS

YOUR CHECKING ACCOUNT BANK

BANK ADDRESS   SIGNATURE

CITY   STATE   YOUR CHECKING ACCOUNT NUMBER

Mr. John Doe Fill-In
123 Main Street
Anywhere, U.S.A.

_____ 1972

PAY TO THE ORDER OF   McGovern for President $_____

THE SUM OF _____ DOLLARS

YOUR CHECKING ACCOUNT BANK

BANK ADDRESS   SIGNATURE

CITY   STATE   YOUR CHECKING ACCOUNT NUMBER

Mr. John Doe Fill-In
123 Main Street
Anywhere, U.S.A.

_____ 1972

PAY TO THE ORDER OF   McGovern for President $_____

THE SUM OF _____ DOLLARS

YOUR CHECKING ACCOUNT BANK

BANK ADDRESS   SIGNATURE

CITY   STATE   YOUR CHECKING ACCOUNT NUMBER

Friends For McGovern

Name_____   Name_____

Address_____   Address_____

City_____ State_____ Zip_____   City_____ State_____ Zip_____

Name_____   Name_____

Address_____   Address_____

City_____ State_____ Zip_____   City_____ State_____ Zip_____

A POTENTIAL CLASSIC, this letter raised $1,000,000 on a $20,000 investment--one of the most successful of the direct mail fund-raising campaign for George McGovern.

ten rules is extremely powerful

4. The offer becomes *irresistible* when the reader is told he can cancel after reading two issues of *Barron's*, or accept a special introductory trial subscription. The ten rules booklet is his to keep, regardless.

THE McGOVERN 'CHECK' LETTER

History is likely to record that the famous fund raising program of all time was the direct mail fund-raising campaign on behalf of George McGovern. Scores of letters were used in the campaign, starting with an incredible seven-page letter announcing the candidacy and soliciting contributions. This letter produced $250,000 in contributions. When the campaign was completed, $15,000,000 had been raised by direct mail.

But of all the great letters Tom Collins wrote for the campaign, one in particular is destined to become a classic, in my opinion. (Letter illustrated on preceding page.)

The mailing cost about $20,000 to execute. It pulled a response approximating 25%. Some respondents sent one check, others four checks, as suggested. Average contribution was $40. Total contributions reached the staggering total of almost $1,000,000. One million dollars on a $20,000 investment!

Let's try to analyze why this letter was so phenomenally successful.

1. There were two great ideas in the letter: (1) All contributors were made to feel very much a part of the campaign through enrolment in the McGovern Million Member Club, and (2) an ingenious plan was developed for precommitment of monthly contributions through the medium of four post-dated checks.

2. The computer was utilized in a unique way to provide the vehicle for making the contributions.

3. The clincher was the offer of the free sterling pin with pre-addressed shipping label provided.

A classic letter in every sense of the word, one which will be adapted, emulated and updated for decades to come, I'm sure.

So here we have three classics. They don't come along very often. But once they do, they never seem to die or fade away!

DISCUSSION QUESTIONS

1. What are the major advantages of direct mail as an advertising medium? Limitations?

2. Which features of a good sales letter are identified in this section?

III-7

PROFITABILITY OF SPECIALTY ADVERTISING

William H. Bolen

Does the use of advertising specialties aid sales? This question is asked either directly or indirectly each time a business buys advertising. And rightly so.

The study presented here deals with one particular ad medium--specialty advertising, which is defined as any useful article imprinted with a promotional message or identifiable with the advertiser in some way which is given without obligation to select groups. Examples include imprinted pens, calendars, key chains, rulers, and wallets.

One technique for studying sales effectiveness makes use of a projection procedure to determine if sales have changed when the only variable is the amount of advertising specialties in the promotion mix.

Thus, the decision rule used in the study states that if the increase in sales is greater than the normal increase in sales using trend line analysis, and this increase is greater than the cost of the specialty promotion, then advertising specialties are said to be achieving sales effectiveness.

CASE STUDY

The firm selected for the study was a drug store, which had re-introduced advertising specialties into its advertising mix in July 1966. Prior to that time, it had used advertising specialties on a very limited basis, omitting them completely during the period from July 1965 to July 1966. To determine the effect on sales of advertising specialties, the sales data of the firm were studied for 13 months after the reintroduction of specialty advertising.

The firm, located in a large Georgia city, was an independent business, affiliated with a major drug franchising operation. Since its beginning in 1921, the drug store has remained in the same location.

Prior to July 1966, the advertising mix of this store consisted of one or more of these three types of advertising: circulars distributed as throwaways; cooperative advertising done with the national drug company affiliate; and advertising specialties on a very small scale. The owner of the store did not use other forms of advertising because his firm was a neighborhood operation and, he felt, could not afford the high

PROFITABILITY OF SPECIALTY ADVERTISING

cost and waste circulation of other media. The store did not promote itself to doctors as some of its competitors did, although prescription blanks with the store name printed on them were available to doctors upon request.

SALES EFFECTIVENESS MEASURES

Since sales effectiveness is when the firm's volume is rising due solely to the use of specialties in the advertising mix, the measurement requires that other conditions remain constant. First, the firm must not make any major changes in its operation other than the amount of specialties used in its advertising mix. Second, competitors must not make any noticeable major changes in their promotional efforts. Finally, the economy of the

area must remain relatively stable.

With the preceding conditions being met by the store, trend line analysis of sales was performed to determine the normally expected increase in sales for the test period. The projected monthly sales are given in Table 1. Then the projected sales data were compared to the actual sales to determine if sales did increase over and above the expected level.

By examining the data in Table 1, sales for the period were shown to be $4,532 above the expected sales level while the total cost of advertising specialties was only $240.

This decision rule may also be used to examine the effect on sales of individual specialty purchases. Table 1 also shows the five specialty purchases made by the store during the test.

Due to the repetitive exposure possi-

Table 1

SALES AND ADVERTISING IN DOLLARS
JULY 1966 - JULY 1967

| Month | Sales | | Advertising | | | |
	Actual	Projected*	Actual over Projection	All except Specialties	Special-ties	Total
July	$11,984	$12,674	$ -690	$ 60	$ 30	$ 90
August	12,901	12,687	214	42	55	97
September	11,184	12,699	-1,515	5	--	5
October	12,976	12,711	265	85	--	85
November	13,137	12,723	414	64	49	113
December	13,693	12,735	958	27	--	27
January	13,432	12,747	685	70	--	70
February	12,758	12,759	-1	11	58	69
March	14,705	12,771	1,934	46	--	46
April	12,240	12,783	-543	36	--	36
May	15,535	12,795	2,740	17	--	17
June	13,564	12,807	757	90	48	138
July	12,133	12,819	-686	25	--	25
Total			$ 4,532	$578	$240	$818

Y*(Sales) = $12,306 + $6,04X
Origin: December 1963 - January 1964

X Units - One Month
Y Units - Sales - Gross in Dollars

Table 2

SALES EFFECTIVENESS OF SPECIALTIES
ASSUMED SIX-MONTH CUMULATIVE EFFECT

Amount of Advertising Specialties in Force Six Months Cumulative		July - $30		Aug.- $55		Nov.- $49		Feb.- $58	
		(1)	(2)	(1)	(2)	(1)	(2)	(1)	(2)
July	$ 30	100%	$-690						
August	85	35%	75	65%	$ 139				
September	85	35%	-530	65%	-985				
October	85	35%	93	65%	172				
November	134	22%	91	41%	170	37%	$ 153		
December	134	22%	211	41%	393	37%	354		
January	104			53%	363	37%	322		
February	107					47%	---	54%	$ -1
March	107					46%	890	54%	1,044
April	107					46%	250	54%	-293
May	58					46%		100%	2,740
June	106							*55%	416
July	106							*55%	-377
Increase in Sales due to Specialty Use			$-750		$ 252		$1,469		$3,529

*Effectiveness allocation includes specialty purchase made in June (Table 1)

Notes: All data rounded to nearest whole number.
(1) Degree of total effectiveness attributed to each specialty item. Allocation based on cost of specialties. (2) Amount of total sales over the expected sales

bilities of specialties and for simplicity, a straight-line six-month cumulative effect for specialties was assumed. Since other specialties were added during the six-month cumulative period for the item under examination, it was necessary to prorate sales effect among specialties.

A direct percentage relationship based on dollar cost of specialties was used to allocate the sales attributed to each item. The June expenditure for specialties was not analyzed as to sales effect since the full six-month cumulative period had not elapsed at the end of the test period.

Results indicate a picture of increas-ing specialty effectivenss, as shown in Table 2. For each specialty purchase, the effect on sales was more favorable than the effect on sales of the previous one, suggesting that they may have a cumulative effect.

It should be noted that the July specialty purchase had a negative effect on sales according to the decision rule. Sales were $750 below the expected level.

Two possible reasons for this low sales level can be cited. First, this specialty purchase represents a relatively lower dollar outlay than the other specialty purchases. Second, the sales data for the past five years showed July to be a low sales month. The other specialty items all achieved sales effectiveness.

The August purchase generated $252 of sales as compared to a specialty cost of $55 for a favorable result under the rule. As shown in Table 2, the findings for the November and February specialty purchases were even more favorable. Taken as a group they created $4,500 in sales above the expected level at a specialty cost of $192.

Studying the individual specialties by means of an assumed six-month cumulative effect: (1) three of four specialty purchases generated sales in excess of their cost; (2) each specialty purchase caused a more positive effect on sales than the previous specialty pur-

chase; and (3) the four specialty purchases taken collectively caused sales to rise above the expected level to the extent that increased sales more than covered the cost of the specialty promotions.

CONCLUSION

Advertising specialties are effective from a sales standpoint. The specialti used by the drug store were found to generate sales over and above the normally expected increase in sales to a level exceeding the cost of the special ty promotion.

DISCUSSION QUESTIONS

1. Discuss the importance of specialty advertising for national versus retail advertisers.

2. What are the advantages and limitations of "specialty advertising" as may be discerned from this article?

Reprinted by permission of JOURNAL OF ADVERTISING RESEARCH; October, 1972, Vol. 12, No. 5, pp. 29-30. Copyright 1972, by the Advertising Research Foundation.

III-8

WHAT ONE LITTLE SHOWING CAN DO

Wendell C. Hewett

Determining the effectiveness of any advertising medium is a complex problem for business management. While there are sophisticated techniques and models in the literature that discuss the problems of measuring media effectiveness, to understand and implement many of these techniques requires extensive knowledge of higher mathematics and operations research.

Fortunately, several less sophisticated experimental designs can be employed by businessmen to test the effectiveness of certain advertising media. One of the less sophisticated experimental designs that holds some promise is the before-after design.

This article presents a case that illustrates how the before-after experimental design can be used to test the effectiveness of an outdoor advertising campaign.

The firm that conducted the experiment is identified as Company Y; the study was conducted in a standard metropolitan statistical area in the Southeast.

METHOD

The independent variable was an outdoor advertising campaign that consisted of a one hundred showing of billboards (24 sheet posters) in a standard metropolitan statistical area. The one hundred showing covered a time period of approximately five weeks.

The dependent variable was the proportion of adults that could identify the 23rd President of the United States. The outdoor advertising campaign focused on the identity of the 23rd President.

Using the SMSA telephone directory as a frame for all samples, interviews were conducted on three Monday evenings between 5:30 and 9:30 over a five-week time period; the first two samples each contained 350 respondents and the third sample contained 340 respondents.

RESULTS

The before measure revealed that, from a sample of 350 respondents, only two persons (.57 percent) could identify

184

the 23rd President.

Several days after the before measure was taken, a one hundred showing of billboards was placed into the SMSA. The copy on the billboards was: "Who was the 23rd President?"

The first after measure was taken a- bout three weeks after the billboards had been introduced into the SMSA. From a sample of 350 respondents, 27 (7.7 percent) could identify the 23rd President.

The outdoor advertising campaign was introduced before the second sample was taken; however, the billboard copy did not identify the 23rd President. A statistical test between the two measures indicated the difference (5.7 percent and 7.7 percent) was statisti- cally significant (less than .01). It was concluded that the proportion of adults who could identify the 23rd President had changed significantly after the experimental variable (the billboard campaign) had been intro- duced.

When a respondent correctly identified the 23rd President in the second sample (the first after measurement), inter- viewers asked: "Why do you know who the 23rd President was?" The respon- dents replied: "I saw the billboards and went home and looked up the answer."

Shortly after the second sample was com- pleted, the billboard copy was changed from "Who was the 23rd President?" to "Who was the 23rd President? Benjamin Harrison."

A third systematic random sample (the second after measurement) of 340 re- spondents was taken approximately two weeks after the answer to the question appeared on the billboards. A total of 121 respondents (35.6 percent) cor- rectly identified the 23rd President.

Statistical tests between the propor- tion of respondents that identified the President in the second sample (7.7 per- cent) and the third sample (35.6 percent) were statistically significant (less than .01).

In addition, the proportion of adults that identified the 23rd President in the third sample (35.6 percent) differed significantly from the proportion of respondents (.57 percent) that identi- fied the 23rd President in the first sample.

The experimental variable (the outdoor advertising campaign) appears to have increased the proportion of adults that could identify the 23rd President in the SMSA by approximately 35 percent. This increase is based upon point esti- mates obtained from the samples.

DISCUSSION

Results indicate that outdoor adver- tising would increase the proportion of adults that were aware of a product or service in the SMSA by as much as 35 percent. However, there should be some reservations about generalizing from the results of this experiment.

The billboard copy in the experiment was unique. The copy, "Who was the 23rd President?" created an unusual amount of respondent curiosity. It is doubtful that more traditional bill- board copy pertaining to a product, firm, etc., would create as much inter- est. The curiosity factor in the ex- periment appears to be significant. Based on point estimates of population proportions from Samples 1 and 2, ap- proximately seven percent looked up the answer to the question posted on the billboards.

This may illustrate the significance of curiosity-creating copy for billboards; however, it appears that the experiment would have been strengthened if more

traditional copy (advertising a fictitious product, etc.) had been utilized
by Company Y. In other words, the experimental variable does not appear to
be comparable with most outdoor advertising campaigns.

Another questionable area of the experiment is the before-after design.
The experiment would have been strengthened if a control group had been added
to the design. For example, during the
same time period a before and after
measurement could have been completed
in a similar SMSA that did not receive
the experimental variable (the advertising campaign). This control group
could have been used to measure the effect of extraneous variables on the
dependent variable in the experiment.

In addition, some questions could be
raised about the sampling methodology
employed in the experiment. An area
type sample would have been superior
to the systematic random sample taken
from a telephone directory. Interviews
should have been conducted each day of
the week at randomly selected times.
The survey results would have been more
objective if interviews had been conducted by personnel that were not employed by the sponsoring company.

DISCUSSION QUESTIONS

1. What are some of the features of effective outdoor advertising identified
in the study?

2. Comment on the suitability of experimental design in the measuring of effectiveness of the advertising media?

Reprinted by permission from MEDIA DECISIONS; May, 1974, pp. 110-112.

III-9

WHO GETS THE MAJOR MEDIA MONEY AROUND THE WORLD

Media Decisions

To secure an accurate picture of the rate of growth of advertising in other countries of the world, *Media Decisions* turned to Wally Ross, new executive director of the International Advertising Association, and to Jay Wilson, president of Starch/INRA/Hooper, which now incorporates International Research Associates, the authority on worldwide advertising dollar expenditures.

The resulting tables on the next two pages give the high points of this remarkable expansion in almost all free-world nations. They are based on preliminary findings of the IAA-sponsored Starch/INRA/Hooper, "World Advertising Expenditures" report.

A word about the tables: The one on the following page shows the expenditures by media (translated into U.S. dollars) within the countries that have reported so far. The table on page 188 shows the share of total advertising dollars invested in each of the major media in the 10 largest advertising countries of the world in the most recent year reported. The final table shows total dollars in 1970 and 1972 for those countries that have reported thus far, including the United States and 20 other active national advertising markets.

The extent to which the U.S. runs ahead of other nations in national advertising expenditures is startling. We're spending about eight times more than any other nation on advertising (over $23 billion in the U.S. compared to almost $3 billion in Japan). In the last few years Japan has moved past West Germany as runner-up.

But there is nevertheless a giant media market outside the United States, it is growing in leaps and bounds, and in such media as TV the growth is phenomenal-- and bound to continue.

The fastest growth advertising markets, as revealed in the data compiled so far, are Japan, France, Switzerland, Spain, and South Africa--each of them showing a 40% or more gain from 1970 to 1972, the most recent year reported.

The differences in favorite media in other parts of the world are striking. Newspapers still hold the lead everywhere (including the United States) except in France and Italy. In these countries a larger percent of total advertising dollars are funneled into magazines than into any other major media.

In Japan, magazines are relatively un-

Table 1

1972 EXPENDITURES IN MAJOR MEDIA WITHIN 16 NATIONS (in millions of U.S. dollars)

	Newspapers	Consumers Magazines	Trade mags	TV	Radio	Outdoor	Cinema	Other	Total
United States	$7,008	$1,499	$781	$4,091	$1,555	$292	*	$7,904	$23,130
West Germany	777	653	104	248	77	*	$19	462	2,340
Japan	1,021	161**		959	145	*	*	672	2,964
Canada	427	32	38	158	147	108	13	335	1,245
France	210	278	111	128	84	104	13	732	1,660
Australia	210	31	33	142	54	54	14	none	538
Switzerland	181	59	35	40	none	29	4	370	618
Spain	153	22	62	78	28	32	6	132	513
Argentina	41	12	8	46	25	15	4	33	184
Belgium	67	53**		1	2	33	4	112	272
Austria	73***			30	10	6	1	117	237
Finland	53	20**		16	none	5	1	59	154
South Africa	64	22	6	none	23	14	9	84	222
Turkey	14	2	1	8	14	13	6	89	147
Taiwan	16	2	*	15	4	6	1	11	55
Philippines	10	2	*	11	10	3	1	none	37

Source: World Advertising Expenditures (jointly sponsored by International Advertising Association and Starch/INRA/Hooper) preliminary findings.

* Included in "other" with point-of-sale media, exhibits, direct, etc.
** Includes trade magazines.
*** Includes consumer magazines and trade magazines.

Table 2

SHARE OF TOTAL AD DOLLARS BY MEDIA
WITHIN 10 TOP NATIONAL MARKETS

	USA	West Germany	Japan	UK	Canada	France	Italy	Australia	Switzer-land	Nether-lands
Newspapers	31%	33%	34%	43%	34%	13%	12%	39%	30%	33%
Consumer magazines	7	28	6	10	3	17	32	6	10	9
Trade magazines	3	4	*	10	3	7	*	6	6	10
Television	18	11	32	24	13	8	16	26	7	8
Radio	7	3	5	*	12	5	8	10	none	2
Out-of-home media	1	*	*	4	9	6	8	10	5	3
Cinema	*	1	*	1	*	1	6	3	1	*
Others	33	20	23	8	26	43	18	none	41	35
	100%	100%	100%	100%	100%	100%	100%	100%	100%	100%

Source: World Advertising Expenditures (jointly sponsored by International Association and Starch/INRA/Hooper) based on 1972 data except for UK, Italy
and Netherlands where 1970 estimates were used because new estimates
have not been completed.

* Included in "other"

Table 3

TOTAL AD EXPENDITURES WITHIN
21 LEADING NATIONS

	1970	1972	Percent Change
United States	$19,600,000,000	$23,130,000,000	+ 18%
West Germany	2,693,900,000	2,339,700,000	- 13%
Japan	2,115,300,000	2,963,900,000	+ 40%
United Kingdom	1,264,800,000	*	
Canada	1,037,200,000	1,245,100,000	+ 21%
France	996,600,000	1,660,000,000	+ 67%
Italy	489,000,000	*	
Australia	456,500,000	538,100,000	+ 18%
Switzerland	428,000,000	617,500,000	+ 44%
Netherlands	410,500,000	*	
Sweden	386,800,000	*	
Brazil	350,000,000	*	
Spain	275,000,000	512,800,000	+ 86%
Argentina	268,600,000	184,000,000	- 32%
Denmark	238,900,000	*	
Mexico	214,700,000	*	
Belgium	207,900,000	272,300,000	+ 31%
Austria	198,400,000	237,000,000	+ 20%
Finland	119,400,000	153,600,000	+ 30%
Norway	112,000,000	*	
South Africa	99,100,000	222,200,000	+124%

Source: World Advertising Expenditures (jointly sponsored
by International Advertising Association and Starch/INRA/
Hooper) preliminary findings.

* 1972 estimates not yet available.

important, but television is a bigger
entity than in any other country.
Television gets 32% of the ad dollars,
and newspapers get 34% in Japan.

DISCUSSION QUESTIONS

1. Explain the differences in media usage in different international markets?

2. How would you describe the rates of
growth of advertising in other countries?

PART IV

ADVERTISING AND ITS MANAGEMENT

Successful advertising does not exist in a vacuum. It must be a part of an overall marketing program. This section presents material on the overall marketing budget, on goals for advertising, on how to determine the total advertising appropriation, and on how top business executives view industrial advertisements.

Although it is impossible to give a "formula" approach to the total marketing budget, Clarence E. Eldridge suggests an outline which can reduce the guesswork that executives now resort to in determining and allocating the marketing budget. He then discusses the methods by which budgets may be assigned.

Roy H. Campbell, in the second selection in this section, discusses the "proper" goals for advertising and

outlines the various responses which an advertiser might expect. One of the important points Campbell makes is that advertising alone cannot insure success for a product or service. Product, price, and distribution strategies must be appropriate as well.

R.S. Alexander deals with one of the perennial problems in advertising: how much advertising is enough. He also discusses objectives and how to measure them.

Last, *Business Week* conducted a survey of top industrial executives and this article reports on the survey's findings. In general, executives representing companies with limited types of markets and customers rated advertising and sales promotion less important than those with widespread markets, customers, and prospects.

From THE ADVERTISING BUDGET, Richard J. Kelly and Herbert A. Ahlgren (ed.)
Association of National Advertisers (New York), 1967, pp. 25-34. Reprinted by
permission of the publisher.

IV-1

THE MARKETING BUDGET AND ITS ALLOCATION

Clarence E. Eldridge

It can be asserted with complete confidence that in a vast majority of cases the marketing budget receives far less attention--from both general management and marketing management--than it deserves. The result is that the allocation of the budget and, even more important, the amount of the budget are determined more by guesswork and instinct than by the application of scientific or even thoughtful analysis.

It can be asserted with equal confidence that management is called upon to make no decisions that are more important, or that can more significantly affect the health, growth and profitability of the business, than those involving the marketing budget. In many companies whose success depends upon effective marketing programs, the cost of marketing is the largest controllable expense; in some companies the cost of marketing the product is even greater than the cost of producing it--including raw materials, labor and packaging costs.

Among packaged goods marketers it is a rarity for marketing costs to be less than 10% of net sales; they are more likely to be much higher--perhaps as much as one third of net sales. This means that marketing costs are in al-most all cases greater than the company's net profit after taxes. Characteristically, the cost of marketing eats up as much as one half of the gross profit, leaving the other half to cover corporate overhead and administrative expense (including technical research and development), taxes *and profits*.

In view of these startling figures, it might naturally be supposed that every aspect of the determination and utilization of the marketing budget would be subjected to the most searching and critical analysis.

ANALYZING THE NEEDS

Of prime importance, of course, is the *amount* of the budget: how *much* money is *needed* to achieve the agreed-upon marketing objectives? How much *is affordable*, consistent with the agreed-upon *profit* objectives? How much of a compromise is permissible between need and affordability--without unduly jeopardizing either the marketing or the profit objectives.

These questions alone, and the difficulty

192

of answering them satisfactorily, would justify allocating an entire chapter of the marketing plan to the subject of the marketing budget. But these questions, vital as they are, are only the beginning. Of almost, if not quite, equal importance are questions such as these:

√ How should the budget be allocated among the several functions of marketing: advertising, selling, promotion, and marketing research?

√ How should the money be divided among individual products or groups of products?

√ How should it be divided among established and new products?

√ How should it be apportioned geographically?

These questions could be sub-divided still further into a veritable maze of permutations and commutations, but this enumeration should suffice for present purposes.

Generally, speaking, top management is likely to concern itself primarily--perhaps exclusively--with the first question: how much money *in total* should be appropriated for marketing purposes? The remaining questions are left to the discretion of the marketing executives in the mistaken belief that they represent mere "details" which can, and should, be delegated to a somewhat lower level of management. But whatever may be said of the wisdom of this delegation, the lack of wisdom in relying on the present methods of answering the first question--the amount of the *total* budget--would seem to be beyond argument.

It must be quickly admitted that finding a foolproof method of determining the marketing budget is not easy, particularly one that gives due consideration to the need for sales volume, the financial and profit needs of the busi-

ness for the immediate future, and the longer-range health of the business. Perhaps a method *cannot be found*, and if so, the more or less fatalistic approach to the subject which is now so typical may eventually be proven to be justified.

Nevertheless, the need for a more scientific determination is so great that defeat should not be conceded until a much greater effort than has yet been made is put behind the search.

HOW NOT TO ARRIVE AT
THE TOTAL ALLOCATION FIGURE

At present there are two *principal* ways--each of which has many variants--by which the amount of the marketing budget is determined. Which of the two ways is used in any given situation depends largely on the relative influence on top management enjoyed by the company controller as compared with the marketing vice president.

a. The Sales--Costs--Profits Formula
If the controller has the ear and the confidence of the chief executive (who must of course approve the marketing budget), the determination is likely to proceed somewhat as follows:

√ The company, in order to continue to show an increase in profits and thereby to satisfy the stockholders and entrench the management, needs to make x-dollars of profit after taxes in the coming year.

√ The estimated sales volume, based *not* on the estimates of the marketing department but on a computerized projection of present sales trends, is y-dollars.

√ The *gross* profit from that sales volume based on the controller's judgment as to what the prices should be--and on his estimate of product costs--will be z-dollars.

√ Other-than-marketing-expenditures-- such as general administrative ex- penses, R & D, interest on borrowed money, and taxes--will take xx-dol- lars.

√ The remainder--z minus x minus xx (gross profit minus GA and taxes minus profit-after-taxes)--represents the *maximum* amount that can be appro- priated or budgeted for marketing.

With a great many chief executives this is likely to be a pretty persuasive ap- proach. The controller, unlike his colleague, the marketing vice president, is a pretty hard-headed fellow. He is not bemused by the blue-sky optimism which sometimes blinds marketing people. He is less persuaded by what someone hopes or expects will happen than by a projection of what has already happened. He bases his approach on facts, not hopes.

He is unlikely to be influenced very much by some things which the marketing vice president may consider highly sig- nificant: a major breakthrough in prod- uct improvement, a price reduction, or an unusually promising marketing or ad- vertising idea.

He considers marketing expenditures-- especially advertising--as an *expense*, and he insists on treating it according- ly. He does not recognize that there *may* be a correlation between the amount of money spent for advertising and the resultant sales volume.

However, in fairness to the controller it must be admitted that in far too few cases has there been any proof that there *is* a correlation between the *amount and quality* of advertising, and the volume of sales.

Nevertheless, with all due allowance for his skepticism about the productiv- ity of advertising, it still remains

true that his method of determining the marketing budget--which was not unfairly outlined above--is *not* the best way to make that determination. It is too inflexible, too mechanical, too impervious to the factors and in- tangibles which keep the *art* of market- ing from graduating into the exactness and predictability of a science. On the other hand, there is this to be said for it: the method is easy to ap- ply. All that is needed is the ability to add, subtract, multiply and divide. It isn't necessary to be able to think.

b. Based on Marketing Department Guesses
The other way is to rely on the recom- mendation of the marketing vice presi- dent. Unlike the controller method, this requires very little in the way of facts. It requires only the more or less instinctive judgement of the mar- keting executive--sometimes slanderously referred to as "guessing." He knows how much has been spent in the current year and he knows what sales volume has been achieved, but he doesn't know what relationship, if any, there is between those two facts.

So he goes about the task of document- ing his budget recommendation is about this way:

√ In this current year we are spending x-dollars for marketing on an esti- mated sales volume of y-dollars.

√ Our gross profit in dollars this year will be z-dollars. Therefore, we are spending x/y% of sales and x/z% of gross profit in marketing.

√ Next year we hope to increase our sales by 10%, and our gross profit by an equal amount. To maintain the same relationship between sales and gross profit on the one hand, and marketing expenditures on the other, we should increase those expenditures by a like amount--namely, 10%.

√ However, Competitor A--on a volume no greater than ours--is outspending us.

This is not a tolerable situation. Therefore, in order to compensate for this factor, we must increase our expenditures by another 10%. Thus, in total, we need an over-all boost in our marketing appropriation of 20%.

It may be assumed that there *is* a correlation between marketing expenditures and sales volume. Ergo, if we spend the recommended amount of money, we can reasonably expect to achieve the projected volume; otherwise, we cannot.

Of course, the two methods depicted here are overdrawn caricatures of the different ways in which this important and difficult problem is actually tackled. But they are only slightly overdrawn. They represent two basically different philosophies--one based entirely on the necessity for making a *predetermined profit*, the other on what is *supposed* to be necessary for the accomplishment of *marketing objectives*.

The methods are different, and they are both wrong. The one is wrong because it fails to ascribe to marketing activities (including advertising) any productive role, or to recognize any relationship between marketing expenditures and sales results. The other is wrong because it assumes, without adequate proof or evidence, that there *is* a predictable correlation between expenditures and results, and that the correlation can be reduced to a mathematical exactness.

Probably no marketing company, certainly no sophisticated one, uses either of these methods to the exclusion of the other. Most companies try to balance the two--seeking to protect the profits which are the overriding concern of the controller, and at the same time giving heed to the marketing vice president's conviction that marketing support, in adequate amount, must be given his products if the business is

to remain healthy, to grow and to produce profits not only for next year but also for the longer future. In other words, a sincere attempt is usually made to balance *need* against *affordability*, sales volume against profits ability.

THE PROFIT RETURN ON ADVERTISING MUST BE SOUGHT

But there must be a better way to solve this transcendentally important problem than has yet been found. And it is incumbent on general management and marketing management alike not to rest until that way has been found.

The principal stumbling block lies in the general inability to state with certitude what results in the form of increased sales are achieved as the result of selling or advertising or promotion. To be sure, there are exceptions to this statement, but in the vast majority of cases it is true. And this applies not only to long-term results but to short-term or immediate results as well. If it were possible to say with any assurance that up to some point of diminishing returns an intensification of marketing acitivity would result in a proportionate increase in sales, the question of how much to spend would answer itself: namely, increase expenditures until that point of diminishing returns had been reached.

Even if the question could be factually answered *after* the fact--after the money had been spent and the returns were in --the answer would provide invaluable guidance for future years. If it were possible to determine how much of any given result had been attributable to advertising, how much to selling effort and how much to promotions, that also would help tremendously. And even if the effect of all marketing effort combined could be isolated and segregated

from the effect of other factors--such
as product quality, product improvements, competitive changes in pricing,
to name only a few--management would
be measurably freed from the present
necessity of flying blind.

AN APPROACH TO SCIENTIFIC ALLOCATION

How then, can the size of the marketing appropriation be more scientifically determined than is now generally the
case?

To that question I have no answer.

But I think it *is* possible to ask, and
to require answers to, a number of
questions which should at least lessen
the amount of guesswork that is now
resorted to:

√ What are the marketing objectives of
the company, product by product; in
what way and to what extent are marketing activities relied upon to
achieve those objectives?

√ How much advertising, how much selling, how much promotion, are needed
to achieve the estimated sales volume
and other marketing objectives? What
reason is there to believe that the
amount of money that is asked for is
the amount that is needed? How much
greater sales could be realized if
more money were spent for marketing;
how much less if less money were
spent? What are the reasons for
thinking so?

√ How important is the *amount* of money
spent for advertising, as compared
with the quality--the effectiveness
--of the advertising? What reason
is there to believe that the product
story which the advertising is intended to transmit is one which will
evoke favorable response and action
by consumers, and that the way it is
intended to tell this story will interest and persuade consumers to buy?

√ How do we know that the amount of
sales work provided for in the budget
is the right amount, that the depth
and intensity of coverage, geographically and by store type, is neither
to great nor too little? Would deeper
or more frequent sales coverage--even
though more costly per unit of sales
than the planned coverage--increase
total dollar profits by adding business which entailed no additional
general, manufacturing or marketing
overhead? Is there, in fact, any
provable relationship between sales
coverage and sales results?

√ How is the allocation of funds between
advertising and promotion arrived at?
What part of the money is to be spent
in the expectation that it will be
fast-acting and product returns trans-
latable into short-term profits; and
what part is designed to build for the
longer-range future? To what extent
has this been considered in the allocation of funds to advertising and to
promotion?

√ What part of the advertising appropriation is designed to *persuade* consumers
of the superiority or desirability of
the advertised product, in terms of
consumer wants; what part is designed
to *inform* consumers--of a new product,
of product improvements, of price
changes, etc.; and what part to merely *reminding* consumers of the product,
its name and its availability? Is the
amount earmarked for "reminder advertising" disproportionate to its probable resultfulness--or to the amount
intended for the two more basic kinds
of advertising?

√ Does the total recommended amount represent a correct relationship to the
expected gross profit? Will it permit
the achievement of an operating profit consistent with the company's requirements? Is it compatible with the
company's cash flow needs?

All these questions are relevant to the determination of the total marketing budget and its allocation among advertising, selling and promotion. Most of these questions will be difficult to answer. Some of them may not be susceptible to factual answers at all. But the mere fact that the questions have been asked and that serious attempts have been made to find the answers will provide some assurance that all facets of the problem have been explored and that the request for marketing funds has not been pulled out of the air or out of a hat.

ASSIGNING BUDGETS BY PRODUCT

But even after the *total* marketing budget has been determined--or perhaps even before as an aid in fixing the total budget--there are other questions that need to be answered. How much should be spent *for each product*, and how should that amount be divided among advertising, selling and promotion? This is surely not done by applying a uniform percentage of net sales, across the board. There are many reasons why this would be an utterly unsound procedure.

a. By Profitability

First, there is a wide variation--even among the products of a single company --in the percentage of gross profit. This figure can run from as low as 12% (or even lower) to as much as 75% (or even higher). In all probability the product with a generous gross profit needs more advertising and promotional support, per dollar of sales, than does the product with a narrow margin. And certainly, since gross profit is the only source of marketing money, the low-margin product cannot afford the lavish expenditure which the wide-margin product needs and can afford. As much as 25% of net sales dollars, or even more, is spent for marketing in the case of

some products. It would be rather suicidal for products with a gross profit of 15% of sales to spend 25% of sales for marketing!

All of this means that quite aside from other considerations, the mathematics and economics involved--and specifically the relationship between marketing expenditures and gross profit--must be considered separately for each individual product.

b. By Responsiveness to Advertising

Second, there is a vast difference between products with respect to their responsiveness to advertising, to promotion, and even to selling. There is likewise a great difference between products as to the *kind* of marketing activity to which they are most responsive. A product which is relatively new and which has yet to reach its sales potential needs and deserves more support than one which is well established, whose sales have reached a plateau and which can hardly hope to do more than maintain its present volume and share of market. The latter product needs only what might be considered a "holding action."

c. By Product Life Cycle

Then there is the product which for one reason or another is on the way out. Perhaps its whole category is becoming obsolete and its eventual demise is therefore inevitable. The need here is for a "delaying action," slowing the retreat as much as possible, liquidating the business in an orderly fashion, and "milking" the business for as much profit as possible in the process.

There is also the new product whose potentialities are as yet unknown. It would be unwise to make a large marketing investment predicated on the assumption that the sky is the limit as far as sales potential is concerned. And it would be equally unwise to assume in advance an ultimate level of sales which may be too low. In such cases the answer would seem to lie in regional testing of various levels of marketing support designed to "feel out" the product's potential in a prudent and affordable way.

Viewing the marketing budget problem for individual products from a different angle, it must also be remembered that there will be a great difference between products in their reliance on advertising as contrasted with promotion.

d. By Differentiation

Generally speaking, a product enjoying an important exclusive feature--whether of utility, convenience, style, economy or what-not--should be responsive to informative and persuasive advertising. All other things being equal, its sales should vary comparably with the success of the advertising in reaching more prospects. The same thing is true of products enjoying demonstrable and/or perceptible--although not necessarily *exclusive*--competitive superiority with respect to a meaningful attribute or consumer benefit.

Here again, except for the desirability of achieving through some form of sampling as high a degree of consumer trial as possible, the emphasis should be on advertising rather than on promotion. In such cases the advertising enjoys the great advantage of having something to say--something significant --and the important thing is to desseminate that "something" as widely as possible.

At the other extreme is the product which has nothing to differentiate it, so far as the consumer is concerned, from any one of a half-dozen or more competitors. True, even in such cases advertising may succeed in creating a pleasant and favorable image of the product or its sponsor, or even in pre-empting in the public mind a feature which is not exclusive at all. But generally speaking in cases such as this, advertising has very little to work on--and can do little more than

keep the product name in the consumer's consciousness.

This is the kind of situation in which, more and more, some form of promotional ingenuity is being relied on to maintain and stimulate sales. Bargain prices, premiums, contests--in which prizes running into the hundreds of thousands of dollars are offered--are resorted to in order to bring people into the filling station, the store, the bank so as to "build traffic." As a rule, these devices have little or nothing to do with the merits of the product being promoted, and there is a serious question as to the permanence of the business generated by the promotion.

This does not automatically condemn such promotions, but it does suggest the absolute necessity of budgeting with a full understanding of what is being done. Serious considerations should be given to such questions as these: how much is the promotion going to cost? How much *additional* business can it be expected to generate? How much additional gross profit will that increased business produce? Will any part of the increased business "stick"--that is, will it be permanent? If so, what reasons, other than wishful thinking, are there for thinking so? Is there any reason to believe that the expenditure of some part of the promotional money, if spent for advertising extolling the *merits* of the product rather than the lure of the promotion, might produce greater results--for the longer term if not for the immediate future?

In other words, all angles should be carefully considered in deciding how to divide the marketing money: the immediate pay-out of the promotion, the likelihood (or unlikelihood) of winning permanent new customers as a result of the sampling effected by the promotion, and the possible disadvantage suffered by diverting advertising money from *product* advertising to *promotion* advertising. The opinion may safely be ventured that not all decisions with respect to promotion are preceded by this kind of consideration

WHEN SHOULD BUDGETS BE CHANGED?

Budgets are an indispensable tool of management. They represent, in fact, a *profit* plan for the period in question, whether it be a year, a quarter, or a month. The estimates of sales volume should be as realistic as possible--if anything underestimating rather than overestimating sales. Product costs can, in most instances, be predicted with almost mathematical accuracy, and marketing expenditures are also subject to absolute and precise determination. Thus, two of the factors that affect profits can be predicted with absolute accuracy; the only *unpredictable* factor is the sales volume.

It goes without saying that once the chief executive has approved the marketing budget, it should be strictly adhered to--unless and until it is changed with his approval. But this does not mean, as is sometimes supposed, that the marketing budget should never be changed during the course of a budget period. Unforseen developments may require a cutback in the appropriation, and this happens with some frequency. Likewise, unforseen developments may justify an *increase* in the budget--and this increase is likely to be approved, or even asked for, with considerably less frequency.

The typical case in which a reduction in marketing expenditures is called for is one where, either for competitive or economic or other reasons, it becomes apparent that the volume budget is going to be missed regardless of the amount of money that is spent for advertising, selling and promotion. To adhere to the original budget figure would jeopardize the profit picture. It would be foolish to spend money that

is unlikely to be productive merely because it has been budgeted and approved.

The reverse situation is one in which the marketing program is working *better* than had been anticipated. The product is showing unexpected responsiveness to advertising, and there is reason to believe that a step-up in the amount of advertising will produce results in the shape of proportionately increased sales and--what is even more important--profits. In such a situation, the budget should be changed and such additional amount of money as can be *productively* employed should be appropriated. The budget should be a tool, not a master, of management. Obviously, such a change as this should not be made without the approval of top management, but the marketing director should not hesitate, when he has reason to believe that the expenditure of more money will produce more sales and greater profits, to ask for a modification of the budget.

TIMING EXPENDITURE RATES

In budgeting advertising expenditures, the timing of those expenditures is also important. It goes without saying, for instance, that mid-winter is not the most ideal time to advertise air conditioners heavily, nor is mid-summer a particularly propitious time to advertise the joys of skiing. But some other equally valid points are not so obvious, nor so universally recognized and acted upon.

For example, it is by no means uncommon for an advertiser to try to counter a sales slump by stepping up the intensity of his advertising; and it likewise sometimes happens that the advertising of a product that is "going like a house afire" is reduced on the ground that the advertising is not needed.

These practices may both be wrong. If

fundamental factors--such as the state of the economy, weather conditions, a competitive breakthrough improvement, or others--are unfavorable, it is extremely unlikely that the situation can be redressed and an increasing number of consumers persuaded to buy merely by spending more money for advertising. If the people who are already being reached by the advertising aren't buying, the people who might be reached by additional advertising aren't likely to buy either. On the other hand, the time to spend money for advertising is when conditions are *favorable*. Advertising cannot counteract unfavorable market conditions, but it can help to exploit the situation when consumers are able to buy and in a mood to buy.

OTHER FACTORS
AFFECTING BUDGET DECISIONS

There are other fundamental factors which should be taken into consideration in determining how much money to spend for advertising. One of these, as pointed out previously, is the product's relative superiority, or lack of it, as compared with competition. The more demonstrable, or provable, or perceptible the superiority may be, the more effective the advertising will be and, therefore, the more justifiable is the beefing-up of the advertising appropriation.

Another factor is the necessity for recognizing the correlation--even though it be a reverse correlation--between price and the size of the advertising budget. Advertising, no matter how brilliant, is no substitute for either an inferior product or a non-competitive price.

It sometimes happens that the most effective way to spend a given amount of money is to reduce the price rather than to spend it in advertising. This is particularly true, of course, when too high a price is proving a deterrent to satisfactory sales.

A number of years ago, a product with which I was familiar was experiencing deep trouble. Analysis and research indicated clearly that it was losing its business to a lower-priced competitor of approximately comparable quality. The situation was not of such a nature that it could be considered a temporary thing. The product was not competitively priced.

A recommendation was made to reduce the price to a point which it was believed would enable the product to compete successfully and at least retain its still dominant share of the market. The recommendation was rejected, the president of the company saying: "I would rather spend an additional million dollars in advertising than to reduce the price."

In vain it was argued that *no* additional amount of advertising--neither one million nor ten--would solve the problem, that it was not an advertising problem. The advertising budget was increased by one million dollars. The decline in sales and the loss in share of market continued without interruption. A year later the decision was reversed: the price was reduced and the advertising budget returned to normal and the sales decline was stopped. But in the meantime, precious time had been lost and a large part of the horse had been stolen.

The amount of advertising, if it is to be wisely determined, must keep in balance a large number of interdependent factors: the problems that are faced, the climate in which the advertising will be working, the strength of the product story, the competitive pricing situation, and many other things.

Sometimes the most productive way to spend "advertising money" is to improve the product or its packaging, to increase its availability and accessibility to consumers, and/or to adjust the price.

Finally, when all has been said and done, the decision as to how much money to spend for marketing and how it shall be spent must be made by individuals whose judgment is not infinte but finite. Neither facts alone, nor computers (in the present state of the art), produce foolproof decisions. But the fullest possible use must be made of *the facts that are available* in order to at least reduce the likelihood of costly wrong decisions.

There is one device, the potential usefulness of which has not yet been even approximately realized. That device is additional testing--"feeling out" the market. The flexibility of media today, which is greater than ever before, makes it practicable to test alternative levels of advertising expenditure on a regional basis. The areas need to be large enough to be significant, and they should be sufficiently isolated as far as media coverage is concerned so that the danger of infiltration can be minimized. A normal level of advertising support can be given in one test area, a saturation level in another, and a lesser amount (or even none at all, if desired) in a third.

In order to provide the necessary information as to the correlation between the *amount* of advertising and the achievement of particular marketing objectives, it is necessary to *eliminate all variables except the weight of the advertising*. The substance and the form of the advertising must be the same. The depth and frequency of sales coverage must be the same. The kind and amount of supplemental marketing support must be the same. And the test

must be run for a long enough time to make possible an assessment of the reasonably long-range as well as immediate results.

This kind of testing would perhaps not be practicable for the relatively small advertiser--one whose advertising budget does not lend itself to this kind of fragmentation; neither would it be of any value in deciding upon the amount of the current budget. But, quite conceivably, it could provide experience that would be valuable when it came time to set the following year's budget.

Granted, the results would be specifically relevant only to the immediate situation, but they could provide an indication as to the point at which, in that particular situation, increased advertising ceased to produce increased results: in other words, they could spot the point of diminishing returns. And from that *specific* experience certain generalizations could be drawn--not infallible generalizations but at least some conclusions that would be far more dependable than today's utter lack of such criteria. It is very doubtful at present whether any marketing director, when asked how his marketing budget was arrived at and how he knew that the amount was neither more nor less than was required to accomplish a given set of marketing objectives, would be able to give a satisfactory answer.

It will cost money to do the testing that is required, and even then the answer will not be so definite as to eliminate the need for expert judgment. But it will cost infinitely *more*--in dollars and in neglected opportunity-- if some way is *not* found to ameliorate, even though it cannot solve, this most difficult of all marketing problems.

DISCUSSION QUESTIONS

1. Based on the article and your judgment, what is the "best" way to determine the size of the marketing budget?
Explain in detail.

2. The article lists seven questions
which help answer the issue of the
size of marketing appropriations.
Evaluate each of the seven questions
listed in the article in terms of its
relevance to determining the marketing
budget and its allocation.

Chapter One of MEASURING THE SALES AND PROFIT RESULTS OF ADVERTISING: A MANAGERIAL APPROACH; Association of National Advertisers (New York), 1969, pp. 1-18. Reprinted by permission of the publisher.

IV-2

THE PROPER GOALS OF ADVERTISING

Roy H. Campbell

Five years of research has revealed that the sales and profits *caused* by advertising can be measured. These vital measurements can be secured through properly designed and executed field experiments. This book tells how to do it. But before we consider the use of field experiments in advertising measurement, we should take a look at the advertising process in operation. It goes like this:

Three months ago a copy requisition was issued in the XYZ Company's advertising agency which read:

Client: XYZ Company
Product: Wife-Saver
Medium: Daily newspaper display
Size: Full page
Copy: Announcement ad

This called for a consumer advertisement to announce an entirely new type of product that would take a great deal of the remaining drudgery out of housework. In the advertising plan, the goal defined for the campaign, of which this was the first advertisement, had been stated as: "Persuade 500,000 housewives to visit 12,000 XYZ dealers for a demonstration of the Wife-Saver, in twenty-six weeks."

Today is A-Day and this announcement advertisement is appearing in newspaper all over the United States. Let's see how this message might be received by a few of the readers of *The New York Times* who perceive the advertisement at home, while commuting, or at their place of work.

A housewife, who was previously aware of XYZ products thinks: "This seems just what I want. I believe I will go into Brown's Appliance Store for a demonstration when I go downtown on Thursday." This response was consonant with the defined goal for this advertising. But there were other entirely different responses, as we shall see.

Mr. Brown of Brown's Appliance Store reads the ad on the train and it reminds him to put in a window display of the Wife-Saver today.

A recently-married housewife, who has never heard of the XYZ Company, becomes aware of the brand for the first time.

An investor reads of the Wife-Saver and thinks: "That wought to increase XYZ's earnings." He calls his broker and places an order for 100 shares of XYZ common even though it is up two points from yesterday's close.

A housewife who now has two other XYZ appliances in her home calls Macy's and orders a Wife-Saver to be sent out and charged to her account.

A prospective dealer whom XYZ's salesmen have been calling on for years, without success, is impressed by the Wife-Saver announcement and finally decides to take on the XYZ line.

A young engineer who has been thinking about looking for a job with a more progressive company is favorably impressed with the design of the Wife-Saver which is illustrated in the announcement ad. He calls the XYZ employment department for an interview.

The purchasing agent for a large hotel chain reads the ad and says to his secretary: "Ask a salesman from XYZ to call." He has an idea that this innovation might reduce their operating costs.

A securities analyst who is writing a report on the XYZ Company, reads the advertisement and it confirms his belief that XYZ represents a sound "growth situation." His report is just a little more bullish than it otherwise would have been.

An employee of XYZ, who is having breakfast with his wife, sees the advertisement and says: "Boy! Look at that ad! I'll bet this new Wife-Saver really increases production. And if it does, I'm in line for a promotion. XYZ is really a good outfit to work for."

And even the senior loan officer of XYZ's principal bank reads the Wife-Saver advertisement and thinks: "The way XYZ earnings have been climbing with their successful new product introductions, we can probably increase their line of credit." He makes a note to discuss this at the next Loan Committee meeting.

ROLES AND GOALS AS MEANS AND ENDS

Thus, every advertising message has different results among its receivers. Each ad plays many different roles simultaneously and simultaneously contributes to many of the firm's goals. These different roles of advertising are means of reaching an end. An end is an outcome worked toward; a target; an objective; the goal toward which effort is directed. Means are intermediary steps or stages by the use of which a desired end is attained. The means-end *chain* as shown in Fig. 1 is a useful way of thinking about the relationship between means and ends within a business enterprise. In this example top management's principal end is to increase profits. This end of top management may be reached by two alternative means: (1) reduce cost, or (2) increase sales. One way would be to assign to middle management throughout the firm the end of reducing costs. This is regularly done by many firms with their cost reduction drives each year. But since we are concerned with measuring advertising as a marketing force, we will concentrate on "increase sales" which, it will be seen, is both an alternative means for top management and an end for marketing management.

MARKETING MEANS

Now, marketing management, in turn, will have alternative means for reaching its end of increased sales. The "Four P's of Marketing" are a succinct way of summarizing the controllable variables in the marketing mix. These are: Product, Price, Place, and Promotion.

Product may be improved by introducing a new product, or a new model or by restyling; or by widening the product line. A new package design is also a

Figure 1

A MEANS-END CHAIN FOR ADVERTISING

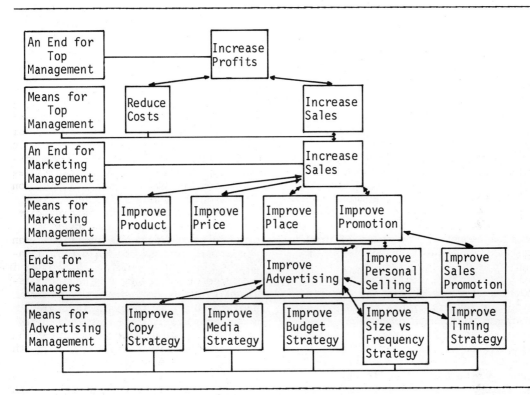

form of product improvement.

Offering a lower price is the usual way of improving price, but occasionally increasing the price, to take advantage of an upward sloping demand curve, is a possible price improvement. A different discount structure or a different system of sales commissions are forms of price manipulation.

Place improvement comes from increasing the product's place utility for the prospective purchaser. This might involve changes in the marketing intermediaries or in widening effective distribution, or in new distribution centers which would cut down out-of-stock and speed delivery.

WORKING DOWN THE MEANS-END CHAIN

Our concern is with the fourth P, promotion. The marketing means of improving promotion automatically becomes an end for the sales manager, the sales promotion manager, and the advertising manager. Translated into their own areas of responsibility the three ends are (1) improve personal selling, (2) improve sales promotion, (3) improve advertising. There are five means available to advertising management to improve advertising. These are: (1) to improve copy strategy, (2) to improve media strategy, (3) to improve budget strategy, (4) to improve size vs frequency strategy, and (5) to improve timing strategy.

Copy strategy may be improved by what is said and how it is said. "Copy" as used in this work refers to all of the physical elements in the finished advertisements; not only the words in headline, text and script, but also layout, artwork, photographic and film techniques, animations and sound effects.

The variables in media strategy are in selecting a media mix from among the alternative offerings of magazines, newspapers, broadcast stations or networks, outdoor and car card representatives, and direct mail services.

Budget strategy, i.e., the amount of money to be spent in advertising during a given time period, may be varied in absolute amounts or by share of product-class or industry advertising expenditures.

Within a given media mix, at a given cost, the advertiser has to make the strategic compromise of size vs frequency. Shall he use ten daytime sixty-second TV commercials per week, or fewer more expensive commercials in prime evening time? Double spreads every other issue vs a full-page in each issue?

Timing or continuity strategy determines the time period within a year during which the advertising shall be exposed, e.g., department store advertising is heavied-up between Thanksgiving and Christmas; canned fish advertising is concentrated during Lent.

SEPARATE GOALS FOR ADVERTISING?

Each organization unit within the company has both implicit and explicit goals. When top management states its explicit goal as "increase profits," this becomes an implicit goal of every subsidiary, division, branch, or depart-

ment of the business; none can escape. Marketing management's explicit goal of increasing sales is, at the same time, an implicit goal of advertising management even though advertising management might prefer to limit its responsibility to a less rigorous task.

It is quite impossible to assign to advertising specific communications tasks that are separate from marketing goals because if the assigned task is an *end* of advertising, it is *ipso facto* a *means* of marketing and thus, inextricably linked to a marketing goal. Rather than having its own goals, advertising has a continuing responsibility to learn more about the ability of advertising to serve as a means of attaining higher-order company goals. Can advertising be used to increase distribution? Will a consumer contest increase market share? Is it possible to change the coverage or frequency of the media schedule so as to increase incremental profit? Does an increase in awareness or an improvement in beliefs lead to an increase in sales? For every product or brand there are literally hundreds of unanswered questions like these. The continuing goal of advertising management should be to learn more about the complex process of using advertising to attain any or all company and marketing ends where advertising can be an effective and efficient force.

WORKING UP THE MEANS-END CHAIN

In the foregoing we have been working *down* the means-end chain starting with an end of top management or marketing management and finishing with an end of advertising. It is equally feasible, and perhaps more desirable, to work *up* the means-end chain in which each stepping-stone goal for one level becomes a means for the next higher echelon until the chain leads to a basic company objective at the top. The chain might be started by advertising management proposing an advertising end that it considered attainable, that would be an acceptable means for marketing management, as was done in the following true example.

A multi-advertising agency, multi-product manufacturer of brands sold through food stores, required as standard operating procedure that the annual *marketing plan* for each brand be prepared by the brand advertising manager and the agency's account executive working as a team. In this example, the marketing plan is for a product which we will identify as Our Brand.

Our Brand was number three in a growing product class which had more than doubled industry volume over the past five years. In this oligopolistic industry the three leading brands accounted for a substantial majority of all industry sales. The market share of Our Brand was 10% nationally and ranged from 1.6% to 18.9%, by geographic regions, while distribution varied from 16% to 87% by regions.

A study of one of the syndicated services reporting on market shares and distribution showed that for Our Brand there was a very high correlation between an increase in effective distribution and an increase in market share. When distribution went up, market share went up.

Special studies conducted by the agency showed that when shelf facings were equalized in height and width for the three leading brands, Our Brand, on the average, sold even with the other two.

This particular company generated its advertising funds for each established brand on the basis of so much per case for merchandise sold in the previous sales period. Thus, Our Brand seemed doomed always to whisper while its two substantially larger rivals could shout. The result, for the past three years, was that Our Brand had been unable to increase its national market share, even though it had kept even with industry growth. The problem was how to use advertising to increase market share within the limits of a rigidly controlled budget which was low man on the advertising funds totem pole.

The *advertising* ends proposed by the brand manager and account executive were: (1) increase distribution, (2) increase floor displays, (3) increase shelf facings. These goals would simultaneously be ends for advertising and means for marketing. How could advertising accomplish this within the limits of its relatively low budget? Here the planning team came up with a daring proposal: Cancel *all* regularly scheduled advertising and concentrate the entire year's advertising campaign in three TV specials of ninety minutes each. These specials would be high-budget shows with big name (and big pay-check) talent which would pre-empt the regular network offering in prime evening time across the country. Each TV special would cost several hundred thousand dollars. The *marketing* reasoning of these two advertising men was as follows:

1. The nine minutes of television commercials permitted in a ninety-minute show would be sufficient to directly induce purchase of Our Brand by millions of housewife viewers *if* the brand had increased distribution with adequate floor displays and adequate shelf facings.

2. The merchandising impact of these three TV specials with adequate support from field sales and sales promotion would secure the increased distribution, displays, and shelf facings which would lead to increased market share and sales volume.

At this point, our advertising team approached the sales manager and the sales promotion manager with their idea. The proposed plan was enthusiastically endorsed. The combined group decided that there would be six weeks of sales

coverage prior to each TV special during which the sales force would offer
a twenty-five cents per case display
allowance.

THE MARKETING SYSTEM

Now we have a complete marketing
plan, an integrated marketing attack,
with advertising, personal selling,
and sales promotion all striving for
the same goals (more distribution,
more displays, more shelf facings) as
a means for marketing management to attain its end of increased sales. In
fact, we have a marketing system in
action. And advertising was the cata-
lytic agent.

A system is a mutually interdependent
set of units combined to form an organized whole. In the case of the marketing system, it becomes a coherent unifi-
cation when the means-end chain binds
it together with each subunit of the
system having an end that is simultaneously a marketing means. There are
three distinct advantages in having all
marketing elements working together:
(1) the dangers of suboptimization are
reduced, (2) effort is concentrated on
the more important goals, (3) the span
of considered alternatives is widened.
Each of these will be considered in
turn.

The word suboptimal, of course, simply
means, "less than optimal." But suboptimization is used here in the more
specific sense introduced by operations
research. In this usage, suboptimization can be thought of as the attain-
ment of one sub-objective without regard to its effect on higher-order objectives. Let us say that we have a
company which is not using the marketing system approach. There is a Vice
President-Sales and a Vice President-
Advertising each reporting to the chief
operating executive. These two vice

presidents have learned the elementary
business lesson that the best way to
increase one's personal income and standing in the company is to preside over a
growing operation with an ever increasing
budget.

We will further suppose that the advertising VP has adopted the philosophy
of "advertising should play in its own
backyard; we will have advertising goals
separate from sales goals." So he a-
dopts the advertising goal of increasing awareness of My Brand by U.S. housewives to 70% next year. His proposal
is to switch from local advertising in
support of market openings to four-
color bleed spreads in national magazines, and a network TV show in prime
time with a big increase in the advertising budget. This advertising VP is
a very persuasive chap and his advertising plan and budget are approved.

Up to now, the market-by-market expansion plan has been concentration in one
market after the other to build a solid
consumer franchise in each market as it
was opened. The sales VP had worked
this out using home-delivered samples,
with a coupon, followed up by mailed
coupons. The sales force concentrated
on getting store demonstrations and increased display. There were thirteen
weeks of newspaper advertising on the
weekly food pages.

The plan had worked, although it was
slow and plodding. Distribution, market
share and volume had increased each
year. But in order to afford the glamorous national advertising, the local
advertising and sales promotion budgets
were drastically cut.

The result was that advertising attained
its objective--even exceeded it. The
measured increase in national awareness
was 84%. But it was attained at a heavy
cost to the company. For the first
time in three years, My Brand's national
market share failed to increase, sales
volume went up only in proportion to
industry volume, and distribution stood

still. That is suboptimization in action!

THE IMPORTANT GOALS

The second advantage of the application of the systems approach to marketing, that of concentrating on the important goals, follows immediately if marketing means are required to be advertising's ends. There are times, as we shall see later, when the most important marketing means is to increase brand awareness, and in that case increasing awareness is the most important end of advertising. But generally, means are closer to the final sale, and advertising management should keep its eye on ends that are more closely related to the pay-off of increased sales.

The third advantage of the marketing systems concept is that it widens the span of considered alternatives. All too often the considered alternatives for next year's advertising budget are: "Shall we increase advertising by five or ten percent next year?" If the firm is operating as an integrated marketing system, wider and more meaningful alternatives can be considered, such as:

1. "Brand A seems to have reached the decline phase of its life cycle curve. Why not withdraw all advertising funds and put them into R & D to develop a successor product?"

2. "The sales of Brand B have started to go up exponentially. Why not pour on the advertising pressure next year to capture first place for Brand B and hold back the introduction of Brand C until the following year?"

These kinds of sweeping alternatives, which can make the difference between great gains and little gains, are never thought of when the marketing operation is fragmented, with each unit intent

upon its own goals without giving any concern to broader goals of the corporation. This is the basic flaw in the so-called "communications effects" measurement of advertising; it focuses attention on the unimportant things.

A MODEL OF THE MARKETING SYSTEM

A marketing system, functioning in the real world, is an exceedingly complex organism. One helpful way of coping with the complexities of reality is to develop a model which is a representation of reality. Fig. 2 shows a schematic model of the marketing system for an individual firm in a free-choice economy. The dependent marketing variables are the things that happen in the marketplace as a result of the interplay of all forces brought to bear on the target market. We call these dependent marketing variables "marketplace outcomes." They may be conveniently classified under the headings of: (1) Advertising Memory Response, (2) Brand Image Response, (3) Marketing Environment Response, (4) Sales Response, and (5) Profit Response.

Variations in marketplace outcomes may be caused by variations in any of the relatively controllable inputs, namely; product strategy, price strategy, place strategy, and promotion strategy. One of the ways of varying promotion strategy is by means of varying advertising strategy. The latter will be our chief concern as we examine the different ways in which marketplace outcomes may vary in their response to advertising.

1) ADVERTISING MEMORY RESPONSE

The most frequently measured result of advertising is the memory of the advertising itself. This may be measured by the recognition method in which the advertising itself is used to stimulate

---

Figure 2. MODEL OF THE MARKETING SYSTEM

Independent Marketing Variables		Dependent Marketing Variables
Relatively Controllable Inputs:	Relatively Uncontrollable Inputs:	Marketplace Outcomes:

Product Strategy
Price Strategy
Place Strategy
Promotion Strategy
	Competitive actions & reactions
	Economic conditions
	Industry conditions
	Government regulations
	War
	Weather
		1)Advertising Memory Response:
		    Recognition
		    Recall
		2)Brand Image Response:
		    Awareness
		    Beliefs
		    Intention
		3)Marketing Environment Response:
		    Purchasers
		    Usage
		    Word of mouth
		    Recommendation
		    Consumption rate
		    Size of sale
		    Timing of purchase
		    Upgrading
		    Intermediaries
		    Distribution
		    Display
		    Promotion
		    Store traffic
		    Inquiries
		    Coupon redemptions
		4)Sales Response:
		    Volume
		    Share
		    Trial purchases
		    Repeat purchases
		5)Profit Response:
		    Incremental contributions
		    to overhead and profit

---

memory of the advertising, or the limited-exposure tachistoscopic technique or the aided-recall method.

2) BRAND IMAGE RESPONSE

Images are the pictures of brands in the heads of people. The term "Brand Image Response" encompasses mental pictures of the company, brand, product or service. As shown in Fig. 2, the dif-

ferent image responses form a continuoum running from awareness through beliefs to intention.

Awareness has several forms and dimensions. A prospective customer can have brand awareness of high or low saliency. High saliency is thought to be indicated by the response to a question of this type: "What brand do you think of when I mention 'cigarettes?'" This response, or top-of-mind awareness, is a composite effect of all previous messages received about the brand plus the experience of use, if any.

Beliefs may be expressed as specific product attributes stated by respondents or classified by the interviewer's assessment of the amount of information possessed by respondents. Beliefs about a company, product, brand, or service can also be expressed as semantic differentials along a pleasant-unpleasant scale. It is an indication of the degree of attraction or repulsion toward the considered object.

Intention may be defined as "a predisposition to act." Within the context of a marketplace outcome, it is a predisposition to buy the product or a predisposition to recommend to others that they buy the product.

3) MARKETING ENVIRONMENT RESPONSE

The literature of advertising measurement has dealt at length with the measurement of so-called communication effects (brand image responses) and the measurement of sales effects, but has largely ignored the intermediate zone of marketing environment response. It is in this area of shaping marketing environment, i.e., of changing the surrounding conditions or influences that lead to sales, where advertising can often make its greatest contribution.

The environmental effect of *"purchasers,"* i.e., of the kind of people who buy the product, can be of paramount importance as a determinant of sales. Experienced advertising and marketing men are aware of the surprisingly large proportion of total industry volume that is purchased by a relatively few "heavy users." It has been demonstrated that advertising, by changing its message strategy or media strategy, can appeal to these heavy users with marked changes in sales as a result.

Sales miracles can occasionally happen

when the product is offered for a *different end use*. One classes case is Listerine. When Listerine was offered for sale as a household antiseptic, it had a continuing but modest sales volume. But when the brand was advertised as a mouthwash to prevent halitosis, its sales volume shot up astronomically. This is now part of the folklore of advertising. A much more recent example of response to a change in *usage appeal* is the current success of Teflon coating for cookware. Teflon was first introduced (by manufacturers of cookware) as a coating that permitted no-fat frying. This limited appeal to food-fadists met with little success. Teflon was dying when Du Pont, with an improved product, decided to re-introduce Teflon coated cookware to be used for non-stick, easy clean-up cooking. Its dramatic success has become a modern-day addition to the folklore of advertising.

Word of mouth is a most powerful marketplace outcome. Favorable word of mouth derives, of course, from memorable satisfaction with product usage. But it can be enhanced by any improvement in the four P's which induce pleased product triers to tell others of their experience.

Recommendation may be thought of as a kind of expert word of mouth. It is very important in affecting the sales of consumer goods when the recommendation comes from an apparently knowledgeable sales clerk. In the industrial field the recommendations of engineers or architects may be crucial. Recommendation trends may be measured as responses to advertising.

Consumption rate and *size of sale* are closely related marketplace outcomes. Pricing, packaging and display strategies, and the advertising of special offers, can often cause larger units of sale with a consequent increase in consumption rate.

Timing of purchase can be affected by advertising. A very large study on the

response to increased levels of advertising for a consumer durable, not yet
released for publication, seemed to
show that larger advertising expenditures had the effect of advancing the
date on which the purchase was made,
i.e., of bringing purchasers of the advertised brand into the market earlier
than otherwise would have been the case.
Consumer desire for the newest model or
current fashion is a powerful environmental effect.

Upgrading is an important response to
advertising. For example, buying the
new car with accessories which have
been made to be essential or choosing
the self-defrosting refrigerator. This
phenomenon of consumer desire seems to
be not so much one of "keeping up with
the Joneses," as of "keeping up with
the advertising."

Changes in the marketing intermediaries
(wholesalers, distributors, brokers,
and retailers) can make a marked environmental change of where and how a product is offered for sale. This is largely
the domain of place strategy and the immediate concern of sales management.
Modern-day scrambled merchandising, where
drug stores sell high-turnover food items
and food stores offer fast-selling drugs,
offers examples of important environmental
changes in the marketing of package goods.

Distribution is greatly affected by advertising. The previously cited example
of the switching to TV specials to force
distribution is a case in point. Experienced marketers of products sold
through food stores feel that the typically heavy newspaper advertising on food
pages which accompanies the introduction
of new food products is as much advertising to the grocery trade as it is
consumer advertising. Advance reprints
of colorful magazine advertising are
wanted by the sales manager for distribution to the sales force so that his
salesmen can have "something to sell
against."

It is equally clear that advertising

promotes increased *product display* and
dealer promotion. Many retailers believe that well-advertised brands lend
themselves to mass floor displays, advertised specials, or loss leaders. The
force of advertising employed in this
area often exerts more differential effect on sales than advertising used to
cause a shift in brand image.

Advertising is also an important means
of increasing *store traffic*. Witness
the sweepstakes which only require
visiting a dealer to qualify for a chance
to win a prize, contests which call for
getting entry blanks at the point of
sale, or lucky license numbers which
encourage motorists to drive in to such-
and-such gas stations to see if they are
the winners. The correlation between
increased dealer traffic and increased
sales has not been overlooked by astute
advertisers.

Inquiries developed through advertising
are an important environmental factor
that leads to sales. The advertising
of encyclopedias, or of correspondence
schools, is devoted almost exclusively
to developing inquiries which salesmen
follow up. Coupons, clipped from ads,
which request catalogs or samples are
important forms of inquiries.

The distribution of cents-off coupons
by mail or in newspapers or magazines
are advertising functions. The display
advertising that accompanies the cents-
off coupon can have a marked effect on
the proportion of the coupons that are
redeemed. A high *coupon redemption* rate
induces high trial, and perhaps increased
repeat purchases, and if the product
rates high on user-satisfaction, can
favorably affect the environment for
future sales.

These changes in marketing environment
are so important that one of the first
things an advertising planner should
ask himself is, "How can we employ advertising to improve the marketing environment for the sale of our product?"

4) SALES RESPONSE

The principal ends for marketing are sales responses. These may be classified by *volume, share, trial purchases,* and *repeat purchases.* Variation in total sales *volume* and in sales *share* are widely used measures of marketing success. These data are the life-blood of the syndicated reporting services such as A.C. Nielsen Company, which measures the flow of goods through certain types of retail stores, Audits and Surveys, with its total-market audits, Market Research Corporation of America, which meters the flow of goods into homes by means of purchase diaries, and Selling Areas-Marketing, Inc., which records the withdrawal of goods from warehouses.

Two specific sales effects of particular interest are variations in *trial purchases* and *repeat purchases.* In this era of low or multiple brand loyalties, these effects are critical. If these are both going up relative to competition, they may be taken as lead indicators of future improvement in sales volume and share. Variations in trial purchases should be a focal point for advertising management's attention, as advertising is capable of greatly accelerating the recruitment of new users. Repeat purchases would seem to be more the result of satisfactory experience in product use, although the reminder effect of advertising must have some effect on rebuying.

5) PROFIT RESPONSE

The most widely articulated end of top management is to increase profits. As advertising costs continue to rise, top management continues to question ever more sharply the profit contribution of advertising expenditures. This, of course, is the most difficult of all marketplace outcomes to measure. The most appropriate measure is some form of incremental profit caused by advertising, i.e., the difference in the

firm's total profits with and without advertising cost in question.

If this incremental contribution can be estimated, it then remains to be seen if this increment is sufficient to cover the other direct costs of manufacturing and marketing the additional number of units of the product sold by advertising, and still leave an overall contribution to overhead and profit. This is difficult to do, but not always impossible.

ADVERTISING GOALS

The goal of an ad may be to increase awareness, but some receivers will rush out and buy. Another ad assigned the goal of increasing store traffic may only induce a low level of awareness among some of its receivers. But whatever the marketplace outcome, *all* advertising effects are *communications effects.* What else could they be, but the result of communication?

If the brand image is made brighter because of an ad, that is a communications effect. If the ad causes the marketing environment to be more conducive to consummating a sale, that is a communications effect. If an advertising campaign causes an increase in sales volume, sales share, trial purchases, or repeat purchases, these are all communications effects. Very simply, all results of advertising *are* the results of communication.

Advertising's principal job is to make sales at more profit than would have been made without advertising, just as it is the job of the sales force to make sales at more profit than would have been made without salesmen. If this is true, then it must also be true that the proper goals for advertising are those that will be profitable means for producing sales. Can there be any other sound reason for spending marketing funds?

ADVERTISING CAN'T DO IT ALONE

In order to have an advertising success, product, price, and place strategies must be right. Personal selling and sales promotions strategies must be right. Then and only then can advertising do its job and multiply a little success into a big success. For some products advertising is the most important single factor in the marketing mix; for others it is the least. Consider the relative importance of advertising in the marketing of toiletries versus the marketing of a commodity like industrial sulphur.

Does this mean that advertising should be withheld until a new product or a new model has actually been put on sale and proved to be viable? Not at all. It may be that heavy consumer advertising should actually precede the physical distribution of the product.

Experienced marketers, time and again, have successfully bet that their total marketing mix was right and launched a product with advertising used first to enthuse the salesmen and force distribution. But for this gamble to turn into a lasting success, all of the marketing P's have to be right, i.e., right product, right price, right place, and right promotion. Only then will the bet pay off.

DISCUSSION QUESTIONS
---

1. Explain how the "Four P's of Marketing work together to achieve a goal.

2. Evaluate the five "responses" the author puts forth to determine the outcome of a marketing expenditure in terms of their validity and reliability.

Reprinted by permission from BUSINESS PERSPECTIVE. Quarterly Journal of the
Business Research Bureau, School of Business, S.I.U., Winter, 1969, Bol. 5, No. 2.
pp. 3-8.

IV-3

HOW MUCH ADVERTISING?

R. S. Alexander

Planning marketing is at best a chancy business, for all planning deals with the future which is forever uncertain. Some business planning seeks to shape the future behavior and the results of such things as machines, materials, and power, most of which are tangible and measureable. The results of their use can be measured with some accuracy and can be predicted.

This is not true of marketing. Its work must be done with means that are largely intangible such as information, ideas, and emotional appeals which are designed to shape man's thinking and patterns of behavior. The fact that these intangible factors must be carried by such tangible tools as the salesman, advertising space, broadcasting time, and promotion pieces, beguiles management into making the mistake of counting or measuring the tools of transmission instead of tackling the seemingly impossible job of measuring the impact and effect of the intangibles transmitted.

This is especially true of advertising and promotion which, of all marketing tools, operate most completely in the realm of the intangible. It explains why most of the attempts to measure the results of advertising and to use the results in planning have fallen so far short of usefulness.

Our understanding of the problem will probably be furthered by a review of the steps by which an advertisement may be transmuted from the words or images in which the sponsor casts it into the effects he desires. A number of systems of such steps have been published. Perhaps the one most useful for our purpose is this:

1. The advertisement must attract the attention of the target public it is designed to influence. Advertisements that fail in this accomplish nothing.

2. The advertisement must capture the interest of its target audience to the point where it is read or listened to. If it fails in this, its message is never delivered.

3. The advertisement must convince or inform. The conviction must be positive rather than negative. For example, a windy, out-of-taste TV commercial may generate negative convictions that cause the listener to want nothing to do with the product or idea featured and to resent the sponsor. The information carried must be that intended by the advertiser.

4. If the advertisement is to be really effective, it must motivate its audience or an economical part of it to act, to modify an attitude, or to adopt an attitude that may lead to future action favorable to the advertiser.

Therefore, we may try to measure attention, understanding, information imparted, action induced, and attitudes or emotions changed or generated. The most widely used methods of checking radio and TV effectiveness really measure none of these but are content with measuring the degree of listener or viewer target exposure. The most widely used method of checking journal advertising measures at best only attention, reading interest, and certain aspects of memory recall.

If marketing planners are to plan advertising effectively, they must go beyond this and develop means to measure the extent to which past advertisements produced the effects desired and use this measurement to forecast the degree to which future advertising will aid them in achieving their objectives.

The phrase "achieving their objectives" provides the key to the greatest weakness of the present approach to measuring advertising effectiveness. The specific objectives of every advertising campaign are, or should be, different from every other. For any firm they should be an outgrowth of the objectives of the general marketing plan and will vary as the product mix, competitive situation, company strengths and weaknesses, and overall firm objectives change. This means not only that the job any firm assigns to advertising during a specific planning period differs from that assigned by other firms over the same period, but also that the advertising objectives of a single firm change with time.

This indicates that the problem of measuring the effectiveness of advertising must be approached piecemeal instead of in total. Many measures must be used instead of a single index. Each marketing manager must do his own measuring, instead of following the easy course of relying on a single index applicable to all firms. Perhaps the biggest mistake made in this area is the idea that we are dealing with one thing, when in fact we are seeking to measure many.

GUIDES TO THE USE OF ADVERTISING

If these observations are sound they suggest an approach to the problem which, while it will not result in an overall index, may provide a series of specific guides to aid the marketing planner in his use of advertising. The steps in this approach may be outlined as follows:

1. Start the process of measuring effectiveness when you plan your marketing operations by defining each objective of your advertising as sharply as possible, stating it as clearly and in as much detail as you can.

2. Estimate the dollar value of achieving each objective as accurately as you can.

3. Develop a method of checking the extent to which each objective is achieved.

4. During the progress or at the end of the campaign, apply these checks and translate the degree of achievement into dollar benefits from each objective and in total.

During the last couple of decades marketing management has come a long way in learning how to use objectives. But it is still by no means common practice to assign clear, sharply defined goal tasks to each of the several marketing functions. This is particularly true of advertising because both its effects and basic tools (appeals) are largely intangible. It is not unlikely that all too often decisions as to the amount and kind of advertising to be used and the part it is to play in achieving the total effect partake more of the nature of nebulous hopes than of sharply drawn plans. But if advertising is to really carry its share of the marketing burden the pieces that make up its load must be carefully selected and clearly described.

TASKS ASSIGNED TO ADVERTISING

As has been observed, the precise tasks assigned to advertising in the marketing plan must vary with each operating situation. But we may single out for illustrative purposes those that are fairly common:

1. To get orders.
2. To get inquiries.
3. To bring a general increase in sales.
4. To open doors for salesmen.
5. To serve as a selling tool for salesmen.
6. To induce a trial use of the product or service.
7. To inform.
8. To create or to change an attitude or opinion.

Probably most advertising plans have as their goals one of these or a combination of several of them, although there may be others imposed by the advertiser's market position, his overall objectives, or the difficulties he must overcome.

Whatever tasks the marketing planner may assign to advertising, it is vital that he envision them as precisely as circumstances will permit and state them as clearly and completely as he can. Only in this way can his plan be realistic. Without this clear understanding there can be no measurement of advertising results, for there would be no definition of what the results should be.

VALUING OBJECTIVES

The cost of advertising is expressed in dollars. To match costs against benefits, therefore, we must seek to express benefits (goal achievement) in the same terms. Only by doing so can we determine whether the advertising is worthwhile. Estimating the dollar value of objective achievement is not easy since some of the most important common advertising objectives are intangible, advertising results are so often delayed and up to a certain point cumulative, and the exploiting of advertising results so often depends on coordinated action of other units of the business.

Let us examine several of the common goals listed above and try to conceptualize methods of putting dollar values on their achievement.

Getting Orders While this is the simplest, in some of its phases it becomes rather complicated. It may be interpreted to include any immediate increase in sales. Such is the objective of much retail advertising. If a firm has a good system of sales records and marketing cost analysis, it should be able to cost out orders brought in by advertising and compute their contribution to net profits or to the aggregate of general overhead and net profits.

If the orders are from new customers, the problem is more complicated. From the past sales records of the firm; it may be possible to compute the average discounted present value of a new customer. If management knows its market, it may be able to sharpen this computation by including in the formula an element to reflect the sales potentials of the customers gained.

If the order is for a new product, it is obviously a trial order and its value can only be estimated on the basis of past experience and judgment as to the probable performance and appeal of the product's use or resalability. Something approaching such a judgment should have been made in the analysis of the new product before the decision to launch it was made.

Inquiries The value of inquiries can be computed by keeping records of the follow-up procedure to determine how many of them are turned into orders and the sales dollars involved. Marketing cost analysis should show the immediate contribution of a typical inquiry to either profits or general overhead costs and profit. If the firm has some experience in handling inquiries, a mathematical analysis of past performance should disclose a present cash value of a typical new customer resulting from the inquiry program. This might be made more accurate in specific cases by including in the formula an allowance for the sales potential of each inquirer if such figures are available.

General Increase in Sales This may be valued by the ordinary techniques of cost accounting and marketing cost analysis. In computing the present value of future volume from a sales increase that promises to continue over a long period, the wise analyst liberally dilutes promise with caution.

Selling Tools for Salesmen This is useful mainly in marketing to mercantile customers--wholesalers, retailers, and industrial distributors--for resale. By showing the customer the supplier's planned advertising portfolio, the supplier's salesman gives assurance of substantial user demand.

The dollar benefit from this is hard to measure. But in practically every sales force there will be some men who use this tool consistently and some who do not. Discreet inquiry among sales supervisors and perhaps among customers should disclose some specimens of both types. Mathematical comparison of their sales volumes and potentials should provide some basis for estimating the dollar value of this advertising benefit to the firm. Specific salesmen might be induced to experiment in matching performance with and without the use of advertising portfolios.

Opening Doors This benefit applies mainly to personal selling efforts directed to big buyers. It has two aspects.

First, it should have the effect of getting for the salesman a more sympathetic hearing from buying executives, such as purchasing officers and mercantile buyers, whose job it is to see him. It is very hard to put a dollar value on this. Probably all we can do is make an estimate based on salesmen's reports and talks with members of the sales force.

Second, it may gain the salesman entry into the offices of customer-firm executives whom he would ordinarily find it hard or impossible to see. This effect is apt to manifest itself in inquiries from these persons and to be reflected in the reports of salesmen if the reporting system is adequate. But in translating this information into dollar benefits, we are probably forced to estimate with little or no solid statistical base.

Informing and Creating or Changing an Attitude The benefits of both of these are very difficult to evaluate in terms of dollars because they are intangible. We must rely on estimates for both. Before deciding to advertise for either of these purposes, the marketing manager must fix at least the minimum dollar-benefit he expects to receive. He is foolish to spend money for such advertising unless the expected benefit exceeds the cost of advertising. From making this estimate it is only a short step to estimating the most-likely dollar return he may expect from it. This most-likely figure is probably the one best adapted to our purposes.

Some of these dollar-benefit figures will lie well within the area of measurable fact. Others are fairly far out in the foggy realm of speculation and estimate. But some attempt to evaluate all of them is necessary if the advertising part of marketing plans is to be comprised of something more realistic than a mixture of fear and hope. No matter how intangible and elusive some of the possible benefit objectives of advertising may be, and no matter how doubtful the accuracy and validity of our attempts to put dollar values on them, our thinking about these objectives will be sharpened and our planning decisions with respect to them will gain soundness from our efforts to do so. The end result we seek is not primarily to find the dollar values of achieving advertising objectives but to improve the planning of advertising.

Checking Achievement The process of checking the achievement of advertising goals must be planned when the advertising is planned. It may be necessary or desirable to build into the advertising program devices to aid in checking its results. Some objectives are specific to the individual company and its situation; the methods of measuring goal achievement must also be specific. No general index will serve the purpose, and even standard techniques will not do the job in all cases.

MEASUREMENT OF COMMON OBJECTIVES

Let us try our hand at suggesting methods of approach to the problem of measuring performance for several of the common objectives listed above.

Getting Orders Much retail advertising is intended to induce sales the day it appears or the day after. Mass retailing firms, especially the department stores and chain systems, have developed and use fairly sophisticated statistical methods for checking the results of such advertising. Such methods are based primarily on the principle of identifying and allowing for the influence of all other factors on sales. Residual change may with some degree of certainty be attributed to advertising.

The manufacturer's problem is somewhat more difficult. Unless positive steps are taken to identify and record orders resulting from advertising, they will be merged with the general flow of orders and lost. The problem of identifying them may be difficult. Some of them, but not all, will probably contain internal evidence indicating their origin. All orders from noncustomers not transmitted by salesmen probably should be investigated to disclose what triggered them, although such investigation will not show conclusive results. In maay cases it may be possible to include matter in the advertisement which will influence the form of the order so its origin can be identified. Even this is not infallible. The analyst will probably be wise to regard any total sales-order figure he comes up with as a minimun rather than as completely accurate.

Drawing Inquiries The time honored method of spotting the inquiries triggered by an advertisement is the inclusion in the copy of a coupon that may be mailed to the advertiser. Many prospective buyers, however, are likely not to use the coupon, but simply to write a letter of inquiry without indicating what prompted them to do so. This is especially apt to be true of the most valuable type of inquiry, that from a technical executive of an industrial firm or from a general executive of either an industrial or mercantile firm whose doors are not ordinarily open to salesmen. Again, the process of identifying the inquiries triggered by an advertisement must start with the planning of the copy so that it includes material that is likely to be repeated or referred to in the inquiry.

Obtaining a General Increase in Sales
It is very difficult to measure the degree of achievement of this advertising objective. The traditional method has been to ascribe to advertising all sales increases occurring within an arbitrary period after the publication of the copy or the conclusion of the campaign under measurement. If no sales increases occur, critics of the effort claim it had no effect while its sponsors ask how much sales would have fallen off had no advertising been done.

Some years ago, M.L. Vidale and H.B. Wolfe proposed a method for attacking the problem.[1] They based their model on the use of three parameters—the sales delay constant, the saturation level, and the response constant. Since these parameters represent only a few of the factors that may influence sales over any particular period, this approach needs to be broadened considerably.

The most promising method of attack seems to be based on the notion of isolating, valuing, and allowing for all factors other than advertising that may affect sales during the period in question. Changes in sales volume can then be ascribed with some degree of assurance to advertising. Possibly the most practical application of this approach consists of two steps:

1. At the expiration of the operating period to be studied, estimate what sales would have been during the period, but without the advertising campaign. In doing this, the usual methods of making a forecast of future sales can be used with the benefit of hindsight.

2. Compare this estimate with actual sales volume. The differences should be due to advertising.

This approach has the advantage of isolating the effect of advertising during periods of generally declining sales as well as when they are increasing. The result is still an estimate and partakes of the inaccuracy of all estimates, but it should be at least as accurate as the sales forecasts on which management builds its annual budget.

Providing Selling Tools for Salesmen
The effectiveness of advertising in serving this purpose may be checked in several ways. Interviews with salesmen should yeild at least some idea of their experience in using it. Admittedly most of the information disclosed is mere opinion and subject to bias, but it should to some extent reflect the facts. Such interviews may also indicate which salesmen are using the advertising portfolio and which are not. A comparison of the sales performance of the two groups and of the portfolio group before and after the portfolio was available may give a measure of its effectiveness. If it is worthwhile to do so, semimotivational research among customers and prospects may be used to get a reasonably accurate appraisal.

Imparting Information or Creating or Changing an Attitude The effectiveness of advertising in achieving any of these objectives can be measured by opinion research techniques which have attained a fairly high degree of development and sophistication. Let us take the development of a company image as an example. Consider the case of an international oil company, which we will call Intropet, which is invading the American market and wishes to establish a company image. Let us say that it takes the company image of Texaco as a standard and estimates that such an image is worth $50,000 000. Before it starts its campaign, it does opinion research to determine the dimensions of the Texaco company image. These dimensions can be expressed numeri-

---

[1] "An Operations Research Study of Sales Response to Advertising," *Operations Research*, Vol. 5, No. 3 (June, 1957).

cally. At the end of the first year of advertising, an Intropet company image opinion research report discloses that the campaign has progressed 10 percent of the way toward achieving the Texaco standard for Intropet. The results of the advertising can then be valued at $5,000,000. While the figures used are guesses, they illustrate the method.

Some of these methods can be used and some of them now are used in a limited way to precheck specific advertising pieces before publication by observation in test-market areas. This should offer sound guidance when the objectives are specific and immediate, such as getting orders, inducing inquiries, and increasing sales, and when the advertising is designed to use local media. When the results of tests with local media are used in planning national campaigns, the procedure is of dubious soundness.

CONCLUSION

If by the method described the dollar benefits of an advertisement or an advertising campaign can be checked with usable accuracy, it will involve much work and expense. In many cases the cost of checking advertising effectiveness may far exceed the losses likely to be sustained from mistakes in using the tool in the traditional manner. But if a firm's advertising budget runs into millions of dollars annually, it probably is a wise use of money to spend the millions more effectively.

Even though a procedure such as we have outlined fails to result in a measure of advertising effectiveness sufficiently precise to provide a reliable guide for marketing planning--and in many, if not most, cases it will not do so until the planner accumulates experience --the attempt to measure is likely to

pay incidental dividends. The process will force the planner to sharpen his thinking about the precise parts of the marketing job he wants advertising to do. It will force him to face the question, "Is what I want advertising to do worth doing?" He must think about these matters with the knowledge that when the hand has been played, a postmortem will be conducted to check the quality of his thinking and the soundness of his decisions. This should lend care, validity, and realism to his planning.

Proponents of advertising may fear that the widespread use of a method such as this will subtract from the volume of advertising used. This is not a foregone conclusion by any means. Certainly, it should reduce the usefulness of fear appeal, and of blind reliance on advertising as a marketing panacea, as tools for selling advertising time and space. But it is not unlikely that if the real dollars and cents benefits of advertising can be checked and forecasted, marketing managers will make more extensive use of it than they now do. It should mean also that the successful vendor of advertising services will be in a much sounder position than he is without such checks. Certainly the added knowledge should vastly improve the soundness and realism of the work of planning the advertising part of marketing.

DISCUSSION QUESTIONS

1. Evaluate the four-step "guides to the use of advertising" in terms of their validity and practicality.

2. In your opinion, how well does the article tell how much advertising to use? Think of topics which would improve the article.

BUSINESS WEEK, May 30, 1970, pp. 92-3, 96. McGraw Hill Publishing Co. (New York).
Reprinted with permission from the publisher.

IV-4

INDUSTRIAL ADS: THE VIEW FROM THE TOP

Business Week

The noblest tenets of modern capitalism hold that advertising builds business. But does it really? Many top
executives of industrial-goods companies are not so sure, and advertising people are grumbling more and more
that their corporate chiefs neither
know nor care enough about the role
that advertising plays in company sales.
This week new light suddenly broke on
the question, and what it reveals will
send shivers down many an adman's spine.
After more than 15 months of study, an
inpartial research firm has confirmed
that top industrial executives do, indeed, place very little faith in advertising.

The study, conducted by the New York
management consultants Cresap, McCor-
mick & Paget, Inc., was commissioned
by the Marketing Communications Research Center, an industry-supported,
nonprofit organization based in Prince-
ton, N.J. To find out what top management thinks of advertising, CMP interviewed key executives of 30 industrial
companies in many lines from printing,
construction, and office equipment to
gypsum products, paper, steel, machine
tools, and scientific instruments. Two-
thirds of the companies gross $100 mil-
lion or more a year in sales, seven are
between $25 million and $100 million,

and the rest have sales of less than
$25 million each. None of the 30 ex-
ecutives are identified by name, which
was CMP's way of getting them to speak
freely and frankly. They held little
back and, while they recognized that
advertising had its occasional uses,
in guilding up a corporate image or
backing up a sales force, they had little else good to say about it:

√ "Advertising as an over-all concept,"
the report notes, "is generally held in
low esteem. The main reason [the execu-
fives] gave were that they lacked satisfactory measurements, that advertising
is an intangible, and that they can see
no relationship between advertising and
profits. In fact, advertising is such
a minor factor in their opinion that
they believe it could be cut off entirely for six months without any loss of
market share."

√ "In only a quarter of the cases does
management set any objectives for advertising. Most of the objectives that
are set are quite vague--usually just
to 'support' the sales force in seeking
marketing objectives."

√ "In discussing the 'ideal ad manager,'
the quality wanted most by the men interviewed was creativity. Their ideal

marketing manager, on the other hand, was a much more broadly and deeply qualified man. They think he should be highly profit-oriented, have a strong knowledge of personal selling, and have a broad understanding of all company functions and the economics of the business--all these in addition to most of the qualities desired in an ad manager."

BACK SEAT

Answers to the key question, "How important are advertising and sales promotion to your company's sales and profits?" were governed largely by the breadth of the company's markets and distribution channels. "As might be expected," the report states, "executives representing companies with limited types of markets and customers generally rated advertising and sales promotion less important than those with widespread markets, customers, and prospects."

Yet even at that, two-thirds of the executives felt that advertising and sales promotion were "not particularly important," and at best played "a supportive role for direct sales activities." Several added that advertising would be among the first expenditures to feel the ax if the company were caught in a major profit squeeze. Chips are already flying, in fact, at some companies.

So why do they advertise at all? "Primarily," says the report, "out of fear of some nebulous, possibly dire, consequences which might befall them if they discontinued or drastically cut advertising and sales promotion expenditures while their competitors continued to advertise." As one steel executive put it: "I honestly feel that we're closer to being obliged to advertise, and I really wonder if it's worthwhile." Added another building-products executive: "We advertise primarily to tell people we're in busi-

ness. The contribution of advertising is small, and it's used mainly to build the corporate image and identity."

A big part of the problem is the difficulty of measuring advertising effectiveness. "I have a tremendous sense of unrest and dissatisfaction on this measurement question," said one executive. "I wish it could be done better, but nobody seems to have the answer." Another compared his company's advertising and sales promotion to shooting blind and putting out "a barrage without really seeing the target." Said a third: "Empirical data in this area are very dangerous and difficult to believe. I evaluate mainly on the basis of the reactions of customers and friends. It's intuitive." The closest thing to empirical measurement is counting ad coupons from prospects seeking information. In only one instance, however, did a company report tracing actual sales that developed from returned coupons.

SCATTERSHOT

Lacking the tools for measuring ad effectiveness, the company cannot set the goals so crucial to any successful sales-promotion program. "As it is now," says the report, "advertising is seen as bits and pieces--a trade show here, a publication there, a direct-mail piece today, a catalogue tomorrow, and so on. It is not felt to be in the mainstream of the marketing effort. Without product advertising goals--goals that are clearly related to marketing objectives--the mouth, so to speak, is separated from the brain, and advertising that seems irrelevant to anything often results. Seeing these results, it is little wonder that the true potential of advertising is not perceived by management."

In contrast to the "amazingly ambivalent" and "inconsistent" management attitude toward advertising, the executives "displayed positive convictions about their over-all marketing and personal-selling activities." These, they feel, are adequately measured by dollar or unit sales, and can be stacked up against goals clearly expressed in units, dollars, or market shares. "It is plain," the report continues, "that [the executives] think 'marketing' is much more important than advertising."

At the heart of such attitudes is an obvious communications gap between advertising management and top management. Of the 30 executives interviewed, 28 were dissatisfied with their advertising and sales promotion, and fully one-third had virtually no contact at all with their advertising and sales-promotion management. "Our major communication problem," admitted one executive, "is that top management doesn't tell ad management the company image which management wants to convey." In the same breath, the executive went on to confide that "unfortunately, the company executives don't know what the image really should be." Another executive complained that "much of the ad manager's presentation is 'canned' and borrowed from media presentations. This is an area where statistics can be manipulated to obtain an end. I'm skeptical."

To a large degree, added another executive, his ad manager is constantly pressured by the company's product managers who, in turn, are vying for a bigger share of the ad budget. "It's the 'squeaky wheel' principle," he said, "and the ad manager doesn't evaluate the alternative use of funds well. Moreover, the ad manager is prone to put lots of money into new products, when in fact these may be the least profitable."

THE PUBLIC

Apart from all the corporate tugging and hauling, there is one hopeful, unifying thread running through the report. That is the fact that top management recognizes that there are certain "communications problems" that clearly require an advertising approach. For instance, the executives voiced support of corporate-image advertising, "perhaps because a consistent company image would be hard to convey solely through the words and bearing of a diverse group of salesmen." Advertising is also the only way to project a corporate image beyond a customer list and to the public at large. Top management recognizes, as well, that advertising can spread the word rapidly about something new--whether a refurbished company image, a new product, or whatever. At the same time, several of the executives feel that mass product advertising provides support or a "door-opener" for salesmen, strengthens the morale of salesmen and other employees, helps in recruiting, and spurs the sale of products through sales representatives who are not under the same company control as regular salesmen.

SCORING

The road to reform, as MCRC sees it, is thus clearly marked. It consists of establishing and restating what most ad people and marketers know already but tend to forget: namely, that a basic part of selling is communicating ideas. "Advertising is selling," as the report notes, "just as personal selling is selling. Each can solve certain communications problems and should be thought of as a coordinated communications effort--each doing the part of the communications job that is easiest and cheapest to do that way." Any final sale, therefore, should be considered the culmination of a long series of communicating acts, performed both by salesmen and advertising working together. "Writing up the order," says the report, "is simply the last putt that wins the golf game. It follows a long afternoon of good and bad strokes with a number of different clubs --all of which went into the final score."

MCRC suggests several ways to start the

ball rolling. First, a company should identify its "communications problems" or the markets it seeks to reach. "Once the problems are defined," the report says, "one has goals for the combined advertising-personal selling communications effort. After these are established, it becomes possible to divide the problems between personal selling and advertising, and decide upon those problems where both activities should be used." With advertising objectives thus established, measurement of results becomes possible, and advertising--as part of the total marketing effort--can be integrated into the broader framework of short- and long-term corporate objectives. The report includes a complex formula for establishing this "hierarchy of objectives."

"None of the 30 companies in this study," the report notes, "appears to come anywhere near having an advertising program geared into a clear hierarchy of objectives. If they do, no one has told the top executives--which means

a serious understanding gap indeed." MCRC concedes that there may be situations where advertising can at best play only a minor role in company performance. "It seems evident, however, that in the great majority of cases, this neglect of advertising and objectives is costing the companies dearly."

The ultimate problem, the report concludes, is that advertising is simply misunderstood at all levels--from top management on down. This means there will be "much that is wasted as well as large opportunities that are missed." And the reasons, as MCRC points out, can be laid at no particular door. The correction can be initiated either from the top down by an insistence on more coordination, or from the bottom up by means of a clearer explanation as to what the corporation's advertising is trying to do. "The indications from this study," the report notes with wry understatement, "are that management would welcome such explanation."

DISCUSSION QUESTION

1. "The noblest tenets of modern capitalism hold that advertising builds business. Many top executives are not so sure..." Do you agree with these top executives or what role do you feel advertising plays in the growth of a business or company?

PART V

ADVERTISING STRATEGY

As the first article in this section indicates, strategy is a design for achieving an end. Advertising strategy is no different, it is the design of the advertising elements, product position, copy, layout, market segment, and others, which achieves the desired end, which may be sales, awareness, or some other goal. How one develops the best strategy for a particular product or service, however, is subject to question. This section presents a number of points of view on how strategy is developed, including some things not to do.

Perhaps the most important thought in the section is expressed in the first article: advertising is an art, not a science. That is not to say that principles are not applied, and that these principles cannot incorporate a scientific approach in them. However, when all is said and done, the "art" of developing advertising strategy will win out over the "science."

The article by Richard S. Lesser covers advertising strategy broadly. Charles F. Adams provides some partly tongue-in-cheek but clearly solid points for developing strategy. One particularly important point is to keep in touch with one's audience. He suggests nine

interesting possibilities, variations of which any student or practitioner of advertising should consider:

1. Ride a bus for ten miles in a metropolitan area twice a year. Talk to people on the bus.

2. Subscribe to *Playboy* and *Esquire* --but also to *Farm Journal*, *Argosy*, and *Grit*. It will cost you only $11.00 more. Then, remember to read them all.

3. Join the PTA.

4. Go to a wrestling match occasionally and watch both the wrestlers and the people watching the wrestlers.

5. Visit your largest department store and stand at the bottom of the escalator for an hour.

6. Listen to a speech at a political rally.

7. Work in a store for a week of your vacation. Actually sell things.

8. Grit your teeth and go see a Jerry Lewis movie, the most popular form of theater entertainment ever devised.

9. Drive leisurely across America

without eating in fancy restaurants.

The Hobson article comes from a book
published for the British advertising
industry, so the English may be somewhat different from that used in most
of the book's articles, but the principles he outlines are interesting and
useful. The remaining articles bring
out specific points about advertising
strategy, including one article questioning the necessity for "positioning"
your product or service.

V-1

WHAT ADVERTISING IS--AND IS NOT

McCann-Erickson, Inc.

Achieving a full understanding of advertising strategy resembles eating an artichoke--you must first peel off and discard the layers of what it is *not* in order to get to the real heart of the matter. Millions of advertising plans notwithstanding, these are the things that advertising strategy is *not*.

Advertising strategy is not a statement of advertising objectives or goals. "We'd like to make people think our product is the best of its type" may be a very basic advertising objective. It describes the intent of the advertising, but it is not advertising strategy.

Advertising strategy is not a statement of facts about the situation. Market share, distribution situation, demographic and psychographic characteristics of the target market, descriptions of competitive pressures in advertising and promotion, however complete and accurate, however fully delineated, do not constitute advertising strategy.

Advertising strategy is not a statement of product benefits. The statement, "Cadillac is regarded as a prestige automobile," is descriptive, but it is not strategic. The statement, "Brand X floor wax dries to a gloss without

polishing," is descriptive, but not strategic. The statement, "The cigarette has less tar," is descriptive, but not strategic.

Advertising strategy is not an isolated element within the totality of the product. For example, Pontiac's "wide track" is not an advertising strategy, even though it may be a key element in an advertising campaign. It is part of a whole product in which many other elements are important.

And, most important:

ADVERTISING STRATEGY IS NOT A SCIENCE, BUT AN ART

There is an unfortunate but widely held belief that disciplined definitions of advertising strategy and the creation of words, pictures and music in advertising are somehow in conflict, or that carefully defined strategy inhibits creativity in the execution of advertising. In fact, they are handmaidens working together. We believe that great advertising professionals are basically great strategies.

Mary Wells told *Ad Age*, "I think my greatest strength in the copy department

229

has really been strategy, because I have, I think, a greater talent for putting information together and coming up with a way to sell a product than I have for actually putting the words together."

We agree, and we believe that great strategy is the heart of great advertising.

What is strategy? To begin, strategy is basically a military word, born out of the most intensive form of human competition. Translated literally from the Greek, strategy means *generalship*. Again, a specific *stratagem* is an "ingenious design for achieving an end."

First, strategy never loses sight of its purpose of "achieving an end." *Strategy is result-oriented.*

Second, strategy is "ingeniously designed," which means it must go beyond a summation of facts and objectives to that *creative insight* leading to a more effective way to sell the product.

Advertising strategy is creativity applied to knowledge for the purpose of finding the most effective way of achieving an end. We believe that advertising strategy must encompass the totality of what a product or service is, and how it is sold to the consumer. It embodies the product's or service's reason for being; it is the product's most important property; it is the differentiating principle that the product embraces. Strategy welds all of the marketing factors into a cohesive unity that will achieve the end.

The development of great advertising strategy is not a mechanistic process. As we noted earlier, advertising strategy development is not a science, but an art. This does not imply that science does not play an important role in the formation of strategy. In fact, adequate and accurate information is essential to the strategist. In arriving at a strategy, all the faces of

the marketing mix can and should play a role: the product itself, with a real understanding of the product in all its dimensions being most important; the current competitive position of the product; competitive trends, including features, expenditures, and so on.

Knowledge of the demographic and psychographic characteristics of the consumer market is also vitally important to the advertising strategist. The same is true for pricing, promotion and all other factors in the mix. The strategist must be aware of the entire marketing framework.

But the sum of all this knowledge is still only knowledge, not strategy.

Translating knowledge into strategy requires application of the most acute insights into facts. Insightful interpretation is the ability to see new configurations. It means viewing a collection of truths with an iconoclastic but searching eye to discern patterns, to sense the fundamental principles that tie the facts together and give them cohesion.

A distinguished British writer, scientist and philosopher in writing on "Art in Science" once said, "The creative mind is a mind that looks for unexpected likenesses. This is not a mechanical procedure, and I believe that it engages the whole personality..." He might well have been describing the creative development of advertising strategy.

We must accept the fact that some minds are more disposed to this kind of thinking than others.

Those who think that facts produce their own conclusions are not strategic thinkers. Paradoxically, perhaps, the true strategic thinker who seeks to perceive the cohesive relationship between the facts is not dependent on absolute accuracy in any specific set of facts, nor is he dependent on having all the facts. While the informed strategist always

has an advantage over the uninformed
strategist, the secret of successful
strategy does not lie in the body of
knowledge or information that is available, but in insightful interpretation.

We can all think of any number of instances in which we have every reason
to believe that agencies, groups or
individuals had the same basic facts
available and had the same fundamental
goals and objectives. The actions they
initiated, however, were different.
That difference is strategy. Differences in performance results are products of those differences in strategy.

For example, we might assume that all
of the major marketers of canned fruits
and vegetables and their agencies have
available very similar information.
Presumably, they all have the objective
of communicating to the consumer the
quality of the product that they sell.

Yet, it was two very basic strategic
insights that made the difference for
Del Monte. First, there was the insight that consumers do not really have
an operating criterion for quality in
canned foods. This afforded an opportunity to educate the consumer about
the product category. However, such
an insight alone might have led to the
portrayal of a perfect peach or string
bean and a story about how such perfect
specimens are selected for canning.
We are convinced, however, that this
would have been a weak strategy.

The second very basic insight was the
opportunity for both candor and greater
meaningfulness inherent in portraying
the peach or string bean that looks
good, but does *NOT* meet the rigid criterion for quality. The strategy of
dramatizing the negatives gives vital
force to the execution of the advertising.

EARMARKS OF EXCELLENCE IN ADVERTISING STRATEGY

While a clear understanding of what
strategy is and what it is not constitutes the first step in achieving excellence in advertising, that understanding does not *guarantee* outstanding advertising any more than a coach's game
plan in football assures a great performance by his team.

A second question is in order: "How do
you recognize great advertising strategy?"

We believe there are at least eight earmarks of great advertising strategy.

Simplicity is the first, and probably
most important, characteristic of great
advertising strategy.

However complex the process that leads
to the generation of a strategy, the
strategy itself should be both simple
and capable of being expressed simply.

If you have a lot of trouble describing
or explaining your strategy, chances
are that you don't have a strategy, or
at least not the right strategy.

Great and simple strategic positionings
are usually easily and effectively
translated into great and simple copy
lines:

"It's the real thing. Coke."

"Come to Marlboro country."

"Wouldn't you really rather have a
Buick?"

"If you think all the good wines in
the world are imported..."

"We try harder."

Specificity is the second identifying
characteristic of great strategy.

The strategy for Swift's Butterball

231

turkey is a model of specificity--
that the Butterball name is an absolute
guarantee of quality, which frees the
consumer from the difficult responsibility of "picking a good bird."

This specific benefit was translated
very directly into a simple and understandable line, "This is all you really
have to know about turkeys."

Eminent advertisability is the third
identifying characteristic of great
strategy.

A strategic idea has little value if
you can't write advertising from it.

We are inclined to believe that one key
objective of Eastern Airlines' advertising has been to increase public
awareness of the importance of Eastern
as an air carrier. We suspect that
there was a carefully formulated strategy to achieve this end by making a
direct tie between Eastern and the
significance of flying. It also seems
reasonable to assume that the "Wings
of Man" campaign, which grew out of
the strategy, was more than ordinarily
difficult to execute.

In contrast, a strategy which achieves
the same objective more easily and
obviously by simply pointing out that
Eastern is the "second largest passenger
carrier in the free world" has, in our
opinion, proved to be eminently advertisable.

The fourth characteristic of great
strategy is *Durability* or the potential
for long life. Great strategies can be
refreshed continually by new emphases,
new executions.

If one studies the changing nature of
Avis advertising as the rent-a-car business has altered and matured, the singular power of the original strategy of
"trying harder" can be easily documented.
The semantics may be different, and the
support behind superior effort--"we're
number two" or "we're *going* to be #1"--

may now carry the credibility load of
the communication. Yet, even with stress
on different consumer service assets--
e.g., more sophisticated computeriza-
tion--the core of the original campaign
still carries a surprising amount of
communications muscle.

Resistance to counterattack is a fifth
distinction shared by superior strategies.

Some strategies are so powerful they
are almost invulnerable to counterattack.

Take the "friendly skies" of United Air
Lines--an unusual preemption of the air-
travel atmosphere, implying service and
safety in an environment of warmth and
understanding. Now, this simple strategy has been extended to include identification with America itself--"your
land is our land"--while still carefully nurturing the "friendly skies" property.

Recognition of limitations is a sixth
distinction of great strategy.

A few strategies for a few products,
such as "The Real Thing" for Coca-Cola,
can come close to being all things to
all people. In an increasingly segmented market, however, many successful
strategies must take the risk in order
to achieve specificity and selling power
of aiming directly at one segment of the
market. In the process of extending a
strategy to adjacent market segments,
it sometimes happens that the strategy
and/or the execution become diffuse and
lose selling power. However powerful
the strategy may be for that segment,
it could, if improperly applied more
broadly, undermine brand strength in
the total market.

For example, Del Monte, a very able
marketer, decided to aim its pudding
cup at the child market, trusting children's requests to influence the buyer
--the mother. This strategy, although
well executed, was a failure. The alter-

nate strategy of targeting to the mother has been successful.

We believe, then, that a key consideration is a realistic appraisal of limitations inherent in the strategy.

Extendability is the seventh hallmark of great strategy.

Great strategy is most effective when it can be carried into the total marketing posture and plans of the company.

Inglenook wine has vigorously asserted that it is the most expensive domestic wine and simultaneously adopted the posture of leadership in wine "education." This has permitted a natural extension of its strategic posture to promotional booklets and other support material of fundamental interest and value to the wine consumer.

High leverage is the eighth earmark of strategic excellence.

It is quite possible for the *direction* of a strategy to be right and still be of limited power. In evaluating a strategic idea, it is vitally important to consider the leverage that the strategy brings to bear.

In the case of Lufthansa, for example, the problem was readily apparent. The image of German businessmen and services was negative--unfun, cold, rigid and humorless. The direction of strategy was equally apparent--to break through the negative attitude of the potential traveler.

The obvious course would be to picture the pretty Frauleins, to stress the friendliness of Lufthansa people from ticket-taker to pilot, from mechanic to baggage handler. But simple negation of an unfavorable image would have had little leverage. The Red Baron strategy gained major leverage, not by negating the existing image, but by putting it to work. The existing belief in rigidity, precision and humorless

efficiency was personified in an interesting way, diffused with relevant humor, and a liability was turned into an asset that made advertising dollars work harder.

We believe that when advertising strategy bears these eight earmarks, we can be confident that it will provide the optimum opportunity for excellence in advertising. When these characteristics are missing, then it is time to pause and examine again whether the strategic underpinnings of the advertising will lead to achievement of its end.

SOME RULES OF THE ROAD IN THE DEVELOPMENT OF ADVERTISING STRATEGY

A clearly defined point of view on the nature of advertising strategy and ability to recognize the key characteristics of good advertising strategy are essential for *evaluation* of strategy.

It is apparent, however, that one cannot insure the achievement of good strategy through evaluation. Development of good strategy is an active process.

We have already described the key to great strategy as insight. It is apparent that some individuals have more innate talent for this kind of strategic insight than others; and that no organization has a monopoly on this kind of talent. Further, it is quite likely that different individuals may prove to be most insightful in different situations.

It is clear, then, that while the first step in development of strategy is choice of talent, the second step is making the most effective use of that talent. We believe that there are some conceptual disciplines which help insure that talent is used effectively.

The remaining section of this White Paper is devoted to a discussion of some of these rules of the road for talent utilization.

STRATEGY DEVELOPMENT REQUIRES THINKING BEFORE WRITING

Henry Ford once said, "Thinking is the hardest work there is, which is the probable reason so few people engage in it." It has also been said, "What no wife of a writer can understand is that the writer is working when he's staring out the window."

The easy thing to do in advertising is to begin writing advertising. But most great copywriters we know do not begin writing as soon as they become aware of a problem or opportunity. They are hungry for the inspiration of information. They value that mental exercise because they are aware of the need to start advertising thinking with a strategic brand positioning concept. This permits the creative process to begin before the thinking about the actual execution occurs.

This process encourages thinking to "start young" and simmer before any commitments are made to visual or verbal expressions. Advertising written too quickly is frequently difficult to "see around" after an initial commitment is made in some physical form. First notions committed to paper tend to take on a life of their own, sometimes unrelated to their merit or relevance to the problem. We believe thought must precede the slogan.

In the professional advertising agency, this "thought" is importantly encouraged --in the developmental process--by exchange, discussion and argument between account "marketing" people and the "creative" groups assigned the critical job of "making" the advertising.

STRATEGIC DEVELOPMENT FORCES EXAMINATION OF ALTERNATIVES

When alternate strategic positionings are defined in advance, there is a better chance that each will be given equal consideration. It sometimes happens that an executional idea or insight disposes the agency team so favorably toward one positioning that alternatives are not adequately examined. We believe that it is important to ensure that all positioning alternatives are inspected, analyzed and evaluated before they are discarded in favor of the final strategic positioning.

STRATEGIC DEVELOPMENT EXPANDS THE OPPORTUNITY FOR CREATIVITY, AND DIRECTS CREATIVE EFFORT IN PRODUCTIVE DIRECTIONS

When the strategic positioning of a product is virtually identical to that of its competitors, there is a temptation (or sometimes a necessity) to turn to devices or borrowed interest to enhance the effectiveness of the advertising campaign. The more creative the basic strategic positioning of the product, the greater the opportunity for creativity in advertising. Uniqueness in product position increases the chances for uniqueness in copy.

Nyquil, Vick's liquid cold remedy, is a good example. Its positioning strategy was to team the potent ideas of taking care of a cold and getting a good night's rest. This unique positioning of the product did more than tap sleep/cold cure needs. It freed the product from the limitation of traditional cold remedy claims ("relieves congestion 10 ways," "fast, fast relief." etc.). The product positioning idea gave the creative people the opportunity and the stimulus to deliver a fresh and distinctive message in a fresh and distinctive way.

STRATEGIC DEVELOPMENT MAKES EFFECTIVE USE OF RELEVANT INFORMATION

We believe that talented professionals learn to let available information wash over them. They learn to incubate the totality of available information. To operate on the basis of a concise summary of the facts is to begin thinking with conclusions, to limit the range of personal insight and creativity in interpretation.

Real "style," in creative strategic thinking, is not to devote yourself, at the outset, to ranking the available factual information in terms of its "hardness." Rather, it is really essential to make "a quick trip" through all the available facts and let them incubate into insight. In a surprisingly short time, patterns begin to emerge out of information. New configurations are formed of old parts. And these new configurations generate new insights.

Insights are not achieved out of the weight of the accumulated facts, but out of a pattern. Even information of marginal validity or only apparent relevance often makes an important contribution as the trigger for reorganizing old information into fodder for new ideas.

"PROJECTIVE POWER" IS AN ESSENTIAL STRATEGIC INPUT

Almost anyone can design an advertising strategy to talk to himself or to others who are exactly like himself. It takes more skill and more experience for a professional to project himself into social frameworks or perspectives other than his own. We call this "projective power."

A dog lover instantly understands why some very high-priced pet products succeed. Someone who does not love dogs must arrive at true empathy with his audience by a sheer ability to project

himself into the moods, needs and perception of those who are targets of his strategic thinking.

We believe it is essential for a strategist to understand, truly and clearly, points of view he does not share or life experiences of which he has not been a part. The strategist need not vote for Wallace, or like Wallace, but he must understand why other people do.

Experience and training are essential ingredients in bringing these personal forces into balance. Just as the strategist must have the sensitivity to generate the new point of view, the different perspective, and act on it, so he must also learn not to fear the obvious. It may be that the soundest strategy is the one that is the most immediately apparent. The courage to implement the obvious is at least as difficult as the courage to implement the new and different point of view.

Then, too, it sometimes happens that information which is readily available is not effectively used in the development of advertising.

For example, for many years Greyhound advertised *economy* relative to other modes of transportation. Everyone *knew* Greyhound was the cheapest way to travel. In fact, awareness of the economy of bus travel became a negative image problem.

When data showed that the main competition to bus travel was the family car, it was time to put that information to work in terms of strategy, as exemplified by "Leave the driving to us." More time passed, and the economy image faded. Research then showed that people had begun to think that Greyhound was more expensive than it was. New information suggested that the small air trunk line was an increasingly popular form of inter-city transportation and thus a growing Greyhound competitor. This could justify a legitimate strategic return to a new form of the traditional "economy" argument used so long by the bus line.

It is the function of strategic monitoring to determine the point in time at which such changes should be made and to insure that they are made.

A professional advertising strategist must be willing, once he has exercised his judgment in selecting a strategy, to accept the price of decisiveness. There is always the risk that a strategy could be wrong or could backfire. But it is inevitable that such risks be accepted. Unwillingness to accept risk most often produces all but invisible advertising.

Confidence also leads to what we believe is a key quality for the advertising strategist: the ability to make effective use of his inner resources, and to keep those inner resources tuned to the world.

For example, the strategic thinker must have the sensitivity to feel the genuine change under way in our society, the acuity to distinguish between fads and superficial shifts and true trends in consumer behavior and tastes. Then, he must have the courage and conviction to make effective use of that understanding to achieve his objectives.

So much advertising sinks without a trace in today's competitive and cluttered environment. The key lesson: advertising that stands out from the crowd, that commands attention and involvement, begins with a distinctinve *idea* and does not depend on a distinctive execution alone.

DISCUSSION QUESTIONS

1. Is advertising an art or a science? Explain.

2. Distinguish between "extendability" and "high leverage" as characteristics of good advertising strategy.

3. Describe the broad steps of designing a good advertising strategy.

American Association of Advertising Agencies, Western Region Convention, Santa Barbara, Calif., Oct. 15, 1969. Reprinted with permission of the author.

V-2

SOME LESSONS UNLEARNED IN TWENTY YEARS OF CREATIVE ADVERTISING

Charles F. Adams

I came into advertising in 1949 as a copywriter. I wasn't too good in the beginning, but I got better, and today I'm the president of the agency. I don't write as much as I used to, because there just isn't as much time for it. Now I talk on the phone a lot--and go to meetings--and call on clients-- and make presentations--and make speeches But writing advertising is still my first love, and I do it at night an on weekends and on airplanes. To me, it remains the great satisfaction in our business, and I still have a school- boy's pride in seeing my efforts in print and on film.

$250 MILLION WORTH OF ADVERTISING

Someone once figured out that I have written a quarter of a billion dollars worth of advertising. I was impressed with myself at the time, but on current reflection, I don't think it means too much. If I had worked on just local accounts, that would be a much smaller figure, and I would have worked just as hard and, perhaps, accomplished just as much. But maybe a quarter of a bil- lion is substantial enough to let me

say a word or two on the subject of creative advertising and the creative mind. And in that belief, I'll proceed, for I do have a few observations I would like to make. Not about things I have learned about creativity, but things I have un-learned about it. Things I thought were probably true when I started out, and which I now be- lieve are not true.

TOO MUCH CREATIVITY CAN SUFFOCATE A GOOD IDEA

The first one is that *it always pays to be creative*. I don't think it does, and I'll tell you what I mean by that. Creative people have a pride in being creative. Someone puts his arm around you and says, "This is our creative director," and you get a shiver right down your back. You're creative. You create things. Like God. So, when you sit down with a product proposition and a blank piece of paper, your juices get going, and you set out to find some great, hidden, clever way of saying it. You want to be dazzling and brilliant. That may be all wrong. In fact, it very frequently is. More often than not, the truth is staring you right in the face and all you have to do is write it down. Frequently the facts are what will sell, and too much creativity will just suffocate them.

It was Macaulay who remarked that the best way to say a thing is to *say* it. This is often true in advertising. If you are fortunate enough to be at work on behalf of a product with some really startling advantages, you might try just telling people what they are. If the news is big enough, too much creativity is just going to louse up your message. If, for example, you have a lawnmower that runs on water instead of gasoline, then you'd better tell your audience what you've got without beating around the bush too much. Some creative people are so accustomed to working with marginal product differences that require artificial dramatization, that they forget that the very idea of the product can be its own best advertising vehicle.

In the fascinating new book "The 400 Best Read Ads in 1968" we see the virtue of forthrightness in advertising in full triumph. Rosser Reeves, who wrote the preface to the book, added this about these best read ads of 1968. "They seemed to be quite humdrum. Quite ordinary. They seemed almost run-of-the-mill. They weren't clever. The brilliance, if there was brilliance, did not peep out. They weren't filled with subtle quips, or naked girls, or startling headlines. These advertisements tell the story of the product-- what it is, how it works, what are its advantages, and what it does for you. They aren't clever, because few of our 200 million people are clever."

The hard truth is that it often doesn't pay to be especially creative. Sometimes non-creativity is the shortest route home.

THE CREATIVE MAN SHOULD WELCOME CRITICISM

The second lesson I have un-learned is that *the creative man should have strong convictions about his ideas*. I used to think you couldn't make a nickel for yourself, your agency, or your client unless you believed in your work like a religion and sold your can off to get it through. I now believe an attitude of humility, and maybe even skepticism, about your own work is healthier and more productive.

This might sound as if I'm recommending a lack of conviction. I'm not. What I am recommending is a healthy respect for the ideas and experience of others-- and an awareness of the fact that you're probably not the only smart guy in the department or in the client meeting. Very frequently, other people can spot holes in your ideas or concepts simply because they are detached from them. The creator is always too close to his own work, too bound up in its success, too committed to it. Once he's had an idea, he can't look at it impartially any more. He needs help. The creative man should always welcome suggestions and comments and criticism. Nine out of ten ad ideas, in my opinion, are better the second time around.

IF YOU LOOK "FAR-OUT" YOU'D BETTER BE GOOD

The third thing I have un-learned is that *you have to look creative to be creative*. When I was in the creative department, I used to wear bow ties, loud suits and suede shoes. Now that I'm in the executive stratosphere, I wear double-breasted suits, silver four-in-hand ties and clean shirts. After all, we all need a little protective coloration, wherever we are. I still wear suede shoes--because they're made by a client.

I noted in those earlier days that the creative staff had a tendency to want to *look* creative, and it seemed sensible. Now, of course, the idea has reached cataclysmic proportions. To be creative, you need a beard, long hair, and bad taste in clothes. The average

238

creative conference today looks like
the Last Supper.

But I tend to side with another agency
president I know who was introduced to
a new member of his creative staff, a
young man with shoulder-length hair,
bell bottoms, a full complement of
chains and medallions, and sandals.
The president rocked back a moment
to drink in the spectacle--and then,
shaking hands vigorously, he said
--"Boy, you better be *good*!"

Or, to put it my way, you'd better
be creative first, and then I don't
give a damn how creative you *look*.
Let me throw out this further thought.
Some of the best creative men I know
come in regular suits, get haircuts
and smell OK at the meetings. But
when they show their ideas, they look
creative as hell!

THE BEARD-AND-BELL BOTTOM SET DON'T ALWAYS KNOW WHERE IT'S AT

The fourth thing I un-learned is that
*the best advertising is done by the
most creative people*. I've changed
my mind. Or, let's say I've changed
my mind to this extent. A great deal
of damn fine advertising is coming out
of the spectacularly creative mind.
But this is more than balanced by a
lot of junk.

Many highly creative, articulate, and
intellectual admen make one terrible
mistake: they confuse their own world
with America. They are often just out
of the mainstream of American life.
Theirs is a tight little island. Culturally, they often look East from New
York, instead of West. They're too hip,
too up-to-date and too contemporary for
the rest of the country. These admakers
tend to move in a narrow world. They
talk to themselves, they write for themselves, and they give awards to one another. They know too much about what's
new and what's in and what's out and
where it's at. They're ahead of every-

body else. They develop their own
little ways of saying things that are
largely foreign to the rest of the nation.

They don't travel, except to hide out.
Their infrequent sallies from the bosom
of the world of creative advertising
usually involve them with artists and
intellectuals and theater people. This
kind of admaker can't any more talk to
a farmer in Iowa than a rabbit can make
love to a chicken. Whenever I see an
ad in the Reader's Digest with wild Pop
Art graphics, I know another admaker
has lost touch. Whenever I read one
of those sharp, hip, clever-funny headlines with a bright play on words--I
smell a writer who's forgotten America.

Rx FOR KEEPING IN TOUCH WITH YOUR AUDIENCE

It's an endemic disease, like malaria,
and you have to innoculate yourself
against it. Here's the way I recommend
doing it.

✓ Ride a bus for ten miles in a metropolitan area twice a year. Talk to
people on the bus.

✓ Subscribe to *Playboy* and *Esquire*--
but also to *Farm Journal*, *Argosy*, and
Grit. It will cost you only $11.00
more. Then, remember to read them
all.

✓ Join the PTA.

✓ Go to a wrestling match occasionally
and watch both the wrestlers and the
people watching the wrestlers.

✓ Visit your largest department store
and stand at the bottom of the escalator for an hour.

✓ Listen to a speech at a political
rally.

✓ Work in a store for a week of your
vacation. Actually sell things.

239

√ Grit your teeth and go see a Jerry
  Lewis movie, the most popular form
  of theater entertainment ever devised.

√ Drive leisurely across America without eating in fancy restaurants.

If you do just a few of these things,
I think you will be considerably so-
bered. For you will be reminded that
the world, despite its growing intellectual affluence, is still filled with
squares--nice, solid, hardworking,
capable, worried people who have no
idea what you're talking about when
you get too clever. The typical reader
of your work is probably not shart, hep,
and brilliant. And if you do not aim
right at his midsection, you're likely
to go completely over his head.

I have many friends in the creative
arena, and I want it understood, God
knows, that I'm not talking about them.
I'm talking about the others.

ONLY YOUR AUDIENCE KNOWS
IF YOUR AD IS EFFECTIVE

The fifth thing I've un-learned is that
research is a pain in the pizazz. Most
creative people seem to think it is.
That's human nature. After all, who
wants the success of his work constantly being probed and measured and dis-
sected? Rembrandt and Shakespeare and
De Vinci didn't have to put up with such
indignities. I used to resent having
to submit my brain children to the slide-
rule boys. Now, I welcome it. I beg
for it. Why?

Research on creative approaches has
kept agencies from monumental errors.
Ideas that seem perfectly sound on the
surface often have nuances and psychological complications that are totally
unpredictable except by advance consumer
soundings. Not infrequently, creative
communications that seem absolutely
right to agency and client alike turn
out to be unintelligible to the public.
Or intelligible but ineffective. And

the stakes are often numbered in the
millions of dollars.

Campaigns have lifespans, and they, too,
must be measured. The question of when
advertising programs have outlived their
usefulness--and when their directions
should be shifted or altered--is far too
important to be left to the whim of the
admaker or the hunch of the advertiser.

My experience has been, in fact, that
the public's tolerance for an ad campaign is infinitely greater than that
of the advertiser. Advertisers usually
weary of an idea long before their prospects and customers, simply because
they are so much closer to it and so
much more conscious of it. A client
once suggested to me that an idea might
have worn out its welcome when, because
of lengthy closing dates, it had not
yet made its appearance!

Used wisely, research can increase the
accuracy of the admaker's decisions
dramatically. But the ultimate responsibility remains always with the man.

Advertising is really just a matter of
opinion. And the opinions that count
the most are the opinions of the people
who read, see and hear the advertising.
Research is the only valid way to stay
in touch with your audience. Never forget to let the people vote.

HOW VALUABLE ARE AWARDS?

The sixth thing I un-learned is that
awards are great. I used to love awards.
Now I've come to the conclusion that
awards are probably rotten. Most of
them, anyway. Bad for our industry, bad
for the agency business, bad for the
people who win them. Most creative
awards are set up largely for the sponsor. The judging is usually sloppy,
without any hard facts about advertising success to guide the selections.
Advertising is, by and large, in this
environment treated largely as an art
form.

Well, advertising isn't largely an art form. It's a selling tool, pure and simple. But the myth is thus created that certain types of advertising are good when they probably aren't. The people who create them are then eulogized, overpaid and imitated. Payrolls skyrocket. The youngsters are misled. Clients are beguiled. And, I believe, our business is the poorer for it.

I once compiled a list of organizations giving awards. When it got over three hundred, I quit. That was five years ago. God knows what it is now. So, rather than fight them, I've decided to join them. I'm organizing, along with a few friends who prefer to remain nameless, SPAAAK. SPAAAK is a new organization that I believe might perform the useful service of putting the whole thing in perspective by making awards available to *everyone*. SPAAAK stands for the Society for the Proliferation of Advertising Awards of All Kinds. Perhaps we can beat the awards people at their own game. Activities of this fine new organization will be announced shortly. I'm sure it will have a brief but fiery life.

Incidentally, if you come to my office in Bloomfield Hills, you'll find a suitable number of awards hanging on my wall. I think I should explain that. These awards are different. They were all well-deserved. The judges who conferred them were all qualified beyond reproach. They stand as well-earned tributes to the fine work that has dribbled from my pen over the years. I am unshakably proud of them.

——— ——— ———

Well, those are some of the things I've un-learned in twenty years of creative advertising. They seem obvious to me now, but I suppose most young creative people won't agree and will just have to un-learn them for themselves.

My final thought is this. There's only one sure formula for getting ahead in this business. Work hard--live clean-- and never stop un-learning!

DISCUSSION QUESTIONS

1. Describe the importance of creativity to advertising as specifically as possible.

2. How valuable is research to creative advertising?

3. Should the advertiser hold any reins on creativity in advertising? Why or why not?

241

From THE SELECTION OF ADVERTISING MEDIA, pp. 174-182. J.W. Hobson. Mercury House, Business Books Limited (London), 1968.

V-3

THREE BASIC PRINCIPLES IN CAMPAIGN PLANNING

J. W. Hobson

The late Sir William Crawford propounded the most concise yet complete recipe for good advertising in a three-word precept: *Concentration--Domination--Repetition*. It applies over the whole field of marketing and advertising. In the choice of advertisng appeal, in the tactics of marketing, in the design of advertising layout--and certainly not least in the media plan for an advertising campaign. In long-hand it may be translated into the three fundamental rules of an advertising plan:

1. Do not disperse your emphasis or your appropriation or your advertising design.

2. Be sure of being the biggest factor in your market at some point; be dominant with one appeal out of the many which your product and its competitors can advance; be dominant in some form of media if you cannot be dominant in all; be sure that some one factor emerges vigorously from your advertisement design.

3. Since advertisements have to create continuing habits if they are to reward the advertiser who invests in them, it is not enough to stop after a single impact or jump about from one

advertising objective to another, or from one product appeal to another, or from one set of media to another.

The precept sounds so simple, as well as so sensible, that it is surprising how often it is not observed or has to give way to some conflict of intentions or some over-ambitious desire to attract everybody all the time.

The consideration of this context is limited to the media plan within the campaign plan, but there is no better way to outline the principles of media planning than to examine Sir William Crawford's three factors.

Concentration   The first of his three elements is probably the most important.

The greatest (and most frequently encountered) mistake in advertising is excessive dispersal of resources. A product may have several good selling points, but it is wise nevertheless to concentrate its advertising campaign on making a thorough conquest of the market with one only: the one that is chosen for its maximum effectiveness in the particular marketing and competitive circumstances of the time. The public does not readily understand two equally good points put to it simultaneously,

242

though it can focus on, and accept, two
points successively. If you throw two
balls to a person he probably will not
catch either of them, when he would
easily have caught one. It is too much
to expect the public to make the mental
effort of concentration for you; you
must do it for yourself. It is the advertiser's job to make it easy for the
public (who, after all, have plenty to
think about apart from his particular
arguments for his toothpaste or his
soap or his store) to understand the
one point which makes his product specially good for a type of customer or
a type of purpose. The trouble is that
advertisers tend to be too greedy in
their objectives. An emollient may be
particularly good for the hands, but
the advertiser cannot also resist saying that it is good for the complexion,
and for sunburn, and for a hundred and
one other uses, for which it is also
quite properly to be recommended.

A hot drink may have its best market
in the evening, but the advertiser finds
it extremely difficult to refrain also
from recommending it at elevenses, for
nursing mothers, on picnics, and for
invalids, having had some direct evidence of its success on all these occasions. In selling a toothpaste it
may be much more valuable to concentrate
on persuading young people of the late
teenage, who are just forming their
adult habits for life, and particularly the young women who are more conscious
of these matters; but the advertiser
cannot resist also the temptation to
try the much more difficult job of changing the settled habits of older people,
or to tackle the quite different and
far more short-term custom of children.

Here are some examples of the risks of
dispersal of aim. The positive side of
the case is the advantage of building
up a product to have, in the mind and
memory of a large public, the complete
answer to one uncomplicated need, and
of concentrating on filling this requirement and on nothing else.

In the field of media selection the
principle of concentration equally applies, partly in carrying out the concentration of the marketing and presentation policy and partly in the quest
for outspending competitors and making
a strong impression on the public in a
given medium.

Taking first the former of these two
contexts, clearly if the marketing and
advertising objective is defined as being a certain type of customer, then
the media planning will concentrate on
reaching this section of the public.
In the sphere of mass advertising, this
is a question of focusing, as well as
the case permits, on a general area
selected from the whole public rather
than picking out a very precisely defined section. The mass media themselves are largely not capable of very
sharp definition; but there is considerable value in narrowing both the target
and the aim as far as possible, so as
to ensure a better and more economical
use of resources. Where the marketing
target takes the form of a specialist
or geographical group, it may prove much
easier to select media so as to achieve
a parallel concentration.

The second, however, of the two contexts
stated above--that of concentrating
media so as to ensure creating a strong
impression on at least one particular
section of the public--is an application
of the principle of concentration which
applies primarily to media selection.
It is of very great importance. Each
medium represents a section of the public either numerically or in terms of
atmosphere, mood, or circumstances.
The mass national morning papers, for
example, have their own particular mood
and circumstances, and within this group
each one of them selects its own section of the total public. Even the
least of these sections represents a
market of considerable size. To select
this one section of media, or any one
of its component newspapers, and to
dominate it thoroughly, may well represent for a given advertiser a fully

sufficient scope for his marketing ambitions.

In a rather different mood and circumstance the same people travel by trans-
port to their jobs and thus the trans-
port media may create their own separate world of advertising, because of
the way in which they are seen, the
colour employed, the shape and positioning of them, and so on. The magazines, again, create a rather different
advertising mood and circumstance from
the daily press, even among the people,
men or women, who read both. The hoard-
ings, television, shop display, the
cinema, and every other medium create
their own particular effects. It is
possible, therefore, for an advertiser
who is outspent by some competitor in
say the daily papers, to turn to another
advertising field and be the most dominant advertiser in his class, within
the type and mood and quality of coverage offered by that field. This second
field may not offer the type and mood
and quality of coverage the advertiser
would have chosen first; but he may
well do better to make his mark effectively in this more limited field than
to be an also-ran in the best field.

The only reservation is that the more
limited field of advertising thus
selected should be large enough to
provide, when properly exploited, a
return which justified the expenditure
on a normal ratio of advertising to
sales. If this equation cannot be
worked out satisfactorily, while at
the same time a more universal coverage
would spread the advertising impact too
thin, then the whole basis of the advertising costing needs re-examining and
possibly a radically different solution
will have to be sought.

The issue which arises at all stages
in media planning can be settled only
by a careful balance of pros and cons.
In a simple case an advertiser may have
the choice of ten insertions of given
size in one newspaper; or five in each
of two; or ten in each of two but only

half the size. The balance of the decision will lie in whether five is adequate frequency, or whether the half-
size will enable him to do the job the
campaign requires; or whether he will
do better to limit himself to the one
newspaper and achieve a full success
among the more limited public so covered.
More complicated examples of the same
issue arise when a larger budget offers
scope for a variety of media of different types.

The rule must be that it is far better
to do a given job--in terms of size and
frequency--in a limited list of media,
than to risk doing an inadequate job in
a long list out of a desire to expand
the total coverage. It is a decision
which is often hard to reach because of
the anxiety to widen the coverage which
always arises. The temptation to make
the resources cover just one more set
of possible customers is difficult to
resist; but it must be resisted. Moreover, there are often conflicting coun-
sels and desires to be reconciled, and
it sometimes seems easier to effect the
reconciliation by giving everyone a little of what they want rather than go
through the labour and trouble of deciding priorities. This is once again an
example of the danger of dispersal of
advertising effort.

The issue particularly calls for good
judgment because if the principle is
applied too far, there is a complemen-
tary risk of wasting resources. In
another context reference has already
been made to the diminishing return
that sets in at a certain point of advertising expenditure on a given medium.
Too great a size of space, too much frequency of insertion, too much money
spent in a single medium, can be a waste
of resources, just as too little can be.
At a certain point of spending in, let
us say, one newspaper, it becomes better to add a second newspaper and thus
broaden the field of total coverage.

The right course is therefore to start
by defining clearly what size and fre-

244

quency of space the tactical situation
requires and ensure that no medium is
included which cannot be afforded an
adequate strength of campaign.

There are various methods of concentrating an advertising budget, and where
concentration is necessary (as it usually is because virtually no budget is
sufficient for everything) the following possibilities may be reviewed:

√ Numerical concentration; i.e., choosing only a few (naturally the most
  economical) media of a certain type.

√ By choice and continuity of position
  within a type of media, pre-selecting
  an even more limited section of the
  whole audience which has particular
  interest in the product.

√ Seasonal concentration; i.e., limiting the advertising to a part (probably the peak period) of the selling
  season.

√ Geographical concentration; i.e., proceeding by intensive coverage of a
  selected area or sequence of areas.

√ Economic class; i.e., not attempting
  to cover all classes equally. Such
  a form of media concentration must
  be linked with parallel concentration
  of marketing and creative effort.

√ Age; i.e., limiting the advertising
  objective to a special age group with
  all the consequent narrowing of the
  media field.

√ Interest groups; i.e., choosing, within the general scope of the product
  appeal, some more limited group of
  interests, e.g., social, religious,
  sporting, etc., which can then be
  reached with a more restricted list
  of media. The creative appeal would
  be limited in parallel.

The scope for deliberate concentration
of objective is almost endless, because
of the vast variety of media available.

These suggestions are only examples of
how a general principle can be worked
out.

In summary, therefore, the need for concentration in media planning lies in:

• the need to focus the media as far as
  possible on the section of the public
  prescribed by the marketing and advertising objective; and

• the need to concentrate on the best
  media for the purpose until a pre-
  defined strength has been achieved in
  each, and not proceed to widen the
  media list until it has.

Domination The advertising complex
may be envisaged as a market place in
which a large number of salesmen are
crying their wares. The resultant hub-
bub is continuous and the public gets
accustomed to it, to the stage where it
discounts it. Moreover, the public is
going about its own affairs which lie
to a large extent outside the field of
buying. It has interests, anxieties,
preoccupations with earning its liveli-
hood, recreations, family affairs, and
other influences far removed from what
the salesmen is trying to sell.

To catch the attention of the public in
these circumstances requires a very skil-
ful technique. There may be a factor of
unusual novelty, or a vast appropriation, or a product of close relevance
to the moment's interests of the public,
or some other element in the situation
which gives an advertiser an advantage.
To suggest that such a factor can be invented if it is not present is to under-
rate the extent to which the public can
subconsciously distinguish between the
real and the false novelty or interest.

There may be some appropriations which
are so great that they can by very volume make themselves heard across the
whole market place. But the average
case is one in which the resources available permit of only a normal volume of
salesmanship. In these circumstances

the salesman must as it were pitch his booth in that section of the market place where from previous knowledge his likeliest customers will circulate in greatest numbers, and at least ensure that within this limited area his resources permit his voice to be heard above the general din.

This is the principle of concentration, already described; its purpose is to *dominate*. So, too, in the choice of media the advertiser must dominate at least for some of the time and in relation to some of the public.

Domination may be achieved by scores of different methods of media planning. The most obvious way is to use large spaces; and even if this cannot be afforded throughout the whole campaign, it will probably be possible for a short period--enough to make its mark on the relevant public for a time. It is often imagined by the inexperienced that novelty and ingenuity are what make advertising successful; and for a short time and in certain circumstances this may be true. But in the long run it is weight of money which generally controls the situation. Therefore to outspend competitors is the surest way to dominate, and once again the argument reverts to the need to concentrate resources in order to do this.

On the other hand, merely to do somethig different from competitors in the sphere of media may go some way to achieve the object; for example, using a medium that is new for the product or an unusual shape of space; or choosing poster sites of noticeable size or quality; or using colour pages where competitors have hitherto used only black and white; or skilfully finding means of getting news printed in the editorial columns; or turning up with a sample offer through the unexpected medium of the consumer's own letterbox.

In a competitive market, domination is particularly necessary, and few markets nowadays are not competitive. But what makes the problem more difficult (and tends to stress the factor of sheer spending power rather than new ideas or ingenuities of presentation) is that an advertisier has to compete not only with others making similar products, but also with manufacturers in other fields who are bidding for the same money with different kinds of interests. Chocolates compete not only with other chocolates or with other sweets, but also with tobacco, and nylons, and cinemas, and biscuits and football pools, and all other forms of recreational spending. Television sets compete not only with other television sets but with washing machines, and household cleaners, and family holidays, and new clothes. To some extent, indeed, competitive products in the same field assist each other because their combined spending tends to outbid competing interests from other fields.

Bigness, as we have already remarked elsewhere, is an important quality in advertising; therefore, to be bigger and more noticeable than competitors is to dominate. But the idea of domination is not only in relation to being better and bigger than other advertisers, but also to taking control of the potential customer's mind and interest for the necessary space of time, and to continuing to control it partly by the quality of the goods sold and partly by repeated domination of his or her subconscious inclinations.

Repetition This brings the argument to repetition. The average advertiser is not aiming to make a single sale; he wants the customer to come back again and again for his product. The investment in advertising cannot otherwise be repaid. All the time other interests are crowding in upon his customer with new ideas and products, and with alternative means of enjoying the pennies or shillings he wants spent on his own product. He must dominate the market and take control of the customer's interests at least once in order to get his own idea or product noticed and tried; but thereafter, he must keep the impression so created alive for ever afterwards. This process requires neither the bigness nor the dominance, but it entails spending advertising resources continuously over a period, and allowance for this continued outlay must be made in deciding what media the budget can afford to use.

The proper frequency and size of this element of repetition are matters which need a chapter to themselves. They depend on a wide variety of factors such as the seasonal peaks of the pruchase of the product, the frequency of consumer purchase, the amount which the buyer is prepared to spend at a single purchase, and similar factors.

The most important point to grasp in this context is the basic factor that, because the only kind of buying that can reward the average advertiser for his outlay involves repetition, therefore repetition is necessary to the selling process which advertising represents. If one may use the alternative description (which the writer prefers) in which advertising is defined as adding a subjective something to the very product itself, then repetition of advertising appeal is clearly as much a necessity to the continuing process of production as is repetition of the labelling process or that of putting into cartons. It is the process of continuing to hallmark the product in which the public places its confidence.

There are many media specially suitable for repetition and generally it is possible (as well as necessary in view of the need to make resources go round) to make do with less expensive forms and sizes of space. This is because:

√ the stage of breaking through the barrier of public ignorance of the product is over, at least for the time being; and

√ it is usually unnecessary, at the repetition stage, to state the sell-

ing points in as much detail as when they are first being put across; and a reminder type of advertising can be adopted.

The process of repetition cannot go on indefinitely. After a stage which must be judged from the tactical circumstances, it will be necessary to create new impact--a new effort of domination--before the repetitive process can be resumed. Repetition is by its very description the *repeating* of something, and each repeat gets a little fainter. The fresh impact may take the shape of a new presentation of the marketing and advertising message, or it may be judged sufficient to use the existing message over again in larger and more dominant spaces.

In the same way too much exact similarity in the medium of repetition may cause the value of it to diminish quicker than would otherwise be the case. It is for this reason that posters which are seen by their public so frequently in the course of a week's normal journeys, are thought by many experts to lose their repetitive value rather quickly. The same poster, or the same hoarding, passed at the same stage of the daily or twice daily journey becomes a mere part of the scenery. Changes of poster design can help to overcome this disadvantage, but it is a factor to consider in relation to what otherwise is the most convincing medium of repetition.

Some variation in the shape, size, and even the actual media of repetition can be very helpful. The same message striking at the viewer from a different angle, in a different context, or catching him in a different mood and circumstance, can almost convey a little of the feeling of a new impact. Repetition must not be allowed to result in a blind spot in the vision of the public.

In newspapers and magazines the risk of this is not so great because the surrounding material--news, features, pictures, and other factors that go to create the context--are constantly changing. An exception may be the earspaces alongside the newspaper titles, which are a favourite repetition medium but which, like the poster sites, can wear a blind spot with the regular reader of the publication. There is no doubt that where repetition is spread over a variety of media each with its different context, it sustains the freshness of the first impact over a longer period.

Concluding this chapter it will be useful to restate the four basic principles of media planning which have been emphasized in this and the previous chapters.

Definition--Getting the campaign objective into clear focus (by methods outlined in the previous chapter).

Concentration--Avoiding dispersal of resources over too many different objectives or media.

Domination--Ensuring that at some part of the market the campaign dominates its competitors, and takes control of the mind and interests of the potential customers.

Repetition--Providing for the continuation of the message in reminder form regularly over a period.

Definition--Concentration--Domination--Repetition. It may be useful thus to expand Sir William Crawford's original precept for sound campaign planning in the field of advertising media.

DISCUSSION QUESTIONS

1. Discuss a particular current advertising campaign that illustrates an effective or ineffective utilization of the three principles described in this reading.

2. What are the significance of size, position, and frequency in media scheduling?

3. Explain what is meant by "concentrating an advertising budget."

V-4

PRODUCT OR INDUSTRIAL ADVERTISEMENTS?

Martin A. Lehman and Richard N. Cardozo

This paper analyzes product advertisements and institutional advertisements in terms of their ability to increase the probability that an unknown industrial supplier would receive an order for particular products. Differences in the relative preference for product and institutional advertisements between high and low risk products and between purchasing agents and managers in other functional areas are also compared.

On the basis of earlier work (Levitt, 1965), the presumption was made that some advertising might help an industrial supplier whose name was not known by prospective buyers. Levitt's finding that an excellent sales presentation might overcome the lack of seller reputation or "image" led to the hypothesis that an unknown supplier might find product advertising more effective than institutional advertising designed to enhance the selling firm's reputation.

In contrast, exploratory studies of industrial buyer behavior carried out through the Center for Experimental Studies in Business at the University of Minnesota indicate that supplier reputation is more critical than product claims in the vendor-choice deci-

sion, particularly for more complex, higher risk products. This preference for information about the supplier, rather than about the product, appeared greater among purchasing agents than among other middle-management personnel.

These data led to four specific hypotheses to be evaluated in this paper:

1. Product advertisements will be more effective than institutional advertisements in low-risk purchase situations.

2. Institutional advertisements will be more effective than product advertisements in high-risk purchase situations.

3. Institutional advertisements will be more effective in persuading purchasing agents than in persuading other managers.

4. Product advertisements will be more effective in persuading middle management personnel than in persuading purchasing agents.

METHODOLOGY

To evaluate these hypotheses, both product and institutional advertisements were created, each for a low-risk and a high-risk product, and purchasing agents and other managers were asked to respond to the advertisements on a variety of measures. The design included three factors, each at two levels, as shown in Figure 1.

The products portrayed in the advertisements were an office desk (low risk). Prior research by Cardozo and Cagley (1971) indicated that purchasing agents considered office desks a relatively low risk item. A pilot study among 33 purchasing and middle management men indicated that electronic calculators were relatively risky purchases.

Names for the companies sponsoring the advertisements were fictitious to assure that no respondent would have had prior experience with the ostensible suppliers. Names were chosen from among those rated by the pilot group as moderately favorable and approximately equal in acceptability to each other and to well-known suppliers of desks and calculators.

Product advertisements pictured the product and described it in detail.

The only information provided about the supplying company was the logo and address. Institutional advertisements prominently featured the company's name and philosophy. The product itself received only one-line mention.

To assure that differences between advertisements would not result from differences in quality of execution, 16 advertisements were prepared, four in each of the four treatment combinations. (See Figure 1.) Based on ratings of the pilot group of purchasing men and managers, one advertisement in each of the four treatment combinations was chosen. The pilot group considered all four chosen advertisements quite effective.

In the study itself, advertisements were presented to participants by an interviewer, who asked each participant to evaluate the advertisement.

Participants in the study included 80 businessmen from the Minneapolis-St. Paul area. Half were in purchasing and half worked in a variety of line management and staff specialist positions. (None of the participants in the study itself had taken part in the pilot tests.) Recent literature (Feldman and Cardozo, 1969; and Weigand, 1968) suggests that middle managers and staff specialists are, along with purchasing personnel, members of the decision-

Figure 1
RESEARCH DESIGN

| Amount of Risk | Type of Advertisement | | | |
| | Product | | Institutional | |
	Mid-Management	Purchasing Agents	Mid-Management	Purchasing Agents
Low	$n = 10$	$n = 10$	$n = 10$	$n = 10$
High	$n = 10$	$n = 10$	$n = 10$	$n = 10$

Table 1

COMPARATIVE EFFECTIVENESS OF PRODUCT
AND INSTITUTIONAL ADVERTISEMENTS BY
MEASURE
(MAXIMUM EFFECTIVENESS = 100)

Measure	Product Ad	Institutional Ad
Probability of soliciting a bid from this supplier	58.0	70.5
Interest in this firm as a future supplier	52.0	70.0
Supplier dependability	56.5	80.0
Quality of product	61.0	84.0
Comparability of product to that of well-known suppliers	56.0	82.5
Unweighted index	56.7	77.4

All differences were significant beyond the .01 level.

making unit for industrial purchases.

Participants were employed by firms which covered a variety of industries, Participants were asked first to look at each advertisement and then to indicate their likelihood of soliciting a bid from the sponsoring company; their interest in the company as a vendor; and their beliefs about company dependability, product quality, and comparison to well-known firms.

Institutional advertisements were generally more effective than product advertisements. Middle management personnel and purchasing agents responded about the same to the advertisements presented. (See Table 1.)

Institutional advertisements generally produced more favorable responses than did advertisements which described the product in detail. This phenomenon was observed for purchasing agents, middle managers and both groups combined. This result also held for the desk (low

risk) and the calculator (high risk), and for both products together. (See Table 2.)

The results suggest that institutional advertisements may be especially effective for low-risk products. On the other hand, advertisements which describe the product in detail may be more effective for high-risk products in conveying messages about product quality and comparability of the supplier to more visible forms. On an unweighted index of all measures combined, the institutional advertisements for the desk produced higher ratings than did institutional advertisements for the calculator, as shown in Table 2.

On both the product quality and comparability to well-known supplier scales, the product advertisements for the calculator were rated more favorably than the product advertisements for the desk.

Middle management personnel and purchasing agents in most instances re-

251

Table 2

COMPARATIVE EFFECTIVENESS OF PRODUCT
AND INSTITUTIONAL ADVERTISEMENTS BY
LEVEL OF RISK AND MEASURE
(MAXIMUM EFFECTIVENESS = 100)

Measure[1]	Level of Risk	Type of Advertisement[2]		
		Product	Institutional	Combined
Quality of product	High (calculator)	65.0	77.0	71.0
	Low (desk)	57.0[3]	84.0	70.5
	Combined	61.0	80.5	70.8
Comparability of product to that of well-known supplier	High risk	60.0	78.0	69.0
	Low risk	52.0[3]	87.0	69.5
	Combined=	56.0	82.5	69.3
Unweighted Index of five measures	High risk	59.2	72.4	65.8
	Low risk	54.2	81.0[3]	67.6
	Combined	56.7	76.7	66.7

[1] On measures not included in this table, no significant difference between risk levels (products) were observed.

[2] All differences between product and institutional advertisements are significant beyond the .01 level.

[3] Differences between high and low risk ads significant beyond the .05 level.

acted to the advertisements in a similar manner. No differences between these two groups of individuals were observed except on the comparability to well-known supplier scale. On that measure, purchasing agents rated both advertisements for both products together less favorably than did middle managers. Purchasing agents may emphasize the source of supply more than the product in such comparisons, whereas middle managers may attempt to evaluate the products on their own merits, rather than weigh heavily supplier capability.

For the group as a whole, the probability of soliciting a bid was higher for the desk than for the calculator. This phenomenon was particularly pronounced for individuals exposed to institutional advertisements. (See Table 3.) The greater willingness to solicit a bid

for a low-risk product is consistent with Levitt's findings.

The results reversed the first two hypotheses and offered no support for the third and fourth. The first two hypotheses predicted that in low-risk purchase situations product ads would be more effective than institutional ads; and that in high-risk situations institutional ads would be more effective. In fact, institutional ads were more effective in both low and high risk situations as defined in this study. The evidence also suggests that, whatever effectiveness product ads may have, it is greater in high-risk purchase situations than in low-risk situations.

It is doubtful that the similarity in results for the two products can be explained entirely by any similarity in risk. The desks included in the adver-

Table 3

PROBABILITY OF SOLICITING A BID FROM
FIRM SPONSORING AN ADVERTISEMENT

Level of Risk		Type of Advertisement	
	Product	Institutional	Combined
High (calculator)	58.0	64.0 ↑	61.0 ↑
Low (desk)	58.0 ← [1] →	77.0 [1] ↓	67.5 [1]
Combined	58.0 ← [1] →	70.5 ↓	64.3 ↓

Level of Risk		Type of Respondent	
	Purchasing Agent	Middle Manager	Combined
High (calculator)	60.0	62.0	61.0 ↑
Low (desk)	71.0	64.0	67.5 [1] ↓
Combined	65.5	63.0	64.3

[1]Difference significant beyond the .05 level.

tisements in this study were standard office desks, a mature, low-risk product approaching commodity status. Electronic calculators, on the other hand, are technically complex, differentiated products still presumably in an early stage of the product life-cycle.

The preference towards institutional advertisements for both desks and calculators can be attributed to decision-makers' interests about the capabilities of prospective suppliers. Individuals involved in industrial buying decisions know that they can obtain extensive knowledge about specific products from salesmen and detailed catalog materials and specification sheets, as well as from examination and trial of the product itself. It is not surprising, then, that industrial buyers and users seek from advertisements information primarily about the qualifications of prospective suppliers. Nor is it surprising that the impact of product ads was greater for the more complex, differentiated product.

What may be surprising, however, is the idea that the best way for an unknown industrial supplier to build a favorable image may be to use institutional ads, rather than product ads. Industrial marketers have traditionally thought that the best way to build a favorable image through advertising was to use ads which described particular products or successful applications. The argument was that prospective buyers would be impressed with the specific product or application and subsequently generalize that favorable impression to other offerings of that supplier. Industrial marketers typically allocate only a small portion of their ad budgets to institutional ads; that portion is generally the first to be cut back in economy drives.

The implication of the results of this research is that an unknown supplier may make more effective use of his advertising budget by spending most of his money on institutional advertising. Such an allocation would contrast sharply with present practice. Emphasis on institutional rather than product ads might in some cases require shifting responsibility for control of ad expenditures from product or market managers to a corporate advertising function.

The observation that purchasing agents and middle managers respond similarly to ads appears to support the argument made by many industrial advertisers that separate ad campaigns need not be developed for the two groups. Results from this study indicate that ads which emphasize supplier capability may be effective toward both groups.

In this study, responses from 40 purchasing agents and 40 middle managers indicated that institutional advertisements were generally more effective than product advertisements for an unknown industrial supplier. Effectiveness was measured in terms of willingness to solicit bids, interest in the sponsoring firm as a future supplier, supplier dependability, product quality, and comparison to well-known suppliers. The results have indicated that for the obscure industrial supplier insti-

tutional or "image building" ads may make more effective use of advertising dollars than advertisements which describe particular products in detail.

REFERENCES

Feldman, Wallace and Richard Cardozo. The "Industrial" Revolution and Models of Buyer Behavior. *Journal of Purchasing,* November 1969, pp. 77-88.

Levitt, Theodore, *Industrial Purchasing Behavior: A Study of Communication Effects*. Boston: Division of Research, Harvard Business School. 1965.

DISCUSSION QUESTIONS

1. According to the findings of this study, how should a relatively unknown supplier spend his advertising dollars? Make any qualifications that seem necessary.

2. Distinguish institutional advertising from product advertising as specifically as possible.

3. How should "level of risk" and "management level" (type of respondent) be taken into account by an industrial advertiser in designing his advertising strategy?

Reprinted by permission from ADVERTISING AGE; 24 April, 1972, pp. 35, 38.

V-5

THE POSITIONING ERA COMETH

Jack Trout and Al Ries

Today it has become obvious that advertising is entering a new era. An era where creativity is no longer the key to success.

The fun and games of the 60s have given way to the harsh realities of the 70s. Today's marketplace is no longer responsive to the kind of advertising that worked in the past. There are just too many products, too many companies, too much marketing "noise."

To succeed in our over-communicated society, a company must create a "position" in the prospect's mind. A position that takes into consideration not only its own strength and weaknesses, but those of its competitors as well.

A TALE OF TWO ADS

If you had to pick an official date to mark the end of the last advertising era and the start of the new one, your choice would have to be Wednesday, April 7, 1971. In the *New York Times* that day was a full-page ad that seemed to generate very little excitement in the advertising community.

But then, an abrupt change in the direction of an industry isn't always accompanied by the blowing of bugles. You sometimes need the vantage point of history to realize what has happened.

The ad that appeared that spring morning in 1971 was written by David Ogilvy. And it's no coincidence that the architect of one era called the tune for the next.

In the ad, the articulate Mr. Ogilvy outlined his 38 points for creating "advertising that sells."

In first place on his list was a point Mr. Ogilvy called "the most important decision." Then he went on to say, "The results of your campaign depend less on how we write your advertising than on how your product is positioned."

√ Blow the bugles, the positioning era has begun.

Five days later, in the *New York Times* and in *Advertising Age*, another ad appeared that confirmed the fact that the advertising industry was indeed changing direction. Placed by Rosenfeld, Sirowitz & Lawson, the ad listed the agency's four guiding principles.

In first place was, you guessed it. According to Ron Rosenfeld, Len Sirowitz and Tom Lawson, "Accurate positioning is the most important step in effective selling."

Suddenly the word and the concept was in everybody's ads and on everybody's lips. Hardly an issue of *Advertising Age* passes without some reference to "positioning."

YOU CAN'T BEAT 'EM HEAD-ON

In spite of Madison Ave.'s current love affiar with positioning, the concept had a more humble beginning.

In 1969, one of us (Jack Trout) wrote an article entitled "Positioning is a game people play in today's me-too marketplace," which appeared in the June, 1969, issue of *Industrial Marketing*. The article made predictions and named names, all based on the "rules" of a game called positioning.

One prediction, in particular, turned out to be strikingly accurate. As far as RCA and computers were concerned, "a company has no hope to make progress head-on against the position that IBM has established."

The operative word, of course, is "head-on." And while it's possible to compete successfully with a market leader (the article suggested several approaches), the rules of positioning say it can't be done "head-on."

Three years ago this raised a few eye-brows. Who were we to say that powerful, multi-billion-dollar companies couldn't find happiness in the computer business if they so desired?

Desire, alas, was not enough. Not only RCA, but also General Electric bit the IBM dust.

With two major computer manufacturers folding one right after another, the urge to say, "I told you so," was irresistible.

Last November, a follow-up article, "Positioning revisited: Why didn't GE and RCA listen?" appeared in the same publication.

WE'RE AN OVER-COMMUNICATED SOCIETY

As GE and RCA found out, advertising doesn't work anymore. At least, not like it used to. One reason may be noise level in the communications jungle.

The per-capita consumption of advertising in the U.S. is approaching $100 a year. And while no one doubts the advertiser's financial ability to dish it out, there's some question about the consumer's mental ability to take it all in.

Each day, thousands of messages compete for a share of the prospect's mind. And, make no mistake about it, the mind of the battleground. Between six inches of grey matter is where the advertising war takes place. And the battle is rough, with no holds barred and no quarter given.

The new ball game can prove unsettling to companies that grew up in an era where any regular advertising was likely to bring success. This is why you see a mature, sophisticated company like Bristol-Myers run through millions of dollars trying to launch me-too products against strongly dug-in competition. (If you haven't noticed, Fact, Vote and Resolve are no longer with us.)

To understand why some companies have trouble playing in today's positioning game, it might be helpful to take a look at recent communications history.

'50s WERE THE PRODUCT ERA

Back in the 50s, advertising was in the "product" era. In a lot of ways, these were the good old days when the "better mousetrap" and some money to promote it were all you needed.

It was a time when advertising people focused their attention on product features and customer benefits. They looked for, as Rosser Reeves called it, the "Unique Selling Proposition."

But in the late 50s, technology started to rear its ugly head. It became more and more difficult to establish the "USP."

The end of the product era came with an avalanche of "me-too" products that descended on the market. Your "better mousetrap" was quickly followed by two more just like it. Both claiming to be better than the first one.

The competition was fierce and not always totally honest. It got so bad that one product manager was overheard to say, "Wouldn't you know it. Last year we had nothing to say, so we put 'new and improved' on the package. This year the research people came up with a real improvement, and we don't know what to say."

IN '60s 'IMAGE' WAS KING

The next phase was the image era. In the 60s, successful companies found their reputation or "image" was more important in selling a product than any specific product feature.

The architect of the image era was David Ogilvy. As he said in his famous speech on the subject, "Every advertisement is a long-term investment in the image of a brand." And he proved the validity of his ideas with programs for Hathaway shirts, Rolls-Royce, Schweppes and others.

But just as the "me-too" products killed the product era, the "me-too" companies killed the image era. As every company tried to establish a reputation for itself, the noise level became so high that relatively few companies succeeded. And most of the ones that made it, did it primarily with spectacular technical achievements, not spectacular advertising.

But while it lasted, the exciting, go-go years of the middle 60s were like a marketing orgy.

At the party, it was "everyone into the pool." Little thought was given to failure. With the magic of money and enough bright people, a company felt that any marketing program would succeed.

The wreckage is still washing up on the beach. Du Pont's Corfam, Gablinger's beer, Handy Andy all-purpose cleaner, *Look* magazine.

The world will never be the same again and neither will the advertising business. For today we are entering an era that recognizes both the importance of the product and the importance of the company image, but more than anything else stresses the need to create a "position" in the prospect's mind.

POSITIONING ERA DAWNS

The great copywriters of yesterday, who have gone to that big agency in the sky, would die all over again if they saw some of the campaigns currently running (successful campaigns, we might add).

Take beer advertising. In the past, a

beer copywriter looked closely at the product to find his copy platform. And he found "real-draft" Piels, and "cold-brewed" Ballantine. Back a little farther he discovered the "land of the sky blue waters" and "just a kiss of the hops."

In the positioning era, however, effective beer advertising is taking a different tack. "First class is Michelob" positioned the brand as the first American-made premium beer. "The one beer to have when you're having more than one" positioned Schaefer and the brand for the heavy beer drinker.

But there's an imported beer whose positioning strategy is so crystal clear that those old-time beer copywriters probably wouldn't even accept it as advertising.

"You've tasted the German beer that's the most popular in America. Now taste the German beer that's the most popular in Germany." This is how Beck's beer is effectively positioning itself against Lowenbrau.

Then there's Seven-Up's "Un-Cola" campaign.

And *Sports Illustrated's* "Third Newsweekly" program.

All of these positioning campaigns have a number of things in common. They don't emphasize product features, customer benefits or the company's image. Yet, they are all highly successful.

OLD WORD GETS NEW MEANING

Like any new concept, positioning isn't new. At least not in the literal sense. What is new is the broader meaning now being given to the word.

Yesterday, positioning was used in a narrow sense to mean what the advertiser did to his product. Today, positioning is used in a broader sense to mean what the advertising does for the product in the prospect's mind. In other words, a successful advertiser today uses advertising to positon his product, not to communicate its advantages or features.

Positioning has its roots in the packaged goods field where the concept was called "product positioning." It literally meant the product's form, package size and price as compared to competition.

Procter & Gamble carried the idea one step forward by developing a master copy platform that related each of their competing brands. For example: Tide makes clothes "white." Cheer makes them "whiter than white." And Bold makes them "bright."

Although the advertising for each Procter & Gamble brand might vary from year to year, it never departed from its pre-assigned role or "position" in the master plan.

√ The big breakthrough came when, people started thinking of positioning not as something the client does before the advertising is prepared, but as the very objective of the advertising itself. External, rather than internal positioning.

A classic example of looking through the wrong end of the telescope was Ford's introduction of the Edsel. In the ensuing laughter that followed, most people missed the point.

In essence, the Ford people got switched around. The Edsel was a beautiful case of internal positioning to fill a hole between Ford and Mercury on the one hand, and Lincoln on the other. Good strategy inside the building. Bad strategy outside where there was simply no position for this car in a category already cluttered with heavily-chromed, medium-priced cars.

If the Edsel had been tagged a "high performance" car and presented in a sleek two-door, bucket-seat form and given a name to match, no one would have laughed. It could have occupied a position that no one else owned and the ending of the story might have been different.

REMEMBER THE MIND IS A MEMORY BANK

To better understand what an advertiser is up against, it may be helpful to take a closer look at the objective of all advertising programs--the human mind.

Like a memory bank, the mind has a slot or "position" for each bit of information it has chosen to retain. In operation, the mind is a lot like a computer.

But there is one important difference. A computer has to accept what is put into it. The mind does not. In fact, it's quite the opposite.

The mind, as a defense mechanism against the volume of today's communications, screens and rejects much of the information offered it. In general, the mind accepts only that new information which matches its prior knowledge or experience. It filters out everything else.

For example, when a viewer sees a television commercial that says, "NCR means computers," he doesn't accept it. IBM means computers. NCR means National Cash Register.

The computer "position" in the minds of most people is filled by a company called the International Business Machines Corp. For a competitive computer manufacturer to obtain a favorable position in the prospect's mind, he

must somehow relate his company to IBM's position.

Yet, too many companies embark on marketing and advertising programs as if the competitor's position did not exist. They advertise their products in a vacuum and are disappointed when their messages fail to get through.

SEVEN BRANDS ARE MIND'S LIMIT

The mind, as a container for ideas, is totally unsuited to the job at hand.

There are more than 500,000 trademarks registered with the U.S. Patent Office. In addition, untold thousands of unregistered trademarks are in use throughout the country.

During the course of a single year, the average mind is exposed to more than half a million advertising messages.

The target of all this communications ammunition has a reading vocabulary of no more than 25,000 to 50,000 words, and a speaking vocabulary of one-fifth as much.

√ Another limitation: The average human mind, according to Harvard psychologist George A. Miller, cannot deal with more than seven units at a time. (The eighth company in a given field is out of luck.)

Ask someone to name all the brands he or she remembers in a given product category. Rarely will anyone name more than seven. And that's for a high-interest category. For low-interest products, the average consumer can usually name no more than one or two brands.

Yet in category after category, the number of individual brands multiply like rabbits. In 1964, there were

seven soft drinks advertised on network television. Today there are 22.

✓ To cope with complexity, people have
learned to reduce everything to its ut-
most simplicity.

When asked to describe an offspring's
intellectual progress, a person doesn't
usually quote vocabulary statistics,
reading comprehension, mathematical
ability, etc. "He's in seventh grade"
is a typical reply.

This "ranking" of people, objects and
brands is not only a convenient method
of organizing things, but also an
absolute necessity if a person is to
keep from being overwhelmed by the complexities of life.

You see ranking concepts at work among
movies, restaurants, business and
military organizations. (Some day
someone might even come up with a rating system for politicians.)

new ladder. This, too, is difficult,
especially if the new category is not
positioned against an old one. The mind
has no room for the new and different
unless it's related to the old.

That's why if you have a truly new product, it's often better to tell the prospect what the product is *not*, rather
than what it is.

✓ The first automobile, for example,
was called a "horseless" carriage, a
name which allowed the public to position the concept against the existing
mode of transportation.

Words like "offtrack" betting, "lead-
free" gasoline and "tubeless" tire are
all examples of how new concepts can
best be positioned against the old.

Names that do not contain an element of
positioning usually die out. The "As-
trojet" name dreamed up by American
Airlines is an example of a glamorous,
but unsuccessful name, because it lacks
a positioning idea.

MIND PUTS PRODUCTS ON LADDERS

To cope with advertising's complexity,
people have learned to rank products
and brands in the mind. Perhaps this
can best be visualized by imagining a
series of ladders in the mind. On each
step is a brand name. And each different ladder represents a different
product category.

Some ladders have many steps. (Seven
is many.) Others have few, if any.

For an advertiser to increase his brand
preference, he must move up the ladder.
This can be difficult if the brands
above have a strong foothold and no
leverage or positioning strategy is
applied against them.

For an advertiser to introduce a new
product category, he must carry in a

LEADING BRAND HAS BIG EDGE

The weather forecast for the old, traditional ways of advertising is gloomy
at best. And nowhere was this more
clearly demonstrated than in the recent
Atlanta study conducted by Daniel Starch
& Staff.

According to Starch, about 25% of those
noting a television commercial attributed
it to the competition. With virtually
no exceptions, high scoring commercials
were the brand leaders in their category.

The also-rans didn't fare nearly as
well. A David Janssen Excedrin commercial was associated with Anacin twice
as often as Excedrin. A Pristeen commercial helped F.D.S., the brand leader,
more than it did Pristeen.

This shattering turn of events is certainly "positioning" at work in our over-communicated society. It appears that unless an advertisement is based on a unique idea or position, the message is often put in the mental slot reserved for the leader in the product category.

Clutter is surely part of the reason for the rise of "misidentification." But another, even more important factor is that times have changed. Today, you cannot advertise your product in splendid isolation. Unless your advertising positions your product in relationship to its competition, your advertising is doomed to failure.

CREATIVITY NO LONGER ENOUGH

In the positioning era, "strategy" is king. It made little difference

how clever the ads of RCA, General Electric and Bristol-Myers were. Or how well the layout, copy and typography were executed. Their strategy of attacking the leaders head-on was wrong.

In this context, it's illuminating to take a look at some recent examples of rampant creativity. The Lone Ranger and REA Express, Joe Namath and Ovaltine, Ann Miller and Great American soups. Even though these programs are highly creative, their chances for success are limited because each of them lacks a strong positioning idea.

Even creativity in the form of a slogan no longer serves much of a purpose if it doesn't position the product.

"If you got it, flaunt it" and "We must be doing something right" achieved enormous popularity without doing much for Braniff and Rheingold. And we predict that "Try it, you'll like it" won't do much for Alka-Seltzer.

DISCUSSION QUESTIONS

1. "The 60s was the image era. The 70s is the positioning era." Evaluate these statements.

2. Describe briefly the steps in the product positioning process.

3. Is positioning at odds with creativity in devising an advertising strategy? Explain.

Reprinted by permission from ADVERTISING AGE; 10 July, 1972, pp. 43-4, 46.

V-6

IS THIS THE ERA OF POSITIONING?
GREENLAND REFUTES STAND OF TROUT, RIES

Leo Greenland

We in advertising take one hell of a lot of abuse. We all know how people feel about advertising and the kind of continuing scathing criticism to which we are constantly subjected. Advertising people are regarded by some as being shallow, glib, superficial and husksterish.

People don't believe us, and sometimes for good reason. All too often one amongst us will rise up and offer a panacea for all that ails products that aren't selling. All too often someone will come along and whittle the practice of advertising down to magic formulas and pseudo-scientific findings.

I admit that it is often a great temptation to embrace a new ghuru when our products aren't selling. It is tempting to look for new buzzwords, new terminology, new analytical techniques, new position papers--in short, anything that will move a product off a shelf.

Advertising Age has devoted a great deal of space to a series of articles that prophetically told us that the answer to advertising in the 70s is positioning (AA, April 24 to May 8). I was sufficiently intrigued by these articles to read them fully. If the biblical and divinely sounding title

was enough to turn me on, the substance of the articles point of view did the exact opposite.

✓ I was amused when I read these articles. It became clear to me that we don't really live in an era of positioning at all. We live in an era of cultists, and each cult has the ultimate answer to the ultimate problem of advertising. In fairness to each cult, both old and new, I think we should begin identifying ourselves by wearing certain clearly recognizable arm bands on our grey flannel suits. One would say "Positionist;" another would say, "Segmentationist;" a third, "psychographicist," and so on. In this way the advertiser will know which cult we belong to and can worship at the altar of the cult of his choice.

And when we go to the mountain and implore our two new ghuru theorists to tell us what to do, a bolt of typewriter ribbon will come down, and a voice will say, "Creativity is dead. Positioning in the 70s is the answer. Long live the king."

A GOOD IDEA STILL HELPS

If I sound cynical, it's because I am. I am bored with prophetic new formulas for successful advertising. Not only bored, but downright embarrassed.

What today's ghuru twins fail to tell us after we have carefully analyzed why our products do not sell is, "Dumb-dumb, what you really need is one hell of a good idea."

I can understand why our profession isn't taken seriously when someone comes along and blurts out in all seriousness that creativity is dead an on to the next solution. Creativity is not only alive and well, but is living here, not Argentina. And contrary to the limited insights of the authors of the positioning series, positioning of products isn't beginning in the 70s. It's been with us for many, many years.

Basically, where I take issue with the positionist cultists--or any cultist for that matter--is in the assessment of one ingredient always being more important to successful advertising than any other ingredient. The cultist becomes dogmatic and inflexible in his approach to advertising because he is saying that it is positioning and nothing else that matters.

Forgive me for saying something you're all probably sick of hearing by now, but sometimes basics need to be said. We all know the ingredients that take a product from inception to a consumer's home. And we all know that a brilliantly conceived message will tip the marketplace in favor of your product.

The magic in advertising is in making the message exciting, breathtaking, provocative, memorable and motivating. Of course strategy is absolutely fundamental and vital--but that's not the only answer. The answer is shaping a creative strategy so that it comes alive.

And why, for heaven's sake, do the positionist cultists signal the end of the importance of product-message advertising as if product features and performance were suddenly of no interest to consumers in their supposed new positioning era? It's a good thing that Timex got in under the gun of the 1940s. If they'd invented the tough little watch during the 1970s, they'd have had to sell it as the timepiece that sits between the sun-dial and Accutron, and totally ignore its incredible performance story.

POSITIONING IS ONLY PART OF IT

The point is that positioning need not be viewed as a technique apart from product message. It isn't either/or. Who can argue that distinctive positioning *plus* a product differentiation message will inevitably be more persuasive than a positioning distinction alone?

For example, you are responsible for a 100mm cigaret. You now must tell the world about the wonders of this new cigaret. That, basically, is the strategy.

The creative strategies for Benson & Hedges and for Pall Mall had to be fairly similar. The execution of the campaign for one of these was brilliant and masterful. It had all of America laughing over, and remembering the name of, the long cigaret which was cut off by closing car windows and elevator doors. It was everything advertising should be: Newsy, memorable, attractive. The execution of the other campaign was competent--very competent-- but competence lost out to creativity. And we're just not talking aesthetics either. Benson & Hedges took over the lion's share of the 100mm cigaret *because* of brilliant creative strategy.

I'm here today to explore with you how

cultists oversimplify and run from basics in advertising. To do so, I'm afraid I must refute the logic of the positionist cult. By so doing, I hope I can symbolically discourage the advent of future cults. Then I'd like to explore the creative elements of some famous campaigns to analyze what made them great and why they sold products. And last, I'd like to do my own assessment of what the 70s really hold in store for us.

POSITIONING THROUGH THE AGES

Let's begin with positioning. Is it new? It's as new as Columbus. Here's a quote from an advertising trade publication on positioning: "The old omnibus advertising began to give way to the advertisement designed as a special tool to reach the special class of people automatically selected by the given publication in which it appeared."

Are we talking about 1972? No. This quote appeared in *Printers' Ink* in 1908.

Here is a description of product positioning in 1926 taken from the same magazine. "This was a device for fastening clothing designed to take the place of buttons, hooks and eyes and other fastening methods. In 1926 the Hookless Fastener Co. (now Talon Inc.) set out upon an advertising and merchandising program to establish the product definitely in the public mind and give it an identity apart from whatever product it might be used on."

And how about this *Printers' Ink* evaluation of a famous cigaret campaign of 1928: "'Reach for a Lucky instead of a sweet' shows positioning of a product for a particular kind of consumer."

These are all examples of an early understanding of positioning. It wasn't new then, just as it isn't new now. It was just as basic to advertising as all the other elements. Even the historically competitive soap market was engaging in positioning advertising as early as 1901. Cuticura soap advertised itself to the athlete who was bothered by "golf rash, heat rash, or any irritation produced by athletics."

UPSTART PLYMOUTH USED IT IN 1932

Almost everybody in advertising will admit that the late J. Sterling Getchell's advertising for Plymouth in 1932 is one of the alltime greats. It is a classic example of creative positioning. For those of you who don't remember it, it's often referred to as the "Look at All Three" ad. It positioned Plymouth with the leaders in the low-price field. Plymouth was entering its third year, having been launched in 1929. It was naturally a very new and a very small contender in the low-price field then dominated entirely by Ford and Chevrolet.

At the time, Chevrolet was in a very good position, having out-styled and out-sold the old Model A Ford, and had obtained a very strong hold on the market while Ford had been out of production retooling. Hardly anyone knew or cared about Mr. Chrysler's new Plymouth --until the ad which broke tradition and referred to the competition. Under the banner headline of "Look at All Three" ran the line, "But don't buy any low-priced car until you've driven the new Plymouth with floating power." Under the subhead was a photograph of Walter P. Chrysler staring earnestly at you from the page, followed by a statement from him.

The day the ad was published in newspapers all over the country, the reaction was unmistakable. Plymouth, over night, had become a real contender in the low-price field, and has remained so ever since. By 1941, sales ran well over 600,000 cars a year.

I could go on and on with these kinds of examples to show that positioning has always been an important factor in advertising. Positioning is no different from any other traditional technique of merely distinguishing a product within its competitive marketplace. Positioning--whether through consumer segmentation, imagery or product distinction, put-up or price-point differentiation, you name it--are all part of the same phenomenon. And none of them can legitimately be described as new.

HOW NO-CAL POSITIONING FLOPPED

I would now like to move on the the subject of positioning without creativity to demonstrate that one without the other equals failure.

No-Cal offers us a classic example. Here's a company (Kirsch Beverages Inc.) that did everything our positionist cultists tell us is their secret for marketing success. They had a beat on the soft drink industry because they were the first to come up with a calorie-free, diet soft drink when we were all becoming very weight conscious. Not only that, but the company did what the positionists tell us can't fail--they named their product after the marketing position they assumed--No-Cal. So there we have it. They were there first with a unique product, and had a great position going for it.

From the positionist point of view, one would think that No-Cal dominated its field the way IBM and Polaroid did theirs. As you know, the answer is no. No-Cal did not. Why? Because No-Cal went through one of the most bland advertising campaigns I've ever seen. Every other diet soft drink that came

along kicked No-Cal's bubbles in with better advertising and execution--a classic example of a company being there first with a product and losing the subsequent market share because of ineffectual execution of the unique selling propositon.

I think you'll agree that the message is just as essential as the position. George Eastman seemed to be aware of that at the beginning of this century when his new product was merchandised to Americans with the promise, "You press the button--we do the rest." As early as 1903, Ford was the "Boss of the Road" and Packard was confidently advising people to "Ask the man who owns one." We started "Watching the Fords go by" in 1907, and the Cadillac of 1912 was already the "Standard of the World."

REMEMBER THESE SLOGANS?

Throughout the history of advertising, literally thousands of catchy phrases made for instant recognition. I'll give you all a little quiz. I'll rattle off a handful of famous advertising phrases and see if you can identify the product:

"We'll take good care of you"; "And away go troubles down the drain"; "Babies are our business ... our only business"; "The best aid is first aid"; "The beer that made Milwaukee famous"; "The biggest should do more. It's only right ..."; "Born in 1820, still going strong"; "Breakfast of Champions"; "The brisk tea"; "The Champagne of bottle beer"; "The coffee-er coffee"; "Come alive"; "A cut above the commonplace"; "Does she ... or doesn't she"; "The extra care airline"; "Filter, flavor, flip-top box"; "Helps build strong bodies 12 ways"; and "Look for this famous name in the oval."

Fun, isn't it? But now, I want to make a point about the role of creativity relative to positioning. And to show why it's so important, let's assume that you've developed a sound marketing strategy for a product, and all signals indicate that the product can't miss. It's a good product, it's positioned well, your consumer testing rates high, and so on... all the signs of strong product life. Now you're ready for the advertising message, the essential ingredient that hits the point home hard and effectively.

But what if you should miss the boat on the proper expression and execution of that all important message? Just as in my earlier example of Benson & Hedges and Pall Mall, the advertising message that is memorable will surely consummate a well-planned marketing strategy.

Seven-Up wisely decided to position itself as an alternative to the cola drinks which had the overwhelming share of the soft drink market. Excellent positioning. But what if its message had been less brilliant? Would the impact have been the same if the message read "7Up Is *Not* a Cola" rather than "7Up. The *Un*-Cola?" Would Heinz have been effective if the line read "Heinz's Ketchup Runs Slowly" rather than "The Slowest Ketchup in Town?"

DO THESE SLOGANS GRAB YOU?

Let's play another little game. Let's see what happens if we alter one or two words in some advertising lines that we have come to accept as classics. Let's see if the impact remains the same. I'll give the "positioning-style" copy lines. See if you can remember the lines as some great writers shaped them. "Let us drive you in our bus instead of driving your own car." "Shop by turning the pages of our directory." "If you're going to drink a lot of beer,

Schaefer is a good beer to drink." "We don't rent as many cars, so we have to do more for our customers." "The luxury standard of bottled beers." "You'll find a sympathetic ear at Chase-Manhattan."

Well, you get the idea.

Another premise developed by the positionist cultists is that when a well-known brand places more products using the same brand name on the market, the less meaning the name has the average consumer. The cultists called this marketing strategy the "line-extention trap," and Scott was used as the victim, and Charmin as the victor. It is claimed that the housewife wasn't going to write the name "Scott" on her shopping list because the name has no meaning in and by itself.

We'll let Scott speak for itself, but the positionists had better start loosening their arm bands if they're going to use logic that can be refuted so easily.

Creative ideas, truly big ideas can do more to establish a position than the product itself, particularly if there is no basic difference in products in the same brand category.

Take the case of Ajax cleanser. As told by Richard Bowman of Norman, Craig & Kummel, the last thing anyone needed in 1964 was another detergent. Colgate had an excellent product, but competitive advertising was spending in excess of $60,000,000. The competition was in many shapes and forms--high sudsers, low sudsers, liquids, powders and pills and packets.

√ The strategy for Ajax was relatively simple. Colgate wanted Ajax to stand for power, to be the strongest detergent the housewife could put in her laundry machine safely, plus take advantage of the Ajax name. Their research showed that it's no surprise that what a woman wants isn't really clean clothes.

She *has* to get them clean because
they're dirty. What the woman wants
is no dirt at all. The problem is,
she *hates* dirt. It was on that premise
that the agency got the line "stronger
than dirt."

Next was not how do we stay clean, but
how do we get on the lady's side and
help her win her fight against dirt
which is really a fight for good versus evil. It was within that framework
that the Ajax White Knight was unlocked
as the mythical helper that turned a
product into a hero. As a result of
the "stronger than dirt" campaign with
White Knight graphics, Colgate's House
of Ajax line climbed to the 20% market
share level of 1967.

DID VW CREATIVITY BOOM OR BUST?

Everyone in this room is familiar
with the Volkswagen success story and
the brilliant advertising by Doyle Dane
Bernbach which will always serve as a
milestone for the advertising industry.
I don't have to recall to you how Doyle
Dane broke new ground by taking such
unprecedented steps that I'm certain
even Volkswagen management was somewhat
skeptical at the beginning. Imagine
assuming a stance that made your product ugly, a bug, a lemon and all sorts
of other epitaphs that must have made
Detroit rub its hands in glee.

What happened is history, of course,
but the real breakthrough in the VW
campaign was Doyle Dane's deep psychological understanding of its consumer
prospect.

✓ Call it psychological positioning
or call it brilliant conceptual creativity; it doesn't matter. The fact is
that it was as bold and daring an advertising approach as it was for Volkswagen
management to attempt to sell a car of
such dimensions and style to an American

market.

In 1949, VW sales in this country totaled
two cars. A year later, 330 cars were
sold. In 1969, U.S. sales topped 569,-
000. The numbers tell the story.

AD 'SCIENCE' WILL FAIL

The 70s are *not* the era of positioning,
nor will the 80s be the era of point of
purchase supremacy, nor the 90s the era
of psychogalvanomic attitudinal reflexi-
bility--whatever the hell that means. I
must warn the cultist that all attempts
to treat basic marketing as a science
can only result in consistent, dismal
failure. For no art form has yet proved
responsive to formularization without
winding up with a paint-by-numbers result.

The 70s will find that creativity lives
and that its influence will be felt by
every single facet of marketing. Creativity will be needed at more levels of
marketing than ever before. The positioning era pundits notwithstanding, the
basics of advertising will remain the
same. They'll simply have to be better
than anything we've ever seen, and the
ad agencies who can rise to the occasion
will sell the products.

DISCUSSION QUESTIONS

1. Which of the following two statements
comes closer to promising advertising
effectiveness? Why?
   a. Creativity is no longer enough.
Product positioning featuring products/
strengths and weaknesses and those of
competitors is the mark of our era.
   b. The creative message is just as
essential as the position.

2. Is it appropriate to view advertising
as a science? Explain.

267

Reprinted by permission from ADVERTISING AGE; 26 October, 1970, pp. 56-58.

V-7

BEWARE THE SEVEN DEADLY C'S OF RETAIL NEWSPAPER ADS

Alan Koehler

Oh, retail advertising *has* stood still all right. You don't have to go out of your way to document it. You just have to open the Sunday paper. Including the supposedly "hot" retail advertising towns, like Dallas, St. Louis, Pittsburgh--or whatever the hot towns are this semester.

Simply sticking out in the paper isn't enough, you know. It's easy to stick out in the paper by being wanton (in your use of space) or silly or odd, instead of selling merchandise. For every exception to the rule, like Bloomingdale's, you've got non-exceptions everywhere. Most stores are advertising just abut the wav they did 20 years ago. Or worse. Twenty years ago, give or take a year, was still the heyday of such famous names in retail advertising as Bernice Fitz-Gibbon, Kenneth Collins, Sarah Pennoyer, Solita Arbib, Bill Howard, Jane Trahey, Margaret Hockaday, Harry Rodman, Margaret Fishback, *et al*. This breed seems either to have vanished, or gone on to other things. If you don't believe it, name a famous incumbent in the retail advertising hierarchy. One springs to mind about as readily as that of a Canadian countess.

If we may risk sounding as glib, pat and adorable as the typical retail

fashion ad, let's put the blame for this inertia on the Seven Deadly Cs. In order, roughly, of their increasing significance, the Seven Deadly Cs are these: Color. Co-op. Contrast. Consistency. Cuteness. Competition. Cost.

---

1 COLOR

Open the "Retail Coloring Book." See the b&w ad. Now, color it purple.

Here is a toy that should be kept from the reach of children. The only really sensible use of color is four-color, that is, complete color. In complete color, things are colored the way they're supposed to be. In less-than-complete color, things are colored the way they aren't supposed to be. Can you imagine owning a two-color TV set?

But only something much less than complete color is widely available in newspapers, except in special sections. Something so much less, in fact, that the richest paper in the world, *The New York Times*, has elected, to date, to exclude color from its news sections. There must be a reason. There is.

268

Color in the newspaper, if you don't keep it under 24-hour lock and key, escapes, and becomes a crutch. A crutch to hobble along on in lieu of creativity and simple thought.

If we color the salesman's necktie, the chandelier, and the end of the lipstick all pink, why, then, we don't have to think! Look through the papers that offer two and three-color r.o.p. Note the abdication, in ads using color, of reason-why. Note frequently, moreover, the abdication of the very reason for retailing: *Something to buy!*

√ The only question to be asked of less-than-total color should be, Here's a really good ad! Now, will color help it? And never: Here's an indifferent ad. Now, will color save it, or at least make it different?

For the answer to the latter question is almost always *"No."* The indifference reaches right through to the reader, despite the difference of color. Only more so, because the difference is superficially and artificially imposed.

So: A run-of-the-mill b&w ad comes off as still more run-of-the-mill--in anything less than total color--than it does in b&w. Only when the very conception of the ad legitimately demands or springs from color can there be an exception.

The advent of color in the main news sections of most newspapers has been relatively recent. Nonetheless, in those papers that have it, color is already well established as one of the Seven Deadly Cs that have kept retail advertising standing still.

2 CO-OP

Only shortsighted stores ever let themselves whore for vendor money.

Longsighted stores insist on remaining ladies. They'll gladly take the vendor's money, but they do with it only as, in all good conscience, they see fit. That is, as they deem appropriate to their considered advertising image.

The circle, otherwise, can be vicious. Particularly since most stores need vendor money and, in doing so, vitiate your image, you decrease, by just that much, the likelihood of further vendor money. However, if you can retain your virtue by refusing vendor money that requires you to compromise your good image, why, then, when that good image is finally mature and secure (if it isn't already), vendors will, ironically, flock to your door. And they'll return each time more eagerly after every rebuff you give them by responsibly advertising their wares your way, rather than their way.

Successful co-op advertising--from the retailer's point of view--always plants the possibility, in even the most hardened competitor's mind, that the store just might have paid for the ad itself--and voluntarily.

(Note to vendors: There's a silver lining here. If you give Bloomingdale's money to advertise, and if the Bloomingdale's ad, perhaps contrary to your wishes, looks as though Bloomingdale's was paying for it, maybe Lord & Taylor won't be after you for equal time.)

There is an opposite side of the co-op coin, of course; a sadder, if not a worse, one. This is when the store is major, and the vendor minor. Or at least when the vendor fancies himself to be more in need of the store than the store of the vendor. Then the vendor may stand helplessly by as the store, lazy with prior success, says, "Oh, what the hell, it's his money." And pulls an ad off the top of its head that wouldn't sell a hot water heater in Spitzbergen in winter.

√ The melancholy rule of thumb is this:

As surely as water seeks its own level, co-op advertising seeks to undermine retail advertising. The two aren't exactly out-and-out natural enemies, like the cobra and the mongoose. But the retailer had better be as wary as those little birds that pick the teeth of open-jawed crocodiles. Especially when the vendor can cause major damage by being comparatively weak, as well as by being comparatively strong.

Without any vendor money at all there would be much less--but surely much more lively--retail advertising. Meanwhile, to round out our metaphoric menagerie, it's really only fun to sleep with the tiger if nobody gets clawed.

3 CONTRACT

In exchange for Marguerite (preferred position, or a lower rate), Faust (the retailer) sells his soul to Mephistopheles (signs a contract with the newspaper). Whether it's for position in the paper, or for lower rate, or for both, most contracts commit most retailers to running advertising when they don't really want to. If you can have Page 7, or the back page of the first section, every day--but only on the proviso that you take it every day --there quickly comes the Tuesday or Thursday when you don't happen to have anything to advertise. Yet you must advertise something, anyway. Your legs, by contract, have to be longer than they need be to reach the ground. You're forced into some coy conceit or caprice, the emptiness of which again comes roaring right through to the reader, reflecting badly on you. (Why is it regarded as cowardly for retailers simply to repeat good previous pages, when national advertisers so frequently and so successfully do?)

How refreshing it would be--for the reader as well as the retailer--if position were no longer guaranteed to any store. If the newspaper, like *The New Yorker*, decided where everybody's ads ran according to how good they were-- with the best ads getting the best positions.

That might tone up the advertising a little, or at least product some incentive for toning it up. That might make the newspaper look a little less inevitable, too. For as it is, you might as well be going through last Sunday's *Times* this Sunday, as far as retail advertising thrills or surprises are concerned. Even the daily *Times* conveys more than an intimation of *deja vu*.

✓ Abolishing position privilege would reduce the major function of the contract to a guarantee of rate, according to linage used over the year. And it's a little more sensible to project in terms of a total number of lines over the year than to commit yourself to a daily, or even a weekly, utterance, in the form of particular pages.

It's possible, of course, successfully to say, "A pox on rate as well as position," and still manage to be so well seen that people think you run much more than you do. The classic example in New York is the Russian Tea Room. The Russian Tea Room surely doesn't run enough linage to earn much of a rate. Yet by interspersing relatively frequent, highly visible, tiny ads, with highly *in*frequent, highly visible full-page ads, the restaurant seems to be running all the time. The ads look so good that they predispose the make-up people at the *Times* to grant favorable position out of the goodness of their hearts.

(We further salute the Russian Tea Room for running full pages, rather than seven-columns, with a column of editorial guaranteed along-side. Most New York stores think that seven-column ads look like pages. Actually, they look more like six-columns. Only pages look like pages.)

4 CONSISTENCY

Rosser Reeves once said he'd rather run a mediocre campaign for ten years than a series of brilliant campaigns that were changed every six months. Such are the rewards of consistency. But note that Rosser chose to use ten years as his outside figure, and not 20. Perhaps consistency, carried on for more than a decade, becomes a rut.

Twenty years and more of unchanging Lord & Taylor advertising have so lulled the eye that perhaps the ads now are slipping by unseen. Perhaps we need some change--if only for change's sake--to start engaging the eye again. We've all heard about the sensitive architect who was so offended by the ugly house he passed on his way to work that finally he bought it, moved in, and before long never saw it again. The same perhaps holds true of houses as lovely as Lord & Taylor's.

Happily, capricious change--change merely for the sake of change--is never necessary if there has been evolutionary change. The world doesn't stay the same. One's appeal to it, therefore, can't either. There must be gradual evolutionary growth, even within the limits of very good. Ohrbach's advertising was very good 20 years ago, and has evolved, while remaining very good. And so Ohrbach's remains, indeed very good today. Lord & Taylor was very good 20 years ago, but has *not* evolved, while remaining very good. And so Lord & Taylor nets out as not nearly so good today.

Insistency on consistency--a refusal to evolve along with the evolving retail environment--is another reason retail advertising is overparked. Slavish consistency, after all, you don't need an advertising department for; you can get it from the milkman.

5 CUTENESS

Advertising people talk about retail advertising and national advertising as though they were two different things. In practice they happen to be. But they needn't, and shouldn't, be. The best retail advertising can look and sound very much like the best national advertising, and very much vice versa. Apart from the bookkeeping detail of whether the ad is being paid for by a store or by a manufacturer, the concept of retail as a separate way of advertising may actually have been hatched by retailers as an excuse for not doing better ads.

Retail advertising certainly is a haven for glib, superficial, poorly-researched copy, that typically tries to squeak by with giving out as little real information as padding will permit. The better stores, or the bigger stores, or any stores embarrassed into a kind of caring, typically attempt to give this inert pill a coat of cuteness. A fun little pun in the headline; a gay little play on words in the lead-in; anything mildly-amusing to set the stage for the puff of vapidity to follow. The retail copywriter is actually encouraged to write ads that say, in effect, "See how good I am," rather than "See how good our goods are."

Corn-fed though it sounds, sincerity, rather than cuteness, will mark the successful retail copy of the 1970s, as it already marked some *avant garde* retail copy of the late 1960s, like Sears in magazines, and Abercrombie & Fitch. Not earnestness, or high-mindedness, but merely a sincere effort to transmit real honest-to-God useful and helpful information, germane to the merchandise. Information, by the way, needn't be dull. Facts shoot far faster to the heart of the matter than the fastest pun in the West. (And beware all you heavily art-over-copy-oriented departments: Copy-less art--or art that might as well be copy-less--won't much longer be enough!)

✓ Superficial copy can no longer successfully gloss over those two hard facts of retailing advertising life: that the volume of new items to be advertised is heavy, and that the average retail copy-writer is either an out-and-out hack or a perhaps-promising beginner, learning how to write (but only to be off to a higher paying agency job).

Miss Fitz-Gibbon had a way of coping with each of these hard facts of life. To cope with the newness of items, she forced the buyer into the copywriter's office, and made the copywriter take a typewritten deposition on every item to be advertised, and why the buyer had bought it for the store to sell. If a typewritten page of facts from which to write the ad didn't result, an ad didn't either.

To cope with the callowness of writers, she made them go to the selling floor and quote their silly or stilted copy, verbatim, to actual customers. You know, the "Where quality and economy walk hand in hand" kind of thing. The embarrassment of doing this encouraged them to learn how to write right, which is simply to write the way people talk.

Because there is usually so little time between the arrival of an item at a store and the store's advertisement of it, the advertising strategy promulgated for each item may leave something to be desired. Here the national advertiser usually has the luxury of time, time that can be well invested indeed, for there is nothing so important to advertising of any kind as strategy. Sure of a sound strategy, you can go on to make a valid emotional, as well as rational, appeal...

Yet, if the buyer is a good one--and if he is rigorously grilled and cross-examined to get the facts--a serviceable strategy should emerge. And if the store head and the advertising director are good ones, a store personality is built to help cast a little

empathy onto those items that seem to remain highly unemotional. Meanwhile, in most retail ads, the facts are too few, the strategy too sketchy, the empathy too empty, and the cuteness is slicked on to hide the barrenness.

✓ In all fairness, though, retail advertising has pulled ahead of national advertising in one area of cuteness or glibness or gloss. That is in the retail rejection of the smashing superficiality of the slogan. Gone is the platitudinous pap of "It's smart to be thrifty"; gone is the abundantly unbelievable "A business in millions, a profit in pennies"; and "Nobody but nobody, undersells Gimbel's." In their stead, we're mercifully more likely to have non-slogans--non-slogans, moreover, that pretend to be something else. Non-slogans like Marshall Field's "There's no place like it back home," which often poses as a sentence of body copy; or Ohrbach's "What a little money can do at Ohrbach's," which poses as a continuation of the headline; or "You've changed a lot lately; so has Sears," which sneaks by as a kind of long logo; or "Did you Garfinckel today?" which sallies forth boldly as a classic question headline, while perhaps still irritating purists by making a verb out of so-unlikely a noun.

By contrast, nothing this side of "Little Women" sounds so prim as still-current national slogans like "Progress is our most important product" or "Better things for better living through chemistry," which should have departed long since down the same track as that cough-free carload.

6 COMPETITION

It's fine to be aware of your competition, but perhaps fatal to be overwhelmed, or mesmerized, by it. By spending too much time contemplating the com-

petition, you can wind up with too little time acting for yourself. Creative
people can be overwhelmed by too-intense
study of competition advertising. It
can make it seem that everything conceivable has been done.

It has.

Better to be underwhelmed, and to think
of something to *do*. Imagine a would-be
fiction writer trying to read all the
fiction. He'd quickly conclude there
was no tale left untold. Unblinking
watch on the competition stifles creativity and a store's individuality.
Competitors trying to stare each other
down grow more and more alike. Unless
they take great care they become look-
alikes in their advertising. Constant
imitation of each other, constant borrowing from each other, buffs the visible differences away.

The more a Macy's and a Gimble's vie
with each other via emulation, the less
distinguishable from one another they
can become. Unless they have the discipline to profit by the example of other
competing neighbors, like Bonwit's,
Bendel's and Bergdorf's. These stores
are just-as-direct competitors. But
these three busy 57th St. Bs bend over
backward to separate themselves from
each other in every visible way. True
these are fashion stores, always more
easily separated in image from promotional stores, regardless of any similarity of merchandise. Yet, when Fitz
was running Gimbel's advertising 20
years ago, Gimbel's managed to come
off in the papers as different from
Macy's as the princess from the goblin.

Again a pragmatic observation of Mr.
Reeves: Every good copywriter is a
good thief. (What Rosser omitted saying is that every good art director is
a *master* thief.) But when we hear something like that, we get all tangled up
in our American puritan ethic, preached
by so many although practiced by so few.
Appropriating ideas from the dead is
learning. Appropriating ideas from the

living is stealing. But since we pretend not to approve of stealing, let's
euphemize, and call it *borrowing*.

√ The fashion industry has no compunction about borrowing. The automobile
industry has no compunction about borrowing. Indeed, no other industry has
any compunction about borrowing, not
even the theological one. Why, then,
should the retail industry have any compunction?

But, when you keep your eye unremitting-
ly on the store next door you wind up
borrowing from the wrong place. By os-
mosis, both of you begin looking more
alike, when you want to begin looking
more different.

Each town has room for only one store
with any one advertising look. Therefore, how foolish it is for an Altman's
to loot a look from Bloomingdale's, when
not many people in New York would know
it, or care, if Altman's shoplifted
from Neiman-Marcus. When pilfering you
would go, for land's sake don't go to
your local competition. Don't stay
anywhere around home. *Get out of town.*
Then, if something you covet catches
your eye, swipe it. I mean borrow it;
maybe modify it a little, if your conscience bothers you. But then use it
to your heart's content. It's not stealing that's bad. It's just bad stealing
that's bad.

√ It's also a good idea not to get
caught up in the cliche of what all the
local stores do, en masse. If you're
Gimbel's, and you have a 127th anniversary sale, don't then, if you're Macy's,
go and have a 111th anniversary sale.
Maybe don't have an anniversary sale
at all. Maybe not even if you're the
only store in town. Hanging a sale pag
on nothing but an anniversary headline
maybe really *is* to hang it. Who *cares*?
Nobody gives a hott it's your birthday
if you're a person, except maybe your
mother. Nobody but *nobody* gives a hoot
it's your birthday if you're a store.
If you're that hard up for a handle to

hang a sale on, how about a "Just For
The Hell Of It" sale?

In the absence of a flow of non-stop,
top-notch ideas from your own store,
immediately fall back on one of retail
advertising's *ten commandments*, no less,
"Thou Shalt Borrow--Well." Bad borrowing from the competition results in
mediocrity, at best. At worst, it results in extinction. Per McCreery's,
Russek's, DePinna, Saks 34th and Stern's,
to name five major retail operations
that have sunk below the bottom line,
in the last decade or so, in Manhattan
alone.

7 COST

Now we can come to the first of the
two really super villains of the piece.

Money--whose absence from the retail
scene never made the heart grow fonder.
Great, if you're a relatively rich
store. Great, if you can afford to
splash a single exquisitely-drawn fashion figure across 2,400 lines of space
that remains mostly pristinely white.
Great, if you can afford to lavish a
sinble eyegrabbing photograph across
the same 2,400 lines to make a single
institutional point. Great, if you can
command the kind of vendor money that
lets you blow your own horn, while blowing a page. Great, if you can afford
to splash a kaleidoscope of color across
a double truck, seething with all the
sell of a TV test pattern.

But, let's assume that this ain't us.
Just because the odds against it are
1,000 to 1. What do we do if we're
really pinched for funds, and if we
live where we don't happen to have the
best artists, photographers, layout
people and copywriters? Above all we
try to develop, borrowing from out of
town advertising as need be, a flexible
format that works in larger space, that

is also highly visible in smaller.
Borders and typefaces and logos and white
spaces are the things that formats are
made of, when excellent art or photography is at a premium. (But don't be
so sure excellent art or photography is
beyond you.)

Big stores have been known to make their
costly art and photography available to
smaller out-of-town stores, for entirely
resonable fees. Write the stores you
admire, to see. If you don't happen to
have similar merchandise, the visuals
can be used in an institutional or the-
matic way.

√ If experieiced layout help isn't
around, or within the budget, perhaps
dig up a local, struggling, so-called
fine artist. They're always around.
Have him try his hand at format, or even
layout. That's what I. Miller did some
years ago with a local, struggling fine
artist whose forte, till then, was drawing cats. He tried his hand at doing
a format for I. Miller's shoes. He did
quite well, then and since. His name
was Andy Warhol.

Borders, in limitless variety, are virtually free for the deciding upon. Many
stores get especially good visibility
by bringing the border into the ad,
and letting the artwork stick out over
it. If the newspaper's typesetting
leaves too much to be desired, how about
hand lettering? You don't even need
an artist. A child-like scrawl can be
charming, or so Bendel's has found.
Even a *motherly* scrawl can be charming,
or so I. Miller found. Andy Warhol
didn't do the lettering for his own
shoe ads. His mother did. How about
actually trying a local child or mother?
Or, if it seems nobody can letter or
print or handwrite or scrawl, how about
being first in your town to use typewriter type, but cheap, right from your
own typewriter?

Look at the new looseness in logos, like
Bloomingdale's big bold magic-marker
script, that looks so contemporary, as

well as so seeable. The days of the
convoluted constipated logo are numbered, among stores that would look
young.

If good finished artwork just cannot
be had, have a reasonably sensible
soul wander about the store snapping
Polaroid shots of merchandise. Abercrombie & Fitch illustrates its highly
successful current campaign with candid,
unprofessional photographs that could
easily be taken by Andy Warhol's *grand-
mother.*

√ As a last resort--if you're the first
in town to do it, thus preempting it--
you can use your ads to publicize, more
or less institutionally, a real or
fictitious character associated with
the operation, who performs good works
there. Betty Crocker is perhaps the
major fictional figure since Mrs. Mini-
ver. But on a smaller, more practical
scale for a store is the Ann Page type
of fictional character, for the A&P.
Or, better, the Julia Waldbaum type of
real-life character for Waldbaum's
supermarkets in New York. Waldbaum's
ads show Julia squeezing the melons
and berating the butcher, and you really get the feeling after a while that
she may personally be doing some good
editing on your behalf.

√ Actually, nothing says that merchan-
dise--or even Julia Waldbaum--has to
be illustrated. All-type ads in a
tasteful, visible format can get good
readership, as Wallach's has proved
over the years in New York. All-type
ads are just fine for getting across
the sincere, helpful message that's
wanted today, too.

If all efforts to produce a format locally fail, there are people who will
evolve one for you. Bill Berta, of
Berta, Grant & Winkler in New York,
evolved the new Bloomingdale's and I.
Magnin formats. If that sounds like
too much money, he also did the format for a small store that nobody outside New York ever heard of--Hirshleifer's

--without apparently bankrupting it.

No matter who does the format, glue a
few layouts at random into the newspaper,
to test the look for visibility, before
you lock it up. Amazing how much advertising that pops on the drawing
board poops in the paper, built-up on
by all the ads for false teeth cleaners
and pile remedies.

Don't despair. Retail budgets, projected nationally, aren't often so small,
after all. Just think, you may be spending more in your community than the
Coca-Cola Co. without really spending
very much at all!

√ One possible economy remains totally
false. Twenty years ago, all of us ink-
stained wretches in the advertising
department at Gimbel's were making $35
a week. Except for ink-stained Miss
Fitz-Gibbon. In 1948 she extracted
$108,000 from the store, or so said her
income tax return, which once I saw.
Well, maybe paying $108,000 a year to
the advertising director is indeed a
bit much for the average retail operation. But you can count on one thing.
Any sizable retail business is missing
plenty if it's not paying about $50,000
to the top advertising cat.

A good, expensive advertising director
will earn the extra dollars you pay him
back for you in about a month. And go
on to put a whole potful of extra bucks
in your pocket for the rest of the year.
Somebody's got to have the incentive to
drive the slave labor on to the heights
that are otherwise ever beyond it. Only
if you pay enough will retail advertising directors become good enough again
to become famous again.

√ A really strong advertising director
can really stand up to the second super-
villain of the piece: The Buyer. The
Big Bad B, who can be bigger and badder
for the advertising than all the Seven
Deadly Cs put together. Whenever you
see a smashing success like Bloomingdale's, you just know that buyers are

barred from meddling with the advertising.

And conversely, whenever you observe
rigor mortis in retail advertising,
you just know the buyers have gotten
right in there, with their jackets off
and their sleeves rolled up.

DISCUSSION QUESTIONS

1. Discuss some of the strengths and
weaknesses of newspapers as a retail
advertising medium.

2. "Co-op advertising seeks to undermine
retail advertising." Do you agree or
disagree? Why?

3. Are the seven C's applicable exclusively to retail newspaper advertising?
Which ones, if any, appear to be applicable to national newspaper advertising
as well?

Reprinted by permission from ADVERTISING AGE; 15 December, 1969. pp. 47-9.

V-8

ADVERTISING IS NO JOKE; DON'T MAKE IT INTO ONE

Fairfax M. Cone

I must say that when I contemplated talking here about advertising and marketing, I felt a certain trepidation.

I haven't made a talk of any kind for several years, because I haven't liked the atmosphere. It has seemed to me that advertising was one of the objects of the revolt that is all around us that was being used with headstrong disregard of the consequences.

The old notion that advertising is at best only a substitute for going somewhere and talking seriously to someone about something of mutual interest was giving way throughout the marketing world, and particularly that part of it whose main street is Madison Ave., to matters of fun and frolic. Straightforward, serious advertising was put down as old-fashioned and frumpy, and for the birds.

And if anyone wanted to argue against the kind of copy and art and mood and tone that had built the great brands of our time, and maintained them, I had no wish to debate.

For one thing, I thought the foolishness would shortly wear itself out. But I was wrong.

√ The whole advertising industry, mistaking Bill Bernbach's candid advertising for Volkswagen and Avis--"Think Small" and "We're only No. 2"--for gags, copied it with incredible lack of understanding.

They thought Bernbach was only another stand-up comedian, moved over from the night clubs: a cleaned-up Lenny Bruce, a thinned-down Jack E. Leonard. And they tried to copy him. Only, of course, they couldn't.

As near as most of them came was, and as near as most of them have come today, is epitomized in the whisky advertising that insists that "people who drink Old Fitzgerald don't know any better."

Or the Lark cigaret advertising that asks you to "tell someone you like about Lark's gas-trap filter. He may remember your anniversary."

The fact that this improbable suggestion is illustrated with a woman kissing a man's bald head is only par for the course.

Rather beating par is a current advertisement for Renault which insists that "The horse if better than most 1970 cars," which, the copy says, are "an affront to progress."

It is this kind of thing that must disturb and distress anyone who is serious about advertising, for it is under great pressure to reform or be destroyed. Unhappily, the pressure is more to destroy it than to reform it.

ADVERTISING CANDIDATES LIKE PUDDING

It is in a similar position to our educational system, of which, in an ancestral way, it is actually a part. The thing is, it is a distant relative and we are allowing it to be characterized as either a crazy distant cousin, or a dishonest one.

And, as I say, sentiment for its destruction seeps down from the intellectual heights where the historian, Toynbee, and the economist, Galbraith, live, to the new centers of what is called relevance where the hippies and the yippies hold forth, not to mention the halls of ivy and the corridors of Congress.

A brand new offender is the advertising of political candidates, packaged and promoted like pudding, or cheese.

But whatever the precise nature may be of the fault finding, make no mistake about it, advertising is under attack from more sides than ever before. For one thing, the attack by young people is something new.

Worst of all, it is a *laughing* attack.

And any attack on advertising is an assault on the strongest force in marketing.

My introduction to marketing took place a long time ago. So long ago, in fact, that it was many years before I ever heard the word "marketing" used. The

term "marketing manager" and, indeed, the marketing function itself, as we know these today, had yet to be introduced.

This was more than a matter of terminology. In 1929, when I came into the business of selling, and until after World War II, although not very much after, the organization of most businesses was relatively simple.

√ In most consumer goods concerns the structure could be charted in three boxes, labeled production, sales and advertising; and these appeared on a line and in equal size beneath the single, superior box entitled "management," which included finance.

Sometimes management meant ownership and sometimes it meant just what it said. But in either case it constituted responsibility for the entire enterprise, and it implied day-to-day involvement in it. All the decisions were the management's.

BACK THEN, YOU DEALT WITH TOP MAN

As late as 1943, when I arrived in Chicago to work for what was probably the largest and most powerful advertising agency of its day, the agency that was operated by the legendary Albert D. Lasker, under the name of Lord & Thomas, at the meetings that I attended as creative director (which is another term that had yet to be invented) I made my advertising proposals to the principals of the companies that were our clients.

I dealt with George A. Eastwood and Frederick W. Specht, chairman and president, respectively, of Armour & Co.; John H. Kimberly and Ernst Mahler, the active menagers of Kimberly-Clark Corp., the makers of Kleenex and Kotex; and Charles Luckman, president of the Pepsodent Co.

And in New York, the dynamic George Washington Hill, president, and chairman, too, of the American Tobacco Co., was my sole contact for the advertising of Lucky Strike, the world's largest-selling cigaret.

√ The oldest graduate school of business in the country was at the University of Chicago, and like Harvard's, and the Wharton School at the University of Pennsylvania, it was soon to be heard from.

But "soon" is a relative term, and professionalism in business, as we know it today, had to wait until some time after the war's end to be accepted other than skeptically.

The school of hard knocks and the university of experience still were the classic institutions and the immediate postwar graduates of the truly professional schools were to be found primarily, if not entirely, in the newly organized (and rather skeptically viewed) research departments, where their chief activity was trying to square the new Nielsen Reports with the hunches that guided (and misguided) their managements.

√ Just here there was another, highly diversionary development in the march toward the marketing concept, and it set back any sensible approach by several years.

This was the discovery and development of a cancerous concept called Merchandising with a capital rather than a lower case "m"; and there was a period of several years in the late 40s and early 50s when it was only a very old-fashioned and out-of-date company that didn't combine its products with some kind of premium, which was sold at a discount, or with an out-and-out giveaway.

SELLING THE PRIZE, NOT THE PRODUCT

Examination of the advertising of the time in magazines and newspapers fails to make clear, for example, whether it was Armour's Star ham that was the object of the sale or whether it was a small bronzed mustard pot, or some other item of marginal worth, blown up in the gaudy advertising illustration to be almost twice the size of the ham.

The Orphan Annie mug overshadowed the powdered Ovaltine with which it was wrapped and offered for 39¢.

And one could question whether it was the toothpaste or whether it was really a hand brush attached to the carton that was the sales objective of a Pepsodent offer.

Ten running pages in *Ladies' Home Journal* or *True Story* might present six or eight such propositions; and advertising agencies like ours had buyers scouring the market for new gimmicks and new gadgets to offer--in terms of values that we, ourselves, established.

Clutch bags were a favorite, close on the heels of flower seeds, and what connection either of them had, or didn't have, with ready-to-eat cereals or kitchen cleaners, made no matter. This was Merchandising, and this was the name of the game. It wasn't the value in the product that counted, but only the prize that came with it!

√ When there weren't any more desirable premiums to pack on or to mail out upon receipt of a quarter (or even as much as $3) and a specified number of box tops, or labels, the contest took the premium's place. And I can't think of anything that wasn't offered to the winners.

One, alone, of our clients set up a series of capital prizes that included a blooded race horse, several choices of automobiles, a producing oil well,

a world cruise for twelve, the winner's
weight in gold, and, finally, a uranium
mine!

Perhaps the strangest of all was a contest promoted in behalf of the ill-
fated Edsel automobile in which
the prizes were ponies. Just what the
connection was no one ever figured out,
and the disgruntled dealers who had
the ponies on display and had to feed
them and clean up their litter, could
be heard screaming from Seattle to Key
West.

What the Edsel people didn't realize
was that it is the primary purpose of
any contest to encourage mass displays
and the sampling of products. In this
case the display space was totally in-
elastic and the would-be samplers were
mostly in their middle teens.

After a breathless run that left the
competitors exhausted (and most of the
prizes, except for the ponies) in the
hands of professionals, the contests
degenerated into today's sweepstakes
which, again, only much more simply,
is a device for the encouragement of
high-piled displays and a competitive
edge for a brief period in the vast
arena of the country's supermarkets.

√ The sweepstakes, I believe (although
I could very well be wrong, the way
these things go), have about run their
course; although, like trading stamps,
that have come and gone and come again
in my own time, their attraction may
prove to be cyclical and everlasting.

Meanwhile, we have the 7¢-off coupon,
and the 10¢-off coupon. And I have no
objection to any of these things, so
long as their place in the marketing
mix is kept in proper relationship with
each of the other elements; and never,
never is allowed to dominate the product promise and the product image.

TV LEADS TO FLAGRANT AD MISUSE

The basic elements of success in marketing, as I understand these, are,
first of all, the product itself, with
its special features; second, its packaging, from both the functional and the
esthetic viewpoints; third, its availability to its best prospects; fourth,
its pricing; and, finally, its advertising.

I put advertising last because a good
product, under favorable competitive
conditions, *could* succeed *without* advertising; or with very little advertising.
A number have. But the road is narrow
and rough. The climb to the top of the
hill is aided very little by word of
mouth; there never is enough of it.

The result is that while advertising is
last in the lineup, it is usually vital
to success. And it is the point of
these remarks to urge you, collectively
and as individuals, to help guard it
from the folly and the flatulence that
threaten it today, and the diminution
of its value that is bound to follow if
these are allowed to predominate.

The trouble is everyone's in marketing,
because they are responsible for advertising; advertising does not stand a-
lone. Moreover, we must remember that
it is a means and not an end.

And it is the current undertaking to
make it an end that I despise and deplore, and that I urge you to resist,
when you consider advertising in your
marketing plans, to the very last ditch.

√ How this flagrant misuse of advertising has become fashionable is one more
evil that must be charged to the de-
bauchery of television. The greatest
medium yet discovered for the dissemination of information has quickly become
an instrument primarily of entertainment; and, I think you must agree, entertainment at a level that is more
often than not witless and absurd.

In the beginning, the marketers used television as a kind of glamorous showcase for their products; and the showcase was the entertainment they sponsored. The value that was involved, and there can be no doubt that this was considerable, was called, as some of you will remember, although it is long since passed almost into limbo, "sponsor identification."

This was a relic of radio. And who, who was around in those days, can forget that Jack Benny's was the voice of Jell-O, that Charlie McCarthy's squeaky tones were broadcast by and for Chase & Sanborn, or that Fibber McGee & Molly were brought to the waiting world by Johnson's self-polishing Glo-Coat.

To be sure, there were commercial announcements, too, and Don Wilson, on the Benny program, and Harlow Wilcox, with Fibber and Molly, who read these announcements, were actually members of the cast.

MUST WE MAKE 30-SECOND MINI-SHOWS?

Television began the same way, but it soon changed. With an audience that was on its way from ten to 20 to 30 to 40-odd million families, at a cost of anywhere from $25,000 to $85,000 per commercial minute, which are the prices today for national coverage, total program sponsorship became out of the question for any but advertisers like General Foods or Bristol-Myers or Procter & Gamble--each with a long line of products to offer.

√ Even for these, sponsorship had to be divided between several products, and so its impact was minimized and diminished until it all but disappeared. And today it is only a few series, like Kraft's Music Hall, Chrysler's Bob Hope programs and Hallmark's occasional Hall of Fame, where sponsorship is an important item in television advertising strategy.

Instead, the advertising burden must be borne entirely by the commercials, which is precisely the way it is with advertising in newspapers and magazines.

The trouble is, the temptation to compete with the programs that carry this advertising, by making the commercials thirty and forty and sixty-second entertainments in themselves, mini-programs, if you please, has been more than either the agents or the advertisers, the *marketers*, have been able to withstand.

√ It seems to me that two of the strongest commercials ever made for television have had the saddest effect upon the business of advertising and marketing since what I have referred to as *merchandising* took the place of *advertising* at the clost of World War II. These were both made for Alka-Seltzer, and I think they have never been surpassed either for ingenuity or for force.

The first was the presentation of a series of disturbed and distorted human mid-sections aching in a duo of paunchy fat men, a writhing belly dancer, a street-worker punishing himself with a pneumatic drill, etc., demonstrating better than any words the anguish of a tormented stomach; until two happily fizzing Alka-Seltzer tablets offered the viewer what clearly seemed to be his own, personal, climactic relief. That was a masterpiece.

And so was the other, also for Alka-Seltzer, which was the hectoring of the distressed over-eater by his sarcastic disembodied esophagus whose accusations had just the authority of a stern old family doctor, touched with his knowledge of both the stomach in question, and the temptations of any good appetite.

TV TORMENT OVER BAD COFFEE

Never, I think, since the demonstration of the electric shaver that was equally effective in removing soft peach fuzz and the stiff bristles of a fingernail brush, have there been more imaginative and more convincing commercials. The mixture was exactly right.

But the result, except for the makers of Alka-Seltzer, who benefited mightily, has been a test of the public endurance. In trying to outdo the Alka-Seltzer success, which they obviously didn't understand, a whole generation of advertising cats, aware of little more than the appearance of things, now is filling the air with inanities that are creeping also into print.

Television advertising is filled with conceits that depend for their effect upon questions that are resolved during the course of the action. Usually, there is a small plot involved in which the product comes to the rescue of the hero or (more often) the heroine of the piece whose problem it quickly and easily solves.

Certainly there is nothing wrong with this pattern. It must be as old as the first printed advertisement; and maybe as old as the advertising hieroglyphics on the walls of Pompeii.

√ But in television it has reached new heights of absurdity, and it is the absurdity that is breaking out in print.

The woman who cried out in torment of equal intensity over the loss of a suitor, her inability to make a decent cup of coffee, or the unpleasantness of bathroom odors, has become a fixture in the folklore of television advertising.

No matter what you think of her, there she is, and you can't get away from her. For by the sheer repetition of her im-

probable fears and failures, and final victories over cruel fate, the product name, if not its promise, is engraved on the constant viewer's mind.

INSIDIOUS, NOT INVIDIOUS

It is the insidious power of television (and please note that I said insidious--which means having more effect than is apparent, and not invidious, which means offensive) that it can make its impressions unconsciously insofar as the viewer in concerned.

This, I hasten to say, is not what Vance Packard called hidden persuasion; it is entirely out in the open. It catches you when you are looking and when you are listening, more often than not simply because it is easier to look and to listen than not.

√ To ignore a commercial of little or no particular interest requires some kind of action, mental or physical; to avoid it one must consciously think of something else, or physically remove himself from the scene. This, I repeat, requires much more effort than accepting the advertising as the price of the entertainment.

Nor do I see anything evil in this; I am only concerned with the use of the medium, with the misuse of advertising time and space--which television has encouraged and which, as I say, is creeping into printed advertising as well. For this could do more than merely blunt the sharpest tool available in marketing; it could destroy its value for an indeterminate period of time, or until a new generation might be approached with a return to reason.

√ What I refer to is the enveloping philosophy, particularly on the part of the tyros in advertisng, and some of the old pros who want to be with it, that advertising is a gas.

The old rules that advertising should, first of all, be clear; and that what is clear should also be important, are being traded away every day for a new concept that makes any serious approach to selling outmoded and unacceptable, partly because, the tyros maintain, nobody believes advertising anyway! To kid it, they say, to treat it lightly, is the only way. The now generation is much too hep, they say, to be taken in by the advertising establishment.

And in a way they are right. The advertising establishment has been responsible for some of the dreariest production I can imagine, and I can find no excuse for the dreadful slice of life commercials with their rumpuses over flaky scalps, stopped-up sinks and loose dentures that fill so much prime time. Nor am I any way edified or instructed by the monilies of Arthur Godfrey or Eddie Albert or Sheila McRae on the subject of enzyme action on ice cream, grease or grass stains.

I don't think either Pat Paulsen or Kay Ballard is funny in commercials (or any other way, for that matter).

And if this is the creative establishment at work, I am against it, too.

ADVERTISING IS NO JOKE

But when it is suggested that I should opt for a cigaret that is uncomfortably long, so long, indeed, that it is caricatured as being snipped off by closing elevator doors, or snuffed out by a falling pizza, I think the alternative is even less than desirable.

In fact, I think it is damned foolishness. By the only possible inference it makes a joke of advertising. And this is something that none of us in

marketing can live with for very long.

It is no more sensible to introduce our selling story with a gag, be this in television or in print, than it would be to redesign our packages to obscure our trade names. This last is something that not even the tyros would suggest. Yet the strategy of disguising advertising, of making it either a game or a joke or, worse still, a mystery, is all around us.

√ Here I should point out that there is a vast difference in what one may do in television advertising and what one *must* do in print. As I have suggested, it is actually easier to *take* television advertising than it is to ignore it; while it requires no effort at all to ignore advertising in print.

Turning the page on an advertisement whose proposition is either unclear or uninteresting has to be one of the easiest of daily exercises. Next time you are riding on an airplane, or in a bus, watch the man or woman across the aisle; watch them turn the pages of a magazine of newspaper; you'll wonder if *any* advertising is read.

But to go back, the ease with which it is taken is not the only difference in television advertising. It is its sequential aspect that is probably the greatest difference from advertising in print.

Whatever is on the screen in a given second or seconds is the total experience for the viewer; there is no contest, no scrambling for the viewer's attention. It is as if, in a printed advertisement, you could force the reader to first become aware of an illustration, then relate this to the headline, follow by reading the argument, and end up by considering the signature and the facsimile of the package.

This is almost exactly what happens in the television advertising sequence;

the viewer is led through it as if by the hand; the problem may be made clear, either as a gag (as in the Alka-Seltzer dialog between the traumatized man and his stomach) or in a real-life situation, as when a litter of puppies climbs all over itself to get at a bowl of Purina dog chow.

NEW AD VIRUS: EXAGGERATION

Unfortunately, neither of these moving sequences lends itself to translation into the static world of print.

Nor does any of the most attractive and effective television advertising. When sequence is removed the best one can do is to snip off a piece of stop action at the height of the drama of the film, and construct the simplest possible story around it.

The real trouble is that there is a virus in the advertising atmosphere that is attacking the fundamental strength and value of the medium, which **is** credibility.

The name of the virus is exaggeration. And it is everywhere.

It ranges from Mister whatever-his-name-is, who can't stop squeezing the packages of Charmin bathroom tissue, to the horde of Amazons that attacks the simple male who has been so foolish as to douse himself with Hai Karate--the after-shaving aphrodisiac that turns them on.

Those are on television.

In print, there is the man; indeed, there are the *men* who pursue their morning shaves clear over the top of their heads to illustrate the ecstasy that comes with a newly-introduced razor blade. And the couples, in equally heroic size, who are quoted as say-

ing only that "Here is a cigaret for the two of you. L&M."

I could go on in TV, to the maniacal driver who wrecks a driving school Rambler just to underscore its name.

As I said, I could go on, and I could go on in *all* media, even in outdoor where Peter Max is exhibited in incomprehensible medleys simply because Peter Max is hot.

His is the exaggeration of form.

'NO ONE BUYS FROM A CLOWN'

But whatever it is that is exaggerated, it is bad for advertising. It is just as bad to make a joke out of advertising as it is to make a lie.

As David Ogilvy has said, and wisely, "The lady in the supermarket is not a moron, she is your wife"; and as Rosser Reeves said very recently, "No one buys anything from a clown."

There has been a great deal written, and a great deal said, about the effect of violence on television, and about the soporific situation comedies, and the news programs that provide little beyond the headlines, and the newly admitted license to turn the late night air blue with so-called adult fun. And I deplore them all.

But most of all, in a time when we need our best marketing skills, in a time when competition for all of us is honed to its finest edge, I deplore making advertising a game. This is something that some of us in advertising have borrowed from show business, and the rest of us should make them give it back.

✓ Here, and in conclusion, I should make it clear that I am not advocating that advertising be devoid of humor. Far from it.

I can't think of any more effective television advertising than the commercials for Maxwell House coffee where whole families beep in time with bubbling percolators. And certainly the television advertising that my own company makes for Raid insecticides uses humor reasonably and effectively.

But this is a far cry from squeezing the bathroom tissue to the squealing delight of a half-dozen blowsy character actors; or the ineffable Durwood Kirby smirking and talking to himself.

I suppose what I am arguing for is restraint in everything we do in advertising and marketing; and just now this is most needed in advertising. Twenty or 30 years ago, this was required to bring down to earth the claims that were made and exaggerated almost as a matter of course.

✓ But the criticism that began with the publication of "100 Million Guinea Pigs," which attacked the high-handed manufacturers, had a salutary effect. Today there is relatively little exaggeration in the claims that are made for any product seriously.

On the other hand, exaggeration in form and presentation, in making advertising a joke, is with us on every side, and if it increases it will be increasingly debilitating.

In making advertising and in approving advertising, it should never be forgotten that the lady in the supermarket or the department store or the specialty shop is a pretty shrewd buyer; for one thing, she is the established and acknowledged purchasing agent for her family in all but a few classifications; and she looks to advertising for assistance and not entertainment.

If I may repeat, it is up to all of us together to see that whatever we have to tell her is made abundantly clear at the outset; that what is clear is also important; that we present it not to amuse her, but solely to help her in her purchaser role. Let us not be caught up in the race to be with it. For the plain unfashionable fact is that it is not *worth* the race, in any way. Indeed, it can only be self-defeating.

DISCUSSION QUESTIONS

---

1. "It is just as bad to make a joke out of advertising as it is to make a lie." Does this advocate that advertising should be devoid of humor? Explain.

2. Define advertising in the light of the author's comments about what it should and should not be.

PART VI

AGENCY OPERATIONS

Although most readers of this book will not be directly involved in agency operations, it is well that all readers be familiar with how an agency is managed, how the agency business is changing, and with some of the important issues facing agency management today.

To give the reader a sense of the history of the advertising agency, Donald R. Holland's article on Volney Palmer, "the nation's first agency man," is presented. Holland's somewhat surprising conclusion is that the advertising agency business has changed very little since its inception in 1842!

Next, Richard C. Christian gives some simple, but certainly not universally followed, principles on how to succeed in the agency business. As he says, this is not an article on how to write ads or develop marketing plans, but is instead a list of day-to-day fundamentals equally necessary to growth and success.

Andrew Kershaw provides some insights into how agency service is changing, partly because of the unprofitability of some services and partly because of the rise of ala carte service agencies, agencies which provide creative talent, media buying, or some other part only

of the services provided by full-service agencies. His conclusion is that agencies rate a "surprisingly clean bill of health."

Howard Fisher delves into his experience in working with advertising agencies to tell us how to work with an agency. His admonitions may seem simplistic, but they can help advertisers avoid problems with their present agencies and pick better agencies.

One of the long-standing issues in the advertising agency business is the question of payment. Should agencies be compensated as most of them are presently at 15% of media billings, at their cost plus a fixed percentage, or by some other method? Maxwell Dane has struggled with this issue for many years and gives us his experience.

The last article in this section discusses a new, somewhat off-beat topic, agency networks. The networks have been founded as a way for small agencies to compete with the larger agencies. Since many of the readers of this book will be involved with small agencies, it should be an informative and helpful reading.

Reprinted by permission from ADVERTISING AGE; 23 April, 1973, pp. 107, 111-12.

VI-1

THE STORY OF VOLNEY PALMER, THE NATION'S FIRST AGENCY MAN

Donald R. Holland

The advertising agency business has changed so little since it was started by Volney B. Palmer in 1842 that if, by some transcendental manipulation, he appeared in a Madison Ave. agency tomorrow, it might take him as long as an hour to fit into the routine of modern agency operation.

The agency's business practices would seem all too familiar to him, although he'd likely raise an eyebrow at the drop in commissions from 25% to 15%; he'd know about copy, layout and production problems; he'd probably remind the media buyers how lucky they are to have only a handful of newspapers and journals to evaluate in comparison to the number in his day; he'd be right at home, rapping with the marketing and research people, lunching with the account executives, and sharing experiences with management about the problem of employes stealing accounts and starting their own agencies.

Admittedly, he wouldn't know anything agout radio or television, but once he discovered they are simply another communications medium, he'd pick up what he'd need to know rapidly. The more things change, as the French say, the more they stay the same.

GENIAL, AFFABLE, WITTY

Mr. Palmer was surely the prototype of the modern account executive. Contemporaries--including employes--stated that he was genial, affable, sociable, fond of telling witty stories, fashionably dressed, lived graciously--in short, the ideal agency account executive.

Mr. Palmer possessed amazing versatility --a versatility that would be the envy of any agency man today. He was, in addition to being a sophisticated account man, a successful copywriter, frequently reminding his clients that they were better off to let him write copy for their ads, since he would make "valuable practical suggestions for improvement in force and style such as are written by unpracticed hands."

And he was, of all things, a "cheerful" media buyer, providing his clients with "reliable explanatory information of places, character and circulation of papers, adaptation of various business pursuits and comparative rates of advertising cheerfully given with every reasonable facility."

Further demonstrating his flexibility, he could shift from copywriter to media buyer to new business presenter with equal aplomb, always making his pitch in phrases selected to mirror the client's own frame of reference.

Who else but Volney B. Palmer has done it all--and done all of it well? From an unpromising beginning in 1842 to a four-office network in Philadelphia, New York, Boston and Baltimore by 1848 --who else has matched that rate of growth since then? He started from nothing 130 years ago, established the agency concepts still accepted today, suffered his accounts to be stolen, created the commission system, and set the advertising agency squarely and profitably between publisher and client. About the only significant difference between the Palmer Agency of the mid-nineteenth century and its direct line descendant, N.W. Ayer & Son, is size. The rest is just about the same.

Palmer was born in Wilkes-Barre, Pa., in 1792, the son of a merchant and politician. Records show that, at the age of 19, the Palmer family moved to Mount Holly, N.J., where they all joined in publishing a weekly newspaper, the *New Jersey Mirror*. Around 1830, Volney left Mount Holly for the anthracite regions of northeastern Pennsylvania, then under development by Philadelphia financier Stephen Girard.

For ten years, Volney Palmer lived in Pottsville, Pa., working mostly in the real estate business. Here he married, accumulated a family and some real estate holdings of his own. Then in 1841, at the age of 42, he left Pottsville for Philadelphia to open a real estate agency.

SELL COAL, SELL SPACE?

Looking back, it's difficult to imagine a more inappropriate place or a more inauspicious time to start a real estate agency than Philadelphia in 1841. The entire country, but especially the East, continued in the throes of a serious depression triggered by the Panic of 1837, and Philadelphia endured more than its share of financial troubles. Palmer himself provided an unintended testimonial to the times in his personal real estate transactions. In 1842, he and his wife sold the building lots in Pottsville, purchased as an investment in 1830, at a loss of $300.

It seems unlikely that a newly established real estate office in Philadelphia in 1841 was greeted with much success, so it isn't surprising to note in the 1842 edition of *M'Elroy's Philadelphia Directory* that Palmer had broadened his business to include selling coal and wood as well as real estate. What is surprising, however, is a half-page ad in the *Directory* containing the first association of Volney B. Palmer and the advertising agency business:

√ "ADVERTISEMENTS and Subscriptions received from some of the best and most widely circulated Newspapers in Pennsylvania and New Jersey, and in many of the principal cities and towns throughout the United States, for which he has the Agency, affording an excellent opportunity for Merchants, Mechanics, Professional Men, Hotel and Boarding-house Keepers, Railroad, Insurance and Transportation Companies, and the enterprising portion of the community generally, to publish extensively abroad their respective pursuits--to learn the terms of subscription and advertising, and accomplish their object here without the trouble of perplexing and fruitless inquiries, the expense and labour of letter writing, the risk of making enclosures of money."

The arrangement of the copy suggests that Palmer in 1842 viewed himself as a real estate man who had a coal business, and who also happened to be agent for advertising and subscriptions for a few nearby newspapers. On the other hand, the copy suggests that Palmer had given some thought to reasons why advertisers might use an agency. The few benefits he listed are hardly definitive, but those included in his first advertising effort reveal that Palmer knew how to sell, and that he was aware that he would have to sell his new service vigorously.

Over-imaginative writers have described the beginning of the first advertising agency as something like Paul's conversion on the road to Damascus. From what we read in Palmer's advertisements, there was nothing sudden about it, no brilliant burst of ideas, no seeing a sudden need and moving into a vacuum with an organization. The idea for an advertising agency was a product of Palmer's long apprenticeship in the newspaper business and the troubled times that must have been hampering his real estate and coal business. Under the pressures of making a living when a living was hard to make, Palmer slowly and tentatively began an ad agency.

HIS NEWSPAPER LIST WAS SECRET

The Sept. 9, 1842, issue of the *New Jersey Mirror* contained an ad by Palmer, headed "V.B. Palmer's Real Estate and Coal Office and Newspaper Agency." The three functions appear for the first time together in an ad, and, although they are set in diminishing type size, there is no doubt from the emphasis of the copy that Palmer was now serious about the agency business.

Beneath the line, "Advertisements and subscriptions received for newspapers published in the following cities," was the first listing of those towns and cities in which Palmer represented a newspaper; only the names of the towns were listed, not the names of the newspapers themselves. The names and rates of the newspapers that were Palmer's principals remained a closely guarded

secret from all but active clients.

√ No attempt was made in this ad to sell either the *concepts* of advertising or a "System of Advertising," which were promulgated frequently in subsequent ads. With this ad, Palmer announced that he was in the agency business.

The term, "advertising agency," was not used by Palmer until he included it in an insert in *M'Elroy's Philadelphia Directory* in 1849. At times he called himself a "newspaper agency," and at times a "business agency," and at least once a "coal agency," but until 1849 he was not running what he called an "advertising agency."

25% COMMISSIONS

The American Newspaper Subscription & Advertising Agency of Volney B. Palmer Esq. claimed to be the sole representative of 1,300 of the estimated 2,000 newspapers published in 1849. A manufacturer or retailer contemplating an advertising program walked into one of the offices Palmer maintained in Philadelphia, New York, Boston or Baltimore, looked over the list of newspapers available to him, examined specific papers from the racks of publications, indicated the particular market area that interested him, described his seasonal preference and revealed the amount of money he intended to spend.

Mr. Palmer then prepared for the potential advertiser a speculative presentation, which included space rates for each newspaper and the total proposed expenditure. To compensate his agency for this work and for the actual preparation of advertisements, Palmer deducted a commission (considered to be 25%, but never publicly stated) from the publisher's bill before payment.

No one had ever done anything quite like

this before. Businessmen were aware of advertising, of course, but hardly in an organized, systematized way. Volney B. Palmer set out to show his clients how they might use this tool "to advertise judiciously, effectively and safely."

"You have only to step into his office with the notice you wish given to the whole people of the United States, and it is done," the publisher of the *Boston Chronotype* declared in 1846. The publisher of the *Baltimore Sun* testified in 1843:

"Mr. Palmer is, we believe, entitled to the credit for originating, and establishing upon a general scale in this country, this new and important public convenience..."

WHAT ADVERTISING CAN DO FOR YOU

How Palmer viewed his agency business can be seen in the following headline and list of advantages of advertising through the Palmer agency, printed in *V.B. Palmer's Business-Men's Almanac* in 1849:

"ADVANTAGES OF ADVERTISING IN THE NEWSPAPERS OF THE CITY AND COUNTRY AT V. B. PALMER'S ADVERTISING AGENCY."

1. "The most widely circulated journals in America are on file for the convenient examination and selection, and the terms for each recorded for the inspection of subscribers and advertisers.

2. "The publishers have appointed and authorized him to make contracts for subscriptions and advertising. His receipts are regarded as payments, and therefore valid and sufficient.

3. "Advertisements are inserted in any one paper or (from a single copy)

in any number, at the lowest cash price, without extra charge, at the earliest practical time, and a copy of each paper furnished to the advertiser, that he may be sure that his order was complied with.

4. "Editorial and business notices inserted on the most favorable terms, calling attention to advertisements.

5. "Reliable explanatory information of places, character and circulation of papers, adaptation of various business pursuits and comparative rates of advertising in different papers cheerfully given with every reasonable facility, for adopting at once a safe, judicious, efficient system of advertising.

6. "Advertisers save the postage and avoid the labor of correspondence with publishers, risk of remittances, unseasonable and repeated calls of strangers with separate bills, the various deceptions of journals of dubious character and losses from contracting with incompetent and irresponsible persons.

7. "To avoid unnecessary expense, concise forms of advertising are written without charge, and valuable practical suggestions made for improvement in style and force such as are written by unpractices hands."

TRY PALMER AND MAKE IT OVERNIGHT

The "advantages" listed above throw an entirely new light on the man and his business, indicating that he was far more than a passive middleman. It is clear that he served the advertiser by providing counsel on media selection, that he handled the physical details of production and billing, that he wrote, or counseled on, advertising copy, and that he did all this at no charge to the advertiser. It is also clear that he earned his commission from the publishers by seeking out and directing the advertiser to the pages of his principals' newspapers, and that he had both their confidence and their authorization to represent them in giving receipts for payment.

The phrase, "system of advertising," appeared frequently in all of Palmer's writings. He urged business men to use advertising on a regular basis, to use it to develop new markets, to take advantage of the flexibility of advertising to specific regions or in specific seasons. The publisher of *Parker's Journal* had this to say about Palmer's advertising system:

"Go into Volney B. Palmer's office... and look over the letters he has received from commercial houses, and then say whether or not this advertising system is productive of benefit. Mr. Palmer, as the Father of American Advertising, may well be proud of his offspring; there are thousands now in prosperous businesses who acknowledge themselves endebted to him for all their wealth; he saw the necessity of increased publicity for the interests of commerce, and organized a system which now can electrify the Union into a knowledge of whatever facts he desires to be generally known.

"An inventor no longer has to fight his way through years of starvation and neglect; he goes to Palmer, and overnight, finds his discovery the topic of discussion in every social circle from Maine to California within a fortnight."

Amid all the hyperbole in the writings of and about Palmer, there is a feeling that something new and significant was in the air. Businessmen who had wallowed through a series of depressions with only occasional glimpses of prosperity for the previous decade ought to be excused if they viewed the zealous Palmer with a feeling bordering on awe.

TENACITY, OR RIGHT MAN, RIGHT PLACE?

In an eight-page, pre-printed insert, the first and only to be bound into *M'Elroy's Philadelphia Directory*, Palmer cited an editorial from the *Gloucester Telegraph*:

"There has sprung up an enterprise which would have been laughed at as impractical a dozen years ago. This originated ...with V.B. Palmer Esq., who is known already wherever an American newspaper finds its way."

In 1846, Palmer was looked upon by some business men as a sort of commercial messiah; and yet, a dozen years before, the *Gloucester Telegraph* reminds us, an advertising agency would have been laughed at as impractical. Was Palmer's success a triumph of personality and tenacity, or simply a case of the right man being in the right place at the right time? The answer is both--and considerably more than both.

By 1846, the advertising agency of Volney B. Palmer included four offices in four eastern cities: Philadelphia, New York, Boston and Baltimore. Palmer maintained his residence in Philadelphia, and supervised the office in that city, hiring managers for the other three offices.

HOW PALMER GOT NEW BUSINESS

S.M. Pettengill, once manager of the Boston office, described in an article in the Dec. 20, 1890, issue of *Printer's Ink* a typical business day with Palmer:

"He would come into his office about 9 am, look over the daily newspapers for new advertisements, which I would cut out and make a list of for calling on. At about 10 o'clock we would sally out, calling on the most important advertisers first.

"He would march into the countingroom of the merchants, calling for the principal partner, and announce himself and hand his card, with a pleasing address and with as much assurance as if he were a customer who was about to purchase a large bill of goods.

"If he found the merchant busy, he would politely excuse himself and inquire when he could have the pleasure of seeing him, and, if possible, would make an appointment for that or the succeeding day. Shaking hands and tipping his hat gracefully, he would leave.

"If he found the party he was calling on willing to listen, he would introduce me and make a well-considered statement on the benefits of advertising in general, and to the party he was addressing in particular. He would mention parties who had made fortunes by the use of judicious advertising. He would show how he (the merchant) could easily double his business and profits by a like course. He would point out the places where he should advertise, and how he should do it. He would generally enforce his words by some well told stories, and get all parties into good humor and laughing heartily. He would end up by asking if he might be permitted to make out an estimate for the merchant's advertising."

HE LEFT DEADBEATS TO PUBLISHERS

Mr. Palmer made no charge for his estimates or for setting up the advertisement for the merchant, and no obligation of any kind was involved so far as the merchant was concerned. He would check off those cities or areas the merchant wanted to reach with his advertising message, and in the next day or two would return with the completed recommendation and a contract to be signed by the merchant.

Mr. Palmer felt that he was the sole agent for the newspapers on his list, and he insisted that they should make a statement to that effect at the head of their editorial column. As their sole and exclusive agent, Palmer charged the newspapers he represented for postage stamps which he used in correspondence for and to them. Palmer also charged publishers for losses he incurred when an advertiser failed for some reason to pay his bill. This was handled simply by deducting the amount from the publisher's bill before paying it. Palmer felt that as the agent for the publishers, his losses were really their losses. On the subject of bill payment, the Palmer agency would not pay a publisher's bill until the agency had first been paid by the advertiser.

✓ There is no reference by name or company to any advertising client of the Palmer agency in any of the brochures or pamphlets published by Palmer. What may seem like a curious omission becomes plausible when the position of the Palmer agency is reconsidered. Palmer was the agent of newspaper publishers; his client was any advertiser who happened to place advertising through his agency on any given day. An advertiser might use the services of the Palmer agency one day and a competitor's agency the next. There was at this stage of agency development no list of loyal clients for whom an agent worked. What loyalty or stability that existed was between agent and publisher, and not between agent and advertiser.

In the late 1850s, Palmer formed a partnership with three men who worked for him as managers of his offices: John E. Joy, J.E. Coe and W.W. Sharpe. No evidence is available to indicate the percentage of partnership owned by each man, but it seems probable that Palmer permitted each to buy increasing shares of the business gradually from earnings.

The year 1858 is a likely date for the

293

partnership, since *M'Elroy's Philadelphia Directory* that year, for the first time, listed the agency as "V.B. Palmer & Co."

After Palmer's retirement, Joy and Coe came to control both the Philadelphia and the New York offices, but removed Palmer's name from the agency. W.W. Sharpe later became manager and then owner of the New York office, and developed it under his own name into one of the best known and most respected advertising agencies in New York at the turn of the century.

HOW THE PALMER AGENCY EVOLVED

The Boston office of the Palmer agency was taken over by S.R. Niles, and he, too, became a successful advertising agent in that city. The Baltimore office apparently closed after Palmer's retirement, since none of the existing advertising agencies claims to be a descendent of that branch of the Palmer agency. After the death of Palmer in 1864, the Philadelphia office became known as Coe, Wetherill & Smith. This name was later changed to Coe, Wetherill & Co. at the death of the third partner, Smith.

It was this agency that Francis W. Ayer bought in October, 1877, and incorporated into his own agency, N.W. Ayer & Son. The purchase of Coe, Wetherill & Co. by N.W. Ayer & Son gave that agency the rightful claim to being the oldest in the U.S., and the only shop that can trace its history in an unbroken line directly to the original agency founded by Volney B. Palmer.

PALMER, THE MAN

The preface to the 1851 edition of the *Almanac* reveals not only Palmer's opinion of advertising, but something about the man himself:

"Advertising is the indispensable and efficient means of securing a liberal share of custom in any department of Trade or Manufacture ... for anyone who has commodities to sell to neglect appraising consumers of the fact through the cheapest, readiest and most penetrating medium, is to lock up his goods and refuse to exhibit them to customers."

There is no doubt, no hesitation, no question of judgment in this quote of Palmer's. He spoke directly in the language of the business man to any and all business men, and suggested that they might be considered somewhat less than brilliant if they ignored advertising.

Throughout the copy in his ads and the various promotion brochures he published, Palmer set a straightforward, self-assured tone. He will perform a certain function or he will not perform it; letters will be post-paid; publishers will imprint his agency's name over their editorial columns; he will not be responsible for the uncollected debts of defaulting advertisers. Palmer was a man of strong opinions who would not permit himself to be pushed around by publishers or advertisers, a trait that would sometimes be interpreted as arrogance and irascibility.

'FAT, JOLLY, HEARTY'

Of those who have written about Volney Palmer, the only man who ever saw him was S.M. Pettengill. He described his former employer as follows:

"...a short, thick-set gentleman of

294

good address, genial and pleasant in manner, and had a good command of language, full of wise saws and modern instances. He was a capital story-teller, wore gold spectacles and carried a gold-headed cane, and was a first class canvasser. He had more self-possession and assurance than any man I ever knew."

The publisher of the *Dayton Gazette*, a principal of Palmer's, had this to say about his new agent:

"We found Mr. Palmer not the gross, surly, uncommunicative individual some agents who have your money in their hands are, but quite the contrary, a fat, jolly, hearty old fellow of about 45 (he was 54; perhaps the figures were transposed in printing) who enjoys a joke and is, withal, quite a wit, in his way."

Only one photograph of Palmer is known to be extant, and it has been reproduced in Ralph Hower's history of the N.W. Ayer agency. The full-page halftone shows a heavy-set man of middle years posed pensively in a chair reading a copy of the *Evening Bulletin*. He is fashionably dressed, wears spectacles, and his thick, graying hair is brushed neatly to one side. His heavy, square chin rests on his clenched left hand and one finger of that hand is laid against his left cheek.

The nose is prominent, the eyes dark and receding, the eyebrows heavy and gray. The mouth is down-turned, but suggests the slight beginning of a smile. The likeness is of a well-established, mature business man of the 1850s.

AT HOME WITH HORACE

There is no available evidence today to determine whether or not Palmer at-tended college, but his writings reveal a man at home among the classics. In the first 30 pages of a pamphlet, *V.B. Palmer's American Newspaper Subscription and Advertising Agency*, he either quotes directly or refers in some way to Horace, St. Paul, Carnot, Frederick the Great, Napoleon, Archimedes, Bacon, Walpole, Hogarth, Newton, Galileo, Cromwell and Dr. Samuel Johnson. The famed politicians, philosophers and scientists are used by Palmer to illustrate a point about advertising or the press, rather than merely serving a decorative function.

As a writer, Palmer possessed the ability to shift freely from straight exposition to an amusing and well-constructed soliloquy by a perplexed and jealous business man:

"There's Tewksbury; he's been off again --down to Newport with his wife, two children and a servant! Where under heaven he gets money to spend in this way is more than I can tell. Look at him now--lives out of town, keeps a horse, drives in and out every day. His expenses must be large--yet he seems to pay as he goes. I hope there's nothing wrong about Tewksbury. Then look at the money he spends on advertising! Why that is enough to ruin any man, I don't care how rich he is...

"Wouldn't I look well taking my wife down to Newport and staying there eight weeks?--eight weeks, indeed! I sent her on a cheap excursion--but I couldn't go myself. I can't afford it--don't take in enough money to do it. And then to see a man spend his money just to let people see his name in the papers, and sending cards and bills about the country. Tewksbury bleeds freely for his vanity, I must confess!"

The sybaritic Tewksbury, Palmer reassured his readers, was not absconding with the company's funds, but was advertising extensively through the Palmer agency, and increasing his sales and profits by doing so.

END OF THE ROAD

There is an air of mystery surrounding the final days of Volney B. Palmer. An article in an early advertising journal, *Fame*, stated that Palmer became violently insane and that Horace Greeley hired a man to take care of him. There is no available evidence to support this atatement, and none has been produced since to back it up.

Unfortunately, the story has received wide circulation by various writers, some of whom choose to view Palmer's insanity as either divine retribution or the natural end of an advertising agency man. At least one advertising textbook writer indulged his sense of humor at Palmer's expense by declaring, "Some people see a moral in the fact that the first advertising agency head went mad."

Palmer's final home at 1323 Franklin St., Philadelphia, is still standing two blocks north of Girard Ave., across the street from St. Luke's Hospital, a crumbling red brick residence trimmed in black wrought iron, with its white marble door-step tilting precariously from the entrance. The area is decaying, but there is a substantial feeling to the house and its surroundings; it must have been, for its day, the home of a moderately successful business man located in a desirable area of the city.

Palmer retired from active participation in the agency business in the latter part of 1862 or the early part of 1863. His final listing in *M'Elroy's Philadelphia Directory* appeared in the 1863 editions.

"Palmer, Volney B., 1323 Franklin, Gentleman." On July 28, 1864, Volney B. Palmer Esq., founder of the first advertising agency in the U.S., died at his home in Philadelphia at the age of 65.

PALMER PUSHED AD CONCEPT, SYSTEM

Palmer from the first assumed that his primary task was selling the *concept* of advertising. In all his writings, he stressed the importance of advertising first, and the services of the Palmer agency second. Service both to publisher and advertiser was the distinguishing mark of the Palmer agency. He made it as easy as possible for an advertiser to come into his office, examine newspapers, plan a campaign around a budget and have all the accounting and bookkeeping details handled efficiently. For his principals, the publishers, he was a vigorous sales force that showed them a source of revenue they hadn't known existed.

No advertising historian had noticed that Palmer was a copywriter, that he understood the power of the written word to convey an idea, a mood, a suggestion. He considered himself skilled as a writer of advertising and offered either to write copy himself or edit the copy of "those unpracticed in the techniques." From the evidence, it seems that the role of Volney B. Palmer was considerably broader than any writer has heretofore indicated, and his contributions to advertising and to the agency business greater than previously suspected. To summarize his many accomplishments:

✓ He was the first advertising agent in this country.
✓ He promoted the concept of advertising to change marketing techniques.
✓ He sold a "system of advertising," instead of simply offering newspaper space for sale.
✓ He wrote copy for advertisers.

SPEEDING THE PACE OF CHANGE

Mr. Palmer was the agent of the news-

paper publishers, and so stated frequently. He provided many services
for advertisers, but his loyalty was
directed to those publishers who paid
him a commission for his services.

The actual functions of the Palmer
agency--assisting with budget planning,
evaluating and selecting media, preparing ads, writing copy and delivering,
checking and billing--are the fundamental functions of a modern advertising agency today.

Taken as a whole, Palmer's chief
contribution was the acceleration of
the concept of systematic advertising.
Advertising, of course, existed before
he set up business, and it would be
folly to suggest that advertising and

the early agents triggered the industrial revolution in the U.S. It is,
however, reasonable to suggest that
Palmer and other early agents served
as a sort of catalyst in the 19th-cen-
tury marketplace.

Through their efforts, merchants, manufacturers and business men of all kinds
were made more aware of the changes
taking place in the marketing structure, and were led, perhaps even pushed,
into raising their sights beyond their
immediate market. The advertising
agents of the mid-nineteenth century
were an accelerator force that quick-
ened the pace of industrial change,
generating results far beyond their
immediate goals or their wildest flights
of imagination.

DISCUSSION QUESTIONS

1. Was Palmer's success attributed to his
personality, or simply a case of the
right man being at the right place at the
right time? Discuss.

2. Palmer once wrote, "Advertising is
the indispensable and efficient means
of securing a liberal share of custom
in any department or trade or manufacture..." Do you agree or disagree with
Mr. Palmer? Why?

VI-2

SOME THINGS WE THINK WE'VE LEARNED ABOUT THE MANAGEMENT OF AN ADVERTISING AGENCY

Richard C. Christian

There are 5000 or 6000 advertising agencies in the United States today. There is probably an equal number in the rest of the world. Very few of these firms achieve real success in terms of client service, company growth and consistent profitability. If there were a surefire formula for success in the agency business, there obviously would be no need for this seminar today. There do appear to be a few fundamentals that seem to work, at least as we observe the most successful agencies in the country. These are the fundamentals that appear to be common to most of them. This is not a dissertation on "how to write great ads" or "how to develop innovating marketing plans" or "how to measure advertising effectiveness." All of those things are obviously important to the success of advertising agencies. On the other hand there are some fairly nitty-gritty day-to-day fundamentals equally necessary to growth and success. Here are a few of them:

HAVE A FINANCIAL EXPERT ON BOARD

No really successful agency has grown and prospered without a very good financial man in the executive suite. One of the weaknesses in many small- to medium-sized agencies is in their accounting and financial operations. When small agencies begin to grow there is great temptation to keep good, old, hardworking Miss Brown, the original bookkeeper. Loyalty is fine, but it can be misplaced if the agency chief executive officer does not free himself of detailed financial housekeeping.

Most agencies are started and run by creative or marketing people, not financial experts. Simple bookkeeping and elementary accounting work okay for the small, stagnant agency, but once growth begins the agency head needs all the financial expertise he can get. Ogilvy & Mather with its Shelby Page, Benton & Bowles with its Bob Lyman, and McCaffrey and McCall with its Jim Manning are outstanding examples of agencies with tough-minded, capable financial men who permit the rest of the top management to concentrate on serving clients and new business.

Our experience tells us that it pays to get a good financial man and pay him well. Supplement his skills with a good outside CPA firm and even consider adding to your board of directors an outside director with some financial experience. Incidentally, 4A Chairman Vic Bloede recently predicted continued growth of the role of the financial officer in agency management. "The agency's key financial man will have a major part in planning, negotiations and most important the agency's profit plan," he said.

marketing and research-oriented agency.

Building a specific personality, character and image is one of the fundamentals that appears to be part of the success of the top agencies in the country today. Be strong, be good at something. Only then the small- or medium-sized agency, once having established itself, can begin if it chooses to broaden its scope of services, the types of products or markets it serves, and its geographical coverage.

BE A BUSINESS

Most really successful agencies, including those with the great creative reputations, are run in a businesslike manner. An agency must succeed as a business, not simply as a creative hot shop or producer of award winning ads. Advertising agencies, just as their clients, need employee policies, profit planning systems, compensation systems, cash flow policies, purchasing and billing programs, etc. There may be a place for the "creative boutique" in our industry, but there is simply no evidence that the sheer gratification of turning out so-called "creative" advertising by wild-eyed and wildly-dressed hotshots succeeds in the long run. Because even those guys have to have some financial stability.

EXERT STRONG LEADERSHIP AT THE TOP

All successful agencies have strong leadership at the top. Those agencies reflect a point of view and a life style of a relatively small group of key executives. This core group of one or two or three or four men sets the pattern, the philosophy, the policies, which gives an agency momentum and sets the pace for everybody else. As agencies grow, naturally delegation of responsibility and authority takes place. But the key leaders can never delegate away the responsibility of providing the spark for growth.

PLAN FOR PERMANENCY TODAY

At various 4A meetings you've heard many times about the need for developing plans for succession. Some years ago the 4A completed a study that indicated of some 15 member agencies that had gone out of business over a particular period of time, 12 of them failed because there was no plan for succession. Top managers should plan for the permanency of their agency today. They should plan forever. Those plans must include how the principals are going to get their money out of the business, who's going to take their place, and when it will

BE BEST AT SOMETHING

Small agencies. Big agencies. New agencies. Old agencies. All should try to be best at something. Trying to be everything to everybody is one of the quickest ways to failure. The top management of an agency should establish itself, if possible from the very beginning, as a company that is really good at something. A good industrial agency. A food agency. Packaged goods agency. An agency with great sales promotional skills. A happen.

place. It pays to make fewer but better new business presentations.

DEVELOP A GROWTH PLAN

Agencies grow through increased client budgets, new business and/or through mergers and acquisitions. Responsible agency managers should develop the growth plan they believe will accomplish the objectives of the management and principal shareholders. Obviously, most succssssful agencies need both increased client budgets plus additional new accounts. More and more agencies are also going the merger and acquisition route. This is terribly time-consuming but our experience indicates that there is much to be learned from occasional merger discussions with other agencies. We have no formula that insures merger success. A merger is good if both parties see financial benefits, see additional growth opportunities, see increased security, and through the combination provide better service for the clients.

RESTRICT NEW BUSINESS EFFORTS

Go after only those accounts you can handle well. Seek the type of clients you are most qualified to handle. Constantly ask the question, "If I were the client would I hire us?" Having the courage to say "NO" to new business opportunities is a lesson which most agencies never learn. Going after every conceivable prospect produces an occasional lucky hit. But the wasted time, effort, money, not to mention possible inattention to present clients, can be a debilitating exercise in futility. Morale is a very fragile thing. It can be easily damaged by constantly running second in new business races in which you don't belong in the first

USE YOUR OWN PRODUCT

Some years ago I was asked by the Central Region of the 4A to give a speech on advertising agencies who advertise themselves. I enlisted the help of a professional from Michigan State who conducted a study among all types and sizes of 4A agencies. Mostly the study showed that very few agencies invest in their own product. Sure, most agencies send out an occasional letter or direct mail piece, but that's about all. We ran an advertisement the day we opened for business on May 1, 1951. We have advertised consistently since then, and according to 4A figures invest a higher percentage of our income in self-promotion than any other 4A member agency. Our new business experience and our own agency recognition and image research indicates that investment has paid off for us. Agencies should use their own product. They may learn something about advertising. And they will surely turn up some new business leads, too.

PLAN THE WORK--WORK THE PLAN

The planning activities in General Motors, IBM, P&G and General Foods are constant and all encompassing. The average agency may not need to do that much planning. But our own observation of successful agencies suggests that another fundamental that seems to work is to "plan the work and work the plan."

We believe we have reasonably scientific profit and budget planning. We use management-by-objectives at each of our 25 profit centers. And we've had a long-range planning committee since 1959. We think planning works for us as well as our clients. Most agencies tend to have frantic atmospheres where seemingly "the business runs the people--the people don't run the business." Proper planning is the only answer.

It's interesting that only within the last year or two has the subject of long-range planning begun to crop up among agency executives. At a 4A Management Seminar at Northwestern University last spring, Leonard S. Matthews, President of Leo Burnett Co., Inc., said: "The future belongs to those who prepare for it. With good future planning you can do your best to anticipate, direct and manage your future. Without it you become the victim of events--both good and bad--and may be forced to make expedient and costly decisions as the events force you into actions you would prefer not to take." About the only useful literature on advertising agency long-range planning in addition to Len Matthew's talk is a speech given by Dr. Melvin Anshen, professor, Columbia University, Graduate School of Business at a 4A seminar in 1970. In the planning stages, however, is a full day 4A seminar on this subject.

AVOID "MANAGEMENT INCEST"

In a personal service business such as ours, most successful agencies tend to be run by nice guys who like each other, who like to do the same things, who think pretty much alike. Perhaps the smartest thing we have done in our short history is to have outside members on our board of directors.

Our first outside board member was our attorney. He's a very tough-minded, sharp guy with an analytical and financial mind. Furthermore, he had been counsel for another larger agency before

he joined us, so he also knew something about our business. The second addition to our board was a professor from Carnegie-Mellon University, in Pittsburgh He later moved to Columbia University, and his name is Melvin Anshen. His work as a consultant to the Rand Corporation, IBM, General Electric, the Department of Defense, permits him to bring to us meaningful experiences and observations. And five years ago we added Joe Wilkerson, Young & Rubicam executive vice president who took early retirement. Obviously his extensive consumer experience, plus his experience as the head of Y&R International, has been helpful to us. Last year, we added our fourth outside board member, Dr. James Hayes, President, American Management Association.

In addition to the particular experience, talent and skills these outside directors bring to us, there is one other vital input. Outside directors bring to a company an objectivity and perspective that is invaluable as an agency analyzes its performance and charts its future growth plans. It's worth your trouble to avoid "management incest."

I am not prepared to call these "Christian's 10 laws of agency success" nor am I prepared to suggest that strict adherence to all ten of these fundamentals will guarantee the elimination of all of your business problems.

I am prepared to suggest, however, that close application of these ten points is a better way to improve profits than constantly cutting people.

DISCUSSION QUESTION

1. The author outlines ten fundamentals necessary for growth and success of an advertising agency. Evaluate each of them as to their probable effect on agency success.

Proceedings of National Conference for University Professors of Advertising, March 11-14, 1973, American Academy of Advertising, pp. 33-39. Reprinted with permission of the author.

VI-3

THE CHANGING FACE OF AGENCY SERVICE

Andrew Kershaw

This talk is bound to be a dismal failure. To be memorable a speaker these days has to make some scandalous revelations about the past, deliver spine-chilling prophecies, or spread gloom with a baleful analysis of the present. All I can offer you are a few crumbs of change, a few problems that will still be problems ten years from now, and a lot of constructive progress.

I must tell you even at the risk of being thought complacent and reactionary, that I am rather fond of advertising as a trade. It provides me with all the intellectual stimulus I require. It is always hard and fascinating work. It pays well.

Advertising continues to attract exceptionally able minds and unusual people: a professional camaraderie flourishes amongst us in spite of the competitive atmosphere. We really respect each other. Well, we respect each other in the same way as lawyers, clergymen, politicians, and academics respect each other.

It is difficult for me to talk about changes in the advertising industry, because I have only worked for Ogilvy & Mather. And I am told we are pecu-

liar. Forgive me if I draw on Ogilvy & Mather for many of my facts.

Three remarkable changes have occurred in the past five years. It is odd that nobody has picked them out for study. But then they are the kind of changes you do not expect from an industry with a reputation for instability and superficiality.

1 REMARKABLE GROWTH

The billings of the 4A agencies have grown, since 1966, by about 30 percent. In the face of a depression, in the face of consumerism, and in the face of government harrassment. That is an extraordinary achievement.

What kind of growth? Well, principally growth of the large agencies. Ten years ago there were eighteen 4A agencies billing over $50 million. Ten years later there are 35. In this period the number of agencies billing between $10 and $50 million went from 42 to only 50. God is on the side of the big battalions; presumably because He has known all along about the economies of scale.

At Ogilvy & Mather, our comestic billings were $97 million in 1966; and in
1972 they were just under $200 million.
Just over 100 percent growth. We may
be pardoned for feeling with Merrill
Lynch not only "bullish about America,"
but also "bullish about advertising in
America."

2 ADVERTISING AGENCIES AS MULTINATIONAL CORPORATIONS

In 1952 the 4A's showed members to
have 44 offices outside North America.
By 1962 the number had grown to 127.
And by 1972 the figure had jumped to
310. If you include offices with
minority ownership the number may well
be over 400. This frenzy of expansion
represents an *outstanding* change.

Foreign billings of the 4A agencies
accounted for $942 million in 1962,
and over $2,000 million in 1971. My
hunch is that by 1972 the billings of
the 4A agencies abroad will have increased by 130 percent in five years.

Foreign billings of the 4A agencies
are now equivalent to about *one-third*
of domestic billings--that is quite
something when you remember that domestic billings themselves increased by
30 percent in five years.

There are few industries that are as
international in scope as the advertising agencies, and none have done it
faster. As an industry we have twice
as many employees abroad as in the U.S.

Ogilvy & Mather's International billings
grew even more dramatically: from $70
million in 1966 to $212 million in 1972
--a three hundred percent increase.

3 THE BURDEN OF DISTRUST

You would think that the advertising
agencies stand out in the minds of government as dynamic, able builders of
the economy at home and abroad. That
Wall Street would find solace in the
stable and remarkable expansion of at
least one of their once-touted favorite
industries. And that economists would
say to themselves: good heavens, there
really must be something to advertising
after all.

The last five years, a period of unparalleled growth in advertising, has
seen a mounting burden of distrust, and
dislike heaped on the advertising agencies. It must be close to a miracle
not only that we survived but prospered.
And also met our critics and detractors
more than half way, without getting even
grudging murmurs of approval.

We rushed to sign consent orders, because the FTC is the law of the land,
and we did not want to be labelled cheats.
Now we find that the courts are not impressed by the windmills of evil the
FTC knights have been trying to attack.

We paid attention to consumerism: some
of us even collected contributions for
Ralph Nader. We discovered that consumerism is not a radical new way of life
for ordinary people, but a narrow pressure group, with special appeal to politicians in search of a non-partisan
cause.

But we listened and changed our ads. We
hired lawyers to interpret what people
in Washington were saying. There were
many in our own ranks who urged us to
reform, and we did.

We were told it was a disgrace that we
did not police ourselves. So we set
up, with extraordinary speed, an organization to do just that. Only to be
told now that we are not policing ourselves well.

Today, seven of the top agencies are publicly owned--and an eighth is waiting for the market to improve. But we are told we are unstable and unpredictable. Well, well. Our earnings increases significantly out-performed the Standard & Poor 500; indeed not many industry groups have done as well as advertising agencies.

Even when in the pillory, advertising agencies can operate both professionally, and financially, with remarkable success. We have done more than most industries to try and get ourselves out of disrepute, but to no avail. Since we got into the mess through a case of mistaken identity, it will take something irrational and unforeseen to get us out of it.

So much for the three remarkable changes. Good growth in the U.S. Remarkable growth abroad--achieved in a hostile climate of opinion. Flexibility and stability.

———   ———   ———

Now I am going to talk about a list of things I was told would interest you.

To my surprise, I learnt you would be interested in *a la carte* service. You must be the only ones left! Both *a la carte* and full service imply a willingness to provide the type and quality of service your client demands. At Ogilvy & Mather our attitude is this: we are prepared to offer any of our services, in any desired combination, provided we can make a fair profit and provided the service can be sensibly executed.

There's the rub. It is almost never possible to do good creative work without some research. Almost never possible to develop a creative strategy without marketing inputs. And it is silly to determine a creative posture without a look at all the media implications. And vice versa. The advertising process cannot be chopped up willy-nilly into many little segments. At

any rate not without a great deal of additional cost, and running grave risks about the quality of output.

You will also remember the trade reports that house agencies and boutiques were destroying the mastodons--the big full-service agencies. Boutiques and house agencies have always existed, both will continue to exist: "you pays your money, and you takes your choice." The share of advertising that goes into house agencies and boutiques--which are nothing but small agencies--has not changed.

I was told you were particularly keen to hear about the organization of account service function at Ogilvy & Mather.

The answer to all organizational questions in a service business is this: don't fit people into jobs, fit jobs to people. This is fundamental in an advertising agency. That is why we have a proliferation of the wildest titles ever invented by man, and why no two agencies function the same way. We must be enormously flexible. We must not impose hierarchical layers for the sake of organization charts--when all we need is one bright person.

If an advertising agency turns into a bureaucracy--i.e., the solemn observation of the rite of levels by passing the buck along the chain of command--you are indeed headed for trouble.

Beware of anyone whose title contains the word "administration," "co-ordination" or "group"--in an advertising agency: he is not likely to have a productive role.

At Ogilvy & Mather we have tried to remove all the routine and semi-clerical functions from account executives. The time-consuming compilation of brand statistics, the regular reports, traffic, policing of internal costs, and the endless post-office duties.

In many agencies this is the job of junior account executives, or assistant accout executives. Frankly, using good college graduates this way is a dreadful waste of time and money: there is nothing more confusing than an over-educated office boy.

We feel the job is better done by less high-powered people, not driven by such ferocious ambition. We call them staff assistants. Some are capable of being promoted to account executives. The staff assistants grade is a way of tapping the potential of people without business school training.

The young accout executive quickly gets bored and disenchanted with plodding routines. We believe he should be spending his time learning from his supervisor, his client, and the creative folks he works with. In our system we can expose the account executive to more varieties of business--he is not started out on a route that leads to specialization.

The account supervisor is the pillar of the account. He is usually a mature, fully experienced guy, someone who has been with our agency for four or five years. Usually a college graduate, with an MBA, and some experience on the client side, or in some totally unrelated business.

The up or out principle operates in all the account executive levels. But when a man reaches the post of account supervisor he can expect--all other things being equal--a decent career opportunity. When we promote, we try to assess whether the person has the potential to make it to the next highest grade. If he does not, he may never be promoted.

How do we know if our account men are any good? Well, there is a formal, written evaluation system. We also ask other departments about them. The views of our creative, media and research people about account executives

weigh with us. We lo
yond the line of duty
we ask: how good is
Yes, that is right.
evaluate the creative
how good are the sales? For, within an advertising agency, the quality of the work must be a *shared* responsibility.

We do not believe that account profitability should be a specific concern below the level of management supervisor or department head. These questions require a delicate balancing of costs and quality of service, and we do not want our working levels to be side-tracked from the ideal of thorough, professional, high quality service.

I am glad to say that in the last five years the exclusive male college club rules of account service have broken down. We now have 7 women account executives. We have 9 women staff assistants with the potential for promotion. We have only one account supervisor who is a woman. If I were to guess about the next five years, I would say that about 35 percent of account executives, about 15 percent of account supervisors, and 3 percent of management supervisors will be women.

Ten percent of our officers are women, including a director, Reva Korda, who is one of our creative heads. All, except Mrs. Korda, became vice presidents in the *last three years*.

The number of women in professional grades has increased by 66 percent since 1966. Notably in account service, art, commercial production, media and research. Equality in numbers? No, not yet. Equality of opportunity? Almost. Resistance is breaking down fast. Equality of pay? Certainly in theory, and almost always in practice.

We are often asked about training. Alas, advertising agencies are rotten at teaching. We have neither the time, nor the resources, nor the technical knowledge. But an advertising agency is a good place to learn. So send me a man who wants to learn--not a man or woman who wants to be taught. We find that people who are students of their craft make the best advertising people: people who have to be taught stay second raters. How do you learn? You are curious, ambitious, and very hard-working. And these three qualities bring me to the question of recruiting.

It seems to have been too readily assumed that in the new social climate young people will not be willing to prostitute their souls by working for advertising agencies. I would like to make the point that we do not need a large army of recruits, but only a tiny elite corps.

For in the wake of the profit squeeze of 1970, and the consequent rethinking of the use of manpower in advertising agencies, the number of people employed has declined by some 3,000 since 1966. The 4A agencies report that their total numbers in 1972 were 2,400 less than in 1966. That meaningless statistic--the number of people employed per million of billing--fell from 7.9 in 1966 to 5.5 in 1972, and is still falling. The drive for productivity was an international phenomenon.

In England too, the number of staff employed by member agencies of the I.P.A. declined by 25 percent between 1966 and 1972. But productivity doubled.

The story is similar in Canada, Germany and Australia.

In the case of Ogilvy & Mather, the industry trends in numbers employed are masked by our rapid growth. Although our numbers grew from 765 in 1966 to 906 in 1972, our numbers per million of billing fell from 7.9 to 4.6. Which is better or worse than the industry average, depending on your point of view.

So when we are talking about entrants into professional categories the ad-

vertising agencies need *hundreds* every year, not *thousands*.

Undeniably, it is more difficult to get the calibre of people we are looking for. They exist all right, and just as interested to get into our business as ever before, but somehow it is more difficult to find them. We have concluded that colleges and business schools are neither the sole, nor necessarily the best recruiting ground for people who put ambition, hard work, and intellectual curiosity ahead of all other career considerations.

One of our agency's innovations was the fee system of agency remuneration, back in 1960. Indeed, we prophecied that by 1970, payment by fee will have driven out the anachronistic commission system. Either our proposal was not as good as we assumed, or the commission system has greater strength and validity than we thought: because the commission system is still the source of the overwhelming proportion of agency income--it accounts for more than three-quarters. Even in our own case, fees amount to only half our income. We may have set out in a new direction, but we have not exactly started a stampede.

There has been a fundamental change, almost unnoticed by all commentators, affecting the anatomy of the major advertising agencies.

Our business used to be run by owner-entrepeneurs, great men, some of them veritable titans. Many of them have faded from the scene. In advertising, as in other businesses, there has been a managerial revolution. Nine of the top ten agencies got new presidents or chief executive officers in the last five years.

We do not pay enough homage to the titans --they built the business, they created a solid, predictable, useful new industry. And they handed to the new management, sound flourishing organizations, with distinct corporate reputations.

I am leaving you with the impression that we are without problems. Not so. But the problems I perceive are not those that the trade press discusses avidly in its daily and weekly outpourings.

A vivid and correct imagination can see the course of future events clearly. But it always underestimates the time required for the changes to work themselves out. I perceive the problems that will plague us, but I am not prepared to guess when they will start to rock the boat.

Client Conflicts For the large agencies, client conflicts are the most serious limiting factor of growth. It is sharpened by advertisers diversifying into each other's businesses. The time will come when it will be necessary to take a new look at what constitutes a conflict, and develop attitudes more like those prevailing in the professions.

Nationalism The fastest growing segment of the major agencies' business will be International. In the case of Ogilvy & Mather it already accounts for half of our income and profit.

Not only is the multi-national corporation we serve going to run into increasing difficulties with the forces of economic and social nationalism, but we, as foreign-owned advertising agencies, will come under increased scrutiny. Sanity suggests that in the long-term extreme forms of nationalism cannot prevail--but in the meantime there will be many anxious moments.

Profits Our system expects us to deliver increasing profits from the enterprise every year. As I have demonstrated earlier, advertising agencies have become much more efficient. But in our search for further improvements we shall look to vertical integration. Increasingly, you will find advertising agencies reaching into work that is now sub-contracted. My guess

is that this inevitable process will not work itself out without a great deal of argy-bargy.

———   ———   ———

Well so much for my review of the changing face of agency services. Let me leave you with two paradoxical observations. I have learnt, much to my surprise, that in our business, established veterans often, for no apparent reason, fail to make runs, but youngsters whose style is crude and untutored sometimes, for inexplicable reasons, hit the ball out of the park.

I have also observed from watching myself and my colleagues that when it comes to breaking rules, innovating, and daring, the middle-aged and respectable have at least as much innocent enjoyment and fun as the youthful and rebellious.

The changing face of the agency business is still very much the same face. Neither vigor nor optimism has drained from it. A few new hard lines around the eyes, a little more grey around the temples. Quite an attractive face really.

Concern for the future? Oh yes. But no terminal diseases. Indeed, a surprisingly clean bill of health.

DISCUSSION QUESTIONS

1. The author writes, "It is almost never possible to do creative work without some research." Do you agree or disagree? Discuss.

2. This article states that all the routine and semi-clerical functions of an advertising agency can be handled better by non-college graduates than by college graduates, referred to by the article as "over-educated office boys." Do you feel this is a valid point? Why?

Reprinted by permission from ADVERTISING AGE; 9 April, 1973, pp. 51-2, 54.

VI-4

HOW TO WORK WITH AN ADVERTISING AGENCY

Howard Fisher

What I have to say is designed for advertisers who don't have big budgets. Let's say up to $500,000 a year.

Half a million is a good cut-off place --under that, you're considered small; over that, you don't solicit or appreciate advice from anyone. So this primer is for small to medium-size advertisers--from the innocents who may never have worked with an agency, to the jaded and cautious who have already worn out several.

There are only four basic questions you want answered when you look for an agency. You already know that the handful of agencies you've selected as finalists for your account can advertise to your satisfaction. You've seen their ads, their TV spots, heard their radio, etc. They know their craft. So what else do you need to know?

1. Do you like them?

2. Do they know anything about your business?

3. What do their present clients think of them?

4. Do they pay their bills?

DO YOU LIKE THEM?

This criterion is so simple and so obvious, too many bosses overlook it. Do you like to be with the people, talk to them? Are they your kind of people? Do they think the way you do? Do you feel comfortable with them? If the chemistry between the people is right, the agency relationship will be right.

It won't work if you're dynamic, think and act fast, etc., and your agency or the account executive assigned is deliberate, thorough, conservative. You both may be smart as hell, but you'll mistake his plodding, sure ways for stupidity, and he'll think you're some kind of con artist. The same thing works in reverse, only more so. Bosses tend to think advertising people are "slick" anyway, and a slow, meticulous boss, paired with a glib, "ad-biz" account executive, spells calamity.

It may be true in marriage that opposites attract (has this ever been proved?), but the agency-client relationship isn't a marriage. It doesn't even come close, and already any number of agencies are crying "foul!" at that remark. Hell, they've sold their clients on the fiction that agency-client relationships are just like marriage. Not so. The purpose of advertising is to sell something. Any boss who thinks of his wife and his account executive in the same framework is in trouble.

He may like his account executive more than his wife; he may have more of a basis for intelligent conversation with him than with her. But it's not marriage. Advertising is a business deal, calculated to sell something.

√ The best way, the only way to determine if you like the people is to talk with them, face to face. Allow as much time as it takes. A good place to start is with the man or woman who runs the agency. You're small to medium-size, and so are they, so this shouldn't be hard to set up. You may find that the agency is only one person.

The first meeting should be exploratory, to look each other over. You'll probably meet two or three of the other top people in the agency. If the personal chemistry is right, you may want to talk an hour or two, maybe the entire morning or afternoon. If you don't like the people, or if you run out of things to say in 15 minutes, another hour of chit-chat won't help anybody. At this first meeting, you outline what it is you want to accomplish, and the agency can indicate whether they feel it's possible, and whether they can help you.

If the conversation lags, you can revive it by asking what new accounts the agency has gained in the past year or two, and what accounts they've lost, if any--and why.

√ After these preliminary talks, you can probably narrow your choices down to a workable number. You may be able to decide on your agency already. But if you still have three or four choices, visit their places again. See how they work.

Agencies have personalities, just as

individuals do. Some are stodgy. Some are bright, young, zingy all the time. Some are well organized; some are Panicsville. Some are all common sense and basic. Others, who knows?

But whatever you do, don't judge an agency by the way the writers dress or the art directors wear their hair. Your only interest is in their talent, their product. That young man with the tight blue jeans, long hair and metal-rimmed glasses, who seems tongue-tied and inarticulate, may be the very person who dreamed up the ads that attracted you to the agency in the first place. Or he may be faking it. Beads do not a brain make. How the people look is irrelevant. How they think and how they produce advertising is what matters.

DO THEY KNOW ANYTHING ABOUT YOUR BUSINESS?

The agency doesn't have to know everything about your business, but they should know something. Maybe someone in the agency worked for a competitor. Maybe they worked on something similar.

If they don't have any experience or knowledge in your field, and you still think they'll do a good job for you, because they're smart, innovative, eager, daring, or whatever, it's your decision, your company's money, and a lot of good advertising has happened because they didn't know it couldn't be done.

Nobody told them what the taboos were, the no-nos, the myths that stifle good work. Many times, all that's necessary to rejuvenate a tired business is for someone to forget everything that's been done before. If the thinking is right, and market conditions are right, the advertising will be right.

WHAT DO THEIR PRESENT CLIENTS THINK OF THEM?

You can find out easily--by picking up the phone. With the agency's permission, call some of their clients. A call is better than a letter, as you'll see in a moment.

Explain who you are and why you're calling.

"I'm the boss of such-and-such, and I'm looking for an agency to handle my advertising. I like the stuff you're doing, and I'm considering hiring your agency to work with me. *Are you happy with them?*"

Now, here's where the phone call will tell you more than a letter ever could. After you've asked the crucial question: *"Are you happy with them?"*...if there's a pause--of any length--at the other end of the line, something's wrong. If a boss has to *think* about whether he likes his agency, there's trouble somewhere.

They either do or they don't.

That considered pause--which can't be in a letter--is your signal to dig deeper. Ask about sales. Most bosses will tell you if their business is good or not. Ask about the agency's people, especially the account executive proposed to handle your business, the writers, art directors, buyers, all the key people who will be working in your behalf. A five or ten-minute phone conversation could be the best investment you make, other than the actual hiring of the agency you ultimately select.

√ A happy client will not be able to conceal his pleasure and enthusiasm. When you ask: Are you happy with your agency? see if the answer comes back spontaneously in any of these forms:

You bet!

Couldn't be happier!

I think they're great!

Yes, we've been very happy!

Then you've struck gold. But beware of pregnant pauses and guarded platitudes that only seem to praise. Holes in the conversation mean holes in the relationship.

Ask about the entire agency, especially about the individuals proposed to handle your account. If these bosses don't know the account executives, creative people, buyers, etc., *they* may prefer it that way--to work only with the *agency boss*--but *you don't want it that way.* You know you'll get better advertising and have more fun if you work with the people who work on your account.

DO THEY PAY THEIR BILLS?

This means, do they pay *your* bills? An advertising agency is an agent. *Your* agent. Some agencies have an impeccable financial reputation, others are always 60, 90, 120 days behind. If you make it a practice to pay your bills on time, you have a right to expect that your agent, acting in your behalf, do the same. An agency's reputation for slow pay can rub off on you, because there's a tendency to assume that an agency that doesn't pay on time has clients that don't pay on time. Because you are a small to medium-size advertiser, talking with small to medium-size agencies, the caution about prompt payment cannot be over-emphasized.

Of course, if you, as the client, string out *your* payments--to hold onto the cash longer, to earn interest on the money, to boost inventory, meet payrolls, or for whatever reason, the agency you want may not want you. An agency relationship can be fun and laughter and excite-

ment--except where the money is concerned. While you're checking out
the agency and their financial reputation, they'll be checking *you* out. An
agency has *its* money on the line--
they've paid the newspapers, radio and
TV stations, magazines, etc., before
they bill you, and a lot of small to
medium-size agencies have been stung--
have been decimated--by clients who
wouldn't or couldn't pay.

That 15% commission can look awfully
small when the client doesn't remit
--and months go by.

WANT MORE FACTS ON AGENCY?
ASK REP

If you're not satisfied that you
have all the information you need,
there's one more excellent source:
The salesmen and representatives who
call on agencies to sell them time and
space. They may not always know how
the agency's *advertising* is working,
but they know how the *agency* and its
personnel work--if they're professionals or charlatans, if they pay their
bills, if they're sharp buyers, if
their management is strong or loose.
Salesmen and reps tell it like it is
--or at least the way they see it--
and their viewpoints can be succinct
and colorful.

Some clients have devised outlandish
questionnaires, many pages long, as an
"aid" to selecting an agency. Fortunately, you're not big enough, yet, to
have fallen into that trap. You only
need to know the four basics:

Do you like them? Do they know something about your business--or can
they learn? Do their present clients
like them? Do they pay their bills?

WHAT NOT TO DO NEXT

Where do you go from here? Let's say
you've narrowed your choices to three
agencies and you want to know what they
can do for you. How can you find out?

You started this search by selecting advertising that appealed to you. You've
talked with the principals, the creative
people, you may even have gotten some
top-of-the-head suggestions that might
work. You probably have a gut feeling
that one of those three agencies is the
one you want to hire, but you don't want
to make the decision strictly on gut
feel. You want to see the kind of advertising they'd do for *you.*

It's very simple. Ask them to prepare
some ads or TV storyboards, or knock
out a campaign. They want your business;
they should be willing to do this, right?

Wrong.

Unless you have a budget of $250,000 to
$300,000 or more, thereby justifying
the gamble on a speculative presentation
of this sort, an agency is reluctant to
take creative people off work they're
doing for existing clients, spend untold
man-hours and untold money gambling on
the possibility that you'll like what
you see.

Many agencies refuse to make speculative presentations, even for accounts
that bill in the millions. They feel,
and rightly so, that their work speaks
for them.

√ For small to medium-size account,
presentations are a monstrous waste.
The agencies that don't win will have
disrupted their entire operation for
nothing but an exercise; the agency that
gets the business may easily take a
year or two--or more--recouping its
presentation costs. If you can possibly
make your decision based on past work
and faith, do so.

But if you feel that a presentation is the only way to be sure, ask your finalists to present--and *pay them for it*. Tell each contending agency they have 30 days and X-number of dollars--$500, $1,000, $3,000--whatever it's worth to you, in relationship to the annual budget you plan to invest in advertising.

Give the competing agencies enough information to do an intelligent job. Each agency should be given the same background information, so everyone is working from the same base. Your market, competitive information, pricing problems, distribution, anything that contributes to your sales effort and problems, should be spelled out. And remember that old premise--you're trying to find an agency to "work with" (not *use*)--so trust these people. If you don't trust them, they shouldn't be on your final selection list. If any of the agencies asks for more information, it should be furnished.

This additional probing can only work to your benefit; an agency may turn up something very valuable to you--vital information that may have been so obvious you overlooked it. And it may be *the* advertising hook you've been seeking.

You may think this kind of briefing is a bit much--sort of putting on airs that your little business doesn't justify. Maybe your company is small--one place of business, one product. There's always something unique about any business, and many times, the small companies present more challenge than the big ones. Your job is tougher because you don't have the dollar clout the big boys do. So if you have enough faith in what you're doing to want to advertise it properly, a good agency will be interested in your business.

BUY PRESENTATION--IT'S EDUCATION

Buying a presentation accomplishes several things: It says you don't expect something for nothing. Also, you can ask the competing agencies to account for your money--which will be an excellent indication of the way they utilize time and cash. What you'll be seeing, when they present to you, is ads, TV storyboards, layouts--rough materials that have some value. You have every right to know what the agencies spent for each item presented, because it's your money.

If they stayed within your budget and got good stuff, that tells you plenty. If they overspent (spent some of money) trying to impress you with how much they want your business, ask them if they'd be willing to do the same thing, should they get the account. A budget should be a budget, and one of the biggest areas for friction between agencies and clients is production cost --the cost of preparing the advertising.

So your speculative presentation (which you're paying for) can be highly educational--you can judge how your future agency performs in meeting a reasonable deadline (30 days). You can judge the caliber of the creative work--and you can see how they spend money.

Make sure the people you're promised are the people you get.

If the agency promises you the personal attention and services of the president or chairman--and that's what you want-- make sure that's what you get.

If they promise you *the* creative director or *the* copy chief or art director-- tell 'em that's who you want. This avoids the possibility (and it happens) of being *sold* by the first string--and then turned over to somebody else.

YOU, NOT GRAPEVINE, MUST TELL WINNER

You've been deliberate. Now decide quickly.

It's important to let your decision be known as soon as possible. No purpose can be served by delay, anxiety, or procrastination. When you've decided, call the runners-up first and tell them which agency you've selected. It's better that they hear the sad news from you rather than someone else. By the time you've made your third call--to the winner--chances are he's already heard it, unofficially. The grapevine again. If advertising could work as fast as the gossip and rumors that permeate the business, it would be one of the major wonders of the universe.

Unfortunately, few such miracles happen.

Don't expect miracles.

If you think advertising is going to perform miracles, forget it. It won't.

When you were searching for an advertising agency, wou were very conscious of the ads that appealed to you. But now a few weeks have gone by, maybe a few months. So here's a good test of the power of advertising.

How many advertisers can you think of whose advertising you like, admire, respect, or remember? You have 10 seconds....

It wasn't a very long list, was it? Not many advertising messages really cut through, did they?

Now, a tougher test: Out of the slim list of advertisers you like, respect, admire, or remember--can you recall what their advertising says about their *products*? You have 60 seconds....

YOU'RE SMARTER THAN MOST PEOPLE

The obvious conclusion has to be: Even companies that spend millions don't always accomplish advertising miracles. They didn't impress *you* that much, and *you're interested* in advertising, and you're smarter than most people because you're a boss and have the job of selling something to people who are not nearly as interested in your sales as you are.

The folks out there in televisionland are not sitting around breathlessly, hanging on every nuance.

They don't buy the newspaper to hunt for your ads. And they have a remarkable talent born of years of practice: They can tune out radio commercials completely.

Somehow, you've got to do better than most advertisers, and you've got to do it with limited money. Your advertising has to be meaningful, intelligent, persuasive. So you've hired the best advertising professionals you could find. They're talented, you like them, and you enter into the advertising relationship with enthusiasm and high hopes.

But don't expect miracles.

You need a written agreement. It can be a letter that spells out the way you'll work together and the terms of your commission/fee agreement. The acceptable markup on production expenses (art, type, studio costs, etc.) should be determined and put in writing.

√ A simple and fair way to handle expenses is: If the agency travels or makes long distance calls or spends its money in your behalf or at your request, they should be reimbursed. Some agencies bill this kind of expense at cost: others add the agreed markup. It's advisable to work out little details like this ahead of time so there's no misunderstanding. Later, if you find you've

agreed to something that's not practical, you can always change it.

You'll need a termination clause. This
is not marriage, it's a business deal.
On small accounts, 30 days is reasonable notice. Bigger accounts, with
more money involved, more contracts to
transfer, more lead time on creative
work, may need 60 or 90 days. Whatever
is fair. You work *with* an agency even
after you've fired them or they've re-
signed you.

DISCUSSION QUESTIONS

1. The questions posed by this article
are designed for advertisers who don't
have big budgets (up to $500,000 a year).
Do you feel large advertisers (with budgets over $500,000) need other questions
answered? If so, what are they?

2. What other questions might be considered by small advertisers?

From THE ADVERTISING BUDGET, by Richard J. Kelly, C.P.A., edited by Herbert A. Ahlgren, C.P.A., 1967, pp. 261-266. Reprinted by permission of Association of National Advertisers, Inc.

VI-5

15%-FACT OR FICTION

Maxwell Dane

In a speech to the House of Commons in 1947, Winston Churchill said, "No one pretends that democracy is perfect or all wise. Indeed it has been said that democracy is the worst form of government except all those other forms that have been tried." With apologies to Mr. Churchill's ghost, I will paraphrase his remark, "The 15% system is the *worst* form of compensation--*except* all those other forms that have been tried."

FEW AGENCIES RELY SOLELY ON MEDIA COMMISSION INCOME

Let me start off by saying that it's fictitious to think that the so-called 15% system is the *sole* source of compensation to the advertising agency. Very rarely is this so. A study made by the 4A's revealed that *less than 1%* of agencies' billings was derived from clients who paid for no services other than gross media costs. The study was made in 1964 and there are no indications that this percentage has changed appreciably despite several highly publicized fee or guaranteed minimum arrangements. Stated another way, there

was almost unanimous agreement between client and agency that the 15% income from media was not adequate compensation to the agency and, therefore, supplementary income had to be derived from percentages added to materials and services purchased and/or fees for inside work such as layouts, storyboards, mechanicals, research, sales promotion, etc.

Among larger agencies (and for the purpose of this paper I will define them as agencies billing $40 million or more) between 75% and 80% of their total income comes from media commission. The remaining 20% to 25% is derived from fees for inside work and percentages added to purchases. The true significance of these figures is that the 15% commission from media is only the foundation, not the entire structure, upon which other charges must be made if the agency is to exist. The percentage of income derived from sources other than media is substantially in excess of the average gross profit margin of any group of advertising agencies.

The trade press gives the impression that changes in patterns of agency compensation have been revolutionary. The *facts* do not support this position. Whatever changes have occurred have been evolutionary, not revolutionary. Almost

315

all agencies are getting paid for more and more services and are receiving compensation over and above media commissions. Accordingly, the total amount of income from charges for services has been rising and, on the average, has become a significantly larger part of the whole income of agencies.

To illustrate, on a total dollar basis, in 1950 media commissions accounted for 81% of agencies' gross income, 19% from all other sources. For 1963, comparable figures were 76% and 24%. Media commissions are still the soul and substance of the agency business.

The words "commission system" or "15% commission system" inaccurately describe the existing, traditional method of compensation. Possibly a more accurate name would be "media commission plus" system. Critics often brush aside as unimportant the fact that this method has worked effectively for advertiser *and* agency in good times and bad. There have been years when the advertiser complained about excessive agency profits but in even more years agencies were concerned with the steadily declining rate of profit. However, the "media commission plus" system provided sufficient flexibility for evolutionary changes which have continued to take place during the past 75 years.

REBUTTAL TO CRITICS OF MEDIA COMMISSION SYSTEM

Critics of the "media commission plus" system exist principally among advertisers but there are also a few agencies in this camp.

Principal criticisms are:

Criticism #1--The agency profits most by recommending increased expenditures to the client. The assumption here must be that the agency has virtual carte blanche to spend the advertiser's money, has no degree of accountability for the results achieved and is dealing with advertisers who don't ask pertinent questions when the agency recommends increased expenditures. An agency does not prosper by proposing larger expenditures--it prospers by creating and producing advertising which brings results.

Criticism #2--An agency provides services that an advertiser doesn't need. Why can't the advertiser pick the services he wants? I can imagine a typical conversation. "Let's see, I'll take one nice, solid supervisor, two account executives--they needn't be too ripe. Art directors? I don't know, we have some pretty bright designers on our own staff. Oh, yes--I almost forgot--copywriters. We're going to need 3 or 4 of them--but don't send any green ones." Seriously, I can recall only one occasion when a client raised this point. But when we went down the list of departments-- copy, art, television, media, account executives research--he nodded in agreement that all were necessary. Sometimes a question arises about an agency's marketing department. How important is it since the client also has a marketing department--often much larger than the agency's. The marketing department is vital in helping an agency *understand* and *independently* evaluate the information which it gets from the client. A client's marketing department is not always as objective as it should be, but we find that where the client has a strong marketing operation, he solicits and welcomes the agency's point of view. Where the client doesn't have a marketing department, the services of an agency's marketing department are indispensable.

Criticism #3--The agency makes too much (or too little) money. Need I add that the first statement is more likely to be the advertiser's, the second the agency's. Well, this is a matter on which there will never be complete agreement. How much is too much--1%, 2%, 3%, 4%? The answer to "too little" is simpler. If it's so little that the agency goes out of business or can't staff properly, it's certainly too little, although I hasten to add that the agency has no one to blame but itself. There are other answers. An agency is being paid *too much* money--regardless of how *little*--if it doesn't create and produce effective advertising. An agency-- whatever it is earning--is a bargain if it is producing results. An advertiser's marketing director who earns $75,000 a year may be a better buy and a bigger bargain than another advertiser's marketing director at $35,000. Is there a better way to evaluate an advertising agency?

Criticism #4--The "15% media commission system" is old-fashioned--let's try something new. As I briefly mentioned earlier, practically no agency which operates on this system derives *all* of its income from the 15% commission it receives from media. There are invariably other charges--we are not talking about a restrictive, inflexible system as some critics would pretend. Something new is not necessarily something better even though something new is always more worthy of press comment.

Criticism #5--An agency can be more objective if it doesn't work on a commission system. An agency can be honest, intelligent and able or it can be dishonest, stupid and incompetent under any system known to man. So can a client. Methods of compensation don't determine ability--although more able people, in any field, ususally earn more than less able people.

OBSERVATIONS ON SOME ALTERNATE METHODS OF COMPENSATION

Now let's talk for a few moments about other methods of compensation which are being tried--and some com-

ments or questions that come to mind about them:

Fees (I'm talking about fees which *entirely* replace media commissions and other agency income). These fees are basically of two types:

√ *A fixed fee* determined at the beginning of the year, with possible adjustments from time to time. Under this method it behooves the agency to keep its costs sufficiently under its income so that a profit can be shown. Weakness of the plan is obvious. The less time spent on the account, the most profit to the agency. Who wants to come hat in hand to the client every year or every six months asking for more money?

√ *A fee based on cost plus.* Never mind whether the work is important or not, the more time spent on a job, the greater the agency's income. Why spend $5 a square foot on space--there's no penalty and perhaps a reward if the cost goes to $6 or $7. Why turn out the lights? It's doubtful that any serious student of cost-plus systems would claim they are efficient or inexpensive.

Another method recently publicized is a guaranteed profit of 1 1/2% of billing (after taxes) with a rebate to the advertiser if it exceeds 2 1/2%. It would seem that there are a few problems which the agency must face:

√ What will the agency do about those accounts which refuse to guarantee the agency a profit of 1 1/2% after taxes?

√ Based on the figures of the advertising agency industry a 1.5% guaranteed *minimum* profit (after taxes) substantially exceeds the average profit of large agencies. If we take another fix on the 1.5% guaranteed *minimum* and compare it with the profit margins which have been published by the five agencies which have gone public (or are in the process of doing so) we find that 4 of the 5 have a total net profit of *less* than the 1.5% guaranteed minimum.

Agencies and advertisers should be violently opposed to any guaranteed minimum *profit*. We don't live in a riskless society. The American economy was not built on guaranteed profits, and the advertising agency business isn't going to thrive or even maintain its independence on *guaranteed profits*.

√ What will happen in periods of recession--national recession, industry recession or individual recession--when the advertiser's own profit (if there is any at all) is substantially below his guarantee to the agency? Is he going to meet the guarantee? Want to make any bets?

In my opinion an agency should be appraised from a "Value Added Concept." What has the agency done to the 85% which is the advertiser's real investment in the white space or broadcast time? Is there too much worrying about the 15% and not enough about the 85%?

New methods of compensation are always being tried--and I say, great--let's never be complacent about what we're doing. For example, several agencies had widely publicized deals with advertisers to share in increased sales. When they vanished, hardly a word was said about them. They didn't work and never will. If sales go up appreciably, the advertiser grumbles that he is paying too much and there are plenty of agencies who will take over the account on a more conventional basis. If sales go down, pity the poor agency.

If an advertiser put a gun to my head and said I could make only one single criticism about fee and *guaranteed* profit agreements, I wouldn't have to think too long. I'd say, over and beyond all else, they rob an agency of its independence. An advertiser who doesn't want independence from his agency is never going to get good work. He may have some part of the 15%, but he'll lose a lot more from the 85%. I am not

saying that independence in itself is enough. It isn't. Independence does not guarantee good work, but it's awfully hard to have good work without independence.

One of the most widely publicized fee tests in recent years was that between General Foods and two of its advertising agencies for seven different products. One of the agencies is the staunchest advocate of the fee system, the other goes along with the more traditional form of agency compensation. So both points of view were represented. General Foods, one of the nation's largest advertisers, has a reputation as a knowledgeable, fair-minded advertiser who knows the problems of client-agency relationships, and knows how the two teams must work together to achieve maximum results. *If it's not a good arrangement for both it's not good for either*.

As you know, the tested fee plan was dropped after a two year comprehensive test with the comment that "the traditional commission form of compensation usually is best when established products are involved, while for new products it sometimes is more suitable to base compensation on an annual fee, plus payment for special services required." Added fees for new products is a subject almost beyond debate. Compensation to agencies for work on new products is indeed a major and growing problem. Whether we like it or not, most new products may require as much and sometimes more agency time and effort than a going product. An agency's role may begin with a suggestion for the product, its purpose, its name, competition and potential market. From six months to a year or more may elapse before there is any advertising. The initial advertising expenditure is small but the results are being carefully checked in several markets. Rarely does the first test check out well enough to warrant immediate expansion on a national scale --changes, refinements and perhaps entirely new approaches are required before there is enough evidence for the

318

go-ahead or the sorry decision to forget about it.

ADDITIONAL COMPENSATION FOR NEW PRODUCT WORK USUALLY WARRANTED

Like most other agencies we have been
confronted with new product problems by
clients but so far we have not been
able to work out a formula that is universally applicable. Should agency profits on going products be diverted to
new products--or should each new product stand on its own feet? Should the
agency take a loss? If so, for how
long? Should the agency be paid only
for out-of-pocket expenses and salaries?
These are questions which eventually
must be answered. Obviously, this is
an area where the "media commission
plus" system can function only if the
"plus" part of the system provides
enough dollars to furnish manpower without straining the resources of the
agency. Currently we are working with
one client on a rather involved compensation plan for new products in which
the agency receives fees for time spent
during the developmental stages in addition to media commission and other normal charges. With this plan there is
some sharing of the risk initially with
the mutual hope of profits for both if
the product succeeds.

A point that must be emphasized and
re-emphasized is that a system, whether
it's a fee, commission or combination
system, is no guarantee of either lower
costs to the advertiser or of better
work.

If there is a seeming inequity in the
prevalent "media commission plus" arrangement, it is that all agencies--
good, fair and mediocre--receive the
same 15% from media. Yet when we stop
to think about it there is a compensat-
ing factor for superior work. The reward for excellence is increased income

from increased advertising, the result
of creating effective advertising which
makes it profitable for the advertiser
to spend more. This is the incentive
carrot, a built-in modest reward to the
agency, automatically and without pro-
tracted negotiation.

Agency billings from advertisers do not
rise because of whims or personal likes.
Normally there is a relationship between
increased advertising expenditures and
increased sales. In reverse, declining
sales usually bring down advertising
budgets--and sometimes the agency's head
with it. Most advertisers believe it is
fair and proper that an agency should
share in the success of a product.

AGENCY GROWTH DEPENDS ON CLIENT SUCCESS

After an agency is established for a
few years, its greatest growth is likely
to come from increased advertising ex-
penditures--part of it the result of a
healthy national economy, a more important part of it the results it helps the
advertiser achieve. Recently we made
an analysis of our 12 largest accounts
who had been with us 2 or more full
years. We compared their expenditures
in the first full year they had been
with us and in 1965. Eleven of the 12
had substantially increased their ex-
penditures--on account A there was an
increase of over 1,300%, account B 1,000%,
account C 800%, account D 500%, account
E 300%, and so on. Only one account
was--down--and that an insignificant 6%.
Doubtless, we contributed to the growth
of these accounts--neither we nor the
client could accurately determine how
much, but our participation in the
growth through the "media commission
plus" system was not unreasonable.

The "media commission plus" system works,
and works well, for most advertisers and
agencies. It's a system which has the
virtue of simplicity--and in a field

319

where everything is becoming more complex, it's a virtue not to be ignored. Whether initially the commission should have been 15% or 12% or 18% is a moot point but hardly debatable at this point in history. Agencies have learned to operate within this area, rendering services year after year which have contributed to the world's most efficient marketing mix.

Who can determine what the profit of an agency should be? Keep in mind that profit can be affected, favorably or adversely, by salaries, rent, travel and numerous other items. An agency which pays higher salaries will have lower profits. Will the client who is paying a fee or guaranteeing a profit be unconcerned with agency salaries? How can he be? It's his money.

The "media commission plus" system makes it possible for an agency to operate with the greatest degree of independence--independence to run its own affairs, even to make its own mistakes and to be rewarded or penalized for its judgment. An agency should have freedom to make its own decisions on manpower, salaries, rent, to turn lights on or off without worrying what the advertiser's opinion may be. But it must be willing to take responsibility for its actions.

Under alternative systems of compensation the advertiser too often will be forced to look over the agency's shoulder--a method which never produces the best work. Don't advertisers have enough of their own headaches? Do they also want to saddle themselves with the agencies'? When advertisers are involved with fees or guarantees there is no choice.

Everyone has his own crystal ball and everyone loves to make predictions. I'll join the parade that A.N.A. started with its question about agency compensation 10 years hence:

√ I predict that commission from media

will continue to be the principal source of revenue for almost all agencies.

√ I predict that an agency which offers clients alternative methods of compensation will find that clients choose the less costly.

√ I predict that agencies which do good work will have no trouble in finding and keeping clients--regardless of the method of compensation.

√ I predict that the subject of agency compensation will be on the agenda of the A.N.A. in 1976. And, later that year, at Greenbrier the members of the 4A's will discuss the same subject--but, strangely enough, from a different perspective.

DISCUSSION QUESTIONS

1. This article offers five criticisms of the media commission system. Do you feel they are valid? Explain. Do you know of any advantages the media commission system offers?

2. The author points out two alternate methods of compensation for ad agencies: (a) fees, and (b) a guaranteed profit of 1 1/2% of billing (after taxes) with a rebate to the advertiser if it exceeds 2 1/2%. Which of the two alternatives do you feel is best or can you devise a better alternative? Discuss.

Reprinted by permission from MEDIA DECISIONS; February, 1973, pp. 60-61.

VI-6

IN UNION THERE IS CLOUT

Media Decisions

Agency networks have suddenly taken on new clout as a media buying force to be reckoned with.

The most significant move was the signing on January second of this year by NAAN (National Advertising Agency Network) of a contract for services with Sam Vitt, the soft spoken and gentlemanly independent media buyer, who was media chief at Ted Bates before he set up his own shop.

This, however, is only one of several steps taken recently by the agency nets to modernize and up-grade their services.

There seems to be a feeling among them that they are in battle for their lives with the big agencies in New York and Chicago that have been setting up "networks" of their own for local media buying--through new branch offices and through mergers with local agencies.

The agency networks have until very recently been loose affiliations of small and medium size agencies. They tended to be run like clubs by gentlemen from member agencies who volunteered their services in the manner of elected officers of media and advertising associations.

Some still operate that way, and apparently very effectively. But now four agency networks have paid, full-time managers, and a fifth is considering the addition of a full-time headquarters man. Furthermore, the managers and the volunteer presidents are experienced, capable admen whose potential for agency services is spread over more than 266 agencies with combined billings of over $935 million. How much of this can be handled through central offices remains to be seen, but the trend is to centralization.

We talked with the agency network managers and presidents about their current activities, but before explaining what we found, a bit of history seems in order.

BACKGROUND

The networks started as associations for less than 4A's-size agencies. They were the place where small agency operators could share their problems, and break bread and play golf once a year with men of like mind and enterprise.

321

PRINCIPAL ADVERTISING AGENCY NETWORKS

	Number of agencies	Combined billings
Affiliated Advertising Agencies International (AAAI)	58	$100 million
Advertising & Marketing International Network (AMIN)	50	320 million
First Advertising Agency Network (FAAN)	25	50 million
Intermarket Association of Advertising Agencies (IAAA)	19	30 million
International Chain of Industrial & Technical Agencies (ICITA)	33	180 million
Mutual Advertising Agency Network (MAAN)	24	35 million
National Advertising Agency Network (NAAN)	29	170 million
Transamerica Advertising Agency Network (TAAN)	28	50 million
Totals	266	$935 million

Then, largely through the activities of Lynn Ellis, an agency management consultant, a very practical business service was added to this for the sharing: an accounting system uniquely suited to small-to-middle size agency needs. The Ellis Plan was bought on a shared basis by three of the first networks. Other shared services followed.

Member agencies also started to trade work assignments on an as-needed basis. In media, for example, an agency with a new account in a field with which it was not well acquainted, sought the advice of mediamen in another agency that had experience in the same market with a non-competing product. These activities grew at first informally (see *Media Decisions*, December 1969, "It Pays to Have Connections").

This kind of media planning and buying exchange continues as a vital and growing part of agency network activity. In fact, it has expanded to such an extent that the networks have formalized the interchange with "start work" sheets, methods of estimating costs on large assignments, systems of payment for services rendered by one agency to another (usually time charges plus a profitable markup).

Currently being laid on top of these activities are a variety of headquarters services that are covered by membership dues or bought through the main office in order to secure the benefits of central office buying (low cost and assured quality). The importance of both of these capabilities in new business solicitation when larger agencies are also competing for the account are, of course, a major factor.

Here's a run-down (in alphabetical order) of what each of the agency networks we talked to had to say;

Affiliated Advertising Agencies International (AAAI) has a new managing director, Bob Griffiths, who became one of the best known figures in advertising during his 17 years as the managing director of the Association of Industrial Advertisers.

Bob finds some things (like setting up meetings and new membership) not too different at AAAI from his old spot at AIA. But he says his new constituents have a wholly new set of interests, and he likes the change.

Griffiths started out in life as a radio newscaster, ran the A&S Club in Kansas City, and then came to New York to head up AIA. He became the agency network's manager only about three months ago, and brought with him the skills of a professional association man.

He rates headquarters services as of great importance. At AAAI these include: SIC classifications for all accounts of

member agencies, many of which have industrial accounts (and this is helpful
in industrial media planning); assistance requests (including the processing of media work by one member for
another), an AAAI Newsletter; a "Net-
worker" magazine (both of which are a
means of exchanging knowhow in media
matters as well as other subjects);
member assistance (in new business,
office management, leasing of equipment); a library of advertising and
marketing research; special research
requests.

"We work on the branch office concept,"
Bob told us. "Members work for each
other, based on written calls for help
that are filed on an Assistance Request
Form."

AAAI has 58 members and about $100 mil-
lion in billings. One immediate objective is to find good new members in
new markets. It wants an effective
"branch" in every important U.S. city.
A couple of new members will probably
be added at the next network meeting
April 2-5 in Palm Desert, Cal.

Three-quarters of Griffith's members
are also members of the 4A's. We
asked him what the network offers that
the 4A's doesn't.

"Interplay," he said. "Our people
handle specific assignments for each
other. Through the network they are
national in scope, and this is essential in pitching some new accounts."

Bob believes the networks have "kept
their light under a bushel for too long."
He hopes he can help them become better known. He also thinks they could
make use of more joint market and media
research.

Advertising and Marketing International Network (AMIN)

has 34 members in
North America and 16 others around the
world (in as many different countries).
Its worldwide network billings are
$320 million. Bob Lando, who has built

his agency in Pittsburgh (Lando, Inc.)
up to a $13 million biller, and who was
president of the network last year, told
us that "one of the major changes in the
network in recent years is the thrust on
media expertise."

He says that is aimed mainly at improving the capability in media work of the
media professionals in member agencies.
The network runs its own seminars on
media, and its mediamen and women get
together in groups of 15 to 18 people
quite frequently. The last meeting was
in November in Atlanta, and the next one
will be in April. "Our people have
found these meetings much more useful
than the big seminars run by others for
all kinds of agencies. Our media people find that in small groups they can
let their hair down, and really discuss
problems and solutions."

At these meetings they also go over such
services as TelMar, Simmons (which was
bought for network use in the past),
TGI (which they are planning to buy for
network use now). And they get their
signals straight on how to use other
agencies in the network for metro market buying away from home.

This latter activity is growing, Lando
told us. Other agencies in the network
do the work at cost--based on time
charges that are standard for the whole
network. The time charges are printed
in advance on intra-network purchase
orders. The amount of time involved
for buys in different markets may vary,
and the time required varies also because of varying buy requirements; but
the price for agency time is standard.

The members take turns at being AMIN
president and headquarters. This year
it's Karl Bishopric, Bishopric & Field,
Miami.

First Advertising Agency Network

has
25 members and billings of $50 million.
Herb Gardner in St. Louis is executive
vp of FAAN, a full-time job. He's been
there since September 1, 1972.

Herb says the greatest call from his members is for help with agency management problems: accounting, contracts, and other forms of paperwork (including media papers). Typically, the accounts handled by the agencies in the network are mixed--some industrial, more consumer; some retail, more national.

The principal channels for exchange of information among members are total network meetings (two a year); direct contact by one member with another; occasionally, a formalized service request for information in a certain field. We asked Gardner for an example of this latter type of work. And he cited a mid-west member who asked the member in Los Angeles for "the best television station in L.A. for such-and-such a product. Normally, the first request of this kind is for free; but later requests are paid for on a regular hourly rate basis."

Herb was aware of the NAAN hook-up with Vitt Media International for broadcast buying. "We have in mind a similar type of thing," he said. "Our concept is different, but it involves an outside service. The group we're thinking of dealing with can offer all kinds of media advice and information. Our objective is to set up an all-media service and information program.

He said that FAAN has wanted a central office for some time. Gardner is their first full-time chief. The elected officers this year are Wendell Montgomery of Beals Advertising Agency in Oklahoma City, Alex Bealer of McCrea & Bealer in Atlanta, and Gerald Brady of West & Brady, Washington, D.C.

"One unique thing about FAAN," Gardner added, "is that we have started soliciting new clients as a network. Batz-Hodgson-Neuwoehner, our flagship station in St. Louis, sets the creative and overall media plan and handles the solicitation. Then other members handle the local media work. They are each paid via hourly rates, fees, and split commissions."

We asked Herb whether they had secured any new business in this way as yet. He cited the A&W Root Beer fast foods operation on the west coast as their first client brought in from an all-network pitch. He pointed out that this chain of fast food units was the type of thing that a network is ideally suited to handle because it can match the advertiser with local agency contacts in the markets he's in.

The Intermarket Association of Advertising Agencies (IAAA) is a group of 19 agencies in various U.S. markets that bills approximately $30 million.

George Johnson is its president, and he operates "a communications center in his office" for the network. He's the president of George Johnson Advertising, St. Louis, and is a charming gentleman who, when we called, said he'd just been reading our last issue--and proved it by commenting on something in the issue.

IAAA has a working agreement with Trans Canada, a network north of the border, that extends its activity across Canada's southern tier of major markets. There'll be a joint meeting of both groups in Canada next June.

Johnson told us that an exchange of media know-how has become one of the principal services agencies within the network offer each other. "Our media work is growing," he said; and spoke with scorn of the efforts of major agencies headquartered in New York to establish branch offices for buying in local markets across the country.

"When one of these agencies sends out a buyer from New York with a rate book in his pocket, it doesn't mean that he really knows the local media scene," he said. We asked him for an example of how an IAAA agency might do the job.

"One of our members, Ed. Lewis in Penn Plaza in New York," he replied, "wanted to buy radio here in St. Louis for a record album of Hits of the 1950s. He told us he wanted to reach World War II types. So we told him to buy adjacencies to Buddy Marino, who has a program of the right type, on WNEW. It was exactly the right show for him, because Buddy plays that kind of music. A rating book buyer wouldn't have bought that. We pay attention to what's happening--not to the rating books."

We told him about NAAN's association with Vitt Media International, and his comment was: "I think they're wrong. They won't get the local buys that way, and that's the big advantage the agency network members have.

"This applies both to the unusual values you get if you're really local, and to price," he added. "We have one member who calls himself The Grinder. This guy boasts, and I think any local agency can make the same boast: 'I have never seen a buy that I can't grind down.' We're not in this business to serve the media, you know; we're in it to get the best price/value relationship for the clients."

The International Chain of Industrial & Technical Agencies (ICITA) is an 11-year old network of 33 agencies (6 in the U.S.) that have a worldwide billing of $180 million. The president of ICITA is Melville Morris, who is president of his own agency in Newark, N.J., Black, Russell, Morris. The members have some consumer accounts, but they specialize in industrial work.

Morris runs the headquarters activities for the net, carefully cost accounting for expenses and operating costs, for which he is reimbursed. This includes the cost of two formal meetings a year for the whole network in Europe. "We really work hard at these meetings for three days," he says, "and then have one social evening before we return to our own shops."

Morris says that help in media selection and placement is "what we use each other for more frequently than anything else." He points out that some media problems are easy to solve for the agencyman on the spot--and these are not charged for. But when considerable research is required, or a study is to be made to find out which media may be most suitable there would be a charge for it.

"The reason for banding together is to do everything at as lowest cost as possible as well as effectively as possible," he says, "so we keep costs in line as a matter of course always."

We asked him to describe how special projects were handled. "All the jobs are worked out individually between the agencies involved," Morris said. "I'm planning some ads to run in France, for example. The agency over there gives us the media recommendation. Then I send them the ad in English with the art work. They're asked to reconstruct the ad for readers in the media they have already recommended and to place it for us.

"They do the translation, use our artwork, make the insertion orders, place the ad. There would be a small copy charge. And there might be a split of the 15% commission--sometimes 7 1/2 - 7 1/2, sometimes 5 - 10 depending on how much work is involved."

We asked him if accounts were ever solicited by ICITA as a whole. "Yes indeed," he said, "we find a growing amount of truly international business can use our network. A case in point is Addressograph-Multigraph of Cleveland. We solicited and got the account for ICITA. We turned the control of the account over to our member in Cleveland, Gregory, Inc. And they are able to have the ads placed through our overseas branches in the many countries in which Addressograph operates."

Mutual Advertising Agency Network (MAAN) is considering setting up a separate headquarters office with a paid managing director, but has not done so yet. Its present executive secretary is Fran Faber, who is president of his own agency, Faber Advertising in Minneapolis. MAAN has 24 members with combined billings of $35 million. "If we hire a managing director, our dues will have to go up, of course," Fran points out.

He says the group got together "on the basis of helpful interchange of ideas in agency management and as a mutual aid operation. The work done varies from surveys on which fees are paid to off-hand services done free. It's mostly an inter-agency service without remuneration, handled through a standard inter-agency work request sheet.

We asked him for an example of each kind of work.

"One of our members asked others to survey local dealers to find out which media might be best in order to reach them," he said. "This was charged for. On the other hand, a request will quite often ask which radio station or TV station would be the best to use in an agency's city to reach certain kinds of prospects. For this there would be no charge. I've even been able in several cases to tell them right off about special buys that could be made in our area opportunistically."

Fran says the affiliates have been a lot of help to each other in new business work. "Some of our members are specialized," he commented. "One is in fashion. One handles a lot of automotive products. In some cases, a man from one member's agency will actually go out on the pitch with the group from another agency that is after an account. A case in point, was a member who was pitching for the account of a Buick dealership. Another member, who had worked for a Buick dealer, worked out the campaign, and he got the account."

National Advertising Agency Network (NAAN) has gone further than any of the others in headquarters services. It has 29 members whose combined billing is $170 million. The members vary in size from $2 to $15 million. Fred Mitchell, the full-time president, is located in New York.

Fred is a large friendly mid-westerner who worked for Dancer and Needham in Chicago and New York, and had an audio-visual firm. NAAN asked him to be their central office while he was still operating the audio-visual company, but he soon found that NAAN was a full-time job. In June of 1969 he came to New York and set up a central office on that basis.

The NAAN goal he says is to have 50 members in the top 50 markets. "We want to be the most extensive in the U.S.," he says, "and at our fall conference this year we signed up two of the four guest agencies we invited to the meeting."

Originally the trading of experience was the only purpose of the net, but an array of headquarters services have been added. Mitchell has a creative boutique he can draw on for members who want it. There is a financial p.r. capability, a new products marketing service, marketing research counsel, sales promotion and incentive systems available. NAAN bought BRI for its members; and now it has signed up for TGI's target marketing and media data. This will be supplemented with an operations manual on the TGI data, with basic charts, etc. so members can make good use of it.

The current hook-up with Sam Vitt for broadcast buying for members is the culmination of two years of planning and development. Like all other headquarters services, the use of VMI is optional.

The agency members can either (1) buy directly itself, (2) use another NAAN member agency to do the buying; (3) turn the buying over to VMI. The arrangement is for broadcast buying only, but that could involve 25% of the $170 million in billings of NAAN members (or $45 million). Furthermore, both Mitchell and Vitt expect that the members will increase the dollars in broadcast now that they have the services of Sam's experts to help them. Increases are expected both from retail and national clients.

The new arrangement, if used to its fullest, could double VMI's spot billings; so it's a good deal for VMI as well as NAAN.

We talked to both Sam Vitt and Fred Mitchell about the venture in Fred's comfortable, old-fashioned, and charming office at 20 West 43rd St.

Said Fred: "We'll be able to get Sam to help us with his counsel as well as in buying if that is desired by one of our members. And Sam can do the job for us in both radio and TV, and in network as well as spot. We anticipate, of course, that spot TV is the area in which the NAAN agencies will be most eager to secure expert buying."

Said Sam: "The big advantage in specialization is in getting senior people to do the negotiating and buying. And these are people who are in the market all the time, so they know what kind of spots are available, and what the rates are at any given time. We have so-called 'clout'--sure--but it's not as important to have this in terms of dollars as in terms of knowledge of the market day by day. It's always changing."

Said Fred: "Broadcast being as detailed as it is, you need a senior surgeon working for you. That's Sam, and in particular our account man at VMI, Pete Berla. We'll also be able to use the VMI systems of setting broadcast weights among markets--both in TV and in radio. VMI will do the buying and

furnish validation and post-buy analysis on every buy. In addition, I'll furnish the members with an audit of the VMI work by an independent source."

Said Sam: "The NAAN agencies will set a par value for their spot TV campaign, and it will be up to us to better that to cover our costs and fair profit. If they'd rather have the work done on a fee basis, that's also fine. In the case of network, it could be on a guarantee basis or with some such arrangement as 15% of the 15% commission."

Said Fred: "We will supply written specs for the buy on standard ordering forms that VMI has worked out for the purpose. We'll be handled the same way as other Vitt clients."

Said Sam: "What we offer is the buying efficiency of a large agency that has a continuing flow of broadcast business 52 weeks a year, so we can take the peaks and valleys off the agency's shoulders. NAAN is way ahead of the pack in the whole agency field on this. This is the most viable solution in the whole business."

Transamerica Advertising Agency Network (TAAN) switched from a network that was completely manned on a voluntary basis to one with a paid president two years ago. This was made possible by the retirement of Charles Ramsey from Phillips-Ramsey in San Diego, which was--and is--one of the key agencies in TAAN. He is still listed as chairman of the board of the agency he founded in 1938, but spends all his time in the network.

Ramsey sees great virtue in keeping the size of a network small but well positioned in major world and U.S. markets. "Our by-laws limit us to 30 members," he says proudly. "If you get too big you lose the personal touch. I made a trip last fall, and was able to spend a day with each of half our members. I'll be doing the same thing with the other half this year."

Requests for services among members are handled via a PAAN Intermember Service Request form. Payments may or may not be involved. There are two meetings a year at which all the members get together. Currently there are 28 members (four overseas) with combined billings of $50 million.

We asked Ramsey if he could give us an example of how PAAN works. He said that Mr. Steak a franchise chain that is headquartered in Colorado might be typical. It's a Phillips-Ramsey client for the creative and general marketing plan. But other members of PAAN administer the advertising locally. Another example is a development company in the mid-west that has a new building to rent in Orlando, Florida. The Florida member was asked to recommend radio, TV, and outdoor to reach both young marrieds and older people, and furnished its recommendations on an hourly rate basis. The rates are standard for all members, and revised annually.

Ramsey said the only service bought for the whole network by headquarters was AMRL, the Advertising Marketing Research Library, Los Angeles, that has turned out to be very helpful to all members, and which they get at a low rate through the network.

THE DROP OUTS

We also talked with a couple of drop-outs from agency networks to get their point of view.

Alfred Edelson, president of Henry Kaufman Advertising in Washington, D.C., said that they still believe in the network concept for small agencies and for agencies that are isolated from the large advertising centers, but that in their case it didn't make sense any longer. Kaufman was for years a member of NAAN, and it was costing them about $10,000 a year for direct costs plus participation costs.

"It was an economic decision," Edelson told us. "We were one of the larger firms in NAAN, and our needs today are quite different from what they were years ago. We're in the east, chase up to New York quite frequently, belong to the 4A's, and are located in a key communications center (the most important one editorially, at least). We have 65 people, and many of them come from top agencies. I'm sure the networks are still of great help to the outlanders and the smaller agencies."

Another drop out, who didn't want to be quoted by name said: "The thing that made us drop out was that we found we were competing for certain accounts with other members. The ease of transportation now makes almost any agency as national (at least in its new business activity) as it wants to be."

A New York City agencyman, another who dropped out of one of the networks, and who did not wish to be quoted said: "It was too much of a one-way street. We didn't need them as much as they needed us. There seemed to be more call for help from New York because of our location than calls we made to other cities. And it got so we found ourselves too busy to do justice to what was expected of us."

The New Yorker said the network association and friendships were very nice, and he still values them; but too many of the calls for help were on a courtesy basis, and even the ones his agency was paid for (on a time plus profit basis) interrupted the regular work of the agency too often, and too much.

He said that a goodly percentage of the requests involved ligitimate questions about media in the New York market and nationally. He also said that "quite a few requests were for things that anybody could look up in SRDS, and these were a waste of time."

All of the drop outs made a big point
of saying that they still believe networks are fine inventions for gentlemen
who still need them to extend their
services and capabilities.

In spite of these negatives, however,
the agency networks appear to be solid-
ly placed in the agency business. At
a time when media work, in particular,
is becoming more diversified and the
work of media decision-making organized
along new lines, it is significant that
the media work of the networks is in-
creasing--even to the point of cen-
tralizing the broadcast buying through
an independent media buying service
for an entire network.

DISCUSSION QUESTIONS

---

1. What factors have contributed to the
growth of advertising agency networks?

2. What is likely to be the future of
the agency network? Why?

PART VII

ADVERTISING RESEARCH

One of the most difficult and controversial topics in advertising is that of advertising research. Some people, particularly in creative departments, say that research only confirms the obvious, as when Kraft Foods found that the best advertising approach was to compare their jams and jellies with those that Grandma used to make, and showed Grandma pouring jars of Kraft jellies into her own jars with hand labels! Research people, on the other hand, sometimes are prone to claim that research is the only way to determine what and how to advertise. Obviously, the answer to the question posed above is somewhere between these extremes. The length of this section of the book precludes answering this question, if, indeed, it can be answered. There are, however, a number of articles highlighting some of the current topics in advertising research which should be of interest to students and practitioners of advertising.

Swartz takes the reader through his thinking and develops a program permitting management to evaluate the effects of its communications upon consumers, related to the costs involved

in the communications. Ziff discusses a popular topic today, that of psychographics, the study of the psychological characteristics of a population. Mayer gives us his views on television ratings and takes us through the European ratings and the early U.S. ratings.

The Media Research Committee of the American Association of Advertising Agencies comments on how ad agencies evaluate various types of research provided by television stations. This is in response to the great variety and varied quality of the research data issued periodically by most media. Maneloveg calls for a better determination of who and where are the best customers for our product and service, and how best to get to them. He especially quarrels with the concept of trying to get a "bargain" in media purchases, without considering more than price.

The last article in this section is for the serious student of advertising research, the person who wants to get more deeply into one of its many topics. The author provides his assessment of the leading articles to date on various advertising research topics.

JOURNAL OF MARKETING, Vol. 33, pp. 20-25, April, 1969. Reprinted with permission from the American Marketing Association and David Schwartz.

VII-1

MEASURING THE EFFECTIVENESS OF YOUR COMPANY'S ADVERTISING

David A. Schwartz

Consumers in today's marketplace have the opportunity to choose between several available alternatives in almost every product category. The willingness of consumers to exercise this option is demonstrated in two significant ways--the large market share differences among competitors within product categories and the high failure rate of new product introductions. An indication of the failure rate is reflected in the statistic that about one out of 540 new product ideas ultimately becomes a successful product.[1] Consequently the marketer is literally forced to devote a very considerable amount of money and effort to planning and executing the advertising program that will, hopefully, yield the greatest financial reward. One industry spokesman summed up the role of advertising in today's marketplace when he stated that:

Advertising today is an important item on the top management agenda. The foremost reason, of course, is the increase in size of advertising expenditures. In many cases, advertising has become the third, second, and in a few cases, the largest item in the corporate budget. Keener competition, together with expanded plant capacity, has forced a greater reliance on advertising to maintain or increase volume and profit. In addition, most companies today are dedicated to a program of new product development, and advertising must carry a heavier load in introducing a greater volume of new products coming out of the laboratory.[2]

Various sources suggest that the sum of money spent to communicate a desired message to the consumer is approaching $17 billion in the United States alone, an all-time high. Furthermore, this figure will in all probability continue to rise in the years to come. To put this sum into the proper perspective, it may be noted that the average family of four is reportedly exposed to more than 1,500 separate advertising messages during the course of a single day. And this too may be rising.

Within this context, it is surprising that a large number of advertisers make

[1]   Elizabeth Marting, *New Products, New Profits* (New York: American Management Association, 1964), p. 9.

[2] Stated by Roger H. Bolin, cited in Russel H. Colley, *Defining Advertising Goals for Measured Advertising Results* (New York: Association of National Advertisers, 1961), Foreword.

no attempt to measure the effectiveness of their advertising investment. In fact, a recent National Industrial Conference Board study indicated that a large portion of current advertising efforts are nothing more than "...untested advertising that small groups of agency or company executives *believed* would be effective."[3] (italics added) Sound management practice dictates that all phases and operations of the company be subject to systematic review in order to achieve a maximum level of performance. This should include advertising.

The short-term and long-term benefits of systematically reviewing a firm's advertising efforts are overwhelming. For example:

√ Management will be forced to define specifically what each element of its program is intended to accomplish, *in advance* of actual advertising exposure.

√ An accurate feedback system could be provided to management, assisting them in uncovering what the advertising program--working in conjunction with other marketing forces--is *actually* accomplishing in the marketplace.

√ Management would be able to use and to learn from experience (both successes and failures) in order to create more effective communications in the *future*.

Management's lack of initiative in this area is potentially very costly. In many cases this lack may be due to a basic inability to design and execute an appropriate program, rather than an absence of interest and desire. It may be that management does not have a

valid and reliable measurement model available to use, except for those based upon magic formulas and unsupported assumptions. The goal of this article is to describe how a valid and reliable advertising accountability program can be developed which will enable management to evaluate objectively the effects of its communications efforts relative to their costs.

THE INFORMATION FLOW FROM ADVERTISER TO CONSUMER

Information from various impersonal sources is communicated to the consumer, either directly or by another person.[4] This message is affected by many subtle yet meaningful variables over which the advertiser has little control. For example, several studies have illustrated that the type of message presentation, the attitudes of the audience to the transmitter (whether it is media or human), the order of presentation, and the emotional set of the audience[5] all serve to influence the effectiveness of a product communications. The total of all pertinent information, that is, all information supplied by a variety of sources and affected by many different factors, eventually results in a product-related message of some kind being perceived by the consumer.

The reception of information directed to the consumer is merely the beginning of the communications process. Furthermore, there is no certainty that even this initial step of the advertising communications process will be success-

[3] Harry Deane Wolfe, James K. Brown, Stephen H. Greenberg, and G. Clark Thompson, *Pretesting Advertising--Studies in Business Policy--109* (New York: National Industrial Conference Board, 1963), p. 5.

[4] For a more complete discussion of this point, see Elihu Katz and Paul F. Lazarsfeld, *Personal Influence* (New York: The Free Press, 1955).

[5] Carl I. Hovland, Irving L. Janis, Harold H. Kelley, *Communications and Persuasion* (New Haven, Conn.: Yale Univ. Press, 1963).

ful. An advertising message will be received by the consumer only if it is transmitted through appropriate media. A message which theoretically communicates well (for example, in a test situation it is remembered and understood; it is successful in changing or confirming attitudes, opinions, and preferences) could easily be ineffective when presented by inappropriate media.

Even if appropriate media are used and the consumer does become exposed to the message, it is still unrealistic to expect that he will buy the product at the first opportunity. The message must first attract the consumer's attention in some way (either consciously or subconsciously). Otherwise, no matter how well-constructed and how well-transmitted, the message would be ineffective as an advertising vehicle. The fact that consumers retain only a small portion of what they are actually exposed to--either because of an inability to retain all messages or a lack of desire to do so--suggests that considerable attention should be given to this problem.

Assuming the sales message is received by the consumer, and attracts his attention, the marketer should still not expect changes in purchase behavior. The message must first influence changes in preference by altering or strengthening key attitudes and images about the product. Both in-theater and on-air research tests have demonstrated the possibility that a consumer may be exposed to a message with no resultant change in *any* image or attitude about the product, much less a change in preference. The key issue here is the true *saliency* of the product message from the consumer's point of view, rather than the effectiveness with which the advertiser communicated the product message he judged to be important to consumers. Some experimenters have recently suggested that consumers may alter their behavior without any prior changes in attitude or preference. However, analysis of their findings suggests that perhaps their definition of attitude

may be incorrect, casting doubt on their "findings" of no relationship between attitudes and behavior.[6]

Assume that a message was transmitted through appropriate media, attracted the consumer's attention, and influenced a change in his preferences by altering or reinforcing relevant and important favorable product images. There is still no certainty that sales will increase in spite of any relationship between attitude and behavior. It is possible, for example, that a considerable time lag may exist between exposure to an effective advertisement or series of advertisements and the actual purchase. This alone would make it difficult to correlate advertising with sales. Furthermore, a multitude of other marketing factors are known to affect the sales of a product, including the ability of a salesman, the availability of the product, its price, taste, size, color, style, competitive efforts, in addition to a host of other very influential variables. The sum total of all of these variables frequently serves to "get in the way" of correlating advertising with sales, except under carefully controlled conditions.

A REALISTIC PROGRAM FOR THE MEASUREMENT OF ADVERTISING EFFECTIVENESS

It is within the preceding framework that one can proceed with the development of a systematic method of measuring advertising effectiveness. By understanding how information about a product is transmitted from the advertiser to the consumer and the complex paths it sometimes takes, an evaluative program can be designed. This program must, however, have one basic methodo-

---

[6] Lester Frankel and Solomon Dutka, *Attitudes As Predictors of Purchasing Behavior*, 22nd Annual Conference AAPOR (May, 1967).

logical objective. It must utilize valid and reliable research instruments. There can be no elements of the program which are based upon magic formulas and unfounded assumptions. This section describes such an evaluative system.

A. An important element of the program is to measure consumer exposure to all media in the advertiser's target market segments. The data may be valuable in defining the specific media to which consumers have recently been exposed, and the frequency of such exposure. For example, one could carefully itemize the specific magazines read, television shows seen, or radio shows heard. Such data would help to determine (1) if the target market segment was exposed to the sales messages in the past, and (2) what media selections should be made to insure optimum exposure per dollar spent in the future.

B. It is also important to measure retention of the advertising and other "messages" received by the consumer. Information should be collected for the product under investigation, as well as for all competitors in the appropriate product category. Specific information could be obtained about retention of the individual elements of a sales message and also consumers' explanations and interpretations of what an advertiser is communicating about his product.

C. The level of consumer preference, both for the advertised product and for its competitors, can be developed. Consumers can be categorized into several intensities of preference. For example, the first and lowest level of preference could be a complete lack of awareness for the product. Next might be a general state of product awareness (either with a negative feeling or with no observable

preference). A third, and more intense level of preference, could be an evaluation by the consumer that the product is within a group of products toward which he has some level of favorable feeling. Finally, the highest level of preference could be the single product that is most preferred. (The concept behind these preference levels has application in most product categories. However, many studies of advertising effectiveness suggest that the number and definition of the various levels of preference may vary among different product categories.

D. Salient images and attitudes toward the product under investigation, as well as for all of its competitors, can also be measured. Knowing a consumer's level of preference, as well as his specific attitudes, enables the correlation of attitudinal factors with preference for all products in the category of interest.

E. Recent actual marketing behavior of the consumer should be investigated. Information sought might include such factors as product brand, size and amount usually purchased, various uses and methods of usage, as well as the consumer's current product inventory on hand.

F. The type of data described above can be used only to measure what the advertising for a product is accomplishing *relative* to its competition. However, it cannot tell the marketer the *economic* value of his current advertising strategy. As noted earlier, there are a large number of variables which must be accounted for and controlled in order to provide this type of information. The actual experience of several manufacturers[7] suggests that it is possible to provide management with a series of objective indicators of advertising's economic value. These observations may then

335

be examined in light of current
market conditions, government actions, competitive activities, and
so on, in order to gain insight
into a measure of advertising's
economic value.

It appears that the best way to
gain such information is to measure attitudes, usage, preferences,
and behavior of individual consumers *periodically* over several
points in time. In this way, it
is possible to uncover the changes
in factors that can be specifically associated with changes in behavior.

The type of feedback suggested above
is developed from present theory of
how communications flow from the advertiser to the consumer. These feedback
areas have a common thread. They involve types of information that can
easily be measured by utilizing currently known methods and techniques. Thus,
accurate evaluation of advertising effectiveness can be achieved by using
presently available techniques.

A SPECIFIC APPLICATION OF THE PROGRAM[8]

The following example illustrates
how the program outlined in the preceding pages may be used to evaluate a
company's communications program.

Table 1 presents a group of competitive
makes of automobiles, as they are dis-

---

[7] Most work in this field has been pri-
vately sponsored and therefore is highly confidential. However, one program
has been publicized. See Gail Smith,
"How GM Measures Ad Effectiveness,"
Printers' Ink (May 14, 1965).

[8] Some of the Tables used in this section have been shown previously in
Printers' Ink (May 14, 1965).

Table 1

PREFERENCE LEVELS

	Make "A"	Competitors "X"	Competitors "Y"
"First Choice"	5%	6%	3%
"Consideration Class"	7	5	2
"Buying Class"	8	10	5
"Aware"	14	11	9
"Not Aware"	66	68	81
	100%	100%	100%

tributed by consumers on a preference
continuum.

a. The "First Choice" category is the
highest level of preference. It
consists of people who have a *single* most preferred make of car.
b. The category "Consideration Class"
is comprised of people who would
consider purchasing that make even
though it may not be their favorite.
c. "Buying Class" consists of people
who indicate that the automobile
make competes for their business
(even if they do not give it very
favorable consideration). A consumer who has always purchased a
Chevrolet and is completely satisfied with this make may give a Ford
or a Plymouth this rating.
d. The category "Aware" is comprised
of consumers who are aware of the
automobile make, but do not plan
to purchase it. These may be consumers who are considering a Pontiac
or an Oldsmobile. They are also
aware of Volkswagen although they
do not intend to own one.
e. Finally, there is a group of consumers who are not consciously
aware of the existence of the advertised product.

Having levels of preference for a product
as well as for its competition is, by
itself, information of major importance.
In the present example 81% of the market has no awareness of competitor "Y."

Table 2

VALUE OF PREFERENCE FOR MAKE "A"

	Preference	Probability of Visiting Dealer Showroom
"First Choice"	5%	84%
"Consideration Class"	7	62
"Buying Class"	8	40
"Aware"	14	24
"Not Aware"	66	1

It appears that herein lies a serious problem for this competitor. However, the data have even more far-reaching usefulness. Each respondent's level of preference for every product in the category can be easily related to his current product usage and future usage expectation. Therefore the one preference level at which advertising may be targeted for optimum results may be *selected* rather than randomly aiming at various demographic market segments. It should be noted that this preference level target is not necessarily those consumers who fall in the "First Choice" category.

Table 2 portrays a situation in which those consumers interviewed in Table 1 were reinterviewed at a later time and asked if they had visited a dealer's showroom. Among those consumers who gave the automobile make a "First Choice" rating, 84% were found to have visited a dealer's showroom. Among those who indicated a "Consideration Class" rating and a "Buying Class" rating, 62% and 40% respectively were found at the time of reinterview to have visited a dealer's showroom. One conclusion that could be reached from these results is that under certain circumstances, an attempt to shift the preference of consumers from the "Buying Class" level to the "Consideration Class" level may be as good an advertising strategy as moving them from

Table 3

RATINGS FOR CAR MAKE "A"
(On Scale of 1-100)

	"Buying Class"	"Consideration Class"	Difference
Smooth Riding	86	91	5
Styling	76	89	13
Over-all Comfort	81	87	6
Handling	83	86	3
Spacious Interior	85	85	0
Luxurious Interior	79	85	6
Quality of Workmanship	80	83	3
Advanced Engineering	77	83	6
Prestige	73	82	9
Value for the Money	76	79	3
Trade-in Value	59	77	18
Cost of Upkeep & Maintenance	63	67	4
Gas Economy	58	58	0

"Consideration Class" to "First Choice," since (in the present example) both would increase the likelihood of a dealer visit by 22%. (It should be noted that dealer visits have been selected as the key decision criterion for this example. Although different marketers in different competitive situations will probably select different criteria, this concept of segmenting the market by preference will still be applicable.)

In Table 3, the product image of the automobile in question is presented, as perceived by two classes of consumers. One group is a target group, consisting of consumers in the "Buying Class." The second group consists of ratings by consumers currently at the preference level to which the marketer is hoping to convert the target group.

Previous research has uncovered a number

of important areas which influence preference for one make over another. The list of 13 image items in Table 3 represents some of these relevant areas. A comparison of the ratings for each of the two consumer groups illustrates those items which significantly distinguish them. For example, there is no difference in opinion between the two consumer groups regarding the "Spacious Interior" of the automobile make in question. Therefore, a favorable shift of this image among consumers in the "Buying Class" level of preference may not shift them to the next highest preference level.

On the other hand, both the "Styling" and the "Trade-in Value" for make "A" receive widely different ratings by consumers in the two market segments. Thus, these ratings indicate that it may be a more profitable advertising approach to stress these aspects of the product in order to accomplish the objective of moving consumers from one level of preference to another. However, "Styling" is an image which is difficult to change during the present model year. Consequently, the best alternative among consumers in the "Buying Class" level of preference may be to attempt to improve the car's reputation for "Trade-in Value."

At this point, two aspects of the program have been illustrated. First, it was used as an aid in isolating an optimum market target. It then was utilized to isolate an effective product appeal. The problem now is to relate these findings to actual media selections. This, too, can be solved by making use of the continuing research program. As seen earlier, all of the data are interrelated, and for each respondent a variety of behavioral and attitudinal data are provided. The choice of the media that will reach the consumer most effectively is facilitated by correlating the media information for each respondent with his product preference, product images, recent behavior, or even with standard demographic data. For example,

the marketer would be able to measure accurately the portion of his target group who watch "Bonanza" or "The Thursday Night Movie" each week. The portion of each of these audiences that also reads "*Newsweek*" or "*Playboy*" magazine can also be determined. Similarly, the amount of exposure to other media by the members of the target group could be ascertained.

The usefulness of the proposed program is even broader and more far-reaching than has been indicated thus far. While it aids management in solving present problems and correcting "weak links" in the communication chain, it also helps management to evaluate the effectiveness of its communications decisions to improve its advertising in the future. The program helps to answer questions of this nature through the use of the reinterview technique described earlier. For example, assume that management wishes to evaluate its media allocations. Table 4 illustrates how the program could be used to accomplish this goal. Portions of the target group who were exposed to different media combinations are separated, and the level of awareness for each segment is isolated. Of course, no final decision on a media buy should be made from these data alone. Assuming that the goal is to increase the level of awareness for the test product, it is still up to the media specialists to decide between reach (media A *and* B) and economy (medium B alone). The program is designed only to supply meaningful information to aid these specialists in making the best possible decision in the face of uncertainty.

GOAL STATING FOR OPTIMAL COMMUNICATIONS RESULTS

Thus far, the program described has been shown capable of providing a variety of important marketing and advertising information.

Table 4

MEDIA ANALYSIS

	Media "A" and Media "B"	Media "A" Only	Media "B" Only	Neither
Reach to Target	51%	9%	33%	7%
Projected to Base	9,740,000	1,720,000	6,300,000	1,340,000
Cost to Reach Group	$120,000	$11,000	$39,000	--
"Aware"				
Before	25%	24%	25%	22%
After	40%	27%	36%	22%
"Accomplishment"	15%	3%	11%	--
Accomplishment Projected	1,460,000	50,000	690,000	--
Cost Per Thousand				
Accomplishment	$83	$220	$57	--

✓ It provides information about message registration, attitudes and preferences for the product category in question, as well as the consumer's recent marketing behavior. To some marketers this information alone would be worth the costs of setting up and implementing the program.

✓ The information produced can be used by management to aid in defining its advertising objectives, isolating optimal advertising appeals, and selecting the best media appraoch.

✓ The reinterview process serves the added function of assisting in the evaluation of past advertising decisions in order to improve future decision making.

However, before the program can effectively accomplish its primary objective of improving the effectiveness of a company's communications efforts, management must first state its communications goals--that is, the specific objectives its advertising program is designed to fulfill. Without question, the development of a standardized method for stating communications goals is of prime importance. In order to state these goals it may be helpful to first set up some general guide posts.

Basic rules for stating advertising goals are that they should be in writing and should not hold advertising accountable for more than it can realistically accomplish.[9] For example, an advertisement for automobiles can, at best, get the consumer into the showroom. At this point the salesman must take over. It is also important to identify the prime prospect group which is the target for the achievement of this goal. Almost any segment of the population is a reasonable target as long as it is properly defined. This may be all beer drinkers who consume 14 or more cans per week, all air passengers who travel three or more times per year, or all new car buyers of the past 12 months.

Another important criterion for stating a goal is that the goal must be broken down into measurable elements. For example, the target group's knowledge of taste improvement is an objective that can be measured. The degree to which a taste alteration has changed a brand's image cannot be measured until manage-

[9] This section has drawn heavily from DAGMAR. For additional information see Russell H. Colley, *Defining Advertising Goals for Measured Advertising Results* (New York: Association of National Advertisers, 1961).

Table 5

COMMUNICATION GOAL STATEMENT

OBJECTIVE - To increase ratings of product "X" regarding economy by 20% in the current fiscal year.

TARGET MARKET - All male heads of households who are aware of product "X."

DATES GOAL IS TO BE IN EFFECT - February 1968 to January 1969.

SIZE OF TARGET - 1,910,000 male household heads.

---

ment states the goal more specifically (that is, in terms of one or more particular elements of the brand image). Finally, the goal should be stated in terms of its expected degree of accomplishment and the time period for which the objective is relevant. For example, an airline that is launching a new service might want at least half of all frequent air passengers to be aware of this new service within 16 weeks of its initiation.

Table 5 is an example of a complete goal statement which had been set by one management team. It has an objective that is stated simply, specifically, and in a manner easy to measure. It also defines a target, a minimum level of accomplishment, and a period of time during which it is in effect.

SUMMARY

The use of the program described on the preceding pages permits management to evaluate the effects of its communications upon consumers relative to the costs involved. The basic goal of this investigation should be to improve future communications to consumers. This program, together with the careful statement of communications goals should be viewed as an expression of management's desire to establish an objective accountability system to evaluate its communications investment.

DISCUSSION QUESTIONS

---

1. In many corporate budgets, advertising has become the third largest item. Do you feel such high expenditures in advertising are justifiable? Why or why not?

2. The article outlines a systematic method of measuring advertising effectiveness. How accurate do you think it is? Can you think of an alternative method of measurement?

American Marketing Association, Spring and Fall Conferences, Combined Proceedings, Series No. 34, 1972, pp. 457-61. Boris W. Becker and Helmut Becker (ed.). Reprinted with permission.

VII-2

CLOSING THE CONSUMER-ADVERTISING GAP THROUGH PSYCHOGRAPHICS

Ruth Ziff

New research areas are currently receiving more attention that the subject of *psychographics*. The importance of psychographics as a research tool is suggested by the numerous speeches and papers given at national conferences of the Advertising Research Foundation and the American Marketing Association, by the large number of articles that are being written on the topic, and by a volume solely devoted to the topic of psychographics which is soon to be published by the American Marketing Association.

There are strong arguments, in favor of psychographics, arising primarily from the shortcoming of other techniques in identifying various groups of consumers in meaningful psychological and sociological terms. These arguments are summarized in the following paragraphs.

DEMOGRAPHIC INFORMATION

The first argument is that demographic information alone is insufficient for the development of advertisng strategy and copy. *Demographic data generally provide an "unreal" composite picture*. This becomes apparent once we recognize that demographic data often consist of a series of averages such as the heavy user of "x" is usually from a large family with an average of 2 1/2 children; she is 33 years of age, lives in the suburbs, in a house of 5.3 rooms, has 2.2 baths, 1.7 television sets, 2/3 of a dog, and 1.6 automobiles. While these figures are valid, the profile of the majority of women obviously would not match this description.

In many product classes, particularly those with high saturation levels, *there are not major demographic distinctions* between users and non-users, and aside from the obvious ones due to family size, there are not even major distinctions between heavy and light users. Further, even if there are important differences in product usage according to demographic characteristics, more often than not there are no sharp and consistent demographic skews by brand. Thus, only rarely can it be said that brand "x" appeals to a very unique group in terms of age or income or education.

Still more important, *knowing "how" usage varies by demographic characteristics is far from knowing "why" it varies*.

341

Surely, if certain demographic patterns are observed, it is reasonable to speculate about the reasons for these patterns--but speculations are indeed different from knowledge and it is the 'whys' rather than the 'hows' that provide the key to effective advertising strategy.

Moreover, *demographic groups are by no means homogeneous in the way they think, in what they believe or want.* What may be called the 'homogeneity myth' is, in the author's opinion, responsible for much of the unwarranted obsession with demographics. Thus, reference is often made to the 'working woman', 'the black', the 'teenager'--as though all in these groups were mirror images of each other. While older women have certain things in common, and teenagers do and certainly blacks have, their communality is not all-pervasive; it relates to certain areas more than others and even in those areas where we would expect great homogeneity, unanimity does not exist. Most teenagers may demonstrate some spirit of rebellion and all blacks may oppose discrimination, but they certainly vary in their attitudes regarding the means of redress and they are by no means homogeneous entities insofar as what they buy or why they buy particular products. Moreover, it is unreasonable to expect that any demographic group would be totally alike, when the individuals in it are affected by so many different social and situational factors, of which only a few can be common to all in the group.

It is, however, more than the deficiencies of demographic data that provokes interest in psychographics. A second important set of reasons relates to the limitations of traditional attitude data.

TRADITIONAL ATTITUDE DATA

The second argument is that traditional attitude data, while clearly valuable, also have significant limitations. *Traditional quantified data lack a consumer focus.* Most traditional attitude studies are concerned with product or brand images and perceptions of brand attributes. Thus, they indicate how consumers view products or brands and through appropriate analytic techniques one can infer the perceptions which promote or deter use of particular products or brands. However, they do not define the consumer himself or herself--identify his or her needs, values, wants--the main focus of psychographic studies.

In traditional attitude studies, each measurement is usually treated as an isolated statistic. Hence, one learns little about the pattern of responses that exist--that, for example, some view brand "x" as safe, convenient and sufficiently strong but that most think it is safe, convenient and too mild. In the same vein, even when information on the consumers themselves is obtained, there is generally no attempt to organize this information and provide what the psychologists call a Gestalt, so that what one may learn, for example, is not simply that 50% of the women say they are prone to have colds, and 35% say it's important to stay out of crowds, and that 80% think it's important to get all the rest one can when one gets a cold, but that taking all of these and many other responses together, there are 40% who have a hypochondriacal gestalt and 20% who are skeptics when it comes to medicines. In motivation research this kind of organization or focus is often seen--but here the lack of projectivity of the data is a handicap.

UNDERSTANDING THE CONSUMER

The third argument is that an understanding of the consumer maximizes our chances for effective communication. This is by no means a new idea; the literature on communication theory is replete with the rationale that supports this view. However, it may be worthwhile to review the basic propositions. *Any communication is one link in a chain of communication extending over time, with its effect mediated by the recipient's cognitive and social structure.* Paraphrasing Joseph Klapper, this implies that people will tend to expose themselves to those mass communications which are in accord with their existing attitudes and interests--they will avoid communications of the opposite hue. If they are exposed to such opposing material, they will seem not to perceive it or they will interpret it to fit their existing views, or forget is more readily than sympathetic material.[1] This is what is meant by selective exposure, selective perception, and selective retention. The implications of this have been well summed up by Wilbur Schramm, who said:

"If a communication is successful, it must:

✓ Be designed and delivered to gain the attention of the intended recipient

✓ Employ signs and symbols that are meaningful to the recipient

✓ Arouse personality needs in the recipient and suggest some ways to meet those needs. The ways suggested must be appropriate to the situation in which the recipient finds himself when making a response.[2]

There is considerable support for these contentions, both from academicians and from professionals in the communications industry--Leo Bogart and Russ Haley among others. The consumer is clearly not an indiscriminate target for message bombardment; knowledge of the consumer is, therefore, essential in tailoring messages that will reach, impress and influence one's target.

Often ignored, but also important, is the fact that communicators--known in advertising as creatives or copywriters --are not aseptic individuals either; they *too are affected by their cognitive and social structures*--their aspirations, personalities, values and social affiliations. Lacking research input about the consumer, the copywriters' values are bound to dominate their perceptions and determine their decisions as to what to communicate. Communicators may have a sixth sense, but considering how atypical the average creative man is, one has to be concerned with whether--without sufficient information about the consumer--he would be able to select what would be most persuasive to the consumer, whose life style and background is generally so different from his own. And without imputing any conscious ulterior motives to the creative person, one should perhaps also be concerned about the potential influence of what has been termed secondary audiences. The reference here is to the fact that communicators will often consciously or unconsciously aim their communications, not at the people for whom they are intended, but at other groups who are important to them--critics, potential employees, competitors. For advertising, this focusses on the danger that an advertising man or woman may be more influenced by what he or she believes will impress the advertising community than by what will persuade the recipient. The best way to guard against this danger would seem to lie in adequate knowledge of the consumer, for such knowledge should mitigate against decisions made

[1] Joseph T. Klapper, *The Effects of Mass Communication* (New York: The Free Press, 1966), p. 19.

[2] Wilbur Schramm, *The Process and Effects of Mass Communications* (Urbana: University of Illinois Press, 1954).

solely on the basis of judgment--whether
that judgment be the judgment of the
client, the account man or the copywriter.

THE CURRENT ENVIRONMENT

The last argument is simply that the
current advertising environment strengthens the need for psychographics--and,
it might be added, for research generally. Put very succinctly, the point is
that the current proliferation of advertising makes the competition for
consumer attention greater than ever,
as does the constant influx of new products. Thus, it would seem that every
avenue available should be used to increase one's chances for success. Moreover, the rapidly changing social environment, and consumerism particularly,
make more hazardous than ever before
reliance on one's own preconceptions
of what the consumer wants or likes.

In view of these many cogent arguments,
it might well be wondered why the marketing community has not shown greater
interest in psychographics. In the
author's view, this is largely because
of the manner in which the research
community has handled the subject.

CONFUSION OF TERMS

First, there is no doubt that the term
psychographics has been used too loose-
ly--so loosely that not only is the non-
research community confused, but even
researchers themselves are. This becomes obvious in meetings among researchers where the term psychographics
is used with different meanings by different members. This 'looseness' is
in two areas.

One problem is that *the term psychographics is used for different types of
variables*. Some use the term to connote
basic personality characteristics--ag-
gression, anxiety, extraversion; some
apply it to life style variables such
as community involvement, home entertaining, leisure activities. Others prefer
definitions involving attitudes, values
and beliefs pertinent to the class under study, nutrition or convenience
orientation for foods, concern about
germs or proneness to illness for drugs,
performance or safety values for automobiles. Finally, still others have
given primary emphasis to the specific
benefits individuals specify as most
desirable in a particular product, for
example, decay prevention, whiteness,
taste in a toothpaste; or strength,
flavor, container convenience in a cough
remedy. Using the term psychographics
so loosely results in:

√ People not knowing what to expect

√ People using a type of psychographics
  that is less useful than another
  might be

√ People damning psychographics because
  a particular type was not productive

A clarification in this regard is very
important. This might be done through
the use of a whole new set of catch-
words that are more revealing. Perhaps
copywriters could be helpful here--as
food for thought, the following are offered as possibilities:

√ ego-graphics for personality items
√ life-graphics for life styles
√ value-graphics for needs/values
√ end-graphics for benefits

The other area of confusion stems from
the fact that *the term psychographics
is being used both to describe a type
of variable and a type of analysis*.
That is, not only is psychographics used
with respect to variables as just discussed, but many also use the term to
imply segmentation analysis. This may

344

be understandable since psychographic variables and segmentation analysis both have a consumer focus. However, it should be obvious that one can segment consumers on demographics, perceptions of brands or on *any* set of variables--segmentation is definitely not dependent on the use of psychographic variables. And in reverse, one can certainly obtain measurements on the kinds of variables associated with psychographics and use analytical procedures other than, or in addition to, segmentation.

Again, the looseness in this area has several important consequences, akin to those we mentioned in connection with the variable problem. People do not know what to expect, and people may damn the use of psychographic variables because they are not committed to segmentation or vice versa.

It is necessary that people be made to understand the distinction between the use of psychographic variables and the use of segmentation and that what each seeks to achieve be clearly specified.

CONTENT, RELIABILITY AND VALIDITY

Additionally, *there has been insufficient concern with the content, relability and validity of the processes and techniques of segmentation analysis*. The result is that not only are people confused by the different results obtained with different techniques but even more important, the innocent recipients of research (and many researchers themselves) are not aware of how different the results might have been had different techniques been used or different decisions been made in the implementation of specific techniques. Yet, the consequences of decisions on each of the following will certainly be significant.

The level of data input Here the issue is whether the data used in a segmentation analysis are the scores on individual variables or factor scores derived from a prior factor analysis of the variables. If individual variable scores are used, equal weight is in effect given to each variable. What this means, however, is that excessive weight may be given to certain dimensions just by virtue of the number of variables included relating to that dimension. For example, if there are four items on convenience and two on taste, convenience would automatically be given more weight in the segmentaion. Presumably, then, the use of factor scores is superior, but this has not been demonstrated nor is everyone utilizing factor scores.

The use of adjusted or unadjusted scores Many people may not realize it but, in current practice involving correlation computations as the basis for segmentation, adjusted or standardized scores are in effect being used. The rationale for this has been that the variation resulting from the differences in the way people respond to different scales should be removed, thus making the basis for identifying individuals as high or low in particular respects whether their responses are in essence above or below average. However, when we do this we may be discarding information and reducing variations that should be taken into account in segmenting consumers.

The use of different types of segmentation techniques There have been many articles and dialogues regarding the use of inverse factor analysis versus cluster analysis and many are aware that there are different factoring and clustering techniques. What differences are produced by one or another of these procedures is far from clear, though it is certain that the results produced by them are not the same.

The importance of these decisions makes it imperative that the professional community undertake the responsibility of developing some agreed-upon criteria for assessing various procedures and techniques, and for providing some comparative data on which to assess the various techniques on these criteria. Four suggested possible criteria are the following:

a. The reliability of various techniques--that is, how consistent are the results produced by each technique as determined by the similarity of results obtained via split samples and replication.
b. The homogeneity of the segments identified--obviously, no segment, while distinct from others, is totally homogeneous--but the more homogeneous a segment is, the more valid are any generalizations about that segment. Thus, this is an important parameter to be examined.
c. The heterogeneity of the segments identified--this is the other side of the coin and refers to the need to evaluate how successful the various techniques are in providing groups really distinct from each other.
d. The meaningfulness of the segments provided--this refers to determining to what extent various techniques identify segments which are relevant to the marketing variables the researcher is interested in explaining.

Only with comparative data on parameters such as these, will it be possible in the long run to decide which technique is best--not on the basis of the biases of individual researchers, but on the basis of fact and with full recognition of what only may be gaining or losing by the use of any particular technique.

STUDY SCOPE

A still *further reason for the resistance* on the part of those who foot the bill for research *is the scope of the psychographic segmentation studies* that are *proposed*. Often it is as though the researcher seizes on the psychographic segmentation study to answer all possible research questions. The result is that the real needs are not carefully assessed; what information must be obtained is not distinguished from what is of marginal interest or from what may be useful but could be obtained other ways or at other times. The result is that excessively expensive and time-consuming studies are proposed and voluminous books of results are produced, books which are often more than can be dealt with or comprehended even by those who are not deterred.

LEGITIMACY OF SEGMENTATION CONCEPT

Even more critical is the failure to date to convince the marketing community that segmentation is a legitimate concept. We have all heard tha following questions: "Even if there are differences between groups, don't the various groups have many things in common, and if they do, am I not better off basing my strategy on the common ground than on the differences?" or "We have achieved a good share selling to the average mass market, why should we restrict our opportunities by selling only a portion?" or "How do I know it would be more profitable to get a large chunk of one segment rather than a small share of several?" or "My product is really unique in this and this way; doesn't it make sense that I advertise this unique feature, rather than concern myself with the need or attitude segments in the population?" These are really significant questions and the people who ask them are not easily put off. What are the answers?

To begin with, it should be admitted that there may be cases where a psychographic segmentation study might provide icing on the cake, but less complex and less costly research procedures would yield the information that is needed. For example, if a brand really has a unique feature, more simple research techniques would seem to be adequate for the development of advertising strategy. Reference here is to concept and guided use tests, into which appropriate questions are built to define the best target for the product. Such questions should undoubtedly cover psychographic variables but a segmentation analysis would not seem to be required and it is questionable whether its utility would be sufficient to warrant the effort.

More important, however, is that the professional community must set about getting evidence to determine the results of applying the principles of segmentation. It can certainly be demonstrated that different segments behave differently, and it can certainly be argued--based on many of the points made earlier--that there is good reason to believe that if one attempts to sell to all, one will sell to none, but this is not enough. Somehow or other, the professional community must find ways to demonstrate that segmentation principles pay off in actual sales.

CONCLUSION

In conclusion then, the necessary steps must be taken to eliminate the confusion that exists regarding psychographics, to develop appropriate criteria for evaluating the current technology and most important, to prove that segmentation is a viable and productive marketing concept. Perhaps the American Marketing Association should take on this charge.

DISCUSSION QUESTIONS

1. How effective do you feel psychographics is as a research tool?

2. What advantages and short-comings do you see in psychographics?

347

Reprinted by permission of JOURNAL OF ADVERTISING RESEARCH; August, 1972, Vol. 12, No. 4, pp. 3-10. Copyright 1972, by the Advertising Research Foundation.

VII-3

A WRITER LOOKS AT TV RATINGS

Martin Mayer

FOREWORD

Selling time on a TV station requires two basic steps assuming the prospect is already sold on using the medium: (1) the buyer must be made aware of and sold on the advantages of a particular market; (2) he must be convinced that a particular station in that market is best suited to reach the type of consumer he wants to reach.

Some of the values and advantages of a market and a station are, of course, already known to an experienced buyer of time; some are not and must be brought to his attention--either through trade advertising or mailed sales promotion or via personal contact. While the competing stations have the common goal to promote the market they all serve, in a good many cases there are few hard facts which distinguish one station from another. This necessitates the development of a plus factor that will set apart station A from competing station B.

As a result of the attempt on the part of stations to reach advertising agencies and their clients with meaningful and useful facts and figures and to create a favorable image for themselves,

a veritable torrent of promotion material hits the buyer on any given day. Some of it is read carefully and filed for future reference; much is discarded. If the stations, and their sales representatives knew which kind of promotion material was useful and which was not, much waste in money and manpower could be eliminated. In addition, the danger of producing a negative effect with an inappropriate or ill-conceived piece of promotion could be minimized.

Sales promotion pieces take on many forms. They range from simple facts, such as a station winning the local merit award for public service, to rather serious and extensive primary research investigations.

The concern of this booklet will be only with material that comes under the heading of research. The booklet's sole purpose is to be helpful and constructive by indicating to sellers of TV time how the buyer feels toward the research material he receives from them, what he can use, in which way the data could be improved for greater usefulness, and what kind of information he is not now getting and would like to receive.

In order to create some order out of the

348

many types of research material produced by the stations and sent out as station promotion, an attempt was made to catalogue the material into basic categories. After considerable study, six such groups were developed and it is felt that virtually all of the station-produced research (with one important exception) can be put into one or the other group.

The six groupings, which will be discussed in order of their usefulness to agency researchers and media people, are as follows:

    I. Coverage Data
   II. Special Audience Studies
  III. Qualitative Research
   IV. Product or Brand Sales Information
    V. Marketing Information
   VI. General Market Statistics & Information

The major ommission referred to earlier is the category that could be called "Rating Information." The AAAA Research Committee feels that the Harris hearings, which have done much to focus industry attention on the problems of ratings research, have resulted in so much discussion and remedial action, that little can be said about the do's and don'ts of this type of research that isn't already known to the seller of TV time.

One word about the basis for this report. It represents the opinions of many of the leading media and media research practitioners at agencies of all sizes who were not only personally consulted but were also polled by mail on their opinions. The committee thus feels that the report contains "actionable" information and evaluation.

I. COVERAGE DATA

Coverage information is of vital con-

cern to advertisers and agencies, and all the help the TV industry can provide in this area is greatly appreciated. There is the predominant feeling among media experts and researchers that it is the responsibility of stations to supply this information because coverage and audience are what stations are selling. By "supplying" we mean showing--on a county-by-county basis--where the station has effective penetration. This detailed information will permit agencies to rearrange the material because, usually, the data are most useful when attempts are made by agencies to relate advertising efforts to client sales and marketing areas. Coverage data define the extent to which the area in question can be exposed to the advertising message. Coverage data also permit a finer evaluation of markets, and stations within a market. This sometimes is not possible with mere rating information. As a matter of fact, there is considerable feeling that the proper definition of the coverage area of a station is the most important aspect of media analysis. Once a precise coverage area has been established, all other relevant facts can be made to conform to this area where advertising effectively penetrates the public.

Most of the researchers expect coverage data to be based on accepted sources such as American Research Bureau or Nielsen Coverage Service. Mail-pull or millivolt contour maps are generally unacceptable because the former is an unrealistic indicator of coverage and the latter reflects physical signal strength but not viewer interest.

The few negative aspects of media-supplied coverage information can be summed up under the heading: "We buy this information directly from the research services." Here, the feeling is that all data are available at the agency and can thus be assembled in the most meaningful (to the agency) way. Therefore, the stations are wasting precious time in duplicating (in a less useful way) the same information.

SUGGESTED IMPROVEMENTS

As for suggestions, a definite need for a
a greater standardization of the data
is apparent. Cut-off points should be
defined and coverage level groupings
should be made uniform. Standardization of data and terminology can provide agencies with comparable information from market to market and would
ultimately eliminate the need for
agencies to concern themselves with the
compilation of coverage data.

Frequency of coverage studies also can
be improved--particularly where changes
in power, antenna height or location,
or channel shifts have taken place.

II. SPECIAL AUDIENCE STUDIES

Information shedding light on TV
habits of demographic or ethnic groups
of special interest is the second most
valuable item to the agency researcher.
It is also in this area that a considerable lack of information exists. Often
an advertiser wants to reach the Spanish
or Negro population in a market, talk
to mothers with young children, to
farmers, etc. and yet, only general TV
audience statistics are available to
him.

The conduct of special audience studies
will fill this important void. These
studies are especially valuable in
media buying because they provide an-
other--and often more meaningful--guide
to station selection. And, proper
media selection to eliminate waste in
coverage has become the watchword at
more and more agencies in this era of
rising costs.

SUGGESTED STUDIES

The need is not only for studies among
special audiences but also for studies

that highlight the special quantitative
values of television. For example,
audience accumulation studies, intra as
well as inter-media, are very useful to
the media buyer.

The fact that special audience studies
are much in demand does not imply, however, that stations should willy-nilly
run out and conduct some. As a matter
of fact, unless they are planned and
executed in a thoroughly professional
way, they may well be a waste of time
and money for the station. It probably
does not warrant mention because so
much has been said about it in recent
years, but aids in audience evaluation
need to be based on solid research
techniques more than ever before.

Thus, it is suggested that any studies
of this type be planned and executed by
professional researchers of unquestioned
ability and stature.

III. QUALITATIVE RESEARCH

The general interest in qualitative
media research is presently at its
highest level and will probably continue
to grow. For that reason, one finds the
most intense difference of opinion among
agency researchers when one discusses
the role TV stations should play in this
area.

The camp is about equally split between
those who feel TV stations and networks
should stay away from attempting these
studies and those who feel they should
do them.

Interestingly enough, while some believe
this type of research is not within the
scope of station research and should not
be done by them for that reason, most
individuals on the negative side feel
the stations are ill-equipped--financial-
ly, in terms of objectivity and in terms
of trained personnel--to carry out im-

portant qualitative research. Unless it has "quality" of its own, qualitative station or network research is rejected. While NBC's "Hofstra" studies are often cited as top examples of good, media-produced research, few agency people believe that this kind of study can be done at the lower strata of the TV industry hierarchy.

Again, most of those positively inclined toward media involvement in this type of research are cautious in their positive attitude. They qualify their comments on these studies with terms such as "this is the pay-off area and we need all the help we can get--if they are well-conducted, reliable and projectable." Or: "They'd be most helpful and welcome if we could control what is done." Or: "Qualitative research is very difficult to handle. Most time buyers wouldn't know what to think of it or how to make a buy using this kind of data."

ACCEPTABILITY OF QUALITATIVE STUDIES

The general feeling about qualitative viewer attitudes or viewer behavior or sales effectiveness or inter-media studies seems to be that stations should first find out from the ultimate user of the study what is and what is not acceptable--not only in terms of the the basic data to be developed, but also in terms of sample size definitions, organization to do the work, etc.

There seems to be enough interest in the general subject of qualitative evaluation of TV that the possibility of this type of investigation being handled through a pooled effort of both agencies advertisers and TV media might be investigated.

IV. PRODUCT OR BRAND SALES INFORMATION

This is one area where agencies feel media can be of little help and where, as a matter of fact, media are not expected to lend a hand. Generally, efforts to product sales data--either at the wholesale or retail level--cannot be done by the media with the detail, the frequency, the definitions and the thoroughness which an agency requires. In addition, it is costly research. Certainly from a test marketing standpoint, this type of information is urgently needed. However, it is usually developed according to set specifications by the test marketer.

This is not to say that marketers would not accept sales data produced by a given TV station in a market. As a matter of fact, if sales data were rigorously developed and properly tailored to suit the usual requirements, it is conceivable that a market not now a heavily-used test market, could become another "Peoria." Many advertisers would undoubtedly make use of this facility. They might even help defray the costs. Thus far, the Milwaukee Journal Company's Advertising Laboratory, which produces sales information, has been well accepted by at least some important advertisers who pay for the research costs.

While the usual media-produced data are not considered very useful by many researchers, some feel they provide an important supplement to syndicated sales indexes, provide an approximate guide as to brand share trends, make possible a certain amount of copy testing and aid in test market selection.

SUGGESTED IMPROVEMENTS

Improvements can be made in the material to make it more useful--if a station should decide to produce sales data at all.

First, the information should be produced fairly frequently to permit an
examination of the dynamics of a test
situation. Second, the data should be
rigorously compiled so that they meet
the research standards set by advertisers and agencies. Third, the criteria for measuring brand movement
should be standardized so that comparability can be achieved from one market to the next.

V. MARKETING INFORMATION

Into this grouping was placed all
"intelligence" that has to do with
marketing mechanics, i.e., location
and number of stores of all types,
brand distribution within store types,
location of warehouses, etc.

Reaction to this kind of marketing aid
is mixed. On the one hand, it fills a
need for some of the agencies in planning test market operations or in conducting some other kind of local market investigation where this type of
information is of value in carrying out
the assignment. It is of particular
value to the smaller agencies which
cannot afford to purchase elaborate
source materials from outside suppliers.

On the other hand, there is considerable sentiment against stations supplying this information. Particularly in
the case of brand distribution information, the agency researchers feel
that more qualified sources should be
consulted and used. Often, the media-
produced data are too general to be
of much use. Stations are felt to be
ill-equipped to conduct the research
properly. Agencies expect their clients'
field force to be familiar enough with
any given market to provide store counts
or warehouse locations. Furthermore,
straight numerical counts without
volume classification are not considered
to be of much use.

SUGGESTED IMPROVEMENTS

Despite the apparently limited usefulness of this type of data, some suggestions for improvement can be made
to those stations interested in providing this information.

Accuracy is essential. Therefore, pains
should be taken to make sure the material
is correct, up-to-date, and of sufficient scope.

Completeness is quite important. All
sizes and brands should be covered in
a distribution check. All stores in a
store count should be counted--by type,
size and neighborhood location. All
data should be properly defined so that
the reader is clear on what the numbers
mean.

Frequency (recency) of reporting is of
course desirable. There is nothing more
useless than old information. Standardization is a major problem here, too.
As with all research, if it doesn't fit
in with accepted breakdowns, it is of
limited use. Setting up standards is,
of course, a knotty problem and calls
for industry-wide consideration before
it can become reality.

VI. GENERAL MARKET STATISTICS AND INFORMATION

Least useful--for the reasons stated
below--are media-supplied facts about
the market in which the station operates
--its population, buying power, demographic mareup, etc. Often this information is issued under a heading such
as "This is WXXXland" or "The Hometown
Market." Usually, this type of research
draws on accepted sources such as the
U.S. Census, Sales Management, Munici-
pal departments, and Standard Rate &
Data Service. If it doesn't, it should.
Its purpose is to underline the value of
the market, and the station covering it,

for the media buyer and for the advertiser.

Opinions are well divided on whether stations should produce this kind of information. Those in favor find it of considerable use because it eliminates the necessity for agency researchers having to compile these statistics--if the data suits the needs of the user. This is of particular help to the smaller agency which often does not have the manpower to compile statistics ad infinitum.

There is no question that knowledge of basic market facts is often a must in media selection. Knowing the market is helpful in putting it into proper perspective in deciding whether to go into it at all. Above all, this type of research material will often break away from the confines of a "Metro Area" concept for which much of the Census and other material is reported. In many cases, the standard metro area does not coincide with the marketing or the TV area which often forms the basis for market evaluation.

Those who have a negative viewpoint feel that this type of information is either available in their own files or easily accessible and that, therefore, they can assemble market facts based on client sales territories or other internal geographic sales or marketing subdivisions which media-produced information cannot be expected to duplicate.

To sum up, agencies find no fault with the basic sources of the supplied market statistics because they often coincide with those being relied on by the user himself.

SUGGESTED IMPROVEMENTS

The usefulness of the data is limited by a lack of uniformity in the definition of what constitutes the geographical extent of the station's market or the geographical extent of the marketer's sales area. It is also limited by a lack of standardization of source and data between markets so that station-produced market statistics can rarely be put together to obtain intermarket rankings of any kind. Thus, while one station--in one market--will proclaim itself covering the 17th market of the U.S., another station--in another market--using a different area definition, will claim 17th rank for its market.

One suggestion for improvement can be offered. To eliminate the problem of differing statistics being circulated by various media serving the same market, it may be possible for the media to work together to compile one book which contains all salient facts about the market they all serve. This combined effort may well save everyone time and money and, at the same time, enhance the usefulness of the material. It does not, however, solve the intermarket comparison problem.

SOME OBSERVATIONS

Delving into the subject matter of TV industry produced research and discussing it with many vitally concerned with it, one is left with a few outstanding impressions.

NEED FOR GREATER STANDARDIZATION

There is a great clamor for the standardization of produced data. This standardization is not only necessary from the standpoint of definition and comparability between markets, but also because of the needs of the computer which is being used more and more.

Standardization must start with geographics. In television, this means effective coverage. While Nielsen, for example, has standardized a TV market concept via his Nielsen Station Index area definitions just as the govern-

353

ment has standardized the extent of Metro areas, so must the TV stations attempt to standardize their effective coverage areas.

Standardization must also be achieved in the many areas in which information is produced. While the AAAA Research Committee has recommended standard demographic breakdowns of data which should be adhered to at all times, standards for non-demographics are lacking. For example, at what point does a TV station's effective coverage end? At 25% total weekly audience? At 50%? At the 0.5 mv. contour line? Where? How should special audience studies be conducted to make them comparable with other, similar studies?

The answer to standardization requires the cooperation between agencies and stations. The agencies must let the media know what they want and how they want it. For that reason, it becomes important for the AAAA to continue its work in this area which was so ably started with the setting forth of demographic standards. Once this is done, the stations should adhere to this consensus. This, however, should not be interpreted to mean that the entire standardization load should be carried by the AAAA. The TV industry should also be vitally interested in this project and actively pursue it.

ACCEPTABILITY OF TELEVISION STATION PRODUCED RESEARCH

The general attitude among agency research and media executives about TV station produced research--about all media research--is one of caution. There is always the knowledge that a medium is primarily sales oriented and --in enough cases to create the impression--cares little about the quality of the research it does as long as it shows the underwriter in a good light. This feeling, however, divides itself into various categories. Research done by the networks or by the Television

Bureau of Advertising--in other words at the top of the hierarchy--is generally well regarded. Useful studies such as the NBC-Hofstra Studies plus Dr. Coffin's subsequent work as head of NBC's research department, CBS's "Apples and Oranges" comparison of TV and magazines and TvB's "Selectroniscope" have done much to produce this feeling. Certain station representatives have also built up good will via some fine studies. Yet, much research that has been prepared by representatives seem to have little acceptance. Among stations, there are only a few whose research attempts are taken seriously. They are the ones which have shown quality and objectivity in the past. In order to reverse the feeling of caution or hesitancy about accepting station-produced research among agency people, it will be necessary for the stations to demonstrate with actual examples that good research can be done.

To help overcome at least some of this feeling, TV stations should make sure that all of their research clearly identifies dates and sources of the material used. In case of original work, the study should contain a full description of methodology so that there will be no mystery about how the material was obtained. Too much of the material now submitted to agencies lacks the proper footnotes and explanations. Adherence to the ARF's "Criteria For Marketing and Advertising Research" is urgently recommended.

Agency research and media executives would rather see no research come from a medium at all than to be deluged with useless, or incomplete, or biased data. While they recognize the fact that media must keep themselves in the eyes of their clients, they wish that station promotion did not include often-seen spurious data. In the attempt to prove that they are "first" in some way or another, the stations only defeat their purpose: The data become suspect in the long run, no matter how good they are.

354

SIZE OF SAMPLES

Although ratings--as stated at the out-
set--were not considered in this evaluation, it might be useful to pass on a
feeling expressed in several corners.
And, that is the feeling that perhaps
the best use stations can make of their
research budgets is to concentrate
virtually all of it on the support of
larger sample sizes for the syndicated
rating reports covering their markets.
The advantages of this recommendation
are two-fold. First, the funds are
turned over to a research organization,
such as Nielsen or ARB, enjoying a vast
general acceptance among agencies thus
eliminating any doubts about the source.
Second, and more inportantly, larger
sample sizes will permit not only a
greater confidence in the actual ratings, but will also permit the breakdown
of the data into many more revealing
sub-segments. Larger sample sizes
would permit study of ratings by important demographic factors, by product usage, etc. It would permit the
stations' salesmen to have a lot more
useful and acceptable data at hand with
which to make a sale and, at the same
time, would give the buyer a much
sharper tool for matching audiences
and product users.

CONCLUSION

As a summary, it may be helpful to focus
once more on the priority which agencies
give to the various types of studies
discussed in this report so that the
limited promotion and research budgets
available to the stations can be made
more efficient by concentrating them
on the more desirable endeavours.

In general, the TV industry is looked
to for help in areas germane to media
evaluation and selection. Thus, development of coverage data, special audience studies and qualitative research
investigations are--in that order--of
most help to agency researchers and
media people.

On the other hand, stations are not
really expected to supply sales data,
marketing facts and statistics. This
is not to say that this type of information is not helpful. It is just
that marketing facts and statistics
are relatively easy to obtain from
standard sources, and sales data are
generally best left to the advertiser
or his agency.

DISCUSSION QUESTION

---

1. The article outlines six basic categories in which to catalogue research
material produced by many TV stations.
How useful do you think these categories are to agency researchers and media
people? Why?

Media Research Subcommittee of the American Association of Advertising Agencies, under the direction of Paul Keller, Vice President, Media & Research. Reach, McClinton & Co., Inc. Reprinted with permission.

VII-4

HOW ADVERTISING AGENCIES EVALUATE VARIOUS TYPES OF RESEARCH ISSUED BY TELEVISION STATIONS, NETWORKS, AND REPRESENTATIVES

Media Research Subcommittee of the 4A's

Broadcasting is, in a way, the quintessential modern activity. It is a man-made force which acts invisibly at a distance, and the distance is so great that even the proximate consequences of an action are undiscoverable. The arrow is shot into the air, and God alone knows where it comes down. Ham operators gleefully keep logs of those who respond to their calls (indeed, once they have made contact, they typically have nothing to say to each other save self-identification). But nobody responds as a matter of course to the broadcaster's call. If he is alone in the world, he stands in a dark and soundless room where no amount of groping will bring sensation to his fingertips. Obviously, he needs ancillary services.

"Ratings," which describe the size of the audience for a broadcast, are an almost universal feature of television in the Western world--indeed, the presence of audience research seems a necessary (clearly not sufficient) criterion for deciding whether or not a society is "democratic." Yet a television system in which all program decisions were determined by the vote of the ratings would be the worst kind of democracy, in which minorities always lose. For the ratings are soulless and simple-minded--one man, one vote. A ratings service knows no way to reward intensities of feeling on the other side of the screen. Few common modern comments are so heartfelt as the housewife's lament, "Every time I like something, they take it off the air." The essence of democracy in operation is logrolling, the swap of support by nonconflicting interests to produce transient majorities. But there is no mechanism by which television viewers can logroll.

None of these difficulties is absolute. Even in the complete absence of rating services observers can acquire some notion of how a broadcasting system is working. When Amos 'n' Andy first began in Chicago, in the early 1930s, the telephone company noted that the number of calls in that city dropped by 50 percent between 7 and 7:15 P.M., and even today most American city water departments find that the pressure in their mains drops at station breaks, every hour on the hour. Nor is the measurement of intensities entirely beyond the wit of man. Sometimes gross measurements occur by accident, as when NBC cut short the telecasting of the New York Jets-Oakland Raiders football game to present the opening moments of *Heidi*, and the Circle 7 telephone exchange in New York was put out of business by angry callers. Equally gross is the persistent habit of counting the unsolicited mail (which two decades ago, in the days of *Red Channels* and blacklisting, gave a letter-writing supermarket owner in Syracuse power to destroy the careers of all but the most talented television performers). Somewhat more refined, and for a while quite popular with network researchers, is the TV Q Service, which sends questionnaires to a panel of about two thousand respondents, asking them to say whether a given program is or is not "one of my favorites." A more sophisticated variant of this approach is the W.R. Simmons study of "attentiveness," in which viewers are asked to say whether during a show they were: (1) in the room paying *full* attention; (2) in the room paying *some* attention; or (3) out of the room most of the time. But advertisers use these measurements very rarely, and since the mid-1960s the networks haven't used them at all.

EUROPEAN RATINGS

Each country handles these problems its own way. In Austria the broadcasting authority (ORF) is required by law to gather ratings and to publish the results. (Management, which is deeply conscious of a cultural potential in the medium, is not entirely happy with this provision. "The worse the program," says Intendant Gerd Bacher a little irritably, "the greater the revolution if you try to get rid of it, because people know it is popular.") In four ratings sweeps ranging in length from four weeks (in November and January) to eight days (in June and September), ORF interviews 2,800 people a week to find out how many were watching what, and how much they liked it on a scale from +10 to -10. The second most popular regularly scheduled entertainment program in 1968 was *Solo fur*

O.N.C.E.L.; the best-liked over the course of the year was *Daktari* (consistently better than +8), closely followed by *Flipper*.

In France, by contrast, there were no ratings at all until l'ORTF began broadcasting commercials in 1964, and though the state-controlled company now does buy a rather elaborate continuing service it is strictly against the law for anyone to publish the results. The procedure involves three French market-research firms which maintain panels of respondents to answer questions about purchasing habits. Each supplies diaries of television viewing to random samples of its panels, the diaries (about 1,400 a week) to be returned to and processed by l'ORTF. Though a great deal of French television is in fact rather vulgar, theory insists that public opinion shall not have a determining effect on what is broadcast. Speaking of its nightly three-minute cartoon strip *The Shadoks*, a member of the team at l'ORTF's experimental center reports a comment by director Pierre Schaeffer: "If people don't like *Shakoks*, they are stupid anyway."

In Britain there are two competing ratings systems, as there are two competing broadcasting systems. The noncommercial BBC, broadcasting over two channels, employs year-round some 700 part-time interviewers, who interrogate some 2,250 adults and 450 children every day of the year, asking them what they watched yesterday. There is also a panel of 2,000 homes, one-sixth of them new every month, who supply what Brian Emmett, head of BBC audience research, calls "quick and dirty feedback on television programming." The corporation mails them a questionnaire asking them to mark on a five-point scale (A+ to C-) how much or little they liked certain programs they had had a chance to see in the previous week. In the case of international sporting events, liking correlates very well with how Britain did. In the case of variety shows, it tends to parallel ratings. "But in a series like the Wednesday play," Emmett says, "new dramatists, lot of kitchen sink about it, the correlation between liking and rating is effectively zero." Though an early study by William Belson indicated that the arrival of television tended to drive one or more members of large families out onto the streets of an evening, in general British researchers feel every program will be seen by many people who don't like it--if only "because," as a BBC pamphlet puts it, "the 'set' is often in the one warm room in the house."

Commercial television in Britain is supervised by the Independent Television Authority, which actually owns the towers over which the programs are telecast. ITA is required by law to "ascertain the state of public opinion concerning the programs (including advertisements) broadcast by the Authority." The great advantage of the machine, of course, is that it tells the advertiser how many homes (as a percentage of the panel, for sure; as a percentage of the country, by extrapolation) were tuned to the channel carrying his message during its brief mortality. "Otherwise," says Ian Haldane, director of research for ITA, "I must say I prefer the BBC interviews. Machines don't watch television; people watch." The panel housewife also keeps a diary identifying individual viewers of each program, allowing the service to estimate for advertisers the age, sex, income, etc., of the viewers.

In addition, Haldane runs his own, rather sophisticated surveys of affection and disaffection among viewers. "Partly," he says, "it's the law. The act lays down that we shall broadcast nothing that offends good taste or decency or conduces to crime. So we do studies asking people, 'Have you seen anything recently that you thought should be taken back of the woodshed?' Then, we want to help program-makers. The act lays down that on Sunday evening from six to seven-thirty nothing can be broadcast without the approval

of an external religious board. We call it the Holy Hour. Our research shows that pure religion gets no audience and no liking, but that religion related to personal and world problems *does* interest. We make suggestions. For a while, drama was full of tramps sitting in dustbins and talking of eternity, and our research showed the drama boys that Mrs. Bloggs couldn't be asked to take an interest in that. The TV audience is not the audience for a West End theatre. They listened, and it improved our audience for drama a good bit."

When ITA adopted a machine system in 1968, BBC considered going along; but the asking price was about a million dollars a year, and there were all those employees at Broadcasting House who would be displaced. Thus the two broadcast services measure different things and the results cannot be compared. The BBC 1970 annual report shows the family comedy series *Not in Front of the Children* as the corporation's most popular program, with 13,780,000 *viewers* (many of them, no doubt, children: the title was pretty irresistible to a child, and the show went on at 7:55 P.M. on Fridays). ITA gives this program an audience of 5,353,000 *homes* and shows it trailing no fewer than thirteen ITA programs (three of them being different nights on *News at Ten*, the ITA half-hour nightly news service).

British advertising men seem to agree that when ITA was new, in the 1950s, it outdrew BBC by nearly two to one. This produced a considerable shift in BBC programming policy, which had been perhaps a little stodgy ("The BBC," Fred Allen once remarked, "begins its program day with a lecture on how to stuff a field mouse, and continues in the same vein for the rest of the day"). Tom Sloan, "Head of Light Entertainment" for BBC, remembered his arrival there in 1954, when the director of the television service felt "frivolity on television was a literal waste of time ... We really were regarded as red-nosed clowns and strolling players."

Fear of commercial competition for audience drove BBC to import large numbers of American westerns and action programs (new greatly diminished in volume and appeal), and to develop its own collection of domestic situation comedies, two of which have recently been adapted for American production as *All in the Family* and *Sanford and Son*. By the late 1960s the two BBC channels between them were pulling about as much average nighttime audience as the one commercial channel. Whether this condescension to public tastes was a good thing or a bad thing is a matter of continuing debate in Britain; the most articulate speakers in the debate tend to believe it was awful.

"We have an obligation to maintain some share of the audience." says David Attenborough, inventor of *The Forsyte Saga* and *Civilisation*, the BBC's director of programs. "It's no good going out on the blasted heath and speaking in the most marvelous aphorisms if nobody is listening. We want to have between 40 to 60 percent of the audience, and I don't care if it's 60 in our favor or in theirs. But if week after week we got only 30 percent on our two services combined, I would know we were not the national broadcasting organization. And if we consistently got 70 percent, I would know we weren't braving enough."

EARLY U.S. RATINGS

Ratings in the United States started in March 1930, when a group of national advertisers met together with opinion researcher Archibald Crossley to form the Cooperative Analysis of Broadcasting. The technique employed was the "telephone recall"--interviewers would call people and ask them to run down a list of what they had heard yesterday.

The first improvement on this system was Claude E. Hooper's Hooperatings. His technique was the "telephone-coincidental," in which an interviewer calls a home and asks the person answering the telephone whether the radio (or television set) is playing, and if so what's on. This method is still used, on special order from a customer, by the American Research Bureau, to provide an overnight answer on how well a network show seems to be doing nationally. Its weaknesses are that it can't provide ratings for the early-morning and late-evening hours; not everybody has a listed telephone; and some people lie --a famous *New Yorker* cartoon in the 1950s showed a man telling a telephone he was watching *Omnibus* (the Ford Foundation's first effort at high-prestige programming) while the screen behind him showed men on horses firing guns at each other.

Next came the method still used by the BBC, the "aided recall" interview, where the interviewer comes in the flesh, armed with a roster of yesterday's programming. The weaknesses here were the possible influence of the interviewer's personality, a tendency for people to say they had watched something yesterday because they "always" watch that show, even if they had in fact missed it the night before, and, again, the little ego-building lie when the roster in the interviewer's hand revealed a show the respondent felt he should have seen. It will be noted that because the average interviewer is socially up-scale from the average respondent these biases would tend on balance to boost the ratings for the BBC, but not for any American network.

The self-administered questionnaire, as researchers who ran household "panels" for advertisers were discovering, saves the cost of interviewers at little loss of accuracy, given an appropriate subject matter; and listening to or viewing broadcasts seemed most appropriate. And this is, indeed, the most widespread way of measuring broadcast audiences in

America, used for local station ratings everywhere except in New York and Los Angeles (which are big enough to support their own machine installations). Diaries are distributed (at the rate of 85,000 a month by the American Research Bureau in the three rating months-- October, February and May), and the recipients are asked to note in appropriate places, every day for a week, what members of the family saw what on the tube.

NATIONAL NETWORK RATINGS

For national network purposes, however, American ratings, like the British ITA ratings, come from machines--specifically, the Audimeters of the A.C. Nielsen Company, which began offering the service, for radio, in 1942. This machine, variously and aggressively patented, consists of a timing device set to local time, a cartridge of photo film, and a lamp that exposes the film in an appropriate place to show the time when a set is turned on and the channel to which it is tuned. Such machines are placed in a relatively small sample of homes--just under twelve hundred for the nation as a whole--and most homes stay on the panel about three years. Participants are paid 50 cents every week in the form of two quarters that fall out of the film cartridge when it is inserted in the Audimeter. Some cartridges don't work right or get lost, but between 950 and 1,000 usable film cartridges return in the mail every week to the Nielsen Company, and from the company there issues every other week the magisterial Nielsen Television Index, not just a rating but a kind of revised and annotated bible. (In some key months the NTI arrives every week, with fresh numbers.) For these national reports and associated local reports, Nielsen seems to be receiving--the figures are confidential, except for a world-wide total including receipts in

four other countries--at least $10 million a year, probably $2.5 million from the networks, at least as much again from stations, and most of the rest from advertising agencies, some of which pay upwards of a quarter of a million dollars a year for Nielsen services.

LOCAL STATION RATINGS

Local ratings services have problems national services don't have. The most serious of them is sample size. The mathematics of surveys is such that the size of the "universe" to be measured is very nearly irrelevant to the size of the sample required for the various levels of accuracy. If you need a thousand homes in the sample nationwide, you need a thousand for local ratings in New York or San Francisco or Lubbock, Texas--if you hope to get comparable accuracy in your local ratings. And that, very obviously, inescapably, doesn't pay--the financial importance of the decisions to be made with the information is much too small to justify spending all that money on audience research.

ARB does "ratings sweeps" in 220 markets in the United States. In the smallest of them, the sample is 250 households; in the largest, 1,500 households.

The names and addresses and telephone numbers for the sample come to ARB from the Mail Advertising Corporation of America in Lincoln, Nebraska, which maintains a complete file of current telephone books indexed by county, and plucks individuals out of each book by random selection. (The "frame" for the sample is thus people with listed telephones, cutting out a sizable chunk of poor people who have no telephones and rich people who have unlisted telephones --maybe a fifth of the country all together.) About 100,000 names are pulled for the country as a whole, and the names are forwarded to some 2,000 women all around the country, who call up and ask the lady of the house whether she would be willing to keep ARB's "Diary of Our Television Viewing" for one week. (Each "ratings sweep" lasts four weeks: one-quarter of the sample is keeping a diary in each of them.)

About 15,000 of the 100,000 homes are eliminated on these first telephone calls, because the family has moved or the number is disconnected or MAC got it wrong in the first place. Of the remaining 85,000 homes, about 15,000 don't answer the phone, or slam down the receiver when they hear it's a research outfit, or listen politely to the spiel and then decline to help. These names of non-cooperators are sent to Beltsville, where every night for three weeks before the sweep ten girls get on the WATS (Wide Area Telephone Service) line and try again, telling the householder on the other end that the matter is so important ARB is calling long-distance from Washington. Very nearly half of those who had previously refused accept under these new blandishments.

Whether or not the potential respondent has agreed to keep the diary ARB sends one, a thin pamphlet in an envelope made heavier by the enclosure of two newly-minted quarters. Just before the week for which the diary is to be kept, the ARB field representative telephones again, as a reminder; and during that week the householder receives a letter from ARB, mentioning he need for prompt reply "because we're having trouble with the mails."

Meanwhile, the stations are asked to send ARB their program logs for the weeks in question. This is not really a hard job for them, because ARB sends back a Xerox of what they had reported during the last sweep, and asks them merely to change what has been changed. ARB has all this material on computer tapes, and when the changed logs return, girls sit at a row of ten CRTs--computer

display terminals, looking like television screens with attached typewriter keyboards--to update the tapes for the new sweep. There are a million program titles printed for the 220 ratings books (one book for each market surveyed) issued at the end of each sweep, and they must be printed correctly. This is tricky work, because a single typo can jam the machines and wreck a pamphlet for a city. Sometimes the stations try some tricky work, too, deliberately misspelling the name of a show for a week in which an opposing station has an overwhelmingly popular special attraction. The computer is programmed to break out of the four weeks anything different in that time slot in one of them (thus eliminating a station's *own* specials too). A misspelled entry means that the week in which it appears with its misspelled form will not be averaged into the month, thus preventing the Sunday night rating of an ABC affiliate, say, from being depressed by the CBS *Ben Hur* blockbuster. Childish? Yes, indeed; but it works, sometimes.

Meanwhile, the diaries are coming back to a corps of a few dozen editors. For each fifteen-minute period, the household is supposed to have filled out (separately for each set, by the way, in a multi-set household) the channel watched, its call letter, the program and (by checking appropriate boxes) the members of the family and any visitors who were watching. If the call letter and the channel disagree, the household is registered as Using Television, but no station gets credit for the viewing.

Cable and the FCC rules governing it have given ARB a fearful headache. In theory, the cable company is supposed to "protect" a local station when a more distant station carried on the cable is presenting the same program, by slotting the local station's signal (and commercials) into the slot normally occupied by the distant station. From the viewer's point of view, the set is still tuned to the distant

channel. Local stations send ARB a
list of the time periods for which they
are protected, and in every community
where viewers are on a cable the ARB
editor checks those time periods to
make sure credit goes to the local
station rather than the distant one.
(Incidentally, in cable situations
where the cable company moves stations
onto different channels--which must be
done in many places, because the internal wiring of the set acts as an
antenna and makes ghosts if the cable
brings the signal into the same fre-
quencies--viewers may lose all sense
of which channel they are watching.
Channel 11 in Hamilton, Ontario, which
broadcasts live and successfully into
the Toronto market as well as coming
to Toronto homes through some other
channel number via cable, boosted its
ratings an average of 3 points an hour
by the simple expedient of super-impos-
ing the line "You are watching Channel
11" on program material three minutes
after the start and three minutes before the conclusion of every show.)

About 60 percent of the diaries sent
out return to Beltsville; just short
of 90 percent of those returned are
usable in the tabulation. These proportions are by no means uniform from
neighborhood to neighborhood, and in
fact ARB has been unable to work normal
procedures in the Negro ghettos, where
rewards as high as ten dollars a week
have failed to produce returns from
much more than 10 percent of the diaries
mailed out. In addition to sending
diaries to the homes in the sample in
a dozen such areas, ARB calls the home
every day to get the information on an
immediate recall basis; and a telephone
interviewer makes out the diary for the
family.

Eight days after the end of the ratings
period the processing of returned
diaries begins; another week, and the
first book is in the mail. By thirty
days after the end of the survey, books
have been published for markets accounting for about three-quarters of all the

television advertising dollars. Within
another twelve days, the job is finished.
In 1970-71, the end product consisted
not only of large pamphlets (one for
each market), but also of 700 computer
tapes custom-built for the information-
consumer.

Though stations pay ninety percent of
the bill, the basic use of ARB data is
at the advertising agencies and the
media-buying services. Goods are not
sold nationally, but locally; every
television show is stronger in some
cities than in others--and so is every
brand. It is almost impossible that an
advertiser's network buy should deliver
audience market by market in patterns
that match his sales market by market.

BUT ARE COMMERCIALS AIRED?

Do the commercials actually get aired?
Broadcast Advertisers Reports try to
answer this question each month by telling exactly what each station in that
market carried in the line of non-network advertising during one sample week
in that month. BAR gets this information by taping the sounds that are
broadcast with the pictures on some 265
stations in 50 markets accounting for
about four-fifths of all advertising
revenue in local television. These
tapes, taken off the air by some 500-odd
tape recorders placed in private homes
(two machines are tuned to almost every
station, just in case) are mailed to a
one-story brick building in a slummy
suburb of Philadelphia, where dozens
of women sit at little tape decks, wearing ear plugs, listening, noting on a
printed data sheet every commercial
broadcast on this channel other than
those embedded in network shows. (BAR
publishes a separate every-week service
for the three networks, derived from
direct monitoring of network feed rather
than from broadcast, and supplies a summary of the results--each network's

minutes and BAR's estimate of its receipts, by day part--for *Broadcasting*
Magazine. With experience, the women
learn to run the tape fast through the
program material and to note only the
spot commercials; an experienced girl
will note all the commercials from a
station's 18-hour broadcast day in a
single 8-hour working day.

The data sheets from the listeners
then go to editors who code them--a
separate code number for almost 300
product categories and store categories (for retail advertising), and then
an individual code number for each
brand and each store. The coded data
from listening are punched onto cards,
the cards are fed to a computer, and
then the computer does its thing in a
variety of ways.

For each of the nation's fifty largest
markets, BAR publishes a separate monthly pamphlet, plus a quarterly "cume"
(for cumulative). These "market pro-
files" first list all the brands and
stores that advertised in the market
in this time period, with the number
of messages delivered for each advertiser on each station. Then the list
is broken down into those that advertised only on one station, on two or
on all, enabling a salesman to find at
a glance where he can compete for existing business now in the hands of his
enemies. Then the pamphlet prints the
total schedule of spots for each brand,
day by day, station by station. Finally, BAR provides in the back of the pamphlet a complete log of programs and
commercials for each station in the
market during the sample week. All
this information is in fifty to eighty
pages for a normal three-station or
four-station market, printed by photo-
offset from computer print-out, all
caps, very small type, five columns to
an 8 1/2 x 11-page in the log section.

Stations pay up to $4,000 a year for
their pamphlets, while advertising
agencies pay on a scale that tops out
at $52,000 a year. How many stations

subscribe is something BAR won't say,
but it seems clear enough that not all
of them do: they feel that knowledge of
what the opposition has been carrying is
something a good salesman should have
without wasting time and money on "data
fall-out."

Agencies use BAR in part to keep up with
what their clients' competition is doing
(and by correlating the BAR information
about local campaigns with ARB ratings
data and Nielsen Food and Drug Index
sales reports an agency can get at least
a reasonable idea of the effectiveness of
a competitor's advertising); in part to
police what the stations are doing with
the business the agency has given them.

RATINGS AND PROGRAM DECISIONS

Much of the data available from television audience studies can be stimulat-
ing stuff. Some of the information is
just inexplicable. Why, for example,
did a television special with Diana Ross
and The Supremes draw lots of women over
fifty but very few older men? Why do
most movies draw heavier audiences in
the last half than they do in the first
half? When all the movies on television
were rereleased after theatrical exhibi-
tion, it was believed that the newcomers
to the audience for the latter part of
the show were people who had already seen
the picture at the movie house and were
tuning in to catch some remembered high
points at the end--but the same phenomenon seems to appear in the made-for-
television *World Premieres* and *Movies of
the Week*. Perhaps people just enjoy a
denouement even if they don't know the
situation that sets it up.

Friday night is the weakest night on
television--one almost never finds a
Friday show among the top ten. The reason, probably, is that Friday night is
when the high schools across the country
stage their athletic events. It's also

the night of the paycheck: people go
out more. In any event, the Friday
audience even more than others tends
to be composed of the young and the
old, with fewer than usual representatives from the 25-49 group. Sunday
night, on the other hand, is the heaviest viewing night, and gets all ages.

At any hour of any weekday, there are
more women watching television than
there are men. The age group over
fifty watches more television than any
other. But viewing by older people is
strongly patterned. They constitute
more than half the audience for the
nightly network news shows, for westerns and for variety programs, but
less than a third of the audience for
movies. Among other very popular shows
with a relatively low component of
over-fifty viewers are the doctor shows
like *Marcus Welby, M.D.* and *Medical
Center*, presumably because the subject
matter cuts a little near the bone.
One of the oddities of the fall 1970
burst of "relevant" shows, which were
supposed to draw younger audiences, is
that they did well with the over-fifty
group, but bombed with everyone else.

The best-educated and highest-income
audiences in television are those for
football and for movies, though many
specials and *Laugh-In* also do well at
the upper end of the income distribution. It is not true that light viewers
look for "better," more serious programs; studies done for Group W, the
Westinghouse stations, indicate that
light tend to choose much the same
shows the heavy viewers choose, and it
is the moderate viewer who makes or
breaks a more serious effort. Jim
Yergin, who runs the Group W research
operation, explains these rather tentative findings on the theory that the
heavy viewer has a need for entertainment; the light viewer turns the set on
only when he has nothing better to do,
so he, too, seeks entertainment; but
the moderate viewer has to decide
whether to look or not and thus can be

tempted by something out of the ordinary.
Maybe so? Maybe not.

The first factor in determining whether
a show will do well or badly in the
ratings is the popularity of its competition. The foundation-supported
Omnibus, an effort to bring upper-mid-
dlebrow tastes to television, drew a
larger audience on Sunday afternoons
than it did when moved to prime time,
because the competition in prime time
was much stronger. (Except perhaps for
Sunday morning, there is no "cultural
ghetto"--as the pro football games demonstrate, the small audiences drawn by
more ambitious programs on Sunday afternoons reflected not an unwillingness of
the American people to look at television on Sunday afternoons but the slight
attraction of the shows.) When CBS on
October 21, 1971, programmed three full-
hour documentaries one right after the
other in prime time, two new opposing
ABC shows that had not previously pene-
trated the Nielsen top forty received
the third- and fifth-highest ratings
of all shows telecast that week. ABC,
knowing the CBS plan, promoted the evening heavily, and linked one of the shows
to a plot line in *Marcus Welby*, to help
nature along.

Public-affairs shows in general do not
draw much audience; indeed, live news
coverage at a time when people expect
entertainment is likely not to draw
much audience. On the first night of
the Six-Day War, all three networks carried the UN Security Council emergency
meeting. In New York, where a quarter
of the televison homes are Jewish and
presumably have more than the normal
interest in the fate of Israel, a rerun
of *Alfred Hitchcock Presents* on an independent station drew more viewers than
the three network stations combined.
Nightly, habit-forming news shows do
better, but they are by no means overwhelming winners. In Washington, which
lives on news as Milwaukee lives on
beer, the nightly national news shows
were staggered in fall 1970--Howard K.
Smith at 6, David Brinkley at 6:30,
Walter Cronkite at 7. At 6 in the

364

Washington market, according to the November 1970 ratings sweep by the American Research Bureau, the most widely watched program in Washington was reruns of *I Love Lucy*; at 6:30, reruns of *Petticoat Junction*; at 7, reruns of *Dick Van Dyke*. In New York in early 1971, reruns of *I Dream of Jeannie* on an independent station drew a bigger audience than any of the three network news shows in the same 7 o'clock time slot. During its last two years as a regular Tuesday night feature, the *CBS News Hour* averaged a rating just under 9 points, a share of roughly 15 percent, an estimated audience of between 5 and 5.5 million households--a lot of homes and a lot of people, but less than the circulation of either *Look* or the *Saturday Evening Post.* at the time of their collapse. Moreover, the audiences drawn by both news and documentaries tend to be slightly below average in both education and income, a fact that always shocks people who have not thought much about television.

It is hard to see how matters could be otherwise. Leland Johnson of the RAND Corporation, who did studies for the Ford and Markle Foundations on the prospects for cable televison, was apologetic about his failure to watch the medium at all. "My problem is," he said, "that television is a very low-rate data transmission system, and I just don't have time for that." Despite much assertion to the contrary, television for most reasonably well-educated people is an extremely inefficient way to learn about anything. People really do learn at their own rate, and television is the most hopeless of lock-step classrooms, insisting that everyone in the audience work on the same time scale. As Wilbur Schramm and his associates put it in their book *Television in the Lives of Our Children,* "Watching television, the viewer cannot set his own pace.... This quality, of course, makes for good storytelling, good fantasy, because in those forms the storyteller *should* be in charge, and the viewer *should* surrender himself.

But it makes learning harder. This is why the child, after he learns to read well...tends to seek information more often from print. With print he is in greater control."

None of this is to deny that documentaries have been artistically among the most satisfying and socially among the most important contributions of television, or to accept the idea that the poor ratings and minimal audience quality of documentaries give networks an excuse not to make and air them. But it does suggest that among those who insist Middle America is very stupid there are some who may not be so bright themselves.

Advertising has a flourishing trade press, including publications as specialized as *Media Decisions,* and this very detailed "information" makes copy for the publications and sermon texts for speakers at the many, many advertising and broadcasting trade lunches, dinners and conventions. There is no secret about the fact that many of the detailed breakouts from audience survey data are not much good. Queried about his computer's answers to my questions about Pepsi-Cola drinkers, Bill Simmons said, "Well, we sell our clients tapes of our data, and they can go to tabulating firms, and there's the tape on the tabulating company's machine, and what can we do? I thought we'd better have a service outselves." Henry Rahmel of Nielsen cheerfully admits that many of his customers are chasing a will-o'-the-wisp: "When you refine your demographics, you're putting in more and more statistical dollars to buy thinner and thinner cells and more sampling error." But the figures are there, and in Banks' Law (named for Seymour Banks, research director of the Leo Burnett agency), "Available data drive out necessary data."

When people in television sales talk about their work, however, about what actually happens day by day, they do not in fact stress these arcana. What

they talk about is "$4 television,"
which means an expenditure of $4 to
reach a thousand households, as measured by Nielsen ratings. "We can tell
you," says Burnett's Banks, "about the
viewing habits of beer-drinking housewives whose husbands are professionals.
We do cross-tabs all the time on everybody's data. But none of this is as
important as ratings, simply because
the variations in cost-per-thousand
households are greater than the variations in kinds of households and purchasing habits. We try to get the
thing that is the best buy, with minor
qualifications for kind of audience.
The qualifications are necessary, but
not sufficient. Cost per thousand is
both necessary and sufficient."

DISCUSSION QUESTIONS

1. The article presents a list of rating systems to measure TV programs.
Which do you feel is the most effective?

2. What method do you believe should
be used by (a) advertisers and (b) networks for choosing TV programs? Why?

Reprinted by permission from ADVERTISING AGE; 28 April, 1969, pp. 65-5, 68.

VII-5

DON'T SNEER AT COMPUTERS

Herbert D. Maneloveg

Within the past decade we have become the recipients of an expanding knowledge and all kinds of sophisticated, far-out but definitely "in" planning tools. Yet, after playing with them for short periods of time we often discard the ideas and the tools; we race to return to the safe and warm old ways of planning and buying. Linus-like, the security blanket of past approaches becomes easier to cope with than striking out with new equipment against the complexities of tomorrow.

Take our most exciting, new toy--the computer. Couple with it the information explosion. And what do you have? A veritable cornucopia of revolutionary data that could help guide a marketer toward sounder manufacturing and advertising decisions. Our ever increasing bank of knowledge is an essential component in order to understand the new world of product proliferation, market segmentaion, automated distribution, population shifts and the profit squeeze. The computer, if utilized properly, permits us to factor all these items together and the picture thus becomes clearer, the direction more concise.

But too often many of us seem to run away from reasoned analysis and an orderly sifting of information; too

many times we almost refuse to program our computers properly. Rather we cling to intuition, to hunch, to guessing to get us through the day.

Or, because we are aware that there is so much new information at our fingertips we somehow expect to find the answer readily at hand, flashing away without any work on our part in big neon lights on our Honeywell 8200s or our IBM 360-92s. Too many of us have become lazy; we cease to experiment. We seem to leave it to the computer or to ourselves, but seldom to the computer plus ourselves, working together.

Yet the marketing world of tomorrow can only be fathomed if we do experiment, if we do examine, if we do study and relate, if we use all our brain power in conjunction with these new tools of marketing. It's time we stopped kidding around. Our present marketing problems are too pressing to be handled by the old "top-of-the-head" approach. Those who seek the easy, the expedient route to sales success will find themselves detoured and chugging along, far, far behind the leaders.

√ Examine food and grocery products, for example. Between 1963 and today, in only five years, the number of frozen food items in the average super-market locker increased from 126 to 182; fats and shortening brands on the shelf jumped from 20 to 59; the number of cigaret brands and sizes from 39 to 116; soaps and detergents from 61 to 81. Thus, the average American house-wife has dozens of more soaps, many more shortenings, all kinds of frozen items to choose from. And she must make her buying decisions when she visits her supermarket. It's no easy task for her; certainly it's no easy task for the man marketing the product either.

The same holds true in the industrial marketplace. Today's industrial pur-chasing agent is faced with brand and company proliferation and an incredible array of new products made possible by the new technology. The number of chemical companies has grown by nearly 50% in the last five years from just under 11,000 in 1964 to over 15,000 in 1968. And that number is expected to increase by another 6,000 by 1972. New products now feasible would take all day to list. They range from room temperature superconducting materials to plastics in building structures to holographic photography to...the list is almost endless.

BUYERS ARE CHOOSIER

And if the decision task is difficult for the housewife choosing between brands of peanut butter that cost 59¢ a jar, how much more difficult the job of the industrial purchaser dealing in hundreds of thousands or even millions of dollars at a time. And how critical each purchase in each field is to the industrial seller; how critical to cor-porate profit each item becomes.

If a manufacturer is to compete in this cluttered, heavily competitive world, he must look to new ways to

sell, new ways to produce profitably, new ways to get his product idea across to a more choosy, more discerning pub-lic. He's got to make that woman buy his product over thousands of others on the supermarket shelf. He's got to con-vince his buying influences that the company's products are more viable and valuable than any others available.

And with it all the population is con-stantly changing, too. Today, our na-tion has zoomed over the 200,000,000 mark. And it's going to grow greater by leaps and bounds. In the next 20 years it will rise over 40,000,000 in population, a whopping 20%! And these increased numbers are going to be busy shoehorning themselves into specific areas of the country. While the nation as a whole will jump by 20%, the South Atlantic states will rise 31%, the Mountain states 38%, and the North Paci-fic a whopping 49%. And if one dares to look on a worldwide basis, the awe-some fact is that our present global population of 3.4 billion will almost double--double, mind you--within the next 30 years.

CALIBRATED ADS

Harvard University conducted an inter-esting study of business management a few years ago. Talk about changes! In 1950, the per cent of business executives with at least one college degree stood at about 60. In 1964 that per cent had jumped to over 70. And among the young-er executives--the top men in the up-coming 1970s, 78% had a degree and over a third--almost 40%--had done graduate work. Thus, the future and the present call for a new kind of sophisticated "sell" to a highly talented group of new and inquiring buyers.

As marketers and advertisers and agency people and media sellers, we need to adjust rapidly in order to cope with these changes, these problems, these opportunities. Plant sites will have to be shifted; distribution and sales patterns changed; timing of product introductions will undergo deeper scrutiny; and advertising pressure will have to be calibrated and analyzed in order to reach the right prospects, at the right place, at the right moment in time.

Each company needs to work harder at trying to "work against the averages." Instead of blithely attempting to reach everyone with our sales messages, we must now learn how to target in on the right prospect and key buying influences for our products. The advertiser must know how to concentrate, the media must demonstrate their ability to do that concentrating. Certainly that's the job of the business press.

When one realizes that we are now over 200,000,000 population, and talking to a management group pressing close to 10,000,000 people, finding inventive ways to zero in on the prime, prime 15% or 20% of each key group is not an unsound avenue to travel. A 20% chunk of top management today is still over 2,000,000 people; and with concentration, amalgamation and acquisition a fact of business life, that 20%--properly defined--could effect 70% or 80% of your over-all sales. That's where you need to lay your efforts; that's where media must demonstrate their powers. That's where the business press can fit in.

NFL GAME OR TOP 1%?

Let me cite an example. Take the U.S. crude oil industry. It's huge, huge, indeed. If I were selling valves or fittings to this industry you can bet I would do well to settle for but 1% of the over 1,000 companies in refining--if they were the right 1% like

Shell, Mobil, Standard Oil, Texaco, Sun Oil, Gulf and maybe three or four more. That's where the business is. That's where I'd want my sales pressures to go. Instead of *Wide World of Sports*, or the *NFL Game*, or *Mission: Impossible*, how about concentration against the 1% that counts?

In the future it is going to be much, much wiser to talk to the right 20% of a market, over and over again, than to reach everybody just a few times. Inflationary media costs make it imperative to do that concentrating...

I can put it yet another way. We're going to have to aim at smaller groups, whether we want to or not; our large affluent consumer population and industrial population are busily dividing themselves into sub-markets for many products.

For example, within the toothpaste market they now break up into regulars, the fluorides, the whitener users, and now the combination of groups augmented by mint. Gain leadership in any one category and you're in business, solid business. But you must carve out the market that is right for you, and you must find media that will give you a large share of that market by talking to the people who will buy.

We fall so easily into the use of general terms to describe our marketing objectives. We've got to stop those generalities--we've got to say, not toothpaste, when we mean fluoride toothpaste, not diesels when we mean just truck or marine, or train or automobile diesels; not plastics when we mean PVC, not the retail trade when we mean or should mean discount and variety chains which could account for 75% of product X's total volume.

369

CONCENTRATE, CONCENTRATE!

Let's dwell on this point for a moment and talk about channels of distribution. Take the category of car waxes and polishes. Traditionally this was a business for the service stations and the red front auto accessory stores. Not any more. Discounters, variety, hardware, others have crept in. Today, only 15% of this business is from service stations; over 30% is accounted for by discount stores. Another growing outlet is food stores, with 15%.

The distribution mix is changing and we have to choose the most profitable route to take. We must buy the right amount of advertising in vehicles we never thought of using in the past. Identifying the prime prospect has become critical; conducting business in profitable sub-markets makes good sense; knowing how and where your products are being distributed, is a key marketing need for us all--and the principal factor tomorrow's media man must study. It's what the business press should demonstrate: Its ability to pinpoint where and to whom we should be selling.

The aspect of concentration makes additional sense when one considers the avalanche of advertising going against the public today. Today the average consumer is witness to up to 1,200 advertising messages a day. Our engineer or plant foreman or company president sees and reads an almost like amount of advertising. Thus, if we blithely spread our pressure across the land, we are less likely ever to be heard. For that reason, the job of finding the key market for products and banging away with messages against that group is going to be our goal in order to gain a lock on the marketplace. *The answer is advertising frequency as much as the message itself.*

√ Out of all these sobering facts one point is clear. *We must now have the data to tell us who these housewives are, who these engineers are, who these plant foremen and company presidents are, and how to reach them.* It's all available if we work at it. And luckily we are just beginning to find out how much pressure is necessary to stir these people to purchase. We're learning what is needed to make them aware, how awareness leads to product trial and usage. And, hopefully, how it eventually relates to sales.

Yet knowing now that all this material can be developed while understanding the complexities involved, how do many advertisers and their agencies and the advertising media react?... [in all too many cases] they keep the techniques and information and expertise at the far end of the headquarters building. They, in effect, quarantine their on-premise talent, as if mathematical problem solving *for advertising* was a disease rather than a hopeful remedy. As if today's complex marketing was, in effect, a mystical world that only a seer can fathom and totally separate from the copy and media world.

'TO HELL WITH RESEARCH'

Agency people stroke their creative beards and say, "To hell with the research; the ad's the thing. I'm looking for an idea that wins awards." Okay. I buy that. But too often they end up developing an agency look for their clients rather than a unique selling proposition. They forget to write to the problem; instead, they write to themselves.

In industrial advertising they hardly ever look at what the competition is saying and dare to be different. They forget that there even are competitors; they present ads as if an adoring public was anxious to devour every single word. Often the basic sales point is hidden at the bottom of the ad where no one will even see it. They forget that one has to excite the reader as well as reach him.

Both these groups, client and agency, cling to the old ways, introducing new products without proper testing, bringing out new items that offer no meaningful difference over others already in the marketplace, building advertising efforts that offer a shotgun approach rather than an on-target rifle barrage, blithely selecting media and forgetting what the competition is doing. And each year their share of market gets smaller and smaller, they wonder why.

One could justify it all if the data for sound marketing decisions and on-target creative were not available. *But it is available.* We now possess the facilities to make it even more meaningful--if only we're willing to bring science as well as art into the marketing and advertising picture.

IT ONLY TAKES SCIENCE AND ART

What we need to do is to adjust our sights to the whole of the problem, rather than to concentrate on a single piece of it. Turn marketing men into complete marketing men, turn agency people into full-service people; use the talents of all--together--not at one person's whim. Devote as much time to the advertising problem as one does to R&D. Don't examine salesmen's call reports on how many visits were made, but design a cost accounting program that actually shows business secured per dollar expended; and factor in advertising to the total cost of marketing. It can be done. And must be.

Certainly a computer that can figure out how to tie together two orbiting

spheres out there in the universe can somehow show us how to figure out a profitable price for a new tube of toothpaste. Or rheostats. Or turbines, or generators. Certainly a computer that can take and relay crystal-clear pictures from the moon can help us in determining how the American housewife might react to a campaign for a new breakfast cereal, or a personal care product, or electrical appliances. Or flooring material and lawn care items.

What we need is a new course in the care and feeding of information, a willingness to experiment by relating pieces of marketing data to the whole. We need to know what to ask for and we need to know how to interpret from the answers we get. *The data is there. Or can be gotten there*--if we work at it. We need to know how advertising works and how much is needed to make it work. The basic responsibility is the client's and his agencies'. But the media can help too. Just a suggestion: Why not devote 0.5% of total ad revenue to mount research on proving the business press effectiveness against today's new breed of management. Do it on an industrywide basis. With only 0.5% you'll have over $2,000,000 or $3,000,000 to prove your point. That's money that will do the job and maybe make us forget broad-based TV thrusts or warm-image ads in *Sports Illustrated* and *Playboy*.

CPM AND THE PROCURERS

But it isn't only prime prospect problems that plague us today. Look at the darlings of today's media world, the barter and outside buying groups. A number of very respectable clients, consumer *and corporate advertisers,* are suddenly fascinated with their claims and we're continually asked what we think of the outside buying groups; perhaps they, (the clients) should utilize them in order to come in with a better cost-per-1,000 for their broadcast *and print purchases*. Print is now being peddled by the barter people. After all, they argue, in this competitive advertising world, CPM is the basic criterion that can be measured.

"You don't seem to condemn them, Maneloveg, so why shouldn't we explore them?" That's what they throw at me.

Well frankly, I don't condemn them, *because they are not the ones that need to be tarred in public*. To my way of thinking the true culprits are the TV and radio stations and--this is why I bring it up today--growing lists of magazines who offer the deals in the first place. These fast-buck media owners should be horsewhipped! And most important, the other villains are agency and advertiser who are willing to forget about sound marketing strategy, proper prime target concentration and respectable frequency and sound editorial compatibility in order to take advantage of a so-called favorable cost-per-1,000 carted around by the outside seller.

CPM CAN DESTROY YOU

These groups, these middlemen, could well be called the procurers (or in a nastier way, the pimps) of today's media world. But it's not fair to paint big red A's on their chests alone. Not if one leaves the prostitutes, those who happen to own the vehicles, plus the other party who is eager for action and is supplying the money, unscathed and unmarked.

If these funny sellers do come in at a 15% or 20% better deal, as they so advertise, they have to be slicing something from the total package. And in truth, efficiency in media does not ever guarantee product sales--hardly

ever. Nor does a slew of audience numbers in SIC classifications or a listing of manufacturing outlets by size of employment. *Effectiveness* is the key word, rather than efficiency. One can logically reason that the cheaper the price, the less likely the value, and the less on-target the audience delivered. Here again, *in my view, clinging to cost-per-1,000 as a major determinant is a specious, specious bit of reasoning. And a trend that could destroy advertising rather than move it forward.*

√ What concerns me about the rising tide of specialized buying groups is that clients and their agencies appear to be returning to CPM as the end-all, rather than looking ahead to deeper, more important measurements. An advertiser should be much more aware of timing. He should become more concerned about his weight in relation to competition. He should be more cognizant of how often he's reaching his prime prospect and with what frequency at key buying periods.

He should make certain that his effort has sales force impact as well as customer influence. He should be sure that it all ties in properly with his manufacturing schedule, and that all are related to the purchase cycle of the product. *These* are the essential elements that should be included in structuring a sound media plan. *These* are the elements that need to be incorporated rather than flow charts, efficiency comparisons and a six-paragraph write-up on the editorial compatibility of a batch of diverse trade publications.

EARLY WARNING SYSTEM

My agency (hopefully other agencies) is hard at work trying to program for this future, in media and in marketing. We're not dragging our feet. We're trying to move with the information tide that's sweeping the country. We've developed a concept called NEWS (New Product Early Warning System), a model that tells us early in the test market stage whether we're on target in our sales objectives in relation to advertising pressure.

We've experimented on a new media model so that we can build plans and schedule our media in relation to desired reach and frequency goals against prime prospect groups. And we're discovering that it makes as much sense for industrial and corporate efforts as it does for consumer campaigns. Maybe even more.

We're now keeping track of all our product gross impression delivery on a quarterly basis for every account in the agency, and we're measuring that weight against quarterly advertising awareness scores secured through a 4,000 panel group across the nation, consumer *and* business groups. We think we're on the way to answering the $18 billion question of how much advertising is enough.

We've developed a sophisticated focus group interview technique wherein we are now able to measure the effect of pricing and of product innovation, the effect of copy concepts and the result of promotional impetus as sales incentives on a prime prospect group. This research is done on as many business people as housewives.

All these developments can soon, hopefully, be blended together via the computer in order to examine the whole of the marketing problem. It will take time and money but it must be done if we are to succeed in the marketplace.

Our sophisticated clients are working along similar lines. They are facing up to the problems attendant with the timing of their introductions, they're looking at pay-out levels, the awesome effect of automated distribution, they're developing a strong product advantage

allied to their copy appeal; they're trying to find out what the public wants and they're trying to give it to them. They're conducting sound media research like protem client Harold Hoffman is doing.

TOGETHERNESS IN FUTURE

They and we are more and more into the facts and data of Nielsen Sales Information, of SpeeDATA's Warehouse Withdrawal Material, of BRI and Simmons Product Uses Data, of sales forecasting and proposal preparation, of distribution and logistics studies, of PERT techniques and production control, of more and more information. With it all, we can *together* plan for the years ahead.

The seat-of-the-pants advertiser, on the other hand, the let's-not-monkey-with-the-computer marketing "expert," the play-it-by-ear man, the let's-reach-all-those-18-to-55, making-over-$5,000-a-year media mogul, the I-can-get-it-for-you-wholesale, image oriented entrepreneur, maybe, will be able to make it for the next couple of years. But his years are numbered. They're dwindling down to an unprecious few.

My advice today is simple to say, but admittedly complicated to accomplish. We must embrace the new tools of the trade, not toss them aside after a quick perusal. And we should blend those tools in with the information explosion in order to paint and comprehend the fuller mosaic of tomorrow's marketing world. Not retreat to the early toys that we feel more comfortable with. We're adults in a mature marketing world, not three-year-olds, in the land of make-believe.

Someone once said, "Get the facts, all the facts, or the facts will get you." If you're an advertising man or a marketing man, it's a phrase to ponder,

whether you're dealing with media, or
advertising, or marketing, or the whole
American industrial system. So ponder.

DISCUSSION QUESTIONS

---

1. Evaluate CPM (cost per thousand) as
a means for choosing an advertising
medium.

2. Maneloveg states: "Today the average
consumer is witness to up to 1,200 advertising messages a day." Evaluate
this statement.

VII-6

KEY ARTICLES IN ADVERTISING RESEARCH

Neil Holbert

Jacob Burkhardt says in *The Civilization of the Renaissance in Italy* that, "When the body of St. Luke was brought from Bosnia (to Venice), a dispute arose with the Benedictines of Santa Giustina at Padua, who claimed that they already possessed it, and the Pope had to decide between the two parties."

Advertising research is a little like that.

Everyone claims to have the body, and --in a quest for maintaining reputations and/or profits--we revile others whose bodies seem not so undefiled as ours. And we spew forth a lot of occult talk, often times ignoring the fact that many useful papers have been published. Such papers are lost sight of again and again in a welter of tradition, stubbornness, and obfuscation.

This paper is an attempt to call up some useful contributions to the periodical literature since 1960. It is limited to four Journals: *Journal of Advertising Research, Journal of Marketing, Journal of Marketing Research,* and *Public Opinion Quarterly*. Even in that list, a favorite piece has probably been overlooked or perhaps misinterpreted--and other pieces in other books may have been strikingly neglected.

A total of 40 articles (almost all with useful bibliographies of their own) were selected. They are discussed under headings which seem to follow customary thinking about advertising research.

ATTITUDE MEASURES

The advocates of attitude-shift as a measure of the effectiveness of advertising suggest, explicitly or implicitly, that it is important because it can presage behavior, or, rather, behavior-shift in favor of the product to which attitude has shifted.

The writer found little in the way of predictive validity to prove this and little on the discriminatory power of the single-exposure attitude-shift measure. Disinterested contributions to the literature along these lines would be welcome.

The key issue in the attitude area, perhaps somewhat simplified, seems to be: Is attitude or attitude-shift--as a presager of behavior (buying)--a useful measure of the effectiveness of advertising?

As noted already, it appears that the key issue should be predictive validity: take a group who were "moved" and another not "moved" and see what their subsequent behavior are. Clearly, there are procedural difficulties, such as contamination and matching. Yet until a major work comes forth, one can remain open-minded about the apotheosis of attitude shift.

In the literature, Axelrod (1968), in an important study, tested ten intermediate criteria between exposure and behavior. These included both attitude and recall measures. The attitude measures were: a lottery question; +5 to -5 scale; predisposition-to-buy scale; constant sum scale; paired comparison; forced switching; first and second choice if buy now; and a buying game.

The recall measures were unaided recall and awareness.

Axelrod subjected each measure to tests of sensitivity (discrimination), stability (reliability), and predictive power (predictive validity). One attitude measure and one recall measure proved the most effective.

"In those situations," Axelrod noted, "where the interest is in prediction of short-term trends in purchase behavior, first brand awareness is the best measure to date.... With a brand that has a substantial share of market and the problem...one of holding customers rather than gaining new customers...the constant sum scale would be considered best.... It is quite possible to use both...(scales)...in the same interview. The first brand awareness can be asked followed by the constant sum scale, using the brands mentioned by the consumer."

For its rigor and expansiveness, the article merits the reader's careful attention.

Assael and Day, in an article not specifically on advertising testing, have offered useful insights by a well-disciplined effort to assay the usefulness of attitudes over time and awareness over time to predict sales over time. The implications for copy testing are clear.

The authors suggest that (1) results vary by product class; (2) attitude and awareness--more so attitude than awareness--do seem to predict behavior, at least for "volatile market situations ...(in which)...brand switchers may be more quick to translate an attitudinal change to a behavioral change." The article is very technical, but, for its rigor, is worth study.

Next is a celebrated series of articles, rebuttals, and re-rebuttals by Buzzell (1964); Fothergill and Ehrenberg (1965A); Buzzell, Kolin, and Murphy (1965); Fothergill and Ehrenberg again (1965B); and Murphy and Buzzell (1965).

The brouhaha is about the Schwerin attitude shift measure to predict sales. The exchanges are partly ego-trip and partly angels-on-heads-of-pins, and they would be fun if not so opaque. Attacks are made on what was seemingly not really intended, among other things.

From them all, we may conclude at least that higher-scoring commercials do better than lower-scoring commercials (albeit not for the same brand) in terms of sales effectiveness. To look for ironclad rules correlating market shares to point-differences in results seems more futile than ever after reading the exchange.

The preceding articles all suggest that there is some relationship between attitudes and behavior.

Festinger (1964) does not begin with this premise. In his article, he wants to know "whether or not an attitude *change* brought about by exposure to a persuasive communication will be reflected

in a *change* in subsequent behavior."
This seems to be what we mean by pre-
post attitude shift.

Three studies (out of a very few available on this subject) are cited, and
none supports the contention, according
to Festinger. He concludes: "We have
essentially persuaded ourselves that
we can simply assume that there is, of
course, a relationship between attitude
change and subsequent behavior.... But
the few relevant studies certainly show
that this 'obvious' relationship probably does not exist...."

Festinger hypothesizes that "in order
to produce a stable behavior change
following opinion change, an environmental change must also be produced
which, representing reality, will support the new opinion and the new behavior. Otherwise, the same factors
that produced the initial opinion and
the behavior will continue to operate
to nullify the effect of the opinion
change." This might suggest such things
as sampling, couponing, and other involving actions at the time of a campaign really designed to shift attitude.

Krugman (1965), in his famous article,
suggests that commercials--as part of
a class of trivial communications which
attempt to engage the viewer--do not
necessarily change attitudes that then
result in behavior modification.

Rather, comprehension may ultimately
alter the structure of parts of the
attitude-mix, bringing certain different
ones to the fore. Ultimately, "the
purchase situation is the catalyst that
reassembles or brings out all the potentials for shift in salience that have
accumulated up to that point. The product or package is then suddenly seen
in a new, 'somewhat different' light
although nothing verbalizable may have
changed *up to that point.*"

Summing up, Krugman suggests, in considering low-involvement communications
like television that "one might look

for gradual shifts in perceptual structure, aided by repetition, activated by
behavioral-choice situations, and *followed* at some time by attitude change."

Again, one may wonder if sampling, couponing, in-store displays, etc., are
not necessary to really translate attitude modification, in a situation of
low interest, into reasonably stable
subsequent behavior modification.

Crespi (1971) takes a middle ground by
stating that attitude shift can presage
behavior shift, but in limited circumstances.

He believes that measures of cognition
and behavioral intentions must be included in any useful measure of attitude
shift, not merely general predispositions.

Writes Crespi, "By measuring specific
dimensions of attitudes with respect
to a specific point in time among persons with a high likelihood of having
to make a behavioral decision, it becomes possible to obtain moderate to
high correlations" between attitude and
behavior.

It works, he suggests, in situations
where the "behavior under investigation
is either highly institutionalized or
routinized. Voting, movie attendance,
and food buying (used to illustrate the
points in the article) are types of
behavior that occur in structured situations characterized by well-defined role
expectations."

On the face of it, this finding seems
to differ from Assael and Day's finding
that brands in flux appear to produce
the closest congruence between attitude
shift and behavior shift.

Rokeach feels that when attitude shift
and behavior shift produce incongruen-
cies, it is because they are not stringent enough in measures of the former.
For Rokeach, change in attitude (as opposed to merely expressed opinion) must
encompass attitude towards *situation* as

well as *object*.

This suggests more extensive testing
than just preexposed-post, including;
(1) repeated posts in different situations to assay longer-term effects;
(2) several opinions to see if relationships are consistent with each
other pre and post, suggesting underlying stability for the change;
(3) tests for behavioral change accompanying change of opinion.

When attitude shift is investigated as
a relevant measure, the author suggests
that we not only talk about things in
the abstract, but also in a given situation. Some empirical work is presented.

This is not an easy article, but, unlike
some critics' views of Wagner's music,
it is probably better than it sounds.

Greene and Stock (1966) describe an ex-
posed-unexposed test of reactions to
the brand after running (withholding)
ads. The article's emphasis on the
product and not the ad (after the diag-
nostic stage), makes it well worth
reading.

In the area of attitude measures, one
nets out from readings such as the above
that, unsurprisingly, research suggests
that more research is needed. There
is neither the certainty that attitude
shift does all that its proponents
claim for it, nor that it lacks any
virtue, as its detractors believe.

In what situations does it work best,
poorly? What about single exposure vs
multiple exposure? More studies with
measures of predictive validity? What
types of specific behavior measures
(and their importance seems indicated)
should be asked in ascertaining attitude shift measures that will best relate to future real-world behavior?
These are the unanswered attitude questions for the Seventies.

RECALL

There is a strong recall school in advertising testing and also a strong
anti-recall school. The former say that
if people don't remember the ad or commercial, it can't have done anything for
the advertiser. The latter say that
people don't have to remember to be
moved, that you aren't necessarily moved
if you do remember.

The literature provides interesting
reading on these and similar views.

Stapel (1971) nets out that recall stimulates intent-to-buy and that intent-to-
buy is a valid predictor of sales. Empirical evidence is offered.

Beyond Stapel, in the literature surveyed, evidence that recall is associated
with behavior was not observed in terms
of predictive validity.

One milestone article in the area of recall, recommended without reservation,
is a well-documented effort by Haskins
(1964). After reviewing 28 advertising
and non-advertising studies, he concludes
that while "learning-type" responses
("what-it-means-to-me") seem to bear
somewhat on behavior, "teaching-type"
responses ("the-things-I-remember-are")
do not particularly do so.

The facts stubbornly suggest to Haskins
that meaning can be transmitted without
conscious learning, that meaning can be
transmitted without conscious recall,
that recall can take place without the
transmission of knowledge, that meaning
can come about very incidentally and not
fronta-ly at all, and other testable
hypotheses too numerous to cite here.

They also suggest to Haskins that engagement and irrationality and suggestion may be more vital than "facts"
for many products (old, established,
parity) and that the communication is
far from the decision-making area, such
as the point-of-purchase.

Concludes Haskins: "Learning and recall of factual information from mass
communications does occur. However,
recall and retention measures seem, at
best, irrelevant to the ultimate effects desired, the changing of attitudes and behavior.... Why have communicators been so resolute in presenting facts, and why have researchers
been so persistent in measuring factual
recall? One reason is that it's so
easy to do: it's easy to write a factual ad and it's easy to measure recall of facts. Another: the primary
emphasis in our education system has
been to implant facts, through rote
memorization, and so on, rather than
to teach students to think, reason,
and relate. As the products of that
system, we consciously or unconsciously build that approach into our efforts
at mass communication."

In line with the suggestion that "learning" rather than "teaching" is the really vital element in recall, two articles
by Leavitt (1968), and Leavitt, Waddell,
and Wells (1970), offer some useful insights.

Leavitt, basing his views on information
theory and calling his approach "structural analysis," suggests that recall
coding attempts to measure the number
of recall references that are "related."
By this he means a count of the number
of "inside" (within-the-commercial)
references that are "related" (connected to each other by verbs or pre-
positions). The key additional recall
question he suggests is "What went
through your mind?"

Leavitt's data show that this method
tends to correlate with standard recall
scores, while being more useful. Content validity for the concept is also
adduced.

Leavitt, Waddell, and Wells (1970) suggest another useful measure to determine
saliency of recall and integration of
the recall with personal needs, plans,
and life-style: the Personal Product

Response.

This is a reference to favorable personal behavior involving the product
outside the context of the commercial.
Note the authors: "The response must
refer clearly to the advertised product either by name or by description;
it must involve favorable personal ex-
periences--past, present, or future;
the first person singular or plural
must be used; the preceding three criteria must be contained in a single
statement or series of consecutive sen-
tences." Reliability and predictive
validity data for the notion are given.

Wells, Leavitt, and McConville (1971)
have also suggested that the relevance
of the commercial to the viewer is a
useful determinant of the effectiveness
of the commercial, and that it relates
to Personal Product Response. Again,
what is emphasized is the need for the
message to be consonant with the expectations of its audience, and the way
that audience sees things: "learning,"
not "teaching."

"Back in the days when copy research
was primitive," notes the article,
"researchers were allowed to ask consumers what they thought of the advertisement being tested. When copy research became precise and scientific,
this practice became illegal because
science is objective and consumers'
opinions are not." But the article
suggests, that unscientific bugaboo:
does the viewer "like" the commercial--
may indeed have some usefulness after
all.

USE OF RECALL

Maloney (1961) suggests that in portfolio tests, variability among the control ads should be noted to see whether
it is greater than the variability among
the test ads.

The author's evidence suggests that in portfolio tests, recall scores are largely functions of memory that, in turn, depend upon respondent's interest in and awareness of the products being advertised. He suggests that such recall scores are not valid if the variability among the control ads exceeds that of the test ads.

Barclay (1962) recommends, among other things, larger sample sizes in portfolio tests to combat the difficulties Maloney suggests, and a measure of interest/knowledge of the product as a cross-tab variable.

Along the same lines, Clancy and Kweskin (1971) suggest that those who like the program vehicle for on-air recall tests are more likely to give recall. This suggests that a rating of the degree of liking of the program might be used as a standard for on-air tests, and that the overall results perhaps be weighted to a standard on the percentages who express various degrees of liking. At least, similar liking groups should be analyzed from test to test.

DIAGNOSTICS

We speak a great deal about the communications value of advertising. In order to assay this, we usually make an effort to test for diagnostics, some probed-for components of the advertising. Such efforts usually include areas like clarity and credibility.

Maloney (1963) has written a major piece whose theme is that "no advertising is likely to be completely 'believable' when its purpose is to change people's minds. Moreover, an advertisement need not be believed completely to be effective." "Reminder" messages are easy to believe; messages meant to persuade less so. When persuasion is the goal,

curiosity ("Can it really do that?-- I'm not sure that..."), which may look like disbelief, may actually be a necessary first step towards eventual adoption of the advertised product, especially if something else must be displaced. But whatever, the advertising must be congruent with the frame of reference and repertory of experiences that the reader brings to the ad.

We have already discussed the notion that "learning" (comprehension) rather than "teaching" (recall) might receive more of our attention in advertising testing.

Grass, Winters, and Wallace (1971) offer us another useful concept in measuring effectiveness, the "message link" idea.

Objectives, as always, should be set as to what the advertising sets out do do. Three types of "message links" are cited: those of *primary importance*-- "the ad is not considered to be a success unless the link is learned by the reader;" *secondary importance*--"a message link that can be sacrificed, if necessary, in order that the primary links can be learned;" *tertiary importance*--"does not really matter whether the message link is learned or not." The need for clear *objectives* is obvious.

Finally, we may cite the useful piece by Abruzzini (1967) which summarizes many standard and probably too-seldom-used measures of the communications effectiveness of the advertising in terms of language difficulty.

FORMS AND TECHNIQUES

Notations abound about forms and techniques for advertising research. Some useful contributions are offered for examination and/or re-examination.

We use scales in advertising testing as

elsewhere in research. There are two well-researched studies worth noting, which attempt to get at familiar things: propensity-to-buy and attitude-shift.

Rothman (1964) included some predictive validity work in his study. He used four scales: *Self-rating*: definitely will buy, etc.; *Gift Method*: drawing, year's supply; *Guttman Scale*: positive response to one item predicts positive response to any lower item; *Distance*: respondent draws in own point on scale (Good.....Bad).

The mail follow-up offer showed the gift method to have the greatest relationship to the answer on propensity-to-buy (external validity).

"The gift scale method has the greatest likelihood of yielding satisfactory results for a variety of brands and products.... (The) self-rating method, because of its high correlation with the gift scale method, can still be applied satisfactorily in circumstances where a question offering the opportunity to win a free gift cannot be employed."

Hughes (1967) used the Thurstone, the semantic differential, and a check-list scale to measure attitude shift. The latter two were effective in detecting it; the former was not. Some useful and clever research-disguise techniques are contained in the article.

What we should test is an issue, too. If we wish to test for overall effective communication power, the experiment by Venkatesan and Haaland (1968) suggests that we should measure the grabbing power of the opening of the commercial.

Non-verbal techniques, like skin and eye measurements, are frequently offered as viable advertising methodology and frequently accepted or rejected out of hand.

In both Blackwell, Hensel, and Sternthal (1970) and Krugman (1964), pupil dila-

tion is held to probably measure emotional engagement, or at least awareness. But Blackwell, et al., conclude that it is not known exactly what it measures, while Krugman, with predictive validity evidence, indicates that pupil dilation is related to sales measures.

We clearly need more empirical evidence in the literature about the saliency of pupil dilation and eye-movement as measures of effectiveness.

Kohan (1968), writing on the galvanic skin response, offers good face validity for the technique (levels highest at moments of apparent dramatic peaks), but low correlation with verbal measures of interest. The need for predictive validity studies is indicated: which of these, the GSR or words, really seems to be more closely associated with meaningful action?

Three interesting and serious articles speak to specific technique questions often propounded. Brown and Gatty (1967) show that scores on rough commercials predict scores from finished commercials. Achenbaum, Haley, and Gatty (1967) report that in-home testing gives better reliability than on-air testing. And Wallerstein (1967), describing a long-term, split-cable experiment, suggests the merits of such an approach for campaign-length testing.

Finally, there is a useful, council-of-elders-type article, "What Big Agency Men Think of Copy Testing" (1965) that deals with forms and techniques, and is worth study for its breadth and authority.

Everything is offered to the titular subjects for evaluation: recognition, recall, attitude comprehension, believability, persuasion, buying predisposition, ad rating, and behavior. *Comprehension* seemed most important to test for in *any one ad* while attidue, behavior, and recall were also deemed valuable. For *campaigns*, recall was judged most important; awareness and attitude of use, but less so than recall. (There was an even split on whether sales results should or should not be used to measure campaigns.) *Natural exposure* was favored over forced. Incremental measures were favored over absolute (although one panelist wondered whether one viewing could really produce a useful increment measure. He said: "If a viewer's attitude really changed as much as the usual incremental measure indicates, he would be a mental basket case after watching an evening's worth of TV commercials.").

Opinions were about equally divided between 12/24 hour recall and more immediate recall.

The overall conclusion to the piece was that "among leading agency research directors there appears to be no universally accepted theory of how advertising works."

Moreover, the need for objectives was stressed as well as the ultimate need to eschew revelation for relevance and emotion for evidence: "There is a wide range of objectives for which different techniques are applied, and the value of a technique depends to some extent on the importance of the feature to which it is applied.

BROAD CONCEPTIONS AND BROAD VIEWS

Advertising research (unlike, say, name testing or store auditing) lends itself well to views about the world and society and about the whole great machine itself: advertising...the machine that may be conceived of as the usually great stoned interface between thee and me.

Six articles may be cited as offering some useful and serious broader-scaled views.

Bogart (1969) seems to be saying that advertising is too important to be left only to the advertiser, and advertising research too important to be left only to the advertising researcher. He questions the communicator's assumptions that only positive things are usually transmitted and that the symbolism behind advertising, for the product, the consumer, and for the entire social fabric are not as important as the simple message. Values, goals, and a lot of deep things are explored in this article which is less prescriptive than indicative, and less indicative than subjunctive.

Stewart (1968), Rohloff (1966), and Kelman (1961), in various ways, suggest theoretical underpinnings for our labors.

Stewart's contribution is concise and precise and should not be lightly passed over. "In an age where social experimentation with the institutional symbols of society seems to be the order of the day." he notes, "it will be of great interest to find out where the impetus will come to provide unfettered theoretical investigations into the problems of advertising evaluation or communication research. Such investigations will necessarily involve a critical re-examination of deeply entrenched psychological and philosophical points of view."

Rohloff raises further basic issues which are worth more thought than they are usually afforded. Among other things, Rohloff urges, in addition to standard data reporting, "structured relationships providing a framework for stating theories and concepts; constraints on the general applicability of structural relationships and associated theories and concepts; synthesis with other accepted relationships, theories and beliefs; specific applications in marketing planning."

In specific areas, he treats such things as the successful brand whose commercials never score well, and we wonder why. Maybe, he suggests, it is just a lot of exposure and enormously high pre-levels of decision. Previous studies are cited.

There are intriguing statements, too, about wearout. As the target audience becomes familiar with the commercials and the campaign, "incremental return will not usually rise greatly by sub-stituting a new commercial. With this audience, the advertiser can increase his incremental return per exposure by reducing the frequency of exposure. He can increase his overall return on his advertising investment by attempt-ing to reach another or broader audi-ence."

Kelman's article is of the sort frequent-ly seen in the pararesearch literature, and one that brings up a theme too often ignored. And this is simply--this mat-ter has been discussed above--that real change (and, no matter how we measure advertising, we all do want to move the beholder in some way) is not that easy to come by. He cites three levels of seeming change: compliance, identi-fication, internalization. The first is assent to achieve favorable reaction, as to an interviewer. The second in-volves a satisfying "role-relationship that forms a part of the person's self-image." In the third case, influence is accepted by one because the result is "congruent with his value system." Do we know what level we are getting, and how to measure each?

Barnett (1968) looks at advertising from the standpoint of objectives and notes that by the time advertising is created--at least for a new product--it should be able to be created from almost a blueprint of consumer wants, needs, and perceptions. Against this background, rational advertising test-ing for communication power seems sim-ple indeed.

Finally, Kassarjian and Nakanishi (1967) and their study of techniques of opinion

measurement. The reader may wonder why this is here, and not under the "Forms and Techniques" rubric. Indeed, here again many alternate scales are chosen for study: Likert, open-choice scales, limited-choice, order-of-merit, and paired comparison.

Much experimentation is done, and we read that "all methods...result in about the same order of preference.... The selection of a research method might best be determined by reasons other than concerns about intermethod differ-ences, the method in fashion or accept-able by clients and colleagues." So once again the one-right-technique-of-advertising-research school is shown to be chimerical.

ENVOI

The promise of the sciences for mar-keting and marketing research has prob-ably been oversold. With all the best of wills, rigid theoreticians preaching cold formalism seldom are able to make useful contributions to the mainstream of the efforts of the field.

Yet must we bow to revelation and super-stition and myth to guide us in research --especially advertising research? Rev-elation has its place in the world for many people, and researchers surely seek it in the process of generating ideas and brushing away the cobwebs of the mind. But how dangerous it is when it poses as hard fact.

We suggest that what we read tends to say that nothing in advertising research is as yet set in stone.

Attitude shift maybe, if we know what attitudes really are and which ones we are trying to shift and then tie it all to reality measures. Recall maybe, if we take it to involve a learning and not a teaching, and if there are signs that what is recalled has reduced the cognitive dissonance that would accompany a move from "theirs" to "ours." Diagnostics, of course, if we understand what we want to diagnose. Sales measures perhaps, and other measures of attack, both esoteric and exoteric, if founded on reason and not acronymic pitchmanship.

And above all, a need for objectives, to help keep the repetitive nature of advertising testing from degenerating into a mindless exercise in technique.

As Young (1972) has noted in a recent brilliant review of copy testing:

> No other type of research, whether product testing, package testing, penetration studies, or strategy research, suffers from the burden of having to provide uniform techniques and simplistic scores to determine a course of action.... If copy research is to cease being the "problem child" of research, the first step is to put it back into the family of market research by applying to it the same systematic definition of *objectives* and *criteria*.

We can get better work, I believe, by reading, thinking, getting involved early enough to effect modifications, shunning witchcraft, and sharing knowledge with our colleagues.

If that be classified as revelation, it is the only revelation I ask the reader to accept in his empiricist's search for better methods to test advertising.

REFERENCES

Abruzzini, Pompeo. Measuring Language Difficulty in Advertising Copy. *Journal of Marketing*, Vol. 31, No. 4, pp. 22-26.

Achenbaum, Alvin A., Russell I. Haley, and Ronald Gatty. On-Air vs In-Home Testing of TV Commercials. *Journal of Advertising Research*, Vol. 7, No. 4, pp. 15-19.

Adler, Lee, Allan Greenberg, and Darrell B. Lucas. What Big Agency Men Think of Copy Testing Methods. *Journal of Marketing Research*, Vol. 2, November 1965, pp. 339-345.

Assael, Henry and George S. Day. Attitudes and Awareness As Predictors of Market Share. *Journal of Advertising Research*, Vol. 8, No. 5, pp. 3-10.

Axelrod, Joel N. Attitude Measures that Predict Purchase. *Journal of Advertising Research*, Vol. 8, No. 1, pp. 3-17.

Barclay, William D. Why Aren't Portfolio Tests Here to Stay? *Journal of Marketing*, Vol. 26, No. 3, pp. 73-75.

Barnett, Norman L. Developing Effective Advertising for New Products. *Journal of Advertising Research*, Vol. 8, No. 4, pp. 13-18.

Blackwell, Roger D., James S. Hensel, and Brian Sternthal. Pupil Dilation: What Does It Measure? *Journal of Advertising Research*, Vol. 10, No. 4, pp. 15-18.

Bogart, Leo. Where Does Advertising Research Go from Here? *Journal of Advertising Research*, Vol. 9, No. 1, pp. 3-12.

Brown, Nigel A. and Ronald Gatty. Rough vs. Finished TV Commercials in Tilpex Tests. *Journal of Advertising Research*, Vol. 7, No. 4, pp. 21-24.

Buzzell, Robert D. Predicting Short-Term Changes in Market Share As a Function of Advertising Strategy. *Journal of Marketing Research*, Vol. 1, August 1964, pp. 27-31.

Buzzell, Robert D., Marshall Kolin, and Malcolm P. Murphy. Television Commercial Test Scores and Short-Term Changes in Market Shares. *Journal of Marketing Research*, Vol. 2, August 1965, pp. 307-313.

Clancy, Kevin J. and David M. Kweskin. TV Commercial Recall Correlates. *Journal of Advertising Research*, Vol. 11, No. 2, pp. 18-20.

Crespi, Irving. What Kinds of Attitude Measures Are Predictive of Behavior? *Public Opinion Quarterly*, Vol. 35, No. 3, pp. 327-334.

Festinger, Leon. Behavioral Support for Opinion. *Public Opinion Quarterly*, Vol. 28, No. 3, pp. 404-417.

Fothergill, J.E. and A.S.C. Ehrenberg. Concluding Comments on the Schwerin Analysis of Advertising Effectiveness. *Journal of Marketing Research*, Vol. 2, November 1965B, pp. 413-414.

Fothergill, J.E. and A.S.C. Ehrenberg. On the Schwerin Analysis of Advertising Effectiveness. *Journal of Marketing Research*, Vol. 2, August 1965A, pp. 298-306.

Grass, Robert C., Lewis C. Winters, and Wallace H. Wallace. A Behavioral Test of Print Advertising. *Journal of Advertising Research*, Vol. 11, No. 5, pp. 11-14.

Greene, Jerome D. and J. Stevens Stock. Brand Attitudes As Measures of Advertising Effects. *Journal of Advertising Research*, Vol. 6, No. 2, pp. 14-22.

Haskins, Jack B. Factual Recall As a Measure of Advertising Effectiveness. *Journal of Advertising Research*, Vol. 4, No. 1, pp. 2-8.

Hughes, G. David. Selecting Scales to Measure Attitude Change. *Journal of Marketing Research*, Vol. 4, February 1967, pp. 85-87.

Kassarjian, Harold and Masao Nakanishi. A Study of Selected Opinion Measurement Techniques. *Journal of Marketing Research*, Vol. 4, May 1967, pp. 148-153.

Kelman, Herbert C. Processes of Opinion Change. *Public Opinion Quarterly*, Vol. 25, No. 1, pp. 57-78.

Kohan, Xavier. A Physiological Measure of Commercial Effectiveness. *Journal of Advertising Research*, Vol. 8, No. 4, pp. 46-48.

Krugman, Herbert E. The Impact of Television Advertising: Learning Without Involvement. *Public Opinion Quarterly*, Vol. 29, No. 3, pp. 349-356.

Krugman, Herbert E. Some Applications of Pupil Measurement. *Journal of Marketing Research*, Vol. 1, November 1964, pp. 15-19.

Leavitt, Clark. Response Structure: A Determinant of Recall. *Journal of Advertising Research*, Vol. 8, No. 3, pp. 3-6.

Leavitt, Clark, Charles Waddell, and William Wells. Improving Day-After Recall Techniques. *Journal of Advertising Research*, Vol. 10, No. 3, pp. 13-17.

Maloney, John C. Is Advertising Believability Really Important? *Journal of Marketing*, Vol. 27, No. 4, pp. 1-8.

Maloney, John C. Portfolio Tests--Are They Here to Stay? *Journal of Marketing*, Vol. 25, No. 5, pp. 32-37.

Murphy, Malcolm P. and Robert D. Buzzell. A Further Clarification. *Journal of Marketing Research*, Vol. 2, November 1965, pp. 415-416.

Rohloff, Albert C. Quantitative Analyses of the Effectiveness of TV Commercials. *Journal of Marketing Research*, Vol. 3, August 1966, pp. 239-245.

Rokeach, Milton. Attitude Change and
Behavioral Change. *Public Opinion
Quarterly*, Vol. 30, No. 4, pp. 529-
550.

Rothman, James. Formulation of an
Index of Propensity to Buy. *Journal
of Marketing Research*, Vol. 1, May
1964, pp. 21-25.

Stapel, Jan. Sales Effects of Print
Ads. *Journal of Advertising Research*,
Vol. 11, No. 3, pp. 32-36.

Stewart, Daniel K. Some Theoretical
Considerations of Coherent Advertis-
ing Research. *Journal of Advertising
Research*, Vol. 8, No. 4, pp. 49-51.

Venkatesan, M. and Gordon Haaland.
Divided Attention and Television Com-
mercials: An Experimental Study.
Journal of Marketing Research, Vol. 5,
May 1968, pp. 203-205.

Wallerstein, Edward. Measuring Commercials on TV. *Journal of Advertising Research*, Vol. 7, No. 2, pp. 15-19.

Wells, William D., Clark Leavitt, and
Maureen McConville. A Reaction Profile
for TV Commercials. *Journal of Advertising Research*, Vol. 11, No. 6, pp.
11-15.

Young, Shirley. Copy Testing Without
Magic Numbers. *Journal of Advertising Research*, Vol. 12, No. 1, pp. 3-
12.

DISCUSSION QUESTION

1. The author refers to several articles
written on the subject of advertising
research. Can you find any similarity
among them?

PART VIII

THE FUTURE OF ADVERTISING

This last section of the book provides some opinions on how advertising will change in the future. *Kaiser News* and E.B. Weiss discuss the coming changes in communications (some of the changes are here already). Unwin tells us that advertising of services, instead of products, will be most important in the future; and Bogart outlines how technical advances in media, changing purchase patterns, and new life styles will profoundly change future advertising.

Two articles deal with television. First, Cawelti prognosticates about our "videoculture," and what continual simultaneous communications are likely to mean to our society. Scott gives a more technical analysis of the growth of cable television to date and its likely growth to 1980. He predicts a growth from CATV covering about 10 percent of the U.S. television audience in 1972 to between 25 and 38 percent in 1980.

Last, Paul Harper, Jr. outlines the agency business in 1980. His conclusion is that the agency business will undergo many changes, but will survive and grow in the eighties, but only those agencies will grow which have: (1) identified what they do *best* better than anyone else against a knowledge of client needs, and (2) submitted each of their present functions to the profit test.

None of these authors is "correct," of course, in the sense that everything they say will come true. They are, however, presenting their opinions based upon assumptions stated and unstated, and it is up to the reader to determine which of the predictions make sense and which are "pie in the sky."

From DIMENSIONS OF CHANGE, Don Fabun, 1971. Kaiser Aluminum & Chemical Corporation. Reprinted with permission of MacMillan Publishing Co., Inc.

VIII-1

CRYSTAL SET

Kaiser News

The research notes for this section, typed on 4 x 6 cards, are stacked in neat piles on a table. Each stack has a title card on top, identifying the subject covered in the cards below.

Let's scan the array and see if against this background, a figure emerges; for the discernment of a figure is the difference between message and noise.

The first thing that comes across is that there are fourteen stacks of cards under the loose title "Electronic," and only one stack under the title "Print." To one raised on printed matter, the message of the pattern is loud and clear. Books, magazines and newspapers, as we know them, are, as McLuhan has said, dead.

Another scan, at a different interference angle, produces another figure. Most of the subject titles on top of the stacks of cards are almost entirely new to the English language. They are composed of acronyms, capital letter abbreviations, and unusual associations of older words. They all represent fields of technology that did not exist prior to World War II; some of them entered the public domain only within the last few years. Below, in no particular order, are the subject titles:

Kinaesthetics
PBC-TV
Pay-TV; CATV
EVR
Laser; Sonar
Unifor Facsimile
Quadrasound
Synaesthetic Cinema

Holography
Magnetic Tape
  Cassettes
Microfiche
Plasma Crystals
Computer Graphics
Voice Recognition

Here, it appears, may be the shape of things to come. Indeed, already here. Communication is the basis on which all segments of a society--business, industry, education, government, religion-- are founded. For nearly all of their time on earth, humans have communicated by spoken or written words. That day is almost gone.

The "new" language is excited phosphors on an oscilloscope or TV screen; turned-on molecules of silver chloride on film; on-off magnetized molecules; displays of various sensory stimuli; coherent light beams; the pulsing of electrons in crystal lattices; the beat of unseen electromagnetic waves.

Someday, perhaps well before the year 2000, the description of "illiteracy" may be "the ability to read words." The Chinese, though they invented printing, have known this for more than 2,000 years. "A poster is worth ten thousand tracts." Artists, musicians, dancers and other practitioners of the lively art in all cultures have known this, too. The only humans who didn't were writers.

(Not that words on a page are not "pictures." Take a look at this page. The one right in front of you. It is a pattern made up of molecules of black against a background of white. The only way it differs from a photograph or painting is the degree of resolution. The degree of resolution is a projection of yourself. There simply is more "information" in a photograph than there is in printed words because the degree of resolution is at a finer level and, therefore, transmits more messages within the field of observation.)

The verbal world will rapidly disappear as a means of any but highly personal communication (as in "Pillow Talk") in a relatively short time. Even that will disappear with the development of telepathy (which will be discussed in the next section). The electronic non-verbal revolution might well be a sort of "half-way house," a transition, between verbalism and extra-sensory perception in all its modes.

All of the electronic and electromagnetic communications systems listed earlier already exist, although at different stages of development. The rather obvious task of the next three decades is to create a grand orchestration of those systems (and others still to be discovered) into an intermedia synthesis. It will be done because these systemic waves are mutually reinforcing. They may crest before the turn of the century into a wave of the magnitude of a cave painting, the invention of spoken language, and later of written and printed communication, sweeping all that we know before it and creating a world we can only dimly imagine now.

Let's play a game and see (out of the

infinite number of possible syntheses of varying degrees of probability) whether we can put a pattern of systems together. It will not be easy, but if one thinks of words as ideographs, and ideographs as cave paintings at a time when verbal language was but a grunt, then it may be possible.

It might be best, in a compartmentalized world, briefly to describe some of the systems available now. Then, as in a jigsaw puzzle, we can attempt to assemble the parts into some sort of pattern of things to come, as we may experience it in our lifetime.

We may begin very simply with an "either/or" experiential distinction between particles and waves. The distinction appears to be a verbal one and what is experienced quite possibly may be the same phenomenon observed with different interference waves in the scanning process. What does seem to matter is that humans can, technologically (and perhaps psychically) control the motion of particles and waves in time and space (to use four old-fashioned words now out of vogue). The continuum is maneuverable.

Once we begin to discern the systems of particles/waves, as we observe them in "nature" (possibly only a projection of our psychoneural arrays), then it becomes possible to control them technologocally. We can construct simulated systems, or build "models" of natural processes which we can then manipulate to create an environment or "surround" that appears to meet our needs at the time.

It should be observed that these developments were seldom the result of "tinkering" in the laboratory or workshop but were the projections of intuitive minds --Newton, Planck, Heisenberg, Bohr, Fermi and others. What is important is that the intuition was projected into the hands--quite literally--of the tinkerers who translated them into "things" or "processes" that humans could use.

And that is perhaps the highest form of communication we now have.

So, now we have all these new systems and processes and we will describe a few of them here. If we've left some out, it's simply a combination of being kind of dumb and short of space.

Where to start? Hard choice.

Say films, as we now know them. Photons striking molecules of silver chloride suspended in a film laminate, react in such a way as to give the human eye the impression of varying shades of darkness within the field being observed... Once it was found this process could be manipulated, we got Charlie Chaplin, and W.C. Fields, and Marilyn Monroe and--you name them. The recorded film, itself, was composed of frozen slices of time which, through sequential patterning, gave the illusion of motion and through repetition, reinforced images, which ultimately became the visual symbols on which our mythology is based.

KINAESTHETICS/SYNAESTHETIC CINEMA

These big words are just a way of saying that movies are better than ever. They are not necessarily better in content, but the technology is there.

Says Youngblood, who insinuates ubiquitously through these pages, "When we say expanded cinema we actually mean expanded consciousness... Expanded cinema isn't a movie at all; like life, it's a process of becoming, man's ongoing historical drive to manifest his consciousness outside of his mind, in front of his eyes. This is especially true in the case of the intermedia network of cinema and television, which now functions as nothing less than the nervous system of mankind."

Michael S. Laughlin (*Easy Rider*) says, "Films are to communicate, to say something. Our generation has gone beyond mere entertainment. We are too well educated, too intelligent to be just entertained. We want to be moved emotionally, intellectually and sensually." ("New Kind of Movie Shakes Hollywood," *Business Week*, January 3, 1970.)

Robert Kaufman, a screen writer, put it this way: "We are approaching today a kind of film journalism. We want to record, reflect, discuss the most immediate problems facing our culture. Our audiences insist that we make our reflections honestly and unflinchingly. The kids can see a copout a mile away."

And in seconds.

Youngblood flows again, "...through synaesthetic cinema man attempts to express a total phenomenon--his own consciousness.

"Synaesthetic cinema is the only aesthetic language suited to a post-industrial, post-literate, man-made environment with its multi-dimensional simulsensory network of information sources. It's the only aesthetic tool that even approaches the reality continuum of conscious existence in the nonuniform, nonlinear, nonconnected electronic atmosphere of the Paleocybernetic Age..."

So, now we have at least two voices crying in the cybernetic wilderness--McLuhan and Youngblood, or vice versa.

Youngblood ("Yes, sir! Here and countable." Okeh, sound off!) "It is quite clear that human communcation is trending toward these possibilities. If the visual subsystems exist doday, it's folly to assume that the computing hardware will not exist tomorrow. The notation of 'reality' will be utterly and finally obscured... We're entering a mythic age of electronic realities that exists only in the metaphysical plane."

Youngblood? Where are you? "Not here,

390

sir. On leave for another reality."
They call it "R&R!"

There is not only a new generation of
technological film-producing devices,
but also a whole new generation of
young film makers who are trying (and
often succeeding) to make film a communication medium instead of an entertainment box office medium.

As Peter Fonda has said (in "The New
Communicators," TV Special, April 14,
1970), "The new communicators are every-
where--in grammar schools, high schools,
colleges, film institutes, and in what
is often referred to as the underground.

"These new film makers are making personal statements about themselves and
about the world around them. And in
most cases, they're doing it with very
little money and with very little equipment.

"But what they lack in money, they make
up with ingenuity."

Said Francois Truffaut about his recent
film, *L'Enfant Sauvage*, "I simply wanted
to make a film in praise of communication between people--in praise of the
unspoken language. It is my answer to
all those films about noncommunication
that keep filling our cinemas."

A replay of the Hallelujah Chorus would
be most appropriate here.

E.V.R.

The Acronym stands for Electronic
Video Recording. It simply means that
images (and sound) can be impregnated
on a reel of magnetic tape, and then
played back through a home television
set. This is the audiovisual counterpart of paperback books. It may very
well completely destroy television as
we know it now. Commercial TV, CATV

and Pay-TV may join the nickelodeon and
the player piano in some honky-tonk joint
where a girl with a painted face gives
an ersatz smile, and makes change of
dubious value for a quickie-look at "What
it used to be like."

A number of highly placed manufacturers
are working on EVR--CBS, Sony, Motorola,
Westinghouse, Phillips (in England) and
Nordemande (in Germany), and perhaps
many others. Although most of the systems are based on the same concept (i.e.,
the EVT is a briefcase sized-unit with
wires that clamp onto the antenna terminals of standard TV sets), they are
not yet "compatible" so that cartridges
from one manufacturer will not fit some
other manufacturer's system, but no
doubt something will be worked out.

Meanwhile, it does appear that EVT systems will be mass-produced and marketed
worldwide shortly. The systems are in
sound and color and the image can be
stopped, replayed for discussion or
review as needed. It also can be erased,
at your friendly neighborhood EVT shop,
and something else put on it. As someone has said, "it's like a returnable
milk bottle." TV conversion costs are
low, and the cartridges ultimately will
cost no more than LP records do today.

Because of the initial high cost, EVR
systems will probably be used mostly by
business and government; for providing
sight-and-sound reports, recording personnel interviews, for training programs,
and to present a new product, service,
or political candidate. As the price
drops, EVR's will move into the educational systems (perhaps making teachers
and instructors unnecessary) and then
into private homes.

The recording of books, periodicals,
plays, opera, ballet and sports already
existing will create an enormous industry. The introduction of new material,
specially designed for EVR, will be even
more enormous.

In the comfort and privacy of one's own

home, through EVR, one may enjoy the visual and audial panorama of the world, selecting his own experience as one does in a book from a library shelf.

It will be a different world--and very, very soon.

LASER

Light Amplification (by) Stimulated Emission (of) Radiation. This is the acronym used for "coherent light," i.e., it does not scatter from the source. Or, as the *American Heritage Dictionary* defines it, "Any of several devices that convert incident electromagnetic frequencies to one or more discrete frequencies of highly amplified and coherent visible radiation." Got it?

Next to nuclear power, the laser is probably the most significant technological "breakthrough" of our century. Its capacity of information carrying is enormous, compared to any systems now in use.

"One of these days," says *The German Tribune*, Nov. 7, 1970, "the entire flow of information of a large office block may pass spontaneously through a single thread of glass fiber thinner then a human hair.

"The carrier will be a laser ray capable of transporting telephone calls, teleprinter messages, data and TV programs, yet will follow every turn made by the 0.05 cable. (The message) is trapped in the core of the glass fiber by the laws of refraction."

Up until recently, laser was considered a "line of sight" phenomenon, which greatly limited its use for everyday terrestrial communication. (Real good for satellite and interplanetary communication, though). Now this new development, by AEG-Telefunken and ex-

pected to be operational within a few years, changes the whole ball game.

The consequences of this advance are almost incomprehensible to us now. It's like the invention of the wheel.

One stumbles from laser to holography.

HOLOGRAPHY

——— (from the Greek holos--whole, entire). It may be defined as "the technique of producing images by wavefront reconstruction, especially by using lasers to record on a photographic plate the diffraction pattern from which a three-dimensional image can be projected." (Or, at least that's the way it is described in "Seeing by Radio Waves...the Promise of Radio Frequency Holography," *Mitre Matrix*, March-April, 1969)

"A hologram, whether produced by light or radio waves--is basically an elaborate record of the pattern of interference created by the intersection of two beams of radiated energy." (Interlude: what happens if three--or more--beams intersect?) Back to *Mitre Matrix*. "The entire picture is contained on a sheet an eighth-of-an-inch thick...and every part of a holographic picture is always in focus, no matter how far the subject was from the film."

The extraordinary thing about a hologram is that the entire picture can be reproduced from any part of the film, and, when projected (by laser) it is fully three-dimensional.

According to Richard Kahlenberg and Chloe Aaron ("The Cartridges are Coming," *Cinema Journal*, Spring, 1970), "'Selectavision,'" RCA's answer to EVR, is a holographic, rather than a photographic system. Original images in color, are converted into embossed holograms from which a master can be made that presses the copies onto vinyl--a material as cheap as paper and similar to the plastic used to wrap meat in supermarkets. Playback requires that the beam from a low-powered laser pass through the vinyl strip into a simple TV camera. The playback mechanism, the laser and the TV camera are all housed in the player (about the size of the CBS EVT machine) which is wired to the antenna terminals of a standard color or black-and-white TV set."

The prospects are almost beyond our ken. ("Dear Ken: How are you? I am fine.")

Home entertainment in full glorious sound, color and available dimensions is certainly going to change things around the old home scatter. The moppets will never leave the living room floor, mama will never get any meals fixed, and daddy won't go to work at all. They'll be caught and transfixed in the amber of an electronic experience; trapped in the waves.

"Eventually," says John Tebbel ("TV and the Arts," *Saturday Review*, April 26, 1969), "an entire library may be carried on a holographic crystal the size of a matchbox, or a thick volume on one no bigger than an aspirin."

Through the use of laser it should be possible to transmit "matter," in the sense that 3-D information can be sent from one place and assembled at another from the molecules available there. Patent applications for this have been filed in a number of countries, and the process has been demonstrated on a laboratory scale in Europe. Not, alas in the U.S. Intersecting laser beams, inside a plastic block, recreate the transmitted object. It may mean, not too long from now, that furniture need not be manufactured in Grand Rapids but only be transmitted from there. The computers will take over, send the instructions by laser through optical fibers (or bounce them off a communications satellite) and the physical object recreated wherever there is a market for it. "Dial-a-chair," or any other physical object may become the new life style. Most of the technology is already here.

PLASMA/LIQUID CRYSTALS

There's a new boy on the communication block; he may change the whole neighborhood.

Technicians call it liquid crystal; a fluid that behaves as a liquid in almost every way, yet has a molecular structure similar to a crystal. There are several kinds of liquid crystals, and some of them have the ability to receive, store (and when scanned) transmit photoelectric images.

The image can be implanted in the liquid crystal by a direct current and erased by an alternating current. Meantime, the image can be stored as long as needed.

According the Hughes Aircraft Company, "When energized, crystal images appear almost instantaneously and they can be short-lived or long-lived; they can be stored indefinitely or stored temporarily or left to decay (become transparent) normally, or they can be erased immediately, only to be recalled at a later time.

"The liquid crystal itself is about a thousandth-of-an-inch think and is sandwiched between two glass plates, held there by capillary action... The substance is clear until photoactivation is used to initiate sufficient current in it to produce the light-scattering phenomena, or mode, which agitates the molecules and causes certain sections to become opaque. By controlling the shape and size of the areas in agitation, the opaque areas can be formed as desired." (*Vectors*, Summer, 1970.)

How can they be used? Well, obviously, for information storage and retrieval in the scientific and business worlds, where they may outperform most electronic computers. For home use?

"The plasma crystal panel," (says Youngblood), "makes possible billboard or wall-sized TV sets that could be viewed in bright sunlight. The Japanese firms of Mitsubishi and Matsushita (Panasonic) seem to be leaders in the field, each having produced workable models."

The communication future is as clear as a crystal.

COMPUTER GRAPHICS

These are visual arrays or displays produced by computers from programmed instructions. This may well be one of the most exciting art-forms of the future, and artists will abandon canvas and easel in order to sit before an electronic console, projecting their dreams, much as a musician or composer works out his music by manipulating a piano keyboard.

"In 1963," (says San VanDerBeek, "New Talent--the Computer," *Art in America*, Jan.-Feb., 1970), "computers began to develop possibilities for making graphics. An electric microfilm was introduced; it can plot points and draw lines a million times faster than a human draftsman. This machine and the electronic computer which controls it thus make feasible various kinds of graphic movies which heretofore would have been prohibitively intricate, time-consuming and expensive.

"The machine can compose complicated pictures or series of pictures from a large number of basic elements; it can draw ten thousand to one hundred thousand points, lines or characters per second...

"The image revolution that movies represented has now been overhauled by the television revolution, and is approaching the next visual stage--to computer graphics to computer controls of environment to a new cybernetic 'movie art,'"

What is exciting here is that computers, which usually have been used to run off payrolls or to construct simulation models of future expectancies, have now emerged as a new medium for the visual arts.

Youngblood says, "The computer amplifies man's intelligence in about the same ratio that the telescope extends his vision. The man/computer symbiosis is developed to the point where the machine instructs its user and indicates possibilities for even closer interaction. One needn't read the manual but may consult the machine directly with the order, 'I want to do somethin; instruct me.' It is not even necessary to be in the presence of the computer to do this. One can carry out one's work thousands of miles away, linked to the computer through remote viewing and operating consoles."

John Whitney, Jr., who has worked on computer graphics for thirty years and produced the magnificent film *Permutations*, which is now widely used on television, has this to say: "we don't know how to integrate realist and nonobjective images yet. But I think our computerized optical printer will help show the way. The use of the realist image is just a basis, a starting point. Working with optical scanning you transform the images, and this seems to be a key to bringing nonobjective and realist imagery together. And why bring them together? Because it may lead to new insights and new experience."

Back to Youngblood. "The computer does not make man obsolete. It makes him fail-safe. The computer does not replace man. It liberates him from specialization. The transition from a culture that considers leisure a 'problem' to a culture that demands leisure as a prerequisite of civilized behavior is a metamorphosis of the first magnitude. And it has begun. The computer is the arbiter of a radical evolution; it changes the meaning of life. It makes us children. We must learn how to live all over again."

———   ———   ———

Due to a natural disinclination to work and a shortage of space, we cannot go into a description of microfiche, voice profiling, Unifor facsimile, CATV, nor a number of other electronic techniques that are already here.

Now we turn, in all too short a compass (ever seen a short compass? Probably imported by some Lilliputian Columbus) to electrostatic printing and the outlook for the printed media.

ELECTROSTATIC PRINTING

The printed word is not dead; he's just pinned to the floor by 300 years of tradition. But he'll get up and go to his corner, and come out fighting against radio and television. And in a very few years. Dr. Herbert Krugman, a General Electric scientist has said, "Print is something you *do*, television represents something done *to* you."

"Now we learn--rather flatteringly I think," says Dick Nolan (*San Francisco Examiner*, Nov. 1, 1970), "that when you read this you are awake, but if I were to sing you the same song on color television, gorgeous as I am, you would be essentially asleep.

"Print clearly involves use of the headbone and brain, the exercise of which is necessary if the culture is to survive. Television, dreamily and drearily flashing its message, turns the brain to cabbage."

The printed word is a participative ideograph. In order for it to have any meaning at all, the reader must make some sort of personal effort to communicate with it. Television and film are, on the contrary, explicit; short of moving the eyeballs they require virtually nothing of the observer. The same appears to be true of radio. Keeping one's ears unplugged is about all that is required. And keeping a closed mind.

So, print media may be around for a long time to come. But the expensive, archaic, utterly inefficient method by which print is now produced will end.

Speaking of typesetting by electronic beam, Gerard O. Walter ("Typesetting," *Scientific American*, May, 1969) says, "In the days of setting type by hand, highly skilled compositors achieved remarkable speeds as high as one character per second; mechanical typesetters built since the turn of the century cast about five characters per second. Nowadays photographic typesetting machines that select the characters mechanically are capable of setting as many as 500 characters per second. In contrast, the new electronic method can produce up to 10,000 characters per second... Electronic typesetting will undoubtedly foster a considerable increase in the demand for and volume of printed material, since it reduces the cost of printing and speeds up the output...news can become available in print almost as quickly as the bulletins on radio or television."

Along the same line, Lawrence Lessing ("The Printed Word Goes Electronic," *Fortune*, Sept. 1969) says, "Around the year 1450, Johann Gutenberg spent about five years casting and composing the movable type for his historic Bible, and three years printing some two hundred copies of it... Today, through use of a radically new kind of computerized machine, the entire Bible can be set in type and composed into pages electronically in 77 minutes flat.

"... researchers are working on various methods of introducing roll film into the cathode-ray tube for direct exposure by its electron beam to get top speeds up to 60,000 characters or more per second... Before words and pictures can be carried by electronic impulses straight through from computer to printed page, some entirely different printing system must be adopted, a system compatible with the electronic generation of type and images. The likeliest prospect, most investigators agree, is some form of electrostatic printing...a process in which dry or fluidized pigment particles...place an image on paper, not by impact or pressure but by electrical attraction."

While it is quite possible that mass printed periodicals as we now know them will disappear, electronic printing systems may make possible the proliferation of many smaller circulation periodicals aimed at specific audiences, thus greatly broadening the spectrum of choice in printed material.

Recipe for the communications future:

1	cup	LASER
2	cups	EVR
1	tbsp.	HOLOGRAPHY
1/2	cup	Liquid Crystals
2	tsps.	Microfiche
1/3	cup	Electrostatic Printing

Mix liberally with computers, COMSAT, advances in communication theory and systems analysis, to taste. Put in a nuclear oven until done.
Result: Global Mind. But make sure it doesn't come out half-baked.

Eye, there's the rub. For in that sleep, what dreams may come? For the same mortals who control mass media today, may very well control them tomorrow, and tomorrow, and will creep in their petty pace from day to day.

Oh, what fuels these mortals be!

DISCUSSION QUESTION

1. In your judgment, what will be the effects of the communications advances discussed in "Crystal Set" on advertising? Discuss in detail.

Reprinted by permission from ADVERTISING AGE; 19 March, 1973, pp. 51-2, 54, 56.

VIII-2

ADVERTISING NEARS A BIG SPEED-UP IN COMMUNICATIONS INNOVATION

E. B. Weiss

The explosion of mass communication through the printed word started with Gutenberg about 1450, more than 500 years ago.

About 60 years ago, David Sarnoff brought Marconi's wireless to world attention when he radioed the news of the Lusitania's sinking. That episode ushered in the era of electronic communication.

Between 1960 and 1972, a 12-year span, mass communication technology innovated on a vastly more dynamic scale than over the preceding 500 years since Gutenberg first used movable type, and over the preceding 60 years of electronic communication.

Between 1973 and 1977, a four-year span, satellite communication will change society more significantly worldwide than all of the remarkable advances in electronic communication between 1960 and 1972. (I will get to the details later in this piece.)

INNOVATIONS WILL COME IN YEARS, NOT DECADES

Yet between 1977 and 1980 the pace of communication innovation will show *still faster* acceleration--and will involve still more sophisticated technology. For example, late in 1972, a technological breakthrough in communication was announced that actually may rival the satellite in its ultimate impact on society--and therefore on advertising. It offers a fascinating (and almost terrifying) insight into the dimensions and speed of the innovations in communications with which advertising will have to contend year by year.

That communication breakthrough was reported in the *New York Times* last Nov. 25: "A microfilming method that can record 625 book-size pages on a single sheet of film no larger than one of those pages has been invented. They can be displayed, one page at a time, in a portable viewing device no larger than a book.

"It is believed the viewer can be made in plastic for as little as $5, and that a film sheet, representing an entire book, can be copied from a master sheet for about 25¢.

397

NEW SYSTEM CHEAP ENOUGH FOR GENERAL USE

"The system was demonstrated recently at the National Science Foundation to a group of high officials and information specialists from various government departments. The acting director of the Office of Science Information Services at NSF said that the system presented a chance for the United States to offer the world a new communication technology with the capability of disseminating knowledge that is 'cheap enough for almost any human being.'

"It might replace or greatly supplement paperback books, eliminate 'central files' in large bureaucracies, and bring the costliest textbooks to any student at nominal cost."

If that were the only communication breakthrough that might logically be expected over the next five to seven years (in addition to the satellite, the audio-visual cartridge, hotel-motel movies, cable TV, etc.), it would still suggest that advertising faces change of extra-ordinary dimensions, since advertising is communication. But the blunt probability is that, by 1980, *several* communication breakthroughs of equal dimensions may become ready for commercial exploitation. Laser communication technology could be one.

MORE SIGNIFICANT THAN RADIO AND TV

That is now advertising's future: One communication breakthrough after another. The kinds of innovations in advertising necessitated by radio and television over several decades will now occur over several *years*--not decades.

Further:
1. Several may be introduced practical-

ly simultaneously.
2. Each will be of more monumental significance to advertising than radio-television combined.

For these (and so many other predictions) I am entirely willing to be labeled a crackpot visionary by those who govern the American Assn. of Advertising Agencies and the Assn. of National Advertisers. Yet ANA and Four A's members have been reading my writings for years. I estimate that over 50% of these members have written me for additional copies of my AA columns and studies.

I have been invited to talk before almost every consumer industry association represented by ANA members. I have even been invited to address the U.S. Chamber of Commerce and the National Assn. of Manufacturers. How much more conservative is it possible to become?

Society is molded by communication-- yet those who govern the Four A's and the ANA are not leading their members into the new era of communication. Instead, they are fighting consumerism and corporate social responsibility-- both exercises in futility. Perhaps this is why *Ad Age* reported that the ANA meeting in Puerto Rico in late 1972 was considered dull by many who attended.

Gutenberg changed society perhaps to the same degree as the great religious leaders. So did Marconi. And now scientists and technologists are reshaping world society, probably in similar degree, through revolutionary communication innovations.

Since society, communication and advertising are indivisible, advertising will be profoundly restructured by the amazing new communication technology and the new society it will create.

It is difficult to believe that television was an infant only 25 years ago, and that color television really began to grow only about ten years ago. Similarly, it is difficult to comprehend the totality of the coming impact of the fantastic new information-communication technology on both traditional and new media used for advertising--*and on the message itself.*

EVEN BIGGER THINGS LIE AHEAD

This would be true even if the new communication technology were close to maturity. But information-communication technology is still in its infancy. What science knows in 1973 about information-communication is merely threshold knowledge. Vastly more awesome developments lie immediately ahead.

This is not a remote probability. It is a near certainty. And by near, I refer to 1973-1977 and 1977-1980. In a mere four to seven years, advertising's public, as well as the media for reaching that public, will have been restructured to an unmatched degree.

I predicted precisely this in a study in 1966--seven years ago--entitled: "The Communications Revolution and How It Will Affect All Business and All Marketing." Much of what I forecast then is no longer prediction; it is already present or near reality.

I pointed out then that, under the new communication technology, there will no longer be any technological distinction in communication between the various forms of communication. Voice or picture, wire, electronic broadcast or print--each will pass through identical electronic pulses and will then be converted into any desired form.

News, information, entertainment will pass through a single integrated system that will combine all of the separate means of communication today. That includes not only television, audio-visual cassette, radio, stereo, holography,

microfilm, telephone, laser, computer and satellite; it also includes newspapers, magazines, business/industrial/professional publications, books, direct mail and catalogs.

The end result at times may be a familiar "printed" document, but the storage, retrieval, transmission and printing (instant facsimile) processes will be totally revolutionary in the home and in offices.

We face a wholly new era best described as an "audio-visual environment"--all traditional media will become adapted components of that new communication-information environment. Moreover, because of the satellite, we are now advancing with incredible speed toward global audiences, global enterprises, global markets--and therefore global marketing and advertising programs.

About seven years ago, in my communications study, I concluded: "communication is synonymous with information, and advertising is (or should be) information. Both create new social values and therefore new life patterns.

"Gutenberg's movable type did that, but it required centuries. Marconi's invention of wireless did that, but it required over half a century. The new communication technology will produce social change on a vastly larger scale --and in no more than 10 to 15 years."

CONSUMERISM, WOMEN'S LIB AND REVOLT

Well, seven of those "10 to 15" years have passed. The communications revolution of those seven years has brought about consumerism, corporate social responsibility, the youth revolt, the feminine revolt, the fashion revolt, the era of individual judgment, a new society-- and the death of the *Saturday Evening Post, Look* and now *Life.*

Seven years ago in my communication study I (very daringly) predicted; "Through communication satellites and other remarkable communications breakthroughs, it will be possible to communicate with anyone, anywhere, at any time, by voice, sight or written message--instantaneously.

"Moreover, all communications will be instantly recorded--instantaneously retrievable--and instantly reproducible.

"Hundreds of millions of individuals will be in full sight and sound of one another. Ultimately, individuals equipped with miniature TV transmitter-receivers will communicate directly with one another worldwide, using personal channels similar to today's personal telephone--and just as simply.

"Overseas mail will be transmitted through facsimile reproduction via satellites. Satellite television could mean that several hundred million viewers may be watching the same program aided by instantaneous language translation."

Only four years later, about one-sixth of the human race saw or heard the first astronauts land on the moon! Perhaps one-third of the human race saw or heard the Apollo 17 flight. In 1975, the exploration of Mars may be heard by 50% of all humans--through satellite communication.

SATELLITES WILL CHANGE EVERYTHING

Between 1972 and 1975, satellite communication will leap into use. That's because in June, 1972, the Federal Communications Commission set rules for the ownership and operation of communication satellites that will be in use by 1975, possibly earlier. (Canada put a communication satellite into successful operation late in 1972. It is

being used through special arrangement here in the States.)

Satellites have relatively large capacities; even the smallest proposed satellite can transmit simultaneously 12 television programs to as many on-ground stations as may want to pick them up. Moreover, transmitting a signal from New York to a distant point will cost the same as from Manhattan to Brooklyn. (Also, the satellite will finally push cable-television into high gear, because it will provide mass distribution capabilities.)

General Electric is even talking about using the satellite for comprehensive *internal* communication services, for video conferences and videophone use, for tying their computers together, for facsimile.

Communications Satellite Corp. (Comsat) has proposed a $248,000,000 satellite system designed to transmit television programs, telephone calls, computerized data, and a range of other communications. Each of the three satellites proposed by Comsat would have the capacity to handle 14,000 telephone circuits, or 24 color TV channels, or combinations of both. One part of this program includes a $100,000,000 satellite system jointly sponsored by AT&T and Comsat.

Last Jan. 4, Western Union won government approval for a $92,400,000 three-satellite system providing ten TV channels plus telegram, teletype, Telex, private line services, data and voice circuits. Negotiations started last January with the three television networks to carry their programs when Western Union's satellite system goes into operation about mid-1974 (it will be called Westar).

Hughes Aircraft Co. plans a $75,000,000 system with two satellites. One part would link together the company's large holdings of cable television systems. It would also carry the Hughes Sports

400

Network, specializing in sports broadcasts of all kinds. In addition, Hughes
has worked out a deal with General Telephone & Electronics, the nation's largest
independent phone system, to provide
channels for telephone, data transmission
and other services.

evitability has been proved by segmented
periodicals, segmented radio, segmented
marketing.) Narrowcasting suggests that
what we now call the era of individual
taste and judgment will soon become
still further fractionated.

HELP FOR EDUCATION AND SCIENCE

Other potential satellite competi-
tors include RCA Global Communications
Inc., Fairchild Industries, Western
Tele-Communications Inc. and the MCI
Lockheed Satellite Corp.

"Within this decade," predicts Comsat's
president, "electronic libraries in
one country could be instantly available to scholars in another. Newspapers,
magazines and books sent by facsimile
from central editorial offices could
be published in a dozen distant cities
simultaneously. School children in
developing nations will have available,
on command, the most advanced educational materials and techniques."

Already, doctors sitting in an amphi-
theater in Switzerland have watched
the famed Dr. Michael DeBakey perform
open-heart surgery in Houston, Tex.
They were able to ask him questions
and receive answers as the operation
proceeded. (Satellite communication
is unaffected by natural cosmic or
terrestrial disturbances.)

It is an extraordinary fact that, as
communication technology achieves a
global reach, it tends simultaneously
to make technologically feasible a
greater degree of control by the individual over the choice of messages he
will tune in. The new technology will
permit, and therefore actually create,
social conditions that will demand individual determination of message.

I call this "narrowcasting." (Its in-

NARROWCASTING TO PASS BROADCASTING

Narrowcasting is a term that will become even more common than broadcasting.
This is because communication will come
under the complete control and discretion of an increasingly sophisticated
user. (The audio cassette and the audio-
visual cassette are, of course, two
giant steps in this direction.) The
"on-off" knob will no longer constitute
the sole range of the public's options--
to the contrary, it will become a tertiary option.

I suggest that, for newspapers, the next
three to five years will not only bring
the first models of a newspaper instantly printed in the home or office, but
that the satellite, over the next five
to ten years, will bring an international
era of newspaper and periodical publishing. The multi-national newspaper is
inevitable--so are new variations of
multi-national magazines and multi-national direct mail. A more sophisticated
public will demand a new balance between
international news and national news.

The merger trend between publishing and
electronics will now accelerate. The
result may be only a few giant electronic publishing networks, each with global
reach.

In my 1966 communication study, I
sketched what I called "Homecom"--the
home communication center--and predicted
it would become the next great communication medium, much greater than all
present media combined.

I suggested it will bring under panel

board control the following communications facilities:

1. *Television* in new forms, including three-dimensional, worldwide satellite, laser, holography, "narrowcasting."

2. *A facsimile printer* with instant print-out and color capability.

3. *A computer* with instant access to other computers and data banks hat will include a visual screen and will "understand" English and be as easy to use as the telephone which will be developing its own intelligence--a potentiality I will be returning to.

4. *A copier* offering instant copying in full color.

5. *Radio-stereo*.

6. *Sound-sight recorder* and playback audio-visual cartridge.

7. *Touch-tone telephone* with remarkable new uses. By 1980, the telephone will be a totally new communication facility.

8. *Picturephone*.

9. *CATV*.

How will the advertising message get through that multi-media complex? How will the advertising message itself be *shaped* by this multi-media complex? Is the medium indeed to be the message?

Homecom is unlikely to be "supported" by advertising to the degree true of traditional media. Its major revenues may come from subscribers. Several magazines are now tending in this direction. For example, Time Inc. announced in connection with its new magazine, *Money*: "What we hope to do is, in effect, to depend on the reader for the bulk of our revenue. That's not to say we're ignoring the advertiser, but we're asking readers to pay $12-a-year charter (initial) rate for subscriptions, and we're banking on strong reader re-

sponse. The reader has to be interested in the magazine to pay the money."

Ms, with its $12 annual subscription price, is another example of this trend. There are several others. The new segmented-circulation magazines appear to be particularly slanted in this direction. The end of the era of advertising's domination of major media may already be at hand! In Europe, television advertising in some of the major nations has tended to be quite restricted. Here at home, rising public clamor about television clutter could lead to similar restrictions.

Fundamentally, both of the two major electronic communication innovations of recent decades--radio and television--broadened advertising's potential enormously. On balance, the new communication technology typified by Homecom also will offer growth potentials for advertising--especially worldwide. But not automatically. Not for the plucking.

Does my Homecom concept sound too much like Jules Verne? Then read this excerpt from *Fortune* for October, 1972 (six years after my 1966 communication study, in which I predicted Homecom.)

RCA BUCKS FOR HOME INFO CENTER

Said *Fortune*: "Bob Sarnoff (of RCA) seems to keep feeling the tug to rival his father, General Sarnoff, and to come up with "another color TV." When asked what that will be, now that his dreams for computers are shattered, Sarnoff answers: *'The home information center.'*

"The term actually refers to the high-capacity coaxial cables that carry TV signals into many homes, and to all the vaguely defined devices that Sarnoff sees attached to the cables' ends. In addition to transmission equipment, the devices might include machines to print newspapers in the home, and keyboards that could be used to order merchandise after viewing it on a TV screen.

"Most important, the home information center involves neither a tremendous gamble nor a major breakthrough in technology. The know-how to produce most of the equipment is in hand, and large research investments are not needed. RCA already has the capability to manufacture, distribute and service most of the communication units."

Can you feel Homecom breathing down your back?

The first mass medium to be radically changed by the new communication technology will be the newspaper. It will be in the early to intermediate stages of being "printed" in the home by 1978.

The second medium to be radically changed within the next decade will be the professional, technical and business press. The trend is already clearly in evidence in professional journals.

KODAK FORECASTS A NEW WAY TO READ

The third medium to be radically changed: Direct mail. Computerized, automated direct mail leaped ahead in the 1972 political campaign.

And as a small example of how even traditional reading will change, consider a recent Kodak ad. It shows a man, a cup of coffee in his hands, seated in a chair and looking at an electronic screen. The headline reads: "This guy is not watching TV. He is reading."

Then the copy proceeds: "There is an awful lot to read that does not get read. At considerable cost, information has been put together.

"Micropublishing on those little sheets of film called microfiche would lighten the overstuffed attache case to the advantage of all... There are many places already--appliance service counters, airline maintenance shops, libraries--where huge compendia of detailed information are consulted on microfiche. Now, if many homes and private offices had a microfiche reader that weighed less than 5 lbs., made no noise, and could be used in broad daylight..."

Is Kodak making a forecast? Don't doubt it!

Newsweek, in a 1972 analysis of CBS, made the basic point that CBS is loosening its dependence on broadcasting. *Newsweek* stated: "In 1965, CBS in rapid succession picked up a group of musical instrument and electronic amplifier companies; Creative Playthings, a small producer of quality educational toys; and a pair of educational film makers. It also launched a theatrical motion picture company from scratch, thus violating its normal rule of purchasing only going companies.

"In mid-1967, it acquired Holt, Rinehart & Winston, one of the top five educational publishers and the largest ever acquired by another company.

"Since then, CBS has added W.B. Saunders, the nation's largest publisher of medical textbooks; a group of West Coast cable television systems; a manufacturer of high-fidelity audiotape; and a medical technicians' school.

"Despite the range of its acquisitions, the company is not quite done with its expansion, and its ambitions are not necessarily limited to its basic franchise in entertainment and education software. The aim is to reduce broadcasting to no more than half of corporate revenues."

I suggest that the potential changes in communication technology for home, office, etc., that will be generated by

Homecom are behind the diversification program of CBS.

Radio did not put the phonograph into the ash heap--but the phonograph had to go through vast change to survive, and it certainly bears little resemblance to the Victrola of the 1920s.

Television did not make radio a museum piece--but radio today and radio circa 1950 bear little resemblance.

TV MUST INNOVATE TO SURVIVE

Now Homecom will compel "traditional" television to innovate on a grand scale if it is to do better than merely survive. RCA is already advertising: "You become the new dimension in television with the introduction of magnetic-tape equipment for home video recordings and the planning of pre-recorded video cartridges."

Sony has been advertising: "No longer does the sales manager have to tour the country for kick-off meetings; never again will you set up a product demonstration at a trade show; no more need for grueling instruction trips by the training director.

"All changed. Your whole world is changed. From now on, you'll do all these things and more--much more--on television. Instant, cassette television.

"Put your demonstration on a Sony Color Videocassette. Shoot it under controlled, bug-proof conditions right in your showroom. Copy it and equip your booth with players and TV sets: Let your audience run your demo for you."

In 1972, Sony turned out 60,000 to 70,000 U-Matic machines, and was working hard to fill heavy back orders from educational, commercial and some con-

sumer users. Sony projects that it will double this rate schedule every year for the next several years!

Darryl F. Zanuck, chief executive officer of 20th Century-Fox Film Corp., said in late 1972 that he recommends that all of the company's film library be put on electronic video recording cartridges five years after initial theatrical release. Will the time come when films are committed to cartridges after one year--or immediately? (Remember when hard-cover and soft-cover editions of a book were not brought out simultaneously?) Isn't it likely that hotel-motel movies will lead toward a market for movies in which the movie theater will become a secondary or tertiary outlet?

CASSETTE TV WON'T BE EXPENSIVE

The compatability problem for the TV audio-visual cassette obviously is being studied deeply by the industry. The rich rewards that await the problem's solution assure considerable progress. Standardization of adequate dimensions may be achieved before 1975. If so, cartridge TV will leap to success as fast as did color TV.

Moreover, there was trade talk in late 1972 about a technological breakthrough that will provide a new tape that could lengthen the playing time of audio cassettes to four or five hours.

The cost of audio-visual cassette home equipment will be brought down sharply. In this connection, I should point out that I bought the first RCA all-electric radio console in the early 1930s: $500. In those terrible depression years, $500 represented at least $2,000 in 1973 purchasing power-- probably more.

Obviously, what I am saying is that between 1973 and 1975, the price for cas- sette TV for the home will not repre- sent a serious marketing problem for the initial market--and, after 1975, prices will drop sharply. And discs promise to achieve a large market--MCA may be marketing discs in 1974.

The *Wall Street Journal* gave the fol- lowing report on the MCA disc: "MCA Inc., a diversified leisure products concern, held the first showing of its new video disc system, disco-vision. The system, which is expected to be marketed some day for under $500, can be attached to a regular television set. Its disc albums, which could sell for $1.99 to $9.99, packaged similarly to long-playing record albums, would then be played through a TV channel not used for regular programming.

"The demonstration, the company stressed, was a progress report on research and development of the video disc and not a consumer introduction...

"Joun W. Findlater, president of MCA DiscoVision,Inc., a new MCA subsidiary, said MCA has been developing the sys- tem over the past three years and has an investment in it thus far of 'well over $2,000,000' to emphasize the mass entertainment market, as opposed to the educational and institutional markets that video cassette makers have stressed...

"The discs can be played in either sin- gle-disc players or multiple-disc player- changers. The single-disc player is expected to retail at under $400, MCA said, while the slightly heavier and larger multiple-disc player will prob- ably retail for under $500."

COMMERCIALS ON CASSETTES

Will the audio-visual tape cassette include one or more commercials offered to advertisers on a rate card basis? The industry has, of course, been ex- ploring the potentials of advertising revenue from the tape cassette, along with working on its technological prob- lems.

Very likely, commercials may be sold on a rental cassette, and the rental price lowered for this privilege. Rental cas- settes offered by food advertisers, for example, might feature recipes. This form of advertising could prove quite attractive, especially if the rental price were sharply lowered by the inclu- sion of commercial messages on the cas- settes.

Much the same idea could be developed for home sewing--also for golf, tennis or scuba diving lessons. Ditto for tapes for the home do-it-yourselfer, boat owners, gardeners.

A variety of premium programs will emerge created around the audio-visual tape cassette. These will include spe- cial cassettes similar to the stereo records that have been offered for years. The "club" concept will be adapted for these tape cassettes--commercials in- cluded.

The mail order houses--Sears, Ward's, Penney's --will surely put their cata- logs, at least in part, on audio-visual tape. So will department stores and other retailers.

'ARTIFICIAL INTELLIGENCE'

While Homecom, as I have outlined it up to this point, is of sufficiently awesome dimensions in its potential im- pact on advertising and marketing, I consider an eventual breakthrough in the technology of computer artificial intel- ligence will have equally awesome im- pact on advertising and marketing.

Artificial intelligence? Yes. While you are still around? Yes, for this reason:

The experience of the last two decades indicates that computer capability increases tenfold every seven years. This seems a reliable rule of thumb for projecting the state of the computer art into the future.

The first vacuum tube computer was completed in 1951. The first transistorized computer--ten times larger and faster--appeared in 1958. Today's fastest computers--based on chips--are ten times faster still, and were first put into operation in 1965. More sophisticated chips are now being built into a new generation of computers that will be delivered starting in 1973 and will offer another tenfold increase in capability.

Transistors and other circuit elements are now so tiny and fitted so closely together that it becomes feasible to combine thinking circuits and memory units on a single chip. *Thus, one cell in the computer's memory bank can both remember and reason.*

Said a communication scientist: "The computer generation appearing some time in the second half of the 1970s and containing the new type of memory will be a major step closer to artificial intelligence."

In July, 1971, the Japanese government earmarked $100,000,000 for an eight-year study of artificial intelligence. Japanese industry accepts the conclusion that it could be increasingly dependent on "intelligent" computers.

RIVAL FOR THE HUMAN BRAIN

In a technical report dated February, 1971, whose source I am unfortunately unable to trace, I read:

"The development of these tiny chips presages a time when the electronic brain will rival the human brain in complexity and memory. The identity of the fully educated computer may become blurred with that of its programer-teacher! It may exhibit esthetic and artistic judgments of an interesting degree of subtlety. Responses akin to feeling and emotion need not be excluded from its training if they enhance its performance."

Will artificial intelligence become competent to produce advertising at least equal to some of 1972s advertising? Don't doubt it!

Along with artificial intelligence will come electronic voice recognition. voice recognition by the computer--in other words, a computer that will respond to oral command--is making significant engineering progress. No serious forecast about computer systems or communication systems in the 1970s can omit voice recognition systems.

Several years ago, in national advertising, the Bell System predicted the orally-actuated telephone. RCA reports that its voice command machine responds to 28 of the basic sounds in the English language.

NEW WAY TO TRANSMIT PHOTOS

Researchers for Sandia Corp., a Western Electric subsidiary that specializes in esoteric projects for the Atomic Energy Commission, recently came up with a new wrinkle in the photo-transmission field. Using a new type of ceramic material, the company has devised a way in which an image can be sent over telephone lines and recorded on a postcard-thin sheet. The information on the sheet can be projected on a large screen, photographed, and then quickly wiped out and the material made ready to receive another image.

Ultimately, the new process may replace current systems of transmitting photographs and printed matter by facsimile and wirephoto. What uses will advertising find for it?

In May, 1972, RCA Global Communications Inc. said it had filed a tariff with the FCC for an electronic mail service between three U.S. cities and Hawaii, Puerto Rico and the Virgin Islands. Telepost messages would be filed with RCA Globcom or Western Union Telegraph Co. from Telex subscribers' offices or from public telex facilities in New York City, San Francisco or Washington.

Messages would then be transmitted electronically by RCA Globcom to specially equipped post offices at the overseas points and delivered by the next regularly scheduled U.S. mail. (The proposed overseas service is much like Western Union's domestic Mailgram service, which also uses the U.S. Postal Service for delivery.)

This facsimile communications system is being touted as the mail of tomorrow. Its promoters envision machines installed in private homes to transmit and receive messages that formerly were mailed.

The mini-calculator will be in millions of homes by 1975. (It will be a major component in the entire system I call Homecom.)

The remarkable success of the tiny calculator for the home dramatically demonstrates:

1. How much more sophisticated the public has become and therefore how much more rapidly millions will accept step-by-step introduction of Homecom.

2. How rapidly the public will develop

new uses for each component of Homecom as it comes along.

3. How rapidly the price of each component of Homecom will be brought down for appeal to a mass market.

'HOTELVISION' IN 265,000 ROOMS

I have already referred to hotel-motel movies room service. It is another innovation that dramatically demonstrates the extraordinary rapidity with which new communication technology can explode into a huge new market--and create new advertising-marketing opportunities.

"Hotelvision" is perhaps the fastest-growing phenomenon in the entertainment industry. Some 15 companies are already in the race to keep hotel guests glued to their TV sets watching movies. And by 1974, an estimated total of 265,000 hotel rooms in the U.S. and Canada will have the service available. That will have been accomplished in just three years.

If hotelvision proves a widespread success, the next logical step would be for its promoters to set up closed-circuit systems for showing movies in large apartment-house buildings with master antennas. Its promoters hope eventually to provide individual homes, through cable television, with movies-for-pay.

Computer Cinema points out that its system offers guests more than just movies. Its system includes devices that awaken a guest, keep track of the room (if it has to be made up), detect fires in rooms, and notify guests about messages at the desk.

The July-August, 1972, issue of *Harvard Business Review* reports: "Interactive television is a promising medium for transmitting graphic information. For example, a one-way video, two-way video link can reproduce graphic material in full color as well as provide a voice channel for dissussion. Furthermore, this link can be distributed to as many locations as desired, with some or all of the stations able to talk back...

"The use of interactive television within a single corporate location is possible today, and should be available in the mid-1970s. Services between different companies will depend on the development of compatible equipment standards and a broadband network, probably by the specialized carriers, and should be feasible in major urban centers in the late 1970s."

CHEVY JOINS TV TAPE CARTRIDGE PARADE

An electronic communication training tool that also doubles as a medium to reach the consumer is the new Chevrolet Mini-Theater TV tape cartridge program. Chevrolet began using the Mini-Theaters about a year ago, with about 2,000 dealers signed up to buy or lease the tape players. Now, some 5,700, or 94%, of the 6,100 Chevy dealers are participating. About 6,200 machines are in operation (some dealers have more than one).

The machines project sight and sound, using tapes. They are leased for $21 per month or purchased for $465. For the 1972 model year, dealers received 15 film cartridges--14 on product and one on warranty. The offering will be expanded to 18 cartridges for the 1973 model year--12 on product and six on sales technique and motivation.

In addition, Chevrolet has installed the tape players at shopping centers, airports and other public gathering places.

A Ford division merchandising manager said, "We have been testing the use of videotapes in dealerships not only as a training device for salesmen, but also as a merchandising assist in making a presentation to customers. We have tape installations in 54 dealerships around the country, and in 34 district offices."

As for the advertising agency of the future and the communication revolution: The mathematician, systems expert, operations analyst, sociologist, economist, programer will become still more common in advertising agencies. Other specialists on the agency roster will include psycho-physicists and electronic engineers who specialize in information theory.

Sophisticated information-communication hook-ups will also become more common. Agency personnel on various levels will require technical education so that they can communicate with the technicians.

Moreover, satellite communication, with its one-world connotation, and the developing global reach of the giant multi-national corporations, leave no doubt that the *global ad agency* will become the thing of the future. That is the future direction of major clients --it must, therefore, become the future direction of the advertising agency.

DISCUSSION QUESTIONS

1. Of all the communications innovations mentioned by Weiss, which, in your judgment, will be most dramatic in its effect on marketing?

2. In your opinion, is Weiss too optimistic, on target, or too pessimistic regarding the development of communications innovations? Why?

Reprinted by permission from ADVERTISING AGE; 27 May, 1974, pp. 39-40.

VIII-3

ADVERTISING OF SERVICES, NOT PRODUCTS, WILL BE THE WAVE OF THE FUTURE

Steve Unwin

Advertising, as it is used today, has come under attack because it has not adjusted to the realities of the post-industrial society. Three anachronisms contribute to this effect:

First, most of the current advertising continues to offer product satisfactions in a service economy. Second, in order to relate to new consumer wants, advertising endows products with unreal, non-product satisfactions. And third, advertising has been little used to channel new wants toward real, non-product satisfactions. Advertising finds itself perpetuating the old values, while plagiarizing the new.

Advertising is the tool of the mass persuader, versatile but compliant, expressing exactly the aims and wishes of those who use it. These anachronisms are not, therefore, the fault of advertising itself. The responsibility lies with those who use advertising too much, and those who use it too little; with the manufacturers, who continue to dominate the advertising media in a service economy; and with the service industries, which, undermarketed and underpromoted, still behave like quasi-charitable institutions in the midst of post-industrial plenty.

Material abundance has these results, each of which has profound significance for advertising: It provides the material foundation on which a prosperous service economy can be built. It permits the manufacture of an increasing number of new products. It brings affluence to the consumer, and with affluence, a changed hierarchy of consumer wants.

The literature is full of references, mostly somewhat colored, to consumer distaste for the fruits of affluence. M.W. Thring, in "Man, Machines and Tomorrow," believes that "at the beginning, new-found material wealth leads to actual happiness in its contrast with the straitened and narrow life many of us had led before, but after a while pleasure in possessions reaches a saturation point and there is disillusionment."

TOYNBEE, OTHERS LOOK ASKANCE AT US

One of advertising's fiercest, yet most esteemed critics, Arnold Toynbee, has written in AA (Nov. 21, 1973), "I guess that a hungry and destitute Indian peasant is less unhappy than a western

conveyor-belt worker who eats steak
for dinner and has a refrigerator, a
TV set, an air-conditioning apparatus
and a car." Only the most ardent conservationist would go as far as Mr.
Toynbee.

But it cannot be escaped that, even
with present shortages, western man is
considerably richer in manufactured
artifacts than in non-material comforts.
People are prone to want what they lack,
rather than what they already have.
Frank Knight's analysis of wants (in
"The Ethics of Competition") is truer
today than 50 years ago: "What the
individual actually wants is not satisfaction for the wants which he has, but
more and better wants."

And yet, the newly affluent, and somewhat surfeited, consumer is met at
every turn by a stream of advertising
for new products, most of which are
not much different from those he already has. Last year, 52 new items
went on supermarket shelves in a typical week. In 1971, one food company
was responsible for the launch of 24
new products, AA reported. A.C. Nielsen Co. recorded 1,154 new product introductions in the grocery and health
and beauty aids fields in the same year.
Most of these failed to meet a demand.
Of the 9,500 new supermarket brands
introduced in 1968, only 20% met their
sales goals.

IT'S STILL 3:1 FOR PRODUCT ADVERTISING

This new product casualty rate not
only says something about the present
state of demand for new products; it
also does much to explain consumer annoyance and irritation with advertising. Similarly, the continued three-
to-one ratio in favor of product advertising over non-product advertising can
make little sense to post-industrial
consumers, who, according the the U.S.

Census Bureau, now spend more than half
their income on services.

Americans, for example, now spend as
many dollars ($350,000,000) with one of
the smaller fast-food hamburger businesses as on all brands of toothpaste, and
yet toothpaste advertisers outspend this
fast-food business seven to one. In
1972, 85 of the 100 leading national advertisers were classified as manufacturers in 15 product categoreis. Ethical
drug manufacturers spent $400,000,000
reaching the nation's doctors, whereas
the 50 United States together combined
to spend less than $100,000,000 adver-
tising to all their citizens.

The Gallagher Report estimates that as
much as 85% of today's ad expenditures
are intended to move products. Affluent
consumers still want to be informed
about new products, and reminded about
old products, but not to the exclusion
of all else. The increased share of
consumer expenditure in such non-product service areas as recreation, education, vacation, sport, hobbies, travel,
health and handicraft has not been balanced by an equivalent increase in
share of advertising expenditure. The
product/service persuasion ratio is the
inverse of the product/service spending
ratio.

This is not to say that affluent consumers no longer need products. They
do. They depend on them, but increasingly as items of necessity. They are
valued for their utility as much as their
status. Alvin Toffler says in AA (Nov.
21, 1973): "We are witnessing a decline
in possessiveness. The consumer is no
longer as concerned with possession as
he is with use." Hence the current consumer interest in product performance,
reliability of product claims, and more
informative product advertising.

ADVERTISING OF SERVICES, NOT PRODUCTS, WILL BE THE WAVE OF THE FUTURE

CONSUMER FEELS CHEATED BY AD THEMES

The advertising practitioner knows, however, that the mere repetition of product data does not give a brand much competitive edge in a market already crowded with many very similar products. He, therefore, seeks to differentiate his brand by giving it an added value. The values he selects reflect those wants which affluent consumers feel most strongly, and focus on non-material rewards instead of product benefits. Thus, beer is advertised as if it were a vacation trip or a passport to immortality. A motor oil is euphemized as an initiation to young adulthood. A car wax is transformed into an erotic experience. A tonic permits the carefree, country life of the gentleman farmer. And so on.

These ads sell. They sell because they motivate people to buy. Consumers identify and respond to these themes. But over a period of time they begin to feel cheated and deprived. The psychological rewards advertising has invested in the product seem flimsy counterfeit to the hardened product consumer of today. When needs are advertised as wants, consumers experience an expectation gap between promise and performance. They start to criticize when advertising masquerades their wants.

People are not inclined to resist or resent want-provoking appeals if they harmonize with their predispositions. As Theodore Levitt tells us, "Advertisments are the symbols of man's aspirations." People do not quarrel with embellishments which enhance the goals of their wants. Advertising helped to accomplish the technological revolution. It must now perform a similar role for the service revolution. This is advertising's new horizon. As people demand more and better services, it is advertising's job to seek out, identify, stimulate and guide these newly-felt wants toward their satisfactions by

service industries.

Society expects and receives many excellent products, but only a few excellent services. Some 123 out of the 154 major U.S. corporations are manufacturers, a *News Front* study tells us. The manufacturer dominates the consumer market in size, organization and influence.

On the other hand, most service industries are regarded as inefficient and lacking in prestige. Although allowing for one or two notable exceptions, like the Bell Telephone System, Peter F. Drucker has noted the absence of defined goals and measurable results in the "public service institutions." John Kenneth Galbraith deplores the exclusion of many of the less organized service companies from what he terms the "planning system."

Often overstaffed and usually underpriced, the service industries stagger from one crisis to the next. Despite their overwhelming aggregate dollar volume (the health industry is now the second largest in the country) they still carry a Cinderella image.

Mr. Drucker has pointed to the paradox: People say they want more services, but are not prepared to pay for them, either out of pocket or out of taxes. Services are still somehow seen as the prerogative of the very rich or as charity for the very poor. The pre-industrial image of services lingers on in an era when material abundance has at last made professional services available to all. The affluent consumer earns twice as much as he did 20 years ago.

And yet, despite technical advances in both health care and automobiles, he is happier to pay the dealer $4,000 for a new car than the hospital $1,000 for a new family member. The need to run sweepstakes to subsidize Chicago mass transit tells a similar story in the public sector. The nation cannot long continue to allow 70% of its GNP to be treated as "good works" or "free handouts."

411

James Webb Young in AA cited advertising's ability to "overcome inertia--
the great drag on all human progress,
economic or non-economic, as represented by the sociological term, 'cultural
lag'." Even Mr. Toynbee allowed that
"advertising is the art of persuading,
and persuasion can be used for preaching a new way of life." Creative advertising can articulate the abstract
benefits of services and help convince
the affluent consumer that such intangible satisfactions as freedom, fulfilment, health, love and security are
more faithfully and fully supplied by
services than through the surrogacy of
a product.

WHAT SERVICE ADVERTISING CAN DO

Further than that, advertising can particularize abstract benefits. The bank's
"friendly image" can be spelled out in
terms of receptiveness to inquiries for
loans, a relaxed atmosphere in which to
discuss matters of personal financial
security and risk, and the avoidance
of banking jargon.

Advertising can demonstrate that the
personal involvement of time and effort
required in the "consumption" of many
services and activities, such as education and sport, can be more edifying
than the more immediate, but usually
more superficial, satisfactions of product consumption.

Advertising can raise the social and
economic status of services, and persuade the affluent consumer that service values justify payment. Opportunities for advertising will increase
with the growth of private and personal
services in education, entertainment,
health and other areas. As a result,
the service industries will be encouraged to become goal and consumer oriented,
and advertising will be doing the job
it does best, and which only advertising

can do, which is to stimulate wants,
create demand and motivate action.

The competing claims of advertisers
will act as a spur to services development. The persuasive art of advertising will again be in harmoney with the
economic system.

ADVERTISING CAN'T BE COY

Advertising will not realize its full
potential in the post-industrial economy
so long as there are service industries
that do not recognize advertisng as a
viable medium for curing their awareness
problems, preventing apathy and gaining
public support.

Such coy and defensive attitudes to advertising are exemplified in the self-imposed restrictions on advertising of
pharmacists and architects. The tenuous ethical arguments put forward to
outlaw the advertising of prescription
services and home designing seem incongruous in a society now accustomed to
the advertising of churches, colleges
and schools. Neither does it make much
sense to condone the advertising of the
medical product, but not its dispenser;
the constructed home, but not its designer.

All suppliers of services will hopefully
come to accept advertising as a highly
flexible tool of communication, which
can be adapted, like all modes of communication, to suit their special needs,
and which can lead to higher consumer
expectations and, thereby, to better
qualities of services.

ADVERTISING ISN'T MORALITY PLAY

It is also to be hoped that the shift

of advertising support from products
to services will forestall further attempts to meddle with its synchroniz-
ing capability. Formal disclosure
and other regulatory ploys, which
threaten to turn advertising into a
sort of latter-day morality play, or
legal tort, miss the point of advertising's function. The purpose of
advertising is to accelerate consumption, expedite changes in attitudes,
and to achieve goals in a shorter
period of time. Advertising is the
persuasive use of mass communication
to help men keep pace with all the
other fast-moving elements in a technological society.

Advertising helps to synchronize modern social and economic processes. To
restrict its use to the provision of
information and to muffle its persuasive power would impede its synchroniz-
ing function. It would also be a misuse of the medium. Because of the
vast number of competing messages, advertising has to communicate its meaning fast. It makes at best a fleeting
impression. Because it is fast, it
has to be short. One advertisement
should not attempt to convey more than
one or two basic points. Otherwise,
it will never be noticed, let alone
remembered.

Because it is fast and short, and because it has to maintain momentum behind a product, service or idea, advertising is essentially a medium of repetition. A fast, short and repetitive
medium is neither a suitable nor efficient vehicle for the dissemination
of detailed information. Packages,
leaflets, catalogs and consumer reports,
available immediately prior to and following purchase, are far more appropriate media for this purpose. Mail
order, some industrial and some new
consumer products require informative
advertising, but not established, fast-
moving, consumer brands.

Advertising that was forever informing
people about things they did not want

to know would make media exposure an
almost unbearable experience, especially for those not in the target audience.
Also, the advertising business should
not be misled into thinking the more
informative advertising will pacify the
critics and satisfy the regulators. In
fact, the opposite is more likely, with
more demands for substantiation of product information and further threat of
affirmative disclosure.

REGULATION SLOWS FLOW OF GOODS

Attempts to change advertising into a
purely informative medium are as mistaken as those which seek to curb corporate power by transforming the manufacturer into an agent for social welfare. There are few obvious parallels
between the profitable manufacture and
distribution of products and the professional planning and administration of
social services. Manufacturers do not
have the training, experience or expertise to perform effectively in the social area. For similar lack of qualifi-
cation the military have traditionally
made bad policemen, artists poor admin-
istrators, and faculty indifferent accountants.

Just as corporate deficiencies in the
social area do not deter the corporate
critic, so the ultimate purpose of advertising regulation is not to make an
"honest" medium of it, but to slow down
the flow of goods and services. Advertising people should take note of the
ominous link between consumerism and
the concept of a "no-growth" economy.
Consumerists have shown little interest
in using advertising to boost the service sector. Regulation is not designed
to improve advertising performance for
products or for services. An advertising business castrated by controls has
serious implications for the future
health of the nascent service economy.

ADVERTISING'S ROLE IN NEW SOCIETY

Thriving service institutions, "the real growth sector of a modern society," as Mr. Drucker says, are vital to the further development of western civilization. There are many visions of the future society to which we are headed. Mr. Thring envisions a "creative society" where men find fulfilment through mental and manual creative activity; Mr. Toffler describes the imminence of an "experiential economy," where goods and services are valued according to their psychological reward; and there are other versions ranging from the cultural to the spiritual.

But is is certain that none of these will transpire, unless they can take place within a prosperous and well-ordered service environment. There is a natural progression from the agricultural economy to the industrial economy to the service economy and, soon, to the cultural economy. Each depends on the former for its existence. Each builds on the achievements of its predecessor. Each adds to, but does not subtract from, the wealth of the previous economy. Advertising, which helps to synchronize change and ease transition, has a role to play at every stage.

As the carrier of messages for the industrial economy, advertising has had its wings clipped; its feathers ruffled. It should now take its head out of the sand, and learn to fly in new directions.

DISCUSSION QUESTIONS

1. Evaluate Unwin's forecast as to the growth of service advertising.

2. What consumer service do you believe will benefit most from the development of service advertising? Why?

VIII-4

AS MEDIA CHANGE, HOW WILL ADVERTISING?

Leo Bogart

To speculate about the future of advertising requires that we first consider some of the developments that lie ahead for the mass media with which most advertising has always been linked. This paper intends to raise some questions as to whether that intimate linkage is apt to continue to the same degree as in the past.

The mass media of communication are today in the midst of a technological revolution which is bound to accelerate in the rest of this century, if only through the commercial application of techniques and systems which already exist in the laboratory in prototype form. Consider the innovations that have taken hold in the last 30 years or so: Web offset and color gravure printing, photocopying, teletypesetting, television, wide-screen motion pictures, miniaturized and printed circuitry, communications satellites, Lasers, audio and video tape recording and cassettes, microphotography, electronic data processing. It is not unreasonable to expect that similar inventions of equally striking importance will be coming along, though some of them are impossible to visualize today.

Surely the most portentous development on the immediate horizon is that of

cable television, already an important factor on the media scene and with growth estimates that range between 20 and 60 percent of the households by 1980. Regardless of what cable's growth rate actually turns out to be, it seems rather certain that before the end of the century most homes in the country will have a cable connection that will vastly expand the range of TV choices, lead to more programming specialization, and facilitate the already existing trend for television viewing to become an individual rather than a family affair. As viewing audiences become more selective, the economics of television will change for the advertiser.

The cable connection will ultimately make possible a two-way feedback system that might make possible both the direct ordering of advertised goods and also retrieval and display on demand of information and entertainment from computerized files of both "print" and video. In effect, everyone will have access to the entire existing library of films and television programs and to the inexhaustible treasurehouse of books and periodicals, as well as to all the news reports. The equivalent of wire service news copy can be displayed and individual specialized interests pursued by the "reader" who requests more and more of the optional backup material from the current or historical file. (The typical newspaper now has room to print only 10 to 15 percent of the input it receives each day.) Photocopies can be made selectively not only of text and still pictures, but of moving images caught in a freeze frame. Thus, the new technology will blur the traditional line between broadcast and print media as well as the line between mass communication and the kind of private communication that takes place on the telephone.

The history of communication tells us that as technology changes and new media come along, the old media do not disappear, but simply adapt themselves to their new competitors. Newspapers and magazines as we know them, in their present tangible format, are not about to disappear, if only because we all recognize the need to expose outselves to a great variety of ideas and information that we cannot possibly know we want ahead of time and that we would never dream of summoning out of storage on the basis of a headline summary.

The new communications technology has its greatest impact on the processing of *information*. Computerized retrieval systems, microphotographs, photocopying all facilitate access to data. The vast explosion of data of all kinds has fostered specialization, and thus created new problems of how to sort things out, of how to manage information to permit more efficient selection The new technology provides increased access to information, increased choice, and a vast saving of time.

Information really exists outside of time, in the sense that anyone who wants information wants it instantly. But to be practical, it always takes time to acquire information, and its pursuit may be pleasurable. As the media inform, they also entertain, and *entertainment* must be experienced in a time dimension. It is, in effect, a pastime, a way of spending time agreeably.

Much or most broadcast advertising capitalizes on the timebound character of broadcast entertainment. Commercials are positioned to catch people as they pass through the surrounding programming. Even the most selectively placed broadcast schedule puts the advertiser's story before those who happen to be passing by. Much print advertising also works this way, though a good deal of it starts from another premise, which is that the reader is already looking for the kind of information embodied in the ad. Information-seeking is more easily carried out when the individual moves at his own pace and is not tied to someone else's timetable.

The technological changes that lie ahead appear to work in the direction of reducing the mass audience, as they increase the public's options. But the existence of the mass audience is essential to image-building brand advertising. For most broadly marketed consumer products, brand identity is built over time through the repetition of entertaining messages which create a set of symbolic associations that people at large have with a product.

Changes in media thus inevitably carry implications for the content and targeting of advertising messages. These changes also parallel changes in buying habits and in retailling practice. Just as the informational non-time aspect of advertising is facilitated by the new technology, so shopping increasingly becomes a fast, utilitarian process rather than a recreational activity.

Forty identical stalls sell identical spices next to each other in an oriental bazaar, and the customer with even a small purchase to make enjoys moving from one to the other, trying his bargaining skill against the merchant's. It's fun; it's a way of passing the time. In our own country, the old cracker-barrel grocery with its atmosphere of easy small talk was a community center of gossip and casual recreation. It is a far cry from the computerized checkout

416

counter and the push button supermarket of the imminent future. The busy
customer stopping off at K-Mart or Penney's on her way home from work goes
straight to the display rack. She
wants instant service, or at least she
wants it much of the time, and the
pleasurable aspects of shopping are
reserved for special occasions.

The technological changes ahead will
save time for consumers, but they will
have more time at their disposal. In
1950, the average work week was 39.8
hours; in 1972 it was 37.2 hours. Va-
cations grow longer; retirement is
earlier; the four-day work week looms
as a distinct possibility well before
the end of this century.

A counterweight to the increase in
leisure time for those who work is the
fact that more people will be in the
labor force. Fully 52 percent of the
female population age 18 to 64 is now
working, with consequent changes in
their media habits as well as in their
consumption capacities, needs, and
tastes. The proportion of working women will get larger, since better educated women are more likely to work,
and the educational disparity between
men and women is fast disappearing.
(In 1960, there were nearly twice as
many men as women graduating from college; by 1980 the ratio will be 6 to
5 1/4.) Changes in the position of
women will be significant for advertisers, since such a large part of their
messages are addressed to women as
primary purchasing agents for the
household.

Patterns of consumption and media habits will also be affected by the slowing of the rate of population growth
and by changes in the shape of the age
pyramid. We can anticipate that real
work productivity will keep rising and
that the nation's economic growth will
continue. The shift from blue collar
to white collar jobs (also linked to
the growth in education) has profound
effects on lifestyle and on media use.

(Greater education is linked to greater
use of print and less of broadcast media,
and to greater selectivity and information-seeking in consumer choice.)

Another important trend is the growth
in the government's share of the nation's
total productive efforts. The government sector--federal, state, and local
--accounted for 13.3 percent of Gross
National Product in 1950 and for 22.1
percent in 1972. Although the activist
style of social protest is currently on
the wane, the rise of social concerns
represents a long-term development that
may be expected to continue into the
future. This suggests that there will
be increased competition between the
social goods (like mass transportation,
environmental protection, medical services, public housing, crime prevention,
etc.) that require higher taxes, and
the individually consumed goods and
services that corporate marketers promote. It is not unreasonable to expect
that government agencies will seek to
use advertising techniques to market
social goods. Under their pressure,
Congress may reluctantly approve advertising appropriations for government
agencies. After all, paid advertising
is already used to recruit volunteers
for the Army as well as by public corporations like Amtrak and the Postal
Service. (In the Soviet Union, billboards urge the public to "drink milk.")
The Federal Government already ranks
among the top 100 national advertisers.
There are troublesome political ques-
tionmarks in such domestic propaganda.
In the present context, advertising by
government agencies might be a factor
in the competition for the attention of
the public, as well as a contribution
to the economic base of the advertising media.

All of the developments reviewed thus
far carry implications for advertising
as well as for the media. But a fundamental question must be raised as to
whether advertising can continue to
grow at the same spectacular rate as in
the era since the end of World War II.

As a percentage of the consumer sector of Gross National Product, advertising rose from 3.0 percent in 1950 to a high of 3.7 percent by 1960. The decade of the Fifties marked television's emergence onto the scene. The fact that advertising growth in this period outpaced the total growth of the consumer economy reflects marketers' eager adoption of the new medium. Other forms of selling and promotional expense appear to have been cut back to permit the use of television without compensatory sacrifices of advertising expenditures going into radio and print. In the Sixties, after TV had achieved virtually full penetration, total advertising expenditures dropped from 3.7 percent of the consumer sector in 1960 to 3.2 percent in 1970. They were still at the same level in 1972. This is a difficult kind of trend line to extrapolate.

As the new revolution in communications technology comes upon us, will advertisers have to increase their total promotional investment, as they did in the Fifties? Television added substantially to the total amount of daily hours that people spend with the media, but cable and the home communications system seem destined to divide present audiences rather than generate new ones.

A number of other factors suggest that advertising will not grow at the same pace as it has in the recent past. Local advertising, which has a lower average advertising-to-sales ratio than national, appears to be getting a larger share of the total. Before the coming of mass TV in 1950, local advertising (not including newspaper classified) represented 38.9 percent of all advertising. As TV induced national advertisers to raise their total spending, local advertising represented a decreasing share, dropping to a low of 33.1 percent in 1965. It has since been climbing again, to 37.9 percent in 1972. There is, furthermore, a blurring of distinctions between retail and national as cooperative advertising continues

to flourish, and as private brands represent a larger share of both the grocery and general merchandising business. The net effect is to make more advertising local, and thereby to reduce the overall spending rate.

Services, rather than merchandise, account for a growing share of the consumer economy. (They went from 33 percent of personal consumption expenditures in 1950 to 42 percent in 1972.) But, in general, services have a lower advertising-to-sales ratio than goods.

Engels' Law suggests that as affluence increases, more and more of people's incomes will be spent not only on services, but on durable goods like furniture and applicances, and a smaller part on food and clothing. Paradoxically, in the age of packaged convenience goods and parity brands, the advertising-to-sales ratio tends to be higher on what Engels would have classified a century ago as "the necessities of life." (Advertising-to-sales is 2.4 percent for food, compared to 1 percent for motor vehicles.)

The net effect of all these trends suggests that advertising expenditures will in the near future no longer keep pace with the rate of total economic growth.

Another development to watch is the increasing concentration of power over advertising decisions. The ten top advertising agencies placed 31 percent of national billings in 1960 and 41 percent in 1972. The 100 top national advertisers represented 23.6 percent of national spending in 1960 and 27.4 percent in 1971.

This process of concentration is also mirrored in retailing. In general merchandising, chains represented 54 percent if sales in 1950. In 1972, they were up to 78 percent. Food chains increased their share of the grocery business from 38 percent in 1950 to 56 percent in 1972.

As fewer organizations represent a larger proportion of advertising expenditures, the planning of advertising will become progressively more sophisticated, more dependent on data, but also more uniform, more subject to rule by formula, less spontaneous. Big advertisers and agencies pack more clout in their negotiations with the media. It may become harder for small fry and new competitors to win access to good positioning and preferred programming. When fewer powerful people are involved, there is a more direct interplay and intermingling of the elites of the media, manufacturing, and retailing worlds. But more concentrated control over advertising makes those in power more visible and more vulnerable to criticism and to government intervention.

What are the prospects for a steady increase in such intervention with advertising, spurred by consumer activism? Consumerism is a catchword that covers a number of distinct phenomena that reflect the prevailing social malaise. Better educated consumers are more apt to be information seekers and more skeptical of advertising, but they are unlikely to become a revolutionary force. At the same time, consumer protection is an appealing issue to legislators, and it has developed its own power centers in the regulatory agencies. Even though the forces that have been set in motion are unlikely to be reversed, this should primarily affect the content of ad messages, rather than media choices. Counter advertising, in spite of all the alarms, seems unlikely to become a significant threat in most product classifications.

However, government controls will not represent the main limitation on the growth of advertising. That limitation is more likely to be set by the psychological bounds beyond which consumers find it difficult or impossible to absorb the steadily growing number of messages. When a given ad or commercial is repeated over time, there is a wearout effect: effects are not proportionate to the number of exposures. (Several studies have shown similar levels of brand awareness among people who are exposed to heavy, medium, and light amounts of television advertising for the brands in question.) More media vehicles compete for attention while the amount of time spent with the media has remained substantially the same since TV arrived at maturity. (In this connection, it must be noted that the oft-cited Nielsen data which suggest that households are spending more time with TV merely reflect the rise in multi-set households. "Homes using television" went from an average of 5 hours 24 minutes a day in 1964 to 6 hours 12 minutes in 1972. But in that same period, viewing by the average individual aged 18 and over remained essentially unchanged. Nielsen reports weekly viewing in December--a peak viewing month--was 28 hours 36 minutes in 1964 and 28 hours 43 minutes in 1972.) Thus, there will be more incentive for advertisers to use media in which the messages are sought by people rather than exposed to them randomly.

As media costs have gone up, many advertisers have turned to shorter commercials and smaller ads. Although it is possible to subdivide and subdivide, the resulting fractionation inevitably diminishes the power of any given message. If the return per unit of advertising expenditure gets smaller, advertising is less efficient. The result might be that budgets would have to be increased to compensate for this reduced yield, but it seems just as plausible to suppose that other promotion and selling techniques will receive greater emphasis and that advertising will represent a smaller percentage of sales.

If advertising support of the media drops off or fails to gain at the same rate as media production expenses, it seems inevitable that consumers will have to pay a larger share. Will they be willing to do so? The print media that have died since television came along have died not for lack of audi ences, but for lack of advertising. *Life, Look, Post,* and *Collier's* all retained vast numbers of readers right up to the end. The 30 metropolitan daily newspapers that have died or merged since 1960 were in the aggregate only 15 percent below their former peak circulations at the time they disappeared.

The consumer is already paying as a subscriber to cable television, and there are indications that payment for special programs (like off-color films or special sporting events) will be steadily moved toward a pay-as-you-go basis. Advertising's share of magazines' gross revenues dropped from 69.6 percent in 1966 to 63.1 percent in 1971. A similar though much less marked trend is visible for newspapers. (In 1960, advertising represented 69.8 percent of total expenditures. By 1971, it was 68.5 percent.)

As the consumer is forced to pay a larger share, he may consume fewer media vehicles--watch fewer programs, buy fewer publications. This will accelerate the trend toward smaller audiences for some media and further brake the expansion in the output of advertising messages. It should also result in a shifting of advertising investments among media.

The developments to which I have been referring throughout this paper have profound implications for advertising research. Four areas represent prime opportunities for study: (1) The economics of the mass media and the contribution of advertising both to their financial support and to their audience appeal. (2) The processes of advertising decision-making, and the assumptions--factual, conjectural, emotional, and faddist--that enter into them. (3) The content and characteristics of advertising messages disseminated by different media. (We know what products are advertised, of course, but we know amazingly little about the

vastly more important "hidden" information that advertising communicates about our society and its values.) (4) The communications properties of advertising perceived in different media, different unit sizes, different competitive conditions, by people with different degrees of predisposition to be interested in the message.

All four of these subjects deserve more attention than they have yet received; since they relate to the generalities of advertising, they are unlikely to fit in with the specifics that spell immediate advantage to any advertiser. But the research that is needed should not merely help to prepare us for the future of advertising; it should help us to cope with the present.

DISCUSSION QUESTIONS

1. Evaluate Bogart's estimates of the changes to come in media as well as the changes in advertising.

2. Bogart mentions the increasing concentration of power over advertising decisions. In your opinion, what, if anything, should be done about this concentration of power?

VIII-5

THE VIDEOCULTURE OF THE FUTURE

John G. Cawelti

In 1973, virtually every American has easy and frequent access to a television set. TV sets are in 90% to 95% of American homes and are watched by somebody from about three to six hours a day. This undoubtedly constitutes the largest group of people bound together in a single communications net in history.

Perhaps even more significantly, no large, complex society has ever possessed the potential of continual simultaneous communication to almost everyone--all classes, all ages, all groups--through a medium which can be more or less comprehended by all because it combines the two most widely and easily grasped forms of expression: the spoken language and pictures.

Of course, the level of political, philosophical, or esthetic expression thus far transmitted through this medium has not been more than superficial and manipulative, except in a few major instances. Nevertheless, television has generated a popular culture in the sense of a culture in which most people can and do participate on an unprecedented scale.

In the very near future the massive spread of two further developments of video technology will further extend and intensify the role of television in American culture: inexpensive videotape recording and cable television.

It seems likely that within ten or twenty years the vast majority of American homes will be equipped with a TV set and a videotape machine, possibly with camera, and will be hooked into a cable system with the capacity to disseminate signals on forty to eighty channels, possibly with some form of return signal.

However, while it is fairly easy, on the basis of present technology, to predict the sort of equipment that will be available, it is extremely difficult to imagine what kind of impact these developments will have on American culture. It is possible that the difference will be minimal; that Americans will continue to prefer the traditional popular entertainments, news, and sports turned out by the major networks while the new cable and videotape developments will be used primarily by specialized and elite groups.

On the other hand, it is also conceivable that the new video technologies will bring about drastic cultural changes

421

by opening up a great variety of new channels of communication and expression. In any case, the cultural impact of new communications technology will be at least partly shaped by our own capacity to imagine effective uses for this equipment and by the models of a videoculture with which we approach the problem of organizaing the use and conceiving of the appropriate contents for this new medium.

I would like to suggest some tentative problems we must consider in preparing ourselves to seize upon the potential benefits and to become aware of some of the possible dangers inherent in some of the ways in which the video-culture may develop. To do so, I would like to consider three possible models of such a culture.

GLOBAL VILLAGE

The first is that of the global village, that striking conception of Marshall McLuhan's which, I think, is one of the more tantalizing and also dangerous images of the future of human culture. The vision is that of an electronically unified world in which the different elements are related like the components of the central nervous system, or, in another of McLuhan's striking images, like the closely knit members of a primitive village, but on a world-wide scale.

This model has a certain plausibility through the assumption that communication through television and other electronic media is different in both degree and quality from communication through earlier media. First of all, through electronics technology--at least according to this model--all persons can be linked in a continual communications net with all other persons. Secondly, the McLuhanites assume that

video is a deeper, more involving form of communication than other media because it evokes on a new level the complex web of feeling once carried by speech in smaller primitive communities. Because of this, video can be understood by all men and it has the potential to unify them psychologically and spiritually. Thus the videoculture can re-create on a national or perhaps even global scale the mystical and sacral unity which we like to think characterized many primitive tribes.

It is easy enough to treat this model ironically as another version of the myth of Paradise Regained, or the restoration of the Golden Age when men lived in complete harmony with one another and the world. It is perhaps almost too obvious to point out that before the fall there was only one human being and that when another was created, discord immediately entered the world.

MOMENTS OF COMMUNION

But that is, I think, unfair, for there is evidence that earlier forms of social organization did possess a kind of mystic social unity, and there have been tantalizing examples when television has momentarily created in the vast majority of the American population something that many people felt as a transcendent sense of social communion.

Most strikingly this was the case with the Kennedy assassination and funeral, a video drama and ritual of such profound impact that its political and cultural implications are, I believe, still with us. It is too much to attribute the peaceful succession of President Johnson to the ritual unity which the video presentation of this event evoked, though there are probably few countries in the world where such an assassination would not have led to massive disorders.

But just what might the "global village" be like? Can we conceive of how video technology might be used to bring about a culture of deep tribal unity and communal involvement in a complex, diverse, and increasingly fragmented society like that of the United States? I suspect that in such a culture we would see two major priorities dominating the videostructure.

First of all, there would almost have to be some kind of modern analog to the traditional ritual year, a cycle of annual ceremonies, games, and other rituals participated in simultaneously by all citizens. This ritual year would give a primary structure and identity to the culture thereby making each individual a communal participant in the flow of time. That video might make such mass ceremonies possible seems unquestionable in the light of phenomenon like the Kennedy assassination, the landing on the moon, and the superbowls. Indeed, the television schedule has already developed some of the mystic regularities which might be associated with a ritual year.

In addition to the collective expression of cultural unity through video ceremony, a complex web of individual and group involvements would have to develop, parallelling the rich web of oral interchange between the members of a tribe. One can imagine cable TV taking this role. Its multiple channels could foster a continual dialog which might enable each major group to enter imaginatively into the consciousness of all other groups.

Videotape would probably play a very important role here as well. Already experiments with social tools like video dialog and video confrontation suggest the potential of videotape and cable for creating a new kind of deep psychological and cultural communication between groups, which have heretofore largely avoided the level of per-

sonal involvement with each other.

The vision is attractive. Unfortunately, it is rather difficult to imagine just how such a system might develop out of the present state of affairs. If the great attraction of the global village is its social unity and harmony through individual involvement and fulfilment in the community, such a system would be most unlikely to develop in the very social situation where a prevailing concern with fragmentation and alienation makes the model most attractive.

SUPPRESSION OF DISSENT

It is far easier to see how the video village could be imposed from above by a powerful ruling group seeking to enhance its power by reducing social diversity to the expression of a single ritual cycle and by forcing the expression of varying points of view into a system of continual surveillance of all members of the community in order to identify and suppress any signs of dissent. The Nazis consciously employed the media in these ways in the 1930s and were able to achieve a sort of national village or tribe to a considerable extent. Orwell imagined an even more thoroughgoing system of this kind, and in his brilliant dystopia we can see how plausible it is that the global village might develop into the satanic form of 1984.

The problem of the global village model is the temptation it offers to men of great conviction and power to use the intensity and distribution of video to make their will that of the community. While it is conceivable that men might evolve a less authoritarian form of unity and harmony through a long period of continuous interchange, I see no reason why video communication should bring about a kind of social order that no other form of communication has come near to generating except under conditions of dictatorial power.

Of course if it is really true that "the medium is the message," I am dead wrong about this. However, I have seen no evidence that this slogan is more than a provocative and useful half-truth. Short of this, it seems to me that the evident totalitarian implications of the global village model should lead us to seek the social values it claims to achieve through other means.

COMPUTER CULTURE

Another model which seems to me a far more likely possibility for the videoculture of the future could be labeled that of the computer culture, or the rationalistic utopia.

In the global village, the central dynamic is the flow of attitude and feeling from one person or group toward another, the ultimate result being a transcendent cultural unity out of great social diversity. In the computer culture the dynamic would probably be the flow of information leading toward the highest possible degree of coordination and efficiency in performing the various tasks necessary to the effective operation of the increasingly complex machinery of society.

Since ultimate efficiency lies in total coordination, this could provide a powerful incentive for the increasing use of video technology for such purposes. Indeed, a great many present-day proposals for the use of cable TV involve a variety of such functional roles: coordination of production, direction of police and fire services, rapid exchange of business and medical information, etc.

I would guess that to imagine the further developments of videoculture in terms of this model, we need only extrapolate such present-day tendencies. Thus, the computer culture would be one in which the resources of the electronic media would be primarily employed for the processing, storage and circulation of information. In such a society, each individual and group would presumably have instant access to all the relevant information not only about their own activities, but about the intersecting activities of all other individuals and groups. Such a culture would no doubt achieve a considerable degree of order and harmony based on, one would hope, the priority of the most efficient production and distribution of goods and services possible within the limits of ecological stabilization.

There are, of course, other less attractive possibilities for the computer culture, depending on whether or not a particular group seizes control of the flow of information and uses it for its own advantage against other groups. On an international scale, such a development might well lead to the rise of a set of super-efficient warfare states.

However, since one evident consequence of such a state of affairs would be the further improvement of a technology of destruction already adequate to total annihilation, we would probably not have to worry about the consequences of such a development for very long. One hopes that the human race has enough residual survival instinct to avoid such a fate. If so, the computer culture is much more likely to move toward maximum distribution of the goods and services needed to create an adequate material existence for all.

To accomplish this, it will obviously be necessary to develop means of psychological control and coordination along with the increasing rationalization of the processes of production and distribution. In order to make the flow of information effective in ordering the

manufacture and circulation of goods
and services, men will have to learn
to overcome their present-day indivi-
dualistic competitiveness, irrationality
and ethnocentrism and to accept the
imperatives of reason.

Such a state of affairs may not be as
utopian as it would seem from our
present-day perspective. If B.F. Skinner is correct in his analysis of human
psychology, the development of a "technology of behavior" may well evolve
along with the intensification of the
videoculture. In this case, the proliferation of electronic technology
could lead to the development of a
videoenvironment capable of delivering
what Skinner calls the "schedules of
reinforcement"--i.e., the system of
learning and incentives--necessary to
the rational control of behavior.
Since the videoenvironment could be
centrally controlled by specialists to
a degree that the traditional learning
environments of family, secondary
groups, schools, and other social institutions dependent on the vagaries
of large numbers of individuals have
never been able to, the systematic application of a technology of behavior
on a national scale may become possible
for the first time.

It is difficult to decide just how one
feels about the computer culture or
rationalistic utopia. Major utopian
thinkers in the 19th century--the
Flurierists, Robert Owen, Edward Bella-
my in his *Looking Backward*--viewed the
possibility with a good deal of hopeful anticipation, though they did not
generally envision the technological
developments which would make such a
society on a large scale more than a
utopian dream.

Many experiments on the small-scale
level of utopian communities were tried,
but all floundered on the inability of
such a culture to exist within a larger
society with different institutions and
priorities.

CLASSICAL ANALYSIS

However, in the 20th century, most
intellectuals' attitude toward the computer culture model has been negative.
Huxley's *Brave New World* is the classical analysis from this point of view.
Our sense that contemporary social and
technological developments could easily
evolve toward the computer culture is
backed up by Huxley's own recent argument in *Brave New World Revisited* that
many of the phenomena he imagined in
his original dystopia have actually
emerged in modern industrial America.

Huxley's criticism of the computer culture derived from three implicit assumptions: (1) that human reason is too
limited, fallible or perverse to be en-
trusted with the power of planning a
total society; (2) that autonomous choice
is the essence of human dignity and
therefore to live in a totally planned
society is to be dehumanized or forced
to become like a machine or an animal;
(3) that man's irrationality, his capacity for suffering, and his susceptibil-
ity to evil are primary sources of what
is most characteristic and best in human
life; therefore, to eliminate pain, conflict, suffering and sin would make man
spiritually empty.

These assumptions continue to dominate
20th century imaginative visions of a
rational utopia. Most recently they
were expressed in a powerful and extreme
form in Anthony Burgess' novel *A Clock-
work Orange* and in Stanley Kubrick's
film adaptation of that work. However,
B.F. Skinner's *Beyond Freedom and Dignity* may be the beginning of a considerable change in contemporary intellectual
attitudes toward the potentialities of
a rational utopia, for Skinner eloquent-
ly argues against the basic beliefs implicit in *Brave New World* and in the
20th century artistic and philosophic
tradition of anti-utopian thinking.

Even without being at all sure that I
understand or accept Skinner's line of

argument, I am persuaded that we have been wrong to dismiss this cultural model as inherently inimical to human life and values. It is both possible as a future line of development and conceivably desirable as a solution to many of the problems which beset us.

HUMAN DIGNITY VS. RATIONALITY

Huxley's vision of the computer dystopia suggests that there would be another important use of the new communications technology in this second model society: the provision of exciting modes of vicarious gratification for emotional needs which the rational activities of the computer culture would tend to leave unsatisfied. If, as Huxley suggests, pain and suffering are the experiences which give man his humanity and dignity, to eliminate the possibility of actual tragedy will force society's planners to find some way of giving harmless expression to this side of human existence. Thus, in *Brave New World*, tragedy becomes pornography, works of art and ritual constructed by experts to give maximal vicarious expression to aggressive and erotic feelings thereby relieving the terrible boredom of a totally planned and controlled rational existence.

A good Skinnerian would argue that Huxley's view is simply a rationalization of existing behavior patterns which would be changed in a more rational society, and he might well be correct.

However, the weight of experience would seem to be on Huxley's side. If we look at present-day uses of the mass media, we can see that to a considerable extent they tend toward various forms of pornography in this broad sense. Therefore, in the computer culture, just as the media would be primarily controlled by functional elites

in the process of planning and directing the affairs of society, so the aspect of entertainment and artistic expression would probably be dominated by elites who specialized in the creation of effective pornographies of various sorts.

This state of affairs would probably be no more than an intensification of certain aspects of the contemporary organization of the mass media.

VIDEODIVERSITY

My third model is based on the assumption that the new video technology of cable and tape makes possible the development of TV as a medium of highly diversified communication to many different, smaller publics rather than a mass medium seeking to reach the largest possible audience with standardized forms of communication.

In effect, this model predicts that TV will develop along the same lines of diversification and specialization that have already been followed by publishing, by radio broadcasting and even, in recent years, by film.

Structurally, the complete dominance of the air waves by three major networks with standardized programing would be replaced by a proliferation of cable channels broadcasting to a great diversity of specialized interest groups and subcultures and by the rich development of video cassette recording along the lines of present-day book, magazine and record production and distribution.

Two major forces might provide the motive power for this development: first the possibility that video as a medium is capable of effective communication to a wider range of society than any medium except speech and is conceivably more powerful than the latter; second, the apparent trend of modern industrial societies toward increasing leisure for the population, higher general levels of education, and an increasing variety of individual interests and life styles.

The first assumption is certainly subject to question, though it is clearly just as rational, if not more so, than the related assertion of the unique qualities of video made by the proponents of the global village model.

If it is the case that video is a uniquely effective medium, there seems no necessary reason to believe that it will foster a world of universal mystic involvement. On the contrary, why should it not simply extend to more social groups the kinds of diverse and specialized communication that print now makes possible among regular readers?

Although it could be argued that the standardizing tencencies of modern industrial society are against this kind of development, it seems to me that this argument might well work the other way. For, if we look at recent trends in some areas of modern industrial society, it begins to seem possible that standardization is not an inherent quality of modern industrial economies, but only a necessity of the first stage of their development.

Once industrial societies have reached the point where production has become efficient enough to outstrip demand, there may well be a strong impetus toward the use of leisure to cultivate a variety of interests which will in turn create demand for new kinds of products and services. Video could become a major channel for the cultivation and satisfaction of a vast new variety of interests.

Perhaps the most striking consequence of this model is that it envisages a culture that goes beyond present-day conceptions of a pluralistic culture as emerging from the interplay of di-verse subcultures and interest groups.

This model also implies the emergence of another kind of diversity embodied in the complex and continual process of the choice and cultivation of new interests and associations. In other words, an individual's identity in this culture would be determined not only by the traditional subcultures and interest groups of family, ethnic subculture, occupation, locality, etc., but by a large range of new associations made possible through his continual selection from the manifold groupings he can plug into through cable TV and videotape. Let us call this model the society of video-diversity.

Given the present-day dominance of the principle of mass communication--i.e., use of the media to reach as large an audience as possible--the emergence of a culture of manifold groupings seems, if anything, less likely than the global village or the computer culture.

NON-ACCEPTANCE OF ALTERNATIVES

On the whole, few people have chosen to take advantage of the minimal diversity offered by such present-day attempts to break up the uniformity of network programing as educational TV, public broadcasting, pay TV, or local programing. Conceivably even the proliferation of available channels and the eventual development of video cassette technology to the point where it is economically competitive with paperback books will not lead the majority of the population to change their preference for the traditional forms of mass culture.

The basic question, I suppose, is whether modern industrial societies require a mass medium in the sense of a centralized and standardized network of more or less continual rapid communication of the

427

same basic messages to a large proportion of society.

However, there is a great difference between the need to make certain kinds of information instantaneously available to the great mass of the population, and the need to have a vehicle for advertising. The model of manifold groupings assumes that however diverse a network of video communication might develop, it would still be capable of instantaneous mass communication as needed.

The thing that would change in the culture of manifold groupings would be the dominant use of video to distribute standardized formulaic entertainment conceived as appealing to everyone. Presumably the traditional forms of popular culture would still be available, but, in competition with a vast diversity of other kinds of programing aimed at the particular needs of spedific groups.

COMPONENTS OF DIVERSITY

As I dimly see it, there would be four main kinds of grouping in the culture of videodiversity: (1) existing subcultures; (2) political and economic interest groups; (3) biological and psychological groupings; (4) new forms of grouping along the lines of hobbies and fanship.

1. Presumably one of the most important bases of audience differentiation in an environment of many different channels of communication would be an extension of groupings that already exist. We would anticipate that the various local, regional and ethnic subcultures of the United States would find much richer and fuller expression. Ethnic traditions, rituals and forms of narrative and humor should become one major source of programming.

A whole range of programs appealing to the interests and concerns of specific subcultural groups which now find almost no expression in television could lead to important changes in the individual American's sense of identity and to greater understanding between subcultures.

2. Just as present-day mass media tend to blur the differences between subcultures, they also rarely permit the articulation of the many different economic and political interests which make up our society. This is particularly true in the area of entertainment programing where, until the impact of "*All in the Family*," one would have thought from the situation comedy and drama on television that America had no conflicting social interest groups.

Even the presentation of news and documentary features do not on the whole adequately reflect our different social interests, because they are supposed to be objective (i.e., to reflect the general interest of a mythical middle-class majority). The many channels of the culture of videodiversity will do away with the need for "objectivity" by eliminating the present monopoly of a few groups over the major communications networks.

3. By biological or psychological groupings I mean groupings around some complex of needs, interests, or attitudes growing out of the circumstances of the life cycle (e.g., youth subcultures or senior citizen communities) or out of some widely shared psychological quality (e.g., those with a special need for the exercise of vicarious aggression). We have already seen how important a role the media can play in the process of age grouping, for one of the central vehicles in the formation of the contemporary youth culture has been music communicated through radio and recordings.

Certainty some of the many channels of the culture of videodiversity will be devoted to the ideas, forms of expression and rituals which define and validate the individual's feeling of identity with an age group. Other channels may become part of a process of psychological grouping by communicating materials which meet various patterns of psychological needs and encourage interchange and understanding between those of various psychic constitutions. It seems not impossible, for example, that various forms of psychotherapy through video might well develop.

4. A fourth kind of grouping would be neither cultural, political, biological nor psychological, but esthetic. If the productive capacities of modern societies do in fact increase the leisure time of the majority of the population the need for a variety of satisfying leisure activities will become a vital matter. To some extent we see this trend already under way with the proliferation of televised sports. In the culture of videodiversity we can anticipate many more groupings of this sort growing up around channels which disseminate both presentation of and commentary on many varieties of sports, games, hobbies, works of drama, music, art, etc.

The human values that are at least potentially likely to flourish in the culture of videodiversity are those of variety, toleration and autonomy. The individual will no longer be bound by the life styles available to him through his family background or local peer group.

But there are also real dangers lurking in this model. The negative side of videodiversity is fairly obvious: further extension of the fragmentation, specialization, and privatization long characteristic of American culture.

However, this effect might actually be offset by the precision and complexity of discussion generated by the formation of many articulate interest groups around the multiple channels and group-

ings of videodiversity.

In addition, the intensification of diversity will cause many strains in the social fabric. All groups will have to accept a wider range of differences, life styles and beliefs, for these differences will inevitably find public expression through the channels of the videodiverse society. This would be a difficult experience for many Americans accustomed to the bland uniformity of the mid-20th century suburb and the restrictive moralism of the dominant white, middle-class religiously-oriented subcultures.

Because there are such dangers inherent in the model of videodiversity, we will need to develop a number of creative and technical skills to counteract them. One such skill will involve finding means of encouraging individual autonomy and respect for differences in life styles.

I mentioned earlier the possible use of video for new forms of psychotherapy. If I am correct in thinking that increasing possibilities of cultural choice will create serious psychological strains, then the development of modes of assisting people to deal with these strains without having to resort to large-scale repression of deviance will be an important task for future media specialists and educators.

Actually, the recent flourishing of pornographic films and the ambiguous public reactions to this development provide us with a continuing case study of the problems inherent in a sudden change in what is culturally acceptable.

Another area where great imaginative skills will be needed is in the establishment of rich and complex dialogs between the distinctive groupings of subcultures, interest and taste which will develop. We must create forms of video which will articulate and express diverse interests, encourage sympathetic communication and understanding between different groupings, and serve as a means of resolving the inevitable conflicts of interest which will multiply in a society which fosters such diversity.

DEALING WITH THE FUTURE

I would not like to claim any more than an exploratory interest for the three models I have sketched out. In our discussions we should consider whether these or another set of patterns are the most useful and plausible means for speculating about the future of popular culture. I am convinced, however, that if we can develop a useful set of such models we can not only gain some perspective on the structure of mass culture in our own times, but begin to think about how we might deal more rationally with the future impact of new cultural technology.

In particular, it seems to me that we must begin giving more thought to the education of the future.

How are we to prepare individuals to lead effective and fulfilling lives in the global village, the computer culture, the world of videodiversity or whatever other new cultural structures seem likely to develop?

What sort of education should be given those who will create and organize the new media technology?

These seem to me the most important problems that face us. I hope that by trying to cast our minds ahead to imagine the various shapes which the popular culture of the future might take we will be able to begin thinking effectively about these basic problems of the nature of future scholarship and education.

DISCUSSION QUESTIONS

1. Explain what Cawelti means by the term "videodiversity."

2. In your opinion, what will be the overall effect of the coming "video-culture" on our society? Why?

Reprinted by permission by MICHIGAN BUSINESS REVIEW; July, 1973, Vol. XXV, No. 4.
Published by the Graduate School of Business Administration, The University of
Michigan.

VIII-6

THE FUTURE OF CABLE TELEVISION

James D. Scott

Cable television (CATV) was originally developed to bring a clear television
picture into homes that otherwise could
receive either a poor signal or none
at all. More recently it has been used
to provide viewers with greater program
variety in cities served by only two
or three television stations. The advantages CATV offers to consumers have
been great enough to lead them to pay
an installation fee ranging from nothing to $100 (average $20) and a monthly
subscription fee averaging $5.00. In
1972, CATV provided service to approximately 6 million homes or about 10 percent of the total U.S. television audience. Estimated annual revenues of the
2,750 operating cable systems in the
U.S. were about $360 million in 1971.

What is the outlook for future growth
of CATV? What problems must be overcome if the industry is to achieve its
potential?

Are cable operators likely to offer program originations superior to over-the-
air broadcasting that will attract subscribers? What are the potentialities
for new services growing out the the
availability of two-way communication
between the cable subscriber and the
program source?

Since expansion of advertising revenues
is crucial to profitable operation of
CATV, is cable an advertising medium
that is likely to receive serious consideration by retailers, service institutions, and consumer goods manufacturers? Does CATV offer advertisers an opportunity for improving the effectiveness of their television commercials
through pretesting them while they are
still in the developmental stage?

In view of the outlook for growth in
CATV, what business opportunities are
likely to exist in the construction,
equipment supply, and operation of cable
systems? What is likely to be the impact of CATV upon the over-the-air broadcasting industry? Is this an industry
that individual and institutional investors should consider for inclusion
in their portfolios? These are the
topics that are explored briefly in
this article.

DEVELOPMENT OF CATV

As background for understanding the
potential for the future development of
CATV, it is helpful to review briefly

the nature of CATV service, what it offers to the subscriber, and its present stage of development. Starting in 1949, CATV first developed in communities where there was no local television broadcasting station and where reception from the nearest stations in the area was either impossible or poor because of distance or topographical obstructions.[1] The strong desire of people located in such communities for television entertainment led to the development of community antennae systems for receiving broadcast signals and feeding them through a network of coaxial cables to the homes of individual viewers on a subscription basis. Sensitive antennae were erected on specially selected sites; broadcast signals received were modulated, amplified, and fed to subscribers through a cable system.

Beginning in 1953 this original concept was supplemented by microwave relay systems to bring the broadcast signals of metropolitan area stations long distances to remote communities having little or no television service. This development also made it possible for cable system operators to offer their subscribers a greater variety of programs than could be provided by the community antennae alone. The result of these technical developments was not only to provide a clear television picture to subscribers, but also to provide them with program diversity which is an important feature of present-day CATV.

According to *Broadcasting*, most cable systems offer between 6 and 12 channels; the average for all is 10; in practice they carry an average of 7 signals. Most new systems being constructed have 20 channels; the state-of-the-art maximum is about 48. Tech-

nology exists for two-way cable television that permits subscribers to transmit signals directly back to the originating cable operator. In March, 1972, cable firms in the top 100 markets were required by the Federal Communications Commission to have the capacity for such return communication at least on a non-voice basis.

CURRENT STATUS OF CATV

CATV's growth has been one of the fastest in the communications field. Selected figures published by *Broadcasting* in their *TV Fact Book No. 42*, 1972-73 edition, demonstrate the progress that has been made since 1952 (as of January 1 of each year):

	1952	1962	1972
Number of operating systems	70	800	2,750
Total subscribing households	14,000	850,000	6,000,000
Estimated number of viewers	n.a.	n.a.	18,500,000
Homes per system	200	1,062	2,182
Percent of TV homes subscribing (household penetration)	.1	1.7	9.7

n.a.: not available

Additional growth may be anticipated. Between January 1 and March 30, 1972, the number of operating systems increased from 2,750 to 2,839. These systems served 5,328 communities. Another 1,641 franchises had been approved, however, but were not yet in operation and 2,702 applications for franchises were still awaiting action in 1,530 communities.

---

[1] Adapted from E. Stratford Smith, "The Emergence of CATV: A Look at the Evolution of a Revolution," *Proceedings of the IEEE*, Vol. 58, No. 7, July 1970, pp. 968-970.

Although the average size of the systems operating in early 1972 was approximately 2,182 subscribers, there were 22 systems with 20,000 or more. The largest--San Diego--served over 51,000. The greatest number of systems (805), however, fell in the 50 to 499 class while there were 38 with fewer than 50 subscribers.

Of special significance is the percentage of TV homes served by CATV. Whereas overall household penetration of CATV was 9.7 percent in 1972, this system has its greatest strength outside the major population centers. An A.C. Neilsen survey in 1969, for example, indicated that CATV had a 23.3 percent penetration of TV homes in rural areas, 34.5 percent in small towns, and 1.6 percent of TV homes in major metropolitan areas. Why is CATV penetration so low in large population centers where there would appear to be a sizable potential market? While the high cost of constructing cable systems in metropolitan centers is one deterrent, of greater importance are the regulatory actions of the Federal Communications Commission (FCC). The impact of these regulations on the development of the industry is explained in the following section.

INFLUENCE OF FCC REGULATIONS ON CATV

With the development of microwave relay systems, beginning in 1953, cable operators saw an opportunity to expand revenues by offering program diversity in major markets served by only one or two television stations.[2] Established broadcasters in such markets opposed this move, fearing reduced audiences and advertising revenues. Moreover, they argued that non-payment of copyright fees on program material by CATV operators gave them an unfair

advantage since local broadcasting stations were forced to pay such charges.

The resulting controversy led the FCC, first, to assert control over the importation of distant signals by microwave relays (1965); and second, to assume total jurisdiction over all CATV systems, including microwave operations (1966). Rules were issued prohibiting importation of distant signals into the 100 markets with the largest television household population. Cable operators were also not permitted to duplicate, on the same day, programs carried by local television stations. In December 1968, these rules were replaced by a "freeze" on CATV installations in the top 100 markets pending the adoption of a new set of rules. These actions discouraged the entry of CATV systems into the top 100 markets.

The freeze lasted until March 31, 1972, when the FCC issued a new set of rules designed to permit expansion of CATV into major markets without jeopardizing over-the-air broadcasting.[3] These rules permit CATV systems in the top 50 markets to carry signals of at least three network and three independent stations; those in markets 51-100 may carry at least three network and two independent stations. All systems in the top 100 markets are entitled to carry two distant signals; permission to do this was given to enable CATV to attract the investment capital for the construction of new systems and open the way for the full development of cable's potential.

Protection to over-the-air broadcasting was provided by rules prohibiting cable systems in the top 50 markets from carrying any syndicated program for one year after its first appearance in any market and then for the life of the contract under which it is sold to a local station. In markets 51-100 in size, different kinds of non-network

---

[2] E. Stratford Smith, *ibid.*, 970-971.

[3] "The FCC Delivers on Cable," *Broadcasting*, Feb. 7, 1972, p. 17 ff.

material are protected for varying periods of time up to two years. The "same-day exclusivity protection" that had previously been afforded network programs, however, is reduced to sumultaneous (same time) duplication.

The controversy over whether cable operators should pay copyright royalties to program producers has not yet been resolved.[4] In 1968 the Supreme Court had ruled that CATV incurs no liability for carrying copyrighted programs under present statutes. This led to proposals for revising the U.S. copyright laws and the Senate Sub-committee on Copyrights has been considering such suggestions. It is believed that action on this issue is necessary to eliminate the uncertainty that impairs the ability of the cable industry to attract the capital needed for substantial growth. Hope was expressed by the Chairman of the FCC that issuance of the new rules covering cable television would facilitate the passage of copyright legislation.

OUTLOOK FOR FUTURE GROWTH OF CATV

Now that FCC regulations have been promulgated that are designed to get cable moving without jeopardizing over-the-air broadcasting, what is the future outlook for CATV? Let us examine two estimates of anticipated growth by 1980--one conservative and one more optimistic. (See following table.)

The 1972 household penetration of CATV was approximately 10 percent. The Director of Media of a large consumer goods manufacturer estimates that this figure will probably amount to about 25 percent by 1980. In a 1970 study, however, the Samson Science Corporation forecast the more optimistic figure of 38 percent. Whether we accept fore-

[4] *Ibid.*, p. 18.

	1972	1980 Conservative*	Optimistic**
Number of systems	2,750	3,600	4,391
Number of subscribers (millions)	6.0	18.0	28.5
Homes per system	2,182	5,000	6,000
Household penetration	9.7	25.0	38.0

Sources: *Reported by Director of Media, large consumer goods advertiser.
 **Samson Science Corp., *Cable Television*, 1970.

cast of 25 percent penetration or 38 percent, such gains would indeed by significant when compared to the 10 percent penetration of 1972.

These forecasts take into account the comparative service offered by CATV vs over-the-air broadcasters, growth in the proportion of families with color television receivers, anticipated changes in average household income, the size of installation and subscription fees charged by cable systems, and the offering of specialized consumer services by CATV without competition from traditional broadcasters, among others.

The success experienced by CATV in penetrating the top 100 markets between now and 1980 will have an important influence upon achievement of the forecasts summarized above. A key factor determining the rate of expansion of CATV service in major markets is the strength of consumer demand for the benefits that CATV promises to viewers currently being served by over-the-air broadcasting. Let us examine these benefits briefly.

WHAT CATV OFFERS TO THE CONSUMER

As CATV systems are established in metropolitan markets such as Detroit, they hold out to the potential subscriber a number of benefits. The first is better reception of television channels they already receive without the cable (i.e., greater clarity, absence of "ghosts" and "snow" common in fringe areas of the market).[5] The improvement of reception is especially noticeable on color television sets. The second benefit is the reception of additional channels from other areas, thus increasing the diversity of program material available for viewing.

The third potential benefit is the program material originated by the CATV operator over the channel or channels reserved for his own use. Over 400 CATV systems have the capacity of originating programs, while nearly 300 do so on a regularly scheduled basis--an average of 16 hours a week.[6] Almost 800 have the capability of providing automated originations such as time and weather services and stock reports. In Manhattan, for example, certain cable systems make available a channel showing a variety of special interest programs such as foreign films, live New York Knickerbocker basketball games, Ranger hockey games, kennel club show finals, tennis matches, and other events. Another channel is devoted almost entirely to weather reports. Still another shows stock market reports. A fourth channel features local and neighborhood news and analysis.

The quality of the local programs originated by cable operators varies widely,

---

[5] John Oppendahl, "Are We on the Brink of a New TV Era?" *Detroit Free Press*, Feb. 7, 1971, Sec. B, p. 1ff.

[6] "A Short Course in Cable, 1972," *Broadcasting*, May 15, 1972, p. 45.

of course. The FCC provided a stimulus to the development of such programs by requiring as of January 1, 1971, CATV systems having 3,500 or more subscribers to operate "to a significant extent" as a local outlet by offering programs other than automated services, music, and announcements. Cable systems willing and able to invest in superior local programs will gain subscribers, revenue, and thus be able to enrich their offerings still more. The problem CATV operators face is to break out of the vicious circle of low audience penetration that limits the funds available to support high quality, appealing programming on the system's own channels. Without such original programs, CATV is limited to rebroadcasts of material already available on standard broadcast stations and to inexpensive local programs such as town meetings, local news, and local sports. Such offerings have limited drawing power.

An important potential source of revenue for cable operators is advertising. Accordingly, let us examine the long term outlook for the sale of advertising time on CATV systems.

OUTLOOK FOR USE OF CATV AS AN ADVERTISING MEDIUM

Cable operators may carry advertisements on their own program originations. Only 53 did so in 1972, although another 375 carried commercials on automated service channels such as time, weather, and news ticker. CATV advertised billings in 1972 were estimated at only $3 million by *Advertising Age* while $300 million was being collected from subscribers for such cablecasting service. If CATV penetration grows from 25 percent to 38 percent by 1980, how is this development likely to affect the use of cablecasting as an advertising medium?

Local advertisers who find television

adapted to their promotional needs account for the lion's share of CATV advertising revenues at present and will probably be the major users of this medium in the years immediately ahead. Retailers, banks, and manufacturers with local distribution fall into this category. Such firms are attracted by CATV by the following consideration: (1) The message may be confined to a given community or part of a community. (2) It can be beamed at a limited percentage of television viewers believed to be the prime target market for the advertiser's product or service. (For example, desired ethnic groups, upper-middle income class, senior citizens, and others.) When an advertiser aiming at a selective market computes the cost of reaching 1,000 *prospects* via CATV, accordingly, he may find it is a better buy than over-the-air broadcasting which reaches a mass market (and hence involves the purchase of waste coverage in reaching the target). (3) CATV advertising rates also tend to be lower than those of over-the-air broadcast stations since the audiences for their programs are generally smaller. (For example, a one-minute spot on Cablechannel 10 in Manhattan costs $250 while 60 seconds of prime time on a New York City television station would cost about $5,000.) CATV advertising costs, accordingly, fit more easily into the budget of the local advertiser.

Advertising agencies serving firms with regional markets shy away from CATV because of the time and effort involved in dealing with a large number of individual systems. As regional associations are formed to sell CATV time in the years ahead, however, the use of this medium by regional advertisers will increase. Such networks would quote a single rate for the use of the associated systems and would submit one bill to the advertiser.

The development of regional networks marketing CATV time will also be encouraged by the trend toward merger of

cable systems that began late in 1970. As a result of this movement, in 1972 the 50 largest system owners accounted for 4.1 million subscribers, while 12 firms had slightly more than half of those on the cable.[7]

At present several influences tend to discourage advertisers with national distribution from the use of CATV. Certain of these obstacles may be removed, however, as cable penetration increases in the next few years. These include: (1) Lack of a cable network. The need for a cable network to attract both regional and national advertisers is recognized by CATV operators. Launching of domestic satellites in the next year will permit the creation of another network over which CATV can beam its own programs nationwide.[8] How long it will take to organize a national CATV network is uncertain, but by 1980 it should be an accomplished fact.

(2) Smaller audiences for CATV program originations than are available by buying time on competing broadcast stations. As CATV systems grow, however, they will be better able to provide programs that will attract larger audiences than at present. At some time between now and 1980 this negative factor should be removed.

(3) Lack of reliable audience data broken down into various demographic categories. Without such data, advertisers find it difficult to determine whether the target market for their brands can be reached economically via CATV. Such information can be provided when CATV operators decide it is worthwhile to incur the cost involved in doing so. As audiences grow for CATV

---

[7] *Broadcasting*, March 27, 1972, p. 21.

[8] Sol Schildhause, Chief of the FCC's Cable Bureau, predicts that domestic staellites will be launched in the next year permitting creation of a CATV national network. *Ann Arbor News*, March 25, 1973, p. 19.

program originations and cable networks are formed, the possibility of selling more advertising time will encourage cable operators to provide the needed demographic data.

(4) Low CATV penetration in the top 50 markets (in fewer than 5 percent of television households). This condition now inhibits the use of cable by national advertisers as a supplementary medium to build up advertising weight in key cities. Park estimates that in cities served by three network-affiliated stations household penetration may grow to between 20 percent and 35 percent by 1982.[9] As this occurs, national advertisers may begin to include CATV as a significant supplementary medium.

As the above obstacles are removed, significant use of CATV as an advertising vehicle is likely to be made first to promote products with target markets among a limited segment of consumers. Here the selective possibilities of CATV would, therefore, be a distinct advantage. Anticipated CATV penetration of from 25 percent to 38 percent, however, is not likely to encourage national advertisers with mass markets to make significant use of CATV, except as a supplement to other national media.

OPPORTUNITIES FOR TESTING ADVERTISING

Although an advertiser with regional or national distribution may not make extensive use of CATV until certain obstacles are removed, such firms may find cable a useful vehicle for testing alternative TV concepts. CATV systems in two cities offer split-market

facilities where results of two alternative advertising approaches may be compared in the same market during the same period of time over double-cable facilities. Using complex electronic equipment the cable operator can cut-in test commercials going to one-half of the subscribers while the other half continue to get the normal advertising message. Experiments may be conducted involving alternative messages, commercial length, amounts of advertising, time of day, types of program and others. One firm offering such testing facilities, Ad-Tel, Ltd., reports that it conducted 50 tests in 45 different product categories for advertisers during its first year of operation (1969).

CATV research facilities are also available in markets with only single-cable systems. These are designed primarily for test marketing and for copy testing. In February, 1972, the research department of a leading advertising agency, for example, listed for its clients four CATV systems, among others, offering natural exposure to test commercials in several markets.

Through scientifically designed advertising research using CATV facilities, accordingly, advertisers are able to improve the effectiveness of advertising used on their current over-the-air television programs. At the same time such firms are gaining experience with CATV, keeping a close check on its penetration into major markets, and observing the devleopment and viewer acceptance of CATV program originations. As obstacles are removed that inhibit the use of CATV as a significant medium for the promotion of their brands in the next few years, such firms will have gained the experience to enable them to utilize cable effectively.

[9] R.E. Park, "Prospects for Cable in the 100 Largest Television Markets," *Bell Journal of Economics and Management Science*, Spring 1972, p. 147.

OTHER APPLICATIONS OF TWO-WAY COMMUNICATION SERVICE

The availability of two-way communication makes possible a number of other applications of CATV. Possible services include the following:[10]

1. Education: Educational television providing student interaction with the instructor. Access to library reference materials via video tape.

2. Public safety: Remote monitoring of television cameras used for surveillance in stores, banks, business offices, private homes among others. Fire and police alarm systems. Emergency communication.

3. Preference polling of television audiences.

4. Automatic reading of gas, water, and electricity utility meters via CATV.

5. Communication: Computer accessibility and interaction; videophone.

6. Politics: Low cost local access to CATV subscribers; voting via cable; political polls.

7. Work activity: Information flow by facsimile; delivery of mail.

8. Recreation: Via pay television, availability of movies, plays or sports programs of unusual interest; game interaction on cable.

Listing these possibilities indicates how broad the opportunities for the development of CATV services are. It is reported that cable operators are recognizing that offering distant signals to television viewers in large

cities is not enough to attract a substantial number of them to subscribe for cable service. They recognize that something more is needed. At the National Cable Television Association convention in May, 1972, many cable operators were indicating that the "something more" might well be pay television.[11] This plan would make available full-length movies and major sports events that may be viewed without commercial interruption. Pay cable entertainment of this sort is likely to be made available by leasing one or two cable channels to firms organized to develop such programs, provide equipment to enable only those subscribers who pay to have access to the entertainment offered, and handle the billing and collection of "admission" charges. Tests of pay cable entertainment services scheduled to begin at the end of 1972 have been announced by Optical Systems, Inc., Theatervision Inc., Home Theater Network Inc., among others. These experiments should provide evidence as to whether pay cable entertainment would be purchased by enough subscribers to make it profitable.

IMPACT ON OVER-THE-AIR BROADCASTING

As CATV penetration grows between now and 1980, what is likely to be the impact upon over-the-air broadcasting? It is recognized, of course, that subscribers to CATV will have more alternative programs from which to choose than were available to them before. Subscribers will have not only the network programs they previously received, but also other program material from distant stations as well as programs originated by the cable operator. It is likely that the network programs brought in by cable will still be popular with television viewers, but the

---

[10] For additional background on the two-way communication services listed here, see Tate, Charles, (Ed.); *Cable Television in the Cities*, The Urban Institute, Washington, D.C., p. 13.

[11] *Broadcasting*, Cable Sourcebook 1972-73, p. 3.

competition from additional programs will probably result in smaller audiences than before for network shows, with the result hat advertising rates will have to be reduced to compensate for the change.

The Sloan Commission estimates that network affiliates could lose 10 to 15 percent of their audiences if cable penetration reaches 50 percent and that network profits could drop from 20 to 50 percent.[12] Evidence reviewed here does not indicate that 50 percent penetration is likely by 1980, however. The Samson Report, for example projects a penetration of 38 percent by 1980 and concludes that the threat to broadcasters is real--but small.[13]

In his study of the prospects for cable in the 100 largest television markets, Park estimates that the impact of cable television would be quite small. He estimates that cable would increase the revenues of UHF independent stations by about 20 percent over the period 1971-81, while reducing the revenues of other stations in the top 100 markets by considerably less than 20 percent. He concludes that the new FCC rules will tend to get cable moving without jeopardizing over-the-air broadcasting.[14]

tion and greater program diversity are attractive enough to stimulate a consumer demand for CATV service in major markets, are cable operators likely to be able to raise the capital that is required for the construction of facilities in these cities or for the expansion of limited service already available? According to *Broadcasting* the total cost of an average system is estimated at between \$500,000 and \$1,000,000.[15] The cost of laying cable ranges from \$4,000 per mile in rural areas to more than \$50,000 per mile in large cities. Hence operators tempted by the prospects in major markets are asking themselves, "Where is the money going to come from?"

It is generally assumed that CATV will need to achieve a base of about 25 million homes in the next ten years if technologically advanced applications of cable are to be economically feasible. To reach this goal would require industry-wide investment of over \$1 billion per year for ten years. To achieve this rate of investment is a formidable task. It is estimated that total national savings-to-investment flow of new funds to corporate users is at a rate of only \$25 to \$30 billion a year. Of this, the utilities take over half. No other single industry attracts capital at the rate of \$1 billion per year.

FINANCIAL REQUIREMENT OF THE CABLE INDUSTRY

Assuming that improved color recep-

TREND TOWARD CONSOLIDATION IN CATV

The CATV systems began as small companies. They developed more extensively in medium-sized communities and rural areas than in major markets. Usually these systems served one community and were owned by a small company. Thus, organization of a CATV company to serve a community has offered many individuals

---

[12] Sloan Commission, *On the Cable*, McGraw-Hill Book Co., New York, p. 219.

[13] Samson Science Corp., op.cit., p. 2.

[14] R.W. Park, "Prospects for Cable in the 100 Largest Television Markets," *Bell Journal of Economics and Management Science*, Vol. 3, No. 1, Spring, 1972, pp. 148-9.

[15] "Now...where's the money?" *Broadcasting*, May 15, 1972, p. 45.

with limited capital an opportunity to participate in a growing industry. Out of 1,100 companies in the cablecasting industry in 1972, for example, there were 925 such systems representing perhaps 850 companies, serving over a million subscribers.

Beginning in 1970, however, a trend toward consolidation of cable companies began that has accelerated in the past two years. What has produced this trend?[16] Analysis suggests several possible explanations, (1) Larger firms may find it easier to raise capital needed to exploit the potential now available through expansion into major markets. (2) Scarce management talent in the industry may best be utilized by concentrating corporate resources in the few talented hands. (3) Combining systems offers advertisers a more attractive package with a larger number of subscribers. (4) Consolidations may bring cost savings. (5) Resources for substantial, professional program origination are more readily available to larger, better financed companies. (6) Mergers may provide a "marriage" of needs and strengths of the participating companies.

As a result of the trend toward consolidation, in 1972 the top 10 firms commanded about 40 percent of all subscribers; the top 50 accounted for 75 percent. Thus CATV has been overtaken by the traditional shakeout that occurs in the development of a young and growing industry. The implication of this development is that there will be less opportunity for organizing and operating a new CATV system in the future than has been true up to now. Those who wish to participate in the opportunities that will come from the continued growth of CATV are likely to find their best opportunity in the securities of well-managed firms with a favorable profit outlook.

---

[16] "Will the Mighty Inherit the CATV Earth?", *Broadcasting*, March 29, '72, p.21.

INVESTMENT IN THE CATV INDUSTRY

The impressive and sustained growth of CATV has attracted the attention of investors interested in growth stocks. According to Stnadard & Poors' Industrial Surveys, September 7, 1972, "Continued growth is expected, predicted on: (1) strong customer demand for these services; (2) the introduction of certain specialized consumer services *without* competition from conventional broadcasters; and (3) a more favorable trend of governmental attitudes toward CATV.[17]

Richard A. Connelly, however, sounds a note of caution. He ovserves that investors seem to be overlooking several drawbacks facing CATV operators: (1) Expansion into big cities will be expensive and require heavy financing; (2) program origination will be costly; and (3) CATV must compete with rich networks and stations for programs.[18] It will take adequate resources and good management to deal effectively with these problems.

Participation in the CATV industry is possible through investment not only in companies that install and operate CATV systems, but also through the suppliers of major components such as master antennae, microwave equipment, and coaxial cable.

Obviously, those interested in the possibility of investment in CATV securities would be well advised to make a careful appraisal of the quality of management of leading firms in the field as well as their past earnings records, future prospects, price-earnings ratios, and ability to provide

---

[17] Standard & Poors Industrial Surveys, *Electronics-Electrical*, Sec. 2, Sept. 7, 1972, p. E-29.

[18] Richard A. Donnelly, "The Dimmer View," *Barrons*, Vol. VLL, No. 28, July 10, 1972, p. 5.

necessary capital for expansion into major markets and for program origination. No attempt is made here to provide such information or to indicate which firms might merit consideration.

CONCLUSIONS

Penetration into major markets will offer CATV its major opportunity during the period between now and 1980. Such growth became possible with the adoption of more liberal FCC regulations in March, 1972. The demand of television viewers for improved color reception and greater program diversity will encourage this development.

The trend toward consolidation in the cable industry should result in systems better able to raise the substantial amount of capital needed to construct facilities in major markets. The resulting firms should also be in a better position to provide program originations equal to or better than their over-the-air broadcast competitors. They should also be better equipped to compete for advertising revenues against such broadcasters.

Two-way communication services with strong consumer appeal should be increasingly available on CATV in the years ahead and this will attract subscribers and increase cable penetration.

As CATV program originations improve and household penetration increases in major markets, advertising revenues may be expected to grow. Even with 25 to 38 percent penetration by 1980, however, CATV will be strongest as a selective medium for use to promote products and services marketed to a limited segment of television viewers. At first local firms will be the main users of CATV advertising time. As cable networks become available, and adequate audience

data are provided, first, regional firms and, later, national advertisers are likely to utilize cable as a significant communication medium.

These changes will mean that over-the-air broadcasters will find CATV to be an increasingly strong competitor in contending for audiences and advertising revenues. It is hoped that this may result in improved entertainment for television viewers and better service to the public at large.

In the future, the opportunity to participate in the growth of CATV will probably be found in the judicious investment in the securities of well-managed publicly held firms involved in systems operation, construction, and equipment supply that are in sound financial condition that have a favorable earnings outlook. In view of the problems that lie ahead for this industry, careful analysis, sound judgement, and good sense of timing would appear to be essential if potentialities are to be realized.

DISCUSSION QUESTIONS

1. What influence have regulatory agencies had over CATV? What influence do you believe they should have?

2. Describe what the further development of CATV will have on advertising.

Reprinted by permission from ADVERTISING AGE; 19 November, 1973, pp. 35-6, 40.

VIII-7

THE AGENCY BUSINESS IN 1980

Paul C. Harper, Jr.

In 1980, advertising agencies will be doing the same thing they are doing in 1972. They will be trying to influence human behavior in ways favorable to the interests of their clients.

But there the resemblance will stop. Their services, methods, structure and economics will be different. They may not even be called advertising agencies --because that name may no longer fit.

Any service business is a reflection of the aggregate market for its services. By 1980, the market for agency services will have changed as follows:

By 1980, few parity products--products that offer no clearly defined advantage--will be advertised extensively.

It is in the parity product area in particular that private brands will take over. As distribution becomes more concentrated, and distributors more powerful, the squeeze on advertised me-too products will become unbearable. As shelf space, floor space and showroom space become more and more costly, more and more parity brands will be thrown out. The distributors' incentive to earn a double profit will become overpowering.

Consumers are accepting fungibility. For years they have suspected that all gasolines were alike. Now they are beginning to believe this about many other frequently purchased categories.

PARITY PRODUCTS BOW TO PRIVATE LABEL

Furthermore, when they perceive that products are the same, they increasingly tire of being told that they are different. Advertising money spent this way will become less and less productive.

In addition, there are many in the government who think that the advertising of parity products is deceitful and wasteful. They may have their way.

By 1980, for the above reasons, many companies that are now heavy advertisers of parity products will cease to advertise them at all. They will manufacture parity products for private label. And they will not advertise or market a brand of their own--unless it has a meaningful exclusive that can be clearly communicated in advertising.

Thus, large sectors of the current advertising arena will dry up, leaving the field to those advertisers who have something to say.

This will mean that in many product categories the *primary function* of the advertising agency will be strategic planning and conceptual input in the new product area. Because of the central importance of this function, it will require behavioral and business knowledge of a much higher order than is generally present now among agency "strategists."

In the advertising for service businesses, the same forces will work, but to a lesser degree. Advertising of parity services will decrease. The fungible airline hostesses and gas station attendants with their plastic smiles will disappear from advertising. But the major service industries--airlines, automotive service, fast food, insurance, small loans, banking, business machines, car rentals, hotels and travel and others are the most rapidly evolving sectors of the economy--and the new dimensions of service which they will bring forth will require heavy promotion.

dollars to train their employees to be polite, clear, prompt, accurate, etc. A dollar spent producing a smile on a real attendant's face will be worth far more in repeat business than an advertised smile that doesn't materialize at point of sale. This will require whole new dimensions in employee recruitment, training and continuing indoctrination.

3. In a society which finally recognizes that commercial success and the social good must be reconciled, there will be more communications which address these common interests. (Auto insurance--safe driving; life insurance--good health; oil industry--pollution reduction; fast food-good nutrition.)

Whether or not there is a net *reduction* in service industry advertising, the strategic emphasis will change, and the use of media will become more segmented and specialized. This will require more strategic guidance from the agency, and it will require the extension of agency service into all forms of communication. Because of this, the highest degree of sophistication will be required of those delivering service to accounts.

SERVICE INDUSTRY ADS SHIFT EMPHASIS

However, funds currently used to advertise mere parity service will be diverted to at least three other kinds of activity:

1. On-premise communications. More use will be made of the captive nature of the customer to both entertain and indoctrinate him as he waits, shops, eats, flies, etc. On-premise promotion will extend into a full range of video, audio, as well as print, media.

2. Behavioral training. In an increasingly crowded world, the service industries will spend more communications

THREE KINDS OF MARKET IN 1980

By 1980, the "national advertising market" as we know it, where most products and services are advertisable on a national basis, will not exist.

Instead, there will be three kinds of market:

A. *The "fungibles" market*, composed of product and service categories which are fundamentally satisfactory, and not susceptible to, or needful of, further refinement. This market will be:

• National and homogeneous.
• Dominated by store brands or captive

443

services.
- Heavily price promoted.
- Virtually unadvertised on a national basis.

B. *The "improvables" market.* This market will be composed of products and services which cater to broad, but not universal, markets, and where continued technological refinement is feasible or where fashion and style are important sales factors. This market also includes major new product and service forms, replacements for existing forms.

- Demographically and regionally segmented.
- Dominated by manufacturers' brands and independent services--or by the brands of the stronger national distributors.
- Heavily advertised in local and regional as well as national media--with presentations varied to meet different demographic tastes and needs.

. C. *The "enclave" market.* This market can only be described as a three-dimensional grid--with the axes representing income, geography and life style, and representing, therefore, a wide degree of variation. This will be a diverse, volatile series of smaller markets where the premium is on individuality. Novelty will be a virtue with some, permanence with others, high style with some, homespun style with others. In current terms, it will be composed of a range of tastes and needs represented by *Vogue* on the one hand and the *Whole Earth Catalog* on the other.

Many of these "enclaves" will be viable markets for extensive advertising because of better education, the growing diversity in our society, and the increasing need to express individual identity.

This market will be characterized by:

- Products and services designed to serve specialized tastes.
- Boutique merchandising (within major distributive centers) and mail order merchandising.
- Highly focused advertising in terms of presentation and media. Media usage will take advantage of the new, highly focused forms, such as video cassettes, paperbacks, cable TV. Advertising language will reflect the mode of the sub-market being addressed.

Again, because of these new dimensions, the agency of 1980 will be called on for strategic guidance in a complex marketplace, where the "broad strokes" of the past are no longer economical-- and where highly focused communications with their efficiencies (and their risks) are required.

By 1980, the western world, as well as large parts of Asia, will be homogeneous as far as marketing techniques, product technology and demographic structure.

This means that not only will these markets be economically interdependent, but they will be technologically and culturally interdependent.

In 1980, the world market for product ideas, merchandising and advertising ideas will indeed be one.

The result of this is that, to survive, the advertising agency of 1980 must be international in its outlook, its input and its physical and human resources.

THE GOVERNMENT AS AN ADVERTISER

By 1980, the government will be a major advertiser. As public corporations like the Postal Service and Amtrak prove themselves, others will be spun off. Wherever the government offers a discrete service of economic value to a definable customer group, it should be spun off and charged for. Some will, despite political pressure to the con-

444

trary. These services will be advertised.

The new volunteer armed services will require heavy advertising support, and so will recruiting for certain civilian activities.

Eventually, many of the causes now supported by the Advertising Council will become government funded, when the social cost of certain forms of behavior gets too high.

To compete effectively for government business agencies will have to have:

1. A highly developed sense of the difference between the commercial and bureaucratic worlds.

2. Ability to distinguish between the cruder forms of buying behavior and the more complex forms of social behavior which government will be trying to influence.

THE GOVERNMENT AS A REGULATOR

It is not necessary here to review the growing efforts of government to regulate advertising and marketing. Its net effect by 1980 will be:

1. To restrict competitive claims, which will reduce advertising effectiveness, which, in turn, will reduce dollars spent in many categories.

2. To eliminate advertising in some categories and impose ceilings on others.

3. To limit advertising as a percent of content of certain media.

4. By applying increasingly higher clinical and technical standards, to greatly increase the cost and risks of introducing new products in certain fields.

In this climate, it will be essential that the advertising agency be equipped not only to avoid legal pitfalls, but to help develop corporate strategies that work, while still observing legal and regulatory guidelines.

In 1980, therefore, the advertising agency, if that is what it is still called, will be operating in a world where:

- Many major current categories of advertising will have dried up, due to (a) inroads of private brands, (b) government action, and (c) public skepticism and indifference.
- New major advertised categories will be generated only as real product or service innovations occur. The entire corporate strategy of today's "brand" manufacturers will revolve around meaningful innovations.
- Much service industry advertising will be diverted to on-premise promotion or employee training and indoctrination.
- Much advertising for certain service industries and for the government will address social issues involving complex facets of human behavior.
- The consumer market as a whole will become more complex and segmented.
- Dramatic evolution of audio-visual media as well as print media will allow highly focused attack on market segments that would today be inaccessible.
- The more highly developed world markets will be truly homogeneous.

In this environment, what kind of an advertising agency will be able to grow and prosper?

Any service business is a reflection of its aggregate market. As the market changes, so must the service business.

Today in 1973, it is already within the capability of many advertisers to perform many of the conventional agency services for themselves. The others they can buy outside piecemeal.

Self-sufficiency is already an option for any advertiser with a medium or large communications budget. By 1980, this option will have been exercised by a large number of today's major advertisers.

Agencies who do not prepare for this day will find themselves scratching for project assignments in the creative and media areas. They will become journeymen and little more. To escape this fate, our industry must redifine its product and structure.

THE CUSTOMER AND HIS FUTURE NEEDS

Any agency function that can be performed by others *as well as* the agency is now doing it must be raised to a new level of excellence or scrapped. The *central* function, or product, of the agency (a) must address the basic needs of the marketer of 1980, and (b) must be something he cannot get from any other form of business organization.

Our customers in 1980 will include any type of organization that serves the social good (broadly defined). This will include manufacturers, distributors, service companies, government, other institutions, citizens groups, etc. Each of them will be competing for favorable attention and action in a diverse, complex, noisy and confused arena.

Yet client management then, as now, will continue to have two related problems that can potentially stifle success.

1. Any management must spend much of its time worrying about what goes on in the factory (the hangar, the kitchens, the garage). It must spend part of its

time worrying about finance, material resources and logistics. The greater this internal focus becomes, the more apt the management is to make external mistakes.

2. Marketing departments were created to avoid the above problem. But marketing departments must focus on the problems at hand, and they, too, can develop tunnel vision.

They can be, and sometimes are, overwhelmed by the internal orientation of their own top management.

These are dangers now, and they will persist because they are founded in human nature. But in the market of the '80s, where corporate strategy must be fine-tuned to meet even more complex external realities, they will be no longer affordable.

Advertising agencies have always provided "the outside view" of the marketplace. Many times they have served to refocus basic client thinking--and have thus served as ad hoc management consultants. But this function has only been performed intermittently, usually as the result of some particularly close individual relationship--or the presence of some extraordinary creative talent. By and large (and more and more), agencies have performed routinized communications functions, and the bigger the agencies get, the more internally focused their own managements have become.

HOW AGENCIES CAN SURVIVE IN '80s

To survive in the '80s, the advertising agency must rediscover its real exclusive over time; this real exclusive has become encrusted with administrative and structural barnacles. For future survival it must be scraped clean and remarketed.

The agency's exclusive service is precisely the service its customers will need to survive *themselves* in the '80s. This exclusive is strategic communications counsel on the highest level based on the broadest possible experience. Advertising agencies today possess an unparalleled aggregate of knowledge of what works and what doesn't work in the influencing of human behavior--across the entire spectrum of human activity--and in every medium.

Agencies are the *only* kind of business organization that:

- Work with clients in every sector of the social and economic structure.
- On a continuing basis.
- In every medium of communications.
- Within a pragmatic framework, where work must show results.

The application of this unique insight in the development of product and communications strategy is our exclusive product. Specifically, the surviving agencies of 1980 will be offering:

1. Continuing predictive counsel on all aspects of the client's marketing arena. (Who is likely to do what, when, for what reasons, and with what impact.) This includes a prediction and analysis of government actions and attitudes. Since the world market is the arena, the counsel will be based on worldwide intelligence and input.

2. Basic product strategy. Continuing counsel in depth on what products and services to offer and to whom.

3. Continuing strategic counsel on every aspect of communications, external, internal and on-premise--including fundamental corporate positioning.

4. Implementation of any aspect of the above counsel (exclusive of manufacturing, finance, direct sales and logistics). (Implementation may even include location of supplementary or even primary research/development facilities, and

would certainly include working closely with such facilities.)

THE NEW AGENCY PROFESSIONALISM

The basic product of this new kind of "advertising agency" will *not* be filmed commercials, although we will conceive and produce them; not corporate logos, although we will design them; not sales brochures, although we will write and design them. Our basic product will be *strategic counsel* relating to what values a client offers the public, and how it communicates these values. This new kind of company will comprise an objective strategic adjunct to the management of client organizations. It will offer, on a continuing basis, the authoritative "outside view" that all managements need and will need increasingly in the future.

The agency of the '80s will operate in an environment where:

- Most of its present services can be purchased from other sources, or performed by the client himself.
- Clients will be operating in an "idea arena" where the currents of change are far more swift, subtle, and fragmented than they are today.
- Clients will *not* pay high prices for journeyman media, research, creative and production work.
- Clients *will* pay high prices for continuous high level strategic input.

For survival in the '80s, the advertising agency must offer a new dimension of professionalism. And to do so, it must restructure.

To offer this kind of service to a large, diversified client list requires, in operating terms, a *partnership structure*. The management structure of the agency will be expanded horizontally, like that of a law firm, so that all clients will be able to deal with a partner at regular intervals--a partner sufficiently involved to be able to give thoughtful input on a continuing basis.

Steep pyramidal structures will disappear. They do not permit the intensive high level coverage required. They foster the loss of good ideas, because these ideas tend to be handled at too junior a level or at too many levels. They also foster the "bag handler" syndrome, with its deadening build-up of administrative layers.

The management structure of the agency will be simple. It will consist of several more or less horizontally aligned partners. These men and women will be "creative generalists." They will have a thorough grounding in marketing, communications, and business procedures, but they will have an essentially creative turn of mind.

The partners will have working for them, directly, a few highly trained specialists in the analytical disciplines. They will also be assisted by a few junior partners who are creative generalists by nature, and who are in training for full partnership.

Apart from the necessary business management and housekeeping functions this is all that will be left of the "advertising agency" per se.

The services of this new "agency" will be paid for by fee. The commission system is clearly irrelevant to this structure and will have largely disappeared.

WHO WILL GET THE ADS OUT?

The Account Executive: The agency of the future will seek some of its partners from among its account executive staff. But only those who have

proven themselves as well-rounded, insighted counselors will be selected. The partnership concept requires a complete redefinition of the "contact" function. The partner is not a "contact man," "an account executive," or a conduit for someone else's thinking. He or she must be capable of generating and implementing whole product strategies, communications strategies. The partner should have enough professional stature and acumen to sit on a client's board of directors.

Creative: In the agency of the '80s the creative department as we now know it will have ceased to exist. Creative people as we now know them will (according to their talents and tastes) have chosen one of three careers:

1. Some, with broad talents, will have become full partners in the new structure.

2. Others will move to boutiques or house agencies.

3. Others will join to form the creative subsidiary of the new advertising agency.

The agency of the '80s will have one or more subsidiaries whose sole function will be the translation of strategy into finished communications material. The creative subsidiary will be a separate profit center, whose fees will flow from partnership clients--or from business that it obtains on its own. The agency of the '80s may structure its creative function into more than one subsidiary, in order to avoid problems of conflict--or in order to provide a higher degree of specialization--by media, or by type of communications problems.

In any case, the partner of the "advertising agency" will have an interesting and varied choice of creative resources. This is because the partner will not be required to use the creative subsidiaries of the corporation if he thinks

he can get the job done better somewhere else. It may well be that for a
specific job of corporate design or an
advertising campaign directed toward a
specialized market he will go to an
outside creative resource. Or, if a
partner feels that he can get better
continuing work off-premise, he may do
so. In any case, the corporation's
creative subsidiaries must compete
against the field in terms of creative
excellence and efficient operation.

Research: Much desk research will be
performed by the analysts on the partner's staff. But all field reserach
will be planned and performed by the
corporation's research subsidiary--if
that subsidiary can compete effectively for the partner's business. Here
again the partner will have a choice of
all available research houses, and he
will pick the one best suited for the
job. The corporation's research subsidiary, likewise, will seek and serve
business not handled by the partners.

Media: As the marketplace becomes
more fragmented and complex, the media
function must become more precise, responsive, and fast moving. As more
and more advertisers do their media
planning and buying outside of the
agency framework, it will become harder
and harder for the *conventional* media
department to compete.

The media function, too, will be transformed to meet the new conditions. It
will become subsidiarized, automated,
and centralized. It will compete for
the partner's business. It will also
seek outside business on its own. Like
research, its survival as a function
within the corporation's structure will
depend on its ability to use all the
science and technology available to it,
as well as on the judgment and insight
of its managers.

Other specialized functions: The corporation will offer other services on
a subsidiary basis as those services
offer a profit opportunity. This will
include sales promotion, design, public
relations, government relations, food
science, product development and testing, and others further afield.

The partnership and the corporation:
Above, the terms "partnership" and
"corporation" are used. It is the function of the *partnership* to deliver the
unique product of the corporation--
counsel in product strategy and communications strategy. It will do this with
a minimal staff of its own as described.
It will draw on and pay for the services
of subsidiaries (or others) as its needs
them. It will receive high cost-ratio
fees for its counseling work. It will
receive cost-plus fees with a nominal
mark-up for the implementing services
it delivers from the subsidiaries. The
subsidiaries are then paid appropriate-
ly. The partnership manages client relationships.

The "corporation" is the fiscal and
legal entity which ties the partnership
and the various subsidiaries together
in some kind of business harmony. It
will have over-all profit responsibility
and will decide on what new ventures
should be undertaken and which should
be discarded.

When all is said and done, the advertising agencies which survive and grow in
the '80s will do so because they performed realistically two fundamental
business exercises:

1. They have identified what *they do
best better than anyone else* against a
knowledge of client needs. They will
then restructure so that this service
is rendered as effectively and profitably
as possible.

2. They will have submitted each of
their present functions to the profit
test. If the function cannot compete
profitably against other sources of the
same service, it will be dropped. If
it can compete it will receive further
investment and developments--along with
new profit opportunities the agency may
identify.

DISCUSSION QUESTIONS

1. Briefly describe the advertising agency of 1980.

2. What will be the effect on our society of the increase in advertising by government at all levels?

†